P9-BIG-091

CULTURE AND
CRISIS

•

A College
Reader

Frank J. Warnke

UNIVERSITY OF WASHINGTON

Janice D. Warnke

CULTURE AND CRISIS · A COLLEGE READER

Holt, Rinehart and Winston, Inc.

NEW YORK
CHICAGO
SAN FRANCISCO

Copyright © 1964 by Holt, Rinehart and Winston, Inc.

All Rights Reserved

Library of Congress Catalog Card Number 64–15411

29230–0114

Printed in the United States of America

PE
1122
W28

PREFACE

Any book, whether it is a textbook or a detective story, should and eventually does speak for itself, and its readers will be the ones who judge it. But the editors of a work which is going to be used in the class-room may perhaps be forgiven for speaking briefly about some of their intentions and hopes. In *Culture and Crisis* we have brought together for the student a selection of writings in various forms dealing with some of the major issues which confront modern man. Some of these issues are specifically modern; more of them are versions of universal and recurrent questions of human existence. The selections in Part One deal directly or indirectly with problems raised by our present mass society, but within a framework of larger historical awareness; the selections in Part Two treat the universal theme of freedom, but in terms of immediate con-temporary experience. The selections in Part Three, all concerned with very lively modern problems, show a consistent awareness of the ways in which the universal is pertinent to the particular, the past relevant to the present and the future. And subsequent parts of the book, occupied with such large subjects as science, literature, religion, and the arts, are informed with a sense of the interrelatedness of all fields of knowledge.

The combination of breadth and particularity distinguishes all the pieces in *Culture and Crisis,* whether we think of the historical studies of Wilson, Toynbee, and De Rougemont, Warren's psychologically and historically perceptive treatment of segregation, Galbraith's examination of the economics of equality, Sherrington's precise scientific account, or Sybille Bedford's report on contemporary justice. It is equally evident in some selections which deal with matters often subjected to a super-ficial journalistic handling. Sunday supplements and popular magazines are fond of the subject which has been known, at least since the time of Ibsen, as "the modern woman." Virginia Woolf's essay supplies a serious cultural and psychological basis for discussion of the subject. The con-flict of science and literature is another favorite topic of modern debate, much of it oversimplified or irresponsible. Trilling and Oppenheimer consider the topic on a high intellectual plane, and such selections as those from Sherrington, Erikson, and Forster cast on it an indirect but penetrating light.

The selections in *Culture and Crisis,* widely varied in subject and form, are united by the intellectual liveliness, seriousness, and firmness with which they approach their material. They are united also by the vigorous and stimulating prose styles of their authors—all of them intellectual figures of importance, many of them among the outstanding figures in the world of contemporary thought and artistic creation. Inevitably, much that the student encounters in this volume will be unfamiliar to him, and much of it will make severe intellectual demands on him, but we are convinced that the book can provide him with a context which will bring him both greater understanding of his own immediate world and heightened possibilities of comprehending the larger world of which he is the heir. An important—indeed a central—part of education is to enlarge the understanding by expanding the range of experience with which the student is familiar: the more this happens, in the course of education, the more capable the student becomes of perceiving the complex structure of the indivisible world in which he lives.

Culture and Crisis, we believe, will contribute to this central process of education not only through the quality of the selections which make it up but also through the range of material which it embraces. The student who is majoring in, or contemplating majoring in, psychology, sociology, literature, art, music, physics, biology, economics, or history will find here something that speaks to his special interest—but speaks to it with an awareness of the larger context of knowledge of which any one discipline is only a part. The organization of the volume is in part designed to bring out the implicit connections between specialized interests and the whole universe of *Culture and Crisis.*

The length of some of the selections—unusual in a reader designed for freshman use—has a number of advantages. In addition to allowing for the inclusion of some detailed intellectual treatments which an arbitrary limitation of length would exclude, it introduces the student early in his college career to the kind of demands that will be made of him later and in courses in other subjects. He will, in a variety of contexts, be expected to handle on his own long and complicated works as well as corollary readings. There is much to be said for introducing him to such demands in a situation in which guided analysis of complex material will help him to feel at home among serious ideas seriously treated. Clearly, also, we make certain assumptions about the American student—that he will respond to the challenge of adult material, that he is capable not merely of understanding his own experience but also of seeing the larger connections of his personal experience and performing, on the basis of that perception, the liberating and creative act of thought. We have confidence, in short, not only in the student's intellectual capacities but also in his imagination—that faculty which must come into play together with the intellect to form an educated man.

This confidence has not, however, made us blind to the necessity of providing some assistance to the student, some guides in understanding both the individual selections and the intellectual questions with which they are concerned. We have arranged the selections in groupings designed to be both pedagogically and philosophically useful. Essays on related subjects illuminate each other; kinds of approach take on definition through contrast with other kinds of approach; and the interconnections of various fields of knowledge are demonstrated. Each part is preceded by an introduction and each selection by a headnote, designed to give not only background information, biographical and historical, but also something of the total context of ideas in which both selection and section take their place. At the end of each part introduction is a brief list of suggested readings, chosen especially to propose further types of classroom study. Some of the suggested readings are, like the selections themselves, expository; others are examples of imaginative literature related to the materials of the section. These readings are, we think, especially well suited to the freshman course which combines the study of composition with an introduction to literature.

The selections in *Culture and Crisis* have been selected in part in order to provide models for the student's own writing—models of felicitous and powerful style and of clear and effective organization. The book is as varied in kinds of writing as it is in subject matter: represented are formal and informal essays, journals and reminiscences, biography and autobiography, letters both personal and open, scientific writing, a book review, a drama review, a controversy, an editorial, speeches, and other forms ranging from the polemic to the journalistic report to the formal treatise. Supplemented by a good handbook for matters of grammar, *Culture and Crisis* lends itself readily to the formal study of style and rhetoric. The generic table of contents in Appendix I will provide further suggestions for using the book in this way.

Just as the collection displays a wide range of forms, so too it displays a considerable range in tone, or level of style—from the relatively informal (Wain, Tynan) to the clearly formal (Ortega, Mann), with a few examples of highly individualized style (Benn, Auden) which demonstrate some of the manifold possibilities of language. George Orwell's well-known essay "Politics and the English Language" is included in the book not only for its independent merits but also for its value in making explicit some of the principles of good writing exemplified throughout the book.

The good student who wants to do further reading on his own will find Appendix II helpful. It lists not only additional expository works by the authors represented, but also imaginative works, both poetry and prose, by those authors. Given the present abundance of paperback editions, the bibliographies constitute a kind of brief, practical reference library.

We have organized *Culture and Crisis* in what we think to be the most effective pattern for teaching, but other instructors, after using the book, may find other patterns which they prefer. The instructor may, for example, choose to follow the ramifications of a given theme—"mass society," let us say—as it is treated by Ortega, Canetti, and Huxley, and as it is illuminated by Benn, Orwell, Wilson, and others. Or he may choose to follow such a theme as "art and society," utilizing to that end not only Trilling's direct treatment of the subject but also the essays of Forster, Yeats, Camus, and Mann, the controversy on drama carried on by Tynan, Ionesco, and Dennis, and all the essays of Part Six.

Few of the selections in *Culture and Crisis* have previously appeared in college readers. (Orwell's essay is the only one to have made many such appearances.) But they lend themselves to the traditional purposes of the introductory course in English more vitally, we believe, than do a good many of the intellectually tamer pieces often found in such collections. In working with *Culture and Crisis* the student will inevitably learn something about standards of intellectual rigor (the nature of analysis, for instance, the distinctions among fact, opinion, prejudice, and judgment), but he is also likely to find himself enjoying the process. Our world is, however alarming, an exciting place, the more so the more it is understood, and the authors in this volume communicate the excitement along with the understanding.

Another characteristic of *Culture and Crisis* is the kind of international representation it affords—appropriately enough in a world whose culture is becoming increasingly and necessarily more cosmopolitan. Of its forty-five selections, thirty-one were written originally in English, six are translated from German, five from French, one from Spanish, one from Dutch, and one from Hungarian. The national origins of the authors themselves are even more varied. In addition to the Americans and Englishmen who make up the largest single blocks, two of the authors are Irish, one Australian, one Canadian, three French, three German, two Swiss, two Hungarian, one Spanish, one Dutch, one Danish, one Russian, one Rumanian, and one Bulgarian. This quality of internationalism in itself helps to reflect with fidelity the nature of the modern intellectual world.

Culture and Crisis has been carefully planned, but in one respect it betrays no design at all on the part of the editors: there is no doctrine that it undertakes to inculcate whether political, religious, economic, or cultural—unless intellectual honesty and a belief in intelligence and imagination may be conceived of as doctrine. The authors included vary widely in their beliefs, values, and emphases; the single respect in which they are united is their common faith in the human mind. The book, in short, answers no questions. But it may perhaps help to frame the questions, which is, after all, what education is all about.

F. J. W.
J. D. W.

Seattle, Washington
January 1964

CONTENTS

Part One

THE AGE OF
THE MASSES

The selections which make up the first section of this book have in common their concern with the larger social, political, and economic forces which lie behind the specific problems of our age. Most of them quite distinctly reflect the central fact of our time—that we live in a world which is, to an extent unparalleled in history, a world of mass humanity. That fact has given, throughout the past 200 years, an unprecedented urgency to the age-old human quest for justice, freedom, and equality for all men, a quest which has ceased to be exclusively the speculative task of the philosopher and moralist and now challenges a wide variety of thinkers and ordinary men as they attempt to make theory become reality.

The theory involved has not always been the same one. Democracy had its western European origin in the slow growth in England of such institutions as free speech and representative government, but any consideration of the history of England will reveal that, until relatively recent times, the English emphasis lay upon individual freedom rather than collective equality. It remained for French thinkers of the eighteenth century, Voltaire and Rousseau the most important among them, to associate with the idea of freedom the idea of equality, and it remained for the American Revolution of 1776 and the French Revolution of 1789 to make the association a concrete one. Such documents as Jefferson's Declaration of Independence and such slogans as the French Revolution's "liberty, equality, and fraternity" have bequeathed to us a complex and difficult ideal which we have not yet learned how to achieve.

The great industrial revolution which transformed the face of Europe and North America in the course of the nineteenth century helped to make possible the extraordinary population increase which is the source of our present mass society (this population increase has in itself become a modern problem, one which is given attention in the essay by Aldous Huxley later in this volume). At the same time, nineteenth-century industrialization created a new exploited class of city-dwelling factory workers and thus inevitably caused the quest for freedom and equality to shift its direction from the purely political to the primarily economic (though of course the two concerns can really only be separated for purposes of retrospective analysis). The most successful revolutions

1

of the nineteenth century were of the liberal-democratic (i.e. individualist) sort, but throughout that century a new movement exhibited steady and inevitable growth. That movement was socialism, and whether its growth should be regarded as promising or ominous is still a matter of hot debate today.

Socialism assumed several different forms: the utopianism of Fourier or Owen, the evolutionary socialism of Shaw and the Fabians, the anarchism of Bakunin, the communism of Marx and Engels. The triumphs of Marxist communism in our century have led to the present political situation, in which a world that is democratic at least in part faces a world that is communistic at least in part, and in which both worlds are convinced that they are irreconcilable enemies. The book by Edmund Wilson from which our first selection is drawn reminds us that, historically, the two systems have similar humanistic aspirations, and that both are defined to some degree by their sense of the necessity of developing an attitude toward collective man. To what extent should a man's individual freedom be limited by the needs of his fellowmen? To what extent ought collective security be modified by the ideal of unrestricted individual freedom? Our age, though it has found no answers, is shaped by its struggles with these questions.

The problems which have emerged in the age of the masses are by no means confined to the political and the economic. José Ortega y Gasset, whose *Revolt of the Masses* is one of the earliest as well as one of the most searching of the examinations of mass society, applies himself to the problem of mass culture in its broadest sense, and his observations, however disturbing, must be taken into account in any consideration of the features of modern civilization. Ortega reminds us that the achievement of liberty and equality for all may in practice mean true liberty for none and, for all, only the dubious equality of general mediocrity. His essay may meaningfully be read in connection with the one by Elias Canetti which follows it. Canetti, in his detailed and philosophical examination of the psychology of crowds, explores the idea that the crowd is more than a collection of individuals, that it is in fact an entity with its own distinguishing characteristics. The implications of crowd psychology for mass society are obvious and disturbing: as the events of the last twenty-five years have demonstrated, the crowd, with its mass identity, is often capable of horrors which few individuals could perpetrate.

Mass psychology, as Canetti points out, tends to bring into power demagogic leaders who establish totalitarian states, and such states, Alan Moorehead's report on the concentration camp at Belsen reminds us, have committed the most conspicuous crimes of our century. But, however wicked many totalitarian leaders have been as individuals, the events of our century do not allow us to lay to our souls the flattering unction that their diabolism alone is sufficient to explain completely such hideous phenomena as total war and genocide. To some extent these phenomena are the result of two factors—the sheer size of present world populations, and the existence of a military technology capable of winning victories through the annihilation or near annihilation of enemy populations. Thus, the Nazi massacre of the Jews and others was founded in the corrupt Nazi philosophy, and Stalin's wholesale destruction of uncooperative elements in Soviet society derived from the cruel logic of total collectivism. But the Allied wiping-out of whole enemy cities, culminating at the end of World War II in the British bombardment of the city of Dresden and the American atomic attacks on Hiroshima and Nagasaki, made it clear that mass society and industrial technology have combined to cheapen life to the point at which its extinction is now conceivable. Raymond Aron's appraisal of modern military tendencies recognizes that the "ultimate weapon" is only one of several developments brought about by our combination of huge populations with a hypertrophy of technological resources, and he demonstrates that modern warfare, in its varied forms, has assumed a shape different from, and in some ways more threatening than, anything in recent historical experience.

The foregoing observations may imply that the essays in Section I consistently view modern man as caught in the grip of blind, unprecedented forces which render useless both the study of past history and the purposeful application of intelligence and will to the problems of the future. Such an implication is not intended, for all of these selections, with the possible exception of Canetti's highly pessimistic study, are motivated ultimately by the conviction that man can somehow determine his own fate. Even Moorehead's report on Belsen, the most journalistic and hence the least philosophical of these pieces, clearly aims at documenting an aspect of current history so that the future may take steps to avoid its recurrence. Such a motive is overt in the essay by Toynbee, as it is indeed in that historian's entire life work. Not only does a proper understanding of the past give man an element of potential control over the future—in Toynbee's view it enables man to perceive that the *form* of current events is never really new or unique but follows patterns that characterized earlier cultures. The same point is made in a less systematic, though more entertaining, manner in Shaw's introductory notes to *Caesar and Cleopatra,* in which the dramatist persuasively argues that the human race does not undergo essential change and that significant alterations in its condition are due not to evolutionary progress but to the influence of great individuals.

The crises of our time are not indentical with those of past ages, but they are certainly not wholly without connection to them. Human problems, now as always, need to be viewed simultaneously with a sense of their uniqueness and with a sense of their typicality. Writers as varied as Ortega, Toynbee, and Shaw are aware of that necessity.

Suggested Further Readings:

Thomas Jefferson, *The Declaration of Independence*
Karl Marx and Friedrich Engels, *The Communist Manifesto*
George Bernard Shaw, *Caesar and Cleopatra*

Edmund Wilson

The last hundred years have been a time of incessant and significant social change, manifesting itself sometimes in the peaceful evolution of new political and economic institutions, sometimes in violent revolution and open class conflict. The central political phenomenon of the age has been the rise of the collectivist ideologies, ranging all the way from democratic and evolutionary socialism to revolutionary communism. These ideologies are historically the product not only of the development of industrial civilization but also of a vast increase in the world's population and the consequent emergence of the mass societies in which we live. The following selection concerns itself with one crucial episode in the history of the most powerful and extreme of these ideologies. It is taken from *To the Finland Station*, the first historical work of Edmund Wilson, one of America's foremost men of letters.

The title refers to the railroad station in Petrograd to which Lenin made his triumphal return to Russia at the outbreak of the 1917 Revolution. The subtitle, "A Study in the Writing and Acting of History," points up the unique character of the book, for it is not in any narrow sense simply an account of the history of the socialist movement. Wilson is also interested in the origins of that movement, in the personalities of the chief revolutionary figures, and in his own analysis of the systems with which they hoped to change the world.

Wilson's range, as one would expect, is necessarily wide. He begins with those intellectual and historical events which were the result of man's recognition during the eighteenth century of the fact that society is something created by man rather than the reflection of an absolute order in the universe. He shows how from this recognition there developed the all-important belief in the idea of progress through deliberate change and how this idea in turn lead eventually to the historical events of revolution. He gives attention to nineteenth century socialist thinkers of various persuasions—liberal-democratic, anarchistic, utopian socialist, and so on. Then he turns to his major subject, the development of communism, its inception in the speculative thought of Karl Marx and Friedrich Engels, its nineteenth-century struggles to make itself an active social and political force in the world, its ultimate triumph in Russia under Lenin, its many transformations since then. But Wilson's basic task throughout might be described as the double one of writing intellectual history and at the same time exploring the actual personalities of the dominant actors of that history. The chapter "The Partnership of Marx and Engels" gives a fair notion of how he goes about that task, dispassionately, incisively, showing considerable sympathy with the humanitarian and egalitarian motives of the great socialists but declining to accept any of their ideas as dogma.

THE PARTNERSHIP OF MARX AND ENGELS

In the meantime, Marx had gotten married and had taken Jenny to Paris in October, 1843. He had been reading up with his usual thoroughness on French communism and studying the French Revolution, about which he was planning to write a book.

But early in 1844 there came under his eye an essay which Engels had written from England for the *Deutsch-Französische Jahrbücher,* to which Karl Marx was also contributing. It was an original and brilliant discussion of the "political economy" of the British, which Engels on his side had been reading up. Engels held that the theories of Adam Smith and Ricardo, of MacCulloch and James Mill, were fundamentally hypocritical rationalizations of the greedy motives behind the system of private property which was destroying the British peoples: the Wealth of Nations made most people poor; Free Trade and Competition left the people still enslaved, and consolidated the monopoly of the bourgeoisie on everything that was worth having—all the philosophies of trade themselves only sanctified the huckster's fraud; the discussions of abstract value were kept abstract on purpose to avoid taking cognizance of the actual conditions under which all commercial transactions took place: the exploitation and destruction of the working class, the alternation of prosperity with crisis. Marx at once began to correspond with Engels, and he set himself to master as much of the British economists as he could find translated into French.

Engels arrived back from Lancashire about the end of August and stopped in Paris on his way to Barmen. He immediately looked up Marx, and they found that they had so much to say to one another that they spent ten days together. Their literary as well as their intellectual collaboration began from that first moment of their meeting. They had been

From *To the Finland Station* by Edmund Wilson. Copyright 1940 by Edmund Wilson. Reprinted by permission of Doubleday & Co., Inc.

working toward similar conclusions, and now they were able to supplement one another. Like the copper and zinc electrodes of the voltaic cell of which they used to debate the mystery—the conductor liquid would be Hegel diluted in the politicial atmosphere of the eve of 1848—the two young Germans between them were able to generate a current that was to give energy to new social motors. The setting-up of this Marxist current is the central event of our chronicle and one of the great intellectual events of the century; and even this electrical image is inadequate to render the organic vitality with which the Marx-Engels system in its growth was able to absorb such a variety of elements—the philosophies of three great countries, the ideas of both the working class and the cultured, the fruits of many departments of thought. Marx and Engels performed the feat of all great thinkers in summing up immense accumulations of knowledge, in combining many streams of speculation, and in endowing a new point of view with more vivid and compelling life.

It would not be worth while here to attempt to trace in detail the influence of all the thinkers that Marx and Engels laid under contribution. In a sense, such attempts are futile. The spotlighting method that I have used in this book must not be allowed to mislead the reader into assuming that great ideas are the creations of a special race of great men. I have discussed some of the conspicuous figures who gave currency to socialist ideas; and Professor Sidney Hook in his admirable *From Hegel to Marx* has indicated with exactitude the relation of Marx to his background of German philosophy. But behind these conspicuous figures were certainly sources less well-known or quite obscure: all the agitators, the politicians, the newspaper writers; the pamphlets, the conversations, the intimations; the implications of conduct deriving from inarticulate or half-unconscious thoughts, the implications of unthinking instincts.

It is appropriate, nevertheless, to point this out at this particular moment, because it was precisely the conception of intellectual movements as representative of social situations which Marx and Engels were to do so much to implant; and it may be interesting to fill in a little more completely the background of early nineteenth-century thought out of which Marx and Engels grew as well as to understand the relation of these two thinkers to one another.

The great thing that Marx and Engels and their contemporaries had gotten out of the philosophy of Hegel was the conception of historical change. Hegel had delivered his lectures on the *Philosophy of History* at Berlin University during the winter of 1822-23 (Michelet, it may be remembered, had first come in contact with Vico the next year); and, for all his abstract and mystical way of talking, he had shown a very firm grasp on the idea that the great revolutionary figures of history were not simply remarkable individuals, who moved mountains by their single wills, but the agents through which the forces of the societies behind them accomplished their unconscious purposes. Julius Caesar, says Hegel, for example, did of course fight and conquer his rivals, and destroy the constitution of Rome in order to win his own position of supremacy, but what gave him his importance for the world was the fact that he was performing the necessary feat—only possible through autocratic control—of unifying the Roman Empire.

"It was not then merely his private gain but an unconscious impulse," writes Hegel, "that occasioned the accomplishment of that for which the time was ripe. Such are all great historical men—whose own particular aims involve those large issues which are the will of the World-Spirit. They may be called Heroes, inasmuch as they have derived their purposes and their vocation, not from the calm, regular course of things, sanctioned by the existing order; but from a concealed fount—one which has not attained to phenomenal, present existence—from that inner Spirit, still hidden beneath the surface, which, impinging on the outer world as on a shell, bursts it in pieces, because it is another kernel than that which belonged to the shell in question. They present themslves, therefore, as men who appear to draw the impulse of their life from themselves; and whose deeds have produced a condition of things and a complex of historical relations which appear to be only *their* interest, and *their* work.

"Such individuals have had no consciousness of the general Idea they were unfolding, while prosecuting those aims of theirs; on the contrary, they were practical, political men. But at the same time they were thinking men, who had an insight into the requirements of the time—*what was ripe for development*. This was the very Truth for their age, for their world; the species next in order, so to speak, and which was already formed in the womb of time. It was theirs to know this nascent principle; the necessary, directly sequent step in progress, which their world was to take; to make this their aim, and to expend their energy in promoting it. World-historical men—the Heroes of an epoch—must, therefore, be recognized as its clear-sighted ones; *their* deeds, *their* words are the best of that time. Great men have formed their purposes to satisfy themselves, not others. Whatever prudent designs and counsels they might have learned from others, would be the more limited and inconsistent features in their career; for it was they who best understood affairs; it was they from whom *others* learned and approved—or at least acquiesced in—their policy. For that Spirit which had taken this fresh step in history is the inmost soul of all individuals; but abides in a state of unconsciousness from which the great men in question aroused it. Their fellows, therefore, follow these soul-leaders; for they feel the irresistible power of their own inner spirit thus embodied."

We shall examine a little later the peculiar dynamics of Hegel's conception of historical change. It is enough to note further for the moment that he regarded each of the epochs of human society as constituting an indivisible whole. "We shall have to show," he announces, "that the constitution adopted by a people makes one substance, one spirit, with its religion, its art and philosophy, or, at least, with its conceptions and thoughts: its culture generally; not to expatiate upon the additional influences, *ab extra,* of climate, of neighbors, of its place in the world. A State is an individual totality, of which you cannot select any particular aspect, not even such a supremely important one as its political constitution, and deliberate and decide respecting it in that isolated form."

But where Hegel had tended to assume that the development of history through revolution, the progressive realization of the "Idea," had culminated in the contemporary Prussian state, Marx and Engels, accepting the revolutionary progress but repudiating the divine Idea, looked for a consummation of change to the future, when the realization of the communist idea should have resulted from the next revolution.

They had by this time their own new notions about communism. They had taken stock of their predecessors and, with their own sharp and realistic minds, they had lopped off the sentimentality and fantasy which had surrounded the practical perceptions of the utopians. From Saint-Simon they accepted as valid his discovery that modern politics was simply the science of regulating production; from Fourier, his arraignment of the bourgeois, his consciousness of the ironic contrast between "the frenzy of speculation, the spirit of all-devouring commercialism," which were rampant under the reign of the bourgeoisie and "the brilliant promises of the Enlightenment" which had preceded them; from Owen, the realization that the factory system must be the root of the social revolution. But they saw that the mistake of the utopian socialists had been to imagine that socialism was to be imposed upon society from above by disinterested members of the upper classes. The bourgeoisie as a whole, they believed, could not be induced to go against its own interests. The educator, as Marx was to write in his *Theses on Feuerbach,* must, after all, first have been educated: he is not really confronting disciples with a doctrine that has been supplied him by God; he is merely directing a movement of which he is himself a member and which energizes him and gives him his purpose. Marx and Engels combined the aims of the utopians with Hegel's process of organic development. By the mid-century they were thus able to see quite clearly, as even John Humphrey Noyes did not do, that it was impossible for small communist units by themselves to effect the salvation of society or even to survive in the teeth of the commercial system; that it was not merely unfortunate accidents and disagreeable personal relations which had rendered the American communist movement futile but its ignorance of the mechanics of the class struggle.

Of this class struggle Marx had learned first from his reading of the French historians after he had come to Paris. Augustin Thierry in his *History of the Conquest of England,* published in 1825, had presented the Norman Conquest in terms of a class struggle between the conquerors and the Saxons. Guizot, in his *History of the English Revolution,* had shown, from the bourgeois point of view, the struggle between the middle class and the monarchy.

But it remained to root the class struggle in economics. We have seen how Friedrich Engels had come to appreciate the importance of economics as the result of his experience in Manchester. Karl Marx owed more to his reading. The idea of the fundamental importance of economic interests was not new in the eighteen-forties. A French lawyer named Antoine Barnave, who had been president of the revolutionary Assembly of 1790, had asserted that the difference between classes was the result of economic inequalities, that the class which was in power at any epoch not only made laws for the whole of society in order to guarantee its own hold on its property but also "directed its habits and created its prejudices," that society was constantly changing under the pressure of economic necessities, and that the rising and triumphant bourgeoisie which had displaced the feudal nobility would in turn produce a new aristocracy. Barnave, who was a moderate in politics and compromised himself with the royal family, was guillotined in 1793. A collected edition of his writings was published in 1843; but Marx never seems to have mentioned him, and it is not known whether he had ever read him. In any case, the thought of the period was converging during the first years of the forties toward the Marxist point of view. Friedrich List, the patriotic German economist, had published in 1841 his work on *The National System of Political Economy,* in which he had described the development of society in terms of its industrial phases; and in 1842 a French communist named Dézamy, a former associate of Cabet, published his *Code de la Communauté.* Karl Marx had read Dézamy at Cologne. This writer had criticized Cabet for believing that anything could be done for labor by invoking the aid of the bourgeoisie, and, accepting the brute fact of the class struggle, had projected a somewhat new kind of community, based on materialism, atheism and science. Though Dézamy had not as yet arrived at any ideas about proletarian tactics, he was sure that the proletariat, among whom he included the peasants, must unite and liberate itself. And it may be noted that the importance of the bottom class had already been emphasized by Babeuf when he had declared in the course of his defense that "the mass of the expropriated, of the proletarians" was generally "agreed to be frightful," that it constituted now "the majority of a nation totally rotten."

In the December of 1843, Marx had written for the *Deutsch-Fran-zösische Jahrbücher* a *Critique of the Hegelian Philosophy of Law,* in which he had postulated the proletariat as the class which was to play the new Hegelian role in effecting the emancipation of Germany: "A class in *radical chains,* one of the classes of bourgeois society which does not belong to bourgeois society, an order which brings the break-up of all orders, a sphere which has a universal character by virtue of its universal suffering and lays claim to no *particular right,* because no *particular wrong,* but complete wrong, is being perpetrated against it, which can no longer invoke an *historical* title but only a *human* title, which stands not in a one-sided antagonism to the consequences of the German state but in an absolute antagonism to its assumptions, a sphere, finally, which cannot emancipate itself without freeing itself from all the other spheres of society and thereby freeing all these other spheres themselves, which in a word, as it represents the *complete forfeiting* of humanity itself, can only redeem itself through the *redemption of the whole of humanity.* The *proletariat* represents the dissolution of society as a special order."

Yet even though Marx has got so far, the proletariat remains for him still something in the nature of a philosophical abstraction. The primary emotional motivation in the role which he assigns to the proletariat seems to have been borrowed from his own position as a Jew. "The social emancipation of the Jew is the emancipation of society from Judaism"; "a sphere, finally, which cannot emancipate itself without emancipating all the other spheres of society"—these are the conclusions in almost identical words of two essays written one after the other and published, as it were, side by side. Marx, on the one hand, knew nothing of the industrial proletariat and, on the other hand, refused to take Judaism seriously or to participate in current discussions of the Jewish problem from the point of view of the special case of Jewish culture, holding that the special position of the Jew was vitally involved with his money-lending and banking, and that it would be impossible for him to dissociate himself from these until the system of which they were part should be abolished. The result was that the animus and rebellion which were due to the social disabilities of the Jew as well as the moral insight and the world vision which were derived from his religious tradition were transferred in all their formidable power to an imaginary proletariat.

Perhaps the most important service that Engels performed for Marx at this period was to fill in the blank face and figure of Marx's abstract proletarian and to place him in a real house and real factory. Engels had brought back from England the materials for his book on *The Condition of the Working Class in England in 1844,* and he now sat down at once to get it written. Here was the social background which would make Marx's vision authentic; and here were cycles of industrial prosperity which always collapsed into industrial depressions—due, as Engels could see, to the blind appetites of the competing manufacturers—and which could only result in a general crash: that millennial catastrophe that for Marx was ultimately to dethrone the gods and set the wise spirit of man in their place.

And for Engels, on his side, here in Marx was the backing of moral conviction and of intellectual strength which was to enable him to keep his compass straight in his relation to that contemporary society whose crimes he understood so well, but out of which he himself had grown, and to which he was still organically bound as Marx was not. Besides, Marx had more weight and more will. Engels wrote with lucidity and ease; he had sensibility and measure and humor. He is so much more like a French writer of the Enlightenment—something between a Condorcet and a Diderot—than a philosopher of the German school that one is inclined to accept the tradition that his family had French Protestant blood. This young man without academic training was an immensely accomplished fellow: he had already learned to write English so well that he was able to contribute to Robert Owen's paper; and his French was as good as his English. He had a facility in acquiring information and a journalist's sense of how things were going; his collaborator Marx used to say that Engels was always ahead of him. But Engels had not Marx's drive; it is what we miss in his writing. From the beginning Marx is able to find such quarrel in matters like the wood-theft debates that he can shake us with indignation against all violators of human relations; while Engels, with his larger experience of the cruelties and degradations of industrial life, does not—even in *The Condition of the Working Class in England*— rouse us to protest or to fight but tends rather to resolve the conflict in an optimistic feeling about the outcome. "Marx was a genius," wrote Engels later. "The rest of us were talented at best."

It is perhaps not indulging too far the current tendency toward this kind of speculation to suggest that Marx took over for Engels something of the prestige of paternal authority which the younger man had rejected in his own father. There was always something boyish about Engels: he writes Marx in the September of 1847, when he is twenty-seven, that he does not want to accept the vice-presidency of one of their communist committees, because he looks "so frightfully youthful." Young Friedrich had been rebelling since his teens against old Caspar Engels' combination of the serious crassness of business with the intolerance of religion; but old Engels' decisions for his son had hitherto determined his practical career. And, in spite of Friedrich's final enfranchisement from theology, some of the fervor of his father's faith had nevertheless been communicated to him. He had grown up in Barmen-Elberfeld under the pulpit of the great Calvinist preacher, Friedrich Wilhelm Krummacher, who with an eloquence that Engels had found impressive had used to alternate the legends of the Bible and a majestic oratory drawn from its language with illustrations from ordinary life and who had harrowed and subdued his congregations with the terrible Calvinist logic, which led them either to damnation or grace. Karl Marx was a great moralist, too, and, on occasion, a formidable preacher. He seems to have provided the young apostate from Pietism with a new spiritual center of gravity.

When Engels went back to Barmen, at any rate, to live with his family and work in the family business, he continued to correspond with Marx; and he grew more and more dissatisfied and uncomfortable in an impatience which this correspondence must have fed.

He had evidently contracted some sort of engagement with a young lady of his own class and locality before he had left Barmen for Manchester; and now this seems to involve in his mind—his letters to Marx leave it all rather dark—the obligation to go to work for the firm. "I have let myself in through the persuasions of my brother-in-law and the melancholy faces of my parents for at least an attempt at this filthy trade, and for fourteen days now I've been working in the office—the outlook in connection with my love affair has also brought me to it; but I was depressed before I started in: money-grubbing is too frightful; Barmen is too frightful, the waste of time is too frightful, and above all it is too frightful to continue to be, not merely a bourgeois, but actually a manufacturer, a bourgeois working against the proletariat. A few days in my old man's factory have compelled me to recognize the horror of it, which I'd rather overlooked before. . . . If it weren't for the fact that I apply myself every day to getting down on paper in my book the most dreadful accounts of English conditions, I believe I should have gone to seed already, but this has at least kept the rage in my bones. One can very well be a communist and yet keep up a bourgeois position, if only one *doesn't write;* but to work at serious communist propaganda and at industry and trade at the same time—that's really absolutely impossible."

He was holding working-class meetings with Moses Hess, who had become his ally in the Wuppertal; and they were getting out a communist paper in Elberfeld. As the weeks go on, his letters to Marx become irradiated by his characteristic hopefulness. One found communists everywhere now, he wrote.

But now old Engels became indignant, tragic. He could not stand Friedrich's associating with Hess, he could not stand his preaching communism in Barmen. "If it were not for the sake of my mother, who has a sweet and human nature and is only powerless against my father, and whom I really love, it would never occur to me for a moment to make even the pettiest concession to my fanatical and despotic old man. But my mother is gradually grieving herself sick and gets a headache that lasts for eight days every time she is specially worried about me—so I can't endure it any longer, I must get away, and I hardly know how I'm going to be able to get through the few weeks that I'll still have to stay."

Finally, he learned that the police were lying in wait for him, and he left Barmen in the spring of '45. There is a passage in one of his letters from which it is possible to form the conjecture that he had been rather hoping to get into trouble in order to be forced to part with, as well as perhaps to be compromised in the eyes of, the young lady to whom he was somehow committed.

He joined Karl Marx in Brussels. The latter had himself had to leave Paris as a result of expulsion from France at the insistence of the German government, which was worried by the activities in Paris of revolutionary German refugees, and on an order from that Guizot, now Prime Minister, who had helped teach Marx the mechanics of the class struggle.

Then Engels went straight back to Manchester to find his friend Mary Burns again and to bring her over to France. He took Karl Marx along on the trip—exhibited to him the activities of Manchester and introduced him to the work of the English political economists. He reminded him a quarter of a century later of how they had used to look out through the colored panes of the bay-window of the Manchester library on weather that was always fine. It had been the light of that human intellect which they felt was now coming to maturity and which would vindicate the dignity of man, in the midst of that inhuman horror of filthiness and deformity and disease that hemmed the city in.

José Ortega y Gasset

Ortega y Gasset, one of the most important figures whom twentieth-century Spain has contributed to the world of the spirit, was born in Madrid in 1883, studied philosophy at several universities in Germany, and then became a professor of philosophy in his native country. In 1936, at the time of the Spanish Civil War, his Republican sympathies obliged him to flee the country, but in 1949 he returned to Spain and lived there until his death in 1955.

Ortega has attained distinction both as a philosopher and as a prose stylist, and his masterpiece, *The Revolt of the Masses* (1930), claims attention on both grounds. Simply put, the thesis of this volume, summarized in its opening chapter, "The Coming of the Masses," is that the formidable fact of our time is the rise of mass man to complete social and political domination, a domination which "crushes beneath it" dissent, excellence, culture, or any of the other features peculiar to the gifted minority of mankind — note how important Ortega's careful definitions of such terms as "masses" and "minority" are to a proper understanding of his thought. Like many other heirs to the humanist tradition, Ortega cannot regard the world-wide development of an aggressive mass culture as a simple or desirable triumph of democracy; for him it inevitably denotes, under whatever name it disguises itself, not only totalitarian government of one sort or another but also the destruction of the traditions of responsible and liberal individualism with which Western civilization is largely identified.

In its lucidity, firmness, and precision, Ortega's prose is an excellent example of formal style, and it reminds us that good formal writing is never ostentatious or stilted or lacking in immediacy. Rather, the formal style, in its concentration on the thought to be expressed, is usually less likely to be affected or foolish than are the various types of informality frequently attempted by inexperienced writers. In his mastery of such a style, as in his unflinching willingness to pursue the logical implications of his perceptions, Ortega is true to the finest traditions of the national culture from which he sprang; in the learning and scope of his observations he gives evidence of the enlightened cosmopolitanism which formed him. The thirty years which have elapsed since the appearance of *The Revolt of the Masses* have only served to emphasize the dilemma which he so searchingly examines in those pages.

*T*HE COMING OF THE MASSES

There is one fact which, whether for good or ill, is of utmost importance in the public life of Europe at the present moment. This fact is the accession of the masses to complete social power. As the masses, by definition, neither should nor can direct their own personal existence, and still less rule society in general, this fact means that actually Europe is suffering from the greatest crisis that can afflict peoples, nations, and civilization. Such a crisis has occurred more than once in history. Its characteristics and its consequences are well known. So also is its name. It is called the rebellion of the masses. In order to understand this formidable fact, it is important from the start to avoid giving to the words "rebellion," "masses," and "social power" a meaning exclusively or primarily political. Public life is not solely political, but equally, and even primarily, intellectual, moral, economic, religious; it comprises all our collective habits, including our fashions both of dress and of amusement.

Perhaps the best line of approach to this historical phenomenon may be found by turning our attention to a visual experience, stressing one

Reprinted from *The Revolt of the Masses* by Jose Ortega y Gasset. By permission of W. W. Norton & Company, Inc. Copyright 1932 by W. W. Norton & Company, Inc. and renewed 1960 by Teresa Carey.

aspect of our epoch which is plain to our very eyes. This fact is quite simple to enunciate, though not to analyse. I shall call it the fact of agglomeration, of "plenitude." Towns are full of people, houses full of tenants, hotels full of guests, trains full of travellers, cafés full of customers, parks full of promenaders, consulting-rooms of famous doctors full of patients, theatres full of spectators, and beaches full of bathers. What previously was, in general, no problem, now begins to be an everyday one, namely, to find room.

That is all. Can there be any fact simpler, more patent, more constant in actual life? Let us now pierce the plain surface of this observation and we shall be surprised to see how there wells forth an unexpected spring in which the white light of day, of our actual day, is broken up into its rich chromatic content. What is it that we see, and the sight of which causes us so much surprise? We see the multitude, as such, in possession of the places and the instruments created by civilization. The slightest reflection will then make us surprised at our own surprise. What about it? Is this not the ideal state of things? The theatre has seats to be occupied—in other words, so that the house may be full—and now they are overflowing; people anxious to use them are left standing outside. Though the fact be quite logical and natural, we cannot but recognize that this did not happen before and that now it does; consequently, there has been a change, an innovation, which justifies, at least for the first moment, our surprise.

To be surprised, to wonder, is to begin to understand. This is the sport, the luxury, special to the intellectual man. The gesture characteristic of his tribe consists in looking at the world with eyes wide open in wonder. Everything in the world is strange and marvellous to well-open eyes. This faculty of wonder is the delight refused to your football fan, and on the other hand, is the one which leads the intellectual man through life in the perpetual ecstasy of the visionary. His special attribute is the wonder of the eyes. Hence it was that the ancients gave Minerva her owl, the bird with ever-dazzled eyes.

Agglomeration, fullness, was not frequent before. Why then is it now? The components of the multitudes around us have not sprung from nothing. Approximately the same number of people existed fifteen years ago. Indeed, after the war[1] it might seem natural that their number should be less. Nevertheless, it is here we come up against the first important point. The individuals who made up these multitudes existed, but not *qua* multitude. Scattered about the world in small groups, or solitary, they lived a life, to all appearances, divergent, dissociate, apart. Each individual or small group occupied a place, its own, in country, village, town, or quarter of the great city. Now, suddenly, they appear as an

1 Of 1914-18.

agglomeration, and looking in any direction our eyes meet with the multitudes. Not only in any direction, but precisely in the best places, the relatively refined creations of human culture, previously reserved to lesser groups, in a word, to minorities. The multitude has suddenly become visible, installing itself in the preferential positions in society. Before, if it existed, it passed unnoticed, occupying the background of the social stage; now it has advanced to the footlights and is the principal character. There are no longer protagonists; there is only the chorus.

The concept of the multitude is quantitative and visual. Without changing its nature, let us translate it into terms of sociology. We then meet with the notion of the "social mass." Society is always a dynamic unity of two component factors: minorities and masses. The minorities are individuals or groups of individuals which are specially qualified. The mass is the assemblage of persons not specially qualified. By masses, then, is not to be understood, solely or mainly, "the working masses." The mass is the average man. In this way what was mere quantity—the multitude—is converted into a qualitative determination: it becomes the common social quality, man as undifferentiated from other men, but as repeating in himself a generic type. What have we gained by this conversion of quantity into quality? Simply this: by means of the latter we understand the genesis of the former. It is evident to the verge of platitude that the normal formation of a multitude implies the coincidence of desires, ideas, ways of life, in the individuals who constitute it. It will be objected that this is just what happens with every social group, however select it may strive to be. This is true; but there is an essential difference. In those groups which are characterized by not being multitude and mass, the effective coincidence of its members is based on some desire, idea, or ideal, which of itself excludes the great number. To form a minority, of whatever kind, it is necessary beforehand that each member separate himself from the multitude for *special*, relatively personal, reasons. Their coincidence with the others who form the minority is, then, secondary, posterior to their having each adopted an attitude of singularity, and is consequently, to a large extent, a coincidence in not coinciding. There are cases in which this singularising character of the group appears in the light of day: those English groups, which style themselves "nonconformists," where we have the grouping together of those who agree only in their disagreement in regard to the limitless multitude. This coming together of the minority precisely in order to separate themselves from the majority is a necessary ingredient in the formation of every minority. Speaking of the limited public which listened to a musician of refinement, Mallarmé wittily says that this public by its presence in small numbers stressed the absence of the multitude.

Strictly speaking, the mass, as a psychological fact, can be defined without waiting for individuals to appear in mass formation. In the presence of one individual we can decide whether he is "mass" or not. The mass is all that which sets no value on itself—good or ill—based on specific grounds, but which feels itself "just like everybody," and nevertheless is not concerned about it; is, in fact, quite happy to feel itself as one with everybody else. Imagine a humble-minded man who, having tried to estimate his own worth on specific grounds—asking himself if he has any talent for this or that, if he excels in any direction—realises that he possesses no quality of excellence. Such a man will feel that he is mediocre and commonplace, ill-gifted, but will not feel himself "mass."

When one speaks of "select minorities" it is usual for the evil-minded to twist the sense of this expression, pretending to be unaware that the select man is not the petulant person who thinks himself superior to the rest, but the man who demands more of himself than the rest, even though he may not fulfil in his person those higher exigencies. For there is no doubt that the most radical division that it is possible to make of humanity is that which splits it into two classes of creatures: those who make great demands on themselves, piling up difficulties and duties; and those who demand nothing special of themselves, but for whom to live is to be every moment what they already are, without imposing on themselves any effort towards perfection; mere buoys that float on the waves. This reminds me that orthodox Buddhism is composed of two distinct religions: one, more rigorous and difficult, the other easier and more trivial: the Mahayana—"great vehicle" or "great path"—and the Hinayana—"lesser vehicle" or "lesser path." The decisive matter is whether we attach our life to one or the other vehicle, to a maximum or a minimum of demands upon ourselves.

The division of society into masses and select minorities is, then, not a division into social classes, but into classes of men, and cannot coincide with the hierarchic separation of "upper" and "lower" classes. It is, of course, plain that in these "upper" classes, when and as long as they really are so, there is much more likelihood of finding men who adopt the "great vehicle,"[1] whereas the "lower" classes normally comprise individuals of minus quality. But, strictly speaking, within both these social classes, there are to be found mass and genuine minority. As we shall see, a characteristic of our times is the predominance, even in groups traditionally selective, of the mass and the vulgar. Thus, in the intellectual life, which of its essence requires and presupposes qualification, one can note the progressive triumph of the pseudo-intellectual, unqualified, unqualifiable, and, by their very mental texture, disqualified. Similarly, in the surviving groups of the "nobility," male and female. On the other hand, it is not rare to find to-day amongst working men, who before might be taken as

[1] It is actually the Hinayana, or "lesser vehicle," that is the more rigorous.—*Ed.*

the best example of what we are calling "mass," nobly disciplined minds.

There exist then, in society, operations, activities, and functions of the most diverse order, which are of their very nature special, and which consequently cannot be properly carried out without special gifts. For example: certain pleasures of an artistic and refined character, or again the functions of government and of political judgment in public affairs. Previously these special activities were exercised by qualified minorities, or at least by those who claimed such qualification. The mass asserted no right to intervene in them; they realised that if they wished to intervene they would necessarily have to acquire those special qualities and cease being mere mass. They recognized their place in a healthy dynamic social system.

If we now revert to the facts indicated at the start, they will appear clearly as the heralds of a changed attitude in the mass. They all indicate that the mass has decided to advance to the foreground of social life, to occupy the places, to use the instruments and to enjoy the pleasures hitherto reserved to the few. It is evident, for example, that the places were never intended for the multitude, for their dimensions are too limited, and the crowd is continuously overflowing; thus manifesting to our eyes and in the clearest manner the new phenomenon: the mass, without ceasing to be mass, is supplanting the minorities.

No one, I believe, will regret that people are to-day enjoying themselves in greater measure and numbers than before, since they have now both the desire and the means of satisfying it. The evil lies in the fact that this decision taken by the masses to assume the activities proper to the minorities is not, and cannot be, manifested solely in the domain of pleasure, but that it is a general feature of our time. Thus—to anticipate what we shall see later—I believe that the political innovations of recent times signify nothing less than the political domination of the masses. The old democracy was tempered by a generous dose of liberalism and of enthusiasm for law. By serving these principles the individual bound himself to maintain a severe discipline over himself. Under the shelter of liberal principles and the rule of law, minorities could live and act. Democracy and law—life in common under the law—were synonymous. To-day we are witnessing the triumphs of a hyperdemocracy in which the mass acts directly, outside the law, imposing its aspirations and its desires by means of material pressure. It is a false interpretation of the new situation to say that the mass has grown tired of politics and handed over the exercise of it to specialised persons. Quite the contrary. That was what happened previously; that was democracy. The mass took it for granted that after all, in spite of their defects and weaknesses, the minorities understood a little more of public problems than it did itself. Now, on the other hand, the mass believes that it has the right to impose and to give force of law to notions born in the café. I doubt whether there have been other periods in history in which the multitude has come to govern more directly than in our own. That is why I speak of hyperdemocracy.

The same thing is happening in other orders, particularly in the intellectual. I may be mistaken, but the present-day writer, when he takes his pen in hand to treat a subject which he has studied deeply, has to bear in mind that the average reader, who has never concerned himself with this subject, if he reads does so with the view, not of learning something from the writer, but rather, of pronouncing judgment on him when he is not in agreement with the commonplaces that the said reader carries in his head. If the individuals who make up the mass believed themselves specially qualified, it would be a case merely of personal error, not a sociological subversion. *The characteristic of the hour is that the commonplace mind, knowing itself to be commonplace, has the assurance to proclaim the rights of the commonplace and to impose them wherever it will.* As they say in the United States: "to be different is to be indecent." The mass crushes beneath it everything that is different, everything that is excellent, individual, qualified and select. Anybody who is not like everybody, who does not think like everybody, runs the risk of being eliminated. And it is clear, of course, that this "everybody" is not "everybody." "Everybody" was normally the complex unity of the mass and the divergent, specialized minorities. Nowadays, "everybody" is the mass alone. Here we have the formidable fact of our times, described without any concealment of the brutality of its features.

Elias Canetti

The relationship that exists between crowds and power, one of the most crucial and bewildering of twentieth century phenomena, can be regarded from many points of view: the social, psychological, historical, political. Elias Canetti, in his recent (1963) and controversial book, *Crowds and Power,* attempts to regard it from virtually every possible point of view and to reach a number of conclusions about crowd situations and their tendency to thrust into sudden power leaders who are ill-equipped to rule but who do in fact rule with a despotism unmatched in earlier periods of history.

Canetti's own life has given him an ample basis for direct personal observation of crowd behavior and its connections to power. Born in Bulgaria in 1905, he moved to Vienna as a child and was living there with his family at the outbreak of World War I. (There he and his two brothers were once caught up in a hostile crowd and beaten by it; he believes his interest in crowds may go back to this event.) After the war he lived in Germany; this was during the period of the disastrous inflation, a disrupting social experience which Canetti believes had more to do with the perversion of values represented by Nazism than did the war itself. Later he returned to Vienna and took his Ph.D. at the University. He remained in that city, with frequent long visits to Paris and Berlin, until eight months after the *Anschluss* brought the Nazis to power, when he moved to England, where he now lives.

Crowds and Power, however, is not a personal account. It is based on twenty-five years of research and reflection as well as on observation and is a long and serious formal treatise, difficult to classify, belonging as much to cultural anthropology as to social history. Our selection is taken from the beginning of the book; it is there that Canetti lays down certain basic premises from which he will elaborate his theories. As in the rest of the book, he here divides his material into small sections which he identifies with caption titles, a useful aid to clarity in any extended examination of complicated material. Canetti's comments, nearly always provocative and often original, raise some startling questions about man's nature and indirectly touch on every aspect of the contemporary scene. The quiet, scholarly tone of voice adds an ironic emphasis to the content.

THE CROWD

.........The Fear of being Touched

There is nothing that man fears more than the touch of the unknown. He wants to *see* what is reaching towards him, and to be able to recognize or at least classify it. Man always tends to avoid physical contact with anything strange. In the dark, the fear of an unexpected touch can mount to panic. Even clothes give insufficient security: it is easy to tear them and pierce through to the naked, smooth, defenceless flesh of the victim.

All the distances which men create round themselves are dictated by this fear. They shut themselves in houses which no-one may enter, and only there feel some measure of security. The fear of burglars is not only the fear of being robbed, but also the fear of a sudden and unexpected clutch out of the darkness.

The repugnance to being touched remains with us when we go about among people; the way we move in a busy street, in restaurants, trains or buses, is governed by it. Even when we are standing next to them and are able to watch and examine them closely, we avoid actual contact if we can. If we do not avoid it, it is because we feel attracted to someone; and then it is we who make the approach.

The promptness with which apology is offered for an unintentional

From *Crowds and Power* by Elias Canetti. © Claassen Verlag, Hamburg 1960; © English translation: Victor Gollancz Ltd. 1962. Reprinted by permission of The Viking Press, Inc.

contact, the tension with which it is awaited, our violent and sometimes even physical reaction when it is not forthcoming, the antipathy and hatred we feel for the offender, even when we cannot be certain who it is—the whole knot of shifting and intensely sensitive reactions to an alien touch—proves that we are dealing here with a human propensity as deep-seated as it is alert and insidious; something which never leaves a man when he has once established the boundaries of his personality. Even in sleep, when he is far more unguarded, he can all too easily be disturbed by a touch.

It is only in a crowd that man can become free of this fear of being touched. That is the only situation in which the fear changes into its opposite. The crowd he needs is the dense crowd, in which body is pressed to body; a crowd, too, whose psychical constitution is also dense, or compact, so that he no longer notices who it is that presses against him. As soon as a man has surrendered himself to the crowd, he ceases to fear its touch. Ideally, all are equal there; no distinctions count, not even that of sex. The man pressed against him is the same as himself. He feels him as he feels himself. Suddenly it is as though everything were happening in one and the same body. This is perhaps one of the reasons why a crowd seeks to close in on itself: it wants to rid each individual as completely as possible of the fear of being touched. The more fiercely people press together, the more certain they feel that they do not fear each other. This reversal of the fear of being touched belongs to the nature of crowds. The feeling of relief is most striking where the density of the crowd is greatest.

.........The Open and the Closed Crowd

The crowd, suddenly there where there was nothing before, is a mysterious and universal phenomenon. A few people may have been standing together—five, ten or twelve, no more; nothing has been announced, nothing is expected. Suddenly everywhere is black with people and more come streaming from all sides as though streets had only one direction. Most of them do not know what has happened and, if questioned, have no answer; but they hurry to be there where most other people are. There is a determination in their movement which is quite different from the expression of ordinary curiosity. It seems as though the movement of some of them transmits itself to the others. But that is not all; they have a goal which is there before they can find words for it. This goal is the blackest spot where most people are gathered.

This is the extreme form of the spontaneous crowd and much more will have to be said about it later. In its innermost core it is not quite as spontaneous as it appears, but, except for these 5, 10 or 12 people with whom actually it originates, it is everywhere spontaneous. As soon as it exists at all, it wants to consist of *more* people: the urge to grow is the first and supreme attribute of the crowd. It wants to seize everyone within reach; anything shaped like a human being can join it. The natural crowd is the *open* crowd; there are no limits whatever to its growth; it does not recognize houses, doors or locks and those who shut themselves in are suspect. "Open" is to be understood here in the fullest sense of the word; it means open everywhere and in any direction. The open crowd exists so long as it grows; it disintegrates as soon as it stops growing.

For just as suddenly as it originates, the crowd disintegrates. In its spontaneous form it is a sensitive thing. The openness which enables it to grow is, at the same time, its danger. A foreboding of threatening disintegration is always alive in the crowd. It seeks, through rapid increase, to avoid this for as long as it can; it absorbs everyone, and, because it does, must ultimately fall to pieces.

In contrast to the open crowd which can grow indefinitely and which is of universal interest because it may spring up anywhere, there is the *closed* crowd.

The closed crowd renounces growth and puts the stress on permanence. The first thing to be noticed about it is that it has a boundary. It establishes itself by accepting its limitation. It creates a space for itself which it will fill. This space can be compared to a vessel into which liquid is being poured and whose capacity is known. The entrances to this space are limited in number, and only these entrances can be used; the boundary is respected whether it consists of stone, of solid wall, or of some special act of acceptance, or entrance fee. Once the space is completely filled, no one else is allowed in. Even if there is an overflow, the important thing is always the dense crowd in the closed room; those standing outside do not really belong.

The boundary prevents disorderly increase, but it also makes it more difficult for the crowd to disperse and so postpones its dissolution. In this way the crowd sacrifices its chance of growth, but gains in staying power. It is protected from outside influences which could become hostile and dangerous and it sets its hope on *repetition*. It is the expectation of reassembly which enables its members to accept each dispersal. The building is waiting for them; it exists for their sake and, so long as it is there, they will be able to meet in the same manner. The space is theirs, even during the ebb, and in its emptiness it reminds them of the flood.

. . . . **The Discharge**

The most important occurrence within the crowd is the *discharge*. Before this the crowd does not actually exist; it is the discharge which creates it.

This is the moment when all who belong to the crowd get rid of their differences and feel equal.

These differences are mainly imposed from outside; they are distinctions of rank, status and property. Men as individuals are always conscious of these distinctions; they weigh heavily on them and keep them firmly apart from one another. A man stands by himself on a secure and well defined spot, his every gesture asserting his right to keep others at a distance. He stands there like a windmill on an enormous plain, moving expressively; and there is nothing between him and the next mill. All life, so far as he knows it, is laid out in distances—the house in which he shuts himself and his property, the positions he holds, the rank he desires— all these serve to create distances, to confirm and extend them. Any free or large gesture of approach towards another human being is inhibited. Impulse and counter impulse ooze away as in a desert. No man can get near another, nor reach his height. In every sphere of life, firmly established hierarchies prevent him touching anyone more exalted than himself, or descending, except in appearance, to anyone lower. In different societies the distances are differently balanced against each other, the stress in some lying on birth, in others on occupation or property.

I do not intend to characterize these hierarchies in detail here, but it is essential to know that they exist everywhere and everywhere gain a decisive hold on men's minds and determine their behaviour to each other. But the satisfaction of being higher in rank than others does not compensate for the loss of freedom of movement. Man petrifies and darkens in the distances he has created. He drags at the burden of them, but cannot move. He forgets that it is self-inflicted, and longs for liberation. But how, alone, can he free himself? Whatever he does, and however determined he is, he will always find himself among others who thwart his efforts. So long as they hold fast to *their* distances, he can never come any nearer to them.

Only together can men free themselves from their burdens of distance; and this, precisely, is what happens in a crowd. During the discharge distinctions are thrown off and all feel *equal*. In that density, where there is scarcely any space between, and body presses against body, each man is as near the other as he is to himself; and an immense feeling of relief ensues. It is for the sake of this blessed moment, when no-one is greater or better than another, that people become a crowd.

But the moment of discharge, so desired and so happy, contains its own danger. It is based on an illusion; the people who suddenly feel equal have not really become equal; nor will they *feel* equal for ever. They return to their separate houses, they lie down on their own beds, they keep their possessions and their names. They do not cast out their relations nor run away from their families. Only true conversion leads men to give up their old associations and form new ones. Such associations, which by their very nature are only able to accept a limited number of members, have to secure their continuance by rigid rules. Such groups I call crowd crystals. Their function will be described later.

But the crowd, as such, disintegrates. It has a presentiment of this and fears it. It can only go on existing if the process of discharge is continued with new people who join it. Only the growth of the crowd prevents those who belong to it creeping back under their private burdens.

. . . . Destructiveness

The destructiveness of the crowd is often mentioned as its most conspicuous quality, and there is no denying the fact that it can be observed everywhere, in the most diverse countries and civilizations. It is discussed and disapproved of, but never really explained.

The crowd particularly likes destroying houses and objects: breakable objects like window panes, mirrors, pictures and crockery; and people tend to think that it is the fragility of these objects which stimulates the destructiveness of the crowd. It is true that the noise of destruction adds to its satisfaction; the banging of windows and the crashing of glass are the robust sounds of fresh life, the cries of something new-born. It is easy to evoke them and that increases their popularity. Everything shouts together; the din is the applause of objects. There seems to be a special need for this kind of noise at the beginning of events, when the crowd is still small and little or nothing has happened. The noise is a promise of the reinforcements the crowd hopes for, and a happy omen for deeds to come. But it would be wrong to suppose that the ease with which things can be broken is the decisive factor in the situation. Sculptures of solid stone have been mutilated beyond recognition; Christians have destroyed the heads and arms of Greek Gods and reformers and revolutionaries have hauled down the statues of Saints, sometimes from dangerous heights, though often the stone they wanted to destroy has been so hard that they have achieved only half their purpose.

The destruction of representational images is the destruction of a hierarchy which is no longer recognized. It is the violation of generally established and universally visible and valid distances. The solidity of the images was the expression of their permanence. They seem to have existed for ever, upright and immovable; never before had it been possible to approach them with hostile intent. Now they are hauled down and broken to pieces. In this act the discharge accomplishes itself.

But it does not always go as far as this. The more usual kind of destruction mentioned above is simply an attack on all boundaries. Windows and doors belong to houses; they are the most vulnerable part of their exterior and, once they are smashed, the house has lost its individuality; anyone may enter it and nothing and no-one is protected any more. In these houses live the supposed enemies of the crowd, those people who try to keep away from it. What separated them has now been destroyed and nothing stands between them and the crowd. They can come out and join it; or they can be fetched.

But there is more to it than this. In the crowd the individual feels that he is transcending the limits of his own person. He has a sense of relief, for the distances are removed which used to throw him back on himself and shut him in. With the lifting of these burdens of distance he feels free; his freedom is the crossing of these boundaries. He wants what is happening to him to happen to others too; and he expects it to happen to them. An earthen pot irritates him, for it is all boundaries. The closed doors of a house irritate him. Rites and ceremonies, anything which preserves distances, threaten him and seem unbearable. He fears that, sooner or later, an attempt will be made to force the disintegrating crowd back into these pre-existing vessels. To the crowd in its nakedness everything seems a Bastille.

Of all means of destruction the most impressive is *fire*. It can be seen from far off and it attracts ever more people. It destroys irrevocably; nothing after a fire is as it was before. A crowd setting fire to something feels irresistible; so long as the fire spreads, everyone will join it and everything hostile will be destroyed. After the destruction, crowd and fire die away.

. . . . **The Eruption**

The open crowd is the true crowd, the crowd abandoning itself freely to its natural urge for growth. An open crowd has no clear feeling or idea of the size it may attain; it does not depend on a known building which it has to fill; its size is not determined; it wants to grow indefinitely and what it needs for this is more and more people. In this naked state, the crowd is at its most conspicuous, but, because it always disintegrates, it seems something outside the ordinary course of life and so is never taken quite seriously. Men might have gone on disregarding it if the enormous increase of population in modern times, and the rapid growth of cities, had not more and more often given rise to its formation.

The closed crowds of the past, of which more will be heard later, had turned into familiar institutions. The peculiar state of mind characteristic of their members seemed something natural. They always met for a special purpose of a religious, festal or martial kind; and this purpose seemed to sanctify their state. A man attending a sermon honestly believed that it was the sermon which mattered to him, and he would have felt astonished or even indignant had it been explained to him that the large number of listeners present gave him more satisfaction than the sermon itself. All ceremonies and rules pertaining to such institutions are basically intent on capturing the crowd; they prefer a church-full secure to the whole world insecure. The regularity of church-going and the precise and familiar repetition of certain rites safeguard for the crowd something like a domesticated experience of itself. These performances and their recurrence at fixed times supplant needs for something harsher and more violent.

Such institutions might have proved adequate if the number of human beings had remained the same, but more and more people filled the towns and the accelerating increase in the growth of populations during the last few centuries continually provided fresh incitements to the formation of new and larger crowds. And nothing, not even the most experienced and subtle leadership, could have prevented them forming in such conditions.

All the rebellions against traditional ceremonial recounted in the history of religions have been directed against the confinement of the crowd which wants to feel the sensation of its own growth again. The Sermon on the Mount in the New Testament comes to mind. It is enacted in the open, thousands are able to listen and there is no doubt that it is directed against the limiting ceremoniousness of the official temple. One remembers the tendency of Pauline Christianity to break out of the national and tribal boundaries of Judaism and to become a universal faith for all men. One remembers the contempt of Buddhism for the caste-system of contemporary India.

The *inner* history, too, of the several world religions is rich in occurrences of a similar kind. The Crusades developed into crowd formations of a magnitude no church building of the contemporary world could have held. Later, whole towns became spectators of the performances of the flagellants and these, in addition, wandered from town to town. Wesley, in the 18th Century, based his movement on sermons in the open air. He was perfectly aware of the importance of the enormous crowds which listened to him and sometimes in his Journals he worked out the numbers of those who were able to hear him. Each eruption from a closed locality means that the crowd desires to regain its old pleasure in sudden, rapid and unlimited growth.

I designate as *eruption* the sudden transition from a closed into an open crowd. This is a frequent occurrence, and one should not understand it as something referring only to space. A crowd quite often seems to overflow from some well-guarded space into the squares and streets of a town where it can move about freely, exposed to everything and attracting everyone. But more important than this external event is the corresponding inner movement: the dissatisfaction with the limitation of the

number of participants, the sudden will to attract, the passionate determination to reach *all* men.

Since the French Revolution these eruptions have taken on a form
which we feel to be modern. To an impressive degree the crowd has freed
itself from the substance of traditional religion and this has perhaps made
it easier for us to see it in its nakedness, in what one might call its biological state, without the transcendental theories and goals which used to
be inculcated in it. The history of the last 150 years has culminated in a
spate of such eruptions; they have engulfed even wars, for all wars are
now mass wars. The crowd is no longer content with pious promises and
conditionals. It wants to experience for itself the strongest possible feeling of its own animal force and passion and, as means to this end, it will
use whatever social pretexts and demands offer themselves.

The first point to emphasise is that the crowd never feels saturated.
It remains hungry as long as there is one human being it has not reached.
One cannot be certain whether this hunger would persist once it had
really absorbed all men, but it seems likely. Its efforts to endure, however,
are somewhat impotent. Its only hope lies in the formation of double
crowds, the one measuring itself against the other. The closer in power
and intensity the rivals are, the longer both of them will stay alive.

. . . . .Persecution

One of the most striking traits of the inner life of a crowd is the feeling
of being persecuted, a peculiar angry sensitiveness and irritability directed
against those it has once and forever nominated as enemies. These can
behave in any manner, harsh or conciliatory, cold or sympathetic, severe
or mild—whatever they do will be interpreted as springing from an un-
shakable malevolence, a premeditated intention to destroy the crowd,
openly or by stealth.

In order to understand this feeling of hostility and persecution it is
necessary to start from the basic fact that the crowd, once formed, wants
to grow rapidly. It is difficult to exaggerate the power and determination
with which it spreads. As long as it feels that it is growing—in revolutionary states, for example, which start with small but highly-charged
crowds—it regards anything which opposes its growth as constricting. It
can be dispersed and scattered by police, but this has only a temporary
effect, like a hand moving through a swarm of mosquitoes. But it can
also be attacked from within, namely by meeting the demands which led
to its formation. Its weaker adherents then drop away and others on the
point of joining turn back. An attack from outside can only strengthen
the crowd; those who have been physically scattered are more strongly
drawn together again. An attack from *within,* on the other hand, is really

dangerous; a strike which has achieved any gains crumbles visibly. It is an appeal to individual appetites and the crowd, as such, regards it as bribery, as "immoral"; it runs counter to its clear-cut basic conviction. Everyone belonging to such a crowd carries within him a small traitor who wants to eat, drink, make love and be left alone. As long as he does all this on the quiet and does not make too much fuss about it, the crowd allows him to proceed. But, as soon as he makes a noise about it, it starts to hate and to fear him. It knows then that he has been listening to the enticements of the enemy.

The crowd here is like a besieged city and, as in many sieges, it has enemies before its walls and enemies within them. During the fighting it attracts more and more partisans from the country around. These slip through the enemy lines and collect in front of the gates, begging to be let in. In favourable moments their wish is granted; or they may climb over the walls. Thus the city daily gains new defenders, but each of these brings with him that small invisible traitor we spoke of before, who quickly disappears into a cellar to join the traitors already hidden there. Meanwhile the siege continues. The besiegers certainly watch for a chance to attack, but they also try to prevent new recruits reaching the city. To do this they keep on strengthening the walls from outside. (In this strange siege the walls are more important to the assailants than to the defenders.) Or they try to bribe newcomers to keep away. If they fail in both, they do what they can to strengthen and encourage that traitor to his own cause which each newcomer carries with him into the city.

The crowd's feeling of persecution is nothing but the intuition of this double threat; the walls outside become more and more constricting and the cellars within more and more undermined. The activities of the enemy outside on the walls are open and can be watched; in the cellars they are hidden and insidious.

But images of this kind never convey more than a part of the truth. Those streaming from outside, wanting to get into the city, are not only new partisans, a reinforcement and a support; they are also the *food* of the crowd. A crowd which is not increasing is in a state of fast—there are ways of holding out through such a fast and religions have developed a great mastery of these. I propose now to show how the world religions have succeeded in holding their crowds even when these are not in the stage of fierce and rapid growth.

. . . . **Domestication of Crowds in the World Religions**

Religions whose claims to universality have been acknowledged very soon change the accent of their appeal. In the beginning their aim is to reach and to win all who can be reached and won. The crowd they envisage is universal; every single soul counts and every soul shall be theirs. But the fight they have to sustain leads gradually to a kind of hidden respect for adversaries whose institutions are already in existence. They see how difficult it is to hold one's ground; institutions which offer solidarity and permanence seem more and more important to them. Stimulated by those of their adversaries, they make great efforts to introduce institutions of their own, and these, if they succeed, grow in importance with time. The dead weight of institutions, which have a life of their own, then gradually tames the impetus of the original appeal. Churches are built to contain the existing faithful and are enlarged only with reluctance and circumspection when there is real need. There is, too, a strong tendency to collect the faithful in separate units. When they become many there is always a danger of disintegration, which must be continually countered.

A sense of the treacherousness of the crowd, is, so to speak, in the blood of all the historical world religions. Their own traditions, which are of a binding character, teach them how suddenly and unexpectedly they grew. Their stories of mass conversions appear miraculous to them, and they are so. In the heretical movements which the churches fear and persecute, the same kind of miracle turns against themselves and the injuries thus inflicted on their bodies are painful and unforgettable. Both the rapid growth of their early days and the no less rapid defections later keep their suspicion of the crowd always alive.

What they want in contrast to this is an obsequious flock. It is customary to regard the faithful as sheep and to praise them for their submissiveness. The churches entirely renounce the crowd's essential tendency to quick growth. They are satisfied with a temporary fiction of equality among the faithful—though this is never too strictly imposed—, with a defined density kept within moderate bounds, and with a strong direction. The goal they place in the far distance, in that other world which no man may enter so long as he is alive and which he has to earn by many efforts and submissions. Gradually the direction becomes the most important thing; the more distant the goal, the better the prospect of its permanence. The seemingly indispensable principle of growth has been replaced by something quite different: by repetition.

The faithful are gathered together at appointed places and times and, through performances which are always the same, they are transported into a mild state of crowd feeling sufficient to impress itself on them without becoming dangerous, and to which they grow accustomed. Their feeling of unity is dispensed to them in doses and the continuance of the church depends on the rightness of the dosage.

Wherever men have grown accustomed to this precisely repeated and limited experience in their churches or temples they can no longer do without it. They need it as they need food and anything else which is part of their existence. No sudden suppression of their cult, no prohibition by edict of the state, can remain without consequences. Any disturbance of their carefully balanced crowd-economy must ultimately lead to the eruption of an *open* crowd, and this will have all the elemental attributes which one knows. It will spread rapidly and bring about a real instead of a fictitious equality; it will find new and far more fervent densities; it will give up for the moment that far-off and scarcely attainable goal for which it has been educated, and set itself a goal here, in the immediate surroundings of this concrete life.

All suddenly prohibited religions revenge themselves by a kind of secularization. The character of their adherents' faith changes completely in an eruption of great and unexpected ferocity, but they do not understand this. They think they still hold their old faith and convictions and their only intention is to keep them. But, in reality, they have suddenly become quite different people. They are filled with the unique and violent feeling of the open crowd which they now compose, and at all costs they want to remain part of it.

. . . . Panic

Panic in a theatre, as has often been noted, is a *disintegration* of the crowd. The more people were bound together by the performance and the more closed the form of the theatre which contained them, the more violent the disintegration.

It is also possible that the performance alone was not enough to create a genuine crowd. The audience may have remained together, not because they felt gripped by it, but simply because they happened to be there. What the play could not achieve is immediately achieved by a *fire*. Fire is as dangerous to human beings as it is to animals; it is the strongest and oldest symbol of the crowd. However little crowd feeling there may have been in the audience, awareness of a fire brings it suddenly to a head. The common unmistakable danger creates a common fear. For a short time the audience becomes something like a real crowd. If they were not in a theatre, people could flee together like a herd of animals in danger, and increase the impetus of their flight by the simultaneity of identical movements. An active crowd-fear of this kind is the common collective experience of all animals who live together in herds and whose joint safety depends on their speed.

In a theatre, on the other hand, the crowd inevitably disintegrates in the most violent manner. Only one or two persons can get through each exit at a time and thus the energy of flight turns into an energy of struggle to push others back. Only one man at a time can pass between the rows of seats and each seat is neatly separated from the rest. Each man has his place and sits or stands by himself. A normal theatre is arranged with the intention of pinning people down and allowing them only the use of their hands and voices; their use of their legs is restricted as far as possible.

The sudden command to flee which the fire gives is immediately countered by the impossibility of any common movement. Each man sees the door through which he must pass; and he sees himself alone in it, sharply cut off from all the others. It is the frame of a picture which very soon dominates him. Thus the crowd, a moment ago at its apex, must disintegrate violently, and the transmutation shows itself in violent individual action: everyone shoves, hits and kicks in all directions.

The more fiercely each man "fights for his life," the clearer it becomes that he is fighting *against* all the others who hem him in. They stand there like chairs, balustrades, closed doors, but different from these in that they are alive and hostile. They push him in this or that direction, as it suits them or, rather, as they are pushed themselves. Neither women, children nor old people are spared: they are not distinguished from men. Whilst the individual no longer feels himself as "crowd", he is still completely surrounded by it. Panic is a disintegration of the crowd *within* the crowd. The individual breaks away and wants to escape from it because the crowd, as a whole, is endangered. But, because he is physically still stuck in it, he must attack it. To abandon himself to it now would be his ruin, because it itself is threatened by ruin. In such a moment a man cannot insist too strongly on his separateness. Hitting and pushing, he evokes hitting and pushing; and the more blows he inflicts and the more he receives, the more *himself* he feels. The boundaries of his own person become clear to him again.

It is strange to observe how strongly for the person struggling with it the crowd assumes the character of fire. It originated with the unexpected sight of flames or with a shout of "fire" and it plays like flames with the man who is trying to escape from it. The people he pushes away are like burning objects to him; their touch is hostile, and on every part of his body; and it terrifies him. Anyone who stands in his way is tainted with the general hostility of fire. The manner in which fire spreads and gradually works its way round a person until he is entirely surrounded by it is very similar to the crowd threatening him on all sides. The incalculable movements within it, the thrusting forth of an arm, a fist or a leg, are like the flames of a fire which may suddenly spring up on any side. Fire in the form of a conflagration of forest or steppe actually *is* a hostile crowd and fear of it can be awakened in any human being. Fire, as a symbol for the crowd, has entered the whole economy of man's feelings and become an immutable part of it. That emphatic trampling on people, so often observed in panics and apparently so senseless, is nothing but the stamping out of fire.

Disintegration through panic can only be averted by prolonging the original state of united crowd fear. In a threatened church there is a way of achieving this: people pray in common fear to a common God in whose hand it lies to extinguish the fire by a miracle.

. . . . The Crowd as a Ring

An arena contains a crowd which is *doubly* closed. On account of this curious quality its examination may not be entirely without value.

The arena is well demarcated from the outside world. It is usually visible from far off and its situation in the city—the space which it occupies—is well known. People always feel where it is, even if they are not thinking of it. Shouts from the arena carry far and, when it is open at the top, something of the life which goes on inside communicates itself to the surrounding city.

But however exciting these communications may be, an uninhibited flow into the arena is not possible. The number of seats it contains is limited; its maximum density is fixed in advance. The seats are arranged so that people are not too closely crushed. The occupants are meant to be comfortable in them and to be able to watch, each from his own seat, without disturbing others.

Outside, facing the city, the arena displays a lifeless wall; inside is a wall of people. The spectators turn their backs to the city. They have been lifted out of its structure of walls and streets and, for the duration of their time in the arena, they do not care about anything which happens there; they have left behind all their associations, rules and habits. Their remaining together in large numbers for a stated period of time is secure and their excitement has been promised them. But only under one definite condition: the discharge must take place *inside the arena.*

The seats are arranged in tiers around the arena, so that everyone can see what is happening below. The consequence of this is that the crowd is seated opposite itself. Every spectator has a thousand in front of him, a thousand heads. As long as he is there, all the others are there too; whatever excites him, excites them; and he sees it. They are seated some distance away from him, so that the differing details which make individuals of them are blurred; they all look alike and they all behave in a similar manner and he notices in them only the things which he himself is full of. Their visible excitement increases his own.

There is no break in the crowd which sits like this, exhibiting itself to itself. It forms a closed ring from which nothing can escape. The tiered ring of fascinated faces has something strangely homogeneous about it. It embraces and contains everything which happens below; no-one relaxes his grip on this; no-one tries to get away. Any gap in the ring might remind him of disintegration and subsequent dispersal. But there is no gap; this crowd is doubly closed, to the world outside and in itself.

. . . . The Attributes of the Crowd

Before I try to undertake a classification of crowds it may be useful to summarize briefly their main attributes. The following four traits are important.

1. *The crowd always wants to grow.* There are no natural boundaries to its growth. Where such boundaries have been artificially created— e.g. in all institutions which are used for the preservation of closed crowds—an eruption of the crowd is always possible and will, in fact, happen from time to time. There are no institutions which can be absolutely relied on to prevent the growth of the crowd once and for all.

2. *Within the crowd there is equality.* This is absolute and indisputable and never questioned by the crowd itself. It is of fundamental importance and one might even define a crowd as a state of absolute equality. A head is a head, an arm is an arm, and differences between individual heads and arms are irrelevant. It is for the sake of this equality that people become a crowd and they tend to overlook anything which might detract from it. All demands for justice and all theories of equality ultimately derive their energy from the actual experience of equality familiar to anyone who has been part of a crowd.

3. *The crowd loves density.* It can never feel too dense. Nothing must stand between its parts or divide them; everything must be the crowd itself. The feeling of density is strongest in the moment of discharge. One day it may be possible to determine this density more accurately and even to measure it.

4. *The crowd needs a direction.* It is in movement and it moves towards a goal. The direction, which is common to all its members, strengthens the feeling of equality. A goal outside the individual members and common to all of them drives underground all the private differing goals which are fatal to the crowd as such. Direction is essential for the continuing existence of the crowd. Its constant fear of disintegration means that it will accept *any* goal. A crowd exists so long as it has an unattained goal.

There is, however, another tendency hidden in the crowd, which appears to lead to new and superior kinds of formation. The nature of these is often not predictable.

Each of these four attributes will be found in any crowd to a greater or lesser degree. How a crowd is to be classified will depend on which of them predominates in it.

I have discussed open and closed crowds and explained that these terms refer to their growth. The crowd is open so long as its growth is not impeded; it is closed when it growth is limited.

Another distinction is that between *rhythmic* and *stagnating* crowds. This refers to the next two attributes, *equality* and *density;* and to both of them simultaneously.

The *stagnating* crowd lives for its discharge. But it feels certain of this and puts it off. It desires a relatively long period of density to prepare for the moment of discharge. It, so to speak, warms itself at its density and delays as long as possible with the discharge. The process here starts not with equality, but with density; and equality then becomes the main goal of the crowd, which in the end it reaches. Every shout, every utterance in common is a valid expression of this equality.

In the *rhythmic* crowd, on the other hand (for example the crowd of the dance), density and equality coincide from the beginning. Everything here depends on movement. All the physical stimuli involved function in a predetermined manner and are passed on from one dancer to another. Density is embodied in the formal recurrence of retreat and approach; equality is manifest in the movements themselves. And thus, by the skilful enactment of density and equality, a crowd feeling is engendered. These rhythmic formations spring up very quickly and it is only physical exhaustion which bring them to an end.

The next pair of concepts—the *slow* and the *quick* crowd—refer exclusively to the nature of the goal. The conspicuous crowds which are the ones usually mentioned and which form such an essential part of modern life—the political, sporting and war like crowds we see daily—are all *quick* crowds. Very different from these are the religious crowds whose goal is a heaven, or crowds formed of pilgrims. Their goal is distant, the way to it long, and the true formation of the crowd is relegated to a far off country or to another world. Of these slow crowds we actually see only the tributaries, for the end they strive after is invisible and not to be attained by the unbelieving. The slow crowd gathers slowly and only sees itself as permanent in a far distance.

This is a mere indication of the nature of these forms. We shall have to consider them more closely.

Alan Moorehead

There is no more grimly powerful symbol—in an era that provided many—of the horrors of totalitarian rule than the memory of the Nazi concentration camps. Indeed, they may be said to have become a symbol of that process of dehumanization and disintegration of traditional values which had been going on for some time everywhere and which the war itself climaxed. From the moment when allied military victory laid bare to the world the truth about these camps until now, millions of words have been written on the subject. Few pieces, however, have concentrated so admirably on the essential issues as Alan Moorehead's "Belsen," and few therefore have held up so well. This is the more remarkable when one considers that it was written not at a comfortable distance afterwards but on the scene itself and while, in a sense, it was all still happening.

Alan Moorehead, a young Australian who went to England in 1937, first won an international reputation for his coverage as a war correspondent of the campaigns of World War II. It is easy to see why, for "Belsen" is an example of reporting at the very highest level. The subject matter itself is a highly emotional one, but Moorehead's language is not; on the contrary, it is restrained, simple, and above all exact, and because it is it evokes the scene most powerfully. The author avoids the temptation to make propaganda out of so terrible a spectacle of human suffering, and he does this by concentrating on the concrete, by telling us as plainly as possible *how things really were* at Belsen. He has the observant eye for the small but significant detail as well as for the general scene, the capacity for impartiality, the skill for interweaving with the descriptive passages background material that is relevant to the great issue of "Why?" The tone is never self-righteous. Instead, the modest and unpretentious voice of the narrator is another of the strengths of this essentially informal and personal kind of writing, and the general speculation as to "cause" which Moorehead allows himself at the end convinces by its very quietness.

BELSEN

Just before you get to the main entrance of Belsen concentration camp—or rather the place where the camp used to be before the British burned it down—you come on a farmhouse. I suggested to the others in my party that we should turn in there and eat lunch before— rather than after—we visited the camp.

While the table was being set for us in the dining-room we were interested to know from the farmer what he thought of Belsen. "I don't know very much about it," he said. "Each morning I had to drive up there with a cart full of vegetables—swedes and turnips mostly—and one of the S.S. guards took the horse and cart from me at the gate. After a bit the cart and horse were returned to me and I drove away. I was never allowed inside, and I didn't want to go in anyway. I knew something

From *Eclipse* by Alan Moorehead (London, Hamish Hamilton, Ltd., 1946). Reprinted by permission of the publisher.

horrible was going on but I didn't ask about it lest I should find myself inside."

We finished the meal and drove up to the gate with a special pass which General Dempsey had given the correspondents: from the first Dempsey was very keen that we should see Belsen and write about it. Although the British had only captured the place from the Germans a few days before they seemed to have things well organized. Hungarian guards were still spaced along the barbed wire fence, good-looking men who jumped eagerly to attention when an army vehicle came by. At the gate British soldiers were on guard. There were notices in English: "Danger Typhus", "Car Park", "Powder Room", "Inquiries" and so on.

A young army doctor and a captain from the Pioneers were in charge. The Captain's job was supervising the counting and burial of bodies. Possibly as a form of immunization from the grisly work he appeared to be in particularly jovial spirits.

"I love doing this," he said, picking up the metal syringe filled with anti-louse powder. "Come on."

A squirt up each sleeve. One down the trousers. Two more squirts down the back and front of the shirt and a final shot on the hair. It was rather pleasant.

"We collected the local burgomeisters from the surrounding villages this morning and took them round the camp," the doctor said.

"How did they take it?"

"One of them was sick and another one wouldn't look. They all said they had never dreamed that this was going on."

We were now walking down the main driveway towards the first of the huts and administrative buildings. There were large crowds of civilian prisoners about, both those who strolled about in groups talking many different languages and those who sat silent on the ground. In addition there were many forms lying on the earth partly covered in rags, but it was not possible to say whether they were alive or dead or simply in the process of dying. It would be a day or two before the doctors got around to them for a diagnosis.

"There's quite a different air about the place in the last two days," the doctor said. "They seem much more cheerful now."

"And the burial rate has gone down considerably," the captain added. "I'm handling just under three hundred a day now. It was five hundred to start with. And we are evacuating five hundred every day to the Panzer training school. It has been made into a hospital. Would you like to see the S.S. boys?"

We saw the women guards first. A British sergeant threw open the cell door and some twenty women wearing dirty grey skirts and tunics were sitting and lying on the floor.

"Get up," the sergeant roared in English.

They got up and stood to attention in a semi-circle round the room, and we looked at them. Thin ones, fat ones, scraggy ones and muscular ones; all of them ugly, and one or two of them distinctly cretinous. I pointed out one, a big woman with bright golden hair and a bright pink complexion.

"She was Kramer's girl friend," the sergeant growled. "Nice lot, aren't they?"

There was another woman in a second room with almost delicate features, but she had the same set staring look in her eyes. The atmosphere of the reformatory school and the prison was inescapable.

Outside in the passageway there was a large blackboard ruled off in squares with white lines. Down the left-hand side of the board was a list of nationalities—"Poles, Dutch, Russians" and so on. Spaced along the top of the board was a list of religions and political faiths—"Communist, Jew, Atheist." From the board one might have seen at a glance just how many prisoners were in the camp from each nation, and how they were subdivided politically and religiously. However, most of the numbers appeared to have been rubbed off, and it was difficult to make out the totals exactly. Germans seemed to make up the majority of the prisoners. After them Russians and Poles. A great many were Jews. As far as one could decipher there had been half a dozen British here, one or two Americans. There had been something like fifty thousand prisoners altogether.

As we approached the cells of the S.S. guards the sergeant's language became ferocious.

"We have had an interrogation this morning," the captain said. "I'm afraid they are not a pretty sight."

"Who does the interrogation?"

"A Frenchman. I believe he was sent up here specially from the French underground to do the job."

The sergeant unbolted the first door and flung it back with a crack like thunder. He strode into the cell, jabbing a metal spike in front of him.

"Get up," he shouted. "Get up. Get up, you dirty bastards." There were half a dozen men lying or half lying on the floor. One or two were able to pull themselves erect at once. The man nearest me, his shirt and face spattered with blood, made two attempts before he got on to his knees and then gradually on to his feet. He stood with his arms half stretched out in front of him, trembling violently.

"Get up," shouted the sergeant. They were all on their feet now, but supporting themselves against the wall.

"Get away from that wall."

They pushed themselves out into space and stood there swaying. Unlike the women they looked not at us, but vacantly in front, staring at nothing.

Same thing in the next cell and the next where the men who were bleeding and were dirty were moaning something in German.

"You had better see the doctor," the Captain said. "He's a nice specimen. He invented some of the tortures here. He had one trick of injecting creosote and petrol into the prisoner's veins. He used to go around the huts and say 'Too many people in here. Far too many.' Then he used to loose off the barrel of his revolver round the hut. The doctor has just finished his interrogation."

The doctor had a cell to himself.

"Come on. Get up," the sergeant shouted. The man was lying in his blood on the floor, a massive figure with a heavy head and bedraggled beard. He placed his two arms on to the seat of a wooden chair, gave himself a heave and got half upright. One more heave and he was on his feet. He flung wide his arms towards us.

"Why don't you kill me?" he whispered. "Why don't you kill me? I can't stand any more."

The same phrases dribbled out of his lips over and over again.

"He's been saying that all morning, the dirty bastard," the sergeant said. We went out into the sunshine. A number of other British soldiers were standing about, all with the same hard, rigid expressions on their faces, just ordinary English soldiers, but changed by this expression of genuine and permanent anger.

The crowds of men and women thickened as we went further into the camp. The litter of paper and rags and human offal grew thicker, the smell less and less bearable. At the entrance soldiers were unloading trucks filled with wooden latrines but these had not yet been placed about the camp, so many hundreds of half-naked men and women were squatting together in the open, a scene such as you sometimes see in India— except that here it was not always possible to distinguish men from women and indeed to determine whether or not they were human at all.

We drove through the filth in cars and presently emerging on to an open space of yellow clayey soil we came on a group of German guards flinging bodies into a pit about a hundred feet square. They brought the bodies up in handcarts and as they were flung into the grave a British soldier kept a tally of the numbers. When the total reached five hundred a bulldozer driven by another soldier came up and started nudging the earth into the grave. There was a curious pearly colour about the piled up bodies and they were small like the bodies of children. The withered skin was sagging over the bones and all the normal features by which you know a human being had practically disappeared. Having no stomach for this sort of thing I was only able to look for a second or two, but the S.S. guards and even the British soldiers there appeared to have grown used to the presence of death and able to work in its presence without being sick.

"The doctors are doing a wonderful job," the Captain said: "They are in the huts all day sorting out the living bodies from the dead, and it's not easy sometimes to tell the difference. Of course there are a lot who are just hopeless and they are simply left. But they are saving a lot now. We have got in all the food we want—two meals a day at 10 and 6. Come on and have a look at one of the huts. We will go to the women first."

It was a single storey rectangular building, I suppose about a hundred feet long. Wooden bunks ran in tiers up to the ceiling and there was a narrow passage just wide enough to allow you to pass through. Since the majority of the women there were too weak to move and had no attention whatever, the stench was nauseating. Hurrying through, handkerchief to nose, one saw nothing but livid straining faces and emaciated arms and legs under the filthy bedclothes on either side. Many were using their last strength to moan feebly for help. These animals were piled one on top of the other to the ceiling, sometimes two to a bunk.

An old hag, somewhat stronger than the others, was standing at the further door. "I'm twenty-one," she whispered. "No, I don't know why they put me in here. My husband is a doctor at the front—I'm German but not Jewish. I said that I did not want to enlist in the women's organization and they put me in here. That was eighteen months ago."

"I've had enough of this," I said to the Captain.

"Come on," he said. "You've got to go through one of the men's huts yet. That's what you're here for."

It was, if anything, more rancid than the one I had seen, but this time I was too sick with the stench to notice much except the sound of the voices: "Doctor, Doctor."

As we returned towards the entrance the people around us were noticeably better in health than those at the pits and the huts. As they were able to walk some instinct drew the people away from the charnel houses and up and out towards the entrance and the ordinary sane normal world outside. It was all like a journey down to some Dantesque pit, unreal, leprous and frightening. And now that one emerged into the light again, one's first coherent reactions were not of disgust or anger or even, I think, of pity. Something else filled the mind, a frantic desire to ask: "Why? Why? Why? Why had it happened?" With all one's soul one felt: "This is not war. Nor is it anything to do with here and now, with this one place at this one moment. This is timeless and the whole world and all mankind is involved in it. This touches me and I am responsible. Why has it happened? How did we let it happen?"

We stood there in a group, a major from the commandos, a padre, three or four correspondents, having at first nothing to say and then gradually and quietly asking one another the unspoken question.

Was it sadism? No, on the whole, not. Or, if it was sadism, then it was sadism of a very indirect and unusual kind. Relatively little torture was carried out at this camp. The sadist presumably likes to make some direct immediate act which inflicts pain on other people. He could not obtain much satisfaction from the slow long process of seeing people starve.

Then again the Germans were an efficient people. They needed manpower. Can one imagine anything more inefficient than letting all this valuable labour go to rot? The prisoners in Belsen were not even obliged to work. They were simply dumped in here and left to make what shift they could with a twice daily diet of turnip stew. Incidentally this lack of work probably led to the break-up of the prisoners' morale as much as anything.

The Germans, too, had a normal fear of disease spreading among themselves. And yet they let these thousands of bodies lie on the ground. It's true that there was not a great deal of typhus in the camp, but it had already broken out when the German commanders approached the British and offered to cede the camp under the terms of a truce.

It was not torture which had killed the prisoners. It was neglect. The sheer indifference of the Nazis. One began to see that the most terrible thing on earth is not positive destruction nor the perverse desire to hurt and destroy. The worst thing that can happen to you is for the master to say: "I do not care about you any more. I am indifferent." Whether you washed or ate or laughed or died—none of this was of any consequence any more because you as a person had no value. You were a slug on the ground, to be crushed or not to be crushed, it made no difference.

And having become attuned and accustomed to this indifference the guards were increasingly less affected by the suffering of the people around them. It was accepted that they should die. They were Russians. Russians die. Jews die. They were not even enemies. They were disease. Could you mourn or sympathize with the death throes of a germ?

Now here is where the evidence of Kramer, the camp commandant, comes in. To consider Kramer calmly I think we have first got to rid ourselves temporarily of our memory of that published picture of him shuffling across the yard in shackles. And we have to forget for a moment the title he was given through the world, "The Monster of Belsen." A friend of mine, a trained intelligence officer and interrogator in the British army, went into the whole question very carefully with Kramer and this was Kramer's statement:

"I was swamped. The camp was not really inefficient before you crossed the Rhine. There was running water, regular meals of a kind— I had to accept what food I was given for the camp and distribute it the best way I could. But then they suddenly began to send me trainloads of new prisoners from all over Germany. It was impossible to cope with them. I appealed for more staff, more food. I was told this was impossible; I had to carry on with what I had. Then as a last straw the Allies bombed the electric plant which pumped our water. Cartloads of food were unable to reach the camp because of the Allied fighters. Then things really got out of hand. In the last six weeks I have been helpless. I did not even have sufficient staff to bury the dead, let alone segregate the sick."

Thus Kramer.

"But how did you come to accept a job like this?" he was asked. The reply: "There was no question of my accepting it. I was ordered. I am an officer in the S.S. and I obey orders. These people were criminals and I was serving my Führer in a crisis by commanding this camp. I tried to get medicines and food for the prisoners and I failed. I was swamped. I may have been hated, but I was doing my duty."

There was some truth in this last. Not only were the prisoners fond of hurling missiles at Kramer since we arrived, but his own guards turned on him as well. Kramer asked the British authorities that he should be segregated. He was told that in this event he would have to be shackled and to this he agreed.

Who then was responsible for Belsen and, for that matter, all the other camps? The S.S. guards? They say they were ordered. They hated the work but disobedience to Kramer meant death. Kramer says he was in precisely the same position. And so presumably do all the other Kramers above him until you reach Himmler. What does Himmler say? Himmler says he is serving his Führer. The Führer, of course, was innocent and knew nothing about the vulgar details (quite a number of Germans assured us of that). But—we can imagine Himmler saying—it was vital to protect the Führer from his enemies inside the Reich—the Jewish Bolsheviks who would have cheerfully murdered him. At this dire crisis for Germany and the Party one could not be too nice about the details— possibly some people were treated a little too harshly. But one could not afford to take chances. The Nazis were perfectly prepared to treat these prisoners with humanity, but the enemies of Germany made this impossible. They destroyed communications, they blocked the food supply. Naturally the camps suffered.

But the people of Germany? Why had they allowed this thing to be? Why had they not protested? The average German answers: in the first place we did not know these camps existed. Secondly, how could we have protested? What possibly could we have done? The Nazis were too strong.

Very well then, why did you not protest when the Nazis were rising to power?

They answer: How could we foretell that the Nazis would end with this horror? When they first came to power they embarked on a programme that was excellent for Germany: new roads, modern buildings and machines. It seemed rational and good at the beginning. When we realized that Hitler was turning to war it was already too late. By then the Nazis had claimed our children. They were Nazified in the schools. A parent would be denounced by his own child if he spoke against the Nazis. Little by little we were overwhelmed and in the end it was too late. There was no point at which we could have effectively protested. Why did not foreign countries which had the power check the Nazis soon enough? If only you had attacked us before the Nazis became too strong.

And so the blame is thrown back upon the world. No one anywhere is willing to take responsibility. Not the guard or the torturer. Not Kramer. Not Herr Woolf.[1] They were all ordered. Not Himmler or Hitler (the end justified the means); they were fighting to rid the world of the terrible menace of Jewish Bolshevism—they were ordered by their high sense of duty. Not the German people. They too had to obey. And finally not the world. Is England Germany's keeper?

That is the line of argument which we have heard as observers of this final eclipse of Germany. I write it here not because I accept or reject it, but because we are still too close to the scene to do much more than report personally and directly; and it seems a pity to give way to the downright childishness of saying that all Germans are natural black-hearted fiends capable of murdering and torturing and starving people at the drop of the hat.

If I were compelled to make some sort of direct line at this moment I would say—Yes, all mankind *is* in some way responsible for Belsen but in varying degrees. Herr Woolf, for example, is a cultured European. Surely he could have seen a little more clearly than, say, the average German workman, what the Nazi party was going to mean and have made some protest in time. Clearly, too, the Germans generally and the leading Nazis most particularly are far more embroiled in this monstrosity than anyone else. The Junkers and the Wehrmacht power-through-war class—they too are utterly compromised. But the degree of guilt varies enormously both inside and outside of the Nazi Party, inside and outside of Germany. Probably the least of all to blame is the unpolitical boy who was put into uniform and forced to come here into the German battle-field to support the tardy conscience of the world. And die for it.

1 The German arms manufacturer whose opinions are paraphrased above.

There is only one thing possible that one can do for him now—be vigilant to snap the long chains that lead to the future Belsens before they grow too strong. A shudder of horror went round the world when the news of these concentration camps was published, but only, I think, because of the special interest and the special moment in the war. We were engrossed with Germany and it is perhaps not too subtle to say that since Germany was manifestly beaten, people wanted to have a justification for their fight, a proof that they were engaged against evil. From the German point of view Belsen was perfectly mistimed. Worse camps like Ausschwitz existed in Poland and we took no notice. Dachau was described in the late thirties and we did not want to hear. In the midst of the war three quarters of a million Indians starved in Bengal because shipping was wanted in other parts and we were bored.

The last living patient has been evacuated from Belsen. The hateful buildings have been burned down. The physical evidence of all those horrible places will soon have been wiped out. Only the mental danger remains. The danger of indifference.

Raymond Aron

Born in Paris in 1905, Raymond Aron was educated there and in Germany. He was associated with the exile government of General de Gaulle in London during World War II. After his return to Paris he began to attract attention for his comments on political, social, and economic matters. In *On War*, from which our selection is taken, as in his larger work *The Century of Total War*, Aron addresses himself to a subject which is not often, outside of professional military circles, subjected to so cool and rational an analysis. Yet Aron's purpose is of course quite different from that of a general staff.

As the phrase "polymorphous violence" indicates, the author is struck by the multiple forms which warfare in our time has assumed, and he argues convincingly that this very fact of variety ought to be taken into account by diplomats and statesmen. He bolsters his argument with a wide range of concrete references to the international scene, and, confining himself very strictly to making a rational analysis of his insights, he relies wholly on the power of his logic to persuade his readers. Nevertheless, beneath the austere surface of this essay there lurk implications of a large order—most of all the implication that the forms of violence in our age mask a kind of disintegration of organized society itself, a perverse counter-movement to those social principles on which the idea of progress depends.

POLYMORPHOUS VIOLENCE

The unity of the diplomatic field is real in many ways: the great powers have the material means of acting at any point of the globe. Marshal Tito, Mr. Nehru, Colonel Nasser, and the Prime Minister of Burma exchange visits and pledges of "active neutrality"; at the United Nations, the representatives of the states of Asia and America rub shoulders with the representatives of Europe and Africa. Never have so many states of so many different kinds been in regular contact. Never has the fate of each state been affected, or risked being affected, to the extent that it is today by events on the other side of the world. This unity nevertheless permits the different regional systems an autonomy which the global balance of power tends to increase.

The more unified the planet becomes, the less does diplomacy seem to obey the ordinary calculations of force and the more military technique differs from continent to continent and conflict to conflict. It is as though some artistic genius were trying to reunite in a grand finale every method of warfare practiced by men for thousands of years, on the eve of the day when the progress of science condemns the human race to choose between wisdom and death.

Seldom has the map of the world changed as quickly and as visibly as in the course of the last ten years. Atom bombs, supersonic aircraft, super-tanks have not been responsible for these upheavals. Wherever the big battalions, atomic or conventional, were present (in Europe) or engaged (in Korea), the outcome has been the *status quo*. In Europe, horsepower could have revived the era of the great invasions which ended with the defeat of the mounted hordes of Asia. Outside Europe it is "disimperialism" which triumphs, although it might appear on the surface that would-be conquerors have never had at their disposal such an effective instrument for realizing their ambitions.

It will be objected that the famous dictum, "the impotence of victory,"[1] applies to the United States but not to the Soviet Union. The United States was unable to turn its victory to account either in Europe, since it withdrew its troops and permitted its rival the peaceful occupation of the contested territories (Eastern Zone), or in Asia, since it could

From *On War* by Raymond Aron. Copyright © 1958 by Martin Secker & Warburg, Ltd. Reprinted by permission of Doubleday & Co., Inc.

[1] A phrase of Hegel's, *"die Ohnmacht des Sieges,"* in *The Philosophy of History,* apropos of Napoleon.

not or would not exert a decisive influence over the outcome of the Chinese civil war. The Soviet Union, taking advantage of the German and Japanese defeats, brought under its suzerainty a hundred million Europeans and extended the empire of its creed by six hundred million Chinese.

"Disimperialism," the objector will continue, is simply the liberation of the peoples of Asia and Africa from the colonial yoke, and the Europeans withdrew because they were exhausted by their internecine quarrels. Incapable of agreeing on the division of the spoils, they had to give up pillaging. They were not converted to altruism: they no longer had the strength to maintain their domination. The expansion of Communism proves that the age of empires is not over. The disintegration of the European empires recalls the age-old truth that there can be no empire without strength. The American reverses recall the lesson, also an old one, that strength without the will to use it, without a motivating idea, is sterile.

Nothing would be more absurd than to seek in our century edifying illustrations of the theme of virtue triumphant. The non-violence of our Indian friends was effective against the British but it did not save the Jews of Europe from extermination and it would not have protected the Poles, Balts, or Central Asians from the Russians or the Germans. It was not non-violence, if we are to believe Mr. Khrushchev, which spared the Ukrainians the rigors of deportation, but their numbers.

Let us have the courage to admit that the fear of war is often the tyrant's opportunity, that the absence of war, that is of open conflict between legally organized political units, is not enough to exclude violence between individuals and groups. Perhaps we shall look back with nostalgia to the days of "conventional" wars when, faced with the horror of guerilla warfare and the atomic holocaust, the peoples of the world submit to a detestable order provided it dispels the agonies of individual insecurity and collective suicide.

Let us try to understand the obscure logic of this polymorphous violence, of these unavowable wars, of these irresistible and futile weapons, of these states which are born without the material means to defend themselves. Let us not make history more coherent than it is, but let us not create a pseudo-paradox by disregarding one of the aspects of its reality.

Ever since the end of the First World War, far-sighted observers have been struck by the contradiction between the war's lessons and the territorial situation created, or rather confirmed, by the Peace Treaty. From 1914-18 it had been progressively discovered that a war kindled by national passions and fed by conscription and industry tended to assume enormous proportions. In Europe, only coalitions possessed resources on the scale of twentieth-century technology. France could not fight without the freedom of the seas. which depended on Great Britain. The latter, in turn, could not dispense with at least the benevolent neutrality of the United States. Doubtless at first this amplification of the conflict was attributable to circumstances which could be considered accidental or transitory: the qualitative superiority of the German army, the stalemate of trench warfare, the resort to the strategy of attrition. The industrial character of the war nevertheless contributed, to quote a famous dictum, toward making the big even bigger and the small even smaller, in other words to widen the gap between first-class and second-class powers. The Versailles convention increased the number of the latter. The partition of the Austro-Hungarian and Turkish empires into multiple states ran counter to the new technique of warfare, which was itself a reflection of the technique of production. States were created which, incapable of military independence, fragmented the vast territory indispensable to their common prosperity.

This new convention, an artificial one, since it failed to correspond with the interests of either Germany or the Soviet Union, did not easily lend itself to peaceful revision. Could the frontiers of Poland, Czechoslovakia, Hungary, or Rumania be modified without putting in doubt the very existence of these states? The great powers were alike incapable of agreeing on the terms of revision and of leaving the small powers to settle their differences by force of arms (the more so since some of these differences opposed a big power to a small one—Poland to Germany). A general conflict was the tragic but not unforeseeable outcome.

Once again peace seemed to endorse a multiplicity of states rather than the unification of vast areas. In 1945 there were almost as many European states as in 1939. Lithuania, Latvia, and Estonia had been erased from the map but Germany was cut in two. Yet this Balkanization is more apparent than real. East of the Iron Curtain, the nations of eastern and central Europe continue to exist, each with its own institutions, but they obey a single overlord state. The countries created in 1918 between Russia and Germany have been integrated first with a German, then with a Russian empire. They have never regained complete independence and have little chance of regaining it in the near future (although the modality of Russian domination must progressively change).

West of the Iron Curtain, the independence of the liberated nations is genuine in the sense that each of them regulates its own internal affairs.[2] It is spurious in the sense that none of them any longer controls

2 The objection may be raised that such independence does not include the right to convert to Communism. It goes without saying that the Americans do their utmost to prevent a Communist victory in an Atlantic Pact country. They do not refuse to abandon their base in Iceland after an electoral verdict, but one wonders if, in the event of a left-wing majority in Italy or France, they would defend their bases by force. The Russians do not have to face this kind of difficulty.

its own national defense. The American leaders have neither the capacity nor the desire to organize a formal empire. Nevertheless, American troops are stationed on the marches of the free world from Berlin to Seoul.

The British and French empires, whose "mother countries" were involved in the Western military system, were becoming a sort of anachronism, the remnants of a power which had failed to survive two world wars and which the rise of a new type of state inevitably made somewhat obsolete. What is surprising is not that France, after the defeat of 1940, should have lost her empire, but that the latter should have appeared to survive the shock. Nor is it surprising that Great Britain, in spite of the enormous part she played in the victory over Hitlerite Germany, should have granted independence to India, Burma, and Ceylon. Let us consider one aspect of this historic movement: European "disimperialism," politically explicable, has been accompanied by another military revolution, the counterpart of the atomic revolution: the machine gun against the H-bomb, the spontaneous organization of rebels against mechanized armies. At one extreme we have the laboratories in which the war of machines is being prepared; at the other, a few thousand professional revolutionaries agitate the masses and change the map of the world. Between the two, France (and Europe) has lost control of her national defense, incapable of measuring up either to the technology of the atom or the technique of revolt.

Throughout history, military superiority has been essentially due to armaments and organization which, together, reflected the capacity of the state—a capacity for production and a capacity to maintain order. Not that the conquering nations were always superior in respect to cultural values (assuming one could establish a hierarchy of the latter). If the God of Battles presides over the tribunal of history, it is probably "virtue" in the Machiavellian sense that he judges, not morality in the Platonic, Christian, or Kantian sense. We cannot subscribe to Toynbee's optimism and affirm that civilizations have never been destroyed by force. The legion, such as it emerged from the Punic Wars, was not an accidental accomplishment: it was an expression of the Roman Republic. No one has the right to conclude that the destruction of Carthage coincided with the interests of humanity properly understood. We are incapable of imagining how the ancient world would have evolved if it had not been unified by Rome, or if another city had been the architect of this unity.

We will confine ourselves to a proposition that is almost self-evident. The army which, by its organization or its armaments, triumphed on the field of battle belonged to a society whose institutions were seldom inferior to those of the vanquished. When the fury of the barbarian warriors triumphed, all that their victory proved was that their civilized foes had lost the secret of the disciplined action without which cities and empires are prone to collapse.

In the nineteenth century and at the beginning of the twentieth, the superiority of European arms seemed irresistible. In 1900 a small army composed of contingents from several European nations under the command of a German general had little difficulty in reaching Peking. Some years later the Russo-Japanese War, although it may have given the world at large an excessive notion of Japan's strength, nevertheless proved one thing: that the non-European civilizations were capable of adapting themselves to the military techniques which had given the tiny archipelago hegemony over a great part of the planet.

As soon as she had proved herself on the field of battle, Japan was admitted into the club of the great powers. Because she had opened her doors to Western goods and Western ideas and had accomplished her own revolution, she was soon free from the encroachments of European imperialism. The opposition to reform put up by a fraction of the Chinese intellectuals and the political decomposition of the Middle Kingdom prolonged for half a century a "time of troubles" to which the Communist party put an end. In the perspective of Chinese history, Mao Tse-tung is the founder of a new dynasty which, thanks to the Korean War, had occasion to prove itself worthy of the celestial mandate.

Neither China nor Japan had formally lost their independence. To retrieve the position in world diplomacy to which their history entitled them, they had only to borrow from the "barbarians" the instruments of warfare. This transaction involved profound changes which have not yet been completed. Armed forces of the European type required (before the beginning of the atomic age) factories which could mass-produce artillery, shells, and machine guns—the millions of tons of steel devoured by mechanized divisions. They also need, in research departments and airports, the engineers, mechanics, and specialized personnel without whom a modern air force cannot be maintained. In addition, armed forces on the European model are inconceivable without officers who have received a secondary or technical education and soldiers who can read and write. The Japanese reformers of the Meiji era were right in regarding the spread of education as the prime condition of Westernization.[3]

India, in a sense, has never ceased to be a great power: the British army in India dominated a zone extending from the Suez Canal to the frontiers of Afghanistan and Thailand. Britain's weakness after the Second World War, the influence of the United States and the Soviet Union, the popularity of the Congress party, and the campaign of nonco-

[3] It is curious that the Westerners, whether right- or left-wing, who are so ready to acknowledge their world-wide influence, fail to remember that they have been responsible for spreading the principle of universal primary education.

operation, were enough to convince the Labour government, interpreting a public opinion which believed less and less in the "white man's burden" and which had always acknowledged in principle that the colonizer's duty and ambition must be to make his presence ultimately unnecessary. During the war the British administration had still managed without much difficulty to command obedience. The Indian army fought no less gallantly in the Second World War than in the First. The "liberation" was the climax of a process of evolution which was moral as well as material.

It was in China, during the "time of troubles," and in Indochina between 1947 and 1954, that guerilla warfare, the counterpart of organized violence, emerged as one of the century's demiurges on a par with the atom bomb. Every state not only claims a monopoly of internal power but also tends to subject its conflicts with other states to the rules of law and order. The soldier who loots or kills without orders is executed; civilians are forbidden to fire on men in uniform. Fighting between archaic tribes, however different in other ways, is no less organized than the wars of civilized peoples. Guerilla warfare is not the original form of human hostilities, any more than individuals or families necessarily preceded clans.[4] In our time it is due either to the collapse of a social order, to popular reactions provoked by an invasion, to patriotic uprisings, or, finally, to a deliberate decision taken by the leaders of a state or a counter-state.

The measures taken by a revolutionary government against a traditional way of life unleashed in the Vendée a "partisan war" favored by the nature of the terrain. The Napoleonic armies, which lived off the country, forced the Spanish and Russian peasants to take to guerilla warfare, probably because of the food shortage their exactions provoked. The importance of the respective roles played by hunger, hatred of the foreigner, and attachment to the native soil in popular uprisings has never been calculated with any precision. The bomb throwings, raids, and ambushes, the destruction of civil and military installations *organized* by the Soviet government behind the lines of the German army between 1941 and 1944 and later organized by the Chinese Communist party and the Vietminh over a period of many years, represent an original phenomenon, on a par with the resistance to German occupation in the countries of the West during the Second World War.

All these examples can be seen to have one point in common: the

[4] Historically, states have rarely succeeded in excluding civilians from hostilities. Often, in antiquity, the citizens of defeated cities were put to death or sold as slaves. In the first centuries of our era, the Germanic invasions brought into conflict tribes and peoples rather than armies. War was badly organized, but it was not, spontaneously or systematically, individual.

refusal to allow the regular armies a monopoly on war. The civilians, spontaneously or by orders, combat the armies as best they can. In Western Europe the Resistance was not revolutionary (that is to say, in opposition to the established regime) where it was approved or inspired by the legal government in exile. It was semirevolutionary in France, where it opposed Vichy, a government that was semilegal and semiusurping (or "a prisoner of the enemy"). It was not at all revolutionary in the Soviet Union, where it was directed and led by leaders parachuted behind the lines. Guerilla warfare, as such, is a military technique, not a political action.

But this military technique (individual attacks, surprise raids by small groups, the evasion of pitched battle) is admirably suited to revolutionary action. It is pre-eminently the instrument of "the war of liberation." Even when it is legal in origin, that is, when the legitimate authority has initiated it, it forces the combatants into illegality. Ukrainian partisans who fought against the German army continued the struggle against the Soviet administration. The Resistance fighters of Western Europe, even in Holland and Belgium, became gradually susceptible to extremist slogans. Guerilla warfare, in the twentieth century, tends to assume a political character, just as revolutionary politics spontaneously turns to guerilla warfare.

In recent times, guerilla warfare alone has never defeated a regular army. The Chinese Communists, even before the Second World War, had built up a conventional army with a base in the northwest provinces which they occupied. First comes the phase of individual attacks, ambushes, and brief forays; this spreads insecurity, gradually wears down the administration, and endeavors to stir up the resentment of the masses against the established power, aiming to shake the loyalty of those (the majority) who trim their sails to the wind. To achieve decisive results this method must be accompanied by the creation of a counteradministration and a counter-state. Such was the case in both China and Vietnam.

In both cases, the Communist victory was promoted by external aid. In 1945, the armies of Mao Tse-tung acquired part of the equipment of the Japanese army of Shantung. The Vietminh divisions were trained in China. In the East as in the West, guerilla war between 1940 and 1945 had only a contributory value. But as an instrument of revolutionary action, it is a force liable to alter the map of the world. In the treatise of a twentieth-century Clausewitz, the Communist theory of revolutionary warfare would figure just as prominently as the theory of nuclear weapons.

First of all we must consider the enormous disproportion between the forces of order and the guerilla forces when the nature of the terrain favors the latter—in Malaya, for example, or in Algeria. Some five thousand Chinese held out for years in forest and jungle against tens of thousands of British soldiers. Three hundred and fifty thousand French soldiers have failed to suppress the Algerian insurrection, although the rebels are said to number no more than fifteen thousand. The conviction has gradually spread in the West that it is impossible to stamp out guerillas by purely military means.

The contrast between the European conquests of the last century and the successful anti-European revolts in this century inevitably raises many questions. Did prestige as much as force account for yesterday's conquests? Or are today's Europeans reluctant to use methods which once seemed quite normal? The guerilla warfare of the twentieth cenutry is organized, the fighters are led by officers or political commissars who, even when they are not Communists, have received a military training, and intellectual education. The Vietminh proceeded to educate the masses with a zeal worthy of the Meiji reformers. The people of Vietnam or North Africa are perhaps no more hostile to the invaders than they used to be. But the French are less convinced of their right to colonize, the colonized no longer believe in the legitimacy of colonization, and above all the subject peoples now have leaders capable of commanding them (intellectuals who have graduated from our universities, officers, or N.C.O.'s from our army).

The Europeans' loss of prestige, the weakening of the imperalist will of the British and the French, the enthusiasm of a minority inspired by nationalism, Communism, or both, the vague aspiration of the masses to an independence which promises both the foreigner's departure and the beginning of an era of prosperity: all these facts together prepare the ground on which guerilla action eventually triumphs. True, without the possession of a territorial base and the Sino-Japanese War, the Chinese peasants would never have been formed into an army capable of defeating Chiang Kai-shek's divisions. Chinese aid was indispensable to the formation of the six divisions General Giap engaged at Dien Bien Phu. In Malaya, where no help came from outside, the few thousand Communists held out vainly in the jungle; in Algeria the insurgents cannot, even if they succeed in organizing a clandestine counteradministration, throw the French army into the sea.

Insurgents have no need of decisive successes in order to win, whereas colonial powers need total victory—that is to say, the establishment of order and security—a victory that is almost impossible on the military plane. In cities there is no way of preventing a few terrorists from throwing bombs at random.[5] North African fellahs can find refuge in the mountains; in the delta of Tonkin the Vietminh fighter was indistin-

---

[5] Indiscriminate attacks against civilians constitute a particularly horrible form of guerilla warfare, since it does not choose its victims. This urban terrorism is a means of guerilla warfare mainly psychological in effect.

guishable from a peasant when the French tanks approached. Asian or African guerilla action ultimately triumphs provided it lasts long enough, even without waiting for the last phase of a general counteroffensive. Combined with the propaganda of the Afro-Asian block and the support of anticolonialist opinion within European countries, it erodes the will to resist or to dominate what it would be incapable of destroying in a pitched battle.

In Tunisia and Morocco the psychological repercussions of terrorism were out of all proportion to the number of victims. Materially the French were capable of "holding on." To put an end to terrorism there was probably no other solution, apart from blind repression, except negotiation with the nationalists. The British too, at the end of a quasi-victorious struggle against a Communist guerilla force, granted independence to Malaya.

Perhaps counterguerillas are the only answer to guerillas. But European soldiers are not equipped for such warfare in the midst of populations of other races. Nothing can eliminate the inferiority of the European in this sort of fighting. Human life has a different value in the West, with its low birth rate, than in countries where fecundity remains the same while medicine and hygiene have reduced mortality. Every French soldier or worker represents an investment of hundreds of thousands if not millions of francs, whereas countless Algerians live on the edge of subsistence, making little or no inroads on the collective resources of the country. On the plane of history, this inequality created by the overlapping of civilizations, weighs more powerfully than the equality of human souls before God.

Guerilla warfare is not a return to anarchy. It is a form of organized combat, although the organization is at the opposite extreme from nuclear war. In the latter, nothing is on the human scale: pilotless planes herald rockets carrying thermonuclear explosives hundreds if not thousands of miles. Guerilla organization, on the other hand, depends constantly on individuals: the resolution of each man, the initiative of a few, the endurance of all, remain decisive. Ambushes which cost the lives of women and children, bombs which kill customers on café terraces, do not represent "a fair fight" any more than saturation bombing. The discipline of clandestine war requires more brutality and terror than that of regular troops. There is always a danger that partisan warfare will degenerate into anarchy, and the revolutionary government, having triumphed through guerilla methods, is condemned for a period to use violence to re-establish order and restore its troops to legality.

The machine gun and the thermonuclear bomb, individual murder and mass slaughter: the two extremes of warfare are now encroaching on the terrain which fifteen years ago seemed the exclusive preserve of regular motorized and mechanized armies. What function remains for those steel monsters that from 1940-45 swept like a whirlwind across the plains of Europe from Brest to Rostov? This is a question for the experts, and we shall not presume to answer it here. The fragmentation of the diplomatic field has a military equivalent in the diversity of wars possible in our time. In the Middle East, Israel and the Arab countries plan a mechanized war comparable to the desert campaigns of Rommel and Montgomery. In North Africa, the Algerians are waging a guerilla war based on the teachings of Communist doctrine. In Europe, East and West face one another under the shadow of the ultimate war—the war of atomic weapons, rockets, and supersonic aircraft. These three types of war, Western in origin, equally presuppose science, industry, and conscription.

For the moment it is impossible to rule out any of them, impossible to shape political units to a single model. If there is normally a correlation between military techniques and the size of political units, three military techniques coexist in our time. Only the technique of 1940-45 condemned, or appeared to condemn, the small power. Guerilla warfare does not require big battalions. The atom bomb will tomorrow be within reach of the so-called second-class states and will narrow the gap between great and small powers, which was originally widened by the discovery of the nuclear weapon.

Arnold Toynbee

Arnold Toynbee's philosophy of history, as conveyed in his monumental *Study of History,* holds that all human civilizations tend to follow a similar pattern and that our own civilization, like others before it, may ultimately destroy itself. He differs, however, from many who subscribe to cyclical theories of history in that he does not regard this process as inevitable; his firm belief in "the message of Christianity and the other higher religions" leads him to a cautious optimism about the future, and to the idea that man is at least capable of learning from past cultures and of thereby avoiding certain of their mortal errors.

Toynbee expresses his own highly original thought in almost a nineteenth-century manner. Particularly notable is his fondness for making his theoretical conceptions concrete through retrospective metaphor and also through personal reminiscences such as the one which begins "The Present Point in History." Equally characteristic is the remarkable breadth of his general view and his easy, unpretentious use of his prodigious learning. He manages also to be strikingly free of the myopia of the merely timely; the fact that America is no

longer the sole atomic power, as she was in 1947, when Toynbee wrote this
essay, does not detract from the over-all accuracy of his analysis of Soviet-
American rivalry in terms of analogy with earlier historical events. It is not
surprising that the particular developments of recent years have not substantially
altered this historian's estimate of our culture's chances for survival. He continues to affirm his faith in man's capacity for understanding—and hence con-
trolling—his destiny.

$\mathcal{T}$HE PRESENT POINT IN HISTORY

Where does mankind stand in the year 1947 of the Christian
era? This question no doubt concerns the whole living generation
throughout the world; but, if it were made the subject of a world-wide
Gallup Poll, there would be no unanimity in the answer. On this matter,
if any, *quot homines, tot sententiae;* so we must ask ourselves in the same
breath: To whom is our question being addressed? For example, the
writer of the present paper is a middle-class Englishman of fifty-eight.
Evidently his nationality, his social milieu, and his age, between them,
will in large measure determine the standpoint from which he views the
world panorama. In fact, like each and all of us, he is more or less the
slave of historical relativity. The only personal advantage that he can
claim to possess is that he happens also to be a historian, and is therefore
at least aware that he himself is a piece of sentient flotsam on the eddy-
ing surface of the stream of time. Realizing this, he knows that his fleeting and fragmentary vision of the passing scene is no more than a caricature of the surveyor's chart. God alone knows the true picture. Our
individual human *aperçus* are shots in the dark.

The writer's mind runs back fifty years, to an afternoon in London
in the year 1897. He is sitting with his father at a window in Fleet Street
and watching a procession of Canadian and Australian mounted troops
who have come to celebrate Queen Victoria's Diamond Jubilee. He can
still remember his excitement at the unfamiliar, picturesque uniforms of
these magnificent "colonial" troops, as they were still called in England
then: slouch hats instead of brass helmets, grey tunics instead of red. To
an English child, this sight gave a sense of new life astir in the world; a
philosopher, perhaps, might have reflected that, where there is growth,
there is likely also to be decay. A poet, watching the same scene, did, in
fact, catch and express an intimation of something of the kind. Yet few

From *Civilization on Trial* by A. J. Toynbee. Copyright 1948 by Oxford University Press,
Inc. Reprinted by permission.

in the English crowd gazing at that march past of overseas troops in London in 1897 were in the mood of Kipling's *Recessional*. They saw their sun standing at its zenith and assumed that it was there to stay—without their even needing to give it the magically compelling word of command which Joshua had uttered on a famous occasion.

The author of the tenth chapter of the Book of Joshua was at any rate aware that a stand-still of Time was something unusual. "There was no day like that before it or after it, that the Lord hearkened unto the voice of a man." Yet the middle-class English of 1897, who thought of themselves as Wellsian rationalists living in a scientific age, took their imaginary miracle for granted. As they saw it, history, for them, was over. It had come to an end in foreign affairs in 1815, with the Battle of Waterloo; in home affairs in 1832, with the Great Reform Bill; and in imperial affairs in 1859, with the suppression of the Indian Mutiny. And they had every reason to congratulate themselves on the permanent state of felicity which this ending of history had conferred on them. "The lines are fallen unto me in pleasant places; yea, I have a goodly heritage."

Viewed from the historical vantage point of A.D. 1947, this *fin de siècle* middle-class English hallucination seems sheer lunacy, yet it was shared by contemporary Western middle-class people of other nationalities. In the United States, for instance, in the North, history, for the middle class, had come to an end with the winning of the West and the Federal victory in the Civil War; and in Germany, or at any rate in Prussia, for the same class, the same permanent consummation had been reached with the overthrow of France and foundation of the Second Reich in 1871. For these three batches of Western middle-class people fifty years ago, God's work of creation was completed, "and behold it was very good." Yet, though in 1897 the English, American, and German middle class, between them, were the political and economic masters of the world, they did not amount, in numbers, to more than a very small fraction of the living generation of mankind, and there were other people abroad who saw things differently—even though they might be impotent and inarticulate.

In the South, for example, and in France, there were in 1897 many people who agreed with their late conquerors that history had come to an end: The Confederacy would never rise from the dead; Alsace-Lorraine would never be recovered. But this sense of finality, which was so gratifying to top dog, did not warm a defeated people's heart. For them it was nothing but a nightmare. The Austrians, still smarting from their defeat in 1866, might have felt the same if the stirrings of submerged nationalities inside an Empire whose territory Bismarck had left intact had not begun, by this time, to make the Austrians feel that history was once more on the move and might have still worse blows than Königgratz in store for them. English liberals at the time were indeed talking freely, and with approval, of a coming liberation of subject nationalities in Austria-Hungary and the Balkans. But, in spite of the spectre of Home Rule and the stirrings of "Indian unrest," it did not occur to them that, in South-Eastern Europe, they were greeting the first symptoms of a process of political liquidation which was to spread, in their lifetime, to both India and Ireland and, in its irresistible progress round the world, was to break up other empires besides the Hapsburg Monarchy.

All over the world, in fact, though at that time still under the surface, there were peoples and classes who were just as discontented as the French or the Southerners were with the latest deal of history's cards, but who were quite unwilling to agree that the game was over. There were all the subject peoples and all the depressed classes, and what millions they amounted to! They included the whole vast population of the Russian Empire of the day, from Warsaw to Vladivostok: Poles and Finns determined to win their national independence; Russian peasants determined to gain possession of the rest of the land of which they had been given so meagre a slice in the reforms of the eighteen-sixties; Russian intellectuals and business men who dreamed of one day governing their own country through parliamentary institutions, as people of their kind had long been governing the United States, Great Britain, and France; and a young and still small Russian industrial proletariat that was being turned revolutionary-minded by living conditions that were grim enough, though perhaps less so than those of early nineteenth-century Manchester. The industrial working class in England had, of course, improved their position very notably since the opening of the nineteenth century, thanks to the factory acts, the trades unions, and the vote (they had been enfranchised by Disraeli in 1867). Still, in 1897, they could not, and did not, look back on the Poor Law Act of 1834, as the middle class did look back on the Reform Bill of 1832, as history's last word in wisdom and beneficence. They were not revolutionary, but, on constitutional lines, they were resolved to make the wheels of history move on. As for the Continental European working class, they were capable of going to extremes, as the Paris Commune of 1871 had shown in an ominous lightning flash.

This deep desire for changes and the strong resolve to bring them about by one means or another were not, after all, surprising in the underdog, as represented by underprivileged classes and defeated or unliberated peoples. It was strange, though, that the apple-cart should be upset, as it was in 1914, by the Prussian militarists' (who in truth had as little to gain and as much to lose as the German, English, and American middle class) deliberately tearing open again history's insecurely closed book.

The subterranean movements that could have been detected, even as far back as 1897, by a social seismologist who put his ear to the ground, go far to explain the upheavals and eruptions that have signalized the resumption of history's Juggernaut march during the past half-century. To-day, in 1947, the Western middle class which, fifty years ago, was sitting carefree on the volcano's crust, is suffering something like the tribulation which, a hundred to a hundred and fifty years ago, was inflicted by Juggernaut's car on the English industrial working class. This is the situation of the middle class to-day not only in Germany, France, the Low Countries, Scandinavia, and Great Britain, but also in some degree in Switzerland and Sweden, and even in the United States and Canada. The future of the Western middle class is in question now in all Western countries; but the outcome is not simply the concern of the small fraction of mankind directly affected; for this Western middle class —this tiny minority—is the leaven that in recent times has leavened the lump and has thereby created the modern world. Could the creature survive its creator? If the Western middle class broke down, would it bring humanity's house down with it in its fall? Whatever the answer to this fateful question may be, it is clear that what is a crisis for this key-minority is inevitably also a crisis for the rest of the world.

It is always a test of character to be baffled and "up against it," but the test is particularly severe when the adversity comes suddenly at the noon of a halcyon day which one has fatuously expected to endure to eternity. In straits like these, the wrestler with destiny is tempted to look for bugbears and scapegoats to carry the burden of his own inadequacy. Yet to "pass the buck" in adversity is still more dangerous than to persuade oneself that prosperity is everlasting. In the divided world of 1947, Communism and Capitalism are each performing this insidious office for one another. Whenever things go awry in circumstances that seem ever more intractable, we tend to accuse the enemy of having sown tares in our field and thereby implicitly excuse ourselves for the faults in our own husbandry. This is, of course, an old story. Centuries before Communism was heard of, our ancestors found their bugbear in Islam. As lately as the sixteenth century, Islam inspired the same hysteria in Western hearts as Communism in the twentieth century, and this essentially for the same reasons. Like Communism, Islam was an anti-Western movement which was at the same time a heretical version of a Western faith; and, like Communism, it wielded a sword of the spirit against which there was no defence in material armaments.

The present Western fear of Communism is not a fear of military aggression such as we felt in face of a Nazi Germany and a militant Japan. The United States, at any rate, with her overwhelming superiority in industrial potential and her monopoly of the "know-how" of the atom bomb, is at present impregnable against military attack by the Soviet

Union. For Moscow, it would be sheer suicide to make the attempt, and there is no evidence that the Kremlin has any intention of committing such a folly. The Communist weapon that is making America so jumpy (and, oddly enough, she is reacting more temperamentally to this threat than the less sheltered countries of Western Europe) is the spiritual engine of propaganda. Communist propaganda has a "know-how" of its own for showing up and magnifying the seamy side of our Western civilization and for making Communism appear a desirable alternative way of life to a dissatisfied faction of Western men and women. Communism is also a competitor for the allegiance of that great majority of mankind that is neither Communist nor Capitalist, neither Russian nor Western, but is living at present in an uneasy no-man's-land between the opposing citadels of the two rival ideologies. Both nondescripts and Westerners are in danger of turning Communist to-day, as they were of turning Turk four hundred years ago, and, though Communists are in similar danger of turning Capitalists—as sensational instances have shown—the fact that one's rival witch-doctor is as much afraid of one's own medicine as one is afraid, oneself, of his, does not do anything to relieve the tension of the situation.

Yet the fact that our adversary threatens us by showing up our defects, rather than by forcibly suppressing our virtues, is proof that the challenge he presents to us comes ultimately not from him, but from ourselves. It comes, in fact, from that recent huge increase in Western man's technological command over non-human nature—his stupendous progress in "know-how"—which was just what gave our fathers the confidence to delude themselves into imagining that, for them, history was comfortably over. Through these triumphs of clockwork the Western middle class had produced three undesigned results—unprecedented in history—whose cumulative impetus has set Juggernaut's car rolling on again with a vengeance. Our Western "know-how" has unified the whole world in the literal sense of the whole habitable and traversable surface of the globe; and it has inflamed the institutions of War and Class, which are the two congenital diseases of civilization, into utterly fatal maladies. This trio of unintentional achievements presents us with a challenge that is formidable indeed.

War and Class have been with us ever since the first civilizations emerged above the level of primitive human life some five or six thousand years ago, and they have always been serious complaints. Of the twenty or so civilizations known to modern Western historians, all except our own appear to be dead or moribund, and, when we diagnose each case, *in extremis* or *post mortem,* we invariably find that the cause of death has been either War or Class or some combination of the two. To date, these two plagues have been deadly enough, in partnership, to kill off nineteen out of twenty representatives of this recently evolved species of human society; but, up to now, the deadliness of these scourges has had a saving limit. While they have been able to destroy individual specimens, they have failed to destroy the species itself. Civilizations have come and gone, but Civilization (with a big "C") has succeeded, each time, in re-incarnating itself in fresh exemplars of the type; for, immense though the social ravages of War and Class have been, they have not ever yet been all-embracing. When they have shattered the top strata of a society, they have usually failed to prevent the underlying strata from surviving, more or less intact, and clothing themselves with spring flowers on exposure to the light and air. And when one society has collapsed in one quarter of the world it has not, in the past, necessarily dragged down others with it. When the early civilization of China broke down in the seventh century B.C., this did not prevent the contemporary Greek civilization, at the other end of the Old World, from continuing to rise towards its zenith. And when the Graeco-Roman civilization finally died of the twin diseases of War and Class in the course of the fifth, sixth, and seventh centuries of the Christian era, this did not prevent a new civilization from success-fully coming to birth in the Far East during those same three hundred years.

Why cannot civilization go on shambling along, from failure to failure, in the painful, degrading, but not utterly suicidal way in which it has kept going for the first few thousand years of its existence? The answer lies in the recent technological inventions of the modern Western middle class. These gadgets for harnessing the physical forces of non-human nature have left human nature unchanged. The institutions of War and Class are social reflexions of the seamy side of human nature—or what the theologians call original sin—in the kind of society that we call civilization. These social effects of individual human sinfulness have not been abolished by the recent portentous advance in our technological "know-how," but they have not been left unaffected by it either. Not hav-ing been abolished, they have been enormously keyed up, like the rest of human life, in respect of their physical potency. Class has now become capable of irrevocably disintegrating Society, and War of annihilating the entire human race. Evils which hitherto have been merely disgraceful and grievous have now become intolerable and lethal, and, therefore, we in this Westernized world in our generation are confronted with a choice of alternatives which the ruling elements in other societies in the past have always been able to shirk—with dire consquences, invariably, for themselves, but not at the extreme price of bringing to an end the history of mankind on this planet. We are thus confronted with a challenge that our predecessors never had to face: We have to abolish War and Class—and abolish them now—under pain, if we flinch or fail, of seeing them win a victory over man which, this time, would be conclusive and definitive.

The new aspect of war is already familiar to Western minds. We are aware that the atom bomb and our many other new lethal weapons are capable, in another war, of wiping out not merely the belligerents but the whole of the human race. But how has the evil of class been heightened by technology? Has not technology already notably raised the minimum standard of living—at any rate in countries that have been specially efficient or specially fortunate in being endowed with the riches of nature and being spared the ravages of war? Can we not look forward to seeing this rapidly rising minimum standard raised to so high a level, and enjoyed by so large a percentage of the human race, that the even greater riches of a still more highly favoured minority will cease to be a cause of heartburning? The flaw in this line of reasoning is that it leaves out of account the vital truth that man does not live by bread alone. However high the minimum standard of his material living may be raised, that will not cure his soul of demanding social justice; and the unequal distribution of this world's goods between a privileged minority and an underprivileged majority has been transformed from an unavoidable evil into an intolerable injustice by the latest technological inventions of Western man.

When we admire aesthetically the marvellous masonry and architecture of the Great Pyramid or the exquisite furniture and jewelry of Tut-ankh-Amen's tomb, there is a conflict in our hearts between our pride and pleasure in such triumphs of human art and our moral condemnation of the human price at which these triumphs have been bought: the hard labour unjustly imposed on the many to produce the fine flowers of civilization for the exclusive enjoyment of a few who reap where they have not sown. During these last five of six thousand years, the masters of the civilizations have robbed their slaves of their share in the fruits of society's corporate labours as cold-bloodedly as we rob our bees of their honey. The moral ugliness of the unjust act mars the aesthetic beauty of the artistic result; yet, up till now, the few favoured beneficiaries of civilization have had one obvious common-sense plea to put forward in their own defence.

It has been a choice, they have been able to plead, between fruits of civilization for the few and no fruits at all. Our technological command over nature is severely limited. We have at our command neither sufficient muscle-power nor sufficient labour to turn out our amenities in more than minute quantities. If I am to deny these to myself just because you cannot all have them too, we shall have to shut up shop and allow one of the finest talents of human nature to rust away buried in a napkin; and, while that is certainly not in my interest, it is surely not in yours either on a longer view. For I am not enjoying this monopoly of amenities exclusively for my own benefit. My enjoyment is at least partly vicarious. In indulging myself at your expense, I am in some sense serving as a kind of trustee for all future generations of the whole human race. This plea was a plausible one, even in our technologically go-ahead Western world, down to the eighteenth century inclusive, but our unprecented techno-logical progress in the last hundred and fifty years has made the same plea invalid to-day. In a society that has discovered the "know-how" of Amalthea's cornucopia, the always ugly inequality in the distribution of this world's goods, in ceasing to be a practical necessity, has become a moral enormity.

Thus the problems that have beset and worsted other civilizations have come to a head in our world to-day. We have invented the atomic weapon in a world partitioned between two supremely great powers; and the United States and the Soviet Union stand respectively for two oppos-ing ideologies whose antithesis is so extreme that, as it stands, it seems irreconcilable. Along what path are we to look for salvation in this parlous plight, in which we hold in our hands the choice of life or death not only for ourselves but for the whole human race? Salvation perhaps lies, as so often, in finding a middle way. In politics, this golden mean would be something that was neither the unrestricted sovereignty of parochial states nor the unrelieved despotism of a centralized world gov-ernment; in economics it would be something that was neither unre-stricted private enterprise nor unmitigated socialism. As one middle-aged middle-class West European observer sees the world to-day, salvation cometh neither from the East nor from the West.

In A.D. 1947, the United States and the Soviet Union are alternative embodiments of contemporary man's tremendous material power; "their line is gone out through all the Earth, and their words to the end of the World," but in the mouths of these loud-speakers one does not hear the still small voice. Our cue may still be given us by the message of Chris-tianity and the other higher religions, and the saving words and deeds may come from unexpected quarters.

George Bernard Shaw

Prodesse et delectare—to teach and to delight—was a Roman ideal of what the artist should do. In this sense no modern writer has been more Roman than the great Anglo-Irish dramatist Bernard Shaw (1856-1950), whose superbly entertaining plays aimed always at curing "the ordinary citizen's ignor-ance." In fact, Shaw's urge to instruct was so strong and his opinion of his

audience so low that when his plays were published he could seldom resist
adding a Preface or "Notes" in the hope of driving home his points still once
more. In the Notes to *Caesar and Cleopatra*, which can be read independently
of the play, Shaw's ostensible purpose is to defend the play against charges of
historical inaccuracy. But his real purpose, like that of Toynbee and other
serious thinkers of the century, is to examine the lessons of history and to formulate from these certain theories about the nature of man and of human society
and to persuade the reader to accept them. A Fabian socialist in politics, Shaw
nevertheless espouses a notion which has not been very fashionable in this
century: that it is great men who make history, and not the other way around.

Shaw's methods of persuasion could hardly be more different from those
of a formal thinker or professional historian. He makes no attempt to prove
his points through closely reasoned argument but relies on the brilliance of his
wit and the prolific and rich variety of his ideas, most frequently expressing
themselves in a series of polemical attacks. In order to move the reader to *his*
point of view, he must manage to destroy a number of conventional ideas and
attitudes which the ordinary citizen uncritically—and often tenaciously—clings
to. His targets are many—the military, the church, the royal family, provincialism,
faith in technology, patriotism, and so on. He has at his command all the
classic weapon devices of the comic spirit: ridicule, spoof, exaggeration, mock
solemnity, hyperbole, wit, irony. But the major and unifying device he uses
here is the wilful disassociation of his own self from the most favored popular
notions of his own time. This disassociation creates the useful illusion that the
twentieth century is as distant in time from us as, say, the fourth, and that its
doctrines and dogmas are often no worthier of respect than many shibboleths
from the past. Shaw, more than most of his contemporaries, knew how to be
serious without being solemn.

*N*OTES TO CAESAR AND CLEOPATRA

. . . .**Apparent Anachronisms**

The only way to write a play which shall convey to the general public
an impression of antiquity is to make the characters speak blank verse
and abstain from reference to steam, telegraphy, or any of the material
conditions of their existence. The more ignorant men are, the more convinced are they that their little parish and their little chapel is an apex
to which civilization and philosophy has painfully struggled up the pyramid of time from a desert of savagery. Savagery, they think, became
barbarism; barbarism became ancient civilization; ancient civilization
became Pauline Christianity; Pauline Christianity became Roman Catho-

From *Caesar and Cleopatra* by George Bernard Shaw. Reprinted by permission of the
Public Trustee and The Society of Authors.

licism; Roman Catholicism became the Dark Ages; and the Dark Ages were finally enlightened by the Protestant instincts of the English race. The whole process is summed up as Progress with a capital P. And any elderly gentleman of Progressive temperament will testify that the improvement since he was a boy is enormous.

Now if we count the generations of Progressive elderly gentlemen since, say, Plato, and add together the successive enormous improvements to which each of them has testified, it will strike us at once as an unaccountable fact that the world, instead of having been improved in 67 generations out of all recognition, presents, on the whole, a rather less dignified appearance in Ibsen's Enemy of the People than in Plato's Republic. And in truth, the period of time covered by history is far too short to allow of any perceptible progress in the popular sense of Evolution of the Human Species. The notion that there has been any such Progress since Caesar's time (less than 20 centuries) is too absurd for discussion. All the savagery, barbarism, dark ages and the rest of it of which we have any record as existing in the past, exists at the present moment. A British carpenter or stonemason may point out that he gets twice as much money for his labor as his father did in the same trade, and that his suburban house, with its bath, its cottage piano, its drawing room suite, and its album of photographs, would have shamed the plainness of his grandmother's. But the descendants of feudal barons, living in squalid lodgings on a salary of fifteen shillings a week instead of in castles on princely revenues, do not congratulate the world on the change. Such changes, in fact, are not to the point. It has been known, as far back as our records go, that man running wild in the woods is different from man kennelled in a city slum; that a dog seems to understand a shepherd better than a hewer of wood and drawer of water can understand an astronomer; and that breeding, gentle nurture, and luxurious food and shelter will produce a kind of man with whom the common laborer is socially incompatible. The same thing is true of horses and dogs. Now there is clearly room for great changes in the world by increasing the percentage of individuals who are carefully bred and gently nurtured, even to finally making the most of every man and woman born. But that possibility existed in the days of the Hittites as much as it does today. It does not give the slightest real support to the common assumption that the civilized contemporaries of the Hittites were unlike their civilized descendants today.

This would appear the tritest commonplace if it were not that the ordinary citizen's ignorance of the past combines with his idealization of the present to mislead and flatter him. Our latest book on the new railway across Asia describes the dulness of the Siberian farmer and the vulgar pursepride of the Siberian man of business without the least consciousness that the string of contemptuous instances given might have been saved by writing simply "Farmers and provincial plutocrats in Siberia are exactly what they are in England." The latest professor descanting on the civilization of the Western Empire in the fifth century feels bound to assume, in the teeth of his own researches, that the Christian was one sort of animal and the Pagan another. It might as well be assumed as indeed it generally is assumed by implication, that a murder committed with a poisoned arrow is different from a murder committed with a Mauser rifle. All such notions are illusions. Go back to the first syllable of recorded time, and there you will find your Christian and your Pagan, your yokel and your poet, helot and hero, Don Quixote and Sancho, Tamino and Papageno, Newton and bushman unable to count eleven, all alive and contemporaneous, and all convinced that they are the heirs of all the ages and the privileged recipients of THE truth (all others damnable heresies), just as you have them today, flourishing in countries each of which is the bravest and best that ever sprang at Heaven's command from out the azure main.

Again, there is the illusion of "increased command over Nature," meaning that cotton is cheap and that ten miles of country road on a bicycle have replaced four on foot. But even if man's increased command over Nature included any increased command over himself (the only sort of command relevant to his evolution into a higher being), the fact remains that it is only by running away from the increased command over Nature to country places where Nature is still in primitive command over Man that he can recover from the effects of the smoke, the stench, the foul air, the overcrowding, the racket, the ugliness, the dirt which the cheap cotton costs us. If manufacturing activity means Progress, the town must be more advanced than the country; and the field laborers and village artisans of today must be much less changed from servants of Job than the proletariat of modern London from the proletariat of Caesar's Rome. Yet the cockney proletarian is so inferior to the village laborer that it is only by steady recruiting from the country that London is kept alive. This does not seem as if the change since Job's time were Progress in the popular sense: quite the reverse. The comman stock of discoveries in physics has accumulated a little: that is all.

One more illustration. Is the Englishman prepared to admit that the American is his superior as a human being? I ask this question because the scarcity of labor in America relatively to the demand for it has led to a development of machinery there, and a consequent "increase of command over Nature" which makes many of our English methods appear almost medieval to the up-to-date Chicagoan. This means that the American has an advantage over the Englishman of exactly the same nature that the Englishman has over the contemporaries of Cicero. Is the

Englishman prepared to draw the same conclusion in both cases? I think not. The American, of course, will draw it cheerfully; but I must then ask him whether, since a modern negro has a greater "command over Nature" than Washington had, we are also to accept the conclusion, involved in his former one, that humanity has progressed from Washington to the *fin de siècle* negro.

Finally, I would point out that if life is crowned by its success and devotion in industrial organization and ingenuity, we had better worship the ant and the bee (as moralists urge us to do in our childhood), and humble ourselves before the arrogance of the birds of Aristophanes.

My reason then for ignoring the popular conception of Progress in Caesar and Cleopatra is that there is no reason to suppose that any Progress has taken place since their time. But even if I shared the popular delusion, I do not see that I could have made any essential difference in the play. I can only imitate humanity as I know it. Nobody knows whether Shakespear thought that ancient Athenian joiners, weavers, or bellows menders were any different from Elizabethan ones; but it is quite certain that he could not have made them so, unless, indeed, he had played the literary man and made Quince say, not "Is all our company here?" but "Bottom: was not that Socrates that passed us at the Piraeus with Glaucon and Polemarchus on his way to the house of Kephalus?" And so on.

Part Two

THE BURDEN
OF FREEDOM

Anyone who shares in the conception of freedom as a desirable human state is aware of the constant attacks to which that idea has been subjected—by tyrants and armies, by dictators of the spirit who are sure that they know what is best for the human race, by intolerant mobs unwilling to endure the existence of the lone dissenter. It is unwise to assume, as do many people of our time, that the enemies of freedom can be simply identified with political philosophies or ideologies which we are opposed to. The essays in Section II—notably Koestler's account of his life as a communist, Benn's expressionistic diatribe against the vices of Nazi Germany, and Brenan's description of life in Falangist Spain—demonstrate that tyranny may come from either the Right or the Left, and Mary McCarthy's analysis of the fear-laden atmosphere of America in the early 1950's suggests the ease with which people may be tempted to surrender their freedom, even amid institutions which, like ours, are traditionally committed to the defense of that ideal.

Although these essays draw our attention to various aggressive threats to freedom, most of them are also concerned with the equally insidious threat posed by the traitor within, by that element in every personality which instinctively regards its own freedom as a troublesome burden to be shuffled off with one excuse or another so that the personality may doze in the comfortable torpor of orthodoxy, conformity, or servitude. This internal threat may be activated by psychological considerations, as Arthur Koestler suggests in relating his willing acceptance of the shackles of Communist Party membership to feelings of inferiority developed in his childhood. It may be, as George Orwell points out, the result of intellectual laziness, or, as Mary McCarthy argues, of a panicky and dishonest refusal to face unpleasant facts. One implication of these essays is that the effective defense of freedom lies in self-knowledge rather than belligerent rhetoric, in intellectual honesty rather than oaths of loyalty.

To some extent the menaces to freedom, both internal and external, have been intensified by the mass features of modern society, the features examined by many of the writers in Section I. A world in which vast numbers of people live crowded together cannot, by its very nature, allow the degree of uninhibited freedom of individual action both permitted and encouraged by frontier societies or even predominantly rural societies. The chief danger is that the kind of cooperation and mutual consideration required by urban society may become a mask for indefensible encroachments upon basic freedoms, and this danger in turn is heightened by the development of what one might call "mass-emotions." Koestler, in describing the pleasure he found in losing his personal identity in the collective mass of his fellows, may well recall to our minds Canetti's observations on the psychology of crowds. And the fascism which both Benn and Brenan take as their subject would have been inconceivable before our century. But in a deeper sense the struggle for freedom has now the same form it always has had, and its enemies show a consistent family likeness: there is an eerie resemblance between the activities of the sixteenth century inquisitor Lucero, recounted by Brenan in an historical anecdote, and the activities of the twentieth century Senator McCarthy, referred to in the course of Mary McCarthy's essay.

Freedom makes strenuous demands on those who are interested in keeping it, and perhaps that is why its effective defenders have never been terribly numerous. Its demands—not merely emotional, not simply identifiable with the willingness to resist tyranny—are specifically related to intellectual and imaginative capacities. Orwell's analysis of the disease of language in the modern world points out, to be sure, that the deliberate corruption of style is a major weapon of oppression, but he also contends that intellectual sloppiness in itself renders human beings incapable of defending, or even exercising, their freedom. Only the effort to think clearly and to find language to express that thought can supply that contact with reality without which freedom is no more than a dishonest word. One of the central points of Mary McCarthy's address is that a free society depends on a belief in ideas and in the power of true ideas to maintain themselves against false ones: a nation that is afraid to permit the expression of any and all ideas, in her view, cannot really be a free nation. Again, the demand is on one's intellectual energy, the willingness to allow accepted views to be tested by contact with views which one may find alien or even detestable. Judged by such rigorous standards, even the freest of societies are still a long way from the ideal, but the survival of the idea of freedom depends upon keeping the ideal in mind.

If the ability to test one's beliefs by allowing them to be exposed to beliefs of a different sort is an intellectual ability, it is at the same time an imaginative ability. For it requires us implicitly to imagine ourselves as other than we are (a necessary condition, perhaps, for all intellectual growth). It requires us to imagine that our earlier beliefs may in fact be wrong, and human laziness is always inclined to resist the effort required by such imaginings. It is worth noting that most of the following essays have as a recurrent theme the intimate relationship between true freedom and the creative imagination. Four of the five authors represented are at least as well known for their creative work as for their political and social commentary: Orwell, Koestler, and Mary McCarthy have all written fiction of considerable merit, and Gottfried Benn is one of the most important of modern German poets. It is not only man's capacity for exercising energetic intelligence which makes him need freedom as he needs air; it is also his possession, to at least some extent, of the creative faculty which belongs to being human. So it is that Koestler's innate gifts as a writer led to his initial disenchantment with communist discipline, and that Benn's poetic talent forced him to turn from the Nazis in revulsion. George Orwell's essay, although directly concerned not with literary art but with a humbler and more utilitarian sort of writing, makes it clear that there can be no good writing without the participation of the imagination in the intellectual act. The theme of the imagination in Section II thus relates these essays not only to each other but also to essays in later sections of this book, notably those in Sections IV and VI.

Suggested Further Readings:

John Milton, *Areopagitica*
Arthur Koestler, *Darkness at Noon*
George Orwell, *Animal Farm* or *1984*

George Orwell

The following essay, one of the most frequently reprinted of Orwell's works, demonstrates, among other things, the inaccuracy of the popular belief that the active life and the intellectual life are somehow mutually opposed. Eric Blair (1903-1950), who wrote under the pseudonym "George Orwell," was born in India in 1903, served with the Imperial Police in Burma, and worked at a variety of jobs in Paris and London. In 1937 his political sympathies led him to Spain, where he fought on the side of the Loyalists in the Civil War and was wounded. A willingness to commit his life to action in the name of his beliefs underlies his subsequent work as a writer, whether in political commentary, essays, or imaginative fiction.

A radical in his political and social thought, Orwell opposed the remains of the class system and economic injustice in his own country as consistently as he fought fascism abroad. He found it impossible, however, to embrace communism as did many leftist intellectuals of his generation: he recognized that tyranny and cruelty do not change their nature when disguised under attractive names. A refusal to mistake words for things permeates Orwell's writings as it permeates his life and thought. Like Koestler, he regards abstraction as the enemy of life, and like Benn, despite the great differences in their prose styles, he sees responsible language as the basis of responsible thought.

Orwell's hatred of slovenly and platitudinous language comes partly from his aesthetic concerns as a writer, but it comes more directly from his conviction that careless language leads to political deceit, oppression, and the breakdown of a healthy society. His analysis of the diseases of language shows much of the satiric wit which is found in more elaborate form in his novels *Animal Farm* and *1984,* but the piece derives most of its force simply from its clarity.

$\mathcal{P}$OLITICS AND THE ENGLISH LANGUAGE

Most people who bother with the matter at all would admit that the English language is in a bad way, but it is generally assumed that we cannot by conscious action do anything about it. Our civilization is decadent and our language—so the argument runs—must inevitably share in the general collapse. It follows that any struggle against the abuse of language is a sentimental archaism, like preferring candles to electric light or hansom cabs to aeroplanes. Underneath this lies the half-conscious belief that language is a natural growth and not an instrument which we shape for our own purposes.

Now, it is clear that the decline of a language must ultimately have political and economic causes: it is not due simply to the bad influence of this or that individual writer. But an effect can become a cause, reinforcing the original cause and producing the same effect in an intensified form, and so on indefinitely. A man may take to drink because he feels himself to be a failure, and then fail all the more completely because he drinks. It is rather the same thing that is happening to the English language. It becomes ugly and inaccurate because our thoughts are foolish, but the slovenliness of our language makes it easier for us to have foolish thoughts. The point is that the process is reversible. Modern English, especially written English, is full of bad habits which spread by imitation and which can be avoided if one is willing to take the necessary trouble. If one gets rid of these habits one can think more clearly, and to think clearly is a necessary first step towards political regeneration: so that the

From *Shooting an Elephant* by George Orwell, copyright, 1945, 1946, 1949, 1950, by Sonia Brownell Orwell. Reprinted by permission of Harcourt, Brace & World, Inc.

fight against bad English is not frivolous and is not the exclusive concern of professional writers. I will come back to this presently, and I hope that by that time the meaning of what I have said here will have become clearer. Meanwhile, here are five specimens of the English language as it is now habitually written.

These five passages have not been picked out because they are especially bad—I could have quoted far worse if I had chosen—but because they illustrate various of the mental vices from which we now suffer. They are a little below the average, but are fairly representative samples. I number them so that I can refer back to them when necessary:

(1) I am not, indeed, sure whether it is not true to say that the Milton who once seemed not unlike a seventeenth-century Shelley had not become, out of an experience ever more bitter in each year, more alien [sic] to the founder of that Jesuit sect which nothing could induce him to tolerate.

PROFESSOR HAROLD LASKI (Essay in *Freedom of Expression*)

(2) Above all, we cannot play ducks and drakes with a native battery of idioms which prescribes such egregious collocations of vocables as the Basic *put up with* for *tolerate* or *put at a loss* for *bewilder*.

PROFESSER LANCELOT HOGBEN (*Interglossa*)

(3) On the one side we have the free personality: by definition it is not neurotic, for it has neither conflict nor dream. Its desires, such as they are, are transparent, for they are just what institutional approval keeps in the forefront of consciousness; another institutional pattern would alter their number and intensity; there is little in them that is natural, irreducible, or culturally dangerous. But *on the other side,* the social bond itself is nothing but the mutual reflection of these self-secure integrities. Recall the definition of love. Is not this the very picture of a small academic? Where is there a place in this hall of mirrors for either personality or fraternity?

ESSAY ON PSYCHOLOGY IN POLITICS (New York)

(4) All the 'best people' from the gentlemen's clubs, and all the frantic fascist captains, united in common hatred of Socialism and bestial horror of the rising tide of the mass revolutionary movement, have turned to acts of provocation, to foul incendiarism, to medieval legends of poisoned wells, to legalize their own destruction of proletarian organizations, and rouse the agitated petty-bourgeoisie to chauvinistic fervour on behalf of the fight against the revolutionary way out of the crisis.

Communist pamphlet

(5) If a new spirit *is* to be infused into this old country, there is one thorny and contentious reform which must be tackled, and that is the humanization and galvanization of the B.B.C. Timidity here will bespeak canker and atrophy of the soul. The heart of Britain may be sound and of strong beat, for instance, but the British lion's roar at present is like that of Bottom in Shakespeare's *Midsummer Night's Dream*—as gentle as any sucking dove. A virile new Britain cannot continue indefinitely to be traduced in the eyes or rather ears, of the world by the effete languors of Langham Place, brazenly masquerading as 'stand-

ard English'. When the Voice of Britain is heard at nine o'clock, better far and infinitely less ludicrous to hear aitches honestly dropped than the present priggish, inflated, inhibited, school-ma'amish arch braying of blameless bashful mewing maidens!

Letter in Tribune

Each of these passages has faults of its own, but, quite apart from avoidable ugliness, two qualities are common to all of them. The first is staleness of imagery: the other is lack of precision. The writer either has a meaning and cannot express it, or he inadvertently says something else, or he is almost indifferent as to whether his words mean anything or not. This mixture of vagueness and sheer incompetence is the most marked characteristic of modern English prose, and especially of any kind of political writing. As soon as certain topics are raised, the concrete melts into the abstract and no one seems able to think of turns of speech that are not hackneyed: prose consists less and less of *words* chosen for the sake of their meaning, and more and more of *phrases* tacked together like the sections of a prefabricated hen-house. I list below, with notes and examples, various of the tricks by means of which the work of prose-construction is habitually dodged:

DYING METAPHORS

A newly invented metaphor assists thought by evoking a visual image, while on the other hand a metaphor which is technically "dead" (e.g. *iron resolution*) has in effect reverted to being an ordinary word and can generally be used without loss of vividness. But in between these two classes there is a huge dump of worn-out metaphors which have lost all evocative power and are merely used because they save people the trouble of inventing phrases for themselves. Examples are: *Ring the changes on, take up the cudgels for, toe the line, ride roughshod over, stand shoulder to shoulder with, play into the hands of, no axe to grind, grist to the mill, fishing in troubled waters, on the order of the day, Achilles' heel, swan song, hotbed.* Many of these are used without knowledge of their meaning (what is a "rift," for instance?), and incompatible metaphors are frequently mixed, a sure sign that the writer is not interested in what he is saying. Some metaphors now current have been twisted out of their original meaning without those who use them even being aware of the fact. For example, *toe the line* is sometimes written *tow the line*. Another example is *the hammer and the anvil*, now always used with the implication that the anvil gets the worst of it. In real life it is always the anvil that breaks the hammer, never the other way about: a writer who stopped to think what he was saying would be aware of this, and would avoid perverting the original phrase.

OPERATORS OR VERBAL FALSE LIMBS

These save the trouble of picking out appropriate verbs and nouns, and at the same time pad each sentence with extra syllables which give it an appearance of symmetry. Characteristic phrases are: *render inoperative, militate against, make contact with, be subjected to, give rise to, give grounds for, have the effect of, play a leading part (role) in, make itself felt, take effect, exhibit a tendency to, serve the purpose of, etc., etc.* The keynote is the elimination of simple verbs. Instead of being a single word, such as *break, stop, spoil, mend, kill,* a verb becomes a *phrase,* made up of a noun or adjective tacked on to some general-purposes verb such as *prove, serve, form, play, render.* In addition, the passive voice is wherever possible used in preference to the active, and noun constructions are used instead of gerunds (*by examination of* instead of *by examining*). The range of verbs is further cut down by means of the *-ize* and *de-* formations, and the banal statements are given an appearance of profundity by means of the *not un-* formation. Simple conjunctions and prepositions are replaced by such phrases as *with respect to, having regard to, the fact that, by dint of, in view of, in the interests of, on the hypothesis that;* and the ends of sentences are saved from anticlimax by such resounding common-places as *greatly to be desired, cannot be left out of account, a development to be expected in the near future, deserving of serious consideration, brought to a satisfactory conclusion,* and so on and so forth.

PRETENTIOUS DICTION

Words like *phenomenon, element, individual* (as noun), *objective, categorical, effective, virtual, basic, primary, promote, constitute, exhibit, exploit, utilize, eliminate, liquidate,* are used to dress up simple statement and give an air of scientific impartiality to biased judgments. Adjectives like *epoch-making, epic, historic, unforgettable, triumphant, age-old, inevitable, inexorable, veritable,* are used to dignify the sordid processes of international politics, while writing that aims at glorifying war usually takes on an archaic colour, its characteristic words being: *realm, throne, chariot, mailed fist, trident, sword, shield, buckler, banner, jackboot, clarion.* Foreign words and expressions such as *cul de sac, ancien régime, deus ex machina, mutatis mutandis, status quo, gleichschaltung, weltanschauung,* are used to give an air of culture and elegance. Except for the useful abbreviations *i.e., e.g.,* and *etc.,* there is no real need for any of the hundreds of foreign phrases now current in English. Bad writers, and especially scientific, political and sociological writers, are nearly always haunted by the notion that Latin or Greek words are grander than Saxon ones, and unnecessary words like *expedite, ameliorate, predict, extraneous, deracinated, clandestine, subaqueous* and hundreds of others constantly gain ground from their Anglo-Saxon opposite numbers.* The jargon peculiar to Marxist writing (*hyena, hangman, cannibal, petty bourgeois, these gentry, lacquey, flunkey, mad dog, White Guard,* etc.) consists largely of words and phrases translated from Russian, German or French; but the normal way of coining a new word is to use a Latin or Greek root with the appropriate affix and, where necessary, the -ize formation. It is often easier to make up words of this kind (*deregionalize, impermissible, extramarital, non-fragmentatory* and so forth) than to think up the English words that will cover one's meaning. The result, in general, is an increase in slovenliness and vagueness.

MEANINGLESS WORDS

In certain kinds of writing, particularly in art criticism and literary criticism, it is normal to come across long passages which are almost completely lacking in meaning.† Words like *romantic, plastic values, human, dead, sentimental, natural vitality,* as used in art criticism, are strictly meaningless, in the sense that they not only do not point to any discoverable object, but are hardly ever expected to do so by the reader. When one critic writes, "The outstanding feature of Mr. X's work is its living quality," while another writes, "The immediately striking thing about Mr. X's work is its peculiar deadness," the reader accepts this as a simple difference of opinion. If words like *black* and *white* were involved, instead of the jargon words *dead* and *living,* he would see at once that language was being used in an improper way. Many political words are similarly abused. The word *Fascism* has now no meaning except in so far as it signifies "something not desirable." The words *democracy, socialism, freedom, patriotic, realistic, justice,* have each of them several different meanings which cannot be reconciled with one another. In the case of a word like *democracy,* not only is there no agreed definition but the attempt to make one is resisted from all sides. It is almost universally felt that when we call a country democratic we are praising it: consequently the defenders of every kind of régime claim that it is a democracy, and fear that they might have to stop using the word if it were tied

---

* An interesting illustration of this is the way in which the English flower names which were in use till very recently are being ousted by Greek ones, *snapdragon* becoming *antirrhinum, forget-me-not* becoming *myosotis,* etc. It is hard to see any practical reason for this change of fashion: it is probably due to an instinctive turning-away from the more homely word and a vague feeling that the Greek word is scientific.

† Example: "Comfort's catholicity of perception and image, strangely Whitman-esque in range, almost the exact opposite in aesthetic compulsion, continues to evoke that trembling atmospheric accumulative hinting at a cruel, an inexorably serene time-lessness . . . Wrey Gardiner scores by aiming at simple bull's-eyes with precision. Only they are not so simple, and through this contented sadness runs more than the surface bitter-sweet of resignation." (*Poetry Quarterly.*)

down to any one meaning. Words of this kind are often used in a consciously dishonest way. That is, the person who uses them has his own
private definition, but allows his hearer to think he means something
quite different. Statements like *Marshal Pétain was a true patriot, The
Soviet Press is the freest in the world, The Catholic Church is opposed to
persecution,* are almost always made with intent to deceive. Other words
used in variable meanings, in most cases more or less dishonestly, are:
class, totalitarian, science, progressive, reactionary, bourgeois, equality.

Now that I have made this catalogue of swindles and perversions,
let me give another example of the kind of writing that they lead to. This
time it must of its nature be an imaginary one. I am going to translate
a passage of good English into modern English of the worst sort. Here
is a well-known verse from *Ecclesiastes:*

I returned and saw under the sun, that the race is not to the swift, nor the
battle to the strong, neither yet bread to the wise, nor yet riches to men of
understanding, nor yet favour to men of skill; but time and chance happeneth
to them all.

Here it is in modern English:

Objective considerations of contemporary phenomena compels the conclusion that success or failure in competitive activities exhibits no tendency to be
commensurate with innate capacity, but that a considerable element of the
unpredictable must invariably be taken into account.

This is a parody, but not a very gross one. Exhibit (3), above, for
instance, contains several patches of the same kind of English. It will be
seen that I have not made a full translation. The beginning and ending
of the sentence follow the original meaning fairly closely, but in the middle
the concrete illustrations—race, battle, bread—dissolve into the vague
phrase "success or failure in competitive activities." This had to be so,
because no modern writer of the kind I am discussing—no one capable
of using phrases like "objective consideration of contemporary phenomena"—would ever tabulate his thoughts in that precise and detailed
way. The whole tendency of modern prose is away from concreteness.
Now analyse these two sentences a little more closely. The first contains
forty-nine words but only sixty syllables, and all its words are those of
everyday life. The second contains thirty-eight words of ninety syllables:
eighteen of its words are from Latin roots, and one from Greek. The first
sentence contains six vivid images, and only one phrase ("time and
chance") that could be called vague. The second contains not a single
fresh, arresting phrase, and in spite of its ninety syllables it gives only
a shortened version of the meaning contained in the first. Yet without a
doubt it is the second kind of sentence that is gaining ground in modern
English. I do not want to exaggerate. This kind of writing is not yet

universal, and outcrops of simplicity will occur here and there in the worst-written page. Still, if you or I were told to write a few lines on the uncertainty of human fortunes, we should probably come much nearer to my imaginary sentence than to the one from *Ecclesiastes*.

As I have tried to show, modern writing at its worst does not consist in picking out words for the sake of their meaning and inventing images in order to make the meaning clearer. It consists in gumming together long strips of words which have already been set in order by someone else, and making the results presentable by sheer humbug. The attraction of this way of writing is that it is easy. It is easier—even quicker, once you have the habit—to say *In my opinion it is a not unjustifiable assumption that* than to say *I think*. If you use ready-made phrases, you not only don't have to hunt about for words; you also don't have to bother with the rhythms of your sentences, since these phrases are generally so arranged as to be more or less euphonious. When you are composing in a hurry—when you are dictating to a stenographer, for instance, or making a public speech—it is natural to fall into a pretentious, Latinized style. Tags like *a consideration which we should do well to bear in mind* or *a conclusion to which all of us would readily assent* will save many a sentence from coming down with a bump. By using stale metaphors, similes and idioms, you save much mental effort, at the cost of leaving your meaning vague, not only for your reader but for yourself. This is the significance of mixed metaphors. The sole aim of a metaphor is to call up a visual image. When these images clash—as in *The Fascist octopus has sung its swan song, the jackboot is thrown into the melting pot*—it can be taken as certain that the writer is not seeing a mental image of the objects he is naming; in other words he is not really thinking. Look again at the examples I gave at the beginning of this essay. Professor Laski (1) uses five negatives in fifty-three words. One of these is superfluous, making nonsense of the whole passage, and in addition there is the slip *alien* for akin, making further nonsense, and several avoidable pieces of clumsiness which increase the general vagueness. Professor Hogben (2) plays ducks and drakes with a battery which is able to write prescriptions, and, while disapproving of the everyday phrase *put up with,* is unwilling to look *egregious* up in the dictionary and see what it means. (3), if one takes an uncharitable attitude towards it, is simply meaningless: probably one could work out its intended meaning by reading the whole of the article in which it occurs. In (4), the writer knows more or less what he wants to say, but an accumulation of stale phrases chokes him like tea leaves blocking a sink. In (5), words and meaning have almost parted company. People who write in this manner usually have a general emotional meaning—they dislike one thing and want to express solidarity with another—but they are not interested in the detail of what they are saying. A scrupulous writer, in every sentence that he writes, will ask himself at least four questions, thus: What am I trying to say? What words will express it? What image or idiom will make it clearer? Is this image fresh enough to have an effect? And he will probably ask himself two more: Could I put it more shortly? Have I said anything that is avoidably ugly? But you are not obliged to go to all this trouble. You can shirk it by simply throwing your mind open and letting the ready-made phrases come crowding in. They will construct your sentences for you— even think your thoughts for you, to a certain extent—and at need they will perform the important service of partially concealing your meaning even from yourself. It is at this point that the special connexion between politics and the debasement of language becomes clear.

In our time it is broadly true that political writing is bad writing. Where it is not true, it will generally be found that the writer is some kind of rebel, expressing his private opinions and not a "party line." Orthodoxy, of whatever colour, seems to demand a lifeless, imitative style. The political dialects to be found in pamphlets, leading articles, manifestos, White Papers and the speeches of under-secretaries do, of course, vary from party to party, but they are all alike in that one almost never finds in them a fresh, vivid, home-made turn of speech. When one watches some tired hack on the platform mechanically repeating the familiar phrases—*bestial atrocities, iron heel, bloodstained tyranny, free peoples of the world, stand shoulder to shoulder*—one often has a curious feeling that one is not watching a live human being but some kind of dummy: a feeling which suddenly becomes stronger at moments when the light catches the speaker's spectacles and turns them into blank discs which seem to have no eyes behind them. And this is not altogether fanciful. A speaker who uses that kind of phraseology has gone some distance towards turning himself into a machine. The appropriate noises are coming out of his larynx, but his brain is not involved as it would be if he were choosing his words for himself. If the speech he is making is one that he is accustomed to make over and over again, he may be almost unconscious of what he is saying, as one is when one utters the responses in church. And this reduced state of consciousness, if not indispensable, is at any rate favourable to political conformity.

In our time, political speech and writing are largely the defence of the indefensible. Things like the continuance of British rule in India, the Russian purges and deportations, the dropping of the atom bombs on Japan, can indeed be defended, but only by arguments which are too brutal for most people to face, and which do not square with the professed aims of political parties. Thus political language has to consist largely of euphemism, question-begging and sheer cloudy vagueness. Defenceless villages are bombarded from the air, the inhabitants driven out into the countryside, the cattle machine-gunned, the huts set on fire with incendiary bullets: this is called *pacification*. Millions of peasants are robbed of their farms and sent trudging along the roads with no more than they can carry: this is called *transfer of population* or *rectification of frontiers*. People are imprisoned for years without trial, or shot in the back of the neck or sent to die of scurvy in Arctic lumber camps: this is called *elimination of unreliable elements*. Such phraseology is needed if one wants to name things without calling up mental pictures of them. Consider for instance some comfortable English professor defending Russian totalitarianism. He cannot say outright, "I believe in killing off your opponents when you can get good results by doing so." Probably, therefore, he will say something like this:

"While freely conceding that the Soviet régime exhibits certain features which the humanitarian may be inclined to deplore, we must, I think, agree that a certain curtailment of the right to political opposition is an unavoidable concomitant of transitional periods, and that the rigours which the Russian people have been called upon to undergo have been amply justified in the sphere of concrete achievement."

The inflated style is itself a kind of euphemism. A mass of Latin words falls upon the facts like soft snow, blurring the outlines and covering up all the details. The great enemy of clear language is insincerity. When there is a gap between one's real and one's declared aims, one turns as it were instinctively to long words and exhausted idioms, like a cuttlefish squirting out ink. In our age there is no such thing as "keeping out of politics." All issues are political issues, and politics itself is a mass of lies, evasions, folly, hatred and schizophrenia. When the general atmosphere is bad, language must suffer. I should expect to find—this is a guess which I have not sufficient knowledge to verify—that the German, Russian and Italian languages have all deteriorated in the last ten or fifteen years, as a result of dictatorship.

But if thought corrupts language, language can also corrupt thought. A bad usage can spread by tradition and imitation, even among people who should and do know better. The debased language that I have been discussing is in some ways very convenient. Phrases like *a not unjustifiable assumption, leaves much to be desired, would serve no good purpose, a consideration which we should do well to bear in mind,* are a continuous temptation, a packet of aspirins always at one's elbow. Look back through this essay, and for certain you will find that I have again and again committed the very faults I am protesting against. By this morning's post I have received a pamphlet dealing with conditions in Germany. The author tells me that he "felt impelled" to write it. I open it at random, and here is almost the first sentence that I see: "(The Allies) have an opportunity not only of achieving a radical transformation of

Germany's social and political structure in such a way as to avoid a nationalistic reaction in Germany itself, but at the same time of laying the foundations of a co-operative and unified Europe." You see, he "feels impelled" to write—feels, presumably, that he has something new to say— and yet his words, like cavalry horses answering the bugle, group themselves automatically into the familiar dreary pattern. This invasion of one's mind by ready-made phrases *(lay the foundations, achieve a radical transformation)* can only be prevented if one is constantly on guard against them, and every such phrase anaesthetizes a portion of one's brain.

I said earlier that the decadence of our language is probably curable. Those who deny this would argue, if they produced an argument at all, that language merely reflects existing social conditions, and that we cannot influence its development by any direct tinkering with words and constructions. So far as the general tone or spirit of a language goes, this may be true, but it is not true in detail. Silly words and expressions have often disappeared, not through any evolutionary process but owing to the conscious action of a minority. Two recent examples were *explore every avenue* and *leave no stone unturned,* which were killed by the jeers of a few journalists. There is a long list of flyblown metaphors which could similarly be got rid of if enough people would interest themselves in the job; and it should also be possible to laugh the *not un-* formation out of existence,* to reduce the amount of Latin and Greek in the average sentence, to drive out foreign phrases and strayed scientific words, and, in general, to make pretentiousness unfashionable. But all these are minor points. The defence of the English language implies more than this, and perhaps it is best to start by saying what it *does not* imply.

To begin with it has nothing to do with archaism, with the salvaging of obsolete words and turns of speech, or with the setting up of a "standard English" which must never be departed from. On the contrary, it is especially concerned with the scrapping of every word or idiom which has outworn its usefulness. It has nothing to do with correct grammar and syntax, which are of no importance so long as one makes one's meaning clear, or with the avoidance of Americanisms, or with having what is called a "good prose style." On the other hand it is not concerned with fake simplicity and the attempt to make written English colloquial. Nor does it even imply in every case preferring the Saxon word to the Latin one, though it does imply using the fewest and shortest words that will cover one's meaning. What is above all needed is to let the meaning choose the word, and not the other way about. In prose, the worst thing one can do with words is to surrender to them. When you think of a concrete object, you think wordlessly, and then, if you want to describe the

* One can cure oneself of the *not un-* formation by memorizing this sentence: *A not unblack dog was chasing a not unsmall rabbit across a not ungreen field.*

thing you have been visualizing you probably hunt about till you find the exact words that seem to fit it. When you think of something abstract you are more inclined to use words from the start, and unless you make a conscious effort to prevent it, the existing dialect will come rushing in and do the job for you, at the expense of blurring or even changing your meaning. Probably it is better to put off using words as long as possible and get one's meaning as clear as one can through pictures or sensations. Afterwards one can choose—not simply *accept*—the phrases that will best cover the meaning, and then switch round and decide what impression one's words are likely to make on another person. This last effort of the mind cuts out all stale or mixed images, all prefabricated phrases, needless repetitions, and humbug and vagueness generally. But one can often be in doubt about the effect of a word or a phrase, and one needs rules that one can rely on when instinct fails. I think the following rules will cover most cases:

(i) Never use a metaphor, simile or other figure of speech which you are used to seeing in print.

(ii) Never use a long word where a short one will do.

(iii) If it is possible to cut out a word, always cut it out.

(iv) Never use the passive where you can use the active.

(v) Never use a foreign phrase, a scientific word or a jargon word if you can think of an everyday English equivalent.

(vi) Break any of these rules sooner than say anything outright barbarous.

These rules sound elementary, and so they are, but they demand a deep change of attitude in anyone who has grown used to writing in the style now fashionable. One could keep all of them and still write bad English, but one could not write the kind of stuff that I quoted in those five specimens at the beginning of this article.

I have not here been considering the literary use of language, but merely language as an instrument for expressing and not for concealing or preventing thought. Stuart Chase and others have come near to claiming that all abstract words are meaningless, and have used this as a pretext for advocating a kind of political quietism. Since you don't know what Fascism is, how can you struggle against Fascism? One need not swallow such absurdities as this, but one ought to recognize that the present political chaos is connected with the decay of language, and that one can probably bring about some improvement by starting at the verbal end. If you simplify your English, you are freed from the worst follies of orthodoxy. You cannot speak any of the necessary dialects, and when you make a stupid remark its stupidity will be obvious, even to yourself. Political language—and with variations this is true of all political parties, from Conservatives to Anarchists—is designed to make lies sound truthful and murder respectable, and to give an appearance of solidity to pure wind. One cannot change this all in a moment, but one can at least change one's own habits, and from time to time one can even, if one jeers loudly enough, send some worn-out and useless phrase—some *jackboot, Achilles' heel, hotbed, melting pot, acid test, veritable inferno* or other lump of verbal refuse—into the dustbin where it belongs.

Arthur Koestler

The European novelist Arthur Koestler (he was born a Hungarian, lived for long periods in Berlin, Palestine, and Paris, and is now a British subject and writes in English) has been an eloquent and articulate opponent of communism ever since he left the party in the late 1930's. His opposition is not, like that of many former party members, based on any sort of religious or specifically economic counterfaith. It is rooted rather in his simple conviction that in practice communism is an aspect of the massive assault on traditional humanistic values which has characterized our century—an assault that has been mounted from both the Left and the Right. Koestler's account of his early experiences as a communist conveys vividly a sense of the party's rejection of the idea of free inquiry and of the idea that the individual as such has any intrinsic worth whatever. The world which his autobiographical narrative recreates is one in which the self and all human relations—love, for example—are subordinated to an ideal which is totally, rather than simply economically, collectivist, a world in which vital human feelings have surrendered to abstractions. As Koestler points out, it is a world with a peculiar attraction for those who, for some personal psychological reason, are trying to flee from their own identities.

Language, as the expression of the self, has a special importance to the humanistic tradition. As Orwell has stated in a more theoretical context, the proponents of totalitarianism know very well that to control language is to control thought. Of particular interest in Koestler's account is his inability, even during his period of most intense devotion to the party, to debase the written word. As a literary artist, he was the involuntary heir of Western civilization; the seeds of his own liberation were already within him.

PORTRAIT OF THE AUTHOR AS A COMRADE

Having lost my job, I was free from the fetters of the bourgeois world; having lost my usefulness for the *apparat,* there was no longer any reason for keeping my Party-membership secret. I gave up my flat in the

Reprinted with permission of The Macmillan Company from *The Invisible Writing* by Arthur Koestler. Copyright 1954 by Arthur Koestler.

expensive district of Neu-Westend, and moved into an apartment-house on Bonner Platz known as the Red Block, for most of the tenants were penniless writers and artists of radical views. There I joined the local Communist cell and was at last permitted to lead the full life of a regular Party member.

Our cell was one among several thousand in Berlin, and one among the several hundred thousand basic units of the Communist network in the world. Cells exist in every country where the Party is legally tolerated; in countries where Communism is outlawed, a system of "groups of five" or "groups of three" replaces the larger legal units. The term "cell" is not purely metaphorical; for these are living, pulsating units within a huge, sprawling organism, co-ordinated in their function, governed by a hierarchy of nervous centres, and susceptible to various diseases—to the Titoist virus, to bourgeois infection or Trotskyist cancer. The part of the white phagocytes is played by the various defence mechanisms of the Party, from the Central Control Commission to the G.P.U.

Our cell comprised about twenty members. The consciousness of being one unit among millions in an organised, disciplined whole was always present. We had among us several *litterateurs,* such as Alfred Kantorowicz and Max Schroeder, who are now both back in Communist Eastern Germany; a psychoanalyst—Wilhelm Reich, who broke with the Party in 1933 and is now the director of the Institute for Orgone Research in Rangeley, Maine; several actors from an *avant-garde* theatre called The Mouse Trap; several girls with intellectual ambitions; an insurance agent and a number of working men. In so far as the majority of us were intellectuals, our cell was untypical in its structure, yet entirely typical in its function—that is, in our daily work and routine.

Half of our activities were legal, half illegal. The cell met officially once a week, but the more active members were in daily contact with each other. The official meeting always started with a political lecture by an instructor from District Headquarters (or by the cell leader after he had been briefed at H.Q.), in which the line was laid down concerning the various questions of the day. This was followed by discussion, but a discussion of a peculiar kind. It is a basic rule of Communist discipline that, once the Party has decided to adopt a certain line regarding a given problem, all criticism of that decision becomes deviationist sabotage. In theory, discussion is permissible before a decision has been reached; in practice decisions are always imposed from above, without previous consultation with the rank and file. One of the slogans of the German Party said: "The front-line is no place for discussions." Another said: "Wherever a Communist happens to be, he is always in the front-line." So our discussions always showed a complete unanimity of opinion.

During that fateful spring and summer of 1932, a series of elections took place which shook the country like a succession of earthquakes—the Presidential elections, two Reichstag elections, and an election for the Prussian Diet; all in all four red-hot election campaigns within eight months in a country on the verge of civil war. We participated in the campaigns by door-to-door canvassing, distributing Party literature and turning out leaflets of our own. The canvassing was the most arduous part of it; it was mostly done on Sunday morning, when people could be expected to be at home. You rang the door bell, wedged your foot between door and post, and offered your pamphlets and leaflets, with a genial invitation to engage in a political discussion on the spot. In short, we sold the World Revolution like vacuum cleaners. Reactions were mostly unfriendly, but rarely aggressive. I often had the door banged in my face, but never had a fight. However, we avoided ringing the bells of known Nazis. And the Nazis in and round our block were all known to us, just as we were all known to the Nazis, through our rival nets of cells and *Blockwarts*. The whole of Germany, town and countryside, was covered by those two elaborate and fine-meshed drag-nets.

That last summer of Weimar Germany was for the Party a period of transition; we were preparing to go underground, and accordingly regrouping our cadres. We might be outlawed overnight; everything had to be ready for this emergency. The moment we were forced into illegality, all Party cells would cease to function, and would be superseded by a new, nation-wide structure, the "Groups of Five." The cells, whose membership ranged from ten to thirty comrades, were too large in size for underground work, and offered easy opportunities for *agents provocateurs* and informers. The breaking up of the cadres into Groups of Five meant a corresponding diminution of risks. Only the leader of the Group was to know the identity and addresses of the other four; and he alone was to have contact with the next higher level of the Party hierarchy. If he was arrested, he could only betray the four individuals in his group, and his contact-man.

So, while the cell still continued to function, each member was secretly allotted to a Group of Five, the idea being that none of the groups should know the composition of any other. In fact, as we were all neighbours in the Block, we each knew which Group was secretly meeting in whose flat; and, on the night of the burning of the Reichstag, when Goering dealt his deathblow to the Communist Party, the Groups scattered and the whole elaborate structure collapsed all over the Reich. We had marvelled at the conspiratorial ingenuity of our leaders; and, though all of us had read works on the technique of insurrection and civil warfare, our critical faculties had become so numbed that none of us realised the catastrophic implications of the scheme. These preparations for a long underground existence in decentralised groups meant that our leaders accepted the victory of the Nazis as inevitable. And the breaking up of the cadres into small units indicated that the Party would offer no open, armed resistance to Hitler's bid for power, and was preparing for sporadic small-scale actions instead.

But we, the rank and file, knew nothing of this. During that long, stifling summer of 1932 we fought our ding-dong battles with the Nazis. Hardly a day passed without one or two being killed in Berlin. The main battlefields were the *Bierstuben*, the smoky little taverns of the working-class districts. Some of these served as meeting-places for the Nazis, some as meeting-places *(Verkehrslokale)* for us. To enter the wrong pub was to venture into the enemy's lines. From time to time the Nazis would shoot up one of our *Verkehrslokale*. It was done in the classic Chicago tradition: a gang of S.A. men would drive slowly past the tavern, firing through the glass panes, then vanish at break-neck speed. We had far fewer motor-cars than the Nazis, and retaliation was mostly carried out in cars either stolen, or borrowed from sympathisers. The men who did these jobs were members of the R.F.B. *(Roter Frontkämpfer Bund)*, the League of Communist War Veterans. My car was sometimes borrowed by comrades whom I had never seen before, and returned a few hours later with no questions asked and no explanations offered. It was a tiny, red, open Fiat car, and most unsuitable for such purposes; but nobody else in our cell had one. It was the last relic of my bourgeois past; now it served as a vehicle for the proletarian revolution. I spent half my time driving it round on various errands: transporting pamphlets and leaflets, shadowing certain Nazi cars whose numbers had been signalled to us, and acting as a security escort. Once I had to transport the equipment of a complete hand-printing press from a railway station to a cellar under a green-grocer's shop.

The R.F.B. men who came to fetch the car for their guerrilla expeditions were sometimes rather sinister types from the Berlin underworld. They came, announced by a telephone call or by a verbal message from District H.Q., but the same men rarely turned up twice. Sometimes, on missions of a more harmless nature, I was myself ordered to act as driver. We would drive slowly past a number of Nazi pubs to watch the goings-on, or patrol a pub of our own when one of our informers in the Nazi camp warned us of an impending attack. This latter kind of mission was unpleasant; we would park, with headlights turned off and engine running, in the proximity of the pub; and at the approach of a car I would hear the click of the safety-catch on my passengers' guns, accompanied by the gentle advice "to keep my chump well down." But I was never involved in any actual shooting.

Once the R.F.B. men who came to fetch the car disguised themselves in my flat before starting out. They stuck on moustaches, put on glasses, dark jackets and bowler hats. I watched them from the window driving off—four stately, bowler-hatted gents in the ridiculous little red car, looking like a party in a funeral procession. They came back four hours later, changed back to normal, and made off with a silent handshake. My instructions, in case the number of the car was taken by the police during some action, were to say that it had been stolen and that I had found it again in a deserted street.

From time to time a rumour got round that the Nazis were going to attack our Red Block, as they had attacked other notorious Communist agglomerations before. Then we were alerted, and some R.F.B. men turned up to mount guard. One critical night some thirty of us kept vigil in my tiny flat, armed with guns, lead-pipes and leather batons, like a huddle of stragglers from a beaten army. A few weeks later, von Papen staged his *coup d'état:* one lieutenant and eight men chased the Socialist government of Prussia from office. It was the beginning of the end.

The Socialist Party, with its eight million followers, did nothing. The Socialist-controlled trade unions did not even call a protest strike. Only we, the Communists, called for an immediate general strike. The call fell on deaf ears. Like inflated currency, our verbiage had lost all real meaning for the masses. We lost the battle against Hitler before it was joined. After the 20th of July, 1932, it was evident to all but ourselves that the K.P.D., strongest among the Communist parties in Europe, was a castrated giant whose brag and bluster only served to cover its lost virility.

A few months later everything was over. Years of conspiratorial training and preparations for the emergency proved within a few hours totally useless. Thaelmann, leader of the Party, and the majority of his lieutenants were found in their carefully-prepared hide-outs and arrested within the first few days. The Central Committee emigrated. The long night descended over Germany.

I threw myself into the activities of the cell with the same ardour and complete self-abandonment that I had experienced at seventeen on joining my duelling fraternity in Vienna. I lived in the cell, with the cell, for the cell. I was no longer alone; I had found the warm comradeship that I had been thirsting for; my desire to belong was satisfied.

Only gradually did I become aware of certain under-currents that existed beneath the free and easy surface. I noticed that individual friendships within the cell were, though not exactly reprehensible, yet regarded as slightly ambiguous and suspect of political "factionalism." "Factionalism"—the formation of groups with a policy of their own—was a capital crime in the Party, and if two or more comrades were known to be often together and to take the same line during discussions, they inevitably became suspect of forming a secret faction.

As in boarding-schools and convents intense personal ties are sus-pected of having an erotic background, so friendships within the Party automatically aroused political suspicion. This attitude was not unreason-able, for between people whose life was entirely dedicated to and filled by the Party, nonpolitical friendships were hardly possible. The slogans of the Party emphasised the diffuse and impersonal "solidarity of the working class" instead of individual friendship, and substituted "loyalty to the Party" for loyalty to friends. Loyalty to the Party meant, of course, unconditional obedience, and meant, furthermore, the repudiation of friends who had deviated from the Party-line, or for some reason had fallen under suspicion. Almost unconsciously I learnt to watch my steps, my words and my thoughts. I learnt that everything that I said in the cell or in private, even to a girl comrade whose pillow I shared, remained on record and could one day be held against me. I learnt that my rela-tions with other members of the cell should not be guided by trust but by "revolutionary vigilance"; that reporting any heretical remark was a duty, failure to do so a crime against the Party, and that to feel revulsion against this code was a sign of sentimental, *petit-bourgeois* prejudice:

> *You and I can make a mistake. Not the Party. The Party, comrade, is more than you and I and a thousand others like you and I. The Party is the embodi-ment of the revolutionary idea in history. History knows no scruples and no hesitation. Inert and unerring, she flows towards her goal. At every bend in her course she leaves the mud which she carries and the corpses of the drowned. History knows her way. She makes no mistakes. He who has no absolute faith in History does not belong in the Party's ranks. . . . The Party's course is sharply defined, like a narrow path in the mountains. The slightest false step, right or left, takes one down the precipice. The air is thin; he who becomes dizzy is lost. ("Darkness at Noon").*

I learnt that the rules of common decency, of loyalty and fair play were not absolute rules, but the ephemeral projections of competitive bourgeois society. Antiquity had one code of honour; the feudal era another; capitalist society still another, which the ruling class was trying to sell us as eternal laws. But absolute laws of ethics did not exist. Each class, as it became dominant in history, had re-shaped these so-called laws according to its interests. The Revolution could not be achieved accord-ing to the rules of cricket. Its supreme law was that the end justified the means; its supreme guide the method of dialectical materialism.

> *The true revolutionary is cold and unmerciful to mankind out of a kind of mathematical mercifulness. . . . A conscience renders one as unfit for the revo-lution as a double chin. Conscience eats through the brain like a cancer, until the whole of the grey matter is devoured ("Darkness at Noon").*

The intense fascination of the dialectical method can only be understood through a study of its masters—by reading, say, Engels' *Feuerbach,* Marx' *Eighteenth Brumaire,* or Lenin's *State and Revolution.* I now lived entirely in a mental world which earlier I have described as a "closed system," comparable to the self-contained universe of the mediaeval Schoolmen. All my feelings, my attitudes to art, literature and human relations, became reconditioned and moulded to the pattern. My vocabulary, grammar, syntax, gradually changed. I learnt to avoid any original form of expression, any individual turn of phrase. Euphony, gradations of emphasis, restraint, nuances of meaning, were suspect. Language, and with it thought, underwent a process of dehydration, and crystallised in the ready-made schemata of Marxist jargon. There were perhaps a dozen or two adjectives whose use was both safe and mandatory, such as: decadent, hypocritical, morbid (for the capitalist bourgeoisie); heroic, disciplined, class-conscious (for the revolutionary proletariat); *petit-bourgeois,* romantic, sentimental (for humanitarian scruples); opportunist and sectarian (for Right and Left deviations respectively); mechanistic, metaphysical, mystical (for the wrong intellectual approach); dialectical, concrete (for the right approach); flaming (protests); fraternal (greetings); unswerving (loyalty to the Party).

However, certain refinements of language were permitted and even encouraged. Thus irony was a desirable method in polemics, but its application was restricted to the use of inverted commas; e.g.: the "revolutionary" past of Trotsky; the "progressive" measures of the "Socialist" government; and so on. Equally popular was the use of what one may call semantic spoonerisms, initiated by Marx's famous pamphlet against Proudhon, *The Philosophy of Poverty and the Poverty of Philosophy.* This delightful game could be varied endlessly: "the war on profits and the profits of war," "the psychology of adolescence or the adolescence of psychology," "the laws of terror and the terror of the law," and so on. There were also certain luxury words whose use was regarded as good form. For instance, in one of his works Lenin has mentioned Herostratus, who burnt down a temple because he could think of no other way of achieving fame. Accordingly, one often heard and read phrases like "the criminally herostratic madness of the counter-revolutionary wreckers of the heroic efforts of the toiling masses in the Fatherland of the Proletariat to achieve the second Five Year Plan in four years."

Few among the intellectuals in the Party realised at the time that their mentality was a caricature of the revolutionary spirit; that within the short span of three generations the Communist movement had travelled from the era of the Apostles to that of the Borgias. But the process of degeneration had been gradual and continuous, and the seeds of corruption had already been present in the work of Marx: in the

vitriolic tone of his polemics, the abuse heaped on his opponents, the denunciation of rivals and dissenters as traitors to the working class and
agents of the bourgeoisie. Proudhon, Dühring, Bakunin, Liebknecht,
Lassalle, had been treated by Marx exactly as Trotsky, Bukharin, Zinoviev,
Kameniev *et alia* were treated by Stalin—except that Marx did not have
the power to shoot his victims. During these three generations, the uses
of the dialectic had also been vastly simplified. It was, for instance, easy
to prove scientifically that everybody who disagreed with the Party-line
was an agent of Fascism because (*a*) by disagreeing with the line he
endangered the unity of the Party; (*b*) by endangering the unity of the
Party he improved the chances of a Fascist victory; hence (*c*) *objectively*
he acted as an agent of Fascism even if *subjectively* he had his kidneys
smashed in a Fascist concentration camp. It was equally easy to prove
that charity, public or private, was counter-revolutionary because it
deceived the masses regarding the true nature of the capitalist system,
and thereby contributed to its preservation.

Our literary, artistic and musical tastes were similarly reconditioned.
The highest form of music was the choral song because it represented a
collective, as opposed to the individualistic approach. The same argument led to a sudden and unexpected revival of the Greek chorus in the
Communist *avant-garde* plays of the 'twenties. Since individual characters
could not be altogether banished from the stage, they had to be stylised,
typified, depersonalised. The Communist novel was guided by similar
principles. The central character was not an individual, but a group: the
members of a partisan unit during the Civil War; the peasants of a village
in the process of being transformed into a collective farm; the workers of
a factory striving to fulfil the plan. The tendency of the novel had to be
"operative," that is, didactic; each work of art must convey a social message. And here again, as individual heroes could not be entirely dispensed
with, they had to be made into typical representatives of a given social
class, party or political attitude.

Stripped of its exaggerations this conception has, of course, a certain
validity in the field of the political and ideological novel. In later years
I have written several essays criticising the Marxist theory of art, and
trying to reconcile the striving for social relevance with the conflicting
claims of aesthetics and psychology. But such critical exercises did not
prevent me from falling into the very errors that I had pointed out. The
effects of years of indoctrination reached deeper than the conscious mind,
and are easily traceable in my novels even ten years after the break.

Nevertheless, the Marxist approach has produced valuable results
both in literary criticism and in creative writing. At least two among the
leading contemporary critics, Edmund Wilson and Lionel Trilling, owe
much to it. The orthodox "proletarian" literature of the 'thirties appears

to-day shallow and dated; but a whole generation of poets and novelists, who took Marx in small and digestible quantities, have added an essential feature to the civilisation of the twentieth century. Among them are Auden, Isherwood, Spender and Day Lewis in England; the early Dos Passos, Steinbeck, Caldwell and Sinclair Lewis in the United States; Barbusse, Rolland, Malraux, Sartre and Sperber in France; Becher, Brecht, Weinert, Renn, Seghers, Regler, Plivier in Germany—to mention only a few.

My own development was different from that of the enthusiastic "fellow-travellers" of the 'thirties. I began to write my first novel when I was already disillusioned, and on my way out of the Party. The reason is that emotionally and in artistic taste I remained an adolescent to my late twenties. But this retarded development is again partly due to my seven years in the Communist Party. So long as I remained a true believer, my faith had a paralysing effect on my creative faculties, such as they are. The Marxist doctrine is a drug, like arsenic or strychnine, which in small doses have a stimulating, in larger ones a paralysing effect on the creative system. The large majority of "socially conscious" writers of the 'thirties were stimulated by it because they did not enter the Party, and remained sympathisers from a safe distance. The few of us who actually took the plunge—such as Victor Serge, Richard Wright, Ignazio Silone—felt frustrated during their active Party career, and only found their true voice after the break. One wonders what would have happened to Catholic novelists like Mauriac, Evelyn Waugh, or the late Bernanos, had they accepted the discipline of monastic life, or at least taken holy orders.

The Russian writers belong to a different category. They could not remain distant sympathisers; from the early 'thirties onward literature in Soviet Russia was regimented, and literary criticism wielded by the Party as a disciplinary weapon, with punishments ranging from the silencing of the discordant voice to the liquidation of its owner. A number of our Russian colleagues—among them the greatest, Alexander Blok—saw long before us where the régime was drifting and committed suicide. The majority, who made Soviet literature great during the first decade of the Revolution, were officially or secretly liquidated during the Purges. Those who survived have either lost their voices, or become Stalin-prize court jesters. The same is true of those non-Russian Communist writers who have remained in the Party—e.g., Johannes R. Becher and Louis Aragon.

My fanatical allegiance to the Party did not cause complete mental blindness to the more absurd phenomena in my new environment. I noticed that the political instructors sent by District Headquarters to the meetings of our cell knew nothing of the world outside the narrow field of working-class politics—that is, strikes, demonstrations and trade union developments. They did not know or believe that the Christian-Democratic Chancellor Bruenning was genuinely opposed to Hitler, or that there was a difference between a British Tory and a German Nazi. For them, democracy was "a camouflaged form of the dictatorship of the capitalist ruling class" and Fascism "its overt form," while "the class-content" of both régimes was the same. The political struggles between the various "bourgeois" parties were merely a symptom of the "internal contradictions of the capitalist system"; the real alignment of social forces was along the class frontier. All this to my mind was both true and untrue. It was untrue because it was a crude oversimplification of a complex reality; but in the long view of History nuances did not matter, and my sophistication did not matter, and the dialectical telescope revealed the essential truth.

There were things even more difficult to swallow, particularly in the field of language and literature. After a speech in the cell, in which I had repeatedly used the word "spontaneous," a well-wishing comrade tipped me off that I had better avoid it in the future, because "spontaneous manifestations of the revolutionary spirit" were part of Trotsky's theory of the Permanent Revolution. I was at the very beginning of my party career, and though I agreed that such semantic purism was part of the necessary "revolutionary vigilance," I did so, for the first time, with my tongue in my cheek. This reaction was soon to become more frequent.

A comrade, on his return from the Soviet Union, quoted to me the contents of a lecture he had heard, given by a Party instructor to a literary circle of workmen in a Russian factory. "To regard poetry as a special talent which some men possess and others don't," the instructor had explained, "is bourgeois metaphysics. Poetry, like every other skill, is acquired by learning and practice. We need more class-conscious proletarian poetry; we must increase our poetry output on the literary front. Beginners should start with five or ten lines a day, then set themselves a target of twenty or thirty lines, and gradually increase the quantity and quality of their production."

Later on I myself heard a Russian lecturer explain that the vogue of excessively long poems in Germany during the 'twenties was the ideological reflection of the currency inflation with its floods of printed paper. I constantly came across nonsense of this kind in Russia, but told myself that it didn't matter; it was merely a touching symptom of the exuberance and enthusiasm of a backward people awakening from centuries of apathy and oppression. The "backward masses" could not be expected to develop overnight the sophistication of an ex-editor of Ullstein's.

After a few months in the Party my faith began to assume a more supple and lasting form. Everything that I disliked I explained to myself as "the heritage of the Capitalist past," or as "the inevitable measles of

the Revolution," or finally as "temporary expedients." The higher interests of revolutionary strategy often necessitated tactical measures which
seemed cruel, absurd or downright despotic. But Marxists must not
judge "mechanistically" by appearances, as the bourgeois Press did; their
duty was to discern the hidden dialetical meaning; and their public
utterances must be kept on the level of the backward masses.

Thus my originally naïve faith gradually changed into a private,
esoteric creed which was more malleable, and shock-proof against reality.
If the outsider asks how intelligent people could stand the wild zigzags
of the Party line, the answer is that every single educated Communist,
from the members of the Russian Politbureau down to the French literary côteries, has his own private and secret philosophy whose purpose is
not to explain the facts, but to explain them away. It does not matter
by what name one calls this mental process—double-think, controlled
schizophrenia, myth addiction, or semantic perversion; what matters is
the psychological pattern. Without it the portrait of the author as a
comrade would not be comprehensible.

There existed, however, a barrier beyond which I was unable to
carry self-deception. My language and reasoning became reconditioned
to the Party's jargon; but this mimicry remained confined to the spoken
word. When it came to writing, I encountered an unconscious resistance.
Though a seasoned journalist, I was unable, during my whole Communist career, to write a single article for the Party Press—even when I
found myself on the verge of starvation. At the beginning I composed
broadsheets and leaflets for our cell, but though correct regarding the
line, they were too unorthodox in style, and the District Committee
stopped them. Much later, during the Saar campaign of 1934, I edited
a comic Party paper, but this too was stopped after the first issue. I was
capable of making speeches in the orthodox Party manner and of keeping
them strictly on the level of the "backward masses," while my esoteric
truth and private opinion remained locked away in an air-tight compartment of the mind. But when I tried to apply the same process to writing,
I became paralysed: I got involved with the syntax, made inkblots on the
paper, was unable to concentrate, and caught myself drawing arabesques
or a naked goddess holding up a hammer and sickle to the sun.[1]

Thus there were limits to my capacity for double-think. I had been
unable to argue with Von E. though my job was at stake; I was unable
to write in the Party's style; later on, as will be seen, I failed at other
tasks. Perhaps, despite my ardour, I was only a mediocre Marxist. The
fact that in spite of my growing misgivings I stuck to the Party through
seven years, seems to indicate that my limitations as a Communist were

[1] I have tried to describe this mental torment in the chapter "Fatigue of the Synapses"
in *The Age of Longing*.

of an unconscious rather than of a rational order. I was still chasing after the arrow in the blue, the absolute cause, the magic formula which would produce the Golden Age. Arrows may drift with the wind, and apparently change their direction relative to the rotating earth; but, unlike guided missiles, they cannot be forced into a zigzag course.

A special feature of Party life that had a profound and lasting influence on me was worship of the proletariat and contempt for the intelligentsia. Intellectuals of middle-class origin were in the Party on sufferance, not by right; this was constantly rubbed into us. We had to be tolerated, because during the transition period the Party needed the engineers, doctors, scientists and litterati of the pre-revolutionary intelligentsia. But we were no more trusted or respected than the so-called "useful Jews" in Hitler's Germany, who were given a distinctive armlet and allowed a short respite before their usefulness expired and they went the way of their kin. The social origin of parents and grandparents is as decisive under a Communist régime as racial origin was under the Nazi régime. Accordingly, Communist intellectuals of middle-class origin were trying by various means to give themselves proletarian airs. They wore coarse polo-sweaters, displayed black finger-nails, talked working-class slang. It was one of our undisputed articles of faith that members of the working-class, regardless of their level of intelligence and education, would always have a more "correct" approach to any political problem than the learned intellectual. This was supposed to be due to a kind of instinct rooted in class-consciousness. There is again a distinct parallel here with the Nazis' contempt for "destructive Jewish cleverness" as opposed to the "healthy and natural instinct of the race."

This atmosphere provided wonderful nourishment for my chronic inferiority complex. In the chapters dealing with my childhood I have explained the depths and tenacity of this affliction, and its ties with anxiety and guilt. In later years I gradually managed to build up a brash façade, but this still further deepened the conviction that I was a sham who deserved his failures and humiliations, and obtained his successes by fraud. I felt a constant longing to be "myself and nothing else beside"; yet for a person suffering from this type of affliction it is easier to climb Mount Everest than to be his own self. We know that Demosthenes, the stammerer, practised speech with his mouth full of pebbles until he became the foremost public orator of Greece; but we are not told whether he ever learnt to speak with a natural voice to his friends.

Now the working-men with whom Party-life threw me into contact did speak in their slow natural voice, and did more or less behave as their natural selves. That a truck-driver or a dynamo-fitter can be just as neurotic as a literary critic, and that he merely lacks the articulateness to express it, was a much later discovery. At the time it seemed to me that the proletarian members of our cell were all strong, silent, hard and kindly men, not only appointed by History to inherit the earth from the decadent bourgeoisie, but also mentally more hale and sane than the clever phoneys of my type. In short, the class-conscious proletarian was the Marxist equivalent of Rousseau's Noble Savage, of Nietzsche's Superman, of Hitler's *Blut und Bodenmensch,* and became a kind of collective super-ego for the Communist intelligentsia. For reasons that I have just explained, my own responses in this respect were particularly deep and lasting.

It is relatively easy to explain how a person with my story and background came to become a Communist, but more difficult to convey a state of mind that led a young man of twenty-six to be ashamed of having been to a university, to curse the agility of his brain, the articulateness of his language, to regard such civilised tastes and habits as he had acquired as a constant source of self-reproach, and intellectual self-mutilation as a desirable aim. If it had been possible to lance those tastes and habits like a boil, I would gladly have submitted to the operation.

A recent American study, embracing people from all social classes and races including Negroes, has shown that the majority of young Americans who joined the Communist Party were prompted not by economic distress, but by some conflict within the family. I have said before that such psychological facts neither prove nor disprove the validity of Marxist theory. But *vice versa,* it is not Marxist theory in itself which turns people into rebels, but a psychological disposition which makes them susceptible to revolutionary theories. The latter then serve as rationalisations of their personal conflict—which does not exclude the possibility that the rationalisation may be a correct one.

To sum up this aspect of the story. As a child I had been taught that whatever I did was wrong, a pain to others and a disgrace to myself. At the age of five, the permanent awareness of guilt and impending punishment resulted in a mild attack of persecution mania, described in an earlier chapter. A few years later, the feeling of inferiority manifested itself in paralysing shyness, then focused on my slow growth and juvenile appearance. Now, at twenty-six, this floating mass of anxiety and guilt, always ready to fasten on the first peg in sight, turned against my bourgeois background, my powers of reasoning and capacity for enjoyment. To bask in the sun, to read a novel, to dine in a good restaurant, to go to a picture gallery, became guilty exercises of a privilege that others could not share, frivolous diversions from the class struggle. True Communists, like Catholics, live in a constant awareness of original sin.

I deplore the logical error that led me into the Communist Party; but I do not regret the spiritual discipline that it imposed. Purgatory is a painful experience; but no one who went through it is likely to wish that it should be erased from his past.

Mary McCarthy

Mary McCarthy's defense of intellectual freedom, written at a time (1952) when that freedom was under especially strong attack in our country, is a good example of high-level controversial writing. Treating an emotionally loaded subject, the essay aims not to arouse emotions but to engage minds. The author first makes a series of sharp intellectual distinctions and follows them with a logical sequence of common-sense arguments. Freedom, as Miss McCarthy points out, is a value to which most people in our civilization pay lip service, but she demonstrates in her opening pages that the older concept of innate, God-given rights, although still nominally maintained, has actually yielded to an unadmitted concept of state-granted privileges, arbitrarily revocable. Having thus cleared the air of rhetorical phrases designed to evoke stock responses, Miss McCarthy goes on to test various other ways of conceiving of freedom—first as enforceable "powers," then as socially desirable "goods." Rejecting the brutal anarchy implied by the "power" conception, she allows the full weight of her defense of freedom to rest on the idea of freedom as a "good," recognized as such by a mature society. Only when she has established a firm positive position does she move openly to attack the rightist opponents of free speech and thought; only then does she bring into play the weapons of ridicule and scorn which have made her one of the deadliest of contemporary controversialists. Deftly exposing the weak points of the rightist position—inconsistency, illogicality, hysteria—she probes more deeply to examine the guilt and fear which lie beneath the opposition to intellectual freedom. Like a much earlier defense of free speech, John Milton's *Areopagitica* (1644), Miss McCarthy's essay ends on a note of emotional eloquence. In both cases the eloquence has been earned by the kind of rigorous argumentation which is the heart of honest controversy.

THE CONTAGION OF IDEAS

Summer, 1952

The Declaration of Independence speaks of certain unalienable rights given to Man by God—the rights to life, liberty, and the pursuit of happiness. Yet nothing is clearer than that these rights are far from unalienable. They can be taken from a man by other men; they

Reprinted from *On the Contrary* by Mary McCarthy, by permission of Farrar, Straus & Cudahy, Inc. Copyright © 1952, 1961 by Mary McCarthy.
This was a speech delivered to a group of teachers.

can be surrendered by a whole people to the state; if they are to be preserved at all, the state, presumably, must secure them. In the days of the
Founding Fathers, these rights had a certain sacred character that flowed
from a belief in God; they were hallowed in the individual by the supposed intention of the Creator and were hardly to be distinguished from
the sacredness of life itself. God meant man to be free, paradoxically, to
obey his conscience; indeed, man's freedom imposed on him the *duty* of
obeying the inner voice, in defiance, if necessary, of law and common
opinion.

Today, in a secular society that no longer believes in God, we retain
a lip-belief in the doctrine of inherent rights without knowing what we
mean by them or where they are supposed to come from. In practice, we
look to the state as the source of rights and the patenter of new rights
that have suddenly come to light—the right to teach, the right to a government job, and so on, though it is evident that no one has the right to
teach inherent in him as a human being. But when we look to the state
as the source of rights, these rights lose their sacred character and become
mere privileges which the state can withdraw at any time from individuals or groups that displease it. This is the situation of the Communists
in the United States today; their liberty is looked upon by the public
as a privilege accorded them by the government that they have misused
and that therefore ought to be taken away from them. Liberty, as it is
conceived by current opinion, has nothing inherent about it; it is a sort
of gift or trust bestowed on the individual by the state pending *good
behavior*. We see this notion applied not only to Communists but to
racketeers like Frank Costello and Erickson, who are deprived of their
freedom to remain silent before Congressional committees; their Constitutional rights are suspended, as long as they remain uncooperative. Thus
a Communist is free to testify to his party-associations; Costello is free to
testify to his illegal gambling transactions; but neither is free to be silent.
In the same way, other, more parvenu rights fade overnight into privileges—the right to strike, for example, or the right to teach in the public
schools turns out to depend on the teacher's or the trade union's "good
behavior," i.e., on political criteria. In short, these so-called rights are
not, realistically speaking, rights at all but resemble, rather, licenses, like
hunting licenses, licenses to carry firearms, or driving licenses, which keep
having to be renewed and are subject to all sorts of restrictions and limitations. This is very clear in the case of a passport: nobody, it is claimed,
has a right to a passport inherent in him as a citizen, and if this right
does not exist, then a passport becomes simply a travel permit which can
be canceled for infractions of discipline, exactly like a license to drive.

Once the state is looked upon as the *source* of rights, rather than their
bound protector, freedom becomes conditional on the pleasure of the
state. You may say that in practice this has always been true and always

will be: the state has always decided how much freedom shall be had and by whom. Yet the difference between a democracy and a tyranny or despotism is that in theory the citizen of a democracy possesses inherent rights, and this theory becomes the working hypothesis, i.e., the practice of a democratic state. However, without a belief in a Creator as the divine provider of rights, the theory tends to shift and to be stood, even, on its head, i.e., to turn into a doctrine of privileges vested in the state and dealt out by it to citizens who can prove their worthiness to enjoy them. That is what is happening today; rights and privileges have become so confused that to talk of rights at all is to invite a demonstration that there are none, for every right can be shown to be contingent and not absolute. If you argue today's vexed cases in terms of rights, you will lose the argument every time, strangely enough, to advocates of "freedom." Nobody, they will tell you, has a right to a Hollywood swimming pool, nobody has a right to perform on television or the radio, nobody has a right to a government job, nobody has a right to a passport, nobody has a right to teach in a public school, nobody has a right to conspire against the government. Conversely, a Hollywood screen-producer has a right to fire whom he chooses, radio and television companies have a right to be responsible to their advertisers, and the advertisers have a right to be responsible to the public, and the public has a right to complain of Communist performers on the air; a school board has the right to refuse to allow subversives to teach the children in its care; the government has the right to keep Communists out of its services, to refuse passports to citizens according to its own judgment, to revoke visas of entry, and in general to withhold the rights of citizenship from those who would take them from others. Agreed, but what exactly are these "rights" we are speaking of? Closely examined, they seem to be not rights but powers. What is meant is that nobody has the power to keep the government from denying a passport or to keep an employer from firing a Communist, to prevent a school board from screening the teachers it selects for its children; and, conversely, no schoolteacher or radio-performer has, in himself, the power to retain his job. Powers, once they have been weakened, cease to be thought of as rights, or a right, on the defensive, is an enfeebled power. Take the right of an employer to hire and fire; this right, once universally recognized and seemingly, almost, a "natural" right, now exists chiefly in small business and in households, where no union power is massed to limit it; similarly, the "right to work," which a few years ago meant the right to a job, now has shifted to mean the right of a worker *not* to belong to a union and is really the old employer's right to hire and fire presented in a proletarian disguise. Rights which appear natural and unquestioned take on a highly unnatural look when the power that bred them wanes. I might like to assert the right of a Communist to perform on the radio, but I lack the power to implement it, a power that could only be created by a *demand* for Communists on the air. Since there is not likely soon to be a demand for Communists, on the air, or in the schools, or in the government service, it becomes rather futile to urge their "right" to be employed in these fields. In default of a real demand, can a synthetic one be improvised, in the interests of pluralism? Is a university president with liberal ideas obligated by his principles to hire a token Communist on his faculty—in fairness to minorities? Should a breakfast-food company be obliged to keep a Communist artiste on its payroll, to show that it does not discriminate? No. Communism is not a commodity that we can force entrepreneurs to stock. When the argument is put this way, scarcely anyone today would defend the right of a Communist, qua Communist, to a job in entertainment or education. Where the problem really presents itself is not in terms of general propositions but in specific cases. For example, should Paul Robeson be allowed to sing on the radio? Here it is easy for the liberal to answer yes, the more so since there is a real demand for Robeson as a singer. And the question for the university president is not whether he should hire new Communists in order to prove himself a liberal, but whether he should get rid of the ones he already has on his staff. Here again, the answer is not difficult. Most liberal college presidents would object to firing a teacher simply because he was a Communist, though few would be likely to insist, in public, on the college's "right" to keep him. The usual course is to deny that the teacher concerned is a Communist, thus avoiding the whole question of the "right to teach," since this right, openly invoked, will be disputed and the college will probably lose its right, i.e., its power, to harbor him.

To my mind, this situation would be greatly clarified if we thought, not just in terms of rights, but of goods, if we endeavored to treat individuals not in terms of what was owing to them by society or the state, but in terms of what an open society owed to its own image. If we thought of liberty not only as a right but as a good, we would be more hesitant to deprive people of it than we are when we think of it as a privilege or license within the bestowal of the state. If liberty is a good, a primary, axiomatic good, then the more that can be had of it, the better, and we should tend, even in situations of danger, to think of maximums rather than minimums. When weighing such questions as that of the right to a passport or of the right to Communists to teach or even of Frank Costello not to testify, we would ask ourselves how much liberty our free society ought to extend, if it is to live up to its name, rather than how much liberty was owing to this or that individual. Advocates of the curtailment of liberties tend to reason in broad scholastic syllogisms; they seldom feel it necessary to show, concretely, how the exercise of a given liberty will endanger the body politic. The Communist conspiracy, in theory, menaces the internal security of the United States; therefore, it is reasoned, every Communist is a dangerous conspirator, potentially, and must be treated as though he were one in fact. The case of Dr. Fuchs, a *secret* Communist sympathizer, who transmitted atomic information, is used as an argument for jailing *open* Communists, who would never, in any case, be employed on an atomic energy project. Or it is maintained that though the Communists are not an internal danger now, they would be duty-bound, in wartime, to disrupt the armed services and sabotage defense industries; what is overlooked in this chain of reasoning is that we *are* at war with Communist forces in Korea, and yet Harry Bridges' powerful West Coast maritime union, admittedly Communist-dominated, has been unable to halt a single shipment of war materials to the battlefront.

To argue these questions on theoretical grounds is to lose sight of common sense—the common sense which, after all, is the rationale of a democracy; a belief in common sense is the informing spirit of all democratic institutions, from the jury system to universal suffrage. No emergency can justify the national suspension of common sense, yet just that is being urged on us as a necessary measure to cope with Communism. We are told, for instance, that Communists' minds are not free and that therefore they are not "fit" to be teachers, but no attempt is made to show this on a common-sense level or to indicate, in contrast, for that matter, what minds are free. The same argument could be used against permitting Catholics to teach. I myself would think it a poor idea to have our schools staffed by large numbers of Communists, but nobody is proposing that. The question is whether, in our energetically anti-Communist society, it is worthwhile to construct a whole apparatus of repression to stamp out the few Communist teachers who have managed to survive in our school systems. Those who would say yes would pretend that the infection of a single school child's mind ought to be avoided, for moral reasons, at the cost of a whole society. But this is the purest scholasticism. In the thirties, when the Communists were a genuine power in the intellectual world, we liberals thought it our duty to expose them in the schools and colleges where they pontificated. I do not think we were wrong, but I think we are wrong today if we fail to acknowledge that the situation has changed and that the student today, far from being in danger of being indoctrinated by Communism, is in danger of being stupefied by the complacent propaganda for democracy that accompanies him to school, follows him through school, goes home with him, speaks to him in the movies and on television, and purrs him to sleep from the radio. The strange thing is that this current indoctrination for democracy has very much the same tone—pious, priggish, groupy—that we objected to in the Stalinism of the popular-front period.

Advocates of "realism" (as opposed to "idealism") in the treatment of Communists seem bent on ignoring the realities of the current situation. Those who, like Sidney Hook, advocate the refusal of teaching jobs to avowed Communists while insisting that mere fellow-travelers should have the right to teach, are courting the very result they deprecate—the growth of an underground Communism that does not acknowledge its name. Clearly, it would be more sensible to ban fellow-travelers from the schools while allowing avowed Communists, under that label, to have their representative say. In my academic experience, the fellow-traveler is far more insidious to deal with than the Party member, for the fellow-traveler invariably calls himself a "liberal" and points to some small difference he maintains with official Marxism to certify his claim to that title; students are frequently taken in by him, to the point where they become fellow-travelers themselves while imagining that they are liberals or else conceive a lasting repulsion for what they suppose to be liberal attitudes. When a science instructor recently left her job at a woman's college, the housekeeper found her Party card in her bedroom safe; no one had ever suspected her of Communism because she had never expressed any political views, though there were a number of vocal fellow-travelers on the faculty, which was considered very "pink." Now a policy that would guard students from this woman's influence while permitting fellow-travelers to teach has only one merit: that of bureaucratic simplicity. It is easier, from an administrative point of view, to clean out "card-carrying" Communists, whose names are known to the FBI, than to draw a line between a fellow-traveler and a liberal. And it might be easier, then, to fire all liberals, to avoid making mistakes. Easiest of all, finally, would be to use machines to teach—a solution not so remote as it sounds.

There is a great deal of talk today about the "dilemma" confronting the liberal. He must choose, it is said, between his traditional notions of freedom and the survival of the free world. This dilemma is totally spurious—the invention of illiberal people. If there were a strong Communist Party in America, allied to the Soviet Union, the choice for the liberal might be painful, as it might have been had there been a strong Fascist Party allied to the Nazis during the last war. As it is, the liberal's only problem is to avoid succumbing to the illusion of "having to choose."

To heighten this illusion, which common sense rejects, the strength of the Communists is claimed to lie not in their numbers but somewhere else, somewhere less evident to the ordinary, uninitiated person. The initiated anti-Communists subscribe to a doctrine that one might call Gresham's Law as transferred to the field of ideas—the notion that bad ideas drive out good. According to this notion, Communism is an idea that is peculiarly contagious. The Communists may be few in number, but their ideas are felt to have a mysterious potency that other ideas do not possess. Nobody contends, for instance, that Communist teachers constitute a majority or even a considerable minority in our schools. Nor does anybody point to a single primary school child who has been indoctrinated with Communism or suggest how, even in theory, such indoctrination might be accomplished. No; it is enough to show that a primary school teacher belongs or has belonged to a subversive organization; from this, I quote, arises "the danger of infection," as if Communism were a sort of airborne virus that could be wafted from a teacher to her pupils, without anybody's seeing it and even though the whole hygiene of school and family and civic life today was such, one would think, as to sterilize the child against such "germs."

Everyone who has had any experience of teaching knows how difficult it is to indoctrinate a pupil with anything—with the use of algebraic symbols, the rules of punctuation, the dates of American history; yet a Communist teacher, presumably, can "infect" *her* pupils with Marxism-Leninism-Stalinism by, to quote one writer, "the tone of her voice." She is able, moreover, to cite another popular image, to "plant the seeds" of Communism, undetected by parents or school superintendents or principals or fellow-teachers; she does it "by suggestion." The inference is that a single Communist teacher has more persuasion in her little finger than a school system consisting of ninety-nine others has in its whole organized body, more persuasion than all the forces of radio, movies, television, and comic books combined.

Yet no one, as I say, has produced (so far as I know) a single case history of a primary school child in the United States who has been indoctrinated with Communism. "Tragic cases," however, are often alluded to of somewhat older young people whose lives have been ruined by being exposed to a Communist teacher or professor. There may have been a few such cases in the thirties, tragic or not, yet we do not hear that such well-known figures as Hiss or Chambers or Remington or Elizabeth Bentley "got that way" because of a teacher. The most Elizabeth Bentley can say, in her autobiography, is that at Vassar she was exposed to godless and atheistic influences that softened her up for Communism. But to save the soul of one Elizabeth Bentley, or a dozen, should all non-believing teachers be eliminated from our colleges? The direct "causation" of Communism cannot be established, but surely a large number of Communists, present and ex-, would claim that they became so in reaction against their conservative parents and teachers; the revolutionary as rebel against authority is a familiar psychological cliché. Then should conservative teachers be eliminated?

The truth is that most young people who become Communists in the United States in the thirties and early forties did so either in response to the misery of the depression or in response to the threat of fascism as exemplified by Hitler. The few in this country who become Communists today probably do so in the mistaken hope that Communism offers protection against a third world catastrophe: war. It is not a question, really, of the contagion of ideas but of a relation that is felt to exist between certain ideas and an actual situation, to which the ideas seem applicable. When an anti-Communist argues that Communist ideas are highly contagious and that mere contact with a Communist is therefore dangerous for a school child or student, he is making an implicit confession. He is admitting to the fear that Communist ideas are catching, not just because they are "bad" and tend to drive out "good" ideas, but because they have a more evident correspondence with the realities of social inequity than he suspects his own ideas have. If Communist ideas are contagious or, rather, if we feel uneasily that they are, is not this precisely because they contain a "germ" of truth? We can laugh at Soviet "equality," Soviet "justice," Soviet "economic democracy," but only in the Soviet context; in France, Italy, China, Indonesia, the American South, these words have the power to shame us. We are afraid of export Communism, though not of the Soviet domestic article, because our own export, democracy, is competing under the same labels, and we know that our own capitalist society to a Chinese peasant or a Sicilian peasant or even an American Negro might appear even more unjust and unequal than the Soviet product.

The fear and hatred of Communism expressed in America today is not just a revulsion from the crimes of Stalin, from the deportation camps and forced labor and frame-up trials; it is also a fear and hatred of the original ideals of Communism. In a certain sense, the crimes of Stalin come as welcome news to America: they are taken as proof that socialism does not "work." Inequality, we would like to believe, is a law of nature, and by "we" I do not mean only wealthy businessmen or blackguards like Senator McCarthy or Southern racists. As the richest nation in the world, we have developed the psychology of rich people: we are afraid of poverty, of "agitators," of any jarring notes in the national harmony. The behavior of our local Communists outrages our sense of majesty, while abroad, all over the globe, our Congressmen are filling satchels with instances of foreign ingratitude. Like all rich people, we feel we are not appreciated, and we suffer from ideas of reference; if anybody speaks about "privilege" or "exploitation," we think they must mean us; if we see a film in which the poor are good and the rich are bad, we wonder whether it is not Communist-inspired. We do not like to hear attacks on segregation, on the use of the atomic bomb, on NATO, unless we are sure that the person talking is "on our side."

It is this guilty fear of criticism, at bottom, this sense of being surrounded by an unappreciative world, that is the source of our demands for loyalty, from teachers, from public performers, from veterans getting subsidized housing, from all those, in short, whom we regard as our pensioners. Certainly, the administration of loyalty oaths, like a mass vaccination against Communism, does not make any practical sense. And if we are particularly sensitive about our schools, it is because we fear that children, with their natural lack of bias, their detached and innocent faculty of observation, will be all too ready to prick up their ears if they hear our society criticized, even implicitly, in the "tone" of a teacher's voice. Our children, we feel, may listen to *her* more than they will listen to us, because they have already noticed the injustices of our society and want to know the why of it, instead of being told that "God made it that way." People with bad consciences always fear the judgment of children.

We did not behave this way toward fascists and fascist sympathizers during the war. We did not make a national effort to root them out of our schools and colleges or demand that they take loyalty oaths; on the whole, we did nothing to disturb them or to prevent the spread of their ideas. This was not because we found their doctrines more tolerable than we find the doctrines of Communism. On the contrary. Their ideas seemed to us so crazy and disgusting that we could not imagine anybody's being taken in by them, though in fact some people were. But this was, as we used to call it, the "lunatic fringe." The proof that we do not regard Communists as lunatics is precisely this fear we have that their ideas may be catching, this fear, as I say, of the "germ" of truth. And this germ phobia will be with us as long as we ourselves try to sell the white lie of democracy abroad, to the starving nations who in fact are the "children" —the ignorant and uneducated—whose allegiance we question, rightly, and whose judgment of us we, rightly, dread.

Gottfried Benn

When Hitler came to power in 1933, many outstanding German intellectual leaders went into voluntary exile. One of the few prominent figures who was temporarily deceived by the Nazis was the poet Gottfried Benn, who expressed a cautious faith in the future of the new Germany in a number of writings which were duly publicized by the Nazi authorities. Within a short time, however, Benn (who had never become a member of the Nazi party) was thoroughly disillusioned, and his private writings from the middle of the 1930's on are filled with a bitter hatred for Hitler and his followers.

"Art and the Third Reich" remained unpublished until after World War II. As it indicates, Benn's hostility toward the Nazis derives from his own nature as an intellectual: what most appalls him is the ignorance and vulgarity of the rulers of his country and their determination to destroy the complex, finely bred, and international unity of European culture. To express his sense of the contrast between European culture and Nazi pseudo-culture, he employs a form which is both idiosyncratic and difficult: a circumstantial and detailed evocation of European high culture in its elaborate pre-World War I development, followed by a condensed and vitriolic description of the Nazi attempt to substitute for it a synthetic, primitivistic, "Germanic" culture. His essay derives added force from the fact that it is itself written in a complex and international style— the "expressionism" of which Benn was one of the founders. In expressionist writing the artist deliberately distorts his materials, including the categories of time and space, in order to project his private vision in its completeness. Thus Benn's style itself becomes a demonstration of the intellectual insufficiencies of those who were his enemies and the enemies of civilization.

ART AND THE THIRD REICH

. . . . 1. General Situation

Life is beyond doubt inextricably bound up with necessity, and it does not release man, the attempted deserter, from the chain; but the chain need not clank at every one of his steps, need not drag its whole weight on every breath. Such a moment, when the chain temporarily loosened, came at the end of the last century, when, for instance, the English Queen's Diamond Jubilee in 1897 gave the whole rest of the world a chance to see the immense riches of the Empire. The white race's two continents were both enjoying a high degree of prosperity: new oil fields, depth-drilling in Pennsylvania, forest conservation, winter-hardened wheat—all this had brought it about. Those who organized and enjoyed this prosperity had for years been in the habit of meeting for the Season in London, the Grande Semaine in Paris, the salmon-fishing in Canada, or in the fall in the valley of the Oos. Some events overlapped in the calendar: on the first of September the bathing season began at Biarritz, lasting till exactly the thirtieth of that month, followed by the after-cure at Pau in the gigantic hotels on the Boulevard des Pyrénées with its incomparable view over the panorama of the Monts-Maudits, or in the shadow of the sixteen rows of plane trees bordering the avenues at Perpignan. In England the thing was to go North on August 12th, to shoot grouse in Scotland, and to return South on September 1st, for

From *Primal Vision* by Gottfried Benn, edit. by Ernst Ashton (New York, New Directions, 1960). All rights reserved. Reprinted by permission of New Directions, Publishers.

partridge-shooting. In Germany those were the great days of Baden-Baden, which came alive in Turgeniev's *Smoke* and a remarkably large number of other Russian books. There were certain families from the old nations, and the intruders from the new ones. The Ritz concern had a special card-index to deal with them. Such items as, "Herr X sleeps without a bolster.... Madame Y takes no butter on her toast.... Lord G. must have black cherry-jam every day," were telegraphed back and forth between London, Lucerne, and Palermo.

The modern nomad was born. About 1500, painting conquered landscape, the day in the country and the long journey. The voyages around the world had begun, and with them came the sense of distance and vast spaces. The religious and eschatological hue of man's sense of infinity was overlaid by the geographical and descriptive. Now, about 1900, the luxurious note was added, and what had sprung from necessity was turned into a source of sensory experience and enjoyment. How much history there is in the Blue Trains and the Golden Arrows! Those luncheon-baskets, a specialty of Drew's at Piccadilly Circus, with their little spirit-stoves, those flasks for distilled water and boxes for meat and butter, were now transformed into the dining-car; the luggage-racks, where for several decades the children had been put to sleep, into Pullman cars and *wagon-lits*. The hotels far surpassed the town halls and cathedrals in significance, taking on their century's identity as the town halls and cathedrals had betokened theirs. At the laying of the foundation-stone for Claridge's in the Champs Elysées, Lady Grey performed the symbolic ceremony with a silver trowel. When the Ritz was furnished, the artistic legacy of Mansard and his masons—which the Place Vendôme still exemplified, uniquely undisturbed from the 18th century down to the present day—was faithfully preserved in months of inventive toil by a staff of architects, interior decorators, artisans, art historians, and other experts. The differences between *petit-point* and tapestry, between porcelain and *faience,* between the styles of the Sung and Tang dynasties had to be no less precisely observed than the subtle distinctions between the Italian and the Spanish Renaissance. It took careful research to discover and select the right shop for silver, for glass, for carpets, brocades, and silks, for table linen, sheets, and pillowcases. In Rome there was a first-rate place for Venetian lace and embroidery, and as for lighting, the novelty was indirect light, casting no shadow. How many tones were compared until it was settled at last: a muted apricot in alabaster bowls, the beams cast up onto the warmly tinted ceilings. A Van Dyck portrait in the Louvre, in which luminous brown tones contrasted with a matt turquoise, served as the model for harmonizing the color scheme of blinds, carpets, and wallpapers. Escoffier, the chef, did not permit gas in the kitchen: "A faultless pie can be baked only with the old, tested fuels."

Coal and wood were vastly superior to gas, in the opinion of Escoffier, who was Sarah Bernhardt's sole guest at a birthday party she gave at the Carlton in London—Escoffier, who named his creations after Coquelin and Melba.

It was the age of the great dinners, meals of fourteen courses, with the sequence of wines following a tradition that went back four hundred years to the pheasant banquets of Burgundian days, of the fleur-de-lis princes. A banker who had successfully brought off an important trans-action handed the paladins of the Ritz a check for 10,000 francs for a meal with a dozen friends. It was in winter, and fresh young peas, asparagus, and fruit were hard to obtain: but it was done. The Jeroboam de Château Lafitte 1870 and the Château Yquem 1869 were brought from Bordeaux by a special messenger, who had to make the night-long journey with the priceless casket on his knees lest the sensitive old wine should suffer any jolting. Among the 180,000 bottles the house had in its own cellars, of which 500 different varieties could be ordered from the wine list every evening, there was nothing fit to go with the *bécassine* and the truffles *en papillottes.*

The restaurant trade becomes out-and-out aristocratic and industrial-ized. The inaugurators and main pillars of the "Ritz idea" are Colonel Pfuffer of Altishofen in Lucerne, Baron Pierre de Gunzburg in Paris, Lord Lathom in London, the last board chairman of the Savoy Company. Marnier Lapostolle, an industrialist in St. Cloud, concocted a cordial whose march of triumph, under the name of *Le Grand Marnier,* doubled its inventor's fortune. Apollinaris was to start on its career with a cele-bration at the new spring, the Johannisbrunn. Among the guests were the Prince of Wales, who happened to be in Homburg, Russian grand dukes and Prussian princes, twenty in all. A special freight-train had to transport food-stuffs, plates, cups, glasses, potted plants, armchairs, ice, and a kitchen-stove from Frankfurt am Main to the remote valley of the Ahr. The twenty covers cost 5,000 Swiss francs, but the Derby victory of his horse, Persimmon, combined with the presence of attractive women, put the prince in one of his most charming moods. Socially and, as the concern foresaw, commercially, it was a great success.

The second third of the last century had witnessed the rise of the great gambling casinos—forever linked with the names of the Blanc brothers from Bordeaux—above all in Homburg and in Monaco. *Grand joueurs* like Garzia, Lucien Napoleon, Bugeja, and Mustapha Fazil Pasha lost or won half a million in a few hours: dangerous people, the terror of the management that had to keep in constant telegraphic communica-tion with three big banks while they stayed. *Trente-et-quarante* was the game for high stakes; they played with a cool million in cash piled before them on the table. But also playing were Adelina Patti, by marriage Marquise de Caux, Madame Lucca, Madame Grassi, and Jules Verne. Rubinstein scarcely stopped to bow to his audience after the last notes had faded away at his concerts, so eager was he to get back to the tables. Paganini gambled away two millions. Dostoievsky at roulette—probably the most famous and most incomprehensible of gamblers, a gambler to the point of degradation, a real addict. The Rothschilds, Bismarck's son, Gortschakoff, Gladstone, gambled at Homburg. Then, for political reasons, Homburg had to close down, and the last game was announced: "Messieurs, à la dernière forever."

On July 1, 1869, an edict was issued, declaring that henceforth the district of Saint-Devote on the cape of Monaco, Les Speluges, was to be known as "Le Quartier de Monte Carlo." A quay was built, the harbor of Condamine enlarged, the Hôtel de Paris smothered in flowers. The railway and the road from Nice were completed, the Casino was built. As early as 1869 all taxes were abolished in the territory, and made up by the gamblers. In 1874 the fourth roulette table had to be set up. When Saxon-les-Bains in Switzerland was closed, too, the only casino left in all Southern Europe was this one at "the Dives," Les Speluges, on the Côte d'Azur. Secure in its monopoly, it could now afford to admit only gamblers holding tickets made out in their names, to permit only play with *refait*, to present building-plots to newspapermen, and to hand considerable sums and a railway ticket to suicide suspects. The environs were organized: golf matches at Cannes, horse-racing at Nice, pigeon shooting. One Blanc was dead, the other, François, was the main shareholder; out of his private fortune he lent the city of Paris five millions to restore the Opéra, for which the Ministry of Transport gave him faster trains to the Mediterranean. One of his daughters married a Prince Radziwill, the other a Bonaparte, and her daughter a son of the King of Greece. Blanc's godfathers back in Bordeaux had been a stocking-weaver and a shoemaker. He left his family eighty-eight millions, made in Homburg and Monte Carlo and soon to be squandered on racing stables, yachts, castles, hothouses for orchids, and *bijouterie*. What is remarkable is how little the persons of this circle and their institutions were moved by the events of the time. It is known that the last Czar did not break off his game of tennis when he received the news of the fall of Port Arthur. The day after Sadowa there was an open-air masquerade in the Prater, with a Venetian *corso*; beer-gardens and wine-gardens were filled to overflowing, and in the Volksgarten, where Strauss was conducting, all seats were sold out. The Casino of Monaco kept open during the war of 1870-'71, and its profits were only two millions less than in the preceding year of peace; it still paid out a dividend of five per cent. In Homburg the profits were lower, but exceeded half a million even during the year of war.

One can look at world history from inside and from outside, as a

sufferer or as an observer. Art is expression, and since its last stylistic
transformation, it is more so than ever. It needs means of expression, it
goes in search of them, there is not much can be expressed by potato-
peelings—not so much, anyway, as a whole life tries to express. More can
be expressed by gold helmets, peacocks, pomegranates; more can be associated with roses, balconies, and rapiers; princes can be made to say what
coopers cannot, and the Queen of the Amazons what a factory-girl cannot; people who have had the experience of Antiquity, who have spent
years observing forms and styles, people who travel, whose nerves are
sensitive and who have a weakness for gambling, may well be more complex and more fractional than savages, and with their modes of expression
they will do more justice to their era than the partisans of Blood and
Soil, who are still close to totemism. The more austere the artist is, the
deeper is his longing for finesse and light. His participation in an era of
squandering and sensual enjoyment is existentially moral; Balzac could
write only within the daemoniacal orbit of high finance; Caruso's voice
became perfect only when he sang before the Diamond Horseshoe at the
Metropolitan. Thus we see the artist play his part in the epochs we are
concerned with, and the public, in its turn, took note of the things that
art produced, including their peculiarities and their inner meaning.

.... 2. Art in Europe

Those were the decades of Duse as Camille, of Bernhardt as l'Aiglon,
of Lily Langtry as Rosalind, and large sections of the nations shared in
that. Remember, there is the press, criticism, essayism. Capitalism can
afford a public; it does not compel valuable conponents of the nation to
emigrate, its *Lebensraum* has not been limited to torture and extermination. When Zola entered the dining room of the Grand Hotel in Rome
and a puritanical Englishwoman jumped up indignantly at being expected to lunch in the same room with the author of *Nana,* there was a
public to notice it, full of alertness and warmth and that fluid which
goes to create the flair of an era—undoubtedly trivial things, too, at times,
but how deep a background it built for achievement and rank to stand
out against! How much brilliance it cast round Kainz, for instance, not
because he hobnobbed with a king, but because by giving a word the
right emphasis he could make people feel the powers of the deep, could
make men and women, lemurs and masks, grow pale merely by the way
he descended a flight of steps or slung his arm round a pillar! There was
one nation in which literature had long been a public power that even
the government had to reckon with: the French. Now they had created
a new rank, that of *grand écrivain,* successor to the great *savants universels*
of the 17th, 18th, and 19th centuries, and socially the successor to the

gentilhomme—a blend of journalism, social criticism, and autochthonous art: *grandseigneurs*, marshals of literature: Balzac, the Goncourts, Anatole France; in England, Kipling. A new form of modern creativeness. In Germany the type was largely rejected, the musical-metaphysical factor remaining the core of the "unreal" German endeavors. In Norway, by contrast, Björnson came close to becoming king.

An age in motion: inflation of themes, chaos of stylistic attitudes. In architecture: glass and iron displacing wood and brick, concrete displacing stone. The age-old problem of rivers was solved by the suspension-bridge; hospitals abandoned the palatial style for that of the barracks. Public gardens, Boy Scouts, dancing schools.

The Third Estate at the zenith of its power: the bourgeoisie advancing into rank and title, into commanding positions in army and navy. The great cities: the proletariat lives in them, too, but did not build them. Modern international law, the mathematical sciences, biology, positivism—all this is bourgeois; so is the countermovement: modern irrationalism, perspectivism, existentialist philosophy. The white bourgeois colonizes, sends the sahib to take charge of the yellow, brown, and black riff-raff. European art turns in the opposite direction, regenerating itself in the tropics: Gauguin on Tahiti, Nolde in Rabaul, Dauthendey in Java, Pierre Loti in Japan, Matisse in Morocco. Asia is opened up mythologically and linguistically: Wilhelm devotes himself to China, Lafcadio Hearn to Japan, Zimmer to India.

A spiritual intensity pervades Europe; from this small continent a spiritual high tension makes the unspeakable, the undreamed-of, take shape. It is hard to say which is more remarkable, the way the public follows and takes an interest, or the harshness, the dedication to truth—brutal, if necessary—on the part of its creators, those great intellects which bear the responsibility for the race's destiny. Immensely serious, tragically profound words about that work: "To say Poetry is to say Suffering" (Balzac); "To say Work is to say Sacrifice" (Valéry); "It is better to ruin a work and make it useless for the world than not to go to the limit at every point" (Thomas Mann); "Oft did I weary wrestling with Thee"—the line that a galley-slave had carved in his oar, now carved by Kipling in the table he worked at in India; "Nothing is more sacred than the work in progress" (d'Annunzio); "I would rather be silent than express myself feebly" (Van Gogh).

Cracks in the positivist picture of the world; influx of crises and menaces. Postulation of the concept of the bio-negative (intoxication, the psychotic, art). Doubts about the meaning of words: for instance dissolving and destructive; and for a substitute: creative and stimulating. Analysis of schizophrenia: in the oldest evolutionary centers of the brain, there survive memories of the collective primal phases of life, which may manifest themselves in psychoses and dreams (ethnophrenia), primal phases! Pre-lunar man comes upon the scene, and with him the ages of geological cataclysm, world crises, doom by fire, moon disintegration, globe-girdling tides; secrets from the beginning of the Quarternary: enigmatic similarities between the gods, the world-wide legend of the Flood, the kinship between linguistic groups in the Old and the New Worlds— problems of cultures, prehistorical cultures, pre-Atlantean links; the complex of problems posed by Negro sculpture, by the cave drawings of Rhodesia, the stone images on Easter Island, the great deserted cities in the primeval forest near Saigon.

Deciphering of the Assyrian clay cylinders; new excavations at Babylon, Ur, Samara; the first coherent presentation of Egyptian sculpture—an analysis of composition methods in the reliefs leads to the surprising perception that they correspond exactly to the theories of Cubism: "the art of drawing consists in establishing relations between curves and straight lines." Promiscuity of images and systems. Forming and re-forming. Europe is on the way to new glory, the shining examples from the past being the grandeur of the fifteenth and the fulfillment of the eighteenth century. Germany hesitates, for here intellectual talents are few and far between, yet an élite answers across the borders, stirred by the truth of an ethos now revealed, manifest for the first time in this insistence on clarity, craftsmanly delicacy, brightness, audacity, and brilliance—the "Olympus of Appearances"; within Germany it means discarding the Faustian urge in favor of work with defined limits.

Ever new throngs of ideas come charging in, the problems become inflated, remote distances draw nearer, displaying their miseries and their splendors, worlds lost and forgotten loom into view, among them some that are cloaked in twilight, equivocal, deranged. The amount of real intellectual discovery during these fifty years is unequalled, and, all in all, it really expands the pattern. Rembrandt, Grünewald, El Greco, long neglected, were rediscovered, the strange and disquieting phenomenon of Van Gogh was given a place in the world of the intellect; the riddle of Marées' Arcadian dream was solved, the unrecognized Hölderlin was conquered for that circle to which his bio-negative *problematik* was intelligible ("If I die in shame, if my soul is not avenged on the brazen ...") Bertram's book appeared, and, in an unending sequence of analytical works transforming themselves in their own dialectics, Nietzsche was placed among the very greatest of Germans. Conrad's fascinating novels were translated. Hamsun became "the greatest among the living." The North had long established its supremacy with Ibsen, Björnson, and Strindberg; by producing Niels Lyhne the small provincial town of Thisted in Jutland had helped to form the taste of at least one of our generations. The New World came—Walt Whitman's lyrical monism had a great influence—and conquered; everyone knows the situation today; Europe's last great literary form, the novel, has largely passed under American control.

Diaghilev appears, the real founder of the modern stage. Composing music for his ballet are Stravinsky, his own discovery, Debussy, Milhaud, Respighi. His dancers are Pavlova, Karsavina, Nijinsky. His stage designers are Picasso, Matisse, Utrillo, Braque. Moving through Europe, he revolutionizes everything. The intellectual novelty of his ideas is the concentration and toughening of all the arts. This is how Cocteau put it: "A work of art must satisfy all nine Muses."

Slavonic and Romance elements combined here in a distinct trend: *against* mere feeling, against everything inarticulate, romantic, amorphous, against all empty planes, against mere allusions in punctuation; and *for* everything perfected, clarified, tempered by hard work; *for* precision in the use of materials, organization, strict intellectual penetration. What it comes to is a turning against inner life, mere good will, pedagogic or racial side issues, in favor of the form-assuming, and thus form-compelling, expression.

Everyone knows how this new style suddenly appeared simultaneously in all the lands of the white race. Today its implication is clear: producing art means purging the inarticulate, nationalistic inner life, dissolving the last residue of Post-Classicism, completing the secularization of medieval man. That is to say: anti-familiar, anti-idealistic, anti-authoritarian. The only authoritarian factor left is the will to express, the craving for form, the inner restlessness that will not leave off until the form has been worked out in its proper proportions. This will take absolute ruthlessness toward the beloved, time-tested, sacred things. But what we might then see is the epiphany of a new image casting its radiance over the anxieties of life, a new image of man's fate, which is so hopelessly, disconsolately laden.

These were not "artists of talent" tipping each other the wink; there was no conspiracy between Montmartre, Bohemian Chelsea, the ghetto, and the barnyard; it was a secular surging of life, racially and biologically founded, a change of style brought about by a mutational *ananke*. Scheler somewhere speaks of "feelings that everyone nowadays is aware of having in himself but which it once took men like poets to wrest from the appalling muteness of our inner life." Such wresters come to the fore now. After all, the whole nineteenth century can today be interpreted as an upheaval within the gene, which saw this new mutation ahead. Things had lost their old relevance, not only in morals but in physics; they even broke out of the mechanical world view that had been held inviolable since Kepler. When this happened the public realized that something had been going on secretly for a long time. For centuries all the great men of the white race had felt only the one inner task of concealing their own nihilism. This nihilism had drawn sustenance from a variety of spheres: with Dürer from the religious, with Tolstoy from the moral, with Kant from the epistemological, with Goethe from the universally human, with Balzac from the social—but it had been the basic element in the work of every one of them. With immense caution it is touched again and again; with equivocal questions, with groping, ambiguous turns, they approach it on every page, in every chapter, in every character. Not for a moment are they in doubt about the essential nature of their inner creative substance: it is the abysmal, the void, the cold, the inhuman. The one who remained naive the longest was Nietzsche. Even in *Zarathustra,* what meaningful disciplined élan! It is only in the last phase, with *Ecce Homo* and the lyrical fragments, that he admits it to his consciousness: "Thou shouldst have sung, oh, my soul!"—not: believed, cultivated, thought in historical and pedagogical terms, been so positive—: and now comes the breakdown. Singing—that means forming sentences, finding expressions, being an artist, doing cold, solitary work, turning to no one, apostrophizing no congregation, but before every abyss simply testing the echoing quality of the rock-faces, their resonance, their tone, their coloratura effects. This was a decisive finale. After all: artistics! It could no longer be concealed from the public that here was a deep degeneration of substance. On the other hand, this lent great weight to the new art: what was here undertaken in artistic terms was the transference of things into a new reality, a new, authentic relevance, a biological realism proved by the laws of proportion, to be experienced as the expression of a new spiritual way of coming to terms with existence, exciting in the creative tension of its pursuit of a style derived from awareness of inner destiny. Art as a means of producing reality: this was the productive principle of the new art.

Undeniably: this art was capitalistic, a ballet demanded costumes, a tour had to be financed. Pavlova could not dance unless she was lodged in rooms filled with white lilac, both winter and summer, whether in India or in the Hague. Duse suffered much, everything around her had to be hushed, far away from her, with the curtains drawn. For some of his paintings Matisse received sums in six figures. Some went to bathe at Lussin-piccolo even at the height of the season; composing a new opera paid for a new car. The high-tension, condensations, oscillations of intensified life were part of this order of things, but so were the sufferings, the hag-ridden dread of losing the inner voice, the vocation, the visions overbrimming with imagery. Exhibitionism and breakdown alike were filled with truth, they were sovereign. The intellectual nonsense about the esthetic sense of the common people had not yet been trotted out to idealize the microcephalic; Bronze-Age barter was not yet proclaimed an economic dream full of possibilities for the future; people could travel, spend their money, take on the imprint of many skies, be transformed in many cities.

There were also some perfectly successful representations of the social milieu: Van Gogh's "Potato-Eaters," Hauptmann's *The Weavers,* Meunier's sculptures of miners, Käthe Kollwitz's drawings; and, for the rural milieu: Millet's "Sower," Leibl's "Forester." But compassion and an intimate sense of one's own country were not all the emotional content and formal motif, no more than "The Return from Hades," or a woman bathing or a jug filled with asphodels. The human and humane was only one of the currents flowing toward the distant shore. And what peopled that shore was goddesses or orange-pickers or horses, girls from Haiti, postmen, railway-crossings, also flute-players and army officers—but all craving for the life of shadows. A very selective, exclusive start. A vocation. A great peculiarity. It meant elevating everything decisive into the language of unintelligibility, yielding to things that deserved to convince no one. Yet art should not be said to have been esoteric in the sense of being exclusive; everyone could come in and hear, open doors and see, draw closer, join, or go away. The tragic distances between man and man are felt a thousand times more as a result of other phenomena: the cruel accumulation of power, justice corrupted by politics, unbalanced passions, senseless wars. This is, perhaps, the place to point out that we had successful novels that were German in the good sense, best sellers such as *Ekkehard, Debit and Credit, Effi Briest, Jörn Uhl.* There was nothing remotely like a bar to German production in any foreign or racially alien works. It is one of the countless political lies to assert that only now was there any guarantee that the true-blue German would get true-blue German books. Rather, what made certain groups loathe the modern style was its exciting, experimental, controversial quality—in short, the intellectual quality of what was going on, and what their own meager talents could not cope with. Besides, there was the hatred of seeing the public reached by anything at all, other than their own political and nationalistic belly-aching. Thus the intellect in itself became "un-German," and at its particularly abominable worst: "European." The rest of Europe thought that a general paganization of form might perhaps reconsecrate the race whose gods had died; it did not expect this from fairy tales and dialect and Wotanisms.

It was this concept of "Europe" that in 1932 gave birth to the notion of a Mediterranean Academy, the Académie Méditerranéenne which was to have its seat in Monaco. All the riparians of that "narrow sea," the directly and indirectly Mediterranean countries, were asked to join. D'Annunzio, Marshal Pétain, Pirandello, Milhaud took the lead. The Royal Italian Academy, the Gami-el-Azhar University in Cairo, and the

Sorbonne were among the cooperating institutions. All that the pagan and then the monotheistic generations had produced in esthetic and conceptual values was here to be clarified anew, for the enrichment and edification of today's world. All that had created and formed us, too, up in the North: the enigma of the Etruscans, the lucid centuries of Antiquity, the inexhaustibility of the Moors, the splendor of Venice, the marble tremors of Florence. Who would deny that we, too, were formed by the Renaissance and the Reformation—whether in devotion or in battle—that the monks, the knights, the troubadours, that Salamanca, Bologna, Montpellier, that botanically roses, lilies, wine, and biographically Genoa and Portofino and the Tristan palace on the Grand Canal, down to this hour of our life—that by all this breathless creativity Rome and the Mediterranean left so indelible an imprint upon us that we, too, belonged to it? But the invitations sent to Germany fell into the hands of the Gestapo. Art was closed down. "Messieurs, à la dernière forever!"

. . . . 3. Art and the Third Reich

It is only against this background situation that one clearly sees what was special about the "German awakening." A nation broadly speaking without any definite taste, as a whole untouched by the moral and esthetic refinement of neighboring civilized countries, philosophically embroiled in confused idealistic abstractions, prosaic, inarticulate, and dull, a practical nation with—as its evolution demonstrates—only a biological way to spirituality: i.e., by Romanization or universalization; such a nation elevates an anti-semitic movement that demagogically conjures up before its eyes the meanest of its ideals: low-income housing developments, with subsidized, tax-favored sex life, home-made rape-oil in the kitchen, self-hatched scrambled eggs, home-grown barley, homespun socks, local flannel, and, for art and the inner life, S.A. songs bellowed in radio style. A nation's mirror of itself. Parallel bars in the garden, and St. John's fires on the hills—there's your pure-bred Teuton. A rifle range and the pewter mug filled with bock, that was his element. And now they gaze questioningly at the civilized nations and wait with childlike naiveté for their amazement and admiration.

A remarkable process! Inside a Europe of high brilliance and joint intellectual endeavors there evolves an inner-German Versailles, a Germanic collective based on a society of criminals, and whenever there is a chance they belabor the Muses. They are not content with the big cars, the hunting lodges where the bison roar, the stolen island in the Wannsee—Europe has to marvel at their culture! Haven't we talents among us with the resonance of tin cans and the pathos of waterlogged corpses, and painters whom we need only show the direction: say, His Nibs at the end of a shoot, the gun still smoking, one foot on the felled sixteen-point stag, the morning mists rising from the ground, furnishing a touch of the primeval woodland murmurs? And the block warden goes in for colored saucers—they will make Europe sit up! But above all one must exterminate: all that is Eastern, or Southern, or Western, not to speak of what is Latin, Gothic, Impressionist, Expressionist, the Hohenstaufen, the Hapsburg, Charlemagne—till they alone are left, perhaps with Henry the Lion and Snow White thrown in. On these odds and ends they base their Chambers of Culture, their esthetic Sing-Sing.

The artist is reincorporated in the guild order from which he freed himself about 1600. He is regarded as an artisan, a particularly senseless and corruptible artisan, patronized by the cell leader or the Soldiers' Home. Artisans are not supposed to care about the era's political or social decisions; only Kultur-Bolsheviks and traitors do. Anyone daring to say that artistic creation presupposes a measure of inner freedom is called before the Chamber; anyone mentioning the word style gets a warning; mental hospitals and institutions are consulted on the question of contemporary art. As filling station attendant for vital contents, the Propaganda Minister is the authority on line and counterpoint. Music must be folksongish, or else it is banned. Only generals or Party officials are subjects for portraiture: in clear, simple colors; subtle nuances are discouraged. For establishing a bridgehead in the East you get an oil portrait, 8-12, rated according to defense value—*i.e.,* value in defending the boss's job. Genre paintings showing fewer than five children are not to be marketed. Tragic, somber, extravagant themes are matters for the Security Police; delicate, high-bred, languid ones for the Racial Health Court.

Personages one could never object to if they confined themselves to fattening pigs or milling flour step forward, hail "man" as ideal, organize song-fests and choir contests, and set themselves up as the measure of things. Lübzow, Podejuch County, disputes the alliterative laurels with Piepenhagen in Pomerania, while the hamlets with a population below 200 in the Schwalm valley vie for the jubilee song of the Xaver Popiol S.A. Brigade. "Terpsichorean," says clubfoot; "melodious," murmurs earwax; skunks claim to smell of roses; the Propaganda Minister takes up relations with poetry. "Strong outlines"—no truck with the sublime! Obvious! Compared with shooting people in the neck outdoors or chair-leg fighting indoors, sublimity has a sissified, un-German look. Of course, flattening is not quite formative, but the gas station attendant does not notice. What does not take on expression stays prehistoric. Art is a buoy marking deep and shallow spots; what the Minister wants is relaxation and dash. Art among all gifted races is a profound delimiting of enhancement and transition; here they order four new pirates à la Störtebeker and three freedom-fighters à la Colonel Schill. Whatever style and expression a few inspired individuals achieved, over slights and abuse, among these ponderous, divided people, they have debased and falsified in their own image: the jaws of Caesars and the brains of troglodytes, the morality of protoplasm and the sense of honor of a sneak thief. All nations of quality create their own élite; now it has come to the point where being German means being hostile to any sort of differentiation and, in matters of taste, betting always on the clumsiest horse; the sensitive are given the third degree by the Gestapo. It also looks after art studios: great painters are forbidden to buy canvas and oils, and at night the block wardens go round checking on the easels. Art comes under the heading of pest control (Colorado beetle). A genius is chased screaming through the woods at night; when an aged Academy member or a Nobel Prize winner finally dies of starvation, the culture guardians beam with glee.

Vengeful underdogs, perspectival *formes frustes*—but, although the occasion scarcely justifies it, one must look at it even more comprehensively. It is the centuries-old German problem that here has the chance to manifest itself so clearly, under the protection of the nation's armed criminals. It is the German substance, something outside differentiation and esthetic transformation. An historically not uninteresting, in spots even distinguished work about conditions in the pre-Reformation era points out that Dürer endangered his Germanness by turning to those mathematical problems in painting that Italian painters had formulated under the impact of the Renaissance. So Dürer was concerned with formal processes of orderly consciousness—studies in proportion—and this was already un-German, already too much. The clear sky of abstraction, which arches over the Latin world without any dehumanizing or sterilizing effect, is here unhealthy and harmful to production. This is the voice of an urge for illiteracy—but here it is genuine. It is part of their *"Lebensraum,"* their "evolution," their thought-shunning dash. The resolution of inner tensions by esthetic means is alien to them. The cathartic nature of expression in general they will always deny, for lack of any corresponding inner experience. What they lack is impressions of the constructive form of the sublime. Spiritually held down by low-grade ideas, such as that of a single, mechanical causality, they will never be able to grasp an essential, productive causality of the creative principle. What they can experience is history, a result of bacteriological research, an experiment, an economic process—they are incapable of experiencing the questing and agonized motions of a productive gene inherent even in the white race and that gene's escape into a structural element. That is why their writers wind up even short paragraphs, trivial dicta, on a moral, didactic, and, if possible, absolute note; they can find no other way of getting themselves off-stage. Their lack of any tendency towards artistic abstraction is complete—for that would require hard work, objectivity, discipline. Objectivity in turn demands decency and detachment, a moral, personal decency that is beyond riff-raff. So wherever they see things raised to the level of consciousness and find an artist revealing his own productive processes, they work off their feelings in hatred against "artistics," in rambling balderdash about formalism and intellectualism. For this people, uni-ovular twins are more important than geniuses: the former lend themselves to statistics, the latter contain lethal factors. This people spews out its geniuses as the sea spews out its pearls: for the inhabitants of other realms.

And so this people is caught up in the Awakening, in the "German miracle," the "recuperative movement," according to E. R. Jaentsch's book, *The Anti-Type*. (The anti-type consists not of the awakened but of the undaunted, those who go on striving for more refinement.) This movement would have us believe that the Great Migrations have just come to an end, and that we are now called upon to clear the forests. It is a miracle whose most unique and sincere quality appears when the cities have to be blacked out, when people fall silent, mists billow, and only they talk and talk and talk, until their stinking breath rolls like vast cow-pats over the suffocated fields. It is a rising, the essence of which—apart from their get-rich-quick schemes, which come so naturally to them—is a lie of lies and an anthropological unreality, excluding the achievement of any sort of identity with any age, race, or continent. This movement purges art. It does so by means of the same concept with which it glorifies and justifies itself and which thus looms gigantically, programmatically, into our field of vision: history.

Five hoplites armed with machine-guns attack a boy they had promised not to harm; then they march in somewhere—: history. Mahomet began as a robber of caravans; the ideology was a later addition. He even poisoned the wells in the desert—for centuries an unimaginable crime, but now ennobled by divine and racial needs: first theft, then religion, finally history. Under Nero, in 67 A.D., private correspondence in Rome had ceased entirely, since all letters were opened; the postmen came to the houses in the mornings bringing news by word of mouth about the latest executions: world history.

And this means: at breakfast, on mountain-tops, while breaking and entering, with filmstars—Colleoni! Before rabbit-hutches, cloakrooms, extra distributions of synthetic honey—Alexander! At mass murders, lootings, blackmail: geopolitics and fulfillment of destiny! Now, history may have its own methods, and one that our eyes can clearly discern is undoubtedly its use of microcephalics, but art has also proved itself in forty centuries. This essay is art's rejoinder; these are the expressions it has found to fit the epoch. It finds them as naturally and sharply as the

Gestapo aims its shots. It collects them and hands them on to those who will always exist, during every historical victory and during every historical doom, and whose influence will outlast both victory and doom. Art now records these expressions in the belief that there will some day be a European tradition of the mind, which Germany will also join, a tradition from which it will learn and to which, having learned, it will contribute.

(Written 1941, published 1949) Translated by Ernst Kaiser and Eithne Wilkins.

Gerald Brenan

Gerald Brenan, who had spent a good part of his youth in Andalusia and who was living with his wife in Malaga when the Spanish Civil War began, returned to Spain for the first time in thirteen years in 1951. In his own words, he was "tired of politics"; his interest in Spanish history and culture had already borne fruit in two books of great general as well as scholarly interest, and he wanted, on this trip, to "give attention to the more permanent and characteristic features of the country." He found, however, that these features could not leave out of account the contemporary facts of Falangist rule. Although the other authors in this section begin with an avowed interest in political problems, Brenan's interest is forced on him by his journey. Nevertheless "Cordova," and the book, *The Face of Spain,* from which it is taken, tell us a good deal about life in a totalitarian state.

The form Brenan has chosen, the journal, is a very useful one for the traveler. It is really a diary that is intended for the eyes of others, and like all such diaries it appeals by its flexibility and variety. Brenan is left a good deal of latitude in organization; for example, he can ignore conventional transitions and can shift mood as abruptly as place as long as he remains faithful to some unifying purpose, which in this instance is the author's search after a deeper understanding of Spain. A strong basic element in all travel literature is that pleasurable sense the reader is given of being taken on a vicarious journey. At the same time, travel literature may serve a variety of other purposes, ranging from the mere imparting of useful information to serious reflections upon history, art, manners, mores, national culture, psychology, and so on. It has been an extremely popular form of literature in the past century, and two famous examples may help suggest the range that is possible: in *Etruscan Places* D. H. Lawrence, true to his evangelical and reforming temper, uses his visits to the site of Etruscan remains as a way of inveighing against the shortcomings of his own society; and in *Mont St. Michel and Chartres* Henry Adams finds that his explorations of the great cathedrals of France lead him into a deep search of the self. The number and kinds of possibilities depend of course upon the author. Note here how Brenan, whose style is deceptively simple, moves in the section on the mosque from a description of a beautiful building to a disquisition on history and comparative cultures and religions.

CORDOVA

In our carriage, as we traveled slowly southward, there were three other people besides ourselves. One was a fat man with a large white head like an egg and two little, plumply lidded eyes set transversely in it. As soon as the train had started, he put on a soft traveling cap, spread a handkerchief over his face, and went to sleep. Next to him sat a lean, nervous man in the middle thirties, with one of those thin, eyebrow-like moustaches often worn by Fascists, and his pretty wife. They talked in monosyllables, while the man kept taking up and putting down his newspaper and moving restlessly from one side of the carriage to the other. Since he avoided my eye, it was obvious that he did not wish for conversation.

We passed Aranjuez with its tall elms, silent in the morning light, and entered the dreary, reddish yellow steppe that prepares the way for the equally dreary plain of La Mancha. At a station the fat man woke up suddenly and got out. Through the window I could see him cross the platform and climb into a diminutive horse bus, which apparently connected the station with the town. Where it could lie was a mystery, for we could see for miles in every direction.

My wife had started a conversation with the smiling woman who sat opposite her, and I joined in. Her husband listened in a moody silence. The conversation languished. Then Valdepeñas came and we decided to have lunch. The hotel had provided a lavish four-course meal and we pressed our companions to share it. They yielded, and over a cold omelet, red mullet, and a bottle of wine the man's hostility broke down and he began to talk.

He had plenty to say for himself. He was a doctor who, while still a *practicante* or medical assistant (a rank we do not have in England) had joined the Blue Brigade and gone to Russia. Here he had spent two years. He said that he liked the Russians: they were a good-natured, simple people, easily imposed on by their rulers and at bottom more sym-

Reprinted from *The Face of Spain* by Gerald Brenan, by permission of Farrar, Straus & Cudahy, Inc. Copyright 1951 by Gerald Brenan.

pathetic than the Germans. But their standard of life was terribly low. The Ukrainians, who lived rather better, hated Communism and for that reason had deserted in large numbers. When the brigade returned to Spain many of them had begged to come with them; we should find two or three in Málaga. I asked him how he had liked the Germans. Not much, he said. They were too technical and too fanatical. That was why they had failed, in spite of their many great qualities.

He questioned me about England. Like all the other Spaniards I had met, he was full of curiosity to know what the conditions of life were in our country. But there was resentment mingled with his rather grudging admiration. Why had we outlawed Spain? I said that we had no wish to outlaw Spain (it is odd how when traveling abroad one becomes the official spokesman of one's country), but that it was impossible for us to have close or friendly relations with its present regime. Our foreign policy was governed by the political struggle with Russia and if we admitted General Franco's government to the union of West European nations, many people in France and Italy who at present supported that union would give their votes to the Communists. We could not afford to make such a gift to Russian propaganda.

This was a point of view that seemed entirely new to him and he sat brooding over it for a few moments in silence. But when I added that if a monarchy were to come in in Spain, we might feel that the position had altered, he became very excited.

"This Don Juan," he said, "with his talk of elections and of friendship with Prieto will never rule in this country. Never—you may take my word for it. For if he were to, in a few years' time we would be back where we were in 1936 and all the work of the Liberation would have to be done over again. That would mean another Civil War."

As we talked, we were passing out of the flat tableland of La Mancha into a different region. Round sage-green hills, topped by whitish rocks, began to collect round us—at first in ones and twos and at some little distance from the track, as if to prepare us for the change that was coming, then crowding close about us in massed formations. In the brittle air the rocks glittered faintly and patches of broom, which the Spanish peasants call *novia de los pastores,* or shepherds' sweetheart, made yellow smears upon the grey-green hillsides. All at once, as we crawled up a little pass, the train began to move faster and looking out we saw that we were racing down a steep grassy valley; jagged cliffs and rock pinnacles sprouting ilex and umbrella pine stood up on either side, rising above one another in distant recession. In an instant the whole scene had changed from the motionless and classical to the picturesque and romantic. We were in the Pass of Despeñaperros, the only breach in the three-hundred-mile wall of the Sierra Morena.

I went out into the corridor to look at the view and the doctor joined me.

"Is it true," I asked, "that there are bandits in the Sierra?"

"You bet there are," he replied. "All those rocks and peaks you see are full of them. Some people call them the Maquis, but you can take my word for it that they are nothing else but bandits and murderers. When they want food, they come down from the mountains to raid farms and then they shoot everyone they see. They spare no one. If, as they pretend, they sought out their personal and political enemies, I should respect them. One knows where one is with people who fight for their ideals; either you kill them or they kill you, but the fight is pure. But these people—no. They have no ideals, they just kill for money and love of bloodshed."

"Are there many of them?"

"Their numbers vary. Sometimes there are only a few, at other times there are thousands. When the police press them in one place, they move to another. They travel where they like and the towns are full of them. While they are in the mountains they live in caves and fire from behind bushes at the civil guards who try to close with them. Then they raid the farms and villages and carry off the cattle and pigs. As they kill any landowners or bailiffs they can catch, the estates are not supervised and agriculture suffers. The whole of the river valley above Cordova is terrorized by them."

"This is the classical region of Spanish brigandage," I remarked. "José María made himself famous here a century ago."

"Yes, but these are not *caballeros* like José María," the doctor insisted. "They kill, kill, kill. And they don't defend the poor against the rich as he did. They rob for their own pockets."

We had come out of the pass into a rolling country planted with olives. Soon we saw on our left a slow, muddy stream bordered with tamarisks and oleanders; it was one of the headwaters of the Guadalquivir. Periwinkles and yellow marigolds were in flower in the hedges and the farmhouses we passed looked white and clean with their pots of geraniums and their iron *rejas*. Everywhere we saw horses, mules, asses, and ragged children. There was no need to be told we were in Andalusia.

We began to talk of the conditions on the land.

"They are not good," my fellow traveler said. "It's the old, old story—the landowners won't pay a living wage. We do all we can to press them in the syndicates, but they refuse to budge. Yet they are some of the richest people in the country. Look at Espejo, for example. The whole town and all the country round it are owned by the Duchess of Osuna, yet the workers on her estates are starving. The Reds ought to have shot those people."

I told him that at Málaga, where I had been living when the Civil

War began, the Reds had not shot the landlords, but only the indus- trialists and the small people.

"That's just it," he said, very excited. "The Reds didn't shoot the right people. They left the landowners alone, and now we have to pay the price for it."

The train drew up at Andújar and a crowd of miserable, starving creatures, dressed in rags, stood on the platform.

"Did you see Russians who were poorer than that?" I asked.

He admitted that he had not, but added that whereas all the Rus- sians in the country districts were miserable, except the commissars, only a few people in Spain were undernourished.

"It's what I'm telling you," he went on. "This is the fault of the landlords. They pay wages that no family can live on. And for half the year they pay no wages at all."

"But why can't you do something about it?" I asked. "After all, Spain is a dictatorship. Franco can do anything he pleases."

"Ah, Franco!" he broke out. "Don't talk to me of Franco! He's the best man Spain ever had. He's a saint, that man is. He's so good his image ought to be on all the altars. If anyone ever had a heart of gold, it's he. But he doesn't know what's going on round him. Poor man, he's always surrounded by his guards, has to travel in a bulletproof car and see Spain from hoardings and balconies. If only he could step just once into a bar or café and listen to what people were saying, the country would change overnight. And then he's so unjustly blamed. If it doesn't rain and the crops fail, they say '—It's Franco's fault. It's all because of Franco. If we had a king, we should be better off—' Is that fair?"

"No," I said. "But they do say that some of the people round him are robbing the country."

"And so they are. Look at X." (He named a well-known political figure.) "He made a pile by pure swindling, ran off to America and lived there for a year. Yet now he's back again and more influential than ever. But Franco doesn't know this. He is *muy caballero*, a very great gentle- man and trusts the people round him. And this is how they repay his confidence!"

The train drew into Cordova and we got out. The doctor shook hands and gave me his card. From it I could see that he was one of the leading figures in the Falange of the province. Something neurotic in his bearing told me that during the Civil War he had been responsible for many disagreeable things, and this impression was confirmed later. Yet I left him with a feeling of respect for his honesty and frankness, as well as with pity for the disillusion he had suffered. It is strange that fanatics, because they live tragically, should often be more likeable than reasonable and balanced people.

I have been carried away this evening by the beauty of Cordova. Our hotel is an eighteenth-century house in the middle of the city, built like all old houses in Cordova round a patio. It is quite a modest place—we pay only 40 pesetas a day—and bears the time-honored name of the Hotel de Cuatro Naciones. From the moment when I went upstairs to the corridor and bedroom and smelled the sour smell of washed tile floors that is so characteristic of Andalusian *fondas,* I felt completely at home here. This was the Spain that I knew.

Our window opens onto the fretted stone balustrade of the Romanesque church of San Miguel, built toward 1240, immediately after the Reconquest. Yellow moldering walls, yellow peeling wash, for yellow is the prevailing color of this city. Its harsh, jangling bell, angry and hurried like a bird's alarm chatter and lasting only a few moments, is calling the devout to evening service.

After a coffee in the plaza we went for a stroll in the warm air given off by the houses. The sun was just setting and we let ourselves be carried by the crowd down one of the narrow, winding streets that lead to the river. Soon we came to the mosque with its long blank walls of yellow stone and its lovely Renaissance minaret. Beyond it lay the river. *O gran río, gran rey de Andalucía,* as Góngora addressed it: the river of Tartessos, whose roots, said the Greek poet Stesichorus, lie among silver. Here, below the stone parapet, it rolled slowly by, a brownish yellow current spotted with white bubbles, and beyond it a low sandy shore, scattered with washerwomen and donkeys and girls carrying pitchers; further off still, the white village of the Campo de la Verdad.

February 19

The Mosque of Cordova is certainly the first building in Spain—the most original and the most beautiful. From the moment of entering the great court planted with orange trees, one gets a feeling of peace and harmony which is quite different from the mood of religious holiness and austerity imparted by Christian cloisters. The small reddish oranges cluster among the dark green leaves, butterflies chase one another, birds flit about and chirp, and the great marble cistern for ablutions seems to be there to say that the warmth and richness of Nature and the instinctive life of Man are also pure because they have been willed by God.

When one enters the mosque itself one is likely to suffer at first from conflicting impressions. The Renaissance choir built in the center disturbs one's view of the forest of columns; some of the restorations, especially the rather garish painting on the ceiling, clash with the warm color of the stone and marble; and then the double horseshoe arches, striped buff-white and brick-rose, arrest one by their strangeness and novelty. One has to visit the building several times to allow its magic to sink into one.

This mosque is surely a first rate example of the adage, so true of all the arts, that necessity is the mother of invention. The Arabs, when in 785 they began to build it, had no style of their own. They wished to make use of the Roman and Visigothic columns that littered the city and, since these were too slight to support the heavy pieces of masonry that would be needed to continue them if the roof was to be raised to a sufficient elevation they were compelled to strengthen the arches by inserting above the abaci a second lower range of arches to act as buttresses. This contrivance—so clumsy structurally but so beautiful in effect—paved the way for the later invention of the wonderful intersecting arches of Al-Hakam's *maqsurah,* which is the crowning glory of the building. A new style, put together from the syllables of a Byzantine idiom, had come into existence.

No two modes of architecture could well be more different from one another than the Moslem and the West Christian. West Christian architecture in its early phase is filled with the craving for weight and massiveness; and in its second phase, the Gothic, for a spectacular liberation from that weight in a skyward ascent. In both cases there is an emphasis on the tremendousness of the force of gravity, either in the form of great masses of stone weighing downward, or of lofty columns springing up like trees in defiance of the downpull. The load of original sin that oppresses the human conscience and seeks to drag the world back into the savagery of the Dark Ages is expressed in a load of stone. The sense of duration, too, the confidence in man's firm establishment on the earth is emphasized: the Universal Church has been built on a rock and will last forever, and, while it lasts, it will interpret history in terms of moral profit and loss, as the Old Testament has taught it to do.

Moslem architecture is quite the opposite. A mosque is to be a court, a square, a market place, lightly built to hold a large concourse of people. Allah is so great that nothing human can vie with Him in strength or endurance, and in a society where the harem system complicates the line of descent, the pride or *orgullo* of the feudal ages—which comes from their association of land tenure with family and from the vista of the long line of descendants—is out of place. (In the feudal ages a man thought of his line as stretching forward into the future; in the aristocratic ages he thought of it as stretching back into the past.) Even the Moslem castles, large though they are, give the effect of being light and insubstantial. But a mosque is also a place for the contemplation of the Oneness of Allah. How can this better be done than by giving the eyes a maze of geometric patterns to brood over? The state aimed at is a sort of semi-trance. The mind contemplates the patterns, knows that they can be unraveled and yet does not unravel them. It rests therefore on what it sees, and the delicate color, the variations of light and shade add a sensuous tinge to the pleasure of certainty made visible. This, at all events, is the only explanation I can give of the strange state of mind set up by Al-Hakam's *maqsurah* and *mihrab*.

Another building not to be missed in Cordova is the synagogue. Though erected as late as 1315—that is to say, after the Christian occupation—its arabesque plaster designs are in the purest Moslem style. Close by lived Maimonides, the great Jewish poet and philosopher, whose tomb is still shown at Damascus. A square near by has been renamed after him.

This old Jewish quarter of the city is particularly lovely. The characteristic feature of Cordova, as everyone who has been there knows, is the two-storied house built round a patio. These patios with their pots of ferns and flowers and their fountain in the center have an irresistible charm and since the street doors are left open, one gets a glimpse into them as one passes. The plan of these houses is Roman, but none are older than the sixteenth century and most of them were put up after 1700. A large part of the area of the present city was occupied by ruins and gardens until well on in the nineteenth century.

February 20

This afternoon we set off to see the famous hermitages in the Sierra. To do this one takes the bus a couple of miles as far as Brillante, a garden city built since the war, and then walks. As we got out of the bus, a man came up and offered to show us the way. He was a pleasant, eager little fellow who was enchanted at the idea of speaking to two English people, because he was a regular listener to the Spanish program of the B.B.C. Very soon his history came out. During the war he had been a sergeant on the Nationalist side; then he had been appointed schoolmaster of a village in the Sierra, but, finding the pay insufficient to support him, he had put in a local man as locum tenens and opened a small business in Cordova. He regretted having had to do this because he liked teaching and had a strong sense of its importance.

We were walking up a broad track between limestone boulders and evergreen oaks. Clumps of asphodels with their glossy leaves and elegant, starry flowers were scattered about and among them, under the trees, sat parties of picnickers, dressed in their gayest Sunday clothes, with bottles and slices of ham and cold sausages spread out on napkins. This was the Quinta de Arrizafa, where the caliphs once had their summer place.

Our friend talked a great deal, holding forth on politics and religion. His politics were Monarchist, his religion a sort of liberal Catholicism, tinged with mystical adumbrations. He believed in goodness. The steepness of the climb was alleviated by the frequent pauses he made to gesticulate and explain his views. But when I told him of the Falangist doctor I had met in the train, he stopped short in his tracks and dropped his voice. It is remarkable what a fear these Falangist extremists set up in some people, in spite of the fact that they have today lost most of their power. People dry up when they discover that you know them. One only begins to understand it when one remembers the fantastic number of people that they are supposed to have killed in and after the war; here in the province of Cordova rumor credits them with having shot 28,000. However our friend soon brightened up again and, in answer to my inquiries, told me that the picture that the doctor had drawn of the brigands in the Sierra Morena was greatly exaggerated: they had been a nuisance some time before, but were now of very little consequence. And they rarely killed anyone. They were all of them political men—Socialists or Communists on the run.

The schoolmaster turned back after a mile and we went on alone. The road climbed slowly in long hairpin curves, so we took a short cut. This led us past the mouth of a little cave or rock shelter, whose entrance had been blocked with a few household chattels. Behind these we discovered a woman lying on some sacks, who, when she saw us, got up and came out. She was a woman of under thirty, dressed in a very old and ragged black dress which showed her naked body through its rents. She had been ill, she told us, after the birth of a child, which had died because her milk had dried up. Her husband had been employed on an estate near by, but as the work had come to an end and they could not pay their rent, they had left and come here. Now she could not leave because her clothes were not decent. She was obviously starving, but she did not complain, or ask for money and, when I gave her some, appeared surprised. "Times are bad," she said with resignation. "Let us hope they will soon take a better turn."

We arrived at the hermitage that crowns the rocky hill. Grey rocks, grey trees, white jonquils and asphodels, and no sound but the tinkling of goat bells. Far below we could see the white city, spread out like a patch of bird droppings by its brown river, and beyond it the red and green *campiña,* flowing in bright Van Gogh-like undulations. The hermits strike me as being museum pieces rather than examples of a serious contemplative life. There are ten of them, each occupying his own snug little hermitage, each dressed in a long brown robe and decorated with a bushy white beard that flows down over his chest in the true Carolingian manner. On Sundays they are on view and, as we walked down the path to the chapel, we passed one of them, seated on a chair under an ancient oak tree and reading from a calf-bound folio with the aid of a prodigious pair of cows' horn spectacles. It was obvious that he was fully aware of his own picturesqueness.

These hermits own the mountain on which their cells are built and employ a man to look after their goats; otherwise they depend for their subsistence on alms, which are never wanting. I imagine that this is the oldest colony of hermits in Europe, for they have been here continuously since Visigothic times. But the age is hostile to the sentiment O *solitudo, O beatitudo* and when I praised the beauty and seclusion of this spot to the hermit who was showing us over the chapel, he grunted and said, "*Es mucha soledad.* It's very lonely."

The people of Cordova are exceedingly proud of their city. If, for example, one happens to mention wine, they tell one that the wine of Cordova (which is unknown anywhere else) is the best in Spain. "You have only to carry a bottle of Montilla across the river and it improves at once, and when you take it back again, it gets worse." Yet they know very little about the famous men their city has produced: Seneca they have heard of, but Góngora to them is just the name of a street and no one knows where his house stands. I had spoken about this to our schoolmaster acquaintance, who has a certain liking for poetry, and he promised that he would help me find it. We met therefore by arrangement at a café.

Our first step was to visit the Instituto de Segunda Enseñanza or secondary school in search of the city archivist. This school was housed in a magnificent building with a large interior court. All the children in it were well dressed and came from middle-class families, so I asked our companion whether any working-class children found their way here.

"Very rarely," he replied. "These children all come from the primary schools run by the Church. In most of these one has to pay something, but one gets a fine education. The state primary schools are today so neglected that the children who go to them make no progress. This suits everyone: the Church sees its schools well sought after and the ruling classes are pleased to have the poor kept in their place. Most of the children of the poor grow up without learning how to read or write."

We found the archivist, who gave us the address of Góngora's house and promised to show us other sites connected with him when we returned to Cordova in a month's time. Then we adjourned to a tavern to taste, not Cordovan, but the far better Montilla wine. We discussed bullfights and, after that, religion.

"Yes," said the schoolmaster, "there has been a genuine revival. But you must bear in mind that the Church in Spain is like an old, old tree, some of whose branches have fallen and lie rotting on the ground. Not all the people you see dressed as Catholics are Catholic inside."

He is a pleasant little man, combining gaiety with genuine kindness and a rather ineffectual enthusiasm for the things of the mind. A man with middle of the road opinions. How many there are of them in this country, in spite of the Spaniards' reputation for fanaticism! Yet how little effect they have had!

February 21

This morning we took a taxi to visit Medina al Zahra. This was the palace which the first and greatest of the Spanish caliphs, Abd-er-Rahman III, began to build in 936 and which his successors enlarged and completed. The accounts given of it by the Moslem historians show it as being possibly the largest and certainly the most luxurious palace ever built in any age. Four thousand marble columns were used in its construction and the quantity of gold, bronze and silver employed in decorating it were fabulous. The whole Mediterranean region as far as Constantinople was ransacked for precious materials.

The most splendid of its apartments was the so-called Chamber of the Caliphs, a vast room entered by thirty-two doors, each decorated with gold and ivory and resting on pillars of transparent crystal. The roof was made of sheets of variously colored marble cut so thin as to let the light through, while the walls were of marble, inlaid with gold and silver. But the most astonishing feature of this apartment was the great basin, or perhaps fountain, which stood in the center. It was filled with mercury instead of water and when set in motion it dazzled the onlooker with the flashes of light and colors which it set up.

Thirteen thousand male servants lived in this palace, not to speak of the harem and their attendants, whose numbers could scarcely be counted. The fish in the garden tanks alone consumed 12,000 loaves every day. The quantities required for the human inhabitants can be left to the imagination. And what became of this superb edifice? In the year 1010 the Berbers, who were besieging Cordova, wrecked and looted it, and so complete was its destruction in the course of the ensuing ages that till a few years ago its very site was unknown, and wild bulls pastured and fought one another where once the most beautiful women in the world had yawned on their solitary beds and stuffed themselves with sweets and pastries.

The excavations lie some four miles to the west of the city, on the lower slopes of the long grey-green line of the Sierra. The situation is beautiful. Ilexes and lotus trees stand around in solemn dignity and under them grow daisies, asphodels and that flower of piercing blue—the dwarf iris. The ruins are scarcely worth seeing, since all the stones have been carried off to build a monastery on the hill above, though there are plenty of fragments of stucco arabesques, mostly of acanthus patterns and showing a strong Byzantine influence. The museum contains some interesting pottery with designs of birds, fishes, and animals in pale green. However only a small area of the palace has yet been excavated; beyond it stretch acres of formless mounds, covered with creeping acanthus leaves and low-growing mandrakes and the dried stalks of fennel. The cormorant and the bittern, the screech owl and the satyr still have the place pretty well to themselves.

As we left, the new civil governor of Cordova drove up in his car. I remarked to the chauffeur that he was said to be an energetic man who would attack abuses. But the chauffeur, an ex-sergeant of the Air Force, was a cynic.

"If that's so," he replied, "he won't be here for long. A few years ago we had one who quadrupled the ration by seizing the stores the syndicates were keeping for their black market operations. This allowed the poor to eat, which on the present scale of rationing they can't do. So they got rid of him."

One cannot walk about the streets of Cordova without being horrified by the poverty. The standard of life has always been very low among the agricultural workers of this part of Spain, but this is worse, far, far worse than anything known within living memory. One sees men and women whose faces and bodies are coated with dirt because they are too weak or too sunk in despair to wash in water. One sees children of ten with wizened faces, women of thirty who are already hags, wearing that frown of anxiety which perpetual hunger and uncertainty about the future give. I have never seen such sheer misery before; even the lepers of Marrakesh and Taroudant look less wretched, because, besides being better nourished, they are resigned to their fate. It presents one too at every step with a personal problem: what right has one to eat meals, to drink coffee, to buy pastries when people are starving all round one? No right at all, and yet, being selfish by nature, I could not help doing so.

Most dreadful are those who creep about the streets without arms or legs. The government provides a small pension for persons who lost their limbs on their side, but those who were involved with the Reds, even if they are women or children, get nothing. They ought to have been living in some other place when the war broke out! The insurance scheme only caters to those workmen who have regular employment. Agricultural laborers, small shopkeepers, street vendors, bootblacks get nothing. If they fall ill, they will not even be taken into a hospital unless they can pay. A bootblack said to me:

"When the Civil War broke out, I had some money saved up. Then, after the Nationalist victory, all the currency in the Red zone was annulled and I lost it. Now I am getting old. I have no children and if I fall ill there is nothing left for me but to die of starvation. So I mean to try to get to France, where they treat people more humanely."

The middle-class Cordovans tell one that most of the destitute one sees in the streets are from other provinces. "From all over Andalusia they collect here." But this is their local pride speaking; the truth is that they are unemployed agricultural laborers from the large estates of the *campiña*. The system in use on these large estates is to keep a handful of men on the payroll all the year round and to take on the rest for short spells as the season requires. For every ten that are permanently employed, a hundred will be at the mercy of casual labor. This means that, even in a good year, an agricultural laborer will have to support his family for twelve months on what he earns in six or eight. Before the Civil War it was just possible for him to get along in this way when the season was not too bad, but now, owing to the inflation, the value of wages has fallen considerably. To make matters worse, this has been an exceptionally bad year. The olive crop last Christmas was very poor—and it is on the money made by olive picking that a family dresses itself—while the drought has held up the spring hoeing. The consequence is a famine—a famine too which cannot be mentioned in the press and which the possessing classes shut their eyes to.

A bad mark for the Franco regime? Yes, certainly—but let us in fairness remember that every other regime, including the Republican, refused to grapple with this problem. What is needed is a complete reorganization of the system of cultivating the land, coupled with a severe pressure applied to the landowners. And this is something that the present government, weak and discredited as it is and fearful of making more enemies, cannot do.

I had wished to visit the dungeons of the Inquisition, which are still apparently to be seen in the medieval Alcázar, adjoining the Arab one. This, however, was not possible because the buildings have been converted to military use. Nor were my inquiries very well received. Spaniards are still chary of speaking of this once revered institution and, when a foreigner puts some question about it, profess ignorance.

Its proceedings at Cordova were particularly revolting, or perhaps it would be better to say that we are particularly well informed about them. Take for example the case of Lucero. In 1499 a canon of Cadiz Cathedral called Rodríguez Lucero was appointed Inquisitor of the Tribunal of Cordova, and at once set to work to arrest and burn all persons of Jewish descent against whom allegations of doubtful faith could, rightly or wrongly, be made. When evidence was lacking, he employed professional perjurers. No objections were raised to this by the people at large, for such acts were in the ordinary line of inquisitorial business and the *conversos* were unpopular. But finding that the thoroughness of his operations was exhausting this field, he began to extend them to persons of Old Christian descent, obtaining the evidence he needed by torturing their dependents. The object was money: the property of persons convicted of heresy was confiscated and paid into the Crown, who returned part of it to the Holy Office. Besides this there were the sums obtained by selling dispensations and imposing fines (termed penances), which went straight into the coffers of the Inquisitors, not to speak of what could be got by squeeze and blackmail. Few criminals have ever had greater opportunities.

Of course in arresting persons of impeccable orthodoxy and Christian descent there were certain risks, because the Inquisition had only recently been established and the country was not entirely cowed by it. However *poderoso caballero es Don Dinero*—money speaks—so that by buying one of King Ferdinand's secretaries and, when the need arose, other important dignitaries, not excluding a cardinal, Lucero made sure of his position, and soon the reign of terror he set up was such that no one in the south of Spain was safe. Eminent ecclesiastics were especially attacked, because during their incarceration the income from their benefices was paid into the Inquisition funds, and a moment came when even the saintly Archbishop of Granada, who had been Queen Isabella's confessor and was now eighty years old, was on the point of being arrested.

There is no knowing how far this diabolical man might have gone had not an accident intervened. In 1506 Philip the Fair landed in Castile and, anxious to exert some act of sovereignty, listened to the appeals of the clergy and municipality of Cordova, which both Ferdinand and the Inquisitor General, who had a pecuniary interest in Lucero's extortions, had refused to hear, and suspended him. In the trial that followed two years later his guilt was fully established, in spite of the fact that he had had time to burn most of the hostile witnesses, and he was therefore dismissed to his canonry at Seville (for an inquisitor could not be punished) where he spent the rest of his days in comfort on the proceeds of the money he had accumulated. This is the only case recorded of an inquisitor being either dismissed or brought to trial.

I have mentioned this episode, which is related at length in Lea's abundantly documented *History,* because it has become the fashion of late to whitewash the Inquisition. Both its principles and its methods, it is asserted, were in accordance with the spirit of the age; it was slow in making charges, scrupulously fair in its prosecutions, just in its sentences, and so forth. But whatever may be said of its procedure in other countries, this was not the way in which it operated in Spain. In the lush and fertile soil of the Peninsula, this institution not only reached the extremes of fanaticism and cruelty (we read, for example, of children of ten being prosecuted and imprisoned for life), but those of the most sordid corruption as well. And what is one to say of those scenes in underground chambers where elderly priests looked on while naked women and girls were tortured? Of all the rackets recorded in history, the Spanish Inquisition, during the first hundred years of its career, was perhaps the most mean and repulsive.

This evening we talked to the hermitage church of Nuestra Señora de Fuensanta, on the eastern edge of the town. On the way we passed a convent where two nuns, dressed in white starched caps, were distributing bowls of soup to the poor. A queue of some three hundred people stretched down the road outside. These nuns belong to an order which is confined to the city of Cordova, and those who have the state of the poor on their conscience contribute to their fund.

The church we were looking for stands in a large open space on the edge of the fields. An avenue of plane trees led down to it and the sunlight flooded their grey trunks and lace-like branches, dotted with little red buds that would soon be bursting into leaf. A cantankerous looking fig tree, growing among heaps of rubbish, filled the air around it with its dense, sticky smell, as if to show that it too was feeling the effects of spring and poetry. Entering the courtyard, we came to a long portico hung with ex-votos. Some of these consisted of crutches or tresses of hair, others of little figures cut out in tin and representing limbs, others again of crude paintings or miracles performed by the Virgin, which often had the charm and freshness of children's drawings. There was also a narwhal's tusk and a stuffed crocodile, formerly esteemed for their aphrodisiac properties, though why hung here I cannot say. Possibly the crocodile, which recalls that to be seen in the porch of Seville Cathedral, was at one time regarded as a maiden-eating dragon which some chivalrous saint of the type of St. George had slain.

Passing through into the church, we found its interior cool and dark. The whole of one end was taken up by a vast gilt *retablo,* carved and scrolled and ornamented, in the center of which—an insignificant doll-like figure—stood the miracle-working Virgin. We made our genuflections and whispered our desires, then walked back by the warm evening light along the river.

Part Three

SOME MODERN PROBLEMS

The problems that are subjected to scrutiny in the following essays are of several different sorts. Some of them—overpopulation, segregation, the effects of the machine on human behavior—have made themselves effectively felt for the first time in our own era. Others—the role of woman, the condition of marriage, the position of the artist, the question of the distribution of wealth—are perennial questions which have assumed a particular shape in our time. Still others, such large philosophical issues as education, justice, and crime and punishment, have exercised the minds of men since the beginning of civilization. The authors of Section III, however, like the authors of Section I, are aware that questions truly relevant to human experience can be neither separated from history nor wrenched from their context in contemporary reality. Thus Robert Penn Warren in his report on southern white attitudes toward racial integration and John Kenneth Galbraith in his account of changing attitudes toward economic equality both place their timely observations in a framework of history. And neither Sybille Bedford's treatment of the abstraction "justice" nor Hannah Arendt's treatment of the abstraction "education" has anything in the least abstract about it.

If these essays are linked to each other by a common habit of finding the universal in the particular, they are distinguished from each other by the range of tone and technique which they display—a range which extends from the open letter to the formal treatise, from the autobiography to the essay, from Galbraith's breezy erudition to de Rougemont's sermon-like pronouncements, from Sybille Bedford's masterful use of a technique which resembles that of an impressionist painter to Virginia Woolf's creation of an illustrative fiction to drive home her passionate sense of the injustices from which women have suffered. The serious approach to human problems enforces a certain kind of breadth of view, but it certainly does not enforce anything resembling uniformity of approach. In fact, much of the value of these essays derives from the fact that the authors instinctively know that good writing must be faithful not only to the demands of its subject but also to the personality viewing the subject. Diana Athill's reminiscences of her childhood relate tangentially to the problems of class consciousness, provincialism, and

133

snobbery in a changing and expanding world; but the center of her interest lies, as that of any autobiographer must, in the development of her own personality, and the strongly personal elements apparent in her style are a necessary reflection of that interest. On the other hand, Robert Penn Warren, in his observations on segregation, writes not as an explorer of his own personality but as a responsible intellectual coming to grips with a desperate problem faced by himself, his fellow-southerners, and the entire country of which he is a citizen. The personal note in his style, the sense we derive of a distinctive voice speaking to us, is not a necessary part of his subject, but its presence in his essay makes what he has to say individual and human and hence vastly more compelling.

The authors of Section III present a wide range also in the relationship between author and subject: John P. Conrad writes on prisons as a highly trained and specialized expert; Sybille Bedford writes on law-courts as an impassioned amateur. Galbraith and de Rougemont have devoted lives to the study of the subjects on which they speak; Russell, Huxley, and Hannah Arendt regard their subjects as localized manifestations of larger issues on which their attention has been concentrated. Both the specialist and the nonspecialist, it appears, may have helpful things to say about the problems which plague us—provided, of course, that the specialist has a vision broad enough to see beyond his limited subject, and that the nonspecialist has the rectitude to inform himself as circumstantially as possible about anything he writes on—as Huxley, Russell, and Arendt clearly do.

Seen as a group, these essays present a large number of interesting interrelationships. "Shakespeare's Sister," as an essay on the problems of the gifted woman, casts an indirect but illuminating light in the autobiographical accounts of Athill and de Beauvoir. Russell's essay examines dispassionately, even drily, the question of the dehumanization of man which elicits Wain's passionate diatribe; at the same time it has obvious connections with Galbraith's essay in its concern with the satisfaction of basic human needs. Galbraith, in turn, has points of contact with writers as different from him—and from each other—as Diana Athill and Hannah Arendt. Miss Bedford's impressions and Conrad's reports stand in a number of relationships to each other, among them the simple one of chronology between their respective subjects—what happens before judgment is made, and what happens after sentence is passed. In its larger context—the meaning of justice—Miss Bedford's study is linked with two essays which have a clear relevance to each other: Virginia Woolf's and Warren's poignant evocations of the actual nature of injustice as it has been experienced by an oppressed sex and an oppressed race.

Similar links, of course, may be observed between the essays of Section III and those of other sections. Huxley sees in overpopulation a major threat to individual freedom, and his essay is thus as relevant to "The Burden of Freedom" as it is to "The Age of the Masses." Similarly, both Galbraith and Hannah Arendt may be usefully read in relation to these first two sections of the volume, as John Wain may be read in connection with Sections IV and VI later on. These suggestions are in no sense meant to be exhaustive. The attentive reader will find other points of reference and contact which demonstrate further the indivisibility of human problems and the common features of human attempts at understanding and resolution.

Suggested Further Readings:

Selections from Plato's *The Republic*
Aldous Huxley, *Brave New World*

Sybille Bedford

Law is a highly specialized branch of learning whose workings often bewilder the average individual though they closely affect him. It is also considered by many to be the basis of social order in that it provides the machinery for equitably resolving problems, individual and general, which cannot otherwise be resolved. The law has not been without its detractors, particularly in those cultures most committed to the ideal of a just order based on law, perhaps because in such cultures the failings are more glaringly noted. (Memorable among the detractors were Chaucer, Dickens, and Shelley, who called the law "tomes of reasoned wrong.") But there is no doubt that a nation's system of legal justice, that is, the laws themselves and the actual application of them, may still rightly be taken as a fair indication of that nation's strengths and weaknesses, and of the tone of its own particular culture— "... some people put up with some things and not with others."

The English novelist Sybille Bedford—a "private, unlearned aficionado of the law ... uneasy and much aware of my unprofessional limitations," set out in 1959 to observe without prejudice the workings of justice within the courtrooms of Europe. The distinguished book *The Faces of Justice*, from which we have selected passages, was the result. Mrs. Bedford's approach is based on scrupulous attention to what she has seen and heard in these courtrooms—she is at ease among the technicalities of the law, yet does not overwhelm the reader with them—and on an exact reporting of them. But her techniques are not those of journalism, as the first contact with her highly individualized, elliptical yet polished use of language makes clear. As she moves through trial case after case, skillfully condensing, never, however, distorting the essentials, we are struck by the extraordinary depth of each scene and by the aliveness of the protagonists, and become aware of how much of this is due to Mrs. Bedford's resources as an artist. The terse conveying of a tone of voice, a gesture, the swift calling up of sensuous detail—how a room really looks, what its colors are, its smell—the imaginative awareness of what lies beneath surfaces, the insights into personality, the rhythmic sense of drama: these, the gifts of the novelist, are as evident here as is the clear reasonableness of Mrs. Bedford's intellect. It is inevitable that on occasion her comments, sometimes directly, sometimes implicitly, extend beyond questions of the law and raise even more trying questions.

Some faces of justice*

NOTES: GERMANY

Scene: The Federal Court of Justice in full session, the highest court in the land, housed beyond marbled halls like the head office of a major bank—a lofty room, chandeliers, a crescent of Supreme-Court Judges, robed in purple, portrait-faced; the drone of trained voices. No extraneous presence mars the legal surface. Appellants do not appear. The Presiding Judge, the Chief Justice of the day is a woman. A tiny sound; something has slid on the carpet; the Chief Justice has dropped a pencil, the Chief Justice bends and picks it up.

Women. The Weimar Republic abolished a number of their disabilities; the Nazis sent them back again into the kitchen. The most conscientious of new brooms, the Federal Republic, has promulgated absolute feminine equality in a recent decision of the Constitutional Court at Karlsruhe. Among all other things, this means equal civil-service pay; it means that the father can no longer overrule the mother on a question concerning a child's education (which rather places the child between two bundles of hay); and it means that women may now stand for any—except ecclesiastical—office.

"Members of the jury, you are men and women of the world! Common sense will tell you . . ." One does not often hear a speech made in an English court that does not have recourse to these two stand-bys. In Germany, the men of the world and their common sense are replaced by experience of life, *Lebenserfahrung* and *Erfahrungstatsachen* are great favourites of bench and bar. Their status is quasi-judicial. In a case I heard

* Editors' title.

From *The Faces of Justice* by Sybille Bedford. Copyright (1961) © by Sybille Bedford. Reprinted by permission of Simon and Schuster, Inc.

reviewed, the appellant had been given a stiff prison sentence for running over two very drunk pedestrians and killing one of them. It had been night, the motorist was going along at twenty-five or thirty miles an hour, some distance ahead two men were wobbling arm-in-arm across the road. They reached the further pavement. But no sooner safe than they stepped back again into the road and smack into his car. In the judgment it was held that the motorist was responsible, not because he had not driven with ordinary due care, but because he had failed, if you please, to exercise the extraordinary care incumbent upon him in the circumstances. The day had been Carnival-Monday, *Rosenmontag;* common experience of life must have taught him that if one saw two middle-aged gentlemen arm-in-arm upon the road on Carnival-Monday night, it became one's legal duty to proceed with extraordinary care. (An opinion not upheld on appeal.)

Konstanz. A case of armed robbery with assault had taken place in the tap-room of an inn. How had it started, when did the accused come in? The accused had been there all evening, sitting drinking with the other guests. At midnight the accused, with ten years in sentences for heavy crimes behind him and who might have learnt some discretion, turned off the light switches and began to sing: *Lichter aus—Messer raus!* Lights out—knives out.

Lindau/Bodensee. A customs case. Someone, eighteen months ago, brought 235 cigarettes into the country instead of the allowed 200. The judge and prosecutor who have to cope with this, and who dealt sensibly enough with other matters earlier in the morning, turn into unworldly sticklers. Prompted by the customs representative, they pore over the letter of the regulations but choose to ignore the facts of modern travel.

Almost any kind of case, however trivial, that comes before the courts involves some rudiment of a valid issue, capable (ideally) of a satisfactory and just solution. Not so customs and excise cases. There is something pettifogging and rapacious as well as extremely irritating about these actions anywhere. They are unbecoming to a country, as traffic in wax candles is unbecoming to a great church. It is no help to say that these niggling rules and their techniques of application are the law of the land; they were slipped most likely into some finance bill before anyone could have said Member for Kidderminster. Try to find the M.P., or Deputy or Member of Congress or the *Bundesrat,* who will, or can, do anything about it. "If it please your Lordship—this concerns an attempt to defraud Her Majesty by concealment of four fifths of a pint of fortified fermented beverage known by the trade-name of Dubonnet." Indeed. It sounds more like Shylock *v.* Indifferent Honest Citizen.

Court day at Staufen (market town, 3000 inhabitants) at the edge of the Black Forest. A young judge—first appointment—who is not always certain of the local dialect, sits behind a desk in a small, neat office smelling of fresh paint, hearing a calendar of civil claims. Outside a pig squeals long and loud. These were the litigants, in order of appearance.

1) Two scraggy sisters in alpaca overalls *v.* a slovenly man and wife, refugees from some Prussian hinterland in the East Zone—landladies and (compulsory) tenants engaged in a running row re-enacted here at the top of voices. Coal in the hall—*and* his bicycle—the woman—never switches it off—the filth—at all hours—you cannot please those old bitches —the slut—let me tell you—washing her hair in the middle of the night— Round goes the canon, and in the lulls the young judge tries to insert a mollifying suggestion and is shouted down. Die Frau—der Mann—der Dreck—die ist so—der ist so—die alten Hexen—die Drecksau—erstunken erlogen—immer—nimmer—nie—nein—

After twenty minutes the judge manages to get down a form of resolution: the tenants will try their best to find lodgings of their own (Oh, haven't they!), the court will second their application with the Housing Bureau; meanwhile landladies and tenants will try to live on better terms. This starts another round.

"Live and let live," says the judge. ("Not with those witches!") Perhaps, he says, the Fräulein should try not to scold *all* the time. They pinch their lips.

They shuffled out. "Folk music," the judge said to his scribe; a waiting lawyer called after the sour sisters, "You two ought to drink more wine."

2) Two lawyers, one for a dentist, the other for his patient. The new false teeth don't work; they won't bite. They were not meant to bite, pleads the dentist's man, they were ordered for best, a Sunday-afternoon set. The judge adjourns the case.

3) An almost incomprehensible man, telling a story in deepest gutturals about the man from his village whom he saw and did not see again on the Russian Front. (The least healed of all recent German memories.) That man had been missing these fourteen years; his wife and son are trying to establish his death. The witness is gnarled and used by work, and it comes as a shock to learn that he was born in 1916. Villichichilickey, he says, that's where he saw the dead soldier, only he was not dead then; himself he was only passing through on leave, on his way home, he was off to marry, *d'Hochziet mache.* Oh, yes, that was where he saw him, it was *him* marching by. . . . Judge and scribe tumble to Velikiye Luki; but not much else can be established.

4) Two peasant women, mother and daughter, against a company lawyer with a well-filled briefcase. Breach of contract. They haven't paid

for their washing machine. The lawyer produces the signed documents; the women tell the story. This is how it was, Herr Doktor, the gentleman came with the machine, not this gentleman, another gentleman from the company. He said he would demonstrate a wash. They fetched some sheets. The machine was doing its stuff, the gentleman talked, got out the forms. Mother went off to milk, the daughter stayed and watched. When mother came back from the cows, the sheets had been torn into shreds.

"And grey, Herr Doktor, not a clean wash."

But the contract by then was signed. (They always do, said the judge.) This case, too, was adjourned.

5) Another housing case. There is, as one quickly comes to realize, still a painful shortage in Germany. They build as hard and fast as they can, which is fast, but haven't been able to catch up yet, and this is not made easier by the steady weekly arrivals of refugees from the East Zone. Thus here, a couple quartered on another in a three-room flat. Four grown-ups and five children share this and one kitchen. They have not come to quarrel, they have come to ask the court to assist them with the Bureau.

"Oh, you are agreed?" says the judge. "Good." He arranges for the landlord to make out an eviction order. This will not enable him to evict the tenants, but it might enable *them* to get another place to live. The parties do not entirely like the sound of this stratagem, but bow to departmental logic.

6) Far-fetched witnessses travelled from other towns to give evidence in a small-scale Captain von Köpenik affair. During the war a civil servant had been sent to Poland to administer some department as an undersecretary. The Russians came, the war was lost, so were the files, the official went home, having meanwhile been promoted to deputy-secretary. He had lived respectably ever after, doing the work, drawing the salary, scoring the pension proper to his rank, until some recent bureaucratic treasure trove cast a dubious light. A self-awarded promotion? Suspended, he has now advertised up and down the Occupied and Unoccupied Zones for witnesses of his Polish triumph: the colleague, last heard of at Breslau, who had seen the telegram; the couple, then next door, who had shared the opened bottle. . . .

"There are dozens of these cases," said the judge.

Moses [Heirs] v. *Deutsches Reich.* In every German town of any size there sit, almost continuously, the *Rückerstattungskammern*, the Courts of Restitution. Most of the plaintiffs are dead. Their traceable descendants are settled in the United States, in Israel, in England. The claims are for possessions torn from them between the years of 1933 and 1944. A Turkey carpet driven off by the S.S.; a brooch and two gold rings con-

fiscated in a precious-metals drive; a Bechstein Grand; a wireless set . . .
A boy's motor bicycle . . . A fur coat taken away by the Gestapo after a
morning raid. . . . Anyone who cares to, may walk in and hear, this is the
aftermath of what everybody knew, and here it is going on, in living
memories. And it is as grim and pitiful and unbearable as it ever was.

The plaintiffs in such cases are represented more often than not by
Jewish law firms. Once more, Jewish faces are seen in German courts;
Jewish lawyers move, speak, mix, with apparent smoothness. "Morning,
Herr Colleague—" "Morning, dear sir—" All as before? Better than be-
fore? Whatever lies behind—must lie behind—this is a daily reality.

Is the past then healing? Forgiving and self-forgiving are graces,
mysterious and individual, hard-won or sudden, always incalculable.
There are some explicit signs of acceptance and realisation, of what the
Germans themselves would call insight; there is also much bleating and
shifting of blame—we were misled, we did not know, we had no idea.
Perhaps the past is simply falling behind through the passage and surge
of life, through distraction, the monkey-shift of mind, the plain human
inability to keep it up, the inevitable final slackening of everything.
There is also something more positive. The past is put behind because
men and women have *in fact* turned over a new leaf; there *is* the change.
Recoil from calamity and horror, recoil, also and naturally, from insup-
portable guilt, is taking the form of deeds. There *is* the new regard for
life—it would be hard for a Bismarck to-day to reintroduce the death
penalty—there is the respect of man for man, the tending of liberty and
the decencies and the due process of law, and with it goes a love, an
almost avid love, of normality and all its trimmings.

A change—yes. But is it not a most opportunistic one, a new conformity? Certainly; as far as that goes. Does not social conduct follow
at all times, not perhaps the leader, but the prevailing wind of change?
Social conduct is contagious; there is mass contagion by a good rule just
as there is mass contagion by a bad one, although there are always contributory factors, nobody needs to catch it; a great many always do catch
it. It is an unwise man who is sure of his own immunity.

In Germany there is now another factor. Time. Not time the healer,
but sheer time, quantitative time. When people like myself think of
Germany to-day, they think of post-Nazi Germany, a country of ex-Nazis,
surviving anti-Nazis and victims. In fact, this can only apply to a limited
and diminishing number of people. I have just made some calculations.
Hitler took over in 1933; the régime ended in 1945, twelve years later.
Anyone in Germany to-day under the age of thirty has nothing to forget
(except childhood hardships); anyone between thirty and forty-five was
from three to eighteen years old when Hitlerism began.

What about the rest, the rest that counts, since notoriously we are all run by men of over fifty-five, to put it young. Are there any Nazis left in Germany? Obviously, yes. They cannot all be dead; they cannot *all* have changed. What about the allegations that important Nazis are still or once more in high government positions? I do not know. I have no facts or impressions to speculate on. What about the alleged two hundred Nazi judges still sitting on the bench? Again, I do not know. That among some eleven thousand German judges two hundred—at least!—must have been active Nazis, like it or not, makes common sense. Question, are these two hundred supposed to be Nazis now or Nazis then? Men with a past who have discarded it, or men who think and feel and wish as Nazis still? In that case they must be Nazis in good judges' clothing.

BÂLE

Happy Half-Cantons have no history. On Dr. K.'s advice I spent two weeks in a metropolis; I went to Bâle, that large, industrialised and most prosperous town on the Swiss Rhine. Here, too, the law courts were housed in an old and friendly building; below the windows there grew trees; in the carpeted court-rooms, gold-framed sombre oils hung upon the walls, stags at the brook, the Judgment of Paris, Alpine sunrise. Here, too, the men on the bench had patrician faces and used the same extravagantly homely speech. Here, too, the judges could not do enough for the stranger in their court, opening minds and chambers, offering guidance, answers, questions, books. Here, too, at the hearings the same simplicity, the absence of professional aloofness, the same slow sympathy and care, the natural pace of patience, the concern with individual dignity and communal well-being, the backing of the petty rule as well as the small change of freedom. And here, too, the humdrum dailiness of the cases—mild civil disputes, infringed regulations, small crime. And in every ante-room there ruled a *Waibel,* dressed, at the High Court of Bâle, in morning-coat and white tie, wielding a large stocking-purse full of silver money, proffering comfort and advice, adding his word at times to the proceedings and generally behaving as butlers do in novels.

The absence of mumbo-jumbo, of professional side, goes further than the mere spurning of wig and gown, the tweed jacket on the Criminal Bench, the dark lounge suit in the Court of Appeal, it springs from the Swiss sense of the community of citizens, from their dislike of specialisation, and from a humanistic inheritance, a still living conviction that —outside of science at least—all branches of human activity are open to all men. Their farmer is also a locksmith and a vintner and a shipwright and in the evening mends the clocks; the artisan keeps books; the chartered accountant runs a saw mill and the county council; the woodcutter has a chair of modern history. There's things you do in winter, they say, and things you do in summer, you can't sit in a chair all year. And so the law, too, is felt to be something that can be administered by any able-minded man of good repute. There is also the fact of a long past of political equality: since 1291 every Swiss, unless a cretin, has been a natural member of the ruling class.

The people do not only vote the laws and elect the judges, there is a cordial and adult relationship between bench and public in the courts. Not that there is much public: a rare sensational trial here as elsewhere draws full courts, but there is a complete absence of that penful of people who come for a bit of warmth and a bit of life, to gape and doze, which is a fixture of the criminal courts of England, France and Germany. Here it is more the young and studious, in groups, in clubs, in classes—a dozen baker's apprentices with their master taking in a commercial case, a company of insurance clerks, a sharp-shooters' association on a semi-outing. The judge asks them who they are; they do not hesitate to put him questions. It's like this, he will say, and keep them back after a case to tell them the reason why.

"Now, how would *you* have handled this?" A woman had been kicking up an unholy fuss about her savings account.

The youth thinks hard. *"D'Frue isch v'ruckt."*

Yawyaw, maybe, says the judge, he could see she was a bit touched, but he had had to look at the post-office savings book all the same. *"Der objektive Tatbestand,* young man. We always have to look at the evidence."

The boy drinks it in. All this does not in the least impair the dignity of the court. Perhaps the contrary.

"Now, what would have happened in England?"

I suppose, I said, that if the case had got to court at all, the plaintiff would have been in the dock for attempting to break the peace in a post office.

The judge shook his head. *"S'Postscheckbüchli*—there was something not in order with the little savings book.

Order, out of order, not in order, these are words heard constantly from every bench. Another one is *Recht;* it serves for Right, Just, Justice, Legal, the Law. It must serve for Fair. The term does not exist. Anything like a sporting notion is alien to these parts; not right is wrong—out of order—out of joint—out of repair. There can be no other reaction than to put it right. Swiss justice works in terms of clock-making, you don't give a fast fly-wheel the benefit of the doubt or another chance, you prize up the case, look inside and try to set it back.

And how hard they work! Longer hours, cheerfully, than their proverbially toiling neighbours further up the Rhine. West-Germans, attracted into Switzerland by lower taxes and high pay, are said to slink back after a time crushed by overwork. The Swiss carry on. At Bâle, in grey winter drizzle, there are cases beginning at eight-fifteen; at Zurich in summer the high court regularly opens at seven A.M. But in the evening all sit in the taverns over wine, there is ski-ing, walking, bathing in the lakes, and the country, everywhere, is at easy uncrowded reach. One hears no talk of ulcers, no-one is ever pressed or in a temper or a hurry, and over every phase of living there is spread a soothing layer of deep-bred placidity.

The Swiss are hard-headed. They know the values and are willing to pay the price. They chose material order, moral regularity and that very hard-earned communal good, unconditional non-aggression. There is of course no capital punishment, and has not been, in three-quarters of the Cantons, for over eighty years. There is of course no question of flogging. There is of course no anti-homosexual law. Pragmatists, paragons of enlightened self-interest and—always—humanists, they have known how to keep a man-sized world, and through the sometimes stern, sometimes pedestrian tissue of their life there runs an enduring streak of douceur de vivre.

The Swiss Judges' Rules, the safeguards against primitive or oppressive forms of criminal investigation, are explicitly codified in some of the Cantons. Here is an example.

Article 73.* Personal liberty is guaranteed. No-one may be arrested except in the circumstances and forms prescribed by the law [minutely detailed below]. The law determines compensation due in cases of unlawful arrest.

Article 76. A private house is inviolate. No public servant or employee of the police may enter a private dwelling place except in the cases and forms prescribed by the law. Personal resistance against unlawful entry is permitted.

Article 106. Means likely to induce a suspected person to give evidence, and in particular means calculated to produce a confession, such as the use of force or constraint, threats, promises, misrepresentations or leading questions, are forbidden. Infractions of this rule will be dealt with disciplinarily, and may also be subject of a subsequent criminal prosecution.

Article 115. After arrest the examining justice must immediately notify the family of the arrested man. Should the family find itself in a position of need, the local assistance office must be informed at once.

Bâle is a very rich Canton. There are no poor. Private and public money is spent freely. Taxes are just and not too high. The young are well brought up. God is feared and the family is loved. Crimes against property are committed mainly by psychopaths and foreign workers. Never-

* Gesetz über das Strafverfahren des Kanton's Bern. 20. *Mai*. 1928.

theless the summary courts do not stand idle. The Swiss appear to have a passion, almost equal to the Germans', for dragging their private rows before the courts. Charges of slander, vilification, back-biting and evil-speaking are for ever poured—not reticently—into the patient judge's ear by waitresses, landlords, van drivers, neighbours and meddling passers-by.

"*Brülle muschtz net,*" the Waibel cautions a furious couple who have come to howl a duet about an intolerable smell of cigar in their flat.

"He smokes them through our key-hole."

"Would you mind saying that again?" says the judge.

The defendant, a reasonable-looking man, who lives in the flat across the landing, denies this with a shrug. His wife confirms him.

The couple persists—great cloud of foul smoke puffed into their home out of sheer malice. The *Dreckspeck.*

The judge says, "Really now . . ."

The defendant says that he may well sometimes have smoked on the common staircase.

The judge says there is no law against it. "What brand do you smoke?"

"Toscani."

"*Not* Toscani," says the judge. "*Oh. Oh. Toscani.* My good man. . . . Of course they go through key-holes."

Next is a service daughter complaining she has been unjustly taxed with ironing holes into the table napkins. She did not iron those napkins, that particular lot went to the laundry. She swears it did, she saw the bundle going off.

Unlike Schaffhausen, the courts of Bâle may administer an oath. They use it with economy. The form of words goes like a Schumann Lied, "Niemand zu lieb, niemand zu leid." There is also a form of hand oath.

"Can you give me a *Handgelübdte?*" The judge said, "then give me your hand on it." The girl stepped up and they shook hands.

Then a taxi driver claimed compensation for dismissal without notice. The company manager gave evidence that the man was unpunc-tual, lazy and rude.

The judge said, yaw shoah, but it wasn't enough for a straight dismissal.

There was more to come, said the manager. Herr Aleck would not wear Christian clothes to work, he wouldn't wear his driver's uniform, he objected to the trousers. He had them altered.

Perhaps they didn't fit, said the judge.

Nanei, it wasn't the fit, it was the cut. Herr Aleck said they were too wide. He had them altered—altered, well, into something more à la cowboy.

A bearded professor had been running across the road heading for his tram, he bumped into a schoolgirl on a bicycle, the girl fell, the professor made for the tram; indignant passengers pulled him off and here he is hurled before the bench. The parents are here, too, suing for a pair of stockings and the doctor's bill. *Mit Zins.* Interest.

Next one horrid woman alleged that when she came home one night from the cinematograph another horrid woman had been hanging out of an upper window, spying on her. The other woman said it was well after midnight and she'd been leaning out for a breath of air.

The impertinence, said the first. Cinematograph, my eye, said the second.

Then there came a whole group who complained of a messenger boy who would whistle at them when they went out to hang their washing in the yard. The boy said it was his luncheon hour, and by no means at all of them.

The judge said, "That amounts to an admission, you know." The boy laughed.

There was worse to come.

A black-suited man with the countenance of Mr. Murdstone stood up and handed a letter to the court. It was an anonymous letter, addressed to himself. It was read out. It was not a pleasant letter.

Stop trying to turn your office into a concentration camp. Everyone knows you are a tyrant and a sadist, but they don't respect you. Your employees kotow to you but they laugh at you behind your back. We could unfold a pretty tale to your hard-used wife. Your connection with a girl of nineteen is common knowledge. You ought to be ashamed of yourself! !

Mr. Murdstone now tendered a second letter. It was from his wife and addressed to the court. Her husband, she wrote, had sent police to ask her questions. She preferred to admit that she herself was the author of the anonymous letter. She begged to be excused attendance. "To appear before you opposite my husband is more than I can face." Her allegations about the girl of nineteen, she added, were the truth.

This was a private prosecution, brought by Mr. Murdstone. The judge asked him if he wished to go on with it.

He bowed gravely. Yes.

Presently an elderly stick of a man appeared and stated that he was a bank clerk by occupation; every evening for two years he had gone to the Gasthaus Swan and helped the owner, the widow Swan, to make up her daily accounts, he had never been paid a franc and he now wished to claim his fee.

The widow Swan, round and elderly, stepped forward to say she had understood that he was helping her with the books and correspondence because she was a woman alone and none too good at figures. They had taken supper together evening after evening in the back-room. A *good* supper.

The judge said, "Was there any kind of agreement, was it a business arrangement?"

"No, more of a love arrangement."

In that case, said the judge, the court was not competent.

The Waibel bowed them out. "That," he said in ringing tones, "is what makes the world go round."

PARIS—SUMMARY JUSTICE

The sinews of litigation are papers. There are many contenders, there can't be a nation recent or old that isn't in the race, but for sheer stamina, antiquity and spread the barnacled French bureaucracy may still be in for a prize. Across the road from the Palais de Justice, in the basements of the Tribunal de Commerce, there is an emporium devoted exclusively to the scrutiny, handling and processing of forms, a kind of infernal French post office where alpaca-coated clerks and petitioners labour on blotchy paper with scratching pens. The line of windows begins quite hopefully:

DEMANDS   *REQUESTS*   *CERTIFICATES*

The pilgrim returning at the end of his third week may have to take his place in the queue for *COPIES* or for

MODIFICATIONS   *EXTRACTS*

Further down the path lie,

OPPOSITIONS   *REVERSES*   *RETARDS*

Some people put up with some things and not with others. Much of life in France—the part of life that can be reached and squeezed by pettifogging or puritanical legislation—is easier, more humanised, more civilised, more agreeable. An adult may drink a glass of beer in a public place at four o'clock of a warm afternoon, there is no insuperable difficulty about being served a decent dinner at a decent place after ten P.M.; food can be bought at leisure in the evening instead of having to be scrambled for as the doors are being bolted on the way back from work; people make love in the parks. There is tolerance in practice, speech and print about sexual matters; working people, in particular, are broad-minded, sensible and charitable.

On the other hand, the French put up with a degree of regimentation which the heavens be praised would still be unacceptable to us. They have had some form or other of a long, rough compulsory military service for centuries; French people, all of them, must carry identity cards; they cannot get a passport without first obtaining a certificate of *bonne vie et mœurs* from the local police station; and they have always acquiesced in the wide, vague and vested powers of police. Not all of them, far from it, but the solid bulk of their middle-classes and Establishment after Establishment. The Frenchman in good standing knows all about the clutches of the police and shrugs about them; order and property have been so often threatened since 1789, the clutches are a necessary evil, perhaps not even that: just necessary, and at any rate they are only for the next man, the man beyond the pale. To the right kind of French, the police, like death to small children, is *pour les autres*. It is all as simply logical as that—the police treat people badly; only bad people get into the clutches of the police; bad people deserve what they get. And if the police do make a mistake—*cela arrive*—other Frenchmen in good standing can be counted on to rally and set things right and all will end in apologies and expressions of esteem and the final handshake with *Monsieur le Commissaire*. And what if one doesn't know anyone of substance or position, what if one has neither got *relations* nor *famille* and doesn't even know a *Député*? Well, then, one is simply not a Frenchman in good standing and back we are at the syllogism. The working people, though cynical enough about it all, are patient and resigned; prosperous as they are, they still have the fatalistic resignation of the poor before authority—*ah, c'est qu'ils sont mauvais! c'est qu'ils sont terribles!*, and a thief or murderer is generally referred to as *un malheureux,* and that is that; at least until the next revolutionary rising.

France—in spite of the Revolution, possibly in a measure because of the Revolution—has never been a "free country" in the sense that the English and the United States and the Dutch and the Scandinavians and the Swiss understand it. The surface of life has been good in the good times for a large number of people of reasonable virtue and of reasonable luck.

Everyone who goes to Paris has walked past the law-courts, the *Palais,* that eclectic construction, Third Empire from feudal tower, so massively planted on the Ile de la Cité between the Quai de l'Horloge and the Quai des Orfèvres. Having dinner in the Place Dauphine one sits below one portico'd façade, on one's way across the river from the Boulevard St-Michel one passes by the railings of the other side; one cannot even visit the Sainte Chapelle without coming out through one of the *Palais* yards. The inside is another matter.

Acres of vestibule and audience hall, mile on mile of gallery, stairways, passages—the stately chambers of the Civil Courts, la Première de la Court, la Sixième du Tribunal, near chapels dripping with renaissance carvings, ceilings alight with nymph and cloud; la Chambre des Requètes; la Cour de Cassation, the Courts of Criminal Appeal; the Robing Room of the Ordre des Avocats; la Chambre des Ordonnances; and down meaner aisles the warren of the Correctionnelles. Gilded vistas and greywalled, thick-walled, twisting, narrowing tunnels leading up and down into attics and cellars, turrets, crevasses and dead-ends—to the Greffier's office, the offices of the Procureur, of the Juges d'instruction, of the Huissiers, to the quarters of the Presse Judiciaire, to the Appellate Court of the Conseil de Prud'Hommes, to the Children's Courts, the Police Courts, the Assistance Publique, the Buvette, the cells, to a score of grubby little classrooms fitted with the tricolour and a row of inky forms, and to a hundred stuffy cubby-holes crammed from top to floor with *paperasses*. And everywhere is black, is alive, with lawyers, clusters, swarms of lawyers.

"Marie Dumas, Femme Chapet—you are accused of stealing two nickelplated spoons from the Bazaar de l'Hotel de Ville where you were employed on the second of November of last year. *Qu'avez-vous à répondre?*"

This is *inside*. We are in the X-ième Chambre Correctionnelle, a criminal court.

"I hadn't meant to keep them, Monsieur le Juge, I only—"

"You deny the offence. And furthermore on a subsequent date [in a nimble quaver] you stole from the said *Grand Magasin* an aluminium saucepan valued at 375 francs."

"Monsieur le Juge, I was trying—"

"You persist in your denial. This is not what I read here. Two months—"

"Monsieur le Président—" a lawyer has just hastened to the bar. "I have the honour to represent Madame Chapet. I apologise. I did not hear the call. With your permission, I will now address the court."

"*Ah, bon,*" says the judge.

"I shall be brief and concise." His client has only been married for a short time, they had the good fortune to secure the lease of a room and a kitchen to themselves, their means are but small. . . . The young woman assured him that she had only taken the spoons home from work in order to match them, the same went for the saucepan, she had wanted to try out whether it fitted the new stove. . . . At any rate she had meant to pay for them out of her next wage.... And there is her youth, M. le Président, twenty-two years old....

The judge behind a tome had been talking to his assessor. Now he looked up. "Woman Chapet—two months."

"*Affaire 4—!*"

The next accused is a man who has said *salaud* to a policeman.

"I had just parked my motor-bike, he told me to move on, *he* wasn't very polite, I was late, I'd just got off work, *j'étais énervé—*" Reluctantly, "*Je le regrette.*"

The judge hadn't interrupted because he was talking himself. Now he said, "Fine of 20,000 francs."

No question about means and earnings had been put.

"*Affaire 5—!*"

That man was a grocer who had filled up some empties with plain tap-water and sold them as a well-known mineral water.

He said he couldn't tell the difference himself, and anyway he was not an *épicier de métier,* he was new in the business.

The procureur, who sits in on such cases, asked from his umpire's chair, "What was your former occupation?"

"Wine merchant."

He was not represented and didn't seem to take the whole thing very seriously. He was wrong.

The mineral water company had constituted itself *partie civile* and sent most able counsel who presently conjured up a moving picture of the effects on commerce and on public health if people were allowed to go about selling tap-water under famous labels. Even the bench is listening.

"Two years with *sursis* and a fine of 250,000 frs."

Sursis is the French version of the deferred sentence. If the sentence is long and the deferment *sine die,* a convicted man may find himself on thin ice.

Meanwhile the guards had led in two handcuffed men, handcuffed to each other. One of them was a negro. Inside the dock, the chains were taken off.

Here, the dock, *le box,* is only for people who are already in custody, and they remain inside it while they are giving their evidence. Free people speak from the floor, and sit with their counsel on a little bench behind the bar.

It is still the turn of another man—at liberty—who had lost his temper. This one had kicked a policeman. He has taken a good lawyer.

"What have you got to say?" says the judge.

He bravely tells his story. He went to the cinema last summer with his wife and child. It was a Sunday afternoon, it was hot, during the intermission he stepped out into the boulevard and had a glass of beer. When he went back, the manager at the door—it was a tiny cinema— refused to let him in without buying another ticket. He protested that his family and ticket stub were inside, the manager was extremely rude; our man tried to walk past him, the manager called a policeman and asked him to throw this fellow out. The policeman at once laid hands on him. Outraged, he lost his temper. To-day, he is all meek and mealy mouthed apologies.

The kicked policeman gives evidence; most decently. He says, *il n'y avait pas de mal,* the accused didn't mean any harm, he didn't know what he was doing; when he realised he calmed down at once and allowed himself to be led off to the station like a lamb.

"You would have done better for yourself," says the judge, "if you'd done as the cinema manager told you. This will come more expensive. 40,000 frs. and costs."

The negro in the dock had been in prison for thirteen days, he is in arrears with alimony to a wife and child. He is described as a musician.

"You tried to evade payment," says the judge.

His lawyer is a woman. She says that the amount was 20,000 frs. and that was a great deal for her client to find in any month. His livelihood consisted of playing in small orchestras and nowadays he often found himself without an engagement.

"He disappeared," said the judge, "he concealed his address."

"He did not conceal it, Monsieur le Président, he did not have one." The judge wants to go on to something else, but she keeps up her voice. "My client has been trying desperately to scrape a living and that meant jumping at any work that offered, often at an hour's notice." He had had engagements recently in the provinces, first near Deauville, and then an offer to stand in for a man who had fallen ill at a winter resort in the Savoie. "People in my client's position, Monsieur le Président, do not keep on their room in Paris when they go off to work elsewhere. A permanent address is a luxury they cannot afford."

"He did not leave his address," said the Procureur.

"Pay, or one year," said the judge.

"Monsieur le Président—how can my client pay from prison? He's already lost one engagement, I implore you! How can he *ever* pay if he is unable to take any engagement at all? *Monsieur le Président—*"

"Case has been judged."

The second man in the dock was a young country lout; stocky, fair, very dirty and rather bemused.

He is charged with an attempt to steal. He has no lawyer. The judge tells him that he has the right to say whether he wishes to be tried as he is today or in a week's time with counsel for the defence.

"Oh, now," he said with a caged animal look at the dock, the guard. *"Pour en finir."*

"Very well," said the judge. "You were found sitting inside a Renault motor car which you were intending to drive away and steal."

The boy said, "I was tired, I tried the handle, it was open, I got inside to sleep."

"You have four previous convictions for theft," said the judge.

"I swear I didn't mean to steal the car, I only wanted to sleep."

"You were found sitting in the driver's seat," said the judge. "Why?"

. . . .

"You were found sitting behind the wheel. Why? Why were you sitting behind the wheel? Why?"

"But I can't drive."

"These denials will do you no good."

"I can't drive, I swear I can't, I've never driven a car . . . please find out it's true I can't drive—"

"Eight months," said the judge.

The boy looked simply horror-struck, incredulous—the guards bundled him out.

From then on, I spent more time in the Court of Criminal Appeal.

Cases first tried at Assizes may go to the *Cour de Cassation;* that court either confirms the verdict or it breaks it, which means that the case must go back to the Assizes for a second trial. Cases first tried *en Correctionnelle* go on to the *Cour d'Appel Correctionnelle.* That court sits—after two P.M.—in one of the more ornate chambers of the Palais; there is a bench of three, an Avocat général is present, and there is counsel for every appellant. The hearings are usually brief, and so quite a number of cases came on and went in the course of a month of afternoons. My notes are but pages of lists (I cannot write while I listen, I often cannot read what I write). I am choosing a page at random.

> The Case of the Student who Took Part in a Political Demonstration
> The Man who lived on Immoral Earnings
> The Man who Stole in Métro Stations
> *Confusion Obligatoire*
> The Case of the Two Women who Said it was a Matrimonial Agency
> The Czech Valet who Took 500 Dollars from his Master's safe
> The Young Man who Hid his Face
> "Too Late!"
> The Man who was Advised to Desist

The Student who Took Part in a Demonstration was a university undergraduate and he had marched for something or other three years before when he was seventeen years old. (The reason or political colour of the demonstration did not come out in the hearing, but the judge very likely knew.) They were headed for a meeting near the Porte d'Orléans and there was a clash with other demonstrators which was followed by a clash with the police and a bit of a general *bagarre*. People were picked up and he among them. Unfortunately there was a bicycle chain in his jacket pocket (found, he maintained, in the road a few minutes earlier and picked up more or less mechanically in the spirit of the occasion). He was appealing from a sentence of the Correctionnelle in 1956.

He sat on a front bench, looking a very thin and serious young man next to his more voluminous robed counsel, and he had a clever, lively face.

The presiding judge said testily, "I fail to appreciate the reason for this appeal, the sentence was only fifteen days deferred, your client has behaved himself since—he hasn't had to serve the fifteen days. What does he have to complain about?"

This young man, counsel explained, was a philosophy student of great brilliance, he had passed his *bachot* with extreme distinction, he was destined for an academic career.... A prison sentence—even never served ... surely, M. Le Président must understand ...

The président said he understood that the young man wanted it off his record. I can see him now, hunching his head, glaring at the young man. *"Vous êtes dressé contre l'autorité,"* he said in that paternal quaver so many of them here affected, *"vous êtes dressé contre l'autorité!"*

That appeal was dismissed.

The Man who lived on Immoral Earnings hadn't really lived on them at all; the earnings were his wife's, and some of them had gone towards paying the nursing home he was sent to when he first found out. He was a middle-aged chap, a business manager in a middling way, married, as he believed, honourably; they had one son, aged eleven, whom the father adored. They were not at all badly off, but the wife had preferred to go out to work; she had, she told her husband, an excellent evening job as cashier at a restaurant in the Palais Royal. He found out that she was a prostitute through a routine letter from the Préfecture requesting her to come in for the weekly medical visit.

He took it hard. Despair; disgust. He would have kicked her out had it not been for the boy, the idea of home. He told her flatly that if she did not give it up at once and for good he'd go to the police. She promised. Meanwhile, the business went to pot; he fell ill and spent some weeks in a nursing home. His wife came to see him and paid one bill.

There was no money in the bank just then, he told the Juge d'instruction, and he hated debts.

When he came out of the nursing home he found that his wife had not reformed. He did not know where to turn. His first thought was to get the boy out of her reach. He had no longer any family of his own. He went to the police. "Monsieur le Commissaire, will you help me?" He told the story; they arrested him. He spent three months *en prison préventive*. He was released some months before his trial at the Correctionnelle. There he was sentenced to eighteen months and a largish fine. He had appealed, and so had not yet begun to serve that sentence.

He sat composed, almost listless, seeming to pay no attention to the efforts counsel was making on his behalf.

The court decided—with no further comment—that there were mitigating circumstances in this case, and reduced the sentence to six months with *sursis* and quashed the fine.

The Man who Stole in Métro Stations was an Algerian convicted of stealing and trying to steal from slot machines in the underground. He had been caught at it exactly fifteen times. *"Un spécialiste de ce genre de délit,"* the président said. The sentence he had appealed from was one of thirty months and *interdit de séjour,* expulsion from the Paris area "Il faut que cet individu soit sorti de la région parisienne" (presumably out of reach of the underground railway network), said the Avocat général, and the sentence was confirmed.

Confusion Obligatoire arose in an argument about a conviction that had been appealed from because of some technical defect, several indictments had been taken or not been taken as one, or something of that kind. The Avocat général got heated and kept saying, "No, no, no, maître, there is no *confusion obligatoire!"* It was a technical term, of course, but it sounded engaging.

The Case of the Two Women who Said it was a Matrimonial Agency was the expected farce and none too pleasant. They looked frightful. Fairly young, Toulouse-Lautrec and Mesdames Stonyhearts, all smiles and fingernails. They were the manageresses—still are—of a bureau where men could meet young women, and young women could meet men. Aim—marriage. Receipts—one million francs a month. A young woman complained. Correctionnelle decision—three months and a fine of a hundred thousand francs.

The defence was high and mighty. Two hard-working young business-women doing their best, the world being what it is you can lead men and women to a meeting but you cannot make them become engaged. The bureau had advertisements accepted by the most respectable publications, *France-Dimanche, La Semaine à Paris, Aux Écoutes, The New York Herald Tribune.*

The Avocat général did not concur. He read out the *petites annonces,—"une publicité équivoque et tapageuse."*

The defence read a string of clients' depositions, gentle tales of soporific outings, *des soirées correctes,* at the cinema, at restaurants. —Monsieur Untel qui me fut présenté par l'Agence Colombe est un homme très correct—Monsieur Untel est un homme très bien. J'ai eu depuis le plaisir de le faire connaître à Maman. . . .

The bench retired over that one. Outside, the two young women were joined by their lawyer and a man in a very thick, very new, very yellow camel-hair coat and pointed shoes. Seen at close quarters they looked even more terrifying. They all smoked and chattered and appeared quite unconcerned, while I hung about rather tense and worried about that prison sentence.

It was all right. The court changed it to a fine of half a million francs for each.

The Case of the Czech Valet was hopeless in every way. He had stolen the dollars from his American master who had trusted him; he had four previous convictions for theft. The Correctionnelle had sentenced him to four years and relegation to the country of his origin.

There was a background to it. This rather consumptive looking Czech was once a professional football champion of international renown. When Czechoslovakia played France a decade or so ago, this man left his team and sought political asylum; for a brief hour he made front-page news, he was acclaimed as a fine feather in the Free West's cap. Now the yellowed cuttings repose inside the Correctionnelle dossiers. A small accident, pleurisy, advancing age—within a year or two his career on the field was over. To-day, the faithless servant and the jail-bird is still a political refugee. The fact was evident and counsel pleaded it strongly. In vain. The court—stirred by some half-conscious impulse to do *something?*—reduced the prison sentence to three years, but upheld the relegation.

The Very Young Man who Hid his Face. I shall not forget him either. He was extremely fair, nordic, with a slight viking look, a viking who had lived a long time indoors. As he sat in that dock and saw and heard, counsel going on, and the judge, about the stolen cheque and whether or not he had meant to cash it, and the investigation and the dates, he suddenly put his face into his hands and began to weep. He wept almost silently but with convulsive violence. I have seen many people cry in the dock. Most women, particularly young women, accused of stealing do; some people cry out of general misery or fear, because they feel so low and it's the natural thing to do and perhaps it may even help. That young man wept out of pure shame.

The président said stiffly, *"Vous regrettez? Ah, bon."* It seemed to mollify them. They made a comment: the accused did not appear to be a man of bad intentions; and they reduced the sentence from six months to four.

"Too late!" refers again to *obiter* by the Avocat général. In that case the accused had been tried for some theft in the lower court where he had protested innocence and had been sentenced to ten months. On appeal, he admitted guilt. Counsel pleaded that he had only been an accessory in the matter, was a first offender and might well be given a deferred sentence. "*C'est trop tard!*" the Avocat général had cried, "*Je vois le calcul*—confession in return for deferment, '*je te donne l'aveu, tu me donnes le sursis.*' *Trop tard!*"

The man said, "*J'avais peur.*"

Counsel explained—in so many words—that this was not his client's fault, he was a man of small intelligence and he had been pressed [sic] by his counsel in the lower court to admit nothing.

Judgment confirmed, appeal dismissed—*l'affaire a été bien jugée . . .*

Not well managed, was the comment of the lawyers in the hall; lucky not to have had the sentence raised.

The Man who was Advised to Desist had been brought into the dock for the day, from his prison where he was serving a sentence for rape. When his case was called, there was a minute's whispering between him and counsel as a result of which counsel told the court that his client wished to desist from the appeal.

"An excellent idea, that is the best he can do," said the president, with such a full note of sinister congratulation that it left one wondering.

I remember that at this point I fled again for a breath of air. Not that there was much choice, at the Cour d'Assises they were trying an Algerian who had knifed another in a drunken quarrel, downstairs in the Police Courts they were hammering out fines to motorists and their likes in francs instead of sterling and only a very little faster. I went once more to one of the *Chambres Correctionnelles*. They can be told apart by the numbers on the doors; inside, those tread-mills appear to be one much like the other, the same face, or almost, on the bench, the same crowds and guards, the men clanked in and out of the docks, the lawyers hurtling themselves to and fro. . . .

"Dupont, Jacques—you are charged with behaviour likely to outrage public decency. *Qu'avez-vous à répondre?*"

"The car was parked—if you can call it so—in a remote countryside in Brittany; the car, M. le Président, was standing in a field. It was after midnight, on the 13th of July of the year before the last, the Eve of the National Fête, my client and the young lady were driving home after a dance on the coast.

"Monsieur le Président, *la veille d'un Quatorze Juillet—c'était dans l'air—dans la chaleur de l'été . . .*

"It was dark, there was no-one about. No-one saw, no-one could have seen. No-one's morality was affected, no-one would ever have known if the young lady later on had not talked . . .

"Jealousy, gossip, evil tongues . . .

"My client, as you can see, is not a man in his first youth, he is a married man, a family man, a civil servant, a man of position—for eighteen months now, M. le Président, this charge has been hanging over him."

"Four months with *sursis* and a fine of 20,000 frs."

"Legrand, Gaston—you are charged with being drunk in the street. *Qu'avez-vous à répondre?*"

The defendant is rather a red-nosed fellow, and he has no lawyer.

"I was on the way home from my daughter's First Communion."

One could almost hear the wide-awake London magistrate, *mutatis mutandis,* swooping down: There are no First Communions in January.

"*Quoi—? Ah, bon.*" But it makes no difference, it doesn't make any difference at all. "Fine of 2,000 frs and fifteen days deferred."

John P. Conrad

Problems of crime and punishment, which have so often haunted the moral conscience of man, most frequently present themselves as distressing social facts which must somehow be dealt with by the public officials delegated by society to act for it. Society's primary way of handling the individual whose actions have been judged to be criminal is to isolate him by imprisonment. To what extent this is simply the old idea of punishment as revenge and to what extent it is a genuine if imperfect attempt to protect society are classic questions. The answers to the questions vary from country to country, and in America even from state to state. Only rather recently has the humane idea of rehabilitation of the criminal begun to make some headway, and in practice it is still in the experimental stage.

The following three essays form part of a series which compared the penal systems of a number of countries and were written by the American criminologist John P. Conrad for the English newspaper, *The Observer.* Conrad is unusually well qualified to make such comparisons. He has been with the Department of Corrections of the State of California for many years and is at present Acting Chief of Planning; in 1958-1959 he was a senior Fulbright Fellow in criminology at the University of London and from 1960-1961 Associate Director of the International Survey of Corrections, which studied advanced correctional practice in the United States, western Europe, and the Soviet Union. Primarily informational, descriptive rather than prescriptive, these essays nevertheless reflect Conrad's own views as an enlightened and experienced specialist. Indirectly they also say a good deal about the cultures that have established the prison systems he describes. On the whole, the tone is professionally matter-of-fact; he is aware of the obstacles and limitations that the reformer faces and he does not presume to offer a simple, formula explanation of the ultimate causes of the alarming increase in crime, particularly among the young, in our own country. But his commitment to the need for more enlightened correctional practice is clear. Although of necessity conforming to certain needs of journalism (for example, breaking the material down into easy categories), Conrad writes a traditional prose that lies beyond the writing skill of many sociologists. And his views as a specialist take on an added authority from the fact that he is a man of wide general culture.

THE SWEDISH PARADOX

There are not many Scandinavians in the world, and few of them are criminals. Visitors to the four countries of the north are regularly impressed with an order and an elegance which leave little scope for crime.

But though delinquency may be an anachronism in these civilised lands, it nevertheless persists. Its very existence is a concern, and a surprisingly large social investment has gone into its correction. The Nordic approach to crime and punishment has been applauded by criminologists from all over the earth, as the visitors' register of any Scandinavian prison will confirm. A recent correctional pilgrimage through the north infected me with some of my colleagues' enthusiasm. It also raised some questions that only time can answer.

. . . . **Old Adam***

I leave the riddle of crime in Utopia to students closer to the scene. What actually happens to Scandinavians in whom there somehow lurks the old Adam? A short answer would be that, as in less-regulated societies, he is involved in a special system to control him.

The difference seems to be that Scandinavians worry more than we do in England and America about the harm the system may do. A veteran Swedish professor of criminal law put it succinctly: until he can be sure what good a prison does, the fewer the people committed, and the shorter the time, the better.

This concern for the impact of official systems on troubled human beings has produced few new ideas. What fascinates the American criminologist is the willingness of Scandinavian correctional leadership and the general public to apply in practice the principles which English

From the July 9, 1961 issue of *The Observer*. Reprinted by permission of the author.

* Subheads throughout this selection were inserted by *The Observer*.

and American social scientists have extracted from our research. What falls on deaf ears when presented to American legislatures has already been translated into brightly painted concrete in Sweden. Instead of trying to apply new ideas in dilapidated old structures, new buildings are designed to fit what we think we know about delinquents as individuals and as members of groups.

. . . . .Gifted Leader

This uncompromising attack on the problem of rehabilitating delinquents can be found in all four of the Scandinavian countries. It has been carried furthest in Sweden.

There are three reasons for Swedish progress. First, Sweden, for reasons that mystify the most ingenious theorist, has by a wide margin the most worrying crime problem. Space in Danish and Norwegian prisons goes begging and plenty of vacant beds are to be found in the labour colonies of Finland. Second, Sweden has money to spend on public services and a well-established tradition of spending it. And third, Sweden has the gifted leadership of Torsten Eriksson, one of the most resourceful correctional administrators of our time.

Eriksson is new to the director-generalship of Swedish prisons, but his ideas have been influential in planning and organisation for many years. His touch is everywhere to be seen in the prisons and approved schools. New establishments are going up all over the country to meet the insistent requirements of the rising crime rate. The demolition of old and unserviceable buildings is systematically planned, especially Langholmen, the shabby old bastille of Stockholm.

A tour of the new prisons, borstals, and welfare schools is like a correctional fantasy. Ideas that English and American criminologists have considered and dismissed as fiscally impractical are here expressed in very palpable bricks and mortar.

What are the ruling ideas that are transforming Swedish corrections? Eriksson readily identifies four with which he has worked up to this point. They are neither new, nor surprising, nor tested. They have been applied because they make better sense than trying to make something of the legacy of the past.

. . . . .Work Tempo

First, prisoners must be put to work. Plausibly, Eriksson points out that all of us must work to live; why should prisoners be exempted? So Swedish prisons begin with a factory, a clean, well-lighted, well-equipped factory in which inmates learn to work at the tempo expected by regular industry. They manufacture uniforms for the Swedish Army, furniture for Government offices, and prefabricated houses for prisons, hospitals and Army posts.

. . . . .Playing-Fields

So far the public has been easy to convince of the importance of prison industry because Sweden has a chronic labour shortage. But for the present and the foreseeable future, Swedish prisoners work, and work hard, at occupations which make good economic sense.

Second, a good prison plan must deliberately minimise the psychological unhealthiness of confinement. People feel better in the open air, they work better in good light. They get along better together when not crowded into spaces in which the fact of confinement is emphasised by unnatural and involuntary closeness to others. Privacy must be a part of the plan rather than the object of inmate scheming. Though Swedish prisons have walls, they are not obtrusive, and the space they enclose includes not only the cottages in which prisoners live but also acres of playing-fields.

Third, prisons should take every possible advantage of modern technology. Not a difficult notion to sell to a Swede; I had seen for myself that if penology can be automated, the Swedes will be the first to do it.

At a new prison at Norrtälje, not far from Stockholm, closed circuit television provides surveillance of the walls and gates. In the control centre, a prison officer watches a battery of television screens, with a short-wave radio to patrol officers in the yard, ready for anything suspicious seen in the blinking tubes before him. Two-way intercommunications systems between each cell and the control room eliminate most of the knocking and shouting which make the night hideous in conventional prisons. Eriksson reasons that a staff which is given the tools to be efficient will be much more likely to be efficient than the key-rattling, tower-sitting prison officers to be found in most countries.

And fourth is the principle of the small group. New Swedish prisons house fewer than two hundred prisoners. Eriksson thinks the ideal figure would be about sixty. For young offenders at the new prison of Mariefred and at the well-known psychiatric facility at Roxtuna this standard has been met. But for ordinary prisoners he has had to compromise in the interests of economy.

Through the compromise he has been able to obtain adequate medical, educational and training services. In return, the principle of the small, manageable group is maintained through keeping the cottages small. The prison thus may be too large for the superintendent to know each inmate well, but each living group is small enough—forty at the most—for members of the staff to observe, know, and influence each inmate.

. . . . Formidable Bill

In turn, the number of cottages is small enough for the superintendent to be thoroughly familiar with the reports of his subordinates. The number of problems that can arise is kept to a level at which the superintendent can solve them as well as keeping some purposeful direction of the progress of the institution.

A visitor used to the grubby survivals of the nineteenth century which predominate in the penal landscape of England and America will be dazzled with the impeccable adherence to principles which seem visionary to our harassed administrators. The costs have been formidable. At one establishment the daily cost for each inmate runs to £5. Capital outlay per bed has been as high as £4,000. Even the most visionary penologist will be likely to ask if the Swedish taxpayer is getting his money's-worth.

If the answer is to be reckoned in money, the accounting will give pause to those who think of prison labour as shiftless and unproductive. Norrtälje Prison, built in 1959, for 150 inmates at a cost of £500,000, in its first year of operation produced furniture and Army uniforms worth over £70,000. Improvements in the organisation and the layout of the factories make an increase in this gross product virtually certain. Swedish prisons are not going to become self-supporting, nor should they. But Swedish prisoners are allowed to acquire self-respect as productive members of society.

Five pounds a day is a high price for room, board and treatment for any prisoner. But Eriksson points out that money spent to discover new methods of treating young criminals is an obvious requirement for the improvement of any prison system. Without a laboratory, the prisons of any country will become as obsolete as Dartmoor, no matter how up to date their basic ideas may be to-day.

. . . . Success Rate

If the pay-off is to be reckoned in reduced recidivism, the answer must be, not yet. No one is making any claims for startling changes in crime or recidivism rates as a result of five years of prison modernisation. The impression of 60 per cent. success continues to be the claim for the system as a whole. (Incredible though it may seem in a country so well endowed with electronic gadgetry, Sweden has only begun to develop a modern system of criminal statistics.) Sixty per cent. is about what is claimed for the success of Dartmoor and Wormwood Scrubs.

Is this all that the money and ingenuity which has been poured into Swedish prisons can accomplish? Why not keep the disreputable old Langholmen gaol instead of demolishing it to make room for two new prisons at a cost of nearly £2 million?

. . . . Staff Question

To this hard-headed question, the answer must be that 60 per cent. success simply isn't good enough for a modern prison system. Gaols that pour out hundreds of prisoners each year, only to receive half of them back after new crimes, probably do nearly as much harm as they do good. If the best that can be done with nineteenth-century facilities is 60 per cent. success, a new beginning must be made.

In England and America we have chosen to develop a staff of which more can be expected than from the crew of unschooled warders and illiterate turnkeys who did more than we like to admit to make the modern prison what it is to-day. Slowly we seem to discern some gains.

In Sweden, on the other hand, the possibility of attracting bright new staff to grimy old prisons has seemed too remote. A capable young man choosing a career is not very likely to make a first choice of a job which calls on him to sit eight hours a day in a tower or to engage in the frustrations of keeping prisoners busy at useless tasks. Nor is he likely to be convinced that a realistic challenge to his abilities exists in the opportunity to influence 200 inmates coming and going in a cell-block.

Swedish prisons as they have been redesigned give a staff a realistic job to do and the tools with which to do it. A staff has yet to be assembled which can measure up to the shiny new implements at hand. Psychiatrists are few, far between, and mostly engaged in diagnostic work. There are hardly any psychologists, and the social workers who comprise the bulk of the professional staffs are scarcely a match for the task of bringing therapeutic communities to life in physical settings ideal for their creation. With inadequate professional leadership, the kind of training programme in operation for years at the Prison Commission Staff College at Wakefield has hardly been started in Sweden.

. . . . The Laboratory

Lastly, Sweden relies heavily for after-care services on the benevolent advice of volunteer probation agents rather than the mature professional service to which English cities are accustomed. Until this gap is closed, the contribution of the prisons to the success of the correctional system will be as seriously handicapped as a surgeon without the assistance of a trained nurse.

But Sweden has made a commitment to scientific penal policy and a tremendous start in meeting that commitment. The laboratory for testing the effectiveness of reason and good will in the social restoration of offenders is in Sweden. It should not be many years, a decade at most, before the returns are in on an experiment of grandeur, generosity, and vision.

$\mathcal{T}$HE AMERICAN NIGHTMARE

The American nightmare is the crime problem. It mocks the American Dream, so nearly translated into the Affluent Society. Statistics in superlatives assail our complacency each year, with many a gloomy moral drawn. We are accustomed to hearing a recurring dirge on criminality, ironically echoing our brighter accounts in economics, education, or population. Each year is a record year for crime; no American criminologist can complain of a lack of experience, raw material, or adequate data.

The impact of the brute figures is difficult to convey to outsiders. A rough comparison of the size of prison populations is useful at least to make a point, if not to account for it. In England and Wales the daily population of all prisons and Borstals fluctuates at a figure of around 26,000. In California, a State with a population of about 15 million, the daily population of the State prisons only, confining only felons serving terms of more than a year, is now about 22,000.

This does not include the thousands of men and women, usually about 20,000, in county and city gaols, nor the boys committed to the youth authority who in England would be in a Borstal or detention centre. A few thousand additional Californians serve time in federal prisons. On any given day twice as many Californians as Englishmen are locked up.

. . . .**Shut Away***

The brandishing of these statistics may lead to the conclusion that crime is six times as bad in California as in England; good criminologists will

From the July 16, 1961 issue of *The Observer*. Reprinted by permission of the author.

* Subheads throughout this selection were inserted by *The Observer*.

require more proof. But the comparison does bring home the extent of the problem which the Americans have to face with this immense number of muddle-headed, shiftless, thieving and violent men, shut away from society for periods averaging between two and three years, with many a full term served to the bitter end. For decades it has been a sufficient task to control this mass with a minimum of inhumanity and a maximum of security.

We seem to know how to do this job. Resourceful wardens, at immense bastilles with populations as large as 5,000, have managed to avoid riots and maintain discipline for many years at a time. Nobody knows for sure what good this achievement does. No one has even thought of a convincing way of answering this question.

But the warden is sobered by the effect of his regime on the inmates. At least half the men he releases go out to commit new crimes, in spite of the dreary inevitability of a return to prison, in spite of whatever has been done with the intention of helping them.

To whom should the failures of the American prison be charged? To the imperfections of a highly acquisitive society? To the haphazard administration of criminal justice? To the irrational operation of the prison itself? For the prison administrator the only possible point of attack is the improvement of the prison, and on this assumption many bright plans have sparkled briefly and sputtered into confusion.

For a long time, we fastened our hopes on education and psychiatry. Teachers taught; here and there, the psychiatrist and his minions have treated. The effect on recidivism has scarcely been dramatic. Only during recent years have the social scientists invaded the field to ask whether something should not be done about the system itself. If the methods of the sociologist and the anthropologist could be used to make soldiers more militant, workers more productive and mental patients more accessible, perhaps from this new workshop could be drawn some tools to make the prison community work in favour of rehabilitation rather than against it.

. . . . .Inmate's Life

From the time of Oscar Wilde, sensitive ex-prisoners have told us how little good can be expected from the indiscriminate housing of criminals together in prisons. At long last, the social scientist has brought his researches to support these scarcely disinterested observers. Wherever it has been studied, the impact of the prison community on the prisoner derides rehabilitation and denies its possibility.

In a brilliant article in the January, 1961, *Prison Service Journal,*

Terence and Pauline Morris have described how, in England, "it's the prisoners that run this prison." Such findings have been duplicated in the United States. Adjustment to the prisoners' code and values determine most of the inmate's life, from his survival to the supply of his cigarettes.

. . . . Long Tradition

This code makes no allowance for rehabilitation. In the shapeless community of rejection, thousands of inmates in American prisons mill about uncertainly. Prisoners will try to protect themselves from each other, but this code allows for no mutual aid to prepare the way back to home and independence. Every assumption of the community implies that what happens after an inmate is released is nobody's business but his own. Long tradition supports this culture of sullen resistance to which both staff and inmates must defer.

No one really knows how the 5,000 inmates of San Quentin or similar bastions can be transformed into communities of hope. Social scientists have enough on their hands, with the means now at their disposal, to construct a therapeutic community of fifty or a hundred out of the refractory raw materials of delinquency.

Nevertheless, methods are now being devised and tested, from which hopeful answers may yet come, conceivably even from the largest prisons inherited from a generation of thoughtless master builders. Heavy reliance is placed on the courageous pioneering of Dr. Maxwell Jones of Henderson Hospital at Belmont. His fundamental work has been combined with the ideas of the theoretical sociologists to bring about the correctional community to replace the indiscriminate prison.

Famous throughout the correctional world is the New Jersey Residential Training Centre at Highfields. Based on guided group interaction, a technique originated by a sociologist, Dr. Lloyd McCorkle, a unit of twenty young men is subjected to a four-month regime of hard work and daily group discussion of common problems. No school, no vocational training, no psychiatric interviews, no organised recreation—the results have been startling.

Comparing it to the New Jersey Reformatory for Men, which deals with delinquents from the same streets in the same cities, but keeps them four times as long, the rate of failure is about the same. This is good enough to satisfy the New Jersey taxpayer; three more residential training centres, including one for girls, have been opened. For some youths Highfields is a good enough answer. It will not succeed with all.

Some failures must be charged up to situations too far gone to be influenced by four months of the impact of daily group discussion. There is, after all, a limit to what can be done for people in trouble, though we don't always know what that limit may be. Other failures might have been successes in still other correctional systems. And some failures will always be due to mistakes and oversights in the day-to-day application of the Highfields idea. For any machinery whose moving parts are human beings will always lack the precision of mechanical standards of efficiency.

Across the country, in the Mormon community of Provo, Utah, an imaginative sociologist, Dr. LaMar Empey, has initiated an experiment in group treatment without confinement. Delinquents are committed by the court to a treatment centre, Pinehills, rather than to probation or to a conventional reformatory. Every day, after school, twenty lads go to the centre for three hours and are put to work on various projects of community maintenance and improvement. On Saturday, and throughout school holidays, attendance is for all day. Each day the project members participate in a one-hour group discussion session. Absence is tolerated neither by staff nor group members.

The counselling objective is to enlist the support of the delinquent's comrades, themselves delinquents, in adopting law-abiding lives. The group insists on absolute honesty about delinquent history.

. . . .**New Standards**

Boys are encouraged to see themselves realistically as prospects for a reformatory, who must make major changes in their behaviour if they hope not to be sent away. They learn to govern their behaviour not by the standards of delinquent friends outside the group but by the new standards set by the group itself. To enforce these standards, the group can go so far as to send a boy to gaol for the week-end, to return for additional week-ends until he has decided to measure up to the group's requirements.

Finally, release from the programme is determined by the boys themselves, and the standards of honesty and good behaviour set by the group must be met before release is allowed. There are no results to report yet, but sociologists all over the country are eagerly watching its progress through a five-year study.

In California, the prisons and youth institutions have been subjected to intensive research for the past four years. Around the perpetually dissatisfied leadership of two of the country's most respected administrators, Richard McGee and Heman Stark, research teams have been overturning established practices and putting new ideas to carefully evaluated tests.

. . . . Three Themes

Three basic themes seem to guide the Californian approach. The first has been the principle that crime is the consequence of emotional immaturity, and that there are different levels of immaturity which can and must be treated differently. The second principle is that small therapeutic communities can be constructed, in which special methods for dealing with various immaturity problems can be applied. The third idea is that the results of these methods can be tested by comparing actual recidivism with that predicted on the basis of experience.

This method, referred to as the base expectancy score, was devised by the ingenious English social statistician, Leslie Wilkins. Through the combination of these methods, each inmate on arriving in a Californian correctional institution may some day be tested to discover his maturity level, scored to predict his probable chance of recidivism, and placed in a therapeutic community designed for the problems presented by a particular kind of immaturity. The success of the treatment method can be settled by comparing his expected rate of success, as predicted by the base expectancy score, with the actual successes achieved by various institutions.

. . . . Good Will

All these methods have obvious promise, the promise which is implicit in the replacement of bureaucratic inertia by purposeful problem solving. But human beings are never mere problems to be solved. The annals of the social sciences are full of disappointing answers to mechanically solved problems. This is especially true in the rehabilitation of delinquents. Prescribed treatment is doomed to failure if there is no context of optimism, concern, and good will towards its treatment.

In California, an appreciable dent was left on the hard-boiled correctional system by Dr. Norman Fenton, a psychologist who first saw the simple truth that toughness begets toughness where it is least desired. Harnessing the good will inherent in any staff, he put correctional officers, the hard-faced guards of years gone by, to work at group counselling. This has been going on for seven years. When it was first proposed, there were plenty of seasoned penologists to say that it was impossible. Enthusiasm got it under way and kept it going, but sage predictions that it would do no good persisted. Even now the practice of group counselling still has its detractors.

. . . . Faint Signs

Nevertheless, many correctional officers now show a lively satisfaction in their success as group counsellors, a kind of satisfaction in their work which was not conceivable for the old prison guards. For many inmates it has made a crucial difference. As group counselling continues, and as officers and inmates gain confidence, prisons change from communities of tension to places of hope. Here seems to be the real foundation of a correctional community. With social science to prove the value of good will, the penological face of the nation may yet change.

Until some Messianic social scientist conceives and implements a therapeutic society, crime will continue to thrive wherever there are cities. It is more than likely that American cities will continue to produce the most crime. But there are faint signs in the approaches that I have just described, and in many others, that our investment of money and brains in the social sciences will reward us in the end by a reliable method for the correction of criminals.

The nightmare will haunt us for a long while to come. Persistent good will and intelligence may yet transform its fearful events into closer correspondence with the American Dream.

WHAT LENIN FORESAW

All over Moscow his name, his face, and his sayings pervade its life. From the beauty of Soviet cities, or the lack of it, to the justice of Soviet laws, there was no feature of Russian society that did not receive the attention of Vladimir Ilyich Lenin. So, when I went to Moscow recently to reconnoitre prison services, I was not surprised to find that Lenin had laid down the principles for dealing with criminals in the Socialist State.

One afternoon I sat down with Nikolai Alexeyevich Struchkov, a brisk young lawyer, who expounded the ideas that govern the correction of delinquents. He began with a reverent citation of Lenin's basic thought on the subject. This is contained in a paper grandiloquently entitled: "Summary of the Essence of the Section Concerning Punishment in the Judicial Point of the Party Programme of 1917." The quintessence of the summary was reduced to five remarkable points, here very roughly translated:—

1. Conditional release of the offender should be extended wherever possible.
2. Wherever possible, punishment of the offender should consist of a social reprimand by the court to express society's attitude toward the offence.

From the July 2, 1961 issue of *The Observer*. Reprinted by permission of the author.

3. Wherever possible, obligatory labour without deprivation of liberty should be the basis of punishment.

4. Prisons must evolve into educational institutions.

5. The educational work of the prison must be strengthened through the active, participating interest of the community.

Here was Lenin, forty-four years ago, calling for probation, for minimal punishments, for education as the core of the correctional programme, and for close integration of the prison world with the community outside. Some of these ideas are rather *avant-garde* in the West even now. Others have been generally accepted by our penologists but only during the last two decades. It was not for nothing that Lenin and his associates saw the inside of so many pre-revolutionary prisons.

These are the precepts on which Soviet criminologists have constructed a new variant of penology, Corrective Labour Science. As an exponent of this domain of knowledge, Mr. Struchkov regards it as his task to conceive and test methods of putting Lenin's principles into effective practice. How well have these ideas fared in the forty-four years of Soviet history?

For an answer, I was invited to visit Kryukovo, a Corrective Labour Colony about thirty-five miles from the Kremlin. Far out in the countryside we found it on an inconspicuous, muddy lane. Barbed-wire fencing surrounded a compound consisting mostly of shabby barracks. Like so many buildings in the Soviet Union, they badly needed paint and sprucing up. In sharp contrast to its surroundings stood a new brick heating plant.

At the gate the Colony Chief, Major Boris Artamanov, with his deputy, Captain Mikhail Persheyev, awaited our party. Heels clicked and hands were shaken in order of rank. The major was a plump, affable man of middle age, dressed like most of his staff in tan and blue military uniform. Obviously he was proud of the achievements of his colony. Like every other Russian I met during my sojourn, he seemed to enjoy the visit, laughing jovially over his own witticisms and mine. How well he filled a familiar role, I thought—the paternal prison governor concerned to maintain control of his inmates without severity.

Captain Persheyev had the zealous look of the thoroughly dedicated schoolmaster, which, it transpired, was his profession. Corrective Labour Science calls for an educator in at least the second ranking post of every colony.

We went to the major's unheated office where I asked him the usual questions of a prison official looking into a colleague's affairs. Here is the major's account. Kryukovo is a Corrective Labour Colony of the general regime, with a capacity of one thousand inmates. Because of a decline in

Soviet crime, the place housed only eight hundred on the day of my visit. The average inmate remains at Kryukovo for about four years. The minimum term is one year, the maximum, ten. The colony is operated by a staff of about seventy corrective labour employees, with some additional teachers and work foremen.

Already I was beginning to wonder how the colony was held together. Seventy guards in charge of eight hundred to a thousand inmates, ominously described as "dangerous recidivists"? How could control be maintained with so thin a line of disciplinary officers? The major replied that he was able to enlist the inmates themselves in the solution of the problem of control. Two inmate commissions provided a structure in the community by which discipline and order were powerfully supported.

First was the Sector on Corrective Labour. To this body, each workers' collective in the colony elected a delegate. The sector took responsibility for removing all impediments to the colony's achievement of its monthly work norms. Impediments that it could not remove it was obliged to report to the major. Such obstacles might be a faulty lathe, an insanitary latrine, or a lazy inmate. The sector could not discipline unproductive workers, but it could ridicule them in wall newspapers, in satirical posters—or it could report misbehaviour to the colony management. Not that there was a great deal of misconduct, the major indulgently added. He had to adjudicate two or three rule infractions a week, mostly on such charges as spitting on the footpaths or smoking in prohibited places.

The second arm of inmate participation in the management of the colony is the Sector on Professional and Vocational Education. Before an inmate can be released from Kryukovo, he must complete an apprenticeship in a recognised trade. To help him, the sector studies his progress and advises the major about his shortcomings and achievements. Of course, said Captain Persheyev, the staff also watched each inmate with care, but the opinions of workmates about one another rounded out the picture and provided information which the staff might not get for themselves. It was important, too, that inmates should be concerned about their fellows.

Such busybodiness is discouraged in most English and American prisons. In the West, guards and prisoners will at least agree that each man should "do his own time." But here in Kryukovo each man was expected to keep his brother. The minding of other people's business seems to be an essential Soviet virtue. Whatever an English or American prisoner sectors—and I suspect their thoughts would be unprintable—their effectiveness in keeping order must be the secret to the colony's success.

I was taken into a workshop where all sorts of aluminium products were being stamped out. Spoons, cafeteria trays, oil filter parts poured out of impressive looking machinery gleaming in poorly lit and draughty sheds. Though I must have seemed like a man from Mars to the inmates, they hardly looked up from their benches as I passed. Did they always work so hard? Well, this was the last day of the month, and they were putting forth extra efforts to achieve or surpass their work norms.

All Kryukovo inmates are paid at the standard rates prevailing in civilian factories. Deductions are made for room, board, and services. Most of them sent money home to their families and most laid money by for their return to civilian life.

On to the inmate quarters. First, a club room in which chess and reading were the main leisure activities. An off-duty workers' collective of about twenty-five men was in earnest discussion as we entered. The men snapped to attention, and I noticed their oddly standardised appearance—they all seemed to have the same broad, impassive face, the same close-cropped head, the same wiry figures in grey woollen uniforms. Above them the portraits of Lenin, Gorky, and Makarenko, the last a major saint in the hagiology of Corrective Labour Science—beamed down with inspirational expressions. I asked one inmate whether the principles of Makarenko applied to Kryukovo. Bracing to an even greater rigidity, he replied: "They are obligatory, Sir!"

The adjoining dormitory was filled with double-bunk beds set as close together as possible. Why so crowded if the colony was not filled to capacity? The major bridled at the implied criticism. The requirements of Soviet sanitary law were met. The code prescribed that in any dormitory there must be two cubic metres of air space per man. Clearly there were two cubic metres and perhaps a little more for each of the men in this dormitory.

As we strolled on, I asked about escapes. Kryukovo has never had an escape, I was firmly told. Never? But why would anyone wish to escape from Kryukovo? Here a man had good food, good work, good pay, good quarters, regular conjugal visits, and an opportunity to educate himself. Besides, there were armed guards around the perimeter with orders to shoot any inmate who approached the fence.

In America we have scarcely begun even to prepare public opinion for the idea that conjugal visiting might strengthen tenuous marital ties and prevent the degrading homosexuality that prevails in any prison in which long terms are served. But Corrective Labour Science takes into account the importance of preserving family relations and goes a good deal farther than most Western countries have been able to countenance in fostering marital relations of colony inmates.

I was taken to the colony guest house, in which inmates can entertain their wives for a total of seven days a quarter. This was another converted barracks situated next to the main gate. On one side, a table extended the full length of the building so that supervised visits between inmates and guests could take place, much as in any Western prison. On the other side was a row of cubicles for the private visiting of inmates and their wives. The building reeked of bygone cabbage; the major explained that wives were expected to bring their own food.

One of the cubicles was not in use. Its contents were a sagging bed, a battered dresser, and a straight chair. Farther down the row, the major knocked at another cubicle, and opened to reveal a flustered inmate frantically trying to get into his clothes, while his wife clutched the blankets around her and glared at us. I could imagine the invective which would be heaped on the poor fellow as soon as the door closed behind us—her humiliation, her embarrassment, and all on his account. Whatever the benefits of conjugal visiting, its hazards were obvious.

Finally, I was taken to the recreation hall; there to see that all was not work in a day of corrective labour. The major opened the door, paused, and then turned to explain that the theatre was in use by the Comrades' Court. But I could come in and watch if I liked.

Going in, I saw an auditorium filled with wooden benches on which sat about a hundred inmates. On the platform there were three grim-looking citizens who looked as though they didn't propose to allow their legs to be pulled. Before them, with his back to the audience, there stood a pitiable youth whose knees were shaking, whose teeth were chattering, and whose obvious torment was for the purpose of convincing the Comrades' Court that he was ready for release.

Until about two years ago the major himself had been responsible for deciding when inmates were ready again for civilian life. To his relief, this task had been taken away from him and vested in the Comrades' Court, perhaps in accordance with Lenin's fifth principle of Corrective Labour Science.

The Comrades' Court consisted of a professional magistrate and two reputable lay citizens of the district. For the moral support of the applicant and the edification of his fellows, any inmate off duty was allowed to attend these hearings. With all eyes fixed impassively on the major and me rather than on the inmate and his arbiters, I decided to beat a hasty retreat.

How effective are Kryukovo and the Corrective Labour Science of which it is evidently a prime example? Major Artamanov, with the air of a man picking a random figure, thought that only 2 per cent. of the releases returned for another term. His superior, the Chief Inspector of Corrective Labour for the Moscow District, told me that he had had to shut down four such colonies during the last year. But I am sure that neither I nor any other Westerner is likely to find out the real situation. Criminal statistics in any advanced country present awkward problems in validating information. It seems unlikely that there exists in some recess of the Kremlin a set of statistics which provide information by which we would compare recidivism in England and the Soviet Union.

But there can be no question that the Corrective Labour Scientists are on to something. One could add to Lenin's essential points, but there could hardly be a quarrel concerning their validity not only for Russians but also for Americans and Englishmen. In the simple society to which the Russians have become accustomed the choices are mostly between compliance and resistance. At Kryukovo a man could certainly learn to comply. From the look of the colony, he would also learn to work hard.

Sneering at Soviet institutions for the sake of sneering has become almost a required attitude for returning Westerners in describing what they have seen. But Soviet prisons present a challenge that we would do well to take up. Our task is to prepare offenders for return to an immensely more complex society. We cannot always excuse our obvious ineffectiveness by citing the difficulty of the task. And none of our elegant new buildings or sophisticated therapeutic community programmes are going to do much good until we take one bold step which the Russians took years ago—the installation of real work at real pay in all our prisons.

Bertrand Russell

Ever since Mary Shelley in the early 1800's wrote the novel *Frankenstein*, the motif of man's destruction by his creature, the machine, has been recurrent in Western literature and thought. In our own time Mrs. Shelley's numerous heirs have continued to treat the subject of man and machine in imaginative and symbolic forms (Aldous Huxley's *Brave New World* is a famous example). At the same time a variety of specialists have studied those aspects of the problem that seem to them most crucial—the current debate is largely one of economics, that is, the effect of automation on employment. In the following essay the eminent rationalist philosopher, mathematician, and moralist, Bertrand Russell, argues that the ultimate stresses in a machine-dominated culture are psychological. As a man committed to, though aware of the limitations of, the scientific method, he accepts no premise uncritically. Indeed the validity of his argument here depends on his demolition of two popularly held assumptions, the first that the profit motive is innate, the second that happiness depends upon the amassing of material possessions. Russell is a thinker who is concerned both with ultimate truth and engaged with contemporary reality; he brings the insights of various disciplines to bear on the problem under investigation.

$\mathcal{M}$ACHINES AND THE EMOTIONS

Will machines destroy emotions, or will emotions destroy machines? This question was suggested long ago by Samuel Butler in *Erewhon,* but it is growing more and more actual as the empire of machinery is enlarged.

At first sight, it is not obvious why there should be any opposition between machines and emotions. Every normal boy loves machines; the bigger and more powerful they are, the more he loves them. Nations which have a long tradition of artistic excellence, like the Japanese, are captivated by Western mechanical methods as soon as they come across them, and long only to imitate us as quickly as possible. Nothing annoys an educated and travelled Asiatic so much as to hear praise of "the wisdom of the East" or the traditional virtues of Asiatic civilization. He feels as a boy would feel who was told to play with dolls instead of toy automobiles. And like a boy, he would prefer a real automobile to a toy one, not realizing that it may run over him.

In the West, when machinery was new, there was the same delight in it, except on the part of a few poets and aesthetes. The nineteenth century considered itself superior to its predecessors chiefly because of its mechanical progress. Peacock, in its early years, makes fun of the "steam intellect society," because he is a literary man, to whom the Greek and Latin authors represent civilization; but he is conscious of being out of touch with the prevailing tendencies of his time. Rousseau's disciples with the return to Nature, the Lake Poets with their mediaevalism, William Morris with his *News from Nowhere* (a country where it is always June and everybody is engaged in haymaking), all represent a purely sentimental and essentially reactionary opposition to machinery. Samuel Butler was the first man to apprehend intellectually the non-sentimental case against machines, but in him it may have been no more than a *jeu d'esprit*—certainly it was not a deeply held conviction. Since his day numbers of people in the most mechanized nations have been tending to adopt in earnest a view similar to that of the Erewhonians; this view, that is to say, has been latent or explicit in the attitude of many rebels against existing industrial methods.

Machines are worshipped because they are beautiful, and valued because they confer power; they are hated because they are hideous, and

From *Sceptical Essays* by Bertrand Russell (London, George Allen and Unwin, Ltd., 1960), pp. 56-61. Reprinted by permission of the publisher.

loathed because they impose slavery. Do not let us suppose that one of these attitudes is "right" and the other "wrong," any more than it would be right to maintain that men have heads but wrong to maintain that they have feet, though we can easily imagine Lilliputians disputing this question concerning Gulliver. A machine is like a Djinn in the Arabian Nights: beautiful and beneficent to its master, but hideous and terrible to his enemies. But in our day nothing is allowed to show itself with such naked simplicity. The master of the machine, it is true, lives at a distance from it, where he cannot hear its noise or see its unsightly heaps of slag or smell its noxious fumes; if he ever sees it, the occasion is before it is installed in use, when he can admire its force or its delicate precision without being troubled by dust and heat. But when he is challenged to consider the machine from the point of view of those who have to live with it and work it, he has a ready answer. He can point out that, owing to its operations, these men can purchase more goods—often vastly more —than their great-grandfathers could. It follows that they must be happier than their great-grandfathers—if we are to accept an assumption which is made by almost everyone.

The assumption is, that the possession of material commodities is what makes men happy. It is thought that a man who has two rooms and two beds and two loaves must be twice as happy as a man who has one room and one bed and one loaf. In a word, it is thought that happiness is proportional to income. A few people, not always quite sincerely, challenge this idea in the name of religion or morality; but they are glad if they increase their income by the eloquence of their preaching. It is not from a moral or religious point of view that I wish to challenge it; it is from the point of view of psychology and observation of life. If happiness is proportional to income, the case for machinery is unanswerable; if not the whole question remains to be examined.

Men have physical needs, and they have emotions. While physical needs are unsatisfied, they take first place; but when they are satisfied, emotions unconnected with them become important in deciding whether a man is to be happy or unhappy. In modern industrial communities there are many men, women, and children whose bare physical needs are not adequately supplied; as regards them, I do not deny that the first requisite for happiness is an increase of income. But they are a minority, and it would not be difficult to give the bare necessaries of life to all of them. It is not of them that I wish to speak, but of those who have more than is necessary to support existence—not only those who have much more, but also those who have only a little more.

Why do we, in fact, almost all of us, desire to increase our incomes? It may seem, at first sight, as though material goods were what we desire. But, in fact, we desire these mainly in order to impress our neighbours. When a man moves into a larger house in a more genteel quarter, he reflects that "better" people will call on his wife, and some unprosperous cronies of former days can be dropped. When he sends his son to a good school or an expensive university, he consoles himself for the heavy fees by thoughts of the social kudos to be gained. In every big city, whether of Europe or of America, houses in some districts are more expensive than equally good houses in other districts, merely because they are more fashionable. One of the most powerful of all our passions is the desire to be admired and respected. As things stand, admiration and respect are given to the man who seems to be rich. This is the chief reason why people wish to be rich. The actual goods purchased by their money play quite a secondary part. Take, for example, a millionaire who cannot tell one picture from another, but has acquired a gallery of old masters by the help of experts. The only pleasure he derives from his pictures is the thought that others know how much they have cost; he would derive more direct enjoyment from sentimental chromos out of Christmas numbers, but he would not obtain the same satisfaction for his vanity.

All this might be different, and has been different in many societies. In aristocratic epochs, men have been admired for their birth. In some circles in Paris, men are admired for their artistic or literary excellence, strange as it may seem. In a German university, a man may actually be admired for his learning. In India saints are admired; in China, sages. The study of these differing societies shows the correctness of our analysis, for in all of them we find a large percentage of men who are indifferent to money so long as they have enough to keep alive on, but are keenly desirous of the merits by which, in their environment, respect is to be won.

The importance of these facts lies in this, that the modern desire for wealth is not inherent in human nature, and could be destroyed by different social institutions. If, by law, we all had exactly the same income, we should have to seek some other way of being superior to our neighbours, and most of our present craving for material possessions would cease. Moreover, since this craving is in the nature of a competition, it only brings happiness when we outdistance a rival, to whom it brings correlative pain. A general increase of wealth gives no competitive advantage, and therefore brings no competitive happiness. There is, of course, *some* pleasure derived from the actual enjoyment of goods purchased, but, as we have seen, this is a very small part of what makes us desire wealth. And in so far as our desire is competitive, no increase of human happiness as a whole comes from increase of wealth, whether general or particular.

If we are to argue that machinery increases happiness, therefore, the increase of material prosperity which it brings cannot weigh very heavily in its favour, except in so far as it may be used to prevent absolute destitution. But there is no inherent reason why it should be so used.

Destitution can be prevented without machinery where the population is stationary; of this France may serve as an example, since there is very little destitution and much less machinery than in America, England, or pre-war Germany. Conversely, there may be much destitution where there is much machinery; of this we have examples in the industrial areas of England a hundred years ago and of Japan at the present day. The prevention of destitution does not depend upon machines, but upon quite other factors—partly density of population, and partly political conditions. And apart from prevention of destitution, the value of increasing wealth is not very great.

Meanwhile, machines deprive us of two things which are certainly important ingredients of human happiness, namely, spontaneity and variety. Machines have their own pace, and their own insistent demands: a man who has expensive plant must keep it working. The great trouble with the machine, from the point of view of the emotions, is its *regularity*. And, of course, conversely, the great objection to the emotions, from the point of view of the machine, is their *irregularity*. As the machine dominates the thoughts of people who consider themselves "serious," the highest praise they can give to a man is to suggest that he has the qualities of a machine—that he is reliable, punctual, exact, etc. And an "irregular" life has come to be synonymous with a bad life. Against this point of view Bergson's philosophy was a protest—not, to my mind, wholly sound from an intellectual point of view, but inspired by a wholesome dread of seeing men turned more and more into machines.

In life, as opposed to thought, the rebellion of our instincts against enslavement to mechanism has hitherto taken a most unfortunate direction. The impulse to war has always existed since men took to living in societies, but it did not, in the past have the same intensity or virulence as it has in our day. In the eighteenth century, England and France had innumerable wars, and contended for the hegemony of the world; but they liked and respected each other the whole time. Officer prisoners joined in the social life of their captors, and were honoured guests at their dinner-parties. At the beginning of our war with Holland in 1665, a man came home from Africa with atrocity stories about the Dutch there; we [the British] persuaded ourselves that his story was false, punished him, and published the Dutch denial. In the late war we should have knighted him, and imprisoned anyone who threw doubt on his veracity. The greater ferocity of modern war is attributable to machines, which operate in three different ways. First, they make it possible to have larger armies. Secondly, they facilitate a cheap Press, which flourishes by appealing to men's baser passions. Thirdly—and this is the point that concerns us— they starve the anarchic, spontaneous side of human nature, which works underground, producing an obscure discontent, to which the thought of war appeals as affording possible relief. It is a mistake to attribute a vast upheaval like the late war merely to the machinations of politicians. In

Russia, perhaps, such an explanation would have been adequate; that is one reason why Russia fought half-heartedly, and made a revolution to secure peace. But in England, Germany, and the United States (in 1917), no Government could have withstood the popular demand for war. A popular demand of this sort must have an instinctive basis, and for my part I believe that the modern increase in warlike instinct is attributable to the dissatisfaction (mostly unconscious) caused by the regularity, mo notony, and tameness of modern life.

It is obvious that we cannot deal with this situation by abolishing machinery. Such a measure would be reactionary, and is in any case impracticable. The only way of avoiding the evils at present associated with machinery is to provide breaks in the monotony, with every encouragement to high adventure during the intervals. Many men would cease to desire war if they had opportunities to risk their lives in Alpine climbing; one of the ablest and most vigorous workers for peace that it has been my good fortune to know habitually spent his summer climbing the most dangerous peaks in the Alps. If every working man had a month in the year during which, if he chose, he could be taught to work an aeroplane, or encouraged to hunt for sapphires in the Sahara, or otherwise enabled to engage in some dangerous and exciting pursuit involving quick personal initiative, the popular love of war would become confined to women and invalids. I confess I know no method of making these classes pacific, but I am convinced that a scientific psychology would find a method if it undertook the task in earnest.

Machines have altered our way of life, but not our instincts. Consequently there is maladjustment. The whole psychology of the emotions and instincts is as yet in its infancy; a beginning has been made by psychoanalysis, but only a beginning. What we may accept from psycho-analysis is the fact that people will, in action, pursue various ends which they do not *consciously* desire, and will have an attendant set of quite irrational beliefs which enable them to pursue these ends without knowing that they are doing so. But orthodox psycho-analysis has unduly simplified our unconscious purposes, which are numerous, and differ from one person to another. It is to be hoped that social and political phenomena will soon come to be understood from this point of view, and will thus throw light on average human nature.

Moral self-control, and external prohibition of harmful acts, are not adequate methods of dealing with our anarchic instincts. The reason they are inadequate is that these instincts are capable of as many disguises as the Devil in mediaeval legend, and some of these disguises deceive even the elect. The only adequate method is to discover what are the needs of our instinctive nature, and then to search for the least harmful way of satisfying them. Since spontaneity is what is most thwarted by machines, the only thing that can be *provided* is opportunity; the use made of opportunity must be left to the initiative of the individual. No doubt considerable expense would be involved; but it would not be comparable to the expense of war. Understanding of human nature must be the basis of any real improvement in human life. Science has done wonders in mastering the laws of the physical world, but our own nature is much less understood, as yet, than the nature of stars and electrons. When science learns to understand human nature, it will be able to bring a happiness into our lives which machines and the physical sciences have failed to create.

Aldous Huxley

When Aldous Huxley's *Brave New World* first appeared in 1932, it revealed a new aspect of the brilliant young writer whose satiric novels had both amused and disturbed readers of the 1920's. Set in the future, the novel described a highly organized world in which science and technology controlled the lives and the very thoughts of the human race. The author's knowledge of the potentialities of science (he is the grandson of the great Victorian biologist T. H. Huxley and the brother of the distinguished scientist Sir Julian Huxley) combined with his wit and imagination to create a fantasy as convincing as it was frightening.

Brave New World Revisited, published in 1958, is neither fiction nor fantasy. In a series of essays, Huxley demonstrates the extent to which our world has approached a condition of spiritual regimentation remarkably like that which he had visualized in 1932. He points out, however, that the major threat lies not so much in the mere existence of techniques for thought control as in circumstances which may make such control a virtual certainty—circumstances which spring from what another modern thinker has called "the greatest problem," the terrifying and apparently uncontrollable increase in the world's population. It is this problem, above all, which threatens to make a totalitarian future inevitable. In considering this problem in the first essays of *Brave New World Revisited,* Huxley speaks not in the language of exuberantly imaginative fiction but in the sober and worried accents of an intelligent man who knows the facts of the situation and is compelled by his own integrity to face them.

OVER-POPULATION

On 1931, when *Brave New World* was being written, I was convinced that there was still plenty of time. The completely organized society, the scientific caste system, the abolition of free will by methodical

From *Brave New World Revisited* by Aldous Huxley. Copyright © 1958 by Aldous Huxley. Reprinted by permission of Harper & Row, Publishers.

conditioning, the servitude made acceptable by regular doses of chemically induced happiness, the orthodoxies drummed in by nightly courses of sleep-teaching—these things were coming all right, but not in my time, not even in the time of my grandchildren. I forget the exact date of the events recorded in *Brave New World;* but it was somewhere in the sixth or seventh century A.F. (After Ford). We who were living in the second quarter of the twentieth century A.D. were the inhabitants, admittedly, of a gruesome kind of universe; but the nightmare of those depression years was radically different from the nightmare of the future, described in *Brave New World.* Ours was a nightmare of too little order; theirs, in the seventh century A.F., of too much. In the process of passing from one extreme to the other, there would be a long interval, so I imagined, during which the more fortunate third of the human race would make the best of both worlds—the disorderly world of liberalism and the much too orderly Brave New World where perfect efficiency left no room for freedom or personal initiative.

Twenty-seven years later, in this third quarter of the twentieth century A.D., and long before the end of the first century A.F., I feel a good deal less optimistic than I did when I was writing *Brave New World.* The prophecies made in 1931 are coming true much sooner than I thought they would. The blessed interval between too little order and the nightmare of too much has not begun and shows no sign of beginning. In the West, it is true, individual men and women still enjoy a large measure of freedom. But even in those countries that have a tradition of democratic government, this freedom and even the desire for this freedom seem to be on the wane. In the rest of the world freedom for individuals has already gone, or is manifestly about to go. The nightmare of total organization, which I had situated in the seventh century After Ford, has emerged from the safe, remote future and is now awaiting us, just around the next corner.

George Orwell's *1984* was a magnified projection into the future of a present that contained Stalinism and an immediate past that had witnessed the flowering of Nazism. *Brave New World* was written before the rise of Hitler to supreme power in Germany and when the Russian tyrant had not yet got into his stride. In 1931 systematic terrorism was not the obsessive contemporary fact which it had become in 1948, and the future dictatorship of my imaginary world was a good deal less brutal than the future dictatorship so brilliantly portrayed by Orwell. In the context of 1948, *1984* seemed dreadfully convincing. But tyrants, after all, are mortal and circumstances change. Recent developments in Russia and recent advances in science and technology have robbed Orwell's book of some of its gruesome verisimilitude. A nuclear war will, of course, make nonsense of everybody's predictions. But, assuming for the moment that the Great Powers can somehow refrain from destroying us, we can say that it now looks as though the odds were more in favor of something like *Brave New World* than of something like *1984*.

In the light of what we have recently learned about animal behavior in general, and human behavior in particular, it has become clear that control through the punishment of undesirable behavior is less effective, in the long run, than control through the reinforcement of desirable behavior by rewards, and that government through terror works on the whole less well than government through the non-violent manipulation of the environment and of the thoughts and feelings of individual men, women and children. Punishment temporarily puts a stop to undesirable behavior, but does not permanently reduce the victim's tendency to indulge in it. Moreover, the psycho-physical by-products of punishment may be just as undesirable as the behavior for which an individual has been punished. Psychotherapy is largely concerned with the debilitating or anti-social consequences of past punishments.

The society described in *1984* is a society controlled almost exclusively by punishment and the fear of punishment. In the imaginary world of my own fable punishment is infrequent and generally mild. The nearly perfect control exercised by the government is achieved by systematic reinforcement of desirable behavior, by many kinds of nearly nonviolent manipulation, both physical and psychological, and by genetic standardization. Babies in bottles and the centralized control of reproduction are not perhaps impossible; but it is quite clear that for a long time to come we shall remain a viviparous species breeding at random. For practical purposes genetic standardization may be ruled out. Societies will continue to be controlled postnatally—by punishment, as in the past, and to an ever increasing extent by the more effective methods of reward and scientific manipulation.

In Russia the old-fashioned, *1984*-style dictatorship of Stalin has begun to give way to a more up-to-date form of tyranny. In the upper levels of the Soviets' hierarchical society the reinforcement of desirable behavior has begun to replace the older methods of control through the punishment of undesirable behavior. Engineers and scientists, teachers and administrators, are handsomely paid for good work and so moderately taxed that they are under a constant incentive to do better and so be more highly rewarded. In certain areas they are at liberty to think and do more or less what they like. Punishment awaits them only when they stray beyond their prescribed limits into the realms of ideology and politics. It is because they have been granted a measure of professional freedom that Russian teachers, scientists and technicians have achieved such remarkable successes. Those who live near the base of the Soviet pyramid enjoy none of the privileges accorded to the lucky or specially gifted minority. Their wages are meager and they pay, in the form of high prices, a disproportionately large share of the taxes. The area in which they can do as they please is extremely restricted, and their rulers control them more by punishment and the threat of punishment than through non-violent manipulation or the reinforcement of desirable behavior by reward. The Soviet system combines elements of *1984* with elements that are prophetic of what went on among the higher castes in *Brave New World*.

Meanwhile impersonal forces over which we have almost no control seem to be pushing us all in the direction of the Brave New Worldian nightmare; and this impersonal pushing is being consciously accelerated by representatives of commercial and political organizations who have developed a number of new techniques for manipulating, in the interest of some minority, the thoughts and feelings of the masses. The techniques of manipulation will be discussed in later chapters. For the moment let us confine our attention to those impersonal forces which are now making the world so extremely unsafe for democracy, so very inhospitable to individual freedom. What are these forces? And why has the nightmare, which I had projected into the seventh century A.F., made so swift an advance in our direction? The answer to these questions must begin where the life of even the most highly civilized society has its beginnings —on the level of biology.

On the first Christmas Day the population of our planet was about two hundred and fifty millions—less than half the population of modern China. Sixteen centuries later, when the Pilgrim Fathers landed at Plymouth Rock, human numbers had climbed to a little more than five hundred millions. By the time of the signing of the Declaration of Independence, world population had passed the seven hundred million mark. In 1931, when I was writing *Brave New World*, it stood at just under two billions. Today, only twenty-seven years later, there are two billion eight hundred thousand of us. And tomorrow—what? Penicillin, DDT and clean water are cheap commodities, whose effects on public health are out of all proportion to their cost. Even the poorest government is rich enough to provide its subjects with a substantial measure of death control. Birth control is a very different matter. Death control is something which can be provided for a whole people by a few technicians working in the pay of a benevolent government. Birth control depends on the co-operation of an entire people. It must be practiced by countless individuals, from whom it demands more intelligence and will power than most of the world's teeming illiterates possess, and (where chemical or mechanical methods of contraception are used) an expenditure of more money than most of these millions can now afford. Moreover, there are nowhere any religious traditions in favor of unrestricted death, whereas religious and social traditions in favor of unrestricted reproduction are widespread. For all these reasons, death control is achieved very easily, birth control is achieved with great difficulty. Death rates have therefore fallen in recent years with startling suddenness. But birth rates have either remained at their old high level or, if they have fallen, have fallen very little and at a very slow rate. In consequence, human numbers are now increasing more rapidly than at any time in the history of the species.

Moreover, the yearly increases are themselves increasing. They increase regularly, according to the rules of compound interest; and they also increase irregularly with every application, by a technologically backward society of the principles of Public Health. At the present time the annual increase in world population runs to about forty-three millions. This means that every four years mankind adds to its numbers the equivalent of the present population of the United States, every eight and a half years the equivalent of the present population of India. At the rate of increase prevailing between the birth of Christ and the death of Queen Elizabeth I, it took sixteen centuries for the population of the earth to double. At the present rate it will double in less than half a century. And this fantastically rapid doubling of our numbers will be taking place on a planet whose most desirable and productive areas are already densely populated, whose soils are being eroded by the frantic efforts of bad farmers to raise more food, and whose easily available mineral capital is being squandered with the reckless extravagance of a drunken sailor getting rid of his accumulated pay.

In the Brave New World of my fable, the problem of human numbers in their relation to natural resources had been effectively solved. An optimum figure for world population had been calculated and numbers were maintained at this figure (a little under two billions, if I remember rightly) generation after generation. In the real contemporary world, the population problem has not been solved. On the contrary it is becoming graver and more formidable with every passing year. It is against this grim biological background that all the political, economic, cultural and psychological dramas of our time are being played out. As the twentieth century wears on, as the new billions are added to the existing billions (there will be more than five and a half billions of us by the time my granddaughter is fifty), this biological background will advance, ever more insistently, ever more menacingly, toward the front and center of the historical stage. The problem of rapidly increasing numbers in relation to natural resources, to social stability and to the well-being of individuals—this is now the central problem of mankind; and it will remain the central problem certainly for another century, and perhaps for several centuries thereafter. A new age is supposed to have begun on October 4, 1957. But actually, in the present context, all our exuberant post-Sputnik talk is irrelevant and even nonsensical. So far as the masses of mankind are concerned, the coming time will not be the Space Age; it will be the Age of Over-population. We can parody the words of the old song and ask,

> *Will the space that you're so rich in*
> *Light a fire in the kitchen,*
> *Or the little god of space turn the*
> *spit, spit, spit?*

The answer, it is obvious, is in the negative. A settlement on the moon may be of some military advantage to the nation that does the settling. But it will do nothing whatever to make life more tolerable, during the fifty years that it will take our present population to double, for the earth's undernourished and proliferating billions. And even if, at some future date, emigration to Mars should become feasible, even if any considerable number of men and women were desperate enough to choose a new life under conditions comparable to those prevailing on a mountain twice as high as Mount Everest, what difference would that make? In the course of the last four centuries quite a number of people sailed from the Old World to the New. But neither their departure nor the returning flow of food and raw materials could solve the problems of the Old World. Similarly the shipping of a few surplus humans to Mars (at a cost, for transportation and development, of several million dollars a head) will do nothing to solve the problem of mounting population pressures on our own planet. Unsolved, that problem will render insoluble all our other problems. Worse still, it will create conditions in which individual freedom and the social decencies of the democratic way of life will become impossible, almost unthinkable. Not all dictatorships arise in the same way. There are many roads to Brave New World; but perhaps the straightest and the broadest of them is the road we are traveling today, the road that leads through gigantic numbers and accelerating increases. Let us briefly review the reasons for this close correlation between too many people, too rapidly multiplying, and the formulation of authoritarian philosophies, the rise of totalitarian systems of government.

As large and increasing numbers press more heavily upon available resources, the economic position of the society undergoing this ordeal becomes ever more precarious. This is especially true of those underdeveloped regions, where a sudden lowering of the death rate by means of DDT, penicillin and clean water has not been accompanied by a corresponding fall in the birth rate. In parts of Asia and in most of Central and South America populations are increasing so fast that they will double themselves in little more than twenty years. If the production of food and manufactured articles, of houses, schools and teachers, could be increased at a greater rate than human numbers, it would be possible to improve the wretched lot of those who live in these underdeveloped and over-populated countries. But unfortunately these countries lack not merely agricultural machinery and an industrial plant capable of turning out this machinery, but also the capital required to create such a plant. Capital is what is left over after the primary needs of a population have been satisfied. But the primary needs of most of the people in underdeveloped countries are never fully satisfied. At the end of each year almost nothing is left over, and there is therefore almost no capital available for creating the industrial and agricultural plant, by means of which the people's needs might be satisfied. Moreover, there is, in all these underdeveloped countries, a serious shortage of the trained manpower without which a modern industrial and agricultural plant cannot be operated. The present educational facilities are inadequate; so are the resources, financial and cultural, for improving the existing facilities as fast as the situation demands. Meanwhile the population of some of these underdeveloped countries is increasing at the rate of 3 per cent per annum.

Their tragic situation is discussed in an important book, published in 1957—*The Next Hundred Years,* by Professors Harrison Brown, James Bonner and John Weir of the California Institute of Technology. How is mankind coping with the problem of rapidly increasing numbers? Not very successfully. "The evidence suggests rather strongly that in most underdeveloped countries the lot of the average individual has worsened appreciably in the last half century. People have become more poorly fed. There are fewer available goods per person. And practically every attempt to improve the situation has been nullified by the relentless pressure of continued population growth."

Whenever the economic life of a nation becomes precarious, the central government is forced to assume additional responsibilities for the general welfare. It must work out elaborate plans for dealing with a critical situation; it must impose ever greater restrictions upon the activities of its subjects; and if, as is very likely, worsening economic conditions result in political unrest, or open rebellion, the central government must intervene to preserve public order and its own authority. More and more power is thus concentrated in the hands of the executives and their bureaucratic managers. But the nature of power is such that even those who have not sought it, but have had it forced upon them, tend to acquire a taste for more. "Lead us not into temptation," we pray—and with good reason; for when human beings are tempted too enticingly or too long, they generally yield. A democratic constitution is a device for preventing the local rulers from yielding to those particularly dangerous temptations that arise when too much power is concentrated in too few hands. Such a constitution works pretty well where, as in Britain or the United States, there is a traditional respect for constitutional procedures. Where the republican or limited monarchical tradition is weak, the best of constitutions will not prevent ambitious politicians from succumbing with glee and gusto to the temptations of power. And in any country where numbers have begun to press heavily upon available resources, these temptations cannot fail to arise. Over-population leads to economic insecurity and social unrest. Unrest and insecurity lead to more control by central governments and an increase of their power. In the absence of a constitutional tradition, this increased power will probably be exercised in a dictatorial fashion. Even if Communism had never been invented, this would be likely to happen. But Communism has been invented. Given this fact, the probability of over-population leading through unrest to dictatorship becomes a virtual certainty. It is a pretty safe bet that, twenty years from now, all the world's over-populated and underdeveloped countries will be under some form of totalitarian rule—probably by the Communist party.

How will this development affect the over-populated, but highly industrialized and still democratic countries of Europe? If the newly formed dictatorships were hostile to them, and if the normal flow of raw materials from the underdeveloped countries were deliberately interrupted, the nations of the West would find themselves in a very bad way indeed. Their industrial system would break down, and the highly developed technology, which up till now has permitted them to sustain a population much greater than that which could be supported by locally available resources, would no longer protect them against the consequences of having too many people in too small a territory. If this should happen, the enormous powers forced by unfavorable conditions upon central governments may come to be used in the spirit of totalitarian dictatorship.

The United States is not at present an over-populated country. If, however, the population continues to increase at the present rate (which is higher than that of India's increase, though happily a good deal lower than the rate now current in Mexico or Guatemala), the problem of numbers in relation to available resources might well become troublesome by the beginning of the twenty-first century. For the moment over-population is not a direct threat to the personal freedom of Americans. It remains, however, an indirect threat, a menace at one remove. If over-population should drive the underdeveloped countries into totalitarianism, and if these new dictatorships should ally themselves with Russia, then the military position of the United States would become less secure and the preparations for defense and retaliation would have to be intensified. But liberty, as we all know, cannot flourish in a country that is permanently on a war footing, or even a near-war footing. Permanent crisis justifies permanent control of everybody and everything by the agencies of the central government. And permanent crisis is what we have to expect in a world in which over-population is producing a state of things, in which dictatorship under Communist auspices becomes almost inevitable.

Robert Penn Warren

In a prefatory note to his book on segregation, Robert Penn Warren points out that it "does not pretend to represent a poll-taking or a mathematical cross-section of opinion" on that fiery subject. The writer's center of interest, then, is not so much the opinions he encounters on his tour of his native South as it is the psychological and moral attitudes he senses behind the opinions. His purpose requires the poet's imagination more than it does the journalist's perspicacity, and Warren—a distinguished poet, novelist, and literary critic—possesses the requirement. Although his study takes the form of a series of quasi-journalistic interviews, he uses his knowledge of both the South and himself to make of the interviews a mosaic of opinion and emotion that accurately reproduces the moral-psychological dilemma which he feels is at the root of the race problem.

To that dilemma Warren applies the term *self-division,* and he sees the defense of segregation in the South neither as blind malice nor as curable ignorance but rather as the product of desperately conflicting impulses within the human psyche. Warren's treatment of the problem differs from that of a great many writers in that it avoids oversimplification as rigorously as it avoids facile name calling. At the same time, the subtlety of Warren's perceptions does not lead him to the state of well-meaning paralysis in which many moderates find themselves; he has a moral position, and he knows what it is. He favors integration and the taking of legal steps to bring it about, but he demands of both himself and his readers a recognition of the kind of inner reform which alone can make a change fruitful as well as possible.

SEGREGATION

What's coming? "Whatever it is," the college student in the Deep South says, "I'd like to put all the Citizens Council and all the NAACP in one room and give every man a baseball bat and lock 'em in till it was over. Then maybe some sensible people could work out something."

What's coming? I say it to the country grade-school superintendent. He is a part-time farmer, too, and now he is really in his role as farmer, not teacher, as we stand, at night, under the naked light of a flyspecked

From *Segregation,* by Robert Penn Warren. © Copyright 1956 by Robert Penn Warren. Reprinted by permission of Random House, Inc.

200-watt bulb hanging from the shed roof, and he oversees two Negroes loading sacks of fertilizer on a truck. "I know folks round here," he says, and seeing his hard, aquiline, weathered face, with the flat, pale, hard eyes, I believe him.

"They aren't raised up to it," he says. "Back in the summer now, I went by a lady's house to ask about her children starting to school. Well, she was a real old-timey gal, a gant-headed, barefoot, snuff-dipping, bonnet-wearing, hard-ankled old gal standing out in the tobacco patch, leaning on her hoe, and she leaned at me and said, 'Done hear'd tell 'bout niggers gonna come in,' and before I could say anything, she said, 'Not with none of my young 'uns,' and let out a stream of ambeer."

"Would you hire a Negro teacher?" I asked.

"I personally would, but folks wouldn't stand for it, not now, mostly those who never went much to school themselves. Unless I could prove I couldn't get white." He paused. "And it's getting damned hard to get white, I tell you," he says.

I ask if integration will come.

"Sure," he says, "in fifty years. Every time the tobacco crop is reduced, we lose just that many white sharecroppers and Negroes. That eases the pain."

What's coming? And the Methodist minister, riding with me in the dusk, in the drizzle, by the flooded bayou, says: "It'll come, desegregation and the vote and all that. But it will be twenty-five, thirty years, a generation. You can preach love and justice, but it's a slow pull till you get the education." He waves a hand toward the drowned black cotton fields, stretching on forever, toward the rows of shacks marshaled off into the darkening distance, toward the far cypresses where dusk is tangled. "You can see," he says. "Just look, you can see."

What's coming? I ask the young lawyer in a mid-South city, a lawyer retained by one of the segregation outfits. "It's coming that we got to fight this bogus law," he says, "or we'll have a lot of social dis-tensions. The bogus law is based on social stuff and progress and just creates dis-tension. But we're gaining ground. Some upper-class people, I mean a real rich man, is coming out for us. And we get rolling, a Southern President could repack the court. But it's got so a man can't respect the Supreme Court. All this share-the-wealth and Communist stuff and progress. You can't depend on law any more."

What can you depend on? I ask.

"Nothing but the people. Like the Civil War."

I suggest that whatever the constitutional rights and wrongs of the Civil War were, we had got a new Constitution out of it.

"No," he said, "just a different type of dog saying what it is."

I ask if, in the end, the appeal would be to violence.

"No, I don't believe in violence. I told Mr. Perkins, when we had our mass meeting, to keep the in-ci-dents down. But you get a lot of folks and there's always going to be in-ci-dents."

I ask if at Tuscaloosa the mob hadn't dictated public policy.

"Not dictate exactly." And he smiles his handsome smile. "But it was a lot of people."

He has used the word *progress*, over and over, to damn what he does not like. It is peculiar how he uses this laudatory word—I can imagine how he would say it in other contexts, on public occasions, rolling it on his tongue—as the word now for what he hates most. I wonder how deep a cleavage the use of that word indicates.

What's coming? I ask the handsome, aristocratic, big gray-haired man, sitting in his rich office, high over the city, an ornament of the vestry, of boards of directors, of club committees, a man of exquisite simplicity and charm, and a member of a segregation group.

"We shall exhaust all the legal possibilities," he says.

I ask if he thinks his side will win. The legal fight, that is.

He rolls a cigarette fastidiously between strong, white, waxy forefinger and thumb. "No," he says. "But it is just something you have to do." He rolls the cigarette, looking out the window over the city, a city getting rich now, "filthy rich," as somebody has said to me. There is the undertone and unceasing susurrus of traffic in the silence of his thoughts.

"Well," he says at last, "to speak truth, I think the whole jig is up. We'll have desegregation right down the line. And you know why?"

I shake my head.

"Well, I'll tell you. You see those girls in my office outside, those young men. Come from good lower-middle-class homes, went to college a lot of them. Well, a girl comes in here and says to me a gentleman is waiting. She shows him in. He is as black as the ace of spades. It just never crossed that girl's mind, what she was saying, when she said a gentleman was waiting." He pauses. "Yes, sir," he says, "I just don't know why I'm doing it."

I am thinking of walking down Canal Street, in New Orleans, and a man is saying to me: "Do you know how many millions a year the Negroes spend up and down this street?"

No, I had said, I didn't know.

He tells me the figure, then says: "You get the logic of that, don't you?"

What's coming? And the college student says: "I'll tell you one thing that's coming, there's not going to be any academic freedom or any other kind around here if we don't watch out. Now I'm a segregationist, that is, the way things are here right now, but I don't want anybody saying I can't listen to somebody talk about something. I can make up my own mind."

What's coming? And a state official says: "Integration sure and slow. A creeping process. If the NAACP has got bat sense, not deliberately provoking things as in the University of Alabama deal. They could have got that girl in quiet and easy, but that wouldn't satisfy them. No, they wanted the bang. As for things in general, grade schools and high schools, it'll be the creeping process. The soft places first, and then one county will play football or basketball with Negroes on the team. You know how it'll be. A creeping process. There'll be lots of court actions, but don't let court actions fool you. I bet you half the superintendents over in Tennessee will secretly welcome a court action in their county. Half of 'em are worried morally and half financially, and a court action just gets 'em off the hook. They didn't initiate it, they can always claim, but it gets them off the hook. That's the way I would feel, I know."

What's coming? I ask the taxi driver in Memphis. And he says: "Lots of dead niggers round here, that's what's coming. Look at Detroit, lots of dead niggers been in the Detroit River, but it won't be a patch on the Ole Mississippi. But hell, it won't stop nothing. Fifty years from now everybody will be gray anyway, Jews and Germans and French and Chinese and niggers, and who'll give a durn?"

The cab has drawn to my destination. I step out into the rain and darkness. "Don't get yourself drownded now," he says. "You have a good time now. I hope you do."

What's coming? And a man in Arkansas says: "We'll ride it out. But it looked like bad trouble one time. Too many outsiders. Mississippians and all. They come back here again, somebody's butt will be busted."

And another man: "Sure, they aim for violence, coming in here. When a man gets up before a crowd and plays what purports to be a recording of an NAACP official, an inflammatory sex thing, and then boasts of having been in on a lynching himself, what do you call it? Well, they got him on the witness stand, under oath, and he had to admit he got the record from Patterson, of the Citizens Council, and admitted under oath the lynching statement. He also admitted under oath some other interesting facts—that he had once been indicted for criminal libel but pleaded guilty to simple libel, that he has done sixty days for contempt of court on charges of violating an injunction having to do with liquor. Yeah, he used to run a paper called *The Rub Down*—that's what got him into the libel business. What's going to happen if a guy like that runs things? I ask you."

What's coming? And the planter leans back with the glass in his hand. "I'm not going to get lathered up," he says, "because it's no use. Why is the country so lathered up to force the issue one way or the other? Democracy—democracy has just come to be a name for what you like. It has lost responsibility, no local integrity left, it has been bought off.

We've got the power state coming on, and communism or socialism, what-ever you choose to call it. Race amalgamation is inevitable. I can't say I like any of it. I am out of step with the times."

What's coming? I ask the Episcopal rector, in the Deep South, a large handsome man, almost the twin of my friend sitting in the fine office overlooking the rich city. He has just told me that when he first came down from the North, a generation back, his bishop had explained it all to him, how the Negroes' skull capacity was limited. But as he has said, brain power isn't everything, there's justice, and not a member of his congregation wasn't for conviction in the Till case.

"But the Negro has to be improved before integration," he says. "Take their morals, we are gradually improving the standard of morality and decency."

The conversation veers, we take a longer view. "Well, anthropo-logically speaking," he says, "the solution will be absorption, the Negro will disappear."

I ask how this is happening.

"Low-class people, immoral people, libertines, wastrels, prostitutes and such," he says.

I ask if, in that case, the raising of the moral level of the Negro does not prevent, or delay, what he says is the solution.

The conversation goes into a blur.

What's coming? And the young man from Mississippi says: "Even without integration, even with separate but pretty good facilities for the Negro, the Negro would be improving himself. He would be making himself more intellectually and socially acceptable. Therefore, as segre-gationists, if we're logical, we ought to deny any good facilities to them. Now I'm a segregationist, but I can't be that logical."

What's coming? And the officer of the Citizens Council chapter says: "Desegregation, integration, amalgamation—none of it will come here. To say it will come is defeatism. It won't come if we stand firm."

And the old man in north Tennessee, a burly, full-blooded, red-faced, raucous old man, says: "Hell, son, it's easy to solve. Just blend 'em. Fif-teen years and they'll all be blended in. And by God, I'm doing my part!"

———————•———————

Out of Memphis, I lean back in my seat on the plane, and watch the darkness slide by. I know what the Southerner feels going out of the South, the relief, the expanding vistas. Now, to the sound of the powerful, mag-nanimous engines bearing me through the night, I think of that, thinking of the new libel laws in Misssssissippi, of the academic pressures, of academic resignations, of the Negro facing the shotgun blast, of the white man with a nice little, hard-built business being boycotted, of the college boy who said: "I'll just tell you, everybody is *scairt*."

I feel the surge of relief. But I know what the relief really is. It is the relief from responsibility.

Now you may eat the bread of the Pharisee and read in the morning paper, with only a trace of irony, how out of an ultimate misery of rejection some Puerto Rican school boys—or is it Jews or Negroes or Italians?—who call themselves something grand, The Red Eagles or the Silver Avengers, have stabbed another boy to death, or raped a girl, or trampled an old man into a bloody mire. If you can afford it, you will, according to the local mores, send your child to a private school, where there will be, of course, a couple of Negro children on exhibit. And that delightful little Chinese girl who is so good at dramatics. Or is it finger painting?

Yes, you know what the relief is. It is the flight from the reality you were born to.

———————•———————

But what is that reality you have fled from?

It is the fact of self-division. I do not mean division between man and man in society. That division is, of course, there, and it is important. Take, for example, the killing of Clinton Melton, in Glendora, Mississippi, in the Delta, by a man named Elmer Kimbell, a close friend of Milam (who had been acquitted of the murder of Till, whose car was being used by Kimbell at the time of the killing of Melton, and to whose house Kimbell returned after the deed).

Two days after the event, twenty-one men—storekeepers, planters, railroad men, school teachers, preacher, bookkeepers—sent money to the widow for funeral expenses, with the note: "Knowing that he was outstanding in his race, we the people of this town are deeply hurt and donate as follows." When the Lions Club met three days after the event, a resolution was drawn and signed by all members present: "We consider the taking of the life of Clinton Melton an outrage against him, against all the people of Glendora, against the people of Mississippi as well as against the entire human family. . . . We humbly confess in repentance for having so lived as a community that such an evil occurrence could happen here, and we offer ourselves to be used in bringing to pass a better realization of the justice, righteousness and peace which is the will of God for human society."

And the town began to raise a fund to realize the ambition of the dead man, to send his children to college, the doctor of Glendora offered employment in his clinic to the widow, and the owner of the plantation where she had been raised offered to build for her and her children a three-room house.

But, in that division between man and man, the jury that tried Elmer Kimbell acquitted him.

But, in that same division between man and man, when the newspaper of Clarksdale, Mississippi, in the heart of the Delta, ran a front-page story of the acquittal, that story was bracketed with a front-page editorial saying that there had been some extenuation for acquittal in the Till case, with confusion of evidence and outside pressures, but that in the Melton case there had been no pressure and "we were alone with ourselves and we flunked it."

Such division between man and man is important. As one editor in Tennessee said to me: "There's a fifth column of decency here, and it will, in the end, betray the extremists, when the politicians get through." But such a division between man and man is not as important in the long run as the division within the individual man.

Within the individual there are, or may be, many lines of fracture. It may be between his own social idealism and his anger at Yankee Phariseeism. (Oh, yes, he remembers that in the days when Federal bayonets supported the black Reconstruction state governments in the South, not a single Negro held elective office in any Northern state.) It may be between his social views and his fear of the power state. It may be between his social views and his clan sense. It may be between his allegiance to organized labor and his racism—for status or blood purity. It may be between his Christianity and his social prejudice. It may be between his sense of democracy and his ingrained attitudes toward the Negro. It may be between his own local views and his concern for the figure America cuts in the international picture. It may be between his practical concern at the money loss to society caused by the Negro's depressed condition and his own personal gain or personal prejudice. It may be, and disastrously, between his sense of the inevitable and his emotional need to act against the inevitable.

There are almost an infinite number of permutations and combinations, but they all amount to the same thing, a deep intellectual rub, a moral rub, anger at the irremediable self-division, a deep exacerbation at some failure to find identity. That is the reality.

It expresses itself in many ways. I sit for an afternoon with an old friend, a big, weather-faced, squarish man, a farmer, an intelligent man, a man of good education, of travel and experience, and I ask him questions. I ask if he thinks we can afford, in the present world picture, to alienate Asia by segregation here at home. He hates the question. "I hate to think about it," he says. "It's too deep for me," he says, and moves heavily in his chair. We talk about Christianity—he is a church-going man—and he says: "Oh, I know what the Bible says, and Christianity, but I just can't think about it. My mind just shuts up."

My old friend is an honest man. He will face his own discomfort. He will not try to ease it by passing libel laws to stop discussion or by firing professors.

There are other people whose eyes brighten at the thought of the new unity in the South, the new solidarity of resistance. These men are idealists, and they dream of preserving the traditional American values of individualism and localism against the anonymity, irresponsibility and materialism of the power state, against the philosophy of the ad-man, the morality of the Kinsey report, and the gospel of the bitch-goddess. *To be Southern again:* to recreate a habitation for the values they would preserve, to achieve in unity some clarity of spirit, to envisage some healed image of their own identity.

Some of these men are segregationists. Some are desegregationists, but these, in opposing what they take to be the power-state implications of the Court decision, find themselves caught, too, in the defense of segregation. And defending segregation, both groups are caught in a paradox: in seeking to preserve individualism by taking refuge in the vision of a South redeemed in unity and antique virtue, they are fleeing from the burden of their own individuality—the intellectual rub, the moral rub. To state the matter in another way, by using the argument of *mere* social continuity and the justification by mere *mores,* they think of a world in which circumstances and values are frozen; but the essence of individuality is the willingness to accept the rub which the flux of things provokes, to accept one's fate in time. What heroes would these idealists enshrine to take the place of Jefferson and Lee, those heroes who took the risk of their fate?

Even among these people some are in discomfort, discomfort because the new unity, the new solidarity, once it descends from the bright world of Idea, means unity with some quite concrete persons and specific actions. They say: "Yes—yes, we've got to unify." And then: "But we've got to purge certain elements."

But who will purge whom? And what part of yourself will purge another part?

"Yes, it's our own fault," the rich businessman, active in segregation, says. "If we'd ever managed to bring ourselves to do what we ought to have done for the Negro, it would be different now, if we'd managed to educate them, get them decent housing, decent jobs."

So I tell him what a Southern Negro professor had said to me. He had said that the future now would be different, would be hopeful, if there could just be "one gesture of graciousness" from the white man—

even if the white man didn't like the Supreme Court decision, he might try to understand the Negro's view, not heap insult on him.

And the segregationist, who is a gracious man, seizes on the word. "Graciousness," he says, "that's it, if we could just have managed some graciousness to the race. Sure, some of us, a lot of us, could manage some graciousness to individual Negroes, some of us were grateful to individuals for being gracious to us. But you know, we couldn't manage it for the race." He thinks a moment, then says: "There's a Negro woman buried in the family burial place. We loved her."

I believe him when he says it. And he sinks into silence, feeling the rub, for the moment anyway, between the man who can talk in terms of graciousness, in whatever terms that notion may present itself to him, and the man who is a power for segregation.

This is the same man who has said to me, earlier, that he knows integration to be inevitable, doesn't know why he is fighting it. But such a man is happier, perhaps, than those men, destined by birth and personal qualities to action and leadership, who in the face of what they take to be inevitable feel cut off from all action. "I am out of step with the times," one such man says to me, and his wife says, "You know, if we feel the way we do, we ought to do something about it," and he, in some deep, inward, unproclaimed bitterness, says, "No, I'm not going to get lathered up about anything."

Yes, there are many kinds of rub, but I suppose that the commonest one is the moral one—the Christian one, in fact, for the South is still a land of faith. There is, of course, the old joke that after the Saturday night lynching, the congregation generally turns up a little late for church, and the sardonic remark a man made to me about the pro-integration resolution of the Southern Baptist Convention: "They were just a little bit exalted. When they got back with the home folks a lot of 'em wondered how they did it."

But meanwhile, there are the pastors at Glendora and Hoxie and Oxford and other nameless places. And I remember a pastor, in Tennessee, a Southerner born and bred, saying to me: "Yes, I think the Court decision may have set back race equality—it was coming fast, faster than anybody could guess, because so quiet. But now some people get so put out with the idea of Negroes in church, they stop me on the street and say if I ever let one in they won't come to church. So I ask about Heaven, what will they do in Heaven?

" 'Well,' one woman said, 'I'll just let God segregate us.'

" 'You'll *let* God segregate you?' I said, and she flounced off. But I ask, where is Christianity if people can't worship together? There's only one thing to try to preach, and that is Christ. And there's only one question to ask, and that is what would Christ do?"

Will they go with him, I ask.

"They are good Christian people, most of them," he says. "It may be slow, but they are Christians."

And in a town in south Kentucky, in a "black county," a Confederate county, where desegregation is now imminent in the high schools, the superintendent says to me: "The people here are good Christian people, trying to do right. When this thing first came up, the whole board said they'd walk out. But the ministers got to preaching, and the lawyers to talking on it, and they came around."

I asked how many were influenced by moral, how many by legal, considerations.

About half and half, he reckons, then adds: "I'm a Rebel myself, and I don't deny it, but I'm an American and a law-abiding citizen. A man can hate an idea but know it's right, and it takes a lot of thinking and praying to bring yourself around. You just have to uncover the unrecognized sympathy in the white man for the Negro humiliation."

Fifty miles away I shall sit in a living room and hear some tale of a Negro coming to somebody's front door—another house—and being admitted by a Negro servant and being found by the master of the house, who says: "I don't care if Susie did let you in. I don't care if Jesus Christ let you in. No black son-of-a-bitch is coming to my front door."

After the tale, there is silence. All present are segregationist, or I think they are.

Then one woman says: "Maybe he did take a lot on himself, coming to the front door. But I can't stand it. He's human."

And another woman: "I think it's a moral question, and I suffer, but I can't feel the same way about a Negro as a white person. It's born in me. But I pray I'll change."

The successful businessman in Louisiana says to me: "I have felt the moral question. It will be more moral when we get rid of segregation. But I'm human enough—I guess it's human to be split up—to want things just postponed till my children are out of school. But I can't lift my finger to delay things."

But this man, privately admitting his division of feeling, having no intention of public action on either side, is the sort of man who can be trapped, accidentally, into action.

There is the man who got the letter in the morning mail, asking him to serve as chairman of a citizens committee to study plans for desegregation in his county. "I was sick," he says, "and I mean literally sick. I felt sick all day. I didn't see how I could get into something like that. But next morning, you know, I did it."

That county now has its schedule for desegregation.

There is another man, a lawyer, who has been deeply involved in a desegregation action. "I never had much feeling of prejudice, but hell, I didn't have any theories either, and I now and then paid some lip service to segregation. I didn't want to get mixed up in the business. But one night a telephone call came. I told the man I'd let him know next day. You know, I was sick. I walked on back in the living room and my wife looked at me. She must have guessed what it was. 'You going to do it?' she asked me. I said, hell, I didn't know, and went out. I was plain sick. But next day I did it. Well," he says, and grins, and leans back under the shelves of law books, "and I'm stuck with it. But you know, I'm getting damned tired of the paranoiacs and illiterates I'm up against."

Another man, with a small business in a poor county, "back in the shelf country," he calls it, a short, strong-looking, ovoidal kind of man with his belt cutting into his belly when he leans back in his office chair. He is telling me what he has been through. "I wouldn't tell you a lie," he says. "I'm Southern through and through, and I guess I got every prejudice a man can have, and I certainly never would have got mixed up in this business if it hadn't been for the Court decision. I wouldn't be out in front. I was just trying to do my duty. Trying to save some money for the county. I never expected any trouble. And we might not have had any if it hadn't been for outsiders, one kind and another.

"But what nobody understands is how a man can get cut up inside. You try to live like a Christian with your fellow man, and suddenly you find out it is all mixed up. You put in twenty-five years trying to build up a nice little business and raise up a family and it looks like it will all be ruined. You get word somebody will dynamite your house and you in it. You go to lawyers and they say they sympathize, but nobody'll take your case. But the worst is, things just go round and round in your head. Then they won't come a-tall, and you lay there in the night. You might say, it's the psychology of it you can't stand. Getting all split up. Then, all of a sudden, somebody stops you on the street and calls you something, a so-and-so nigger-lover. And you know, I got so mad not a thing mattered any more. I just felt like I was all put back together again."

He said he wished he could write it down, how awful it is for a man to be split up.

———————•———————

Negroes, they must be split up, too, I think. They are human, too. There must be many ways for them to be split up. I remember asking a Negro school teacher if she thought Negro resentment would be a bar to integration. "Some of us try to teach love," she says, "as well as we can. But some of us teach hate. I guess we can't help it."

Love and hate, but more than that, the necessity of confronting your own motives: *Do we really want to try to work out a way to live with the white people or do we just want to show them, pay off something, show them up, rub their noses in it?*

And I can imagine the grinding anger, the sense of outrage of a Negro crying out within himself: *After all the patience, after all the humility, after learning and living those virtues, do I have to learn magnanimity, too?*

Yes, I can imagine the outrage, the outrage as some deep, inner self tells him, yes, he must.

I am glad that white people have no problem as hard as that.

John Kenneth Galbraith

An inherent difficulty in writing on specialized, technical subject matter for the general reader is how to remain faithful to the subject itself and still make it intelligible. Oversimplification results in distortion and inaccuracies and in offending intelligent readers, who do not like to be "talked down to." To make no concessions to the occasion, however, to use technical language when it is not necessary or without indicating its meaning, to swamp the reader in technical detail—in this instance the complicated one of economics—and to ignore the ever-constant need to write clearly and interestingly is equally ineffective and annoying. The following selection is, among other things, a good example of how to strike a happy balance between the just demands of the subject matter—in this instance the complicated one of economics—and of the reader. The considerable reading public enjoyed by its author, the Canadian-born Harvard economist who also served as United States Ambassador to India from 1960-1963, is perhaps in some measure attributable to his ability to strike this balance.

In "Inequality," a chapter from *The Affluent Society,* Galbraith addresses himself to the history of the idea of achieving greater equality through a redistribution of wealth. He refers us to various important, and often conflicting, theories of economics and to actual social and economic conditions that have characterized organized society, using both as a basis for a fairly sharp, if oblique, critique of the "conventional wisdom" that shapes contemporary thinking on economic and social problems. Although he eschews complicated tables and all graphs, favored tools of the economist, he does make judicious use of statistics to further his argument, particularly in his attack upon the tax structure. (It is obvious that statistics may be nothing more than a manipulative device designed to "prove" anything to a gullible public—*e.g.,* as they are frequently used in poll-taking, advertisements. But it is equally obvious that, responsibly and honestly used, as here, statistics are indispensable to certain sorts of analyses). Galbraith also employs a variety of ironic devices, chief among them cleverly juxtaposed quotations. There is, in fact, along with an impressive marshalling of facts, a vigorous presentation of Galbraith's own judgments and opinions as such. Clearly he does not ascribe to that curious notion that in order to be objective a social scientist must obliterate his own personality. One senses here, and is meant to, Galbraith's characteristic attitudes not only towards general problems but even towards specific figures. One knows frankly where he stands. Some of the references to the rich, for example, or the comments on diamonds or the English aristocracy, have a tone of epic nastiness that is almost worthy of Thorstein Veblen. And, like Veblen, Galbraith has the steady habit of looking through conventional explanations and seeing behind them the discomforting realities that they are meant to obscure.

*I*NEQUALITY

Few things have been more productive of controversy over the ages than the suggestion that the rich should, by one device or another, share their wealth with those who are not. With comparatively rare and usually eccentric exceptions, the rich have been opposed. The grounds have been many and varied and have been principally noted for the rigorous exclusion of the most important reason, which is the simple unwillingness to give up the enjoyment of what they have. The poor have generally been in favor of greater equality.

As the last chapters have shown, the economic and social preoccupation with inequality is deeply grounded. In the competitive society—the society of the central tradition of economics in descent from Ricardo—there was presumed to be a premium on efficiency. The competent entrepreneur and worker were automatically rewarded. The rest, as automatically, were punished for their incompetence or sloth. If labor and capital and land were employed with high efficiency then, *pro tanto*, nothing more, or not much more, could be got out of the economy in the short run by way of product. And longer run progress did not necessarily benefit the average man; in the original doctrine its fruits accrued to others.

So if people were poor, as in fact they were, their only hope lay in a redistribution of income, and especially that which was the product of accumulated wealth. Much though Ricardo and his followers might dissent, there were always some—and the number steadily grew—who believed that redistribution might be possible. (Ricardo and those who followed him in the central tradition were never immune from the suspicion that they were pleading a special interest.) All Marxists took a drastic redistribution for granted. Consequently, throughout the nineteenth century the social radical had no choice but to advocate the redistribution of

From *The Affluent Society* by John Kenneth Galbraith (Boston, Houghton Mifflin Company, 1958), pp. 78-97. Reprinted by permission of the publisher.

wealth and income by one device or another. If he wanted to change things this was his only course. To avoid this issue was to avoid all issues.

The conservative defense of inequality has varied. There has always been the underlying contention that, as a matter of natural law and equity, what a man has received save by overt larceny is rightfully his. For Ricardo and his immediate followers the luxurious income of landlords and of capitalists was the inevitable arrangement of things. One could tamper with it but only at the eventual price of disrupting the system and making the lot of everyone (including the poor) much worse.

This was essentially the passive defense. With time (and agitation) the case for inequality became a good deal more functional. The undisturbed enjoyment of income was held to be essential as an incentive. The resulting effort and ingenuity would bring greater production and greater resulting rewards for all. Inequality came to be regarded as almost equally important for capital formation. Were income widely distributed, it would be spent. But if it flowed in a concentrated stream to the rich, a part would certainly be saved and invested.

There were other arguments. Excessive equality makes for cultural uniformity and monotony. Rich men are essential if there is to be an adequate subsidy to education and the arts. Equality smacks of communism and hence of atheism and therefore is spiritually suspect. In any case, even the Russians have abandoned egalitarianism as unworkable. Finally, it is argued that by means of the income tax we have achieved virtual or (depending on the speaker) entirely excessive equality. The trend for the future must be toward restoring an adequate measure of inequality by well-conceived tax reductions affecting the upper surtax brackets.

The cultural misfortunes from excessive equality cannot be pressed too far. As Tawney observed: "Those who dread a dead-level of income or wealth ... do not dread, it seems, a dead-level of law and order, and of security of life and property. They do not complain that persons endowed by nature with unusual qualities of strength, audacity, or cunning are prevented from reaping the full fruits of these powers."[1] And in fact in the conventional wisdom the defense of inequality does rest primarily on its functional role as an incentive and as a source of capital.

Thus the egalitarianism of the present tax structure is thought to be seriously dampening individual effort, initiative, and inspiration or is in danger of doing so. It "destroys ambition, penalizes success, discourages investment to create new jobs, and may well turn a nation of risk-taking entrepreneurs into a nation of softies...."[2] "It destroys the incentive of

---

[1] R. H. Tawney, *Equality* (4th ed.; London: Allen & Unwin, 1952), p. 85.

[2] "Taxes and America's Future." Address by Fred Maytag II, before National Association of Manufacturers, December 1, 1954.

people to work. . . . It makes it increasingly difficult, if not impossible, for people to save. . . . It has a deadening effect on the spirit of enterprise . . . which has made America."[3]

However, this case is not an impeccable one. Income taxes have been at present levels for approaching two decades. These in general have been years of rapid economic growth. Those who view the taxes with most concern point to this progress with most pride. Nor would many businessmen wish to concede that they are putting forth less than their best efforts because of insufficient pecuniary incentive. The typical business executive makes his way to the top by promotion over the heads of his fellows. He would endanger his chance for advancement if he were suspected of goldbricking because of his resentment over his taxes or for any other reason. He is expected to give his best to his corporation, and usually he does.

To give individuals large incomes to encourage savings also has elements of illogic. The rich man saves because he is able to satisfy all his wants and then have something over. Such saving, in other words, is the residual after luxurious consumption. This obviously is not an especially efficient way to promote capital formation. Moreover, the empirical evidence on the effect of egalitarianism on capital formation is uncertain. England is often cited as an unfortunate example. But Norway, an even more egalitarian country, has had since the war one of the highest rates of capital formation and of economic growth of any country in the noncommunist world.[4] Middle eastern countries where inequality is greatest are among those with the lowest rate of capital formation. All or most gets spent.

The *formal* liberal attitude toward inequality has changed little over the years. The liberal has partly accepted the view of the well-to-do that it is a trifle uncouth to urge a policy of soaking the rich. Yet on the whole the rich man remains the natural antagonist of the poor. Economic legislation, above all tax policy, continues to be a contest between the interests of the two. No other question in economic policy is ever so important as the effect of a measure on the distribution of income. The test of the good liberal is still that he is never fooled and that he never yields on issues favoring the wealthy. Other questions occupy his active attention, but this is the constant. Behind him, always challenging him, is the cynical Marxian whisper hinting that whatever he does may not be enough. Despite his efforts, capitalist concentration will keep on, and the

[3] "The Relation of Taxes to Economic Growth." Address by Ernest L. Swigert, before National Association of Manufacturers, December 6, 1956.

[4] Alice Bourneuf, *Norway: The Planned Revival* (Cambridge, Mass.: Harvard University Press, 1958).

wealthy will become wealthier and more powerful. They lose battles but win wars.

. . . . II

However, few things are more evident in modern social history than the decline of interest in inequality as an economic issue. This has been particularly true in the United States. And it would appear, among western countries, to be the least true of the United Kingdom. While it continues to have a large ritualistic role in the conventional wisdom of conservatives and liberals, inequality has ceased to preoccupy men's minds. And even the conventional wisdom has made some concessions to this new state of affairs.

On the fact itself—that inequality is of declining concern—it is only necessary to observe that for some fifteen years no serious effort has been made to alter the present distribution of income. Although in the semantics of American liberalism there is often a tactful silence on the point, since nothing so stirs conservative wrath, the principal public device for redistributing income is the progressive income tax. Not since World War II has there been a major effort to modify this tax in the interest of greater equality. Loopholes have been opened and a few closed. Liberals have not, however, proposed any important new steps to make the tax more progressive and hence more egalitarian. And conservatives, while they have won numerous secondary victories, have not been able to mount any major attack on the tax itself. On the contrary, although roughly the present nominal surtax rates were put into effect during the war, with the presumption that they were a temporary measure for insuring equality of wartime sacrifice, they are now regarded by many and perhaps by most people as permanent.

As part of the present compromise, liberals do not seek to make current taxes more progressive or even passionately to eliminate existing inequities and loopholes in their application. They would, however, rally in opposition to any general reduction in rates on the higher income brackets. Those who believe the tax has gone too far in enforcing equality are more vocal. Appeals for public sympathy and support, and clarion calls for courage and action, come regularly from the well-to-do. "The hour is late, but not too late. There is no excuse for our hesitating any longer. With all the strength of equity and logic on our side, and with the urgent need for taking the tax shackles off economic progress, initiative is ours if we have the courage to take it."[5] But not even a con-

5 Maytag, "Taxes and America's Future."

servative administration such as that of President Eisenhower thought it wise to tackle the question of surtax reduction on a wide front.

Apart from the income tax almost no legislation has been enacted or even discussed in recent years which has as its main point the reduction of inequality. Fifty years ago, at the height of the debate over socialism and capitalism, it would have been hard to imagine there was any other issue.

The decline in concern for inequality cannot be explained by the triumph of equality. Although this is regularly suggested in the conventional wisdom of conservatives, and could readily be inferred from the complaints of businessmen, inequality is still great. In 1955 the one-tenth of families and unattached individuals with the lowest incomes received after taxes about one per cent of the total money income of the country; the tenth with the highest incomes received 27 per cent of the total, which is to say their incomes averaged 27 times as much as the lowest tenth. The half of the households with the lowest incomes received, after taxes, only 23 per cent of all money income. The half with the highest incomes received 77 per cent. In 1954 only about three per cent of all families had incomes before taxes of more than $15,000. They received, nonetheless, 15.5 per cent of total income. At the other extreme, 16.7 per cent had before tax incomes of less than two thousand and received only 3.6 per cent of the income.[6] Vast fortunes are still being made out of natural resources and especially out of oil—where the famous depletion allowance of $27\frac{1}{2}$ per cent effectively frees that proportion of oil income, and sometimes much more, from all taxation. Present laws are also notably favorable to the person who has wealth as opposed to the individual who is only earning it. With a little ingenuity, the man who is already rich can ordinarily take his income in the form of capital gains and limit his tax liability to 25 per cent of his income. In addition, unlike the man who must earn, he is under no compulsion to acquire a capital stake, either for old age, family, or the mere satisfaction it brings, since he already has one. Accordingly he need not save. Yet none of these matters arouses the kind of concern which leads to agitation and action.

. . . . **III**

The first reason inequality has faded as an issue is, without much question, that it has not been showing the expected tendency to get worse. And thus the Marxian prediction, which earlier in this century seemed

6 U. S. Department of Commerce. *Statistical Abstract of the United States*, 1957, p. 309. The after-tax percentage distributions are from *Board of Governors of the Federal Reserve System* and are based on the surveys of consumer finances. The before-tax data are estimates by the Department of Commerce.

so amply confirmed by observation, no longer inspires the same depth of fear. It no longer seems likely that the ownership of the tangible assets of the republic and the disposal of its income will pass into a negligible number of hands despite the approving sentiment of those who would abandon the progressive income tax or widen its present loopholes. Meanwhile, there has been a modest reduction in the proportion of disposable income going to those in the very highest income brackets and a very large increase in the proportion accruing to people in the middle and lower brackets. While taxes have restrained the concentration of income at the top, full employment and upward pressure on wages have increased well-being at the bottom. In 1928 disposable income, i.e., income after taxes, of the 1 per cent of the individuals with the highest income was estimated to account for 19 per cent of all income. By 1946 it accounted for a little less than 8 per cent. In 1928 the 5 per cent with the highest incomes received over a third of all income; by 1946 their share was about eighteen per cent.[7] The war and postwar years, especially, were a time of rapid improvement for those in the lower bracket. Between 1941 and 1950 the lowest fifth had a 42 per cent increase in income; the second lowest fifth had an increase of 37 per cent. The detailed figures for these years are as follows:

AVERAGE FAMILY INCOME AFTER INCOME TAXES
(In dollars of 1950 purchasing power)[8]

	1941	1950	Per cent change 1941–1950
Lowest fifth of all families	$ 750	$ 1,060	+42
Second lowest	1,730	2,360	+37
Third lowest	2,790	3,440	+24
Second highest	4,030	4,690	+16
Highest	8,190	8,880	+ 8
Highest five per cent	15,040	14,740	− 2

Emulation or, when this is frustrated, envy have long played a large role in the economist's view of human motivation.[9] So long as one individual had more than another, the second was presumed to be dissatisfied with his lot. He strove to come abreast of his more favored contemporary; he was deeply discontented if he failed. It may be, however, that these disenchanting traits are less cosmic than has commonly been supposed. Envy almost certainly operates efficiently only as regards nearby neigh-

[7] The data are from National Bureau of Economic Research. Note that these figures are not for households but for individuals.

[8] From Selma Goldsmith, George Jaszi, Hyman Kaitz, and Maurice Liebenberg, "Size Distribution of Incomes since the Mid-thirties." *Review of Economics and Statistics,* vol. XXXVI (February 1954).

[9] Chapter XI.

bors. It is not directed toward the distant rich. Hence, at a time when the individual's real income is rising, the fact that unknown New Yorkers or Texans are exceedingly wealthy is not, probably, a matter of prime urgency. It becomes easy, or at least convenient, to accept the case of the conventional wisdom which is that the rich in America are highly functional and also much persecuted members of the society. Moreover, as noted, to comment on the wealth of the wealthy, and certainly to propose that it be reduced, has come to be considered bad taste. The individual whose own income is going up has no real reason to incur the opprobrium of this discussion. Why should he identify himself, even remotely, with soapbox orators, malcontents, agitators, Communists, and other undesirables?

Things would be different were the incomes of the well-to-do rising and those of the rest of the people stationary or falling. This has been well illustrated by the reactions of the farmers who, though in many cases not badly off by past standards, during the middle fifties suffered a reduction of their income at a time when the incomes of nearly all other groups were rising. They were not reconciled either to their fate or to a Secretary of Agriculture who sought its acceptance.

. . . . **IV**

Another reason for the decline in interest in inequality, almost certainly, is the drastically altered political and social position of the rich in recent times. Broadly speaking, there are three basic benefits from wealth. First is the satisfaction in the power with which it endows the individual. Second is the physical possession of the things which money can buy. Third is the distinction or esteem that accrues to the rich man as the result of his wealth. All of these returns to wealth have been greatly circumscribed in the last fifty years and in a manner which also vastly reduces the envy or resentment of the well-to-do or even the knowledge of their existence.

As recently as a half century ago the power of the great business firm was paramount in the United States and so, accordingly, was the power of the individual who headed it. Men like Morgan, the Rockefeller executives, Hill, Harriman, and Hearst had great power in the meaningful sense of the term, which is that they were able to direct the actions and command the obedience of countless other individuals.

In the last half century the power and prestige of the United States government have increased. If only by the process of division, this has diminished the prestige of the power accruing to private wealth. But, in addition, it has also meant some surrender of authority to Washington. Furthermore, trade unions have invaded the power of the entrepreneur from another quarter. But most important, the professional manager or executive has taken away from the man of wealth the power that is implicit in running a business. Fifty years ago Morgan, Rockefeller, Hill, Harriman, and the others were the undisputed masters of the business concerns they owned, or it was indisputably in their power to become so. Their sons and grandsons still have the wealth, but with rare exceptions the power implicit in the running of the firm has passed to professionals. Nor has any equivalent new generation of owning entrepreneurs come along.

When the rich were not only rich but had the power that went with active direction of corporate enterprise, it is obvious that wealth had more perquisites than now. For the same reasons it stirred more antagonism. J. P. Morgan answered not only for his personal wealth but also for the behavior of the United States Steel Corporation which he had put together and which he ultimately controlled. As a man of corporate power he was also exceedingly visible. Today shares of the United States Steel Corporation are still the foundation of several notable fortunes. But no sins of the Corporation are visited on these individuals, for they do not manage the company and almost no one knows who they are. When the power that went with active business direction was lost, so was the hostility.

The power that was once joined with wealth has been impaired in a more intimate way. In 1194 the crusading knight, Henry of Champagne, paid a visit to the headquarters of the Assassins at the castle at al-Kahf on a rugged peak in the Nosairi Mountains. The Assassins, though a fanatical Moslem sect, had, in general, been on good terms with the Christians, to whom they often rendered, by arrangement, the useful service of resolving disputes by eliminating one of the disputants. Henry was sumptuously received. In one of the more impressive entertainments a succession of the loyal members of the cult, at a word from the Sheik, expertly immolated themselves. Before and ever since, the willing obedience of a household coterie has been a source of similar satisfaction to those able to command it. Wealth has been the most prominent device by which it has been obtained. As may indeed have been the case at al-Kahf, it has not always endeared the master to the men who rendered it.

In any case, such service requires a reservoir of adequately obedient or servile individuals. The drying up of this reservoir, no less than the loss of wealth itself, can rob wealth of its prerogatives. The increase in the security and incomes of Americans at the lower income levels has effectively reduced—indeed, for many purposes, eliminated—the servile class. And again the reciprocal is that those who no longer work for the rich (or who have done so or who fear that they might be forced to do so) no longer feel the resentment which such dependence has induced.

. . . . **V**

The enjoyment of physical possession of things would seem to be one of the prerogatives of wealth which has been little impaired. Presumably nothing has happened to keep the man who can afford them from enjoying his Rembrandts and his home-grown orchids. But enjoyment of things has always been intimately associated with the third prerogative of wealth which is the distinction that it confers. In a world where nearly everyone was poor, this distinction was very great. It was the natural consequence of rarity. In England, it is widely agreed, the ducal families are not uniformly superior. There is a roughly normal incidence of intelligence and stupidity, good taste and bad, and morality, immorality, homosexuality, and incest. But very few people are dukes or even duchesses, although the latter have become rather more frequent with the modern easing of the divorce laws. As a result, even though they may be intrinsically unexceptional, they are regarded with some awe. So it has long been with the rich. Were dukes numerous, their position would deteriorate. As the rich have become more numerous, they have inevitably become a debased currency.

Moreover, wealth has never been a sufficient source of honor in itself. It must be advertised, and the normal medium is obtrusively expensive goods. In the latter part of the last century in the United States this advertisement was conducted with virtuosity. Housing, equipage, female adornment, and recreation were all brought to its service. Expensiveness was keenly emphasized. "We are told now that Mr. Gould's '$500,000 yacht' has entered a certain harbor, or that Mr. Morgan has set off on a journey in his '$100,000 palace car,' or that Mr. Vanderbilt's '$2,000,000 home' is nearing completion, with its '$50,000 paintings' and its '$20,000 bronze doors.' "[10] The great houses, the great yachts, the great balls, the stables, and the expansive jewel-encrusted bosoms were all used to identify the individual as having a claim to the honors of wealth.

Such display is now passé. There was an adventitious contributing cause. The American well-to-do have long been curiously sensitive to fear of expropriation—a fear which may be related to the tendency for even the mildest reformist measures to be viewed, in the conservative conventional wisdom, as the portents of revolution. The depression and especially the New Deal gave the American rich a serious fright. One consequence was to usher in a period of marked discretion in personal expenditure. Purely ostentatious outlays, especially on dwellings, yachts, and females, were believed likely to incite the masses to violence. They

[10] Matthew Josephson, *The Robber Barons* (New York: Harcourt, Brace & Co., 1934), p. 330. Josephson is paraphrasing W. A. Croffut, Commodore Vanderbilt's biographer, writing in 1885.

were rebuked as unwise and improper by the more discreet. It was much wiser to take on the protective coloration of the useful citizen, the industrial statesman, or even the average guy.[11]

However, deeper causes were at work. Increasingly in the last quarter century the display of expensive goods, as a device for suggesting wealth, has been condemned as vulgar. The term is precise. Vulgar means: "Of or pertaining to the common people, or to the common herd or crowd." And this explains what happened. Lush expenditure could be afforded by so many that it ceased to be useful as a mark of distinction. A magnificent, richly upholstered, and extremely high-powered automobile conveys no impression of wealth in a day when such automobiles are mass-produced by the thousands. A house in Palm Beach is not a source of distinction when the rates for a thousand hotel rooms in Miami Beach rival its daily upkeep. Once a sufficiently impressive display of diamonds could create attention even for the most obese and repellent body, for they signified membership in a highly privileged case. Now the same diamonds are afforded by a television star or a talented harlot. Modern mass communications, especially the movies and television, insure that the populace at large will see the most lavish caparisoning on the bodies not of the daughters of the rich but on the daughters of coal miners and commercial travelers, who struck it rich by their own talents or some facsimile thereof. In South America, in the Middle East, to a degree in socialist India, and at Nice, Cannes, and Deauville, ostentatious display by the rich is still much practiced. This accords with expectations. In these countries most people are still, in the main, poor and unable to afford the goods which advertise wealth. Therefore ostentation continues to have a purpose. In not being accessible to too many people it has not yet become vulgar.

The American of wealth is not wholly without advantages in his search for distinction. Wealth still brings attention if devoted to cultural and technical pursuits or to hobbies with a utilitarian aspect. A well-to-do American may gain in esteem from an admirably run farm, although never from an admirably manicured estate. He will be honored for magnificent and imaginative cow stables, although not for luxurious horse stables. Although wealth aids a public career those who too patently rely on it are regarded as slightly inferior public citizens. A Harriman or a Lehman who is elected to public office enjoys a prestige far in excess of an Aldrich or a Whitney whose appointment to an ambassadorial posi-

11 Cf. C. Wright Mills, *The Power Elite* (New York: Oxford University Press, 1956), p. 117. Mr. Mills suggests that in the depression years this effort to provide protective coloration led to the recruiting of technicians and corporate managers as front men behind which the well-to-do could survive in peace. Not uncharacteristically, I think, Mr. Mills reads too much design and contrivance into such change.

tion, however justified on merit, might have been less certain in the absence of sizable campaign contributions. In sum, although ostentatious and elaborate expenditure, in conjuction with the wealth that sustained it, was once an assured source of distinction, it is so no longer. The effect on attitudes toward inequality will be evident. Ostentatious expenditure focused the attention of the poor on the wealth of the wealthy, for this of course was its purpose. With the decline of ostentation, or its vulgarization, wealth and hence inequality were no longer flagrantly advertised. Being less advertised they were less noticed and less resented. The rich had helped to make inequality an issue. Now they were no longer impelled to do so.

There were similar consequences from the fact that the rich man now had to compete for esteem. Once the intellectual, politician, or man of general ambition saw the rich man achieve distinction without effort and in contrast with his own struggle. He reacted by helping to focus the resentment of the community as a whole. Now he saw the man of wealth forced to compete for his honors. In this competition the rich man retained undoubted advantages, but he did not automatically excel. Nothing could operate more effectively to dry up the supply of individuals who otherwise would make an attack on inequality a career. By graduating into the ranks of the professional managers, and after making his way up through the hierarchy of the modern corporation, the ambitious man could expect to compete on tolerably equal terms with the grandson of the founder.

It would be idle to suggest that the man of wealth has no special advantages in our society. Such propositions are the one-day wonders of the conventional wisdom, and those who offer them have a brief but breath-taking reputation as social prophets. This itself suggests that such findings assuage some sense of guilt. But it does seem clear that prestige and power are now far more intimately identified with those who, regardless of personal wealth, administer productive activity. The high corporate official is inevitably a man of consequence. The rich man can be quite inconsequential and often is.

. . . . VI

In the Ricardian world, as noted, progress required profits, and its fruits accrued to the landlords. Economic advance—expanding output—did not ordinarily help the common man. His only hope lay in reforms that Ricardo and his followers would have considered highly destructive or, alternatively, in a drastic overthrow of the system. Economic advance still holds little promise of betterment for the average man in many if not most countries. On Andean haciendas, in the Arab lands, and in India and China at least until recent times it mattered little to the man who tilled the land whether the product increased. His own share was minute; an increase in product is not important if all but a minute fraction goes to someone else. And matters may be worse: any surplus over the barest need may be absorbed, as the result of an *ad hoc* revision of the rules, by the landlord, merchant, or moneylender. This is still the Ricardian world, and in it the obvious hope for improvement lies in a different distribution of income. For the same reason, until the share of the ordinary man in the product is increased, his incentive to increase production—to adopt better methods of cultivation, for example—is slight or nil. The people of the so-called backward countries have frequently heard from their presumptively more advanced mentors in the economically more advanced lands that they should be patient about social reform, with all its disturbing and even revolutionary implications, and concentrate on increasing production. It can be remarkably inappropriate advice. Reform is not something that can be made to wait on productive advance. It may be a prerequisite to such advance.

In the advanced country, in contrast, increased production is an alternative to redistribution. And, as indicated, it has been the great solvent of the tensions associated with inequality. Even though the latter persists, the awkward conflict which its correction implies can be avoided. How much better to concentrate on increasing output, a program on which both rich and poor can agree, since it benefits both.

That among those who might be subject to redistribution this doctrine has something approaching the standing of divine revelation is perhaps not entirely surprising. For many years the relationship of businessmen to economists in the United States has been characterized by a degree of waspishness. The economist has shown a predisposition to favor low tariffs, the income tax, the antitrust laws, and quite frequently trade unions. This has made him, at the minimum, an inconvenient friend. But increased ouput as a substitute for greater equality has lately become the basis for a notable *rapprochement.* "From a dollars-and-cents point of view it is quite obvious that over a period of years, even those who find themselves at the short end of inequality have more to gain from faster growth than from any conceivable income redistribution."[12]

Some have reacted with slightly more suspicion. Over the centuries those who have been blessed with wealth have developed many remarkably ingenious and persuasive justifications of their good fortune. The instinct of the liberal is to look at these explanations with a rather unyielding eye. Yet in this case the facts are inescapable. It is the increase

[12] "Learning to Multiply and to Divide." Address by Roger M. Blough, Chairman of the Board of the United States Steel Corporation, quoting Professor Henry C. Wallich of Yale University, January 15, 1957.

in ouptut in recent decades, not the redistribution of income, which has brought the great material increase, the well-being of the average man.[13] And, however suspiciously, the liberal has come to accept the fact. As a result, the goal of an expanding economy has also become deeply imbedded in the conventional wisdom of the American left. The beneficent effects of such an economy, moreover, are held to be comprehensive. Not only will there be material improvement for the average man, but there will be an end to poverty and privation for all. This latter, in fact, is suspect. Increasing aggregate output leaves a self-perpetuating margin of poverty at the very base of the income pyramid. This goes largely unnoticed, because it is the fate of a voiceless minority. And liberals have long been accustomed to expect the poor to speak in the resounding tones of a vast majority. To these matters it will be necessary to return.

For the moment we need only notice that, as an economic and social concern, inequality has been declining in urgency, and this has had its reflection in the conventional wisdom. The decline has been for a variety of reasons, but in one way or another these are all related to the fact of increasing production. Production has eliminated the more acute tensions associated with inequality. And it has become evident to conservatives and liberals alike that increasing aggregate output is an alternative to redistribution or even to the reduction of inequality. The oldest and most agitated of social issues, if not resolved, is at least largely in abeyance, and the disputants have concentrated their attention, instead, on the goal of increased productivity. This is a change of far-reaching importance. Our increased concern for production in modern times would be remarkable in itself. But it has also pre-empted the field once occupied by those who disputed over who should have less and who should have more.

Diana Athill

Taken from the opening pages of *Instead of a Letter,* the selection "Beckton Manor" by the English editor and writer, Diana Athill, is in one of the

[13] In the decade 1900-1909 employed workers as a class received an estimated 55 per cent of all income. By the decade of 1930-39 it had increased to 67 per cent since which time it has evidently been more or less stable. A 67 instead of a 55 per cent share of the total income paid out in the first decade would not have meant a very great increase. On the other hand a 55 per cent share of present income would still be a huge advance over what workers received in the first decade. Calculations are from Gale Johnson, "The Functional Distribution of Income in the United States, 1850-1952," *Review of Economics and Statistics,* vol. XXXVI (May 1954). The estimates are rough.

most flexible and yet demanding of forms, the personal reminiscence. All such reminiscence is a searching of the self, but inevitably it is a searching that takes into account many factors outside the self, and this is no exception. To some extent, then, "Beckton Manor" is a personal account in concrete, human terms of those vast social changes which in part have been the result of that redistribution of the wealth which economists and historians describe in more abstract and impersonal terms. "How guilty do I feel," Miss Athill writes, "at having come in at the tail end of such a life and having loved passionately a place founded on privilege the earnings of which had become remote?" The setting is England, but the essential contrasts between the prewar world of Beckton Manor and the one in which Miss Athill—and her readers—now live have validity for most of the countries of the west.

The personal tone of voice is of course the key factor in a recollection piece. Everything is filtered through this voice, both the recreating of a world that is past but that still lives in the mind of the author and the judgments that the author makes on that world. Thus it is Miss Athill's voice that provides unity of tone and point of view, and it is quite unmistakably her own, shaped with language that is simple and modest yet very distinctive. She can evoke scene and person with great vividness (the inset character sketch of Gran, who is the pivot figure, and the sensuous details that bring Beckton itself to life are good examples). But she moves with equal ease into concise and uncompromising analysis of the prejudiced and provincial attitudes which characterized Beckton, attitudes that were founded on an assumption of social superiority, an assumption that in its turn was founded almost entirely on economic privilege. The piece derives its special power from the paradoxical fact that the author is able to write so sympathetically and affectionately about a society whose weaknesses she so clearly sees and whose values she has rejected.

BECKTON MANOR*

........One

My maternal grandmother died of old age, a long and painful process. Heart and arteries began to show signs of wearing out when she was ninety-two years old, but it was not until two years later that they failed her and precipitated her—still lucid, still herself—into death. By the end, pain and exhaustion had loosened her grip on life so that when she "recovered" yet again from a heart attack she would whisper, "Why doesn't God let me die?" but for a long time she was afraid of what was happening to her. She was afraid of death, and she was sorrowful—which was

* Editor's title.

From *Instead of a Letter* by Diana Athill. Copyright © 1962 by Diana Athill. Reprinted by permission of Doubleday & Company, Inc.

worse—because she had much time in which to ask herself what her life had been for, and often she could not answer.

I was not much with her at that time. Her son and her daughters, who lived near or with her, laboured through it at her side, but her grandchildren were scattered and saw her only when they visited their parents. But once I happened to be there when she was very ill and everyone was more than usually worn out, so I took a night watch. I sat in her cold room (if the windows were shut she felt suffocated), watching the dark hollows of her eyes and the shocking dark hole of her mouth— it was unbearable that Gran, always so completely in control of appearances, should lie with her mouth agape. I listened to the rhythm of her breathing. Sometimes it would stop for a whole minute and the winter night would be absolutely still. In the long silences I prayed to her God, "Please, please don't let her start breathing again," and knew that if she died it would not be frightening, that I should feel peace. But each time the harsh, snoring breaths would begin again, hauling her back to another awakening and to more pain and physical humilation. It was some weeks after that, when she had rallied to the extent of writing an angry letter to the local paper about a new road of which she disapproved, and of ordering a dentist to her bedside to make her a new set of false teeth, that she turned her beautiful speckled eyes towards me one afternoon and said in so many words: "What have I lived for?"

It was she who should have been able to tell me that. All her life she had been a churchgoing Christian of apparently unshaken faith. But she was on her own then: not suffering, like Doctor Johnson, from fear of the consequences of her sinfulness according to the teachings of that faith, but simply unsupported by it. I said to her what I believed: that she had lived, at the very least, for what her life had been. The long, hard months of dying could eclipse her life, but they did not expunge it. What she had created for us, her family, by loving and being loved, still existed, would continue to exist, and could not have existed without her. "Do you really think that it has been worth something?" she asked, and I held her hands and told her that I believed it with all my heart. Then I went away, and wondered. For her it might well be the truth. She had created a world for us. Even if I had been the only one of her descendants to have been rooted in that world (and perhaps I was one of the least deeply rooted of them all), something that her love had made would still be alive. But what of a woman who had never had the chance, or had missed the chance, to create something like that? What of myself? That was a question to whistle up an icy wind, and I was out in it. I waited for the shivering to start.

Well, it has not started yet, and I would like to know why. Which is my reason for sitting down to write this.

. . . . **Two**

It is strange to have loved someone like my grandmother, with whom I came to disagree on almost everything of importance. In anyone but her the values she held seem to me absurd or shocking, yet there she is: the dominant figure in my curiously matriarchal family, her memory warm with love, pleasure, and gratitude.

When she was a girl, one of four handsome daughters of a Master of an Oxford college, she swore that she would never be kissed by any man but the one she would marry, and she never was. She met her husband when he was an undergraduate: a man with frosty blue eyes and a trace of Yorkshire accent ("cassel" for castle, "larndry" for laundry), who read for the bar but did not practice for long because he inherited his father's estate, which I shall call Beckton. It was not in Yorkshire but in East Anglia, to which his family had moved because his mother was supposed to be delicate and to need a softer climate. She must in fact have been a hardy woman in spite of delicate looks, for she lived to a good age and if the climate of East Anglia is softer than that of Yorkshire, heaven forbid that I should ever have to winter in the latter.

My grandmother bore her husband four daughters, of whom my mother was the youngest; and at last, when I suspect that a sense of failure was beginning to prey on her, one son. She despised women, or thought that she did. Intelligent herself, happy to send two of her girls to Oxford when it was still uncommon, and proud of any success her female grandchildren might achieve in unwomanly careers, she yet insisted that women's minds were inferior to men's. There was some kind of ambiguity at work here, for although masculine superiority was never questioned, the climate of my grandmother's house was markedly feminine and her daughters' husbands always seemed to be slightly on the fringe of it. On a subject suitable to men—war, politics, a question of local government, the appointment of a clergyman to a living—she would turn to a son-in-law with a formal deference: "I have been wanting to ask you—ought I to write to the bishop . . .?" but if she intended to write to the bishop, that was what she would do, whatever the son-in-law said. It was not that the deference was false, but perhaps it was paid to a figure too masculine, too infallible to exist: a pattern of manhood to which the real men in the family failed wholly to conform.

Whether my grandfather conformed to it or not I do not know, for he died when I was six. If he did not, it was through no fault of his wife's. All I know of their relationship is that their two writing desks in the library at Beckton Manor were so placed that his was near the fire and hers far from it, and that when, after his death, she referred to him it was always as though he were unquestionable in whatever he said or did. The references were infrequent, but they followed a pattern: "Granpapa always said . . ." and so it was; "Granpapa would never let the children . . ." and so they never did; "Granpapa was very fond of . . ." and so it was good. That she had adored him was an article of faith in the family, but during her last illness she disconcerted one of her daughters. They were talking of her fear of death. "I don't understand why you are so afraid," said her daughter. "You have always been religious—surely you believe in an afterlife and that you will meet Dad again?" My grandmother, it seems, said nothing. "But," I was told, "she gave me such a *very odd* look, it quite shocked me." The look may have referred to the afterlife in general, but her daughter had an uncomfortable feeling that it referred to Granpapa.

What do I know about him? That he had blunt, North Country good looks; that he had discriminating taste in silver and wine and built up a large and excellent library with its emphasis on history; that when he enlarged Beckton Manor, making it U-shaped instead of L-shaped, he set up a kiln to make small bricks matching those of the house, which was built in about 1760, and employed skilled workmen to carve stone to a Georgian design round his new front door and to mould plaster swags to crown the Adams chimney-piece he put in his new drawing room. A man of taste, but backward-looking. He would give sixpences to his children for learning *Lycidas* before they were eight, wrote in well-managed Johnsonian cadences a thesis on the Serbs (whom he called Servs), and travelled modestly in Italy and Greece, bringing back stone urns for the terrace wall and insisting that his accompanying children put permanganate in the foreign water with which they had to brush their teeth. He was a good farmer. The estate at Beckton is of a thousand acres, some of the land rented out to tenants but much of it attached to the Manor Farm. My grandfather employed a bailiff from Yorkshire, but he took most of the management on himself and did it well.

I cannot recall any word spoken to me by my grandfather. His children's talk of him has always been as unquestioning as his widow's, and sometimes affectionate. He was not quite a tyrant, perhaps, but they convey that he ruled his roost as though by divine right, and I do not think that I would have liked him. Death lent him a sort of holiness for a time. His soul flew out of open sash windows and "went to Heaven to be with God," which gave him a share of God's benevolence. After that he did a miracle for me, permitting me to walk unstung through a bed of nettles. Each spring, when we made cowslip balls for my grandmother's birthday, we put the best of them on his grave, an austere grey slab with the words "Tomorrow to fresh woods and pastures new" carved on it, but the feeling of piety and love which attended this tribute was engendered by the act rather than directed towards the memory of a real man. And the things I owe him—Beckton as a place in which to grow up, books as an indispensable part of life—soon came to seem Gran's dispensation, not his.

She went on being there. After breakfast she would put on an overall and brush the dogs out on the terrace by the steps which led into the library. Wearing thick leather gloves she would garden in her greenhouse, or the rose beds, would cut flowers for the house and would arrange them in the "flower room," where the vases were kept and where the dogs slept. She wrote many letters on small sheets of black-edged paper, in writing so like shorthand that only her daughters knew the secret of reading it. She went for a long walk every day and took a strong dose of senna pods every night: fresh air and open bowels were, she considered, all that was necessary for health. Her housekeeping, to which she paid vigilant attention, was simplified by custom. Vegetables, milk, eggs, and butter all came from the estate; hams were cured, honey was harvested, or jam was made at fixed times, and the groceries were ordered by post every month, from the Civil Service Stores in London. It was a simple, rhythmical life in which she was only concerned with the management, not the execution, but when much later she moved to a smaller house and staff problems combined with the dwindling of a fixed income forced her to do things herself, she knew how to clean, dust, polish silver, and so on much better than the rest of us, who had been doing it for years as a matter of course.

The pleasures of her life were the place itself, which she adored, her family, and reading: her existence should have been a tranquil one. What was it that made anxiety such a distinct thread in it? Never could anyone go away from Beckton without my grandmother's eyes expressing real unhappiness. The journey might be a short one, made for pleasure, but she still felt a clutch of fear. We were not going to eat enough, and what we ate would be unwholesome; we were going to sleep with our windows shut; we were going to catch some infectious disease; a car was going to skid or a train run off the rails. Bad things were likely to happen to people if they went away. I have noticed this attitude in other people whose lives are secure, comfortable, and sheltered by privilege so that one would expect disaster to be far from their minds. I suppose, whether they recognize it or not, it is an acknowledgment of the forces besieging their position. My grandmother had a good knowledge of history and read *The Times* daily: she knew what was happening in the world. Wars and rumours of war; communists abroad and socialists at home; rising taxes and falling respect for tradition. She, a conservative, a gentlewoman, a devout Protestant Christian and an owner of property, was automatically on the defensive against powers outside her control. She did not trust "outside" and converted her distrust into fear of accident and careless eating. Over and over again I have heard her, or someone like her, say in a voice of real dismay, "But you can't go on that train, you'll miss lunch!" as though they had become obsessed by the value of food because of some experience of hardship or starvation. In their time measured out not by coffee spoons but by dishes of roast beef, steak-and-kidney puddings, apple pie and cream, they have never once felt or expected to feel a pang of true hunger, so from where does this irrational panic come if it is not a symbol of something else?

My grandmother's anxiety increased as she grew older, because she felt that the right, the natural order of things would be for her to be able to provide for us all on her death, and it was clear that she could not do so; but when I was a child it was less explicit. It was simply darling Gran fussing, and if you teased her about it she smiled back ruefully, half amused by herself, half expressing "It is all very well for you to laugh, if only you knew!"

My father had a family, but it did not own Beckton. It owned no land at all. My paternal grandfather, a clergyman in comfortable circumstances, shot himself for no good reason while I was still a baby (the coal had not been delivered on time, I believe: he had high blood pressure and would therefore fly into violent rages over small matters). It was as "good" a family as my mother's and although it had left East Anglia long ago, it had a better claim than hers on our own beloved county, having several tombs and brasses there to prove the existence of rustic Athill knights and one fishmonger at a respectable distance in time. In spite of this my mother felt it to be a family inferior to hers, and somehow, I can no longer remember exactly in what way, conveyed this idea to her children. She always felt that possession by her was nine-tenths of anything's value, even a dog's. A woman who loved animals to the point of absurdity, she rarely admitted charm or breeding in a dog belonging to someone else. "It's not a bad-looking puppy, I suppose," she would say, "but it's going to be leggy"—or, "One of those hysterical dogs, always ready to make a fuss of strangers." In the same way, her husband's family bored and irritated her. It was as though when they were first married and conflicting loyalties emerged—with whom, for instance, should they spend Christmas?—she had said like a child "Bags I my family," and got away with it ever since.

Because of Beckton, this was easy to do. A house with twenty bedrooms, standing in a large garden and park with a thousand acres of land round it, can absorb children far more easily than can a neat six-bedroomed house with a two-acre garden, like that of my paternal grandmother, who lived in Devonshire. It was more *sensible* to go to Beckton for the holidays. And if we or any of our cousins had been ill, or our parents were abroad, Beckton Gran could house us with much pleasure and little inconvenience, while Devonshire Grannie, fond though she was of us, would have had to turn her house upside down. Besides, my father was an Army officer with, during all my childhood, the rank of major, and with private means so small that they hardly counted. He lived above his income, modestly and anxiously, from the day he was married, but even by doing that he could not afford to give his wife and children so good a time as they had at Beckton: he would have felt churlish had he prevented their visits. I doubt, indeed, whether he could have done so if he had tried. My mother was strong-willed and he had the disadvantage of being the one *qui aimait*. So although I and my younger brother and sister knew that our official home was where he happened to be working—Woolwich, or when he retired from the Army and took a job in the city, Hertfordshire—our "real" home, the place to which we "came home" from other places, was Beckton.

Having bought a small glass bottle made in about 1785, club-shaped, with a delicate spiral rib from neck to base, I was looking at it with affection, enjoying the colour of the glass and the hint of irregularity in the shape. Why, I began to wonder, are objects made in England during that period so much my home territory when it comes to aesthetic pleasure? The products of other centuries and of other countries I have learnt to appreciate, but I cannot remember having to *learn* to delight in those of the English eighteenth century. Probably, I concluded, it is because so much of my upbringing took place in an eighteenth-century house. It was a thought with gratifying implications. I am glad that I have not inherited money or possessions, and I *would* be glad if I could be sure that I had not inherited any prejudices or attitudes of mind towards other people, but I like the idea of a child's mind and eye unconsciously trained by graceful shapes, just proportions, and the details of good craftsmanship. It suggested that whatever faults the middling English gentry might have, they would be likely to possess a certain feeling for grace and style: good for us!

Then, unfortunately, I began to remember various objects bought by my relatives, prized by them and admired by myself before I left home and began to sniff round museums and listen to the opinions of people better educated in such matters than myself. I remembered certain lamps and pieces of china and materials for curtains or chair covers. . . . It was true that we were all familiar with one kind of beauty so that if any of us became interested in aesthetics, that kind, being familiar, would be easy to start with; but it was clearly not true that we had gained from it any ingrained, generally applicable sense of quality or style. If the inhabitants of Beckton had to buy something new and were unable to afford to go to the right place for it (the family's fortunes have been coasting downhill all my life), choice would be conditioned not by knowledge, but by familiarity. The new object would be a pitiful, decadent bastard of the old and we would be cheerfully blind to the difference between patina and French polish, cut glass and moulded, a graceful curve and a clumsy one. Only a few members of my family had, if left to themselves, more natural taste than the people they most pitied and despised: the dwellers in suburbia. (The working classes were allowed a few distinct and even endearing merits: suburbanites—no!)

New purchases were not often made, partly because everything in Beckton Manor was certainly "good" in the sense of being solid and enduring, partly because, even early in my lifetime, extravagance was condemned. It was still a rich man's house compared to those of the vast majority, but the family did not feel itself a rich family. There was a strict line drawn between necessities and luxuries, and luxuries were suspect.

During my early childhood, necessities included a head gardener with two men under him, two grooms, a chauffeur, a butler and a footman, a cook and a kitchenmaid with a scullery maid to help them, a head housemaid with two under-housemaids, and my grandmother's lady's maid. They included, too, animals for our pleasure and governesses and schools for our instruction. They included books, and a great deal of wholesome food, linen sheets rather than cotton, and three separate rooms for being in at different times of the day, not counting the dining room, the smoking room, the front hall, in which, for some reason, my grandmother always had tea, and the nursery. Capital being inviolate, there can, indeed, have been little income left over after the maintenance of all this at what was felt to be its proper level.

Clothes for my mother's generation and then for us were almost all made at home or in the village, except for the obligatory coat and skirt, and riding clothes, for which we went to a good tailor. My mother, happily for me, was the extravagant one of the family. She used to make gleeful and guilty forays to London for clothes, but it was an adventure, not routine. My grandfather had travelled a little (since it was before I can remember, I see it as Making the Grand Tour), but after his death it was unusual for anyone to take a holiday abroad, while to buy curtains for your bedroom simply because you were tired of the old ones was unheard of. If the old ones fell to pieces so that you *had* to replace them, you only considered the cheaper ranges of material (even my mother never considered the *most* expensive), and then—alas for that instinctive taste which, for a moment, I attributed to us. If you liked pink roses you chose pink roses, regardless of how the rest of the room was furnished. Sometimes you would recognize aesthetics to the point of saying "The blue in the pattern picks up the blue in the carpet," indicating a tiny blue motif in the design which, if examined closely, could be seen almost to match an equally inconspicuous blue twirl in the carpet's pattern; or sometimes you would speak the words which have sealed the fate of so many British interiors, and of the appearance of so many Englishwomen: "It is a good colour because *it goes with anything.*"

Yet Beckton Manor was a charming house to be in, and so are almost all the English houses of its kind that I have known. Like its fellows, it had plenty of lovely things in it by chances of inheritance or the good taste of individuals, and it had something else as well. Its inhabitants might not be interested in decoration, but they were interested in nature: to flowers, trees, skies, landscapes, and weather they responded with a strong sense of beauty, and without thinking of it they brought into the house as much of nature as they could. The tables loaded with cut flowers, the flowery chintzes, the indifferent water colours of beloved places expressed the life lived from the house, and they pleased.

As a child, of course, I thought it not only lovely but inevitable: that was what a house should be. Any house which did not have those things in it, and which did not look out over terrace and park to a lake beyond which rose the Lake Covert (landscaped by Capability Brown, we all mistakenly believed), was only a poor attempt at a house. When my mother scolded me for bragging to a friend of the number of bedrooms at Beckton and the two islands in the lake, telling me that one should never show off about good fortune to those with less, she may have improved my manners but she did not diminish my sense of superiority. Even the cold was a matter of pride. Warmth did not rate as a necessity, since it was held to be the opposite of fresh air and therefore unhealthy, so everyone was crippled by chilblains from November to February. "My sponge is *often* frozen solid in the morning," I remember boasting to some less hardy, less fortunate child.

How guilty do I feel at having come in on the tail end of such a life and having loved so passionately a place founded on privilege the earning of which had become remote? I do not often refer to it, and when I think about it a figure appears opposite me: that of some faceless friend brought up in a Manchester back street, with a childhood very different from my own stored in his head. At his most charitable, I feel, he would be giving me a quizzical look; and if I were to repeat to him the kind of thing my grandmother, my parents, my other relatives of their generation and even some of my own would say about his accent, his clothes, his attitudes ... Well, how could I repeat that kind of thing? And if he were a Jew or a Negro, or some other kind of foreigner not of noble birth (for a foreigner can only be guaranteed a gentleman by a title), then what could he feel towards my background less than disgust?

That smug, matter-of-fact assumption of superiority! Many landed families were richer and better bred than mine; nuances which mine recognized but which made no difference to their certainty. Except when it came to lords, whose acquaintance gave them a pleasure verging on the undignified, they were convinced that they were the best kind of people to be (indeed there was something a little fishy about anyone not a lord who was richer or grander than they were). When my grandparents dismissed someone as "not a gentleman," their unthinking certainty had the force of a *moral judgment;* while the tinge of apology or defiance that crept into the same judgment when pronounced by my parents' generation was only faint.

This attitude was at the best comic, at the worst repulsive, for with what could that particular family support its certainty of being "the best"? The abilities of most of its members were respectable but ordinary, their achievements no more than commonplace. None of them was unusually intelligent or energetic and most of them lacked imagination to a remarkable degree. Generous and affectionate they could be, but they hardly ever extended these qualities outside the family circle. Like anyone else they had their charms, their interesting quirks, their endearing or impressive aspects, and their standard of behaviour was, within certain limits, civilized and reliable, but it was not just in matters of taste that they were no better than anyone else: physically, intellectually, and morally they were no more than middling. Yet they despised almost all the rest of the world, excepting people as nearly as possible replicas of themselves, as though their status as English country gentlefolk made them exceptional beings; something of which they fell short even by their own standards, for they were not well enough connected, and Beckton was not a large enough estate, for them to come anywhere near the top of the ladder of snobbery.

What made my family so profoundly self-satisfied? That question has puzzled me more with every year of my life. The satisfaction in itself was not objectionable, since people can only function comfortably if they have it; but its obverse—the disdain or distrust of anyone not of their kind—that was stupid, ugly, and pitiful, and it is a curious sensation to be bound by enduring ties of love and habit to a set of people who so stubbornly displayed it. All that money spent on education, and so little thinking done as a result of it! Reactions still triggered by the sound of a vowel, the cut of a coat, the turn of a phrase. . . . "He was wearing what I think he would have called a *sports jacket,*" said one of them, only the other day (he would have called it a tweed coat), and that, as far as the wearer of the sports jacket was concerned, was that. Once imbued with such reactions, it is impossible entirely to escape them: I know that until the day I die I shall be unable to avoid *noticing* "raound" for "round," "invoalve" for "involve" (on that one an Army officer of my acquaintance used to turn down candidates for a commission), because a built-in mechanism will always click, however much I dislike it, "placing" everyone I meet as though for a second it was my parents' eyes and ears at work, not mine. But once it has clicked it can very easily be disregarded. The puzzle lies in the choice not to disregard it.

An old man near death once gave my uncle great pleasure by telling him that a treasured memory—something which had remained for years in his mind as a vignette of the England he loved—had been a glimpse, once caught as he was driving by, of my uncle riding in the park at Beckton. It is a pretty park, well planted with groups of beech and oak trees, sloping gracefully down to the lake beyond which the wood known as the Lake Covert rises, and mildly dominated by the house (to the left of the picture as the old man approached it), standing on its balustraded terrace with a great cedar tree at one corner of it to break its slightly austere Georgian lines. "It was a perfect October afternoon," said the old man. "There was the Lake Covert, all golden in its autumn leaves, reflected in the water, and there were you, cantering along beside the lake on that black of yours—what a beautiful horse he was—with a couple of dogs running behind you. I watched you and I thought, Now that's a lovely scene, that's England, and I've never forgotten it."

Describing the conversation, and the old man's emotion, my uncle gave a slight deprecating laugh, but he was not only touched, he was satisfied. That man had recognized in him and his setting what he himself felt deeply to be their true nature, and as he savoured it he was likable rather than absurd. He was moved by a vision of something which he dearly loved and which had comforted him when, during the war, he was badly wounded: he felt genuinely that it was worth dying for. To have said to him, "But you are not England. You and what you represent are only a tiny fraction of England and an archaic one at that, preserved not by deeds of virtue but by money most of which you yourself did not earn"—to have said that would have been to have attacked not a fancy but a rooted belief. He might have answered, "All right, so it is preserved by money: money in the hands of the right people, of people like us. What further argument do you need for the existence of such people and such money?" He and his like have been snug all their lives, and snugness breeds smugness—but smugness is too small a word for what it feels like *from inside*. From inside, it feels like moral and aesthetic *rightness;* from inside, it is people like me, who question it, who look stupid, ugly, and pitiful—and ungrateful, too. Why admit that the grammar-school boy, the self-made businessman, the artist, the foreigner or whatever are just as likely to be "the best" as we are, when such an admission must attack certainty, the cosiest of all the gifts bestowed by privilege? It is not only ingratitude, it is treachery.

Treacherous I may be, but ungrateful I am not. I consider it good fortune to have been born of Beckton's youngest daughter, not of its son, at a point in time and a position in the family where diminishing resources had brought unthinking certainty up against the facts of life and worn it comparatively thin. Never to have broken through its smothering folds would have been, I have always thought, extremely depressing. But on the other hand, not to have enjoyed a childhood wrapped warmly in those folds—that would be a sad loss. There I used to be, as snug and as smug as anyone, believing with the best that we were the best—and if security is the thing for children, which it surely is, then how lucky I was.

Beckton and Gran: they blur together. When I think of her I may see a handsome woman with crisp, pure-white hair (it turned when she was thirty), wearing a black, black-and-white, or grey dress with a cross-over bodice and a lace collar (she was in her eighties before she forgot her widow's status to the point of wearing a dress made of soft, pinky-red wool). Her eyes, with lids that droop slightly in an odd way at the outer corners, are speckled green and grey, capable of an ironic expression but usually full of affection, and she will be looking at me attentively, ready to be amused or interested by what I am saying (for one did not say to Gran the things which would have shocked or displeased her). I may see this woman, or I may think of getting out of the car to open the white gate between park and lawn, breathing that first, almost drinkable, smell of grass, flowers, and cedar tree which was the assurance that we were home. Then images come crowding in: the stream in the kitchen garden in which the newts and tadpoles lived; the marble children under a tree on the library chimneypiece; the scalloped black-green leather which would pull off from the edges of the nursery bookshelves; the goat-shed in the lower stable yard made into a bower of beech branches by a cousin and myself, because tender young beech leaves on the branch were what our goats liked best (we gave them senna pods, too, when we thought they needed them, and sometimes an aspirin or a spoonful of cough linctus). Very clear is the chasm between the back of the sofa and the bookshelves in the morning room, where I would squat for hours to read bound volumes of *Punch,* and the smell of the plush curtains over the double door between morning room and front hall, in which I had only to muffle myself, at one time, in order to begin writing a play in which a cousin was to take the part of a good, blond and slightly insipid princess while I was to be the dark, wicked one, like Sir Rider Haggard's She-Who-Must-Be-Obeyed. "Go and play in the morning room, darlings," people would say. It was the room to which children graduated from the nursery, where one could bounce on the furniture or litter the floor with meccano or cutting-out.

There was only one unpleasant thing in that house: the ghost in the night nursery, where at our smallest we usually had to sleep. It was not an ordinary ghost but a disgusting presence, a slimy grey thing like a stubby elephant's trunk which reached down over the gutter and groped at the window one morning while I was sitting alone on my pot. No one liked that room, which was at the back of the house, looking out onto a gloomy thicket of yew trees, on the old principle, not otherwise observed, of pushing children out of the way with the servants. But no one thought of telling my grandmother about that, so it was nothing to do with her. Every other sound, smell, and texture in the place I loved quite consciously from the earliest time I can remember, and I loved it so much not only because I felt it to be beautiful, but because its presiding genius, my grandmother, loved me.

In relationships outside her family she was not a loving woman, nor a tolerant one. Her servants she distrusted, not (the older, long-established ones anyway) in terms of honesty so much as of sense. She expected them to be ninnies, and to be dirty, and how they managed not to be the latter is hard to see, considering that it was years before anyone thought of putting in a bathroom on the attic floor where they lived, while they were not allowed to use ours. Of people who differed from her on politics or religion she was fiercely scornful, particularly of anyone who believed that the Pope spoke God's word, or who was a socialist. Of foreigners she was not only scornful, but distrustful as well. If they thought that they could govern their own countries better than we could she considered them both fools and traitors. Outside the ramifications of what might be called the greater family as opposed to the central family—the second cousins and so on, about whose fortunes she was always completely and mysteriously informed and whom she wished well—she had no intimate friends.

Described like this, she sounds a disagreeable woman, yet no one ever met her without being charmed. The charm came from the warmth of her personality, and the warmth came from the dynamo of love at work in her for the benefit of her children and her children's children. She was not soft with them. She mocked them if their politics veered to the left, scolded them if they did not eat properly, and criticized any folly they might get up to unless it was something really grave, like marrying a foreigner or having an extra-marital love affair. About that kind of thing she would either keep silent, or would choose not to know. But although her family could cause her impatience or grief, they could not diminish her love—and the only grief they could have caused her when still young would have been by illness or death. In her house we could be excited by our own misdemeanours, but we could never feel that they put us in peril, so for us this autocratic woman, whose sharp intelligence was deliberately confined to so narrow a range, created a benign air which we could always breathe again, even in middle age, simply by going back to the place where she lived.

I shocked her once. I was about ten years old and had thought of an image for life. I thought that it was as though people were confined in a bowl which was floating on a sea. While snug at the bottom of the bowl they lived their lives complacently, but the bowl spun and tossed on the sea and its spinning sometimes sent one of them up its side until he could see over the rim. All round would be the endless chaos of dangerous, cold grey water, unsuspected till then, and anyone who had seen it and had understood that what he had thought was safety was only a little bowl, would not be able to bear it. That, I decided, was the origin of madness. I was proud of this idea, described it to my grandmother, and was disconcerted to see her so upset. It was not at all clever, she said sharply, to think that life was aimless, and she told me to remember the then Prince of Wales, who had recently made some statement of high purpose and idealism to a gathering of Boy Scouts.

I was disappointed by this response, which did not seem to me to recognize the implications of my idea, but I remember it because in spite of my disappointment, its inadequacy did not matter. I noted that in some ways I would have to differ from Gran but I did not feel betrayed, because there she was as she spoke, wearing the kind of dress she always wore, with her beautiful hair and her dear, kind eyes watching me with the anxiety I thought was a joke and the love which I would never think of questioning. I myself might incline more to the bowl theory than the Prince of Wales theory, but clearly whatever Gran believed was *good,* because it was believed by Gran.

Virginia Woolf

Early in this century the agitation for women's rights, led by the suffragettes and their more liberal adherents among the male population, aroused a great and protracted controversy. Even legally woman's status was that of a second-class citizen, and antifeminists and traditionalists intended to keep things that way. History, however, does not appear to have been entirely on their side in this century. The first important step in a new direction was taken after World War I when women's legal rights were to some extent improved (Ameri-

can women were granted the vote in 1920, and European women—with the
exception of the Swiss, who in all but one canton remain disenfranchised—
were given the vote in the same general era). The next step came after World
War II when, as a result of their having been urged during the war to go out of
the home and take jobs, women came to make up a large permanent part of the
working force in America and an increasing part in Europe. The improvement
in woman's economic situation has opened the way for greater, if less easily
definable, changes in her general position in society. Some old stresses have been
lightened, some new ones have been added; and "woman's role" is a subject
much discussed by psychologists, sociologists, theologians, popular journalists,
and indeed by the public as a whole. Yet while the specifics of the discussion
may change some from decade to decade, the essential issues remain largely the
same, and no one perhaps has dealt more forcefully and elegantly with these
issues than the great English novelist Virginia Woolf (1882-1941) in her long
essay *A Room of One's Own*. (It was based on a series of lectures she delivered
in the late 1920's to the women students at Cambridge University.)

The general thesis of Mrs. Woolf's book is that women have their creative
lives ahead of them if they can first manage the economic independence—
symbolized by that "room of one's own" of the title—which has historically been
so difficult, and often impossible, for them to attain. Much of the book is given
over to a discussion of the reasons for this. In the particular chapter selected,
"Shakespeare's Sister," Mrs. Woolf considers the lot of the woman of unusual
gifts, but by implication much of what she has to say applies to the average
woman, too. Clearly she associates women with other underprivileged social
groups, but the bitter edge of resentment, so common to such discussions, is
controlled by wit, humor, irony. Particularly effective is the lighthearted yet
serious way she makes fun of the most offensive and hypocritical examples of
male chauvinism (see her handling of Trevelyan). Here is nothing of rancor or
harangue, but a deft analysis of those factors which have perpetuated the notion
of the "mental, moral, and physical inferiority of women," a notion which Mrs.
Woolf shows to be as absurd as it is dishonest. But there is passion and pathos,
too, as the little story which she has invented about Shakespeare's sister reveals.
It is natural for the writer of fiction to create character, scene, drama, and Mrs.
Woolf could find no more effective way of illustrating the idea that underlies
this chapter: the talented woman who accepts the traditional notion that she is
inferior is condemned to mediocrity, and the one who defies it risks personal
disaster. The terms of opposition are less extreme than in the Elizabethan age,
but in Mrs. Woolf's view they are still very much in force.

SHAKESPEARE'S SISTER*

It was disappointing not to have brought back in the evening
some important statement, some authentic fact. Women are poorer than

* Editor's title.

From *A Room of One's Own* by Virginia Woolf, copyright, 1929, by Harcourt, Brace &
World, Inc.; renewed, 1957, by Leonard Woolf. Reprinted by permission of the publishers.

men because—this or that. Perhaps now it would be better to give up seeking for the truth, and receiving on one's head an avalanche of opinion hot as lava, discoloured as dish-water. It would be better to draw the curtains; to shut out distractions; to light the lamp; to narrow the enquiry and to ask the historian, who records not opinions but facts, to describe under what conditions women lived, not throughout the ages, but in England, say in the time of Elizabeth.

For it is a perennial puzzle why no woman wrote a word of that extraordinary literature when every other man, it seemed, was capable of song or sonnet. What were the conditions in which women lived, I asked myself; for fiction, imaginative work that is, is not dropped like a pebble upon the ground, as science may be; fiction is like a spider's web, attached ever so lightly perhaps, but still attached to life at all four corners. Often the attachment is scarcely perceptible; Shakespeare's plays, for instance, seem to hang there complete by themselves. But when the web is pulled askew, hooked up at the edge, torn in the middle, one remembers that these webs are not spun in mid-air by incorporeal creatures, but are the work of suffering human beings, and are attached to grossly material things, like health and money and the houses we live in.

I went, therefore, to the shelf where the histories stand and took down one of the latest, Professor Trevelyan's *History of England*. Once more I looked up Women, found "position of," and turned to the pages indicated. "Wife-beating," I read, "was a recognised right of man, and was practised without shame by high as well as low.... Similarly," the historian goes on, "the daughter who refused to marry the gentleman of her parents' choice was liable to be locked up, beaten and flung about the room, without any shock being inflicted on public opinion. Marriage was not an affair of personal affection, but of family avarice, particularly in the 'chivalrous' upper classes.... Betrothal often took place while one or both of the parties was in the cradle, and marriage when they were scarcely out of the nurse's charge." That was about 1470, soon after Chaucer's time. The next reference to the position of women is some two hundred years later, in the time of the Stuarts. "It was still the exception for women of the upper and middle class to choose their own husbands, and when the husband had been assigned, he was lord and master, so far at least as law and custom could make him. Yet even so," Professor Trevelyan concludes, "neither Shakespeare's women nor those of authentic seventeenth-century memoirs, like the Verneys and the Hutchinsons, seem wanting in personality and character." Certainly, if we consider it, Cleopatra must have had a way with her; Lady Macbeth, one would suppose, had a will of her own; Rosalind, one might conclude, was an attractive girl. Professor Trevelyan is speaking no more than the truth when he remarks that Shakespeare's women do not seem wanting in personality and character. Not being a historian, one might go even further and say that women have burnt like beacons in all the works of all the poets from the beginning of time—Clytemnestra, Antigone, Cleopatra, Lady Macbeth, Phèdre, Cressida, Rosalind, Desdemona, the Duchess of Malfi, among the dramatists; then among the prose writers: Millamant, Clarissa, Becky Sharp, Anna Karenine, Emma Bovary, Madame de Guermantes—the names flock to mind, nor do they recall women "lacking in personality and character." Indeed, if woman had no existence save in the fiction written by men, one would imagine her a person of the utmost importance; very various; heroic and mean; splendid and sordid; infinitely beautiful and hideous in the extreme; as great as a man, some think even greater.[1] But this is woman in fiction. In fact, as Professor Trevelyan points out, she was locked up, beaten and flung about the room.

A very queer, composite being thus emerges. Imaginatively she is of the highest importance; practically she is completely insignificant. She pervades poetry from cover to cover; she is all but absent from history. She dominates the lives of kings and conquerors in fiction; in fact she was the slave of any boy whose parents forced a ring upon her finger. Some of the most inspired words, some of the most profound thoughts in literature fall from her lips; in real life she could hardly read, could scarcely spell, and was the property of her husband.

It was certainly an odd monster that one made up by reading the historians first and the poets afterwards—a worm winged like an eagle; the spirit of life and beauty in a kitchen chopping up suet. But these monsters, however amusing to the imagination, have no existence in fact. What one must do to bring her to life was to think poetically and prosaically at one and the same moment, thus keeping in touch with fact— that she is Mrs. Martin, aged thirty-six, dressed in blue, wearing a black hat and brown shoes; but not losing sight of fiction either—that she is a vessel in which all sorts of spirits and forces are coursing and flashing perpetually. The moment, however, that one tries this method with the

---

1 "It remains a strange and almost inexplicable fact that in Athena's city, where women were kept in almost Oriental suppression as odalisques or drudges, the stage should yet have produced figures like Clytemnestra and Cassandra, Atossa and Antigone, Phèdre and Medea, and all the other heroines who dominate play after play of the 'misogynist' Euripides. But the paradox of this world where in real life a respectable woman could hardly show her face alone in the street, and yet on the stage woman equals or surpasses man, has never been satisfactorily explained. In modern tragedy the same predominance exists. At all events, a very cursory survey of Shakespeare's work (similarly with Webster, though not with Marlowe or Jonson) suffices to reveal how this dominance, this initiative of women, persists from Rosalind to Lady Macbeth. So too in Racine; six of his tragedies bear their heroines' names; and what male characters of his shall we set against Hermione and Andromaque, Bérénice and Roxane, Phèdre and Athalie? So again with Ibsen; what men shall we match with Solveig and Nora, Hedda and Hilda Wangel and Rebecca West?"—F. L. Lucas, *Tragedy*, pp. 114-15.

Elizabethan woman, one branch of illumination fails; one is held up by the scarcity of facts. One knows nothing detailed, nothing perfectly true and substantial about her. History scarcely mentions her. And I turned to Professor Trevelyan again to see what history meant to him. I found by looking at his chapter headings that it meant—

"The Manor Court and the Methods of Open-field Agriculture ... The Cistercians and Sheep-farming ... The Crusades ... The University ... The House of Commons ... The Hundred Years' War ... The Wars of the Roses ... The Renaissance Scholars ... The Dissolution of the Monasteries ... Agrarian and Religious Strife ... The Origin of English Sea-power ... The Armada ..." and so on. Occasionally an individual woman is mentioned, an Elizabeth, or a Mary; a queen or a great lady. But by no possible means could middle-class women with nothing but brains and character at their command have taken part in any one of the great movements which, brought together, constitute the historian's view of the past. Nor shall we find her in any collection of anecdotes. Aubrey hardly mentions her. She never writes her own life and scarcely keeps a diary; there are only a handful of her letters in existence. She left no plays or poems by which we can judge her. What one wants, I thought— and why does not some brilliant student at Newnham or Girton supply it?—is a mass of information; at what age did she marry; how many children had she as a rule; what was her house like; had she a room to herself; did she do the cooking; would she be likely to have a servant? All these facts lie somewhere, presumably, in parish registers and account books; the life of the average Elizabethan woman must be scattered about somewhere, could one collect it and make a book of it. It would be ambitious beyond my daring, I thought, looking about the shelves for books that were not there, to suggest to the students of those famous colleges that they should re-write history, though I own that it often seems a little queer as it is, unreal, lop-sided; but why should they not add a supplement to history? calling it, of course, by some inconspicuous name so that women might figure there without impropriety? For one often catches a glimpse of them in the lives of the great, whisking away into the background, concealing, I sometimes think, a wink, a laugh, perhaps a tear. And, after all, we have lives enough of Jane Austen; it scarcely seems necessary to consider again the influence of the tragedies of Joanna Baillie upon the poetry of Edgar Allan Poe; as for myself, I should not mind if the homes and haunts of Mary Russell Mitford were closed to the public for a century at least. But what I find deplorable, I continued, looking about the book-shelves again, is that nothing is known about women before the eighteenth century. I have no model in my mind to turn about this way and that. Here am I asking why women did not write poetry in the Elizabethan age, and I am not sure how they were educated; whether they were taught to write; whether they had sitting-rooms to themselves; how many women had children before they were twenty-one; what, in short, they did from eight in the morning till eight at night. They had no money evidently; according to Professor Trevelyan they were married whether they liked it or not before they were out of the nursery, at fifteen or sixteen very likely. It would have been extremely odd, even upon this showing, had one of them suddenly written the plays of Shakespeare, I concluded, and I thought of that old gentleman, who is dead now, but was a bishop, I think, who declared that it was impossible for any woman, past, present, or to come, to have the genius of Shakespeare. He wrote to the papers about it. He also told a lady who applied to him for information that cats do not as a matter of fact go to heaven, though they have, he added, souls of a sort. How much thinking those old gentlemen used to save one! How the borders of ignorance shrank back at their approach! Cats do not go to heaven. Women cannot write the plays of Shakespeare.

Be that as it may, I could not help thinking, as I looked at the works of Shakespeare on the shelf, that the bishop was right at least in this; it would have been impossible, completely and entirely, for any woman to have written the plays of Shakespeare in the age of Shakespeare. Let me imagine, since facts are so hard to come by, what would have happened had Shakespeare had a wonderfully gifted sister, called Judith, let us say. Shakespeare himself went, very probably—his mother was an heiress—to the grammar school, where he may have learnt Latin—Ovid, Virgil and Horace—and the elements of grammar and logic. He was, it is well known, a wild boy who poached rabbits, perhaps shot a deer, and had, rather sooner than he should have done, to marry a woman in the neighbourhood, who bore him a child rather quicker than was right. That escapade sent him to seek his fortune in London. He had, it seemed, a taste for the theatre; he began by holding horses at the stage door. Very soon he got work in the theatre, became a successful actor, and lived at the hub of the universe, meeting everybody, knowing everybody, practising his art on the boards, exercising his wits in the streets, and even getting access to the palace of the queen. Meanwhile his extraordinarily gifted sister, let us suppose, remained at home. She was as adventurous, as imaginative, as agog to see the world as he was. But she was not sent to school. She had no chance of learning grammar and logic, let alone of reading Horace and Virgil. She picked up a book now and then, one of her brother's perhaps, and read a few pages. But then her parents came in and told her to mend the stockings or mind the stew and not moon about with books and papers. They would have spoken sharply but kindly, for they were substantial people who knew the conditions of life for a woman and loved their daughter—indeed, more likely than not she was the apple of her father's eye. Perhaps she scribbled some pages up in an apple loft on the sly, but was careful to hide them or set fire to them. Soon, however, before she was out of her teens, she was to be betrothed to the son of a neighbouring wool-stapler. She cried out that marriage was hateful to her, and for that she was severely beaten by her father. Then he ceased to scold her. He begged her instead not to hurt him, not to shame him in this matter of her marriage. He would give her a chain of beads or a fine petticoat, he said; and there were tears in his eyes. How could she disobey him? How could she break his heart? The force of her own gift alone drove her to it. She made up a small parcel of her belongings, let herself down by a rope one summer's night and took the road to London. She was not seventeen. The birds that sang in the hedge were not more musical than she was. She had the quickest fancy, a gift like her brother's, for the tune of words. Like him, she had a taste for the theatre. She stood at the stage door; she wanted to act, she said. Men laughed in her face. The manager—a fat, loose-lipped man—guffawed. He bellowed something about poodles dancing and women acting—no woman, he said, could possibly be an actress. He hinted—you can imagine what. She could get no training in her craft. Could she even seek her dinner in a tavern or roam the streets at midnight? Yet her genius was for fiction and lusted to feed abundantly upon the lives of men and women and the study of their ways. At last—for she was very young, oddly like Shakespeare the poet in her face, with the same grey eyes and rounded brows—at last Nick Greene the actor-manager took pity on her; she found herself with child by that gentleman and so—who shall measure the heat and violence of the poet's heart when caught and tangled in a woman's body?—killed herself one winter's night and lies buried at some cross-roads where the omnibuses now stop outside the Elephant and Castle.

That, more or less, is how the story would run, I think, if a woman in Shakespeare's day had had Shakespeare's genius. But for my part, I agree with the deceased bishop, if such he was—it is unthinkable that any woman in Shakespeare's day should have had Shakespeare's genius. For genius like Shakespeare's is not born among labouring, uneducated, servile people. It was not born in England among the Saxons and the Britons. It is not born today among the working classes. How, then, could it have been born among women whose work began, according to Professor Trevelyan, almost before they were out of the nursery, who were forced to it by their parents and held to it by all the power of law and custom? Yet genius of a sort must have existed among women as it must have existed among the working classes. Now and again an Emily Brontë or a Robert Burns blazes out and proves its presence. But certainly it never got itself on to paper. When, however, one reads of a witch being ducked, of a woman possessed by devils, of a wise woman selling herbs, or even of a very remarkable man who had a mother, then I think we are on the track of a lost novelist, a suppressed poet, of some mute and inglorious Jane Austen, some Emily Brontë who dashed her brains out on the moor or mopped and mowed about the highways crazed with the torture that her gift had put her to. Indeed, I would venture to guess that Anon, who wrote so many poems without signing them, was often a woman. It was a woman Edward Fitzgerald, I think, suggested who made the ballads and the folk-songs, crooning them to her children, beguiling her spinning with them, or the length of the winter's night.

This may be true or it may be false—who can say?—but what is true in it, so it seemed to me, reviewing the story of Shakespeare's sister as I had made it, is that any woman born with a great gift in the sixteenth century would certainly have gone crazed, shot herself, or ended her days in some lonely cottage outside the village, half witch, half wizard, feared and mocked at. For it needs little skill in psychology to be sure that a highly gifted girl who had tried to use her gift for poetry would have been so thwarted and hindered by other people, so tortured and pulled asunder by her own contrary instincts, that she must have lost her health and sanity to a certainty. No girl could have walked to London and stood at a stage door and forced her way into the presence of actor-managers without doing herself a violence and suffering an anguish which may have been irrational—for chastity may be a fetish invented by certain societies for unknown reasons—but were none the less inevitable. Chastity had then, it has even now, a religious importance in a woman's life, and has so wrapped itself round with nerves and instincts that to cut it free and bring it to the light of day demands courage of the rarest. To have lived a free life in London in the sixteenth century would have meant for a woman who was poet and playwright a nervous stress and dilemma which might well have killed her. Had she survived, whatever she had written would have been twisted and deformed, issuing from a strained and morbid imagination. And undoubtedly, I thought, looking at the shelf where there are no plays by women, her work would have gone unsigned. That refuge she would have sought certainly. It was the relic of the sense of chastity that dictated anonymity to women even so late as the nineteenth century. Currer Bell, George Eliot, George Sand, all the victims of inner strife as their writings prove, sought ineffectively to veil themselves by using the name of a man. Thus they did homage to the convention, which if not implanted by the other sex was liberally encouraged by them (the chief glory of a woman is not to be talked of, said Pericles, himself a much-talked-of man), that publicity in women is detestable. Anonymity runs in their blood. The desire to be veiled still possesses them. They are not even now as concerned about the health of their fame as men are, and, speaking generally, will pass a tombstone or a signpost without feeling an irresistible desire to cut their names on it, as Alf, Bert or Chas. must do in obedience to their instinct, which murmurs if it sees a fine woman go by, or even a dog, Ce chien est à moi. And, of course, it may not be a dog, I thought, remembering Parliament Square, the Sieges Allee and other avenues; it may be a piece of land or a man with curly black hair. It is one of the great advantages of being a woman that one can pass even a very fine negress without wishing to make an Englishwoman of her.

That woman, then, who was born with a gift of poetry in the sixteenth century, was an unhappy woman, a woman at strife against herself. All the conditions of her life, all her own instincts, were hostile to the state of mind which is needed to set free whatever is in the brain. But what is the state of mind that is most propitious to the act of creation, I asked? Can one come by any notion of the state that furthers and makes possible that strange activity? Here I opened the volume containing the Tragedies of Shakespeare. What was Shakespeare's state of mind, for instance, when he wrote *Lear* and *Antony and Cleopatra*? It was certainly the state of mind most favourable to poetry that there has ever existed. But Shakespeare himself said nothing about it. We only know casually and by chance that he "never blotted a line." Nothing indeed was ever said by the artist himself about his state of mind until the eighteenth century perhaps. Rousseau perhaps began it. At any rate, by the nineteenth century self-consciousness had developed so far that it was the habit for men of letters to describe their minds in confessions and autobiographies. Their lives also were written, and their letters were printed after their deaths. Thus, though we do not know what Shakespeare went through when he wrote *Lear,* we do know what Carlyle went through when he wrote the *French Revolution;* what Flaubert went through when he wrote *Madame Bovary;* what Keats was going through when he tried to write poetry against the coming of death and the indifference of the world.

And one gathers from this enormous modern literature of confession and self-analysis that to write a work of genius is almost always a feat of prodigious difficulty. Everything is against the likelihood that it will come from the writer's mind whole and entire. Generally material circumstances are against it. Dogs will bark; people will interrupt; money must be made; health will break down. Further, accentuating all these difficulties and making them harder to bear is the world's notorious indifference. It does not ask people to write poems and novels and histories; it does not need them. It does not care whether Flaubert finds the right word or whether Carlyle scrupulously verifies this or that fact. Naturally, it will not pay for what it does not want. And so the writer, Keats, Flaubert, Carlyle, suffers, especially in the creative years of youth, every form of distraction and discouragement. A curse, a cry of agony, rises from those books of analysis and confession. "Mighty poets in their misery dead"—that is the burden of their song. If anything comes through in spite of all this, it is a miracle, and probably no book is born entire and uncrippled as it was conceived.

But for women, I thought, looking at the empty shelves, these difficulties were infinitely more formidable. In the first place, to have a room of her own, let alone a quiet room or a sound-proof room, was out of the question, unless her parents were exceptionally rich or very noble, even up to the beginning of the nineteenth century. Since her pin money, which depended on the good will of her father, was only enough to keep her clothed, she was debarred from such alleviations as came even to Keats or Tennyson or Carlyle, all poor men, from a walking tour, a little journey to France, from the separate lodging which, even if it were miserable enough, sheltered them from the claims and tyrannies of their families. Such material difficulties were formidable; but much worse were the immaterial. The indifference of the world which Keats and Flaubert and other men of genius have found so hard to bear was in her case not indifference but hostility. The world did not say to her as it said to them, Write if you choose; it makes no difference to me. The world said with a guffaw, Write? What's the good of your writing? Here the psychologists of Newnham and Girton might come to our help, I thought, looking again at the blank spaces on the shelves. For surely it is time that the effect of discouragement upon the mind of the artist should be measured, as I have seen a dairy company measure the effect of ordinary milk and Grade A milk upon the body of the rat. They set two rats in cages side by side, and of the two one was furtive, timid and small, and the other was glossy, bold and big. Now what food do we feed women as artists upon? I asked, remembering, I suppose, that dinner of prunes and custard. To answer that question I had only to open the evening paper and to read that Lord Birkenhead is of opinion—but really I am not going to trouble to copy out Lord Birkenhead's opinion upon the writing of women. What Dean Inge says I will leave in peace. The Harley Street specialist may be allowed to rouse the echoes of Harley Street with his vociferations without raising a hair on my head. I will quote, however, Mr. Oscar Browning, because Mr. Oscar Browning was a great figure in Cambridge at one time, and used to examine the students at Girton and Newnham. Mr. Oscar Browning was wont to declare "that the impression left on his mind, after looking over any set of examination papers, was that, irrespective of the marks he might give, the best woman was intellectually the inferior of the worst man." After saying that Mr. Browning went back to his rooms—and it is this sequel that endears him and makes him a human figure of some bulk and majesty—he went back to his rooms and found a stable-boy lying on the sofa—"a mere skeleton, his cheeks were cavernous and sallow, his teeth were black, and he did not appear to have the full use of his limbs. . . . 'That's Arthur' [said Mr. Browning]. 'He's a dear boy really and most high-minded.' " The two pictures always seem to me to complete each other. And happily in this age of biography the two pictures often do complete each other, so that we are able to interpret the opinions of great men not only by what they say, but by what they do.

But though this is possible now, such opinions coming from the lips of important people must have been formidable enough even fifty years ago. Let us suppose that a father from the highest motives did not wish his daughter to leave home and become writer, painter or scholar. "See what Mr. Oscar Browning says," he would say; and there was not only Mr. Oscar Browning; there was the *Saturday Review;* there was Mr. Greg —the "essentials of a woman's being," said Mr. Greg emphatically, "are that *they are supported by, and they minister to, men"*—there was an enormous body of masculine opinion to the effect that nothing could be expected of women intellectually. Even if her father did not read out loud these opinions, any girl could read them for herself; and the reading, even in the nineteenth century, must have lowered her vitality, and told profoundly upon her work. There would always have been that assertion—you cannot do this, you are incapable of doing that—to protest against, to overcome. Probably for a novelist this germ is no longer of much effect; for there have been women novelists of merit. But for painters it must still have some sting in it; and for musicians, I imagine, is even now active and poisonous in the extreme. The woman composer stands where the actress stood in the time of Shakespeare. Nick Greene, I thought, remembering the story I had made about Shakespeare's sister, said that a woman acting put him in mind of a dog dancing. Johnson repeated the phrase two hundred years later of women preaching. And here, I said, opening a book about music, we have the very words used again in this year of grace, 1928, of women who try to write music. "Of Mlle. Germaine Tailleferre one can only repeat Dr. Johnson's dictum concerning a woman preacher, transposed into terms of music. 'Sir, a woman's composing is like a dog's walking on his hind legs. It is not done well, but you are surprised to find it done at all.' " [1] So accurately does history repeat itself.

Thus, I concluded, shutting Mr. Oscar Browning's life and pushing away the rest, it is fairly evident that even in the nineteenth century a woman was not encouraged to be an artist. On the contrary, she was snubbed, slapped, lectured and exhorted. Her mind must have been

[1] *A Survey of Contemporary Music,* Cecil Gray, p. 246.

strained and her vitality lowered by the need of opposing this, of disproving that. For here again we come within range of that very interesting and obscure masculine complex which has had so much influence upon the woman's movement; that deep-seated desire, not so much that *she* shall be inferior as that *he* shall be superior, which plants him wherever one looks, not only in front of the arts, but barring the way to politics too, even when the risk to himself seems infinitesimal and the suppliant humble and devoted. Even Lady Bessborough, I remembered, with all her passion for politics, must humbly bow herself and write to Lord Granville Leveson-Gower: ". . . notwithstanding all my violence in politics and talking so much on that subject, I perfectly agree with you that no woman has any business to meddle with that or any other serious business, farther than giving her opinion (if she is ask'd)." And so she goes on to spend her enthusiasm where it meets with no obstacle whatsoever upon that immensely important subject, Lord Granville's maiden speech in the House of Commons. The spectacle is certainly a strange one, I thought. The history of men's opposition to women's emancipation is more interesting perhaps than the story of that emancipation itself. An amusing book might be made of it if some young student at Girton or Newnham would collect examples and deduce a theory—but she would need thick gloves on her hands, and bars to protect her of solid gold.

But what is amusing now, I recollected, shutting Lady Bessborough, had to be taken in desperate earnest once. Opinions that one now pastes in a book labelled cock-a-doodle-dum and keeps for reading to select audiences on summer nights once drew tears, I can assure you. Among your grandmothers and great-grandmothers there were many that wept their eyes out. Florence Nightingale shrieked aloud in her agony.[1] Moreover, it is all very well for you, who have got yourselves to college and enjoy sitting-rooms—or is it only bed-sitting-rooms?—of your own to say that genius should disregard such opinions; that genius should be above caring what is said of it. Unfortunately, it is precisely the men or women of genius who mind most what is said of them. Remember Keats. Remember the words he had cut on his tombstone. Think of Tennyson; think—but I need hardly multiply instances of the undeniable, if very unfortunate, fact that it is the nature of the artist to mind excessively what is said about him. Literature is strewn with the wreckage of men who have minded beyond reason the opinions of others.

And this susceptibility of theirs is doubly unfortunate, I thought, returning again to my original enquiry into what state of mind is most propitious for creative work, because the mind of an artist, in order to achieve the prodigious effort of freeing whole and entire the work that

[1] See *Cassandra*, by Florence Nightingale, printed in *The Cause*, by R. Strachey.

is in him, must be incandescent, like Shakespeare's mind, I conjectured, looking at the book which lay open at *Antony and Cleopatra*. There must be no obstacle in it, no foreign matter unconsumed.

For though we say that we know nothing about Shakespeare's state of mind, even as we say that, we are saying something about Shakespeare's state of mind. The reason perhaps why we know so little of Shakespeare —compared with Donne or Ben Jonson or Milton—is that his grudges and spites and antipathies are hidden from us. We are not held up by some "revelation" which reminds us of the writer. All desire to protest, to preach, to proclaim an injury, to pay off a score, to make the world the witness of some hardship or grievance was fired out of him and consumed. Therefore his poetry flows from him free and unimpeded. If ever a human being got his work expressed completely, it was Shakespeare. If ever a mind was incandescent, unimpeded, I thought, turning again to the bookcase, it was Shakespeare's mind.

Denis de Rougemont

A man of letters and of very wide interests, the Swiss theologian Denis de Rougemont has been since 1950 director of the European Cultural Center in Geneva. He has also been an articulate proponent of European federalism ever since his return to Europe in 1946 from America, where he had spent the war years in charge of French broadcasts of the Voice of America. He has written books on religion, philosophy, literature, and politics and has published a three-volume personal journal. *Love in the Western World,* the book from which our selection is taken, is a work of erudition, but it might be described as applied erudition. In it the author examines the entire complex history of attitudes toward sexual love and marriage in Western civilization. Space does not permit even a summary of de Rougemont's thesis concerning the origin and nature of romantic love, but, as our selection makes clear, he believes that it has to do with the death-oriented impulse toward violent and destructive passion which was first codified by the troubadours of southern France in the twelfth century. Romantic love, intrinsically opposed, de Rougemont finds, both to the ideal of Christian marriage and to the social reality of marital arrangements, has continued ever since that time to exert a coercive force on the Western mind—in the love poetry of the Renaissance, in romantic literature and music in the nineteenth century, in a final debased and degenerate form in Hollywood movies and cheap fiction in our own times.

The greater part of de Rougemont's book is devoted to a learned examination of cultural history, supported by equally learned digressions into literary history and theological speculation. But he also has many forceful and direct things to say about our society. "The Breakdown of Marriage," relatively self-contained, illuminates popular modern conceptions of love by turning on them the dispassionate light of history. To some extent a critique of modern mass culture, one that has connections with the essays of Ortega and Canetti, the study has its larger value in the wealth of new ideas that it brings to bear on the familiar materials of our own life, ideas capable of interesting even those readers who may not agree with all the author's formulations or conclusions. The institution of marriage in the modern world—its condition, purpose, the stresses placed upon it by rapid social change and the needs of the psyche—this is certainly another topic of much current discussion and debate and one which has its connections to several of the other modern dilemmas touched on in this section. De Rougemont's conclusions in "The Breakdown of Marriage," as in the rest of his book, are frankly determined by his convictions as a Christian theologian; but many of his individual perceptions derive their validity from the fact that he is also a man of the world who has a sharp eye for social and psychological deceptions.

THE MYTH v. MARRIAGE

.... 1. The Breakdown of Marriage

The Middle Ages had two rival moral systems—one upheld by Christianized society; the other the product of heretical courtesy. The first took marriage for granted, and even made it into a sacrament; the second promoted a set of values in the light of which—at any rate theoretically—marriage was a mistake. The attitude of each to adultery clearly indicates their mutual antagonism.

In the eyes of the Church, adultery was at one and the same time a sacrilege, a crime against the natural order, and a crime against the social order. For the sacrament conjoined in one and the same act two faithful souls, two bodies capable of begetting, and two juridical persons. It was therefore a sacrament that made holy the fundamental needs of both the species and the community. Whoever broke the triple undertaking given at the altar did not thereby become "interesting," but an object of pity or contempt. The Roman Catholic synthesis was intended to harmonize fire and water, as alike in Scripture and in the Fathers it was possible to find thoroughly contradictory theories regarding the holiness of procreation—the law of the species—and regarding the holiness of virginity—the law of the spirit. The Old Testament, for example, deems a numerous progeny the sign of election, whereas Saint Paul says that it is good for a man not to touch a woman, even if he also says that is better to marry than to burn.

From *Love in the Western World* by Denis de Rougemont (New York, Pantheon Books, 1956). Reprinted by permission of the publisher.

The heresy which was bound up from the beginning with the *cortezia* of the South of France condemned Catholic marriage on each of the three heads just mentioned. It denied that marriage was a *sacrament,* declaring its sacramental character to be established by no single unambiguous text in the Gospel.[1] It declared procreation to be the work of the Prince of Darkness, the Demiurge who, in its view, had created the visible world. It sought to destroy a social order which could countenance and demand war as a manifestation of the collective will to live.[2] But the mainspring of its triple rejection of marriage was in reality a doctrine according to which Love is the divinizing Eros, everlastingly in anxious conflict with the fleshly creature and this creature's enslaving instincts.

Accordingly, the appearance of the *passion* of Love was bound radically to transform the attitude to adultery. Doubtless, unalloyed Catharist doctrine never condoned the fault *per se;* on the contrary, it prescribed chastity. But, as I have pointed out earlier, inextricable misunderstandings were produced by the courtly symbol of love for the Lady, obviously a kind of love incompatible with marriage in the flesh. To an uninitiated reader of the Provençal poems and Arthurian romances, Tristan was no doubt guilty of a fault in committing adultery, but at the same time the fault took on the aspect of a *splendid experience more magnificent than morality.* What for Manichaeans was a dramatic expression of the struggle between faith and the world thereupon became for such a reader an ambiguous and searing "poesy." And this poesy was seemingly altogether secular. Its seductive power was intensified by the reader's own ignorance of the mystical significance of its symbols, for he supposed these to point merely to some *vague* and *pleasing* riddle.

Only thus can we account for the fact that in the twelfth century an adulterer or adulteress suddenly became somebody "interesting." King David, in lying with Bath-sheba, was held to have committed a crime and to have made himself into an object of contempt. But when Tristan carries off Iseult, his deed turns into romance, and he makes himself into an object of admiration. What had hitherto been a "fault" and what could only give rise to edifying remarks on the perils of sin and on remorse now became—in symbol—something mystically virtuous, and later

[1] According to Father B. M. Lavaud, the Roman Catholic sacrament is open to being justified by the account of the miracle at Cana ("a mere hypothesis," he says, however), by the passage in which Jesus states that what God has joined man must not put asunder, or, finally, by the conversations between the risen Jesus and his disciples regarding the Kingdom of God, "which the Evangelists and the Acts mention, but do not describe in detail." Father Lavaud points to nothing more substantial than these three "hypotheses" as ground for attributing to the traditional dogma a *biblical* authority. Vide his article in *Études carmélitaines,* April 1938, p. 186.

[2] The Gnostics (e.g. Carpocrates) often asserted that "crimes are a tribute paid to life." Cf. Schultz, *Dokumente der Gnosis,* op. cit.

on was degraded (in literature) into a disturbing and alluring entanglement.

I do not want directly to suggest that the present breakdown of marriage is simply the latest aspect of the discord between a medieval heresy and orthodoxy. The heresy, as such, exists no longer; and if orthodoxy does still exist, it must nevertheless be admitted no longer to play a direct part in the lives of our contemporary societies, to the formation of which it contributed so much. In my opinion, the present general demoralization reflects a confused strife in our lives as a result of the co-existence of two *moral* systems, one inherited from religious orthodoxy, but no longer sustained by a living faith; the other derived from a heresy of which the "in-essence-lyrical" expression has come down to us in a form altogether profaned and therefore distorted. On the one hand, we have today a morality concerned for the species and the general well-being of society, though none the less bearing some impress of religion—what are called middle-class morals. On the other hand, there is a morality spread among us through our literary and artistic atmosphere and general culture—and this produces passionate or romantic morals. The whole of middle-class youth in Europe was brought up to regard marriage with respect; and yet at the same time all young people breathe in from books and periodicals, from stage and screen, and from a thousand daily allusions, a romantic atmosphere in the haze of which passion seems to be the supreme test that one day or other awaits every true man or woman, and it is accepted that nobody has really lived till he or she "has been through it." Now, passion and marriage are essentially irreconcilable. Their origins and their ends make them mutually exclusive. Their co-existence in our midst constantly raises insoluble problems, and the strife thereby engendered constitutes a persistent danger for every one of our social safeguards.

In bygone times it fell to the myth to restrain this latent lawlessness, and to fit it symbolically into moral categories. The myth provided an outlet, and operated to the benefit of civilization. But it came about that the myth was abased and profaned together with the formal modes which had furnished its physical embodiment. If it were now to strive to rise into existence again, we know that no powers of *resistance* would be strong enough to serve as its mask and excuse. Every month sees a flood of articles and books about the breakdown of marriage. They are not in the least likely to settle the problem; for only the myth—that is to say, our unawareness—could bring about in behalf of passion a kind of *modus vivendi*. In making us more keenly alive to the problem, these articles and books contribute, on the contrary, to hampering the elaboration of a settlement. They are themselves evidence of the breakdown, and signs also of our inability to repair it with things as they are. For the institution of marriage was founded on three sets of values which subjected it to *compulsions,* and it was precisely in the effect and interaction of these that the myth achieved expression.[3] But today the compulsions have been either relaxed or abandoned.

There were, in the first place, sacred compulsions. Pagan races have invariably made marriage the subject of a ritual, vestiges of which long survived in our own customs. The ritual covered the purchase, abduction, and exorcism of the bride. Nowadays, owing to economic uncertainties, dowries (even on the Continent) have lost importance. The customs derived from nuptial abduction now only live on as rustic practical jokes. In France no longer does a mother call on the parents of the girl whom her son wishes to marry and formally ask for her hand. Nowhere now is a betrothal very often the occasion for a lawyer's presence at a full-dress reception. And few couples feel any "superstitious" need of having their union "blessed" by a priest.

There were, in the second place, social compulsions. But today considerations of rank, blood, family interests, and even money, are receding into the background so far as democratic countries are concerned, and hence the mutual choice of a marriage partner tends more and more to depend on individual circumstances. That is why divorce is steadily on the increase. Likewise epithalamial ceremonies have either been greatly simplified or else are dispensed with altogether. Customs of remote and sacred origin such as that of "the semi-publicity of the nuptial bed"[4] were kept up in the French provinces right into the seventeenth century. The original mystery had been forgotten, but the ritual continued to give weddings their social character and to fit them into the life of the community. But in the eighteenth century the ceremony of "bedding the bride" had already become nothing more than an occasion for mild and picturesque gallantries. Nowadays the honeymoon, to the extent that it survives and retains any significance, must be held to indicate a wish for escape from habitual social surroundings and an insistence on the private nature of what is called wedded bliss.

There were, finally, religious compulsions. But the modern mind, in so far as it is still able to distinguish between Christianity and sacred and social compulsions, recoils from it with horror. For a religious vow is taken for "time and eternity," which means that it makes no allowance for temperamental vagaries, alterations of character, and changes in taste and external circumstances, such as every couple must expect to experience. And it is on there being no such ups and downs that modern couples make what they call their "happiness" depend. I shall return to this presently.

[3] Cf. Book I, above.

[4] *The Waning of the Middle Ages,* op. cit.

From such a general decay of institutional obstructions a slackening of tension was bound to ensue, so that it is no wonder that there is now a vast confusion. Adultery has become a topic either for delicate psychological analysis or else for facetious jokes. Fidelity in marriage has become slightly ridiculous: it is so conventional. Strictly speaking, the two hostile moral systems are no longer in *conflict* (and hence no myth is any longer possible), but are approaching a state of mutual neutralization, which will be reached when the old values—not transcended, but abased—have finally dissolved.

. . . . 2. The Modern Notion of Happiness

Now that marriage has ceased to enjoy the safeguards of a system of social compulsions, the only possible basis on which it can rest is individual choice. This means, actually, that the success of any given marriage depends upon an individual notion of the nature of happiness, which at best may be assumed to be identical in the minds of both parties. And yet if in any event it is perplexing enough to define happiness in general, definition becomes impossible when account has to be taken of the contemporary wish to control one's own happiness, or—what doubtless amounts to the same thing—to be able *to experience* the ingredients of one's happiness and to be able to analyse them and roll them over the tongue, so as to give here and there a neat pat of improvement. Your happiness, it is being asserted from the pulpits of magazines, depends on this or on that; and this or that is invariably something that must be *acquired,* usually for cash. The consequence of this propaganda is that we are obsessed by the notion of a facile happiness and at the same time are rendered incapable of being happy. For everything thus suggested introduces us to a world of comparisons in which, until there are men like gods, no happiness can be established. Happiness is indeed a Eurydice, vanishing as soon as gazed upon. It can exist only in *acceptance,* and succumbs as soon as it is laid claim to. For it appertains to being, not to having, as the moralists in all ages have insisted; and our own age brings no new factor to disprove them. Every wish to experience happiness, to have it at one's beck and call—instead of *being* in a *state* of happiness, as though by grace—must instantly produce an intolerable sense of want.

To wish marriage to be based on such "happiness" implies in men and women today a capacity for boredom which is almost morbid, or else a secret intention not to play fair. Perhaps it is only this intention or hope that can account for the readiness of couples to get married "without believing in it." The dream of potential passion acts as a perpetual distraction to paralyse the revulsions of boredom. People are not unaware that passion is a woe, but they imagine that such a woe will be splendid and "vital" in a way ordinary life cannot be, and more exciting than the "happy-go-lucky" present. Either a resigned boredom or else passion—this is the dilemma our lives come up against as a result of the contemporary notion of happiness. In any case this notion threatens the ruin of marriage as a social institution that is defined by its stability.

. . . . .3. "It's Wonderful to be in Love!"

In the twelfth century in Provence love was regarded as a dignity. It not only imparted a titular nobility, but actually ennobled. Troubadours were raised socially to the level of the aristocracy, which treated them as equals. That is perhaps how there has been imposed on us today through the medium of literature the altogether modern and romantic notion that passion is something morally noble, and need know no law and no custom. Whoever loves passionately is supposed to be thereby made one of an exalted section of mankind among whom social barriers cease to exist. A Tzigane may carry off a princess; a mechanic, marry an heiress. Likewise, a beauty queen has some hopes of becoming the wife of an earl or millionaire. This is a modern "adaptation"—to use a cinematographic term, such as is alone appropriate here[5]—of the theory that love is above the established social order.

The profane passion is something absurd, a kind of drug, a "sickness of the soul," as the Ancients supposed, everybody is ready to grant, and moralists have said so *ad nauseam;* but in this age of novels and films, when all of us are more or less drugged, nobody will *believe* it, and the distinction is capital. The moderns, men and women of passion, expect irresistible love to produce some revelation either regarding themselves or about life at large. This is a last vestige of the primitive mysticism. From poetry to the piquant anecdote, passion is everywhere treated as an *experience,* something that will alter my life and enrich it with the unexpected, with thrilling chances, and with enjoyment ever more violent and gratifying. The whole of possibility opens before me, a future that assents to desire! I am to enter into it, I shall rise to it, I shall reach it in "transports." The reader will say that this is but the everlasting illusion of mankind, the most guileless and—notwithstanding all I have said—the most "natural"; for it is the illusion of freedom and of living to the full. But really a man becomes free only when he has attained self-mastery, where as a man of passion seeks instead to be defeated, to lose all self-control, to be beside himself and in ecstasy. And indeed he is being urged on by his nostalgia, the origin and end of which are unknown to him. His illusion of freedom springs from this double ignorance. A man of

---

[5] German films in the days of Hitlerism freely used the Hollywood plot in which a workman or chauffeur comes "to deserve" his employer's daughter.

passion wants to discover his "type of woman" and to love no other. Gérard de Nerval, in one of his poems, tells of a dream in which a noble Lady appears to him in a landscape of childhood memories.

> She's fair, dark-eyed, and in old-fashioned clothes
> That in another life I may withal
> Have seen before, and now but do recall.

Without question this is a mother-image, and psychoanalysis has shown what tragic impediments that may imply. But to quote a poet is either of no value or of too much. I want to confine myself to the illusion which most people in the present century have been *taught:* what obsesses them far more than a mother-image is "standardized beauty." Nowadays —and we are only at the beginning—a man who falls passionately in love with a woman whom he *alone* finds beautiful is supposed to be a prey to nerves. So many years hence he will have to undergo treatment. Admittedly, every generation forms a standardized notion of beauty as a matter of course, even as fashion concentrates at various times on heads, bosoms, hips, or the slim lines of the open-air girl. But nowadays our sheep-like aesthetic tastes exert a greater influence than ever before, and they are being fostered by every possible technical and sometimes political means. A feminine type thus recedes more and more from personal imponderables and is selected in Hollywood or by the State. This influence of standardized beauty is a double one. On the one hand, it preordains who shall be an appropriate object of passion (and to this extent the object is drained of personality); on the other hand, it disqualifies a marriage in which the bride is not like the obsessing star of the moment. In short, the present so-called "freedom" of passion is a question of advertising power. A man who imagines he is yearning for "his" type, or a woman for "hers," is having his or her private wishes determined by fashionable and commercial influences; i.e. by novelty.

. . . . 4. Marrying Iseult?

Now suppose that, in spite of everything, a man succeeds in plumping for a particular type as his type—a type which will be a cross between what naturally appeals to him and what the cinema has taught him to like. He meets a woman of this type, and identifies her. There she is, the woman of his heart's desire and of his most intimate nostalgia, the Iseult of his dreams![6] And of course she is already married. But let her get a divorce, and she shall be his! Together they will experience "real life,"

---

[6] The title of a novel by Max Brod, *Die Frau nach der man sich sehnt*—the women we yearn after, of our nostalgia—supplies the best definition of Iseult. Passionate love wants "the *faraway* princess," whereas Christian love wants "our *neighbour*."

and the Tristan he nurses like his hidden daemon in his bosom will wax and bloom. As regards the revelation of the myth, that is all that matters. There we have the real "marriage for love" of our time—with passion as the bride! But thereupon the onlookers (or the public) display a certain uneasiness. Will the lover with all his desires gratified continue to be in love with his Iseult *once* she has been *wed?* Is a cherished nostalgia still desirable once it has recovered its object? For Iseult is ever a stranger, the very essence of what is strange in woman and of all that is eternally fugitive, vanishing, and almost hostile in a fellow-being, that which indeed incites to pursuit, and rouses in the heart of a man who has fallen a prey to the myth an avidity for possession so much more delightful than possession itself. She is the woman-from-whom-one-is-parted: to possess her is to lose her.

And thereupon begins a new "passion." There is a deliberate effort to renew both obstacle and struggle. The woman in my arms I must imagine as other than she is. I give her another guise, I cause her to recede in my dreams, I strive to disturb the emotional tie that is gradually being formed thanks to the smoothness and serenity of our lives. For I must devise fresh obstructions if I am to go on desiring, and if I am to magnify my desire to the dimensions of a conscious and intense passion that shall be infinitely thrilling. And only suffering can make me aware of passion; and that is why I like to suffer and to cause to suffer. When Tristan carries off Iseult to the forest, where there is nothing any longer to obstruct their union, the daemon of passion sets down a drawn sword between their two bodies. Let us descend a few centuries, stepping down at the same time the whole gamut that stretches from the age of religious heroism to the drab confusion in which men and women of our own profane era are struggling: instead of the knight's sword, it is the sly dream of the husband that comes between him and the wife he can only continue to desire by imagining she is his mistress.[7] In countless nauseating novels there is now depicted the kind of husband who fears the flatness and same old jog-trot of married life in which his wife loses her "allure" because no obstructions come between them. Such husbands are the pathetic victims of a myth the mystical promise of which long ago faded out. In the eyes of Tristan, Iseult was nothing but the symbol of luminous Desire: his other world was the divinizing death that was to release him from terrestrial ties. So Iseult had to be the Impossible, for every possible love recalls us to its bonds, reduces us to those limits of time and space without which there are no "creatures"—whereas the one goal of infinite love is compelled to be the divine: God, our idea of God, or the deified Self. For a man whom the myth now haunts without disclosing its secret, there is no other world beyond passion except another

[7] The recipe was made available as early as Balzac's *Physiologie du mariage* (1828).

passion, which he must pursue in another turmoil of appearances each time more fleeting. Originally it was of the essence of mystic passion to be *without end,* and that is how this passion became distinct from the throb of carnal desire. But whereas infinity in the eyes of Tristan was an eternity from which there could be no return and in which his lacerated spirit would at last dissolve, men and women today can look to nothing but the everlasting return of an ardour constantly being thwarted.

Formerly victims of the myth could not throw off its spell except by escaping out of the finite world. Today a passion calling itself "irresistible" (as an alibi for the discharge of responsibility) cannot even discover how to be *faithful,* since its end is no longer transcendence. One after the other, it exhausts illusions it has found all too easy to grasp. Instead of leading to death, it is broken off by unfaithfulness. How patent the degradation of a Tristan who has *several* Iseults! But it is not he who should be blamed; for he is the victim of a social organization in which the obstructions have been cheapened. They break down too soon, before the undertaking has been completed. A soul that sets out to rise in opposition to, and above, the world, has incessantly to begin its ascent afresh. And thereupon a modern Tristan lets himself turn into the antithetical Don Juan type—the man of successive love affairs. The categories break down, and the experience itself ceases to be outstanding. Alone the mythical Don Juan could evade this consummation. But he knew no Iseult, no unattainable passion, neither past nor future, nor sensual anguish. He lived always in the present, having no time to love, to wait, or to remember; and nothing that he desired could resist him, because he *loved* not what did resist.

To love in the sense of passion-love is the contrary of to live. It is an impoverishment of one's being, an *askesis* without sequel, an inability to enjoy the present without imagining it as absent, a never-ending flight from possession. To love with passion-love meant "to live" for Tristan; as the true life which he summoned was transfiguring death. But we have lost transcendence. Death is but a slow consumption.

It is evident in the light of a knowledge of the original myth that the popular novels and films of the present day are the sign of a decay of the individual person; the sign of a sort of sickness of being. Nearly all the complications to which plots resort do not amount to more than a monotonous arrangement of the contrivances of an enfeebled passion in quest of *secret* obstructions. Passion now only wants somehow to keep going. For instance, there is the psychology of jealousy, a jealousy that has been wished for and that is provoked and surreptitiously encouraged— and not only in "the other"! A man or woman wants the beloved to be unfaithful in order that he or she may once again go forth in pursuit and once again "experience" love for its own sake. Rapture is now no

more than a sensation, and it leads nowhere. Married people are constantly being thrown back into a realm of comparison, which is the realm
of jealousy. Extruding from his or her own self and also from the present
as it is given, unable to take the other as he or she is, because that would
mean being first of all content with oneself, a man or woman now sees
on every side nothing but things to be coveted, qualities that he or she
feels the want of, and grounds for comparison that invariably turn against
the comparer. It hurts a husband to find that other women seem beautiful in a way his wife is not, even when everybody else insists that hers is
the greater beauty. For he does not understand either how to possess or
how to enjoy what reality has given him. He has lost the one essential—
a sense of constancy. For to be faithful is to have decided to accept another
being for his or her own sake, in his or her own limitations and reality,
choosing this being not as an excuse for excited elevation or as an "object
of contemplation," but as having a matchless and independent life which
requires *active* love.

I am not trying to attack passion here. I confine myself to describing
it, well aware that I shall convince not a single victim of the profaned
myth. But it was necessary to show briefly by means of a few features *how*
this passion leads to a number of psychological fates the effects of which
are beyond dispute. It has got to be admitted that *passion wrecks the very
notion of marriage at a time when there is being attempted the feat of
trying to ground marriage in values elaborated by the morals of passion.*
Of course it would be going too far to suggest that a majority of people
today are a prey to Tristan's frenzy. Few are capable of the thirst that
would cause them to drink the love-potion, and still fewer are being
elected to succumb to the archetypal anguish. But they are all, or nearly
all, dreaming about it, or else have mused upon it. And however worn
and faded the mark of the original myth, it still hugs the secret of the
anxiety that is nowadays disturbing married couples. The contemporary
mind recoils from nothing so much as from the notion of a limitation deliberately accepted; and nothing pleases this mind more than the mirage
of infinite transcendence which the reminiscent impress of the myth keeps
up. To try to *grow conscious* of the nature of the situation—that sums up
the ambition that inspired the preceding analyses; but I realize that they
have taken me to the limits of the displeasing. We are too fond of our
illusions to suffer gladly any attempt even to name them.

.... 5. **From Lawlessness to Eugenics**

Nevertheless, modern marriage, which may be said by antiphrasis to be
founded upon the remnants of the myth, amounts to a permanent state
of lawlessness, and this must obviously involve perils such as no *social*

order can tolerate. I say nothing of the spiritual peril to which the morals of escape engendered by the myth must expose a moral being. The social peril is enough to account for the number of attempts made since the first world war "to re-establish" marriage.

There were the respectable efforts of the Churches to define the institution afresh, together with the moral duties which it implies.[8] Humanists restated the arguments of Goethe and Engels in favour of marriage. According to the former, marriage is the greatest achievement of European culture and the solid foundation of any private life; according to the latter, monogamic unions provide the most sensible relation between the sexes in a society that has been emancipated from the restraints of money and class. Others sought to found a science of conjugal relations. Jung analysed the "psychological conflict" and the "neuroses" that lie, in his opinion, at the root of the evil; he hinted that medical psychology could put everything straight. Van de Velde and Hirschfeld suggested that the best course would be to spread a more accurate knowledge of sex.

So many inquiries and so many panaceas indicate how serious the question is, but they have not produced any adequate means of settling it. Curiously enough, too, every one of these learned authors devotes a few lines to extolling passion, or at least to seeming to countenance it. There are obvious reasons for hesitating to offend readers in their most intimate and assured convictions. To do so would seem "puritanical." Some of these writers, however, go further, indulging in the paradox that loving passion may crown a union that has been perfectly achieved (according to their recipe). Nobody, so far as I know, has dared to say that love, *as understood nowadays,* is the flat negation of the marriage to which it is claimed that this love can serve as support. The reason is that nobody seems to know exactly what passionate love may be, and neither where it comes from nor whither it may lead. There is indeed a feeling that something is wrong, but writers also fear (quite correctly) that if they attacked passion they would pass for Philistines. So the fundamental problem is passed over with a simulated lightness. "We must get ourselves read, and win confidence. There is no going against the tide of a whole epoch. Passion has always existed, it therefore always will exist; and we are no Don Quixotes." No doubt! And yet something *must* be done. Hence the one question confronting the historian and sociologist is: *What mechanism* will be released in order to put matters right—what mechanism or what collective reflex?

Two large-scale experiments furnish one kind of answer, and perhaps point to the solution to which we shall all be brought.

8 The encyclical *Casti connubii* replied to the decisions of the Anglican Lambeth Conference. The oecumenical meetings at Stockholm and Oxford of representatives of all the non-Roman Churches also touched on the problem.

Revolutionary Russia was the scene of a youthful "outburst" of sex which it is tempting to regard as unprecedented in European annals.[9] As for marriage, theoretically it was swept away during the early stages of the Soviets. Nihilist or romantic intellectuals had inspired the young Bolshevist leaders with a doctrine that found expression in unmarried cohabitation, abortion, and the desertion of babies—in short, in whatever was imagined to defy reactionary prejudices mistakenly thought to have been fostered by bourgeois capitalism. Lenin, in a famous letter to a woman Bolshevist named Zetkin, describes this collapse of morals, and protests with all the vigour of a "professional" revolutionary—and hence of a Puritan—against the sexual lawlessness which—using the words in their contemptuous Marxian sense—he termed "petit bourgeois." Twenty years later, a "restoration of morals" had been achieved, not owing to any sudden revival of virtue nor thanks to the efforts of some philanthropic society, but as a result of the deliberate action of a dictatorship fully alive to the conditions requisite for its survival. Stalin's immediate aim was to rebuild the framework of his nation. For in the absence of a framework economic life was in danger of collapse, and "national defence" could not be organized without constant appeal to the passion of the early revolutionaries, and it was precisely this passion that Stalin had determined to get rid of. To lay down new social foundations, and especially that most stable and most stabilizing of units: the family, became therefore a vital necessity. The nature of the mechanism of productivist dictatorship compelled the so-called Socialist State to decree a series of laws against divorce—which was made more burdensome—and against abortion and the deserting of babies born out of wedlock. The sudden severity of these laws, the psychological shock which they inflicted, propaganda, and measures enabling the police to keep a watch on private life, transformed the moral atmosphere of Russia round about the year 1936.[10] Marriage was instituted again on strictly utilitarian, collectivist, and eugenic principles; and there was promoted a spirit in which individual problems tended to lose all their dignity, legitimacy, and lawless virulence.[11]

In pre-Hitlerite Germany the level of lawlessness to which sex sank was possibly quite as low as that reached in Russia before Stalin. The gradual decay of social restraints was not accompanied by any outward

[9] Actually, similar happenings occurred among the youth in so-called bourgeois countries. But in Russia principles of "emancipation" were advertised; elsewhere the young were content to put these principles into practice.

[10] Cf. Hélène Iswolsky, *Femmes soviétiques* (Paris, 1937).

[11] When dealing with the U.S.S.R. the words "family," "eugenics," and "abolition of passion" should all be put in inverted commas. The headlong drop in the population compelled Stalin to encourage births. But who can be sure that his plans were carried out? And his motives, I repeat, were not in the least "moral"; rather were they military.

violence, but on that very account the marriage morals of the young were all the more seriously undermined. At the same time the decline of the passion myth in the fatherland of romanticism involved far more complicated consequences than in France, and they seemed of the greatest variety. The morbid shamelessness of the German post-war years, the *neue Sachlichkeit* promoted by advanced writers and artists, the homosexuality so common in the secret societies that were a prelude to Hitlerism, the sadistic outbursts in the Baltic *Freikorps,* the so-called "political" crimes committed by leagues of youth, certain forms of nudism, the "trial betrothals" that became customary among students, the serious manner in which passionate quarrels involving "threes" or "fours" were treated— on the model of Friedrich Schlegel's *Lucinde*—all these were so many signs of the sex stampede that followed the weakening of matrimonial restraints and the decline of the myth of fatal love. Already the elements of despair and of private surrender to impulse, which are implicit in any pseudo-legitimization of a strictly individual "happiness," were rising to the surface.

But Hitler's dictatorship, for the very reason that it claimed to operate for racial and military ends, was bound to address itself at the very outset to repairing this breakdown in the nation's morals. To begin with, the anti-social ideal of "happiness" and that of "living dangerously" were countered by the promotion of a collective ideal. *"Gemeinnütz geht vor Eigennütz!"* The general interest comes before that of individuals! Next, by means of every spectacular, didactic, and even religious instrument that it could devise, Hitlerism effected the extraordinary *transference*[12] which resulted in making the one legitimate and possible object of passion the concept of a Nation symbolized in its Führer. First, woman was bereft of her romantic halo and relegated to the position of wife, her only function being to bear and to bring up children till at the age of four or five they could be handed over to the Party. Next, certain steps in eugenics were taken. A "school of future brides" was opened in order to supply wives to the S.S. *(Schutz-Staffeln),* Nazi protective squads, troops selected as supposedly incarnating the racial ideal. Entrance to this school was confined to girls of fair complexion, of Aryan blood, and at least five feet eight inches in height. Hence, in Germany, a man's "type of woman" was fixed for him, not by the recollections of his unconscious nor by exotic fashions, but by the scientific section of the Ministry of Propaganda. In 1938 similar schools were set up for all German women, and attendance at these schools may well have become compulsory. It was decreed that marriages would henceforth be celebrated "in the name of the State." The ultimate aim is obvious. It was to reach a point at which only eugenic marriages would be legal, and would be allowed to take place

[12] Referred to in Book V, above.

entirely according to social, racial, and physiological data; they would not be affected in any way by individual "taste." Then scientific marriage would have fulfilled the dream of Lycurgus: it would have become a stage in military training.

Stalin's experiment failed, if we can trust the accounts of the present state of the manners of youth in U.S.S.R. Nazi-ism belongs to the past. Yet the totalitarian temptation is still there. We are not forbidden to imagine that our democracies will one day yield to it in the name of some "science" or sociological hygiene. The enforced practice of eugenics *may* succeed there where all moral doctrines had failed, resulting in the effective disappearance of any "spiritual"—and hence artificial—need of passion. The cycle of courtly love would be complete. The Europe of passion would be no more. A new and unforeseeable Europe would be taking its rise in the laboratory.

.... 6. The Significance of the Breakdown

The better to see our situation, let us look at America—that other Europe which has been released from both the routine practices and traditional restraints of the old. No other known civilization, in the 7,000 years that one civilization has been succeeding another, has bestowed on the love known as *romance* anything like the same amount of daily publicity by means of the screen, the hoarding, the letterpress and advertisements in magazines, by means of songs and pictures, and of current morals and of whatever defies them. No other civilization has embarked with anything like the same ingenuous assurance upon the perilous enterprise of making marriage coincide with love thus understood, and of making the first depend upon the second.

During a telephone strike in 1947, the women operators in the county town of White Plains, near New York, received the following call: "My girl and I want to get married. We're trying to locate a justice of the peace. Is it an emergency?" The women telephone operators decided forthwith that it was. And the newspaper which reported the item headed it: "Love is Classified as an Emergency." This commonplace newspaper cutting provides an example of the perfectly natural beliefs of Americans, and that is how it is of interest. It shows that in America the terms "love" and "marriage" are practically equivalent; that when one "loves" one must get married instantly; and, further, that "love" should normally overcome all obstacles, as is shown every day in films, novels, and comic-strips. In reality, however, let romantic love overcome no matter how many obstacles, and it almost always fails at one. That is the obstacle constituted by time. Now, either marriage is an institution set up to be lasting—or it is meaningless. That is the first secret of the present breakdown, a breakdown of which the extent can be measured simply by reference to divorce statistics, where the United States heads the list of countries. To try to base marriage on a form of love which is unstable by definition is really to benefit the State of Nevada. To insist that no matter what film, even one about the atomic bomb, shall contain a certain amount of the romantic drug—and romantic more than erotic—known as "love interest," is to give publicity to the germs that are making marriage ill, not to a cure.

Romance feeds on obstacles, short excitations, and partings; marriage, on the contrary, is made up of wont, daily propinquity, growing accustomed to one another. Romance calls for "the faraway love" of the troubadours; marriage, for love of "one's neighbour." Where, then, a couple have married in obedience to a romance, it is natural that the first time a conflict of temperament or of taste becomes manifest the parties should each ask themselves: "Why did I marry?" And it is no less natural that, obsessed by the universal propaganda in favour of romance, each should seize the first occasion to fall in love with somebody else. And thereupon it is perfectly logical to decide to divorce, so as to obtain from the new love, which demands a fresh marriage, a new promise of happiness—all three words, "marriage," "love," "happiness," being synonyms. Thus, remedying boredom with a passing fever, "he for the second time, she for the fourth," American men and women go in quest of "adjustment." They do not seek it, however, in the old situation, the one guaranteed—"for better, for worse"—by a vow. They seek it, on the contrary, in a fresh "experience" regarded as such, and affected from the start by the same potentialities of failure as those which preceded it. That is how divorce assumes in the United States a less "disastrous" character, and is even more "normal," than in Europe. There where a European regards the rupture of a marriage as producing social disorder and the loss of a capital of joint recollections and experiences, an American has rather the impression that "he is putting his life straight," and opening up for himself a fresh future. The economy of saving is once again opposed to that of squandering, as the concern to preserve the past is opposed to the concern to make a clean sweep in order to build something tidy, without compromise. But any man opposed to compromise is inconsistent in marrying. And he who would draw a draft on his future is very unwise to mention beforehand that he wishes to be allowed not to honour it; as did the young millionairess who told the newspaper men on the eve of her marriage: "It's marvellous to be getting married *for the first time!*" A year later, she got divorced.

Whereupon a number of people propose to forbid divorce, or at least to render it very difficult. But it is marriage which, in my opinion, has been made too easy, through the supposition that let there be "love" and marriage should follow, regardless of outmoded conventions of social and religious station, of upbringing and substance. It is certainly possible to imagine new conditions which candidates for marriage—that true "co-existence" which should be enduring, peaceable, and mutually educative—should fulfil. It is possible to exact tests or ordeals bearing on whatever gives any human union its best chances of lasting: aims in life, rhythms of life, comparative vocations, characters, and temperaments. If marriage—that is to say, lastingness—is what is wanted, it is natural to ensure its conditions. But such reforms would have little effect in a world which retained, if not true passion, at least the nostalgia of passion that has grown congenital in western man.

When marriage was established on social conventions, and hence, from the individual standpoint, on chance, it had at least as much likelihood of success as marriage based on "love" alone. But the whole of western evolution goes from tribal wisdom to individual risk; it is irreversible, and it must be approved to the extent it tends to make collective and native destiny depend on personal decision.

It is also clear that the present breakdown of marriage, in Europe as in America, results from a plurality of profound or proximate causes, of which the cult of romance is but an instance. (But it was my due to myself to insist on it here.) For the quest for individual happiness to have precedence on social stability, and for respect of psychological evolution to have precedence on the meaning of a vow, is something which can be connected with the romantic complex. But there is more to it, and in other domains, or at other levels of reality, at times social and at other times psychical.

Woman's emancipation—her entrance into the professions and her claim to equality of treatment—is a perceptible factor in the breakdown. The popularization of psychological knowledge is another. Men and women of the twentieth century, even with only a smattering of the existence of Freudian complexes, of the play of repressions and inhibitions, and of the origin of neuroses, are inclined to require more than their ancestors did from marriage and from conjugal life. Those demands will go on growing with the diffusion of the "human sciences," the early stammerings of which have already in perceptible measure modified the self-awareness of western man. Finally, there are signs of a more profound event—one possibly comparable to that which invaded the collective psyche in the twelfth century, and which I called in Book II the "Reascent of the Shakti." The strong revival of Mariology in the Roman Catholic Church with its popular millions; the most recent work of C. G. Jung and his school,[13] on the eternal Sophia, Wisdom, and Mother-Virgin; and also (and really otherwise) the revival of interest in Catharism shown by the *avant-garde* of European literature, and in the elevation of the "Child-Woman," saviour of rational man, or the repeated announcement that the feminine principle is about to get even with patriarchal pretensions[14]—all that allows the premonition of a vast evolution of the modern psyche in prospect, and even though the first principle and the implications of such an evolution are withheld from us, nevertheless an evolution that will possibly provide the future historians of our western society with the key to a breakdown of which we so far see but the superficial, sporadic, and incoherent symptoms.

We can feel how vain any attempt would be at present "to resolve" the contradictions which so many men and women put up with in marriage. Harmonization or a new equipoise is being worked out, perhaps—invisibly. Its nature keeps it for the present out of range of individual awareness. Any solution that I might be tempted to offer, even if deemed "it" in the next century, would be stamped today as ineffectual, or, if it could effect anything, would do more harm than good. If I had hit upon it, and had the power to make my contemporaries adopt it, I should carefully refrain from doing so. For a breakdown of this sort is no accident. To try to arrest it as a fever is stopped would be not so much to cure it as to deprive ourselves of any prospect of one day understanding its secret. And it would be at the same time a kind of cheating, either because a solution would mean really no more than an attempt to get back to the former equipoise, and how precarious that was the breakdown itself shows, or else because any solution must cast over the future of the community a theory or precepts reasonable enough in themselves, but the remote effects of which cannot be estimated so long as the general *significance* of the breakdown escapes us.

We shall be better employed in deciphering the message and in patiently decoding the ambiguous tidings which the breakdown brings us concerning ourselves—concerning our secret wishes, the genuine tendency—possibly creative—sometimes betrayed in our rebellions, our ingenuous illusions, and our sins. To seek to repair the breakdown of marriage by means of moral, social, or scientific measures inspired by the sole

13 Cf. C. G. Jung, *Antwort auf Hiob* (1952), where the author does not hesitate to write that the proclamation in 1950 of the Dogma of the Assumption of the Virgin marks the most important religious event since the Reformation. See also Henry Corbin's study of the Eternal Sophia in *Revue de Culture européenne* No. 5, 1953.

14 Cf. notably, and in addition to the works cited above on Catharism and Courtly Love, such books as *Arcane 17* by André Breton, the lyrical novels of Julien Gracq, the studies by Robert Graves concerning the Great Goddess, and by Adrian Turel on matriarchates.

desire to stop further damage, might very well be to deny arbitrarily to this breakdown what seems to be its actual character—namely, that of a quest, as yet carried on blindfold, for *a fresh equipoise* of the married couple—a harmony that will reconcile the invariably simultaneous, contrary, and legitimate demands of the stability and evolution of both the species and the individual, and indeed the needs both of the fulfilment of the person and of the Absolute that alone judges and raises up that person.

Simone de Beauvoir

Memoirs of a Dutiful Daughter, from which "Life at the Sorbonne" is excerpted, is the first volume of the autobiography of the famous novelist and woman of letters who is associated with Jean-Paul Sartre as one of the founders of the modern philosophy of existentialism. As autobiography, it may be compared with the accounts by Arthur Koestler and Diana Athill; as the personal history of an intellectually gifted woman, it has intrinsic connections with Virginia Woolf's essay on that subject. Simone de Beauvoir's book exemplifies the genre of autobiography in its largest and most ambitious form: the author-subject viewing her own individual experience as both unique and yet also, and consciously, as a mirror that reflects the larger issues of history. The genre demands above all an intellectual and emotional honesty which borders on the absolute. In this respect, as well as in several other important ones, de Beauvoir's work, which is still in the process of composition, makes a significant claim on our attention.

This particular section recreates the inner and outer events of one of the author's crucial years of study at the Sorbonne. There is much here of the friendships, the intellectual enthusiasms and perplexities, the emotional crises which fill her life as a student and young woman, and one particularly important confrontation with what she calls "the physical realities" as the result of the scene she witnesses in the Place Clichy. Indeed, the evocation of the cosmopolitan atmosphere of life in the midst of the great city of Paris stands as much at an opposite extreme from the protected bourgeois world that has produced her as does the spirit of free inquiry at the university itself, and in one sense this whole section is really about freedom. Simone, who has been quietly but firmly turning away from her background, is beginning to find herself, to make choices. Although she recognizes the "resistances and prohibitions" that still confuse her, she has an unequivocal longing to take her place freely in the community of the intellect and the confidence that she will in time find her place as a woman as well. Her childhood friend Zaza, with her plaintive "the things I love do not love each other," is not so fortunate; instead of either resolving the conflict between generations or bluntly choosing one set of values or the other, she attempts an uneasy compromise, which results in a "division of personality." Her mother, Madame Mabille, with her hatred of intellectuals, her desire to arrange her daughter's marriage and to manage her life for her, stands in the mind of the author for the old narrow authoritarianism of the "orthodox" bourgeois world which even the young Simone quite clearly regards as the enemy.

LIFE AT THE SORBONNE*

The beginning of this academic year was unlike any other. By deciding to enter for the competition, I had at last escaped from the labyrinth in which I had been going round in circles for the last three years: I was now on my way to the future. From now on, every day had its meaning: it was taking me further on my road to final liberation. I was spurred on by the difficulty of the enterprise: there was no longer any question of straying from the straight and narrow path, or of becoming bored. Now that I had something definite to work for, I found that the earth could give me all I wanted; I was released from disquiet, despair and from all my regrets. "In this diary, I shall no longer make note of tragical self-communings, but only of the events of every day." I had the feeling that after a painful apprenticeship my real life was just beginning, and I threw myself into it gladly.

In October, while the Sorbonne was closed, I spent my days in the Bibliothèque Nationale. I had obtained permission to have my lunch out: I would buy bread and rilletts and eat them in the gardens of the Palais Royal while watching the petals of the late roses fall; sitting on the benches, navvies would be munching thick sandwiches and drinking cheap red wine. If it was raining, I would take shelter in the Café Biard with bricklayers eating out of mess-tins; I was delighted to escape from the ritual of family meals; by reducing food to its essential elements I felt I was taking another step in the direction of freedom. I would go back to the library; I was studying the theory of relativity, and was passionately interested in it. From time to time I would look up at the other readers and lean back proudly in my armchair: among these specialists, scholars, researchers and thinkers I felt at home. I no longer felt myself to be rejected by my environment; it was I who had rejected it in order to enter that society—of which I saw here a cross-section—in which all those minds that are interested in finding out the truth communicate with each other across the distances of space and time. I, too, was taking part in the effort which humanity makes to know, to understand, to express itself: I was

* Editor's title.

From *Memoirs of a Dutiful Daughter* by Simone de Beauvoir (New York, The World Publishing Company, 1959). Reprinted by permission of the publisher.

engaged in a great collective enterprise which would release me for ever from the bonds of loneliness. What a victory! I would settle down to work again. At a quarter to six, the superintendent's voice would solemnly announce: "Gentlemen—we shall—very soon—be—closing." It was always a surprise, after leaving my studies, to come back to the shops outside, the lights, the passers-by, and the dwarf who sold bunches of violets near the Théâtre Français. I would walk slowly, giving myself up to the melancholy of evening and of my return home.

Stépha came back to Paris a few days after me and often came to the library to read Goethe and Nietzsche. With her roving eye and ready smile, she was too attractive to men and they were too much interested in her for her to be able to get much work done. She would have barely taken her place beside me when she would put her coat over her shoulders and go outside to have a chat with one of her boy-friends: the teacher studying German, the Prussian student, the Roumanian doctor. We used to lunch together and although she was not well-off she would treat me to cakes at a pastrycook's or a good cup of coffee at the Bar Poccardi. At six o'clock we would stroll along the Boulevards, or most often have tea in her room. She had a bright blue room in an hotel in the Rue Saint-Sulpice; she had hung reproductions of Cézanne, Renoir and El Greco on the walls, together with some drawings by a Spanish friend who wanted to be a painter. I liked being with her. I loved the soft feel of her fur collar, her little toques, her dresses, her scent, her warbling voice, her loving gestures. My relationships with my other friends—Zaza, Jacques, Pradelle—had always been extremely formal. But Stépha would take my arm in the street; in the cinema she would hold hands with me; she would kiss me on the slightest provocation. She used to tell me all kinds of stories about herself, was enthusiastic about Nietzsche, indignant about Madame Mabille and made fun of the men who were in love with her: she could do imitations very well and would intersperse her stories with bits of acting which amused me vastly.

She was trying to get rid of a religious hangover. At Lourdes, she had gone to confession and taken Holy Communion; back in Paris she had bought a small missal at the Bon Marché and had gone to pray in one of the chapels in Saint-Sulpice: but it hadn't worked. For a whole hour she had paced up and down in front of the church without being able to make up her mind whether to go back inside or to walk away. With her hands behind her back, her forehead deeply furrowed and stamping backwards and forwards in her room, she mimed this spiritual crisis so exuberantly for me that I didn't know whether to take her seriously or not. In fact, the divinities she really worshipped were Thought, Art and Genius; at a pinch, intelligence and talent would do instead. Every time she tracked down an "interesting" man, she would arrange to have herself introduced to him and then would do her utmost to "get him under my thumb." It was, she explained to me, the "eternal feminine" in her. She preferred intellectual conversations and comradeship to these flirtations; once a week she would argue for hours at the Closerie des Lilas with a group of Ukrainians who were journalists or engaged on vague studies in Paris. She saw her Spanish friend every day; she had known him for years, and he had asked her to marry him. I often met him in her room; he lived in the same hotel. He was called Fernando. He was a descendant of one of those Jewish families that had been driven out of Spain by the Inquisition four centuries ago; he had been born in Constantinople and had studied in Berlin. Prematurely bald, with a rounded face and skull, he would talk with romantic intensity about his *daimón*, but he was capable of irony, and I liked him very much. Stépha admired him because, though he hadn't a penny, he managed somehow to go on painting, and she shared all his ideas: these were unshakably internationalist, pacifist and even, in a Utopian sense, revolutionary. The only reason she hesitated to marry him was that she wanted to keep her freedom.

I introduced them to my sister, whom they at once took to their hearts, and to my friends. Pradelle had broken his leg; he was limping when I met him at the beginning of October on the terrace in the Luxembourg Gardens. Stépha thought he was too quiet, and her volubility bewildered him. She got on better with Lisa, who was now living in a students' hostel, the windows of which overlooked the Petit Luxembourg. She made a scanty livelihood by giving lessons; she was studying for a science certificate and preparing a thesis on Maine de Biran; but she had no intention of presenting herself for the competitive examination; her health was too weak. "My poor brain!" she used to say, holding her little cropped head in her hands. "When I think it's all I have to rely on, and that I have to get everything from it! It's not natural! One of these days it's going to give way!" She wasn't interested in Maine de Biran, in philosophy, or in herself: "I often wonder," she told me with a frosty smile, "what pleasure you can get in seeing *me!*" I was always pleased to see her, because she never let herself be taken in, and her mistrustful turn of mind often made her very perspicacious.

I often talked to Stépha about Zaza, who was having an extended holiday at Laubardon. I had sent her a few books from Paris, including *The Constant Nymph;* Stépha told me that Madame Mabille had flown into a temper and had declared: "I hate intellectuals!" Zaza was beginning to cause her serious concern: it would not be easy to make her accept a marriage of convenience. Madame Mabille regretted ever having let her attend the Sorbonne; she felt it was now urgently necessary to get her daughter in hand, and she would have very much liked to have her somewhere where she would not be under my influence. Zaza wrote to me that she had mentioned our plan for playing tennis to her mother, and that she was up in arms against it: "She declared that she didn't hold with that sort of student behaviour and that I was not to go to a game of tennis organized by a girl of twenty where I would come into contact with young men whose families she had never met. I'm not mincing my words; I prefer that you should realize the state of mind I have to contend with all the time and which nevertheless my concept of Christian duty obliges me to respect. But today I'm so upset about it I could weep; the things I love do not love each other; and taking refuge in moral principles I have been listening to opinions that I cannot stomach . . . I made an ironical offer to sign a statement saying I would undertake never to marry either Pradelle, Clairaut nor any of their friends, but that didn't make matters any better." In her next letter, she told me that in order to make her break completely with the Sorbonne her mother had decided to send her to Berlin for the winter, just as in former times the local gentry used to pack their sons off to South America in order to put an end to some scandalous or embarrassing affair.

Never had I written Zaza such expansive letters as in those last weeks; never had she confided so frankly in me. Yet when she came back to Paris in the middle of October our friendship got off to a bad start. When she was not with me, she could write to me about her difficulties and her dislikes and I felt I was her ally; but in fact her attitude was an equivocal one: she still retained all her love and respect for her mother, and remained loyal to her background. I could no longer accept such a division of personality. I had got the measure of Madame Mabille's hostility, and had understood that there could be no possible compromise between the two camps to which we belonged: the "orthodox" catholics wanted to annihilate the "intellectuals" and vice versa. By not coming over to my side, Zaza was throwing in her lot with enemies who were set on destroying me, and that made me feel resentful towards her. She dreaded the journey she was being compelled to make, and was worrying herself sick; I showed my resentment by refusing to share her worries; I let myself go in a great burst of high spirits which disconcerted her. I professed a great intimacy with Stépha, and began to imitate her by laughing and chattering in her own over-exuberant way; Zaza was often shocked by our conversations; she frowned when Stépha declared that the more intelligent people were, the more internationally-minded they became. In reaction against our "Polish student" manners, she set out deliberately to play the part of the "well-bred young French girl," and my apprehensions increased: perhaps in the end she would go over entirely to the enemy; I no longer dared speak freely to her, and so I preferred to meet her when I was in the company of Pradelle, Lisa, my sister and Stépha rather than alone. She certainly sensed this distance between us; she was absorbed in the preparations for her departure. We said good-bye to one another, without regrets, at the end of November.

Lectures started again. I had skipped a year, and, except for Clairaut, knew none of my new fellow-students; there was not one amateur, not one dilettante among them: they were all, like me, grim professionals intent on getting through the competition. I thought they looked a forbidding lot, with their air of great self-importance. I decided to ignore them. I went on working hell for leather. I followed all the lectures in the competitive examination course at the Sorbonne at the Ecole Normale, and, whenever my timetable allowed, I would go and study at Sainte-Geneviève, at the Victor Cousin or the National libraries. In the evenings I would read novels or go out. I had grown up; I would soon be leaving them: that year my parents gave me permission from time to time to go out to the theatre in the evenings, alone or with a friend. I saw Man Ray's *Star-fish*, all the programmes at the Ursulines, Studio 28 and Ciné Latin, all the films with Brigitte Helm, Douglas Fairbanks and Buster Keaton. I frequented the left-wing theatres. Under Stépha's influence, I took more pride in my personal appearance. She had told me that her boy-friend who was studying German thought I was wrong to spend all my time studying: twenty is too young for a blue-stocking, and if I went on like this I'd turn into an ugly little spinster. She had protested against his judgment, but had taken it to heart; she didn't want her best friend to look like an old frump; she assured me that I could do something with a body like mine, and insisted that I should show it off to its best advantage. I began to pay regular visits to the hairdresser and to take an interest in the purchase of a hat, the making of a dress. I made friends. Mademoiselle Lambert no longer interested me. Suzanne Boigue had followed her husband to Morocco; I was quite pleased to see Riesmann again and I took a fresh liking to Jean Mallet who was working as assistant master at the Lycée de Saint-Germain and was preparing a thesis under the guidance of Baruzi. Clairaut often used to come to the Nationale. Pradelle had great respect for him and had convinced me of his exceptional qualities. He was a Catholic, a Thomist and a follower of Maurras; when he talked to me, with his eyes boring into mine, and using a categorical tone of voice that impressed me deeply, I would wonder if I hadn't misjudged St Thomas and Maurras; I still disliked their doctrines; but I should have liked to know how one looked at life and how one felt within oneself when one adopted them: Clairaut intrigued me. He assured me that I was bound to succeed in the competition: "Apparently you succeed in everything you undertake," he told me, and I felt very flattered. Stépha, too, encouraged me: "You'll have a wonderful life. You'll always get just what you want." So I sailed along, confident that I was under a lucky star and feeling very pleased with myself. It was a lovely autumn, and whenever I raised my head from my books I was grateful to the heavens for their smile.

All the time I was trying so hard not to be a little book-worm, I was thinking of Jacques; I devoted entire pages of my diary to him, and wrote him long letters that I never posted. When I met his mother at the beginning of November, she was very affectionate towards me; Jacques, she informed me, was always asking her for news of "the only person in Paris who interests me"; she smiled at me in a conspiratorial manner as she uttered these words.

I was working hard, and amusing myself too: I felt my balance had been restored, and it was with a certain wonder that I recalled the pranks I had got up to in the summer. Those bars and dance-halls where I had whiled away my evenings now only filled me with disgust, and even with a kind of horror. This virtuous revulsion had the same roots as my former dissipation: despite my rationalist mentality, the things of the flesh remained taboo to me.

"How idealistic you are!" Stépha often told me. She took great care not to shock me. One day, Fernando, pointing to a sketch of a naked woman on the walls of his room, told me mischievously "Stépha posed for that." I didn't know where to look, and she cast an indignant glance at him: "Don't say such stupid things!" He hurriedly admitted that he only meant it as a joke. Not for one moment did I think that Stépha might be what Madame Mabille had called her—"not a lady," which meant, of course, "not a virgin." Nevertheless she made some gentle attempts to open my eyes a little: "But I'm telling you, dear, physical love is very important, for men especially...." One night, as we were coming out of the Atelier, we saw a crowd gathered in the Place Clichy; a policeman had just arrested an elegant young man whose hat was lying in the gutter; he was white-faced and trying to struggle free; the crowd were booing him: "Dirty touting pimp...." I thought I was going to faint, and dragged Stépha away; the lights, the noises of the Boulevard, the painted women, everything made me feel like screaming. "But Simone, that's life!" In her brisk, matter-of-fact voice, Stépha explained to me that men aren't angels. Of course, "all that" was rather "disgusting," but after all it was a fact, and even a very important fact; she supported her claims with a host of examples. Her stories made me rigid with disapproval. All the same, from time to time I tried to be frank with myself: where did these resistances and prohibitions stem from? "Is it my Catholic upbringing which has left me with such a fixation on purity that the slightest allusion to fleshly things causes me this indescribable distress? I think of Alain Fournier's Colombe, who drowned herself in a lake before she would sully her purity. But perhaps that is pride?"

Obviously I did not hold that one should languish in perpetual virginity. But I was sure that the wedding-night should be a white mass: true love sublimates the physical embrace, and in the arms of her chosen one the pure young girl is briskly changed into a radiant young woman. I loved Francis Jammes because he painted physical passion in colours as simple and as clear as the waters of a mountain torrent; I loved Claudel above all because he celebrates in the body the miraculously sensitive presence of the soul. I refused to read to the end of Jules Romains' *Le Dieu des Corps* because in it physical pleasure was not described as an expression of the spirit. I was exasperated by Mauriac's *Souffrances du Chrétien* which the *NRF* was publishing just then. In the former triumphant, in the latter humiliated, I found that in both of them the flesh was given too much importance. I was indignant with Clairaut who, in his reply to a questionnaire in *Les Nouvelles Littéraires,* denounced "the rag-bag of the flesh and its tragic tyranny", and also with Nizan and his wife who claimed that married couples should enjoy complete sexual licence.

I justified my repugnance in the same way as when I was only seventeen years old: all is well if the body obeys the head and the heart, but it must not take the first step. This argument was all the more illogical because Romains' heroes were "spontaneous" lovers and the Nizans were apostles of sexual freedom between man and woman. Moreover the reasonable prudery I felt at seventeen had nothing to do with the mysterious "horror" which so often used to chill my heart. I did not feel directly threatened; sometimes I had been momentarily seized by a physical urge: at the Jockey for example, in the arms of certain dancers; or at Meyrignac, when, lying with my sister in the long grass, we would be locked in one another's arms; but I enjoyed these intoxicating sensations which made me feel in tune with my body; it was curiosity, and sensuality, that made me want to discover the resources and secrets of my body; I waited without apprehension and even without impatience the moment when I would become a woman. It affected me in a rather round-about way: through Jacques. If physical love was only an innocent game, there was no reason why he shouldn't indulge in it; but then our conversations ought not to carry much weight with him beside the joyous and violent delights he had known with other women; I admired the pure and lofty tone of our relationship: but in fact it was incomplete, insipid, lacking in body, and the respect Jacques showed me was dictated by the most conventional morality; I was assigned the thankless rôle of the little girl cousin, of whom one is quite fond—what distance lay between such a green girl and a man rich in the full possession of all a man can experience! I didn't want to submit to such an inferior position. I preferred to look upon debauchery as a defilement; then I could allow myself to hope that Jacques had not been contaminated by it; if he had, then I didn't envy him—I pitied him; I would rather forgive him his weaknesses than be exiled from his pleasures. Yet this prospect too frightened me. I yearned for the transparent confusion of our souls; if he had committed murky deeds, I was robbed of his past and even of his future, for our story, wrong from the start, would never fit in with the one I had invented for us. "I don't want life to obey any other will but my own," I wrote in my journal. Here I think lay the root of my anguish. I knew almost nothing of physical reality; in my class of society it was masked by conventions and rituals; these tedious formalities bored me, but I didn't attempt to seize the root of existence; on the contrary, I found escape in the clouds; I was a soul, a pure, disembodied spirit; I was only interested in people's souls and spirits. The advent of sexuality destroyed this angelic concept; it suddenly revealed to me, in all their dreadful unity, sexual appetite and sexual violence. I had had a shock, in the Place Clichy, because I had felt the most intimate link between the pimp's revolting trade and the policeman's brutality. It was not I, but the world that was at stake: if men had bodies that were heavy and racked with lust, the world was not the place I had thought it was. Poverty, crime, oppression, war: I was afforded confused glimpses of perspectives that terrified me.

Nevertheless, in the middle of November I returned to Montparnasse. I suddenly wearied of books, student gossip, cinemas. Was this any way to live? Was it my real self that was living in this way? There had been tears, frenzies, adventure, poetry, love—a life filled with emotions: I didn't want to let them die. That evening, I was to go with my sister to *L'Oeuvre;* I met her at the Café du Dôme and took her off to the Jockey. As the believer at the end of a period of spiritual drought plunges into the smell of incense and candles, I lost myself in the fumes of alcohol and tobacco. They very soon went to our heads. Reverting to our old ways, we exchanged loud-mouthed insults and knocked each other about a bit. I wanted my heart to be rent beyond recall, and I took my sister to the Stryx. There we found Bresson and one of his friends, a middle-aged man who flirted with Poupette and bought her bunches of violets while I talked to Riquet; he warmly defended Jacques: "He's had some hard knocks," he told me, "but he's always risen above them." He assured me that there was great strength behind his apparent weaknesses, and great sincerity beneath his mask of flippancy; that he could talk of grave and painful things while sipping a cocktail—and with what lucidity he had seen through everything! "Jacques will never be happy," he concluded admiringly. My heart sank: "And what if some woman were to give him her all?" I asked. "It would just humiliate him." Fear and hope clutched at my throat again. All the way along the Boulevard Raspail I sobbed into my bunch of violets.

I loved tears, hope, fear. The next morning, when Clairaut, fixing

me with his steady gaze, told me: "You'll do a thesis on Spinoza; there's
no greater thing in life than to marry and write a thesis," I took offence.
Marriage and a career were two ways of throwing in the sponge. Pradelle
agreed with me that work can also be a drug. I was deeply grateful to
Jacques whose memory had delivered me from my brutish enslavement
to my books. Doubtless many of my friends at the Sorbonne were of
greater intellectual worth than he, but that didn't matter too much.
Clairaut's, Pradelle's futures seemed to me to be already mapped out;
Jacques' very existence, and that of his friends, appeared to me like a
series of throws in a game of dice; perhaps in the end they would destroy
or ruin themselves. I preferred such risks to sinking deeper and deeper
into a rut.

Once or twice a week during the next month I went to the Stryx
with Stépha, Fernando and a Ukrainian journalist who was a friend of
theirs and who preferred to spend his free time learning Japanese; I also
took my sister, Lisa and Mallet. I don't quite know where I found the
money that year, because I was no longer giving any lessons. Probably
I saved something out of the five francs a day which my mother gave me
for my lunches, and I managed to scrape up a bit here and there. In any
case, my budget was based on the assumption that I would indulge in
these orgies. I wrote in my diary: "Glanced through Alain's *Eleven Chapters on Plato* at Picard's. It costs eight cocktails: too dear." Stépha would
dress up as a barmaid and help Michel to serve the clients, with whom
she could joke in four languages, and sing Ukrainian folksongs. With
Riquet and his middle-aged friend we talked about Giraudoux, Gide,
the cinema, life, women, men, friendship, love. We would then saunter
down towards Saint-Sulpice in a noisy gang. The next morning I would
make a note: "Wonderful evening!" But I would intersperse my account
with parentheses which struck quite a different note. Riquet had said
about Jacques: "He'll marry one day, out of sheer impetuosity, and perhaps he'll make a good father of a family: but he'll always regret having
done so." These prophecies did not unduly worry me; what disturbed me
was that Jacques should have led practically the same sort of life as
Riquet during the past three years. The latter spoke about women with a
freedom which offended me: could I still go on believing that Jacques was
a brother of Le Grand Meaulnes? I very much doubted it. After all, I
had created this image of him in my mind quite without his authoriza-
tion, and now I was beginning to think that perhaps he did not in the
least resemble it. But I would not give in. "All that is very hurtful to me.
I have visions of Jacques that hurt me." All in all, if work was a narcotic,
alcohol and gambling were no better. My place was neither in bars nor
libraries: then where was it? I could see no other salvation than in books;
I planned a new novel; its protagonists would be a heroine who would

be myself and a hero who would resemble Jacques, with "his overween-ing pride and his mad urge to self-destruction." But I couldn't get rid of my uneasiness. One evening, I saw Riquet, Riaucourt and his friend Olga in a corner of the Stryx; I thought Olga looked very elegant. They were talking about a letter they had just received from Jacques; they were sending him a post-card. I couldn't help asking myself: "Why does he write to *them*, never to me?" I walked all one afternoon along the Boulevards with my heart sunk in despair, then wound up weeping in a cinema.

The next day, Pradelle, who was on excellent terms with my parents, came to dine at our house and then we left for the Ciné Latin. We got right to the Rue Soufflot; then I suddenly suggested that he should come with me to the Jockey; he agreed, without enthusiasm. We sat down at a table like two good and sober customers, and while I drank my gin fizz I tried to explain to him who Jacques was, for I had only mentioned him to Pradelle in passing. He listened to me in a detached way. He was obviously embarrassed. I wondered if he was shocked that I frequented this sort of place. I asked him. No, but personally he found them de-pressing. That's because he hasn't known that utter loneliness and despair which justifies all derangements. Yet as I sat beside him, at a dis-tance from the bar where I had so often behaved with such eccentric abandon, I could look upon the place with a fresh vision: he had seen through it at once, and extinguished all its poetry. Perhaps I only brought him here in order to hear him say aloud what I kept whispering quietly to myself: "What are you doing here?" In any case, I at once told myself he was right, and even began to look upon Jacques with a more critical eye: why did he waste his time killing his finer feelings? I gave up my life of debauchery. My parents went to spend a few days in Arras and I did not profit by their absence. I refused to go to Montparnasse with Stépha; I even rejected her offers with some acerbity. I stayed at home and read Meredith.

I gave up wondering about Jacques' past; after all, if he had made mistakes, the heavens weren't going to fall. Now I hardly bothered to think about him; he had kept silent too long; and the silence in the end was beginning to resemble hostility. When at the end of December his grandmother Flandin gave me the latest news about him, I couldn't have cared less. Yet as I disliked giving anything up I supposed that on his return our love for each other would revive again.

———————•———————

I went on working furiously; every day I spent from nine to ten hours at my books. In January I did my pupil-teacher stint at the Lycée Janson de Sailly under the supervision of Rodrigues, a very sweet old gentleman: he was president of the League of Civil Liberties and killed himself in 1940 when the Germans entered France. My fellow-pupils were Merleau-Ponty and Lévi-Strauss; I knew them both a little. The former I had always admired from a distance. The latter's impassivity rather intimidated me, but he used to turn it to good advantage. I thought it very funny when, in his detached voice, and with a dead-pan face, he expounded to our audience the folly of the passions. There were foggy mornings when I felt it was ridiculous to discourse upon the life of the emotions to forty boys who obviously couldn't care less about it; but when the weather was fine, I used to take an interest in what I was saying, and I used to think that in certain eyes I could catch glimmers of intelligence. I recalled my former emotions when I used to pass by the College Stanislas: all this had seemed so far away, so inaccessible—being in a classroom full of boys! And now here I was out in front of the class, and it was I who was giving the lessons. I felt that there was nothing in the world I couldn't attain now.

I certainly didn't regret being a woman; on the contrary it afforded me great satisfaction. My upbringing had convinced me of my sex's intellectual inferiority, a fact admitted by many women. "A lady cannot hope to pass the selective examination until the fifth or sixth attempt," Mademoiselle Roulin had told me; she had already had two. This handicap gave my successes a prestige far in excess of that accorded to successful male students: I felt it was something exceptional even to do as well as they did; in fact, I hadn't met a single man student who seemed at all out of the ordinary; the future was as wide open to me as it was to them: they had no advantage over me. Nor did they lay claim to any; they treated me without condescension, and even with a special kindness, for they didn't look upon me as a rival; girls were judged in the contest by the same standards as the boys, but they were accepted as supernumeraries, and there was no struggle for the first places between the sexes. That is why a lecture I gave on Plato brought me unreserved compliments from my fellow-students—in particular from Jean Hippolyte. I was proud at having won their esteem. Their friendliness prevented me from ever taking up that "challenging" attitude which later was to cause me so much dismay when I encountered it in American women: from the start, men were my comrades, not my enemies. Far from envying them, I felt that my own position, from the very fact that it was an unusual one, was one of privilege. One evening Pradelle invited to his house his best friends and their sisters. Poupette went with me. All the girls retired to Mademoiselle Pradelle's room; but I stayed with the young men.

Yet I did not renounce my femininity. That evening my sister and I had paid the utmost attention to our appearance. I was in red, she in blue silk; actually we were very badly got-up, but then the other girls weren't all that grand either. In Montparnasse I had caught glimpses of elegant beauties; but their lives were too different from mine for the comparison to overwhelm me; besides, once I was free, with money in my pocket, there would be nothing to stop me imitating them. I didn't forget that Jacques had said that I was pretty; Stépha and Fernando had high hopes of me. I liked to look at myself, just as I was, in mirrors; I liked what I saw. In the things we had in common, I fancied that I was no less ill-equipped than other women and I felt no resentment towards them; so I had no desire to run them down. In many respects I set Zaza, my sister, Stépha, and even Lisa above my masculine friends, for they seemed to me more sensitive, more generous, more endowed with imagination, tears, and love. I flattered myself that I combined "a woman's heart and a man's brain." Again I considered myself to be unique—the One and Only.

John Wain

This open letter attacking the journalistic vulgarization of serious intellectual and artistic effort requires little in the way of preliminary comment. Straightforwardness and simplicity, together with the informality appropriate to the form, are among its most effective features. Wain, who is a poet as well as a novelist, was one of the first young writers to whom the cant phrase "angry young men" was applied, and one has the feeling that the indignation expressed in the letter had been building up for a long time. It is worth noting, however, that Wain expands his critique from the merely personal to the broadly cultural; in the affixing of cheap labels he finds a sign of the failure of the imagination in mass civilization. Worth noting also are the violent metaphors with which, in the last paragraph, he sums up his advice to Joe. They reveal, more than anything else, how strongly the writer's convictions are engaged in the issue.

ANSWER TO A LETTER FROM JOE

The other day I received a letter. It was dated from a town in Pennsylvania, and ran:—

From the April 16, 1961 issue of *The Observer*. Copyright © John Wain 1961. Reprinted by permission of the author.

Dear Mr. Wain,

For my high school thesis I have chosen the topic The Angry Young Men. However, I have found it difficult to obtain information other than the briefest sketch. Since your name appears quite often as a member of this group and since I read and enjoyed your novel *The Contenders* I am writing to you for any information which you would care to send me.

I would be most happy if you would send a history of the movement, a biography of yourself and some of the other prominent members, and basically your complaints and just what you are angry at.

Thank you very much, and I shall be expecting the information if you are able to send it.

(signed) Joe.

Of course the boy's name is not really Joe, but I will call him that because I don't want to embarrass him. Joe's letter is by no means the first of its kind that I have had, but it is the first I am going to answer, and I want to make my answer a public one because his letter does reveal, in fact, certain things about our present-day civilisation that are legitimate matter for public speculation.

So here goes.

Dear Joe,

Thank you very much for your letter. It was short, but in its few lines it told me a tremendous amount. I would even go so far as to say that from this one letter an acute observer could deduce almost every important fact about the "cultural" life of the Atlantic nations to-day.

The first thing your letter told me, Joe, was that the teacher who is supposed to be in charge of your intellectual development isn't very good. The most important thing (the *only* important thing, probably) that you can learn from writing a high school thesis is the use of reference books. The whole exercise should be directed towards teaching you where to find the facts you want—a training that would be useful to you in any profession and also in handling your personal affairs. The information you need, in the way of biographies and the like, is very easily available in reference books, and the large body of critical or pseudo-critical writing on this topic (most of it sludge, admittedly) is readily traceable from bibliographies. So I deduce, Joe, that your teacher is not up to his, or her, job.

The second thing that emerges is that a crude caricature invented by the lower type of English journalist has power to get itself accepted in America; not merely in the corresponding section of the Press, but inside the educational system. I have never described myself as an Angry Young Man, Joe, but everyone is angry at something, and one of the things that angers me is the thought that I am living in a civilisation so completely dominated by the journalist and his cousin the ad man. You, for instance, though you have read one of my books and say (quite sincerely, I am sure) that you enjoyed it, show no interest in me as a writer but only as a member of "a group" that has an immediate social (i.e., journalistic) set of references. You propose to study our books not as books but as representative documents. And you write to me to ask for a statement about what they are representative *of*.

In other words, having decided that the only interest of these books is the journalistic capsule which can be extracted from them, you write to me for the capsule. But why, Joe, do you think I went to the trouble of writing books? If what I wanted to say could be enclosed within a few sentences of quotable "message," I'd have written the message and not bothered to write the books. In other words, I'd have gone into journalism and not into authorship.

None of this is your fault, Joe, I know that. You can't be expected, single-handed, to overturn all the assumptions on which the popular culture of America, and England, too, is based. This kind of radical misunderstanding is not specially American; it is simply a feature of the modern world, in which the imagination is so slighted and despised, the ephemeral and the documentary so exalted, that men have ceased to believe in any values except those of the Press. They can't believe that a writer would imagine a situation, create character, breathe life into figures of clay from the abandoned marl-pits of his imagination, *just for the sake of doing so.* What would be the point? they ask. Surely the only thing worth doing is to make a statement about conditions to-day, about our situation here and now?

———————●———————

You, Joe, have picked up this attitude, and no wonder. If your teacher knew his (or her) job, he (or she) would have suggested this thesis-subject to you in rather different terms. These writers have been lumped together by journalists and given the label "Angry Young Men." What justification is there for this? Have the writers themselves assented? Is their work really similar? Or is the whole thing a fabrication, designed to help tired and hasty gossip-writers, or to facilitate cocktail-party chatter, rather than to focus the work of the writers themselves? But I can tell from your letter that the suggestion was made in no such sceptical form. It was simply handed to you inertly, or (if the original idea was your own) accepted inertly, with no thought for the educative value of a genuine investigation along these lines.

Because you see, Joe, if you really followed this Angry Young Man business to its roots, you would learn a great deal. Not about literature, but about journalism, and finally about the world you and I are living in. The world that has rejected art and imagination, because it has rejected humanity. Instead of the artist, we have the journalist. Instead of the voice, the loudspeaker. Instead of the man, the machine. Productivity instead of work. Sex instead of love. The pop-disc instead of the folk-song. Housing estates instead of villages. Plagiarism, staleness, envy, discontent, gossip, malice, instead of a genuine free play of the imagination.

All this follows, Joe, from your basic premise: that a handful of English writers, whose work is not at all similar except in the broadest outline, are "a group," that they are "The Angry Young Men," and that they are amateur politicians rather than professional writers. Because what your letter is really saying, Joe, is that art not only does not but *cannot* exist to-day. Art is dead: only the representative document and the news story can live.

So tear up your thesis, Joe. If writers are only journalists in disguise, why not drop them and write directly about the men who make the news? Or, if you still want to discuss writers, and still want to do it from the journalistic point of view, choose those who openly accept the new and debased role the modern world has assigned them. You'll find some writers who have welcomed the label.

Better still, take this letter and make it the starting-point of a new thesis, one that will land on your teacher's desk like a grenade. Tell them all to stop combing their dandruff on to the page when you are trying to read. Tell them from now on you are going to read books as art, which is a part of life, rather than as journalism, which is a part of money-making, selling, manipulating, string-pulling, and finally disease, disfigurement and incarceration. Tell them to stop fouling the spring, that you need it to slake a genuine thirst. Throw them your thesis wrapped round a brick, Joe, and good luck to you.

Your sincere friend until the final day of reckoning.

JOHN WAIN.

Hannah Arendt

The continuing debate on the nature and purposes of education promises to go on for some time. Usually, the debate involves two clearly defined groups of champions, each tending toward an extreme position: the liberal-permissive-progressives, dedicated to the goal of "education for life" and the techniques of "learning by doing"; and the conservative-authoritarian-traditionalists, oriented toward the three R's, the good old-fashioned ways, and, all too often, nostalgic reminiscence of an America which, if it ever did exist, assuredly exists no longer. The dialogue between these groups has led to no discernible improvement in a situation which, both would agree, is critical.

Although Hannah Arendt's hard-headed essay delivers its most telling blows against the progressive educators, it would be impossible to fall into the error of seeing her as an orthodox conservative (or, for that matter, even a moderate). Although she does advocate such conservative ideals as authority, tradition, and the teaching of facts rather than life adjustment, she does so precisely because of her awareness of the inevitability and the necessity of change—in the name of the desirable emergence of what she calls "the new": that which comes into the world with every generation.

In an area of thought that tends to be as oversimplified and conformist as any other, Miss Arendt's views are bound to seem paradoxical, but in fact paradox is one of the most effective intellectual devices used in her essay. The product of careful and subtle reasoning, her paradoxes clear our minds of commonplaces and platitudes and force us to perform the difficult act of thought. She points out, for example, that the ideal of equality, when applied in the world of childhood, leads to a stultifying conformity; that the absence of school-room authority imposes unfair burdens on the young; that doctrinaire progressivism ends in the stifling of individual innovation. These are paradoxes which compel at the least our recognition of the complexities to which they point. At the same time, Miss Arendt is equally adept at pointing out the unrecognized and unresolved paradoxes at the heart of most contemporary education—primarily those resulting from the conflicting doctrines that the child in a democracy is the equal of the adult and that the child in a civilized society is a special and specially privileged being.

Miss Arendt's essay is a difficult and a disturbing one, but it promises a way out of the arid arguments of those conservatives and liberals alike who either cannot or will not view education in any frame of reference other than itself. It is precisely Miss Arendt's breadth of context—her awareness of philosophy, psychology, and history, for example, and her firsthand experience of both Europe and America—which enables her to make sense on the problem.

THE CRISIS IN EDUCATION

. . . . I

The general crisis that has overtaken the modern world everywhere and in almost every sphere of life manifests itself differently in each country, involving different areas and taking on different forms. In America, one of its most characteristic and suggestive aspects is the recurring crisis in education that, during the last decade at least, has become a political problem of the first magnitude, reported on almost daily in the newspapers. To be sure, no great imagination is required to detect the dangers of a constantly progressing decline of elementary standards throughout the entire school system, and the seriousness of the trouble has been properly underlined by the countless unavailing efforts of the educational authorities to stem the tide. Still, if one compares this crisis in education with the political experiences of other countries in the twentieth century, with the revolutionary turmoil after the First World War, with concentration and extermination camps, or even with the profound malaise which, appearances of prosperity to the contrary notwithstanding, has spread throughout Europe ever since the end of the Second World War, it is somewhat difficult to take a crisis in education as seriously as it deserves. It is tempting indeed to regard it as a local phenomenon, unconnected with the larger issues of the century, to be blamed on certain peculiarities of life in the United States which are not likely to find a counterpart in other parts of the world.

Yet, if this were true, the crisis in our school system would not have become a political issue and the educational authorities would not have been unable to deal with it in time. Certainly more is involved here than the puzzling question of why Johnny can't read. Moreover, there is always a temptation to believe that we are dealing with specific problems confined within historical and national boundaries and of importance only to those immediately affected. It is precisely this belief that in our

From *Between Past and Future* by Hannah Arendt. Copyright © 1954, 1956, 1957, 1958, 1960, 1961 by Hannah Arendt. Reprinted by permission of The Viking Press, Inc.

time has consistently proved false. One can take it as a general rule in this century that whatever is possible in one country may in the foreseeable future be equally possible in almost any other.

Aside from these general reasons that would make it seem advisable for the layman to be concerned with trouble in fields about which, in the specialist's sense, he may know nothing (and this, since I am not a professional educator, is of course my case when I deal with a crisis in education), there is another even more cogent reason for his concerning himself with a critical situation in which he is not immediately involved. And that is the opportunity, provided by the very fact of crisis—which tears away façades and obliterates prejudices—to explore and inquire into whatever has been laid bare of the essence of the matter, and the essence of education is natality, the fact that human beings are *born* into the world. The disappearance of prejudices simply means that we have lost the answers on which we ordinarily rely without even realizing they were originally answers to questions. A crisis forces us back to the questions themselves and requires from us either new or old answers, but in any case direct judgments. A crisis becomes a disaster only when we respond to it with preformed judgments, that is, with prejudices. Such an attitude not only sharpens the crisis but makes us forfeit the experience of reality and the opportunity for reflection it provides.

However clearly a general problem may present itself in a crisis, it is nevertheless impossible ever to isolate completely the universal element from the concrete and specific circumstances in which it makes its appearance. Though the crisis in education may affect the whole world, it is characteristic that we find its most extreme form in America, the reason being that perhaps only in America could a crisis in education actually become a factor in politics. In America, as a matter of fact, education plays a different and, politically, incomparably more important role than in other countries. Technically, of course, the explanation lies in the fact that America has always been a land of immigrants; it is obvious that the enormously difficult melting together of the most diverse ethnic groups—never fully successful but continuously succeeding beyond expectation—can only be accomplished through the schooling, education, and Americanization of the immigrants' children. Since for most of these children English is not their mother tongue but has to be learned in school, schools must obviously assume functions which in a nation-state would be performed as a matter of course in the home.

More decisive, however, for our considerations is the role that continuous immigration plays in the country's political consciousness and frame of mind. America is not simply a colonial country in need of immigrants to populate the land, though independent of them in its political structure. For America the determining factor has always been the motto printed on every dollar bill: *Novus Ordo Seclorum,* A New Order of the World. The immigrants, the newcomers, are a guarantee to the country that it represents the new order. The meaning of this new order, this founding of a new world against the old, was and is the doing away with poverty and oppression. But at the same time its magnificence consists in the fact that from the beginning this new order did not shut itself off from the outside world—as has elsewhere been the custom in the founding of utopias—in order to confront it with a perfect model, nor was its purpose to enforce imperial claims or to be preached as an evangel to others. Rather its relation to the outside world has been characterized from the start by the fact that this republic, which planned to abolish poverty and slavery, welcomed all the poor and enslaved of the earth. In the words spoken by John Adams in 1765—that is, before the Declaration of Independence—"I always consider the settlement of America as the opening of a grand scheme and design in Providence for the illumination and emancipation of the slavish part of mankind all over the earth." This is the basic intent or the basic law in accordance with which America began her historical and political existence.

The extraordinary enthusiasm for what is new, which is shown in almost every aspect of American daily life, and the concomitant trust in an "indefinite perfectibility"—which Tocqueville noted as the credo of the common "uninstructed man" and which as such antedates by almost a hundred years the development in other countries of the West—would presumably have resulted in any case in greater attention paid and greater significance ascribed to the newcomers by birth, that is, the children, whom, when they had outgrown their childhood and were about to enter the community of adults as young people, the Greeks simply called οἱ νέοι, the new ones. There is the additional fact, however, a fact that has become decisive for the meaning of education, that this pathos of the new, though it is considerably older than the eighteenth century, only developed conceptually and politically in that century. From this source there was derived at the start an educational ideal, tinged with Rousseauism and in fact directly influenced by Rousseau, in which education became an instrument of politics, and political activity itself was conceived of as a form of education.

The role played by education in all political utopias from ancient times onward shows how natural it seems to start a new world with those who are by birth and nature new. So far as politics is concerned, this involves of course a serious misconception: instead of joining with one's equals in assuming the effort of persuasion and running the risk of failure, there is dictatorial intervention, based upon the absolute superiority of the adult, and the attempt to produce the new as a *fait accompli,* that is, as though the new already existed. For this reason, in Europe, the belief that one must begin with the children if one wishes to produce new conditions has remained principally the monopoly of revolutionary movements of tyrannical cast which, when they came to power, took the children away from their parents and simply indoctrinated them. Education can play no part in politics, because in politics we always have to deal with those who are already educated. Whoever wants to educate adults really wants to act as their guardian and prevent them from political activity. Since one cannot educate adults, the word "education" has an evil sound in politics; there is a pretense of education, when the real purpose is coercion without the use of force. He who seriously wants to create a new political order through education, that is, neither through force and constraint nor through persuasion, must draw the dreadful Platonic conclusion: the banishment of all older people from the state that is to be founded. But even the children one wishes to educate to be citizens of a utopian morrow are actually denied their own future role in the body politic, for, from the standpoint of the new ones, whatever new the adult world may propose is necessarily older than they themselves. It is in the very nature of the human condition that each new generation grows into an old world, so that to prepare a new generation for a new world can only mean that one wishes to strike from the newcomers' hands their own chance at the new.

All this is by no means the case in America, and it is exactly this fact that makes it so hard to judge these questions correctly here. The political role that education actually plays in a land of immigrants, the fact that the schools not only serve to Americanize the children but affect their parents as well, that here in fact one helps to shed an old world and to enter into a new one, encourages the illusion that a new world is being built through the education of the children. Of course the true situation is not this at all. The world into which children are introduced, even in America, is an old world, that is, a pre-existing world, constructed by the living and the dead, and it is new only for those who have newly entered it by immigration. But here illusion is stronger than reality because it springs directly from a basic American experience, the experience that a new order can be founded, and what is more, founded with full consciousness of a historical continuum, for the phrase "New World" gains its meaning from the Old World, which, however admirable on other scores, was rejected because it could find no solution for poverty and oppression.

Now in respect to education itself the illusion arising from the pathos of the new has produced its most serious consequences only in our own century. It has first of all made it possible for that complex of modern educational theories which originated in Middle Europe and consists of an astounding hodgepodge of sense and nonsense to accomplish, under the banner of progressive education, a most radical revolution in the whole system of education. What in Europe has remained an experiment, tested out here and there in single schools and isolated educational institutions and then gradually extending its influences in certain quarters, in America about twenty-five years ago completely overthrew, as though from one day to the next, all traditions and all the established methods of teaching and learning. I shall not go into details, and I leave out of account private schools and especially the Roman Catholic parochial school system. The significant fact is that for the sake of certain theories, good or bad, all the rules of sound human reason were thrust aside. Such a procedure is always of great and pernicious significance, especially in a country that relies so extensively on common sense in its political life. Whenever in political questions sound human reason fails or gives up the attempt to supply answers we are faced by a crisis; for this kind of reason is really that common sense by virtue of which we and our five individual senses are fitted into a single world common to us all and by the aid of which we move about in it. The disappearance of common sense in the present day is the surest sign of the present-day crisis. In every crisis a piece of the world, something common to us all, is destroyed. The failure of common sense, like a divining rod, points to the place where such a cave-in has occurred.

In any case the answer to the question of why Johnny can't read or to the more general question of why the scholastic standards of the average American school lag so very far behind the average standards in actually all the countries of Europe is not, unfortunately, simply that this country is young and has not yet caught up with the standards of the Old World but, on the contrary, that this country in this particular field is the most "advanced" and most modern in the world. And this is true in a double sense: nowhere have the education problems of a mass society become so acute, and nowhere else have the most modern theories in the realm of pedagogy been so uncritically and slavishly accepted. Thus the crisis in American education, on the one hand, announces the bankruptcy of progressive education and, on the other, presents a problem of immense difficulty because it has arisen under the conditions and in response to the demands of a mass society.

In this connection we must bear in mind another more general factor which did not, to be sure, cause the crisis but which has aggravated it to a remarkable degree, and this is the unique role the concept of equality plays and always has played in American life. Much more is involved in this than equality before the law, more too than the leveling of class distinctions, more even than what is expressed in the phrase "equality of opportunity," though that has a greater significance in this connection because in the American view a right to education is one of the inalienable civic rights. This last has been decisive for the structure of the public-school system in that secondary schools in the European sense exist only as exceptions. Since compulsory school attendance extends to the age of sixteen, every child must enter high school, and the high school therefore is basically a kind of continuation of primary school. As a result of this lack of a secondary school the preparation for the college course has to be supplied by the colleges themselves, whose curricula therefore suffer from a chronic overload, which in turn affects the quality of the work done there.

At first glance one might perhaps think that this anomaly lies in the very nature of a mass society in which education is no longer a privilege of the wealthy classes. A glance at England, where, as everyone knows, secondary education has also been made available in recent years to all classes of the population, will show that this is not the case. For there at the end of primary school, with students at the age of eleven, has been instituted the dreaded examination that weeds out all but some ten per cent of the scholars suited for higher education. The rigor of this selection was not accepted even in England without protest; in America it would have been simply impossible. What is aimed at in England is "meritocracy," which is clearly once more the establishment of an oligarchy, this time not of wealth or of birth but of talent. But this means, even though people in England may not be altogether clear about it, that the country even under a socialist government will continue to be governed as it has been from time out of mind, that is, neither as a monarchy nor as a democracy but as an oligarchy or aristocracy—the latter in case one takes the view that the most gifted are also the best, which is by no means a certainty. In America such an almost physical division of the children into gifted and ungifted would be considered intolerable. Meritocracy contradicts the principle of equality, of an equalitarian democracy, no less than any other oligarchy.

Thus what makes the educational crisis in America so especially acute is the political temper of the country, which of itself struggles to equalize or to erase as far as possible the difference between young and old, between the gifted and the ungifted, finally between children and adults, particularly between pupils and teachers. It is obvious that such an equalization can actually be accomplished only at the cost of the teacher's authority and at the expense of the gifted among the students. However, it is equally obvious, at least to anyone who has ever come in contact with the American educational system, that this difficulty, rooted in the political attitude of the country, also has great advantages, not simply of a human kind but educationally speaking as well; in any case these general factors cannot explain the crisis in which we presently find ourselves nor justify the measures through which that crisis has been precipitated.

. . . . **II**

These ruinous measures can be schematically traced back to three basic assumptions, all of which are only too familiar. The *first* is that there exist a child's world and a society formed among children that are autonomous and must insofar as possible be left to them to govern. Adults are only there to help with this government. The authority that tells the individual child what to do and what not to do rests with the child group itself—and this produces, among other consequences, a situation in which the adult stands helpless before the individual child and out of contact with him. He can only tell him to do what he likes and then prevent the worst from happening. The real and normal relations between children and adults, arising from the fact that people of all ages are always simultaneously together in the world, are thus broken off. And so it is of the essence of this first basic assumption that it takes into account only the group and not the individual child.

As for the child in the group, he is of course rather worse off than before. For the authority of a group, even a child group, is always considerably stronger and more tyrannical than the severest authority of an individual person can ever be. If one looks at it from the standpoint of the individual child, his chances to rebel or to do anything on his own hook are practically nil; he no longer finds himself in a very unequal contest with a person who has, to be sure, absolute superiority over him but in contest with whom he can nevertheless count on the solidarity of other children, that is, of his own kind; rather he is in the position, hopeless by definition, of a minority of one confronted by the absolute majority of all the others. There are very few grown people who can endure such a situation, even when it is not supported by external means of compulsion; children are simply and utterly incapable of it.

Therefore by being emancipated from the authority of adults the child has not been freed but has been subjected to a much more terrifying and truly tyrannical authority, the tyranny of the majority. In any case the result is that the children have been so to speak banished from the world of grown-ups. They are either thrown back upon themselves or handed over to the tyranny of their own group, against which, because of its numerical superiority, they cannot rebel, with which, because they are children, they cannot reason, and out of which they cannot flee to any other world because the world of adults is barred to them. The reaction of the children to this pressure tends to be either conformism or juvenile delinquency, and is frequently a mixture of both.

The *second* basic assumption which has come into question in the present crisis has to do with teaching. Under the influence of modern psychology and the tenets of pragmatism, pedagogy has developed into

a science of teaching in general in such a way as to be wholly emancipated from the actual material to be taught. A teacher, so it was thought,
is a man who can simply teach anything; his training is in teaching, not
in the mastery of any particular subject. This attitude, as we shall presently see, is naturally very closely connected with a basic assumption
about learning. Moreover, it has resulted in recent decades in a most
serious neglect of the training of teachers in their own subjects, especially
in the public high schools. Since the teacher does not need to know his
own subject, it not infrequently happens that he is just one hour ahead
of his class in knowledge. This in turn means not only that the students
are actually left to their own resources but that the most legitimate
source of the teacher's authority as the person who, turn it whatever way
one will, still knows more and can do more than oneself is no longer
effective. Thus the non-authoritarian teacher, who would like to abstain
from all methods of compulsion because he is able to rely on his own
authority, can no longer exist.

But this pernicious role that pedagogy and the teachers' colleges are
playing in the present crisis was only possible because of a modern theory
about learning. This was, quite simply, the logical application of the
third basic assumption in our context, an assumption which the modern
world has held for centuries and which found its systematic conceptual
expression in pragmatism. This basic assumption is that you can know
and understand only what you have done yourself, and its application to
education is as primitive as it is obvious: to substitute, insofar as possible, doing for learning. The reason that no importance was attached to
the teacher's mastering his own subject was the wish to compel him to the
exercise of the continuous activity of learning so that he would not, as
they said, pass on "dead knowledge" but, instead, would constantly demonstrate how it is produced. The conscious intention was not to teach
knowledge but to inculcate a skill, and the result was a kind of transformation of institutes for learning into vocational institutions which
have been as successful in teaching how to drive a car or how to use a
typewriter or, even more important for the "art" of living, how to get
along with other people and to be popular, as they have been unable
to make the children acquire the normal prerequisites of a standard
curriculum.

However, this description is at fault, not only because it obviously
exaggerates in order to drive home a point, but because it fails to take
into account how in this process special importance was attached to
obliterating as far as possible the distinction between play and work—in
favor of the former. Play was looked upon as the liveliest and most appropriate way for the child to behave in the world, as the only form of
activity that evolves spontaneously from his existence as a child. Only

what can be learned through play does justice to this liveliness. The child's characteristic activity, so it was thought, lies in play; learning in the old sense, by forcing a child into an attitude of passivity, compelled him to give up his own playful initiative.

The close connection between these two things—the substitution of doing for learning and of playing for working—is directly illustrated by the teaching of languages: the child is to learn by speaking, that is by doing, not by studying grammar and syntax; in other words he is to learn a foreign language in the same way that as an infant he learned his own language: as though at play and in the uninterrupted continuity of simple existence. Quite apart from the question of whether this is possible or not—it is possible, to a limited degree, only when one can keep the child all day long in the foreign-speaking environment—it is perfectly clear that this procedure consciously attempts to keep the older child as far as possible at the infant level. The very thing that should prepare the child for the world of adults, the gradually acquired habit of work and of not-playing, is done away with in favor of the autonomy of the world of childhood.

Whatever may be the connection between doing and knowing, or whatever the validity of the pragmatic formula, its application to education, that is, to the way the child learns, tends to make absolute the world of childhood in just the same way that we noted in the case of the first basic assumption. Here, too, under the pretext of respecting the child's independence, he is debarred from the world of grown-ups and artificially kept in his own, so far as that can be called a world. This holding back of the child is artificial because it breaks off the natural relationship between grown-ups and children, which consists among other things in teaching and learning, and because at the same time it belies the fact that the child is a developing human being, that childhood is a temporary stage, a preparation for adulthood.

The present crisis in America results from the recognition of the destructiveness of these basic assumptions and a desperate attempt to reform the entire educational system, that is, to transform it completely. In doing this what is actually being attempted—except for the plans for an immense increase in the facilities for training in the physical sciences and in technology—is nothing but restoration: teaching will once more be conducted with authority; play is to stop in school hours, and serious work is once more to be done; emphasis will shift from extracurricular skills to knowledge prescribed by the curriculum; finally there is even talk of transforming the present curricula for teachers so that the teachers themselves will have to learn something before being turned loose on the children.

These proposed reforms, which are still in the discussion stage and

are of purely American interest, need not concern us here. Nor can I discuss the more technical, yet in the long run perhaps even more important
question of how to reform the curricula of elementary and secondary
schools in all countries so as to bring them up to the entirely new requirements of the present world. What is of importance to our argument is a
twofold question. Which aspects of the modern world and its crisis have
actually revealed themselves in the educational crisis, that is, what are
the true reasons that for decades things could be said and done in such
glaring contradiction to common sense? And, second, what can we learn
from this crisis for the essence of education—not in the sense that one can
always learn from mistakes what ought not to be done, but rather by
reflecting on the role that education plays in every civilization, that is
on the obligation that the existence of children entails for every human
society. We shall begin with the second question.

. . . . **III**

A crisis in education would at any time give rise to serious concern even
if it did not reflect, as in the present instance it does, a more general crisis
and instability in modern society. For education belongs among the most
elementary and necessary activities of human society, which never remains
as it is but continuously renews itself through birth, through the arrival
of new human beings. These newcomers, moreover, are not finished but
in a state of becoming. Thus the child, the subject of education, has for
the educator a double aspect: he is new in a world that is strange to him
and he is in process of becoming, he is a new human being and he is a
becoming human being. This double aspect is by no means self-evident
and it does not apply to the animal forms of life; it corresponds to a
double relationship, the relationship to the world on the one hand and
to life on the other. The child shares the state of becoming with all living
things; in respect to life and its development, the child is a human being
in process of becoming, just as a kitten is a cat in process of becoming.
But the child is new only in relation to a world that was there before him,
that will continue after his death, and in which he is to spend his life.
If the child were not a newcomer in this human world but simply a not
yet finished living creature, education would be just a function of life
and would need to consist in nothing save that concern for the sustenance
of life and that training and practice in living that all animals assume in
respect to their young.

Human parents, however, have not only summoned their children
into life through conception and birth, they have simultaneously introduced them into a world. In education they assume responsibility for
both, for the life and development of the child and for the continuance

of the world. These two responsibilities do not by any means coincide; they may indeed come into conflict with each other. The responsibility for the development of the child turns in a certain sense against the world: the child requires special protection and care so that nothing destructive may happen to him from the world. But the world, too, needs protection to keep it from being overrun and destroyed by the onslaught of the new that bursts upon it with each new generation.

Because the child must be protected against the world, his traditional place is in the family, whose adult members daily return back from the outside world and withdraw into the security of private life within four walls. These four walls, within which people's private family life is lived, constitute a shield against the world and specifically against the public aspect of the world. They enclose a secure place, without which no living thing can thrive. This holds good not only for the life of childhood but for human life in general. Wherever the latter is consistently exposed to the world without the protection of privacy and security its vital quality is destroyed. In the public world, common to all, persons count, and so does work, that is, the work of our hands that each of us contributes to our common world; but life *qua* life does not matter there. The world cannot be regardful of it, and it has to be hidden and protected from the world.

Everything that lives, not vegetative life alone, emerges from darkness and, however strong its natural tendency to thrust itself into the light, it nevertheless needs the security of darkness to grow at all. This may indeed be the reason that children of famous parents so often turn out badly. Fame penetrates the four walls, invades their private space, bringing with it, especially in present-day conditions, the merciless glare of the public realm, which floods everything in the private lives of those concerned, so that the children no longer have a place of security where they can grow. But exactly the same destruction of the real living space occurs wherever the attempt is made to turn the children themselves into a kind of world. Among these peer groups then arises public life of a sort and, quite apart from the fact that it is not a real one and that the whole attempt is a sort of fraud, the damaging fact remains that children—that is, human beings in process of becoming but not yet complete—are thereby forced to expose themselves to the light of a public existence.

That modern education, insofar as it attempts to establish a world of children, destroys the necessary conditions for vital development and growth seems obvious. But that such harm to the developing child should be the result of modern education strikes one as strange indeed, for this education maintained that its exclusive aim was to serve the child and rebelled against the methods of the past because these had not sufficiently taken into account the child's inner nature and his needs. "The Century of the Child," as we may recall, was going to emancipate the child and free him from the standards derived from the adult world. Then how could it happen that the most elementary conditions of life necessary for the growth and development of the child were overlooked or simply not recognized? How could it happen that the child was exposed to what more than anything else characterized the adult world, its public aspect, after the decision had just been reached that the mistake in all past education had been to see the child as nothing but an undersized grown-up?

The reason for this strange state of affairs has nothing directly to do with education; it is rather to be found in the judgments and prejudices about the nature of private life and public world and their relation to each other which have been characteristic of modern society since the beginning of modern times and which educators, when they finally began, relatively late, to modernize education, accepted as self-evident assumptions without being aware of the consequences they must necessarily have for the life of the child. It is the peculiarity of modern society, and by no means a matter of course, that it regards life, that is, the earthly life of the individual as well as the family, as the highest good; and for this reason, in contrast to all previous centuries, emancipated this life and all the activities that have to do with its preservation and enrichment from the concealment of privacy and exposed them to the light of the public world. This is the real meaning of the emancipation of workers and women, not as persons, to be sure, but insofar as they fulfill a necessary function in the life-process of society.

The last to be affected by this process of emancipation were the children, and the very thing that had meant a true liberation for the workers and the women—because they were not only workers and women but persons as well, who therefore had a claim on the public world, that is, a right to see and be seen in it, to speak and be heard—was an abandonment and betrayal in the case of the children, who are still at the stage where the simple fact of life and growth outweighs the factor of personality. The more completely modern society discards the distinction between what is private and what is public, between what can thrive only in concealment and what needs to be shown to all in the full light of the public world, the more, that is, it introduces between the private and the public a social sphere in which the private is made public and vice versa, the harder it makes things for its children, who by nature require the security of concealment in order to mature undisturbed.

However serious these infringements of the conditions for vital growth may be, it is certain that they were entirely unintentional; the central aim of all modern education efforts has been the welfare of the child, a fact that is, of course, no less true even if the efforts made have not always succeeded in promoting the child's welfare in the way that was hoped. The situation is entirely different in the sphere of educational tasks directed no longer toward the child but toward the young person, the newcomer and stranger, who has been born into an already existing world which he does not know. These tasks are primarily, but not exclusively, the responsibility of the schools; they have to do with teaching and learning; the failure in this field is the most urgent problem in America today. What lies at the bottom of it?

Normally the child is first introduced to the world in school. Now school is by no means the world and must not pretend to be; it is rather the institution that we interpose between the private domain of home and the world in order to make the transition from the family to the world possible at all. Attendance there is required not by the family but by the state, that is by the public world, and so, in relation to the child, school in a sense represents the world, although it is not yet actually the world. At this stage of education adults, to be sure, once more assume a responsibility for the child, but by now it is not so much responsibility for the vital welfare of a growing thing as for what we generally call the free development of characteristic qualities and talents. This, from the general and essential point of view, is the uniqueness that distinguishes every human being from every other, the quality by virtue of which he is not only a stranger in the world but something that has never been here before.

Insofar as the child is not yet acquainted with the world, he must be gradually introduced to it; insofar as he is new, care must be taken that this new thing comes to fruition in relation to the world as it is. In any case, however, the educators here stand in relation to the young as representatives of a world for which they must assume responsibility although they themselves did not make it, and even though they may, secretly or openly, wish it were other than it is. This responsibility is not arbitrarily imposed upon educators; it is implicit in the fact that the young are introduced by adults into a continuously changing world. Anyone who refuses to assume joint responsibility for the world should not have children and must not be allowed to take part in educating them.

In education this responsibility for the world takes the form of authority. The authority of the educator and the qualifications of the teacher are not the same thing. Although a measure of qualification is indispensable for authority, the highest possible qualification can never by itself beget authority. The teacher's qualification consists in knowing the world and being able to instruct others about it, but his authority rests on his assumption of responsibility for that world. Vis-à-vis the child it is as though he were a representative of all adult inhabitants, pointing out the details and saying to the child: This is our world.

Now we all know how things stand today in respect to authority.

Whatever one's attitude toward this problem may be, it is obvious that in public and political life authority either plays no role at all—for the violence and terror exercised by the totalitarian countries have, of course, nothing to do with authority—or at most plays a highly contested role. This, however, simply means, in essence, that people do not wish to require of anyone or to entrust to anyone the assumption of responsibility for everything else, for wherever true authority existed it was joined with responsibility for the course of things in the world. If we remove authority from political and public life, it may mean that from now on an equal responsibility for the course of the world is to be required of everyone. But it may also mean that the claims of the world and the requirements of order in it are being consciously or unconsciously repudiated; all responsibility for the world is being rejected, the responsibility for giving orders no less than for obeying them. There is no doubt that in the modern loss of authority both intentions play a part and have often been simultaneously and inextricably at work together.

In education, on the contrary, there can be no such ambiguity in regard to the present-day loss of authority. Children cannot throw off educational authority, as though they were in a position of oppression by an adult majority—though even this absurdity of treating children as an oppressed minority in need of liberation has actually been tried out in modern educational practice. Authority has been discarded by the adults, and this can mean only one thing: that the adults refuse to assume responsibility for the world into which they have brought the children.

There is of course a connection between the loss of authority in public and political life and in the private pre-political realms of the family and the school. The more radical the distrust of authority becomes in the public sphere, the greater the probability naturally becomes that the private sphere will not remain inviolate. There is this additional fact, and it is very likely the decisive one, that from time out of mind we have been accustomed in our tradition of political thought to regard the authority of parents over children, of teachers over pupils, as the model by which to understand political authority. It is just this model, which can be found as early as Plato and Aristotle, that makes the concept of authority in politics so extraordinarily ambiguous. It is based, first of all, on an absolute superiority such as can never exist among adults and which, from the point of view of human dignity, must never exist. In the second place, following the model of the nursery, it is based on a purely temporary superiority and therefore becomes self-contradictory if it is applied to relations that are not temporary by nature—such as the relations of the rulers and the ruled. Thus it lies in the nature of the matter—that is, both in the nature of the present crisis in authority and in the nature of our traditional political thought—that the loss of authority which began in the political sphere should end in the private one; and it is naturally no accident that the place where political authority was first undermined, that is, in America, should be the place where the modern crisis in education makes itself most strongly felt.

The general loss of authority could, in fact, hardly find more radical expression than by its intrusion into the pre-political sphere, where authority seemed dictated by nature itself and independent of all historical changes and political conditions. On the other hand, modern man could find no clearer expression for his dissatisfaction with the world, for his disgust with things as they are, than by his refusal to assume, in respect to his children, responsibility for all this. It is as though parents daily said: "In this world even we are not very securely at home; how to move about in it, what to know, what skills to master, are mysteries to us too. You must try to make out as best you can; in any case you are not entitled to call us to account. We are innocent, we wash our hands of you."

This attitude has, of course, nothing to do with that revolutionary desire for a new order in the world—*Novus Ordo Seclorum*—which once animated America; it is rather a symptom of that modern estrangement from the world which can be seen everywhere but which presents itself in especially radical and desperate form under the conditions of a mass society. It is true that modern educational experiments, not in America alone, have struck very revolutionary poses, and this has, to a certain degree, increased the difficulty of clearly recognizing the situation and caused a certain degree of confusion in the discussion of the problem; for in contradiction to all such behavior stands the unquestionable fact that so long as America was really animated by that spirit she never dreamed of initiating the new order with education but, on the contrary, remained conservative in educational matters.

To avoid misunderstanding: it seems to me that conservatism, in the sense of conservation, is of the essence of the educational activity, whose task is always to cherish and protect something—the child against the world, the world against the child, the new against the old, the old against the new. Even the comprehensive responsibility for the world that is thereby assumed implies, of course, a conservative attitude. But this holds good only for the realm of education, or rather for the relations between grown-ups and children, and not for the realm of politics, where we act among and with adults and equals. In politics this conservative attitude—which accepts the world as it is, striving only to preserve the status quo—can only lead to destruction, because the world, in gross and in detail, is irrevocably delivered up to the ruin of time unless human beings are determined to intervene, to alter, to create what is new. Hamlet's words, "The time is out of joint. O cursed spite that ever I was born to set it right," are more or less true for every new generation, although since the beginning of our century they have perhaps acquired a more persuasive validity than before.

Basically we are always educating for a world that is or is becoming out of joint, for this is the basic human situation, in which the world is created by mortal hands to serve mortals for a limited time as home. Because the world is made by mortals it wears out; and because it continuously changes its inhabitants it runs the risk of becoming as mortal as they. To preserve the world against the mortality of its creators and inhabitants it must be constantly set right anew. The problem is simply to educate in such a way that a setting-right remains actually possible, even though it can, of course, never be assured. Our hope always hangs on the new which every generation brings; but precisely because we can base our hope only on this, we destroy everything if we so try to control the new that we, the old, can dictate how it will look. Exactly for the sake of what is new and revolutionary in every child, education must be conservative; it must preserve this newness and introduce it as a new thing into an old world, which, however revolutionary its actions may be, is always, from the standpoint of the next generation, superannuated and close to destruction.

.........**IV**

The real difficulty in modern education lies in the fact that, despite all the fashionable talk about a new conservatism, even that minimum of conservation and the conserving attitude without which education is simply not possible is in our time extraordinarily hard to achieve. There are very good reasons for this. The crisis of authority in education is most closely connected with the crisis of tradition, that is with the crisis in our attitude toward the realm of the past. This aspect of the modern crisis is especially hard for the educator to bear, because it is his task to mediate between the old and the new, so that his very profession requires of him an extraordinary respect for the past. Through long centuries, i.e., throughout the combined period of Roman-Christian civilization, there was no need for him to become aware of this special quality in himself because reverence for the past was an essential part of the Roman frame of mind, and this was not altered or ended by Christianity, but simply shifted onto different foundations.

It was of the essence of the Roman attitude (though this was by no means true of every civilization or even of the Western tradition taken as a whole) to consider the past *qua* past as a model, ancestors, in every instance, as guiding examples for their descendants; to believe that all greatness lies in what has been, and therefore that the most fitting human age is old age, the man grown old, who, because he is already almost an

ancestor, may serve as a model for the living. All this stands in contradiction not only to our world and to the modern age from the Renaissance on, but, for example, to the Greek attitude toward life as well.
When Goethe said that growing old is "the gradual withdrawal from
the world of appearances," his was a comment made in the spirit of the
Greeks, for whom being and appearing coincide. The Roman attitude
would have been that precisely in growing old and slowly disappearing
from the community of mortals man reaches his most characteristic form
of being, even though, in respect to the world of appearances, he is in
the process of disappearing; for only now can he approach the existence
in which he will be an authority for others.

With the undisturbed background of such a tradition, in which education has a political function (and this was a unique case), it is in fact
comparatively easy to do the right thing in matters of education without
even pausing to consider what one is really doing, so completely is the
specific ethos of the educational principle in accord with the basic ethical
and moral convictions of society at large. To educate, in the words of
Polybius, was simply "to let you see that you are altogether worthy
of your ancestors," and in this business the educator could be a "fellow-
contestant" and a "fellow-workman" because he too, though on a different level, went through life with his eyes glued to the past. Fellowship
and authority were in this case indeed but the two sides of the same
matter, and the teacher's authority was firmly grounded in the encompassing authority of the past as such. Today, however, we are no longer
in that position; and it makes little sense to act as though we still were
and had only, as it were, accidentally strayed from the right path and
were free at any moment to find our way back to it. This means that
wherever the crisis has occurred in the modern world, one cannot simply
go on nor yet simply turn back. Such a reversal will never bring us anywhere except to the same situation out of which the crisis has just arisen.
The return would simply be a repeat performance—though perhaps different in form, since there are no limits to the possibilities of nonsense
and capricious notions that can be decked out as the last word in science.
On the other hand, simple, unreflective perseverance, whether it be pressing forward in the crisis or adhering to the routine that blandly believes
the crisis will not engulf its particular sphere of life, can only, because it
surrenders to the course of time, lead to ruin; it can only, to be more
precise, increase that estrangement from the world by which we are
already threatened on all sides. Consideration of the principles of education must take into account this process of estrangement from the world;
it can even admit that we are here presumably confronted by an automatic process, provided only that it does not forget that it lies within

the power of human thought and action to interrupt and arrest such processes.

The problem of education in the modern world lies in the fact that by its very nature it cannot forgo either authority or tradition, and yet must proceed in a world that is neither structured by authority nor held together by tradition. That means, however, that not just teachers and educators, but all of us, insofar as we live in one world together with our children and with young people, must take toward them an attitude radically different from the one we take toward one another. We must decisively divorce the realm of education from the others, most of all from the realm of public, political life, in order to apply to it alone a concept of authority and an attitude toward the past which are appropriate to it but have no general validity and must not claim a general validity in the world of grown-ups.

In practice the first consequence of this would be a clear understanding that the function of the school is to teach children what the world is like and not to instruct them in the art of living. Since the world is old, always older than they themselves, learning inevitably turns toward the past, no matter how much living will spend itself in the present. Second, the line drawn between children and adults should signify that one can neither educate adults nor treat children as though they were grown up; but this line should never be permitted to grow into a wall separating children from the adult community as though they were not living in the same world and as though childhood were an autonomous human state, capable of living by its own laws. Where the line between childhood and adulthood falls in each instance cannot be determined by a general rule; it changes often, in respect to age, from country to country, from one civilization to another, and also from individual to individual. But education, as distinguished from learning, must have a predictable end. In our civilization this end probably coincides with graduation from college rather than with graduation from high school, for the professional training in universities or technical schools, though it always has something to do with education, is nevertheless in itself a kind of specialization. It no longer aims to introduce the young person to the world as a whole, but rather to a particular, limited segment of it. One cannot educate without at the same time teaching; an education without learning is empty and therefore degenerates with great ease into moral-emotional rhetoric. But one can quite easily teach without educating, and one can go on learning to the end of one's days without for that reason becoming educated. All these are particulars, however, that must really be left to the experts and the pedagogues.

What concerns us all and cannot therefore be turned over to the special science of pedagogy is the relation between grown-ups and children in general or, putting it in even more general and exact terms, our attitude toward the fact of natality: the fact that we have all come into the world by being born and that this world is constantly renewed through birth. Education is the point at which we decide whether we love the world enough to assume responsibility for it and by the same token save it from that ruin which, except for renewal, except for the coming of the new and young, would be inevitable. And education, too, is where we decide whether we love our children enough not to expel them from our world and leave them to their own devices, nor to strike from their hands their chance of undertaking something new, something unforeseen by us, but to prepare them in advance for the task of renewing a common world.

Part Four

SCIENCE, LITERATURE AND CULTURE

The culture of the West has traditionally been a literary culture; that is to say, one in which a very special social, moral, and philosophical value has been ascribed to the work of imaginative writers. The ancient Greeks found in the epics of Homer something vastly more important than entertainment; they found a kind of wisdom and insight which to them verged on the divine. It is worth remembering also that the Greek tragedies were in part religious rituals, a way of doing honor to the gods. The great poets of later national civilizations—Dante in Italy, Shakespeare in England, Goethe in Germany, and others—poets who were able to give expressive form to the ideas and aspirations of their countrymen, have been rewarded by an analogous kind of quasi-divine status. The force of the literary element in Western civilization is suggested further by the fact that the Bible itself, even in the days of the Fathers of the early Church, has been praised for its literary merits—as if the Western sensibility found it altogether to be expected that the word of God should assume aesthetically pleasing form.

"Culture" in our civilization has been identified with "literature" to such an extent that an educated European or American of a few generations ago might well have found it difficult to imagine that there were other civilizations in the world that ascribed unique authority not to imaginative writers but rather to priest castes of one sort or another, to sages, or to formal philosophers. The reaction of the Westerner of today would be less predictable and would depend to a large extent on his individual education and specialized training. For our own age presents in an extreme form a challenge to the dominance of literature, an intensification of a challenge which made itself heard for the first time three centuries ago with the emergence of modern science.

Before turning to the champions of science as a dominant cultural force, one would do well to look at some of the claims which have, over the centuries, been advanced for literature, viewed not as a form of entertainment but as a *magister vitae,* a way of making sense out of experience. To begin with, there is the moral claim in its simplest form, a claim which goes back at least as far as the Roman poet Horace, who maintained that literature, since it delights and instructs at the same time, is a more effective moral instrument than unadorned teaching or preaching (see the introductory note to the selection from George Bernard Shaw, pp. 61-62). This moralistic view of the role of literature, repeated by literary critics and theorists throughout the Renaissance and the eighteenth century, continues to have its exponents today: Lionel Trilling reflects it in his conception of literature as the criticism of life (more specifically the criticism of social and political behavior); Albert Camus, like George Orwell, applies it in his entire creative achievement; Kenneth Tynan, in Section V of this volume, argues for it in an extreme and simplified form with which both Horace and Trilling would be likely to disagree. In the second place, there is the more sophisticated view of literature as a synthesizing power, an agency for creating a world of its own which enables us to understand and experience our own world more completely and wisely. This view, explicitly avowed by E. M. Forster and Carl Jung, may be clearly felt in both examples of literary criticism included in the following pages—as clearly in the textual criticism of Bernard Knox as in the more impressionistic criticism of Thomas Mann. Related to this latter view is the conception of literature as a form of knowledge which, being unspecialized, speaks to all men about the common human condition in a manner impossible for the specialized disciplines. Such a conception is overtly stated by Robert Oppenheimer, although with the questionable implication that the literary artist himself need not be, in terms of his own craft, a specialist. Such a conception also has an effect on the scientific account by Sir Charles Sherrington which opens Section IV, for Sir Charles, initially trained in the older literary culture, is able to draw on that culture in order to communicate more vitally than he otherwise might his very specialized, scientific knowledge.

The first faint challenges to the cultural dominance of literature in the West may be found in seventeenth-century England, in the writings of the philosophers Francis Bacon and Thomas Hobbes. Both were cultivated men of the Renaissance and themselves distinguished prose stylists familiar with classical literature as well as that of their own time. Nevertheless, they imply throughout their writings a kind of affectionate contempt for "mere literature," which they seem to regard as a pleasant ornament to life but one on which serious men ought not to waste too much time. The real business of life, for Bacon and Hobbes, is finding out about the material world and learning how to harness its powers for the material advantage of mankind. Such attitudes, however, were not strongly advanced until two centuries later, by which time enormous strides in both theoretical and applied science had made that mode of thought a serious contender for dominance over man's mind. Lionel Trilling, in the openings pages of his essay, details this first real struggle between science and literature as it found expression in the debates between Thomas Henry Huxley and Matthew Arnold in the nineteenth century. He goes on to analyze the conflict in its modern form, and his analysis may be read in meaningful connection with the statements of Oppenheimer and Forster, which, despite certain shared humanistic values, reveal respectively science-oriented and literature-oriented visions of life.

In our own time science seems to have gained cultural ascendancy, at least in the popular mind. To some extent this ascendancy is the result of the enormous strengths of science as a method—its objectivity, its verifiability, its clarity, its cumulative authority. Oppenheimer, speaking as a scientist, emphasizes these strengths and seems to regard science as the most promising variety of intellectual endeavor. To some extent also, the material accomplishments of science lend it a special prestige in the eyes of society as a whole—its authority, after all, is based on control over the concrete universe, as that of the poet and the philosopher is not. Hence comes, too, the regrettable popular confusion between theoretical science, a way of understanding reality, and technology, a practical occupation. It is probably also true that the necessary specialization of science, leading to an intellectual isolation which is deplored by Oppenheimer and Trilling alike, in itself contributes to the special prestige of science: the fact that the scientist works in terms which are largely incomprehensible except to another specialist makes him, so to speak, a member of a mysterious priest caste, one who is respected precisely because his world cannot be understood.

The prestige of science in the modern world is not, however, confined to the general public alone; it has affected almost every area of nonscientific intellectual activity. The social studies, for example, often seem to have as their aim the achievement of methods and standards indistinguishable from those of the natural sciences, and the often-discussed obscurity of much modern art may be related to an impulse toward specialization comparable to that which science finds unavoidable. Literary criticism also has been influenced by the great claims of science: some contemporary criticism employs a specialized vocabulary and a tortuous method which makes it accessible only to the initiate. Mann's essay on Tolstoi, however, reminds us that criticism is most illuminating when it retains the breadth of literature itself. And Knox's essay on Sophocles shows that criticism can have its own standards of accuracy, penetration, and attention to detail, different from those of science, but equally rigorous.

The discipline of psychology is especially interesting in its relation to natural science. Behavioristic psychology, determined to achieve standards of "scientific" rigor, deliberately refuses to consider psychological phenomena which do not lend themselves to its materialistic approach, and analytic psychology, ever since its beginnings with Freud, has undergone a conflict between its scientific aspirations and its willingness to confront whole areas of possibility not strictly amenable to scientific method. A large part of Freud's greatness, as indicated in Erik Erikson's commemorative essay, is due to his having conquered a vast new area for science, but Freud's life work shows a shift of attention from the physiological to the psychic, and his last contributions, to which Erikson briefly refers, move from the descriptive to the speculative. Carl Jung, who ranks second only to Freud as a force in psychoanalytic thought, initially broke with his master in part over the question of the nature of science and the extent to which psychology might aspire to the condition of the natural sciences. His essay on psychology and literature typifies the breadth of his approach: gifted with the caution and humility of the true scientist, he nevertheless refuses to shut out of his thought the mysterious areas of psychological experience which cannot be summed up in a verifiable formula. At the same time, his sensitive response to literature itself suggests, as cogently as does Sherrington's essay, that the conflict between scientific and literary cultures may be due to regrettable human pettiness rather than to any inherent opposition of the disciplines themselves.

If one conceives of the claims of science and those of literature as complementing each other rather than as opposing each other, the question of the boundaries between the two activities logically poses itself. What can one do that the other cannot? Science, as Sherrington, Erikson, and Oppenheimer demonstrate, can speak with ever-increasing authority about the actual construction of the world of experience, whether that experience be of the atoms which make up all matter, the cells which make up the living body, or certain of the forces which make up the human psyche. Literature, like philosophy and religion, can continue its age-old task of putting all our experience together into meaningful wholes, so that we may respond to it as human beings rather than as fragments of human beings: so it is that Forster and Mann conceive of its function. Science, as Oppenheimer tells us, is the great achievement of man working with his fellow men; literature, as William Butler Yeats tells us, is the equally great achievement of man communing with himself. Yeats, we know, personally held a number of fantastic beliefs about psychology and physiology; these beliefs, necessary as a personal foundation for the poet's great work, are useless to us as science—as useless as the astronomical ideas of Dante or Shakespeare. But by the same token the philosophical and religious ideas of many great scientists—Sir Isaac Newton, for example—are useless to us as a source of religious or aesthetic experience. What we are saying is that science deals with fact, whereas literature deals with value. The good scientist cannot, as scientist, ask what should be; he can only ask what is. The literary artist (see, for example, the essays of Camus, Forster, and Mann) must always implicitly ask what should be, even as he imaginatively explores what is.

But for man as man the two worlds of science and literature can never be wholly separated. Jung suggests some of the ways in which they are related, and his life work indicates the extent to which the study of psychology partakes of both worlds simultaneously. It is impossible, at any rate, to conceive of a true civilization in which both forms of knowledge do not play a part: a society which will not pose questions of value, which will not criticize, is, as Trilling points out, threatened by terrible dangers. A society which will not pursue questions of fact is already on the threshold of decadence. Separate in practice, as they necessarily are, science and literature are both forms of human creativity, united by a common concern for human destiny. Perhaps Oppenheimer is right in thinking that the future holds a new leisure which will make communication between "the two cultures" more nearly possible. Even if he is not, the entire humanistic tradition urges the necessity of mutual respect and cooperation—even at a distance.

Suggested Further Readings:

Matthew Arnold, *Culture and Anarchy*
C. P. Snow, *The Two Cultures and the Scientific Revolution*
F. R. Leavis, *The Significance of C. P. Snow*

Sigmund Freud, *The Interpretation of Dreams*

William Butler Yeats, *Selected Poems*
Any standard paperback anthology of poetry

Leo Tolstoi, *The Death of Ivan Ilytich and Other Stories*
Thomas Mann, *Death in Venice and Other Stories*
E. M. Forster, *Howard's End*
Albert Camus, *The Plague*
Ernest Hemingway, *The Old Man and the Sea*

Sophocles, *Oedipus Rex* (i.e., *Oedipus Tyrannos*) and *Oedipus at Colonos*

Sir Charles Sherrington

As the branches of learning commonly referred to as "the sciences" have become more exact and specialized, the lines of communication between literary and scientific culture have deteriorated, though to exactly what degree and for what reasons are matters that are difficult to determine. Obviously, the materials of the "impure" or social sciences (psychology, sociology, and so on) are more accessible to the man of general culture than are the materials of the natural, or "pure," sciences (physics, biology, and so on). In part, problems of communication are the inevitable result of the private language that physics and chemistry have had to develop and which many of the other sciences draw from, a language which a man who has not been especially trained to read cannot read at all. But in part these problems are also the result of much more complicated forces which are of great concern to the best minds of both the "two cultures," the literary and the scientific, and which several of the essays in this section debate in some detail.

It is still possible, of course, not to conceive of science and humane letters as locked in a state of conflict or rivalry but rather as coexisting, indeed concomitant, aspects of the unity of human knowledge. Such seems to be the underlying assumption of the great English biologist Sir Charles Sherrington, who for most of his long life (1857-1952) was Professor of Physiology at Oxford University. In his speculative work *Man on His Nature* (it first appeared in 1940, and in a revised, new edition in 1950), he explains the physical phenomenon of life itself, as understood by modern biology, and directs his attention toward that most complex and bewildering form of life: man himself. In "The Wisdom of the Body," our selection from this work, Sherrington is concerned with the manner in which single cells combine to form the human mind and body, and the essay is from one point of view an admirable example of clear scientific prose. Yet it also has specifically literary qualities, and it reminds us of the fact that until quite recently this was true of the work of most of the great scientists (*e.g.,* Bacon, Newton, Darwin). Instinctively, Sherrington avails himself of the full resources of the English language and of classical rhetorical devices: literary and historical reference and allusion, analogy, metaphor and imagery of all sorts—the phrase "that subversive change called death" has almost a Shakespearean ring to it. Furthermore, the story he has to tell of cellular development, which reaches its climax in the long section of the human eye, is a dramatic story. The author recognizes this and organizes his material accordingly, conveying to the reader his own sense of excitement as events rapidly succeed each other. Thus, while "The Wisdom of the Body" remains an exact account, technically precise, wholly faithful to the letter and the spirit of the laws of scientific investigation, it also has dimensions that may justly be called poetic, and it has them because they, too, are inherent in the material under examination. The essay itself becomes, then, a demonstration of Sherrington's belief that *wonder* is common both to science and to poetry.

Wonder plays its role in philosophy too (it is significant that the prefatory quotations include statements by a scientist, a poet, and a philosopher). Indeed, the larger philosophical issues are never absent from the author's mind: the enigmatic implications of purpose in cellular behavior, and the recognition of the fact that physical being, in man, has been capable of evolving out of itself values and standards that transcend the physical. Like other philosophers, Sherrington poses for himself the largest of questions; like other scientists, however, he is discontent with answers that are not based on firm and verifiable evidence. As a result, he presents us with more questions than answers, but his work reaffirms the vigor of the humanistic tradition in an age in which science, as well as other forces, have often called the tradition into question.

To read Sir Charles Sherrington is to wonder if perhaps some of the failure in communication between science and letters is not wilfully induced by those of narrow and acrimonious spirit among the adherents of both the "two cultures."

THE WISDOM OF THE BODY

Or a giggle at a Wonder.

KEATS

*Anatomize the eye: survey its structure and contrivance; and
tell me, from your own feeling, if the idea of a contriver does
not immediately flow in upon you with a force like that of a
sensation.*

HUME'S *Dialogues concerning Natural Religion,*
ED. KEMP SMITH, p. 191

*I remember well the time when the thought of the eye made
me cold all over.*

CHARLES DARWIN

L'admiration est toujours une fatigue pour l'espece humaine.
Le Bal de Sceaux

We dismiss wonder commonly with childhood. Much later we
may return. Then the whole world becomes wonderful. But, greatest
wonder, our wonder soon lapses. A rainbow every morning who would
pause to look at? The wonderful which comes often is soon taken for
granted. That is practical enough. It allows us to get on with life. But
it may stultify if it cannot on occasion be thrown off. To recapture now
and then childhood's wonder is a driving force for occasional grown-up
thoughts. Among the workings of this planet, there is a *tour de force,* if
such term befits the workings of a planet.

The body is made up of cells, thousands of millions of them, in our
own instance about 1000 billions. It is a unity which has become multiplicity while keeping its unity (Carrel). At its beginning it is just one
cell, and the whole body is the progeny of that one. Its ancestry converges
back to that one ancestral cell. And that, in its turn, was from the ancestral cell of a next preceding family of cells.

In each generation the impetus for the initial cell to produce its
organized family is supplied by the coming together of it and another
cell, outside its own familial stock, but not too far outside. In our own
case and in the case of all our nearer kind, these two cells come from
individuals of like species. The two individuals have to be complemental
in sex. The fertilization-process which is preliminary to the train of

From *Man on His Nature* by Sir Charles Sherrington (New York, Cambridge University
Press, 1946). Reprinted by permission of the publisher.

growth of a new individual we can dispense with. The story of growth from a rounded microscopic speck to a shaped creature, is what we will glance at in outline. Before the coming of the microscope the earliest chapters of this life-story baffled the wisest. They were mere conjecture. When the microscope did come it set itself to trace this Odyssey, this journey from a pin's-head egg to a grown man. Some saw as the starting-point of it an infinitesimal man. The truth was stranger still. All there was to see was a speck of granular jelly, bearing no likeness to either parent or to man at all.

Then at its outsetting that speck grew and, presently tearing its tiny self in two, made an adhering pair. Then they 4, 8, 16, 32 and so on; only to slow down after reaching millions upon millions. Not to stop altogether until by misadventure or, after years, by natural term, there falls on the whole assembly that subversive change called "death." Each of the cells from the beginning besides shaping itself takes up for itself a right station in the total assembly according to the stage which the assembly has by that time attained. Thus each cell helps to shape, and to construct as by design, the total assembly. So it is that those early thirty-two cells dispose themselves as a little ball, hollow and filled with water. These thirty-two cells then are a beginning stage of the individual to be, and the beginning whether beast or man.

Their visible arrangement taken at that stage gives no obvious hint of what the ultimate will be. Thence quickly, though gradually, change sweeps onward to later stage on stage. Darwin quoted the naturalist who wrote, "I have two little embryos in spirit, to which I have omitted to attach names. I am now quite unable to say to what class of animals they belong." Lizards or birds or mammals, they might be any of them. That kind of thing must have confronted Aristotle as a biologist; it was a *final* cause. He insisted that to know a thing its final cause must have been explored. That was an injunction which Jean Fernel accepted from him and endorsed. In biology to jump at the final causes has many times led to mistakes. It did so notably with Galen. But it has also often solved problems. It opened clues to Harvey. But in following it, Harvey never forgot that its following as a clue demands control by other evidence at every step.

The successive chapters of the story of the little ball of cells is like a serial transformation scene. The little ball can be likened, crudely enough, to a set of magic bricks. The one cell, the original fertilized cell, grows into two and those two each into two, and so forth. When that has gone on in the aggregate some 45 times there are 26 million million magic bricks all of a family. That is about the number in the human child at birth. They have arranged themselves into a complex, which is a human child. Each has assumed its required form and size in the right place. The whole is not merely specific but is a particular individual within the limits of the specific.

Each cell, we remember, is blind; senses it has none. It knows not "up" from "down"; it works in the dark. Yet the nerve-cell, for instance, "finds" even to the fingertips the nerve-cell with which it should touch fingers. It is as if an imminent principle inspired each cell with knowledge for the carrying out of a design. And this picture which the microscope supplies to us, conveying this impression of prescience and intention, supplies us after all, because it is but a picture, with only the static form. That is but the outward and visible sign of a dynamic activity, which is a harmony in time as well as space. "Never the time and the place and the loved one all together." Here all three and always, save for disease.

In its earliest stage the embryo's cells are not notably different one from another. Later a finished muscle-cell and a finished nerve-cell and a finished liver-cell are as far apart in visible structure as in what they do. They become so in spite of being by descent all members of one family. On the other hand, take of each similarly-functioning cells a pair, one from man and one from fish, and, though by descent worlds apart, the observer can read at a glance that members of a pair, alike in what they do, conform to the same pattern. The nerve-cell is as obviously a nerve-cell whether from man or fish. The cells of the various parts of the systematized assembly assume special shapes, octagonal, stellate, threadlike, or what not. They, as the case may require, pour out cement which binds, or fluid in which they shall move free. Some will have changed their stuff and become rigid bone or, harder still, the enamel of a tooth; some become fluid, so to flow along tubes too fine for the eye to see. Some become clear as glass, some opaque as stone, some colourless, some red, some black. Some become factories of a furious chemistry, some become inert as death. Some become engines of mechanical pull, some scaffoldings of static support. Some a system transmitting electrical signs. It might serve as a text for democracy. It is as if the life of each one of all those millions has understood its special part. Thus arises the new integral individual to be.

To this there seems at first sight one exception. One cell-type which, out of all the myriads, alone remains its original self and does not specialize. It retains the old original nature of the ancestral cell. Its sisters and their progeny pass on through chains of metamorphoses to form a world of different shapes and activities. But this one persists still unmodified and true to its own primitive forbear. It must be so, or there would be no future generation of the entire stock. To begin again there must be a return to the beginning. All its sisters with their flights into far-fetched specializations, including the brain with its mysteries of mind, are power-less to produce again a germ such as they sprang from. From no one of them all, let them be ever so human, can any fertilization produce their like again in the shape of man or human child. For that their sister cell, still generalized like the ancestral cell, is the sole means remaining. Hence from the old ancestral cell one narrow derivative line of descendants, nested in the rest of the immense specialized collateral progeny, retains its original germinal and general nature; and even this has to ripen. Sig-nificantly enough it then sets itself free from all the others. And so from generation on to generation. This limited cell-stock which can be called exceptional in that unlike its congeners, it does not specialize away from the parent germinal form, can be thought of as no exception after all. It is specialized for reproduction. It is clearly specialized in so far that only a special fertilizer can fertilize it. Its own specialization, as though by foreknowledge, anticipates among other anticipations what the nature of that special fertilizer will be. The whole astonishing process achieving the making of a new individual is thus an organized adventure in spe-cialization on the part of countless co-operating units. It does more than complete the new individual; it provides for the future production of further individuals from that one.

More than half a million different species of pattern of creature are, I believe, listed as current life. And each, as we say, "breeds true." This particular one we have followed is that to which the pair of cells, which made it, themselves belong, and they will make no other kind. But although of their species it is not quite like any other that ever was. It is not only man but it is the man John Brown, or the woman Mary Smith, whose exact like never was yet.

But that procession of change which for instance abuts in the human child has never come within the role of the actual ancestry of the fer-tilized cell which sets about it. All that has come within the experience of that ancestry has been the launching from generation to generation of that side-adventure which now terminates in fully completed man. An explanation once offered for the evolutionary process traced it to "mem-ory" in the ancestral cell. But such an explanation rests, even as analogy, on a misapprehension of the actual circumstances. It would be imagina-tion rather than memory which we must assume for the ancestral cell; memory could not recall experience it never had.

The few early units which formed the family when it was but a tiny ball take into their counsel water. The ball they form is filled with it. The growing membrane, half-floating, can then fold. It shapes itself, it feeds, water is a generous solvent; and it admits electrical activities, chem-ical compounds separating with opposite charge. Water is the very men-struum and habitat of each and every cell. Water, within and without, allows the cell free scope for action. Water is a wonderful "surround" and the germinal cell seems to appreciate that.

Water within and water without. The cell-surface becomes at once a boundary and a medium of exchange between two chemical worlds, one inside the cell, "alive," the other outside it, lifeless. The cells divide and divide and differentiate and differentiate. The total aggregate of the surface between alive and not alive becomes greater and greater, and endlessly qualitatively graded.

Step by step things shape. There appear, tiny at first, what to the eye of the expert are recognizable as rudiments of parts of the future creature. The brain is a set of three little hollow chambers, and, thrust from the hindmost, a short tube, the spinal cord. They were formed by the membrane folding over right and left, the side-flaps merging and so making a tube. Their membrane will come to be a patterned nest of branching cells all in touch directly or indirectly one with the other and, in man, approaching in number our planet's human population. The tubular chamber with its watery content persists, buried within the greatly enriched membrane. It persists throughout life, a primitive vestige, a dumb witness to far primeval times when not only man, but bird and mammal and even reptile had not yet come to be. That early step of folding to make a tube-like brain belongs to the opening chapter of the story of the human embryo growing into a child, but it is a primordial step, which foreran by aeons the advent of the human form itself.

Yet this swift and sure drama at some detail in some scene occasionally fails of full enactment. Sometimes the child is born with its brain and cord not closed to a tube, but lying open as a furrow. Then the nerves, which from all over the body should grow in and make connection with the roof of the completed tube, may be found looking, as it were, for it; and they look for it in the right place. But they themselves are helpless. It is not here. What kind of co-operation is this? The whole story is not just chemistry and physics. There is a final cause at work. The outcome here is evidently that of a process which sometimes goes wrong. Such instances are not very uncommon. Fingers or toes may misgrow club-like together. One kidney may fail. The head may contain practically no brain. In the heart the window between lung-half and other half may not close at birth, so that the blood goes imperfectly aerated, and the child lives half blue with suffocation. What is the meaning of these failures in the issue of the plan? Where two calves of a birth are of opposite sex, the sex-organ of the female twin is found underdeveloped. Its development is checked by chemical substances which favour the male twin. In the cow the twins in the uterus have a circulation in common and the male hormones circulating through both inhibit the cow-calf. In the human case the circulation is not in common and this does not occur. The blood-supply of each twin is separate. Now, hormones are chemical substances.

We speak of nerves *for* doing this and that. This is the Galen in us. To do so comes unbidden to the lips. And Galen in this was thinking as everyone thinks and was speaking for Mr. Everyman, not merely of his own time but for practically ever since. Muscles seem made for what will be wanted of them. In the foetus a short channel joins the root of the lung-artery with that of the main artery of the body. Immediately following birth the lung enters activity, and this side-tracking of its blood-supply would be disadvantageous. A little before the foetus is actually born this channel is shut by a special small muscle. This muscle "as far as is known never used in the foetus," "springs into action at birth" and shuts the channel. "Having performed its function it degenerates" and disappears, the channel having in due course become obliterated under disuse. Sir Joseph Barcroft adds "it would seem very difficult to claim that the muscle which closes the ductus at birth has been differentiated as the result of any specific conditions to which it has been subjected—much less any specific use which it has subserved." It is an instance of a final cause.

Nerves seem *for* their purpose, constructed in view of what *will* be "wanted" of them. Before ever they function they grow where they *will* be wanted, they make the "right" connections. We all drop into this mode of thought; we adopt it as we dissect. In the particular prodigy before us now, that of a microscopic cell becoming a man, we incline to read the whole story in that way. We say "it grows into" a child. Grows? Levers laid down in gristle, becoming bone when wanted for the heavier pull of muscle which *will* clothe them. Lungs, solid glands, yet arranged to hollow out at a few minutes' notice when the necessary air shall enter. Limb-buds, futile at their appearing and yet deliberately appearing, in order to become limbs in readiness for an existence where they will be all-important. A pseudo-aquatic parasite, voiceless as a fish, yet constructing within itself an instrument of voice against the time when it *will* talk. Organs of skin, ear, eye, nose, tongue, superfluous all of them in the watery dark where formed, yet each unhaltingly preparing to enter a daylit, airy, object-full manifold world which they *will* be wanted to report on. A great excrescence at one end of a nerve-tube, an outrageously outsized brain, of no avail at the moment but where the learning of a world which is *to be* experienced will go forward. Living structure is a mass of Aristotle's final causes. All is remembered; no detail is forgotten, even to the criss-cross hairs at entrance to a cat's ear which keep out water and flies. Had antiquity or the middle ages been acquainted with the facts, they would have been set down to Natural Magic. Fernel's Preface (1542) wrote "as Aristotle says to know the end of a thing is to know the why of it." And similarly today the biologist writes, "we can only understand an organism if we regard it *as though* produced under the guidance of thought for an end," as a final cause at work.

Suppose tentatively, at pause before this riddle, we allow the premise that in this developing embryo there resides some form of mind or psyche, and even in each of its constituent cells, and not inferior to what as human individual it will ever have. Mind so present and intent on producing the child to be, would still be faced at every step with "how." It would be helpless. It is an aggregate of cells doing what they are doing for the first time and the only time they ever will. Yet every step they take seems fraught with purpose toward a particular end. The purpose clear, the "how" of it obscure. Watching the limb-bud enlarge and shape without hitch to an arm, the surprise is not when all goes right but when sometimes something goes wrong. Perhaps it is best to think of it as an inherited final cause.

The microscope merely resolves the mystery into some millions of separate microscopic growing points, each still a mystery. We ask what is the process going on at each of these? Again, how are they all co-ordinated to give a harmony of growth "according to plan"?

Growth? The word in biology, employed I suppose since biology first was, took long in getting to grips with its intimate scientific "how." Its "rapport" with chemistry and physics was not close. Its study consorted rather with that of gross visible shape, the shapes of life. Growth is of course the factor in their shaping. To record shape has been far easier than to understand it. The shaping of the embryo taken at its face-value is an amazing "becoming" which carries "purpose," even as the wing of the insect or the stream-lining of the whale. Because atoms combine on the basis of the arrangement of their sub-atomic parts we do not speak of those constituent parts as there *for* producing molecules.

In the study of biology the integral shape of the living thing has always held a prominent place. Such shape is always specific and of decisive meaning to the life itself. It was a study which as it became subtler and more conscious of its ultimate aim called itself morphology. Its technique, like that of anatomy from which it sprang, was, prior to the microscope, simple, requiring a few cutting tools and the naked eye. Hence it had been accessible to antiquity. Aristotle's genius ranging over the field of animal form practically for the first time in science discovered much and laid down philosophic foundations. He possessed, for his era, an encyclopaedic acquaintance with animal form, and he drew from it profound and far-reaching inferences.

Aristotle treated visible form as an *a priori* concept. Probably, all circumstances considered, that was well. We can think he got further by that means than he would by any other open to him and his time. The "abstraction of structure and function is," happily remarks Professor A. D. Ritchie, "at bottom merely a question of what changes slower or faster."

There is one aspect of life's shaping which has however always pointed plainly to a dynamics of living form. That is growth. An old commonplace of the text-books used to tell us that although growth is a term applied to crystals as well as to living things, crystal growth affords no clue to and no paradigm for living growth. That seems now too hard and fast a saying. New techniques have recently been enlisted for the examination of biological structure. One of them is that developed by the Braggs for their masterly X-ray analysis of crystal structure and growth. The cell not so long since was plausibly regarded as a colloidal droplet. A drop of amorphous colloidal suspensoid seems as remote as anything possibly can be from what we should call architecture. To appraise the living cell as such a droplet was to forget that the cell is always an organized integer. If unified spatial plan is architecture the cell has architecture. As to the stones of its architecture, they are "proteins." It is a protein fabric. The nucleus, centring it, is a nodal point for the cell's synthesis of proteins.

As for colloid, the proteins behave in several ways as do inorganic colloids. They are held back by membranes, they diffuse slowly, and so on. Protein particles were not so long since thought colloidal molecular aggregates, not single molecules. For one thing they seemed too large. The chemist for all his synthetic achievements cannot construct any molecule approaching in mass the protein particle. That particle, when regarded as a cluster of lesser molecules, was therefore supposed indeterminate in mass. But the protein particle is now at least in many instances known to be one giant molecule. It has the definite individuality which is the hall-mark of a molecule, where every constituent atom is indispensable for the completion of the structure. X-ray analysis yields a picture of the atomic architecture of the protein-molecule. Likewise the ultra-centrifuge in a different way gives data of the mass and figure of protein particles, and it too finds them to be giant molecules. Some are thread-like, others practically globular. Their potential variety of pattern runs to astronomical figures. The probability nevertheless holds that one underlying style of architecture obtains throughout them. Their wealth of detailed pattern provides a practically inexhaustible variety for life to build with.

Pure mechanical treatment affects these giant molecules to an extent not evident with smaller and simpler ones. They can be "denatured," that is warped in configuration, reversibly or irreversibly, by mechanical agitation or even by inclusion in the surface-layer at a boundary. The cell, and therefore the living body, are sponge-works of boundary layers. The protein coat of the fertilized egg-cell which restrains the daughter-cells from becoming spherical behaves as a sheet of elastic jelly. It can be cut by the "microneedle" without loss of its rigidity. But mechanical agitation by moving the needle back and forth "dissolves" it locally. In wool-keratin the molecule has an extensible backbone which lengthwise pull unfolds to a more open zig-zag. Hence the wool's reversible extensibility. Again, the immense significance of muscle to life rests on its property of changing length and lengthwise tension. This, it is claimed, is due to a protein-molecule of folding and unfolding type.

The essential service of muscle to life is, quickly and reversibly, to shorten so as to pull. Its shortening is called "contraction." The importance of muscular contraction to us can be stated by saying that all man can do is to move things, and his muscular contraction is his sole means thereto. Each muscle-fibre is a simplified miniature of muscle, in size just visible to the naked eye. A millimetre is $\frac{1}{25}$ inch; a large muscle-fibre may be 15 mm. long and 0.1 mm. across. A muscle is composed of bundles upon bundles of its fibres set lengthwise so as to pull on the muscle's tendon. Each fibre is seen by the microscope to consist of strands of lengthwise-running fibrils arranged in packets and bathed liberally in nutritive juice within the fibre. Beyond that, to further degrees of minute structure, the microscope can hardly carry. X-ray examination then continues the analysis. The unit of measurement is the millionth of a millimetre. The ultimate filament then resolves itself in countless lengthwise lines of giant molecules. Each molecule is about 60 $\mu\mu$ long by about 5 $\mu\mu$ thick. Such a molecule is, as molecules go, immensely large; it weighs about 500,000 times the hydrogen-gas molecule. It is a protein (myosinogen), and it is one of the folding molecules which by buckling back on itself becomes shorter. A cross-section of our sample muscle-fibre would cut 150 millions of them. It is as if for each square millimetre of a muscle's cross-section a set of pullers five times more numerous than earth's entire human population were aligned to pull co-ordinately in one and the same direction. And at the given command they are called into play. It is a command issued through the muscle's nerve. It may be a chemical message but it is transmitted electrically.

How it induces the molecules in their millions actually to buckle, we have still to wait to know. Whatever the device, nature has contrived it on a number of independent occasions; for instance in the thread-stalk of little vorticella as well as in vertebrate muscle.

I have heard Professor Vivian Hill say that the design of a spade or the gearing of a pedal bicycle are found to have worked themselves out duly proportionately to the rates of performance of the human muscle-fibre. These latter were not scientifically known until Hill's own researches determined them. But when we turn to the muscle-fibre it has solved the incomparably more difficult problem of constructing a prime-mover fitting the biological situation. That is a sample of the biological problem. Ross Harrison, a veteran observer, remarks that such mechanical influence is unmistakable. Chambers finds: "Stretching a dividing Arbacia egg longitudinally does not impede its divisions, but stretching it transversely completely stops it."

Certain viruses have been separated in crystalline state—a pledge of purity—and are then found to be proteins of giant molecular weight. These propagate; they reproduce themselves. The mechanism of this multiplication seems a ferment action, e.g. the virus-molecule acting as its own enzyme (ferment). In fine, this protein "grows." Again, as though to demonstrate that the self-fermenting protein gives a clue to biological growth, the "gene," that quintessence of growth, seems to be a self-fermenting protein. It may, with some licence, be styled a quantum of heredity. But it has, with further licence, to be thought of as a seed which planted, though a quantum, grows. Each gene in the egg-cell embodies a unit "character" in the make-up of the individual springing from the ovum. The gene in the growth of the body may multiply to some billions of its original. It is situated in one of the nuclear threads. The nuclear threads are thought of as containing strings of genes. The estimated size of the gene makes it of the same order of size as a giant protein-molecule. A cell-nucleus is known to be a nest of ferments. The gene, thus conjectured to be a self-fermenting protein-molecule, is a master-builder both of plant and animal.

Experiment indicates that the abrupt change in transmitted "characters" spoken of in genetics as "mutation" can be brought about by "radiation" applied to a gene. A modification of the gene-molecule induced by absorption of an energy-quantum would seem then to reproduce itself under the self fermentation of the molecule. The mutation would be a "quantal-step." The rate of production and reproduction of cell-substance under growth can be very high, but in the hands of catalysts (enzymes) that is not surprising. In 10 seconds an organic catalyst will activate nearly 10,000 times its own weight of hydrogen peroxide. In a quarter of an hour the nucleus of an actively secreting cell will yield an amount of "enzyme" nearly equal in volume to itself. Where synthesis, for instance protein-synthesis, is adding to the cell-system itself the cell *has* to multiply, for one thing because the necessary give and take between the cell and its surround sets an upper limit to the ratio cell volume/cell surface.

A motion-picture photographed from cells in growth almost startles us by the intensity of the activity they show. Protein-synthesis is in flood—a riot of activity, but always an ordered riot. The specificity of enzymes is an element of mechanism which carries order far.

The body of a worm and the face of a man alike have to be taken as chemical responses. The alchemists dreamed of old that it might be so.

Their dream however supposed a magic chemistry. There they were wrong. The chemistry is plain everyday chemistry. But it is complex. Further, the chemical brew, in preparation for it, Time has been stirring unceasingly throughout some millions of years in the service of a final cause. The brew is a selected brew.

Can then physics and chemistry out of themselves explain that a pin's-head ball of cells in the course of so many weeks becomes a child? They more than hint that they can. A highly competent observer, after watching a motion-film photo-record taken with the microscope of a cell-mass in the process of making bone, writes: "Team-work by the cell-masses. Chalky spicules of bone-in-the-making shot across the screen, as if labourers were raising scaffold-poles. The scene suggested purposive behaviour by individual cells, and still more by colonies of cells arranged as tissues and organs." That impression of concerted endeavour comes, it is no exaggeration to say, with the force of a self-evident truth. The story of the making of the eye carries a like inference.

The eye's parts are familiar even apart from technical knowledge and have evident fitness for their special uses. The likeness to an optical camera is plain beyond seeking. If a craftsman sought to construct an optical camera, let us say for photography, he would turn for his materials to wood and metal and glass. He would not expect to have to provide the actual motor power adjusting the focal length or the size of the aperture admitting light. He would leave the motor power out. If told to relinquish wood and metal and glass and to use instead some albumen, salt and water, he certainly would not proceed even to begin. Yet this is what that little pin's-head bud of multiplying cells, the starting embryo, proceeds to do. And in a number of weeks it will have all ready. I call it a bud, but it is a system separate from that of its parent, although feeding itself on juices from its mother. And the eye it is going to make will be made out of those juices. Its whole self is at its setting out not one ten-thousandth part the size of the eye-ball it sets about to produce. Indeed it will make two eye-balls built and finished to one standard so that the mind can read their two pictures together as one. The magic in those juices goes by the chemical names, protein, sugar, fat, salts, water. Of them 80% is water.

Water is a great menstruum of "life." It makes life possible. It was part of the plot by which our planet engendered life. Every egg-cell is mostly water, and water is its first habitat. Water it turns to endless purposes; mechanical support and bed for its membranous sheets as they form and shape and fold. The early embryo is largely membranes. Here a particular piece grows fast because its cells do so. There it bulges or dips, to do this or that or simply to find room for itself. At some other centre of special activity the sheet will thicken. Again at some other place it will thin and form a hole. That is how the mouth, which at first leads nowhere, presently opens into the stomach. In the doing of all this, water is a main means.

The eye-ball is a little camera. Its smallness is part of its perfection. A spheroid camera. There are not many anatomical organs where exact shape counts for so much as with the eye. Light which will enter the eye will traverse a lens placed in the right position there. *Will* traverse; all this making of the eye which *will* see in the light is carried out in the dark. It is a preparing in darkness for use in light. The lens required is biconvex and to be shaped truly enough to focus its pencil of light at the particular distance of the sheet of photosensitive cells at the back, the retina. The biconvex lens is made of cells, like those of the skin but modified to be glass-clear. It is delicately slung with accurate centring across the path of the light which *will* in due time some months later enter the eye. In front of it a circular screen controls, like the iris-stop of a camera or microscope, the width of the beam and is adjustable, so that in a poor light more is taken for the image. In microscope, or photographic camera, this adjustment is made by the observer working the instrument. In the eye this adjustment is automatic, worked by the image itself!

The lens and screen cut the chamber of the eye into a front half and a back half, both filled with clear humour, practically water, kept under a certain pressure maintaining the eye-ball's right shape. The front chamber is completed by a layer of skin specialized to be glass-clear, and free from blood-vessels which if present would with their blood throw shadows within the eye. This living glass-clear sheet is covered with a layer of tear-water constantly renewed. This tear-water has the special chemical power of killing germs which might inflame the eye. This glass-clear bit of skin has only one of the four-fold set of the skin-senses; its touch is always "pain," for it should *not* be touched. The skin above and below this window grows into movable flaps, dry outside like ordinary skin, but moist inside so as to wipe the window clean every minute or so from any specks of dust, by painting over it fresh tear-water.

The light-sensitive screen at back is the key-structure. It registers a continually changing picture. It receives, takes and records a moving picture life-long without change of "plate," through every waking day. It signals its shifting exposures to the brain.

This camera also focuses itself automatically, according to the distance of the picture interesting it. It makes its lens "stronger" or "weaker" as required. This camera also turns itself in the direction of the view required. It is moreover contrived as though with forethought of self-preservation. Should danger threaten, in a moment its skin shutters close protecting its transparent window. And the whole structure, with its prescience and all its efficiency, is produced by and out of specks of granular slime arranging themselves as of their own accord in sheets and layers, and acting seemingly on an agreed plan. That done, and their organ complete, they abide by what they have accomplished. They lapse into relative quietude and change no more. It all sounds an unskilful overstated tale which challenges belief. But to faithful observation so it is. There is more yet.

The little hollow bladder of the embryo-brain, narrowing itself at two points so as to be triple, thrusts from its foremost chamber to either side a hollow bud. This bud pushes toward the overlying skin. That skin, as though it knew and sympathized, then dips down forming a cuplike hollow to meet the hollow brain-stalk growing outward. They meet. The round end of the hollow brain-bud dimples inward and becomes a cup. Concurrently, the ingrowth from the skin nips itself free from its original skin. It rounds itself into a hollow ball, lying in the mouth of the brain-cup. Of this stalked cup, the optic cup, the stalk becomes in a few weeks a cable of a million nerve-fibres connecting the nerve-cells within the eye-ball itself with the brain. The optic cup, at first just a two-deep layer of somewhat simple-looking cells, multiplies its layers at the bottom of the cup where, when light enters the eye—which will not be for some weeks yet—the photo-image will in due course lie. There the layer becomes a fourfold layer of great complexity. It is strictly speaking a piece of the brain lying within the eye-ball. Indeed the whole brain itself, traced to its embryonic beginning, is found to be all of a piece with the primordial skin—a primordial gesture as if to inculcate Aristotle's maxim about sense and mind.

The deepest cells at the bottom of the cup become a photo-sensitive layer—the sensitive film of the camera. If light is to act on the retina—and it is from the retina that light's visual effect is known to start—it must be absorbed there. In the retina a delicate purplish pigment absorbs incident light and is bleached by it, giving a light-picture. The photo-chemical effect generates nerve-currents running to the brain.

The nerve-lines connecting the photo-sensitive layer with the brain are not simple. They are in series of relays. It is the primitive cells of the optic cup, they and their progeny, which become in a few weeks these relays resembling a little brain, and each and all so shaped and connected as to transmit duly to the right points of the brain itself each light-picture momentarily formed and "taken." On the sense-cell layer the "image" has, picture-like, two dimensions. These space-relations "reappear" in the mind; hence we may think their data in the picture are in some way preserved in the electrical patterning of the resultant disturbance in the brain. But reminding us that the step from electrical disturbance in the brain to the mental experience is the mystery it is, the mind adds the third dimension when interpreting the two-dimensional picture! Also it adds colour; in short it makes a three-dimensional visual scene out of an electrical disturbance.

All this the cells lining the primitive optic cup have, so to say, to bear in mind, when laying these lines down. They lay them down by becoming them themselves.

Cajal, the gifted Spanish neurologist, gave special study to the retina and its nerve-lines to the brain. He turned to the insect-eye thinking the nerve-lines there "in relative simplicity" might display schematically, and therefore more readably, some general plan which Nature adopts when furnishing animal kind with sight. After studying it for two years this is what he wrote:

> The complexity of the nerve-structures for vision is even in the insect something incredibly stupendous. From the insect's faceted eye proceeds an inextricable criss-cross of excessively slender nerve-fibres. These then plunge into a cell-labyrinth which doubtless serves to integrate what comes from the retinal layers. Next follow a countless host of amacrine cells and with them again numberless centrifugal fibres. All these elements are moreover so small the highest powers of the modern microscope hardly avail for following them. The intricacy of the connexions defies description. Before it the mind halts, abased. *In tenuis labor.* Peering through the microscope into this Lilliputian life one wonders whether what we disdainfully term "instinct" (Bergson's "intuition") is not, as Jules Fabre claims, life's crowning mental gift. Mind with instant and decisive action, the mind which in these tiny and ancient beings reached its blossom ages ago and earliest of all.

The first and greatest problem vision faces is doubtless that attaching to it as part of the matter-mind relation. How is it that the visual picture proceeds—if that is the right word—from an electrical disturbance in the brain? But as a sub-problem of high importance concerning vision comes that of pattern-vision. The study of vision, pursued comparatively in different animal forms, indicates that the primitive vision widely prevalent in simpler forms of life attains merely to the distinguishing of "light" from "no light." It usually reaches the refinement of distinguishing grades of intensity of light. This primitive vision however does not attain to distinguishing shape or figure. It does not arrive at what is called "pattern-vision." Our own seeing makes so rich a contribution to the shapes of our world that it is a little puzzling for us to think of unpatterned seeing. To think of colourless seeing is likewise a little difficult; in many creatures, however, sight is colourless.

Over a great diversity of more highly developed vision, the eye supplies a definite image of what it looks at. There we must suppose "pattern-vision"; without it the optical apparatus would seem wasted. In many cases the eye has means of focussing its image. That gives further development of the well-known relation between nerve and mind, namely that the *"place"* of a stimulated sensual point acts on the mind; whence "sensual space" with "local sign." It holds certainly not least in visual sense. If the sensitive sheet receiving the light-image be arranged as a mosaic of sub-areas corresponding severally with quasi-independent nerve-elements each with its access to "sense," then any light-image affecting two or more such sub-areas simultaneously begins to have "shape," or when affecting them successively begins to "move." The *spatial* pattern of the image thus acts on the mind. Different patterns acting differently enable mental distinction between them. For instance a moving object tends to "catch" vision.

We know enough of pattern-vision in ourselves to recognize that it is the foundation of a perceptual analysis of our visible world which is of supreme service to us. We know enough of our animal kith and kin to judge that in them it serves not greatly otherwise for them. We must think that in each instance a great nervous rallying-place for confluent nerve-impulses from the quasi-independent elements of the ocular-sheet and for reactions between them must be appended to the eye. And that is what is found. Serving the eye there are condensed masses of nerve-structure which examined by the microscope are thickets of seeming entanglement, doubtless replete with meaning could we read their scheme. These great nerve-ganglia of vision are familiar to the zoologist. He knows them in the ant, the bee, the squid, and most of all in our own stock, and especially in ourselves. Their complexity in the insects was what amazed even so veteran an anatomist as Cajal.

The human eye has about 137 million separate "seeing" elements spread out in the sheet of the retina. The number of nerve-lines leading from them to the brain gradually condenses down to little over a million. Each of these has in the brain, we must think, to find its right nerve-exchanges. Those nerve-exchanges lie far apart, and are but stations on the way to further stations. The whole crust of the brain is one thick tangled jungle of exchanges and of branching lines going thither and coming thence. As the eye's cup develops into the nervous retina all this intricate orientation to locality is provided for by corresponding growth in the brain. To compass what is needed adjacent cells, although sister and sister, have to shape themselves quite differently the one from the other. Most become patterned filaments, set lengthwise in the general direction of the current of travel. But some thrust out arms laterally as if to embrace together whole cables of the conducting system.

Nervous "conduction" is transmission of nervous signals, in this case to the brain. There is also another nervous process, which physiology was slower to discover. Activity at this or that point in the conducting system, where relays are introduced, can be decreased even to suppression. This lessening is called inhibition; it occurs in the retina as elsewhere (Granit). All this is arranged for by the developing eye-cup when preparing and carrying out its million-fold connections with the brain for the making of a seeing eye. Obviously there are almost illimitable opportunities for a false step. Such a false step need not count at the time because all that we have been considering is done months or weeks before the eye can be used. Time after time so perfectly is all performed that the infant eye is a good and fitting eye, and the mind soon is instructing itself and gathering knowledge through it. And the child's eye is not only an eye true to the human type, but an eye with personal likeness to its individual parent's. The many cells which made it have executed correctly a multitudinous dance engaging millions of performers in hundreds of sequences of particular different steps, differing for each performer according to his part. To picture the complexity and the precision beggars any imagery I have. But it may help us to think further.

There is too that other layer of those embryonic cells at the back of the eye. They act as the dead black lining of the camera; they with their black pigment kill any stray light which would blur the optical image. They can shift their pigment. In full daylight they screen, and at night they unscreen, as wanted, the special seeing elements which serve for seeing in dim light. These are the cells which manufacture the purple pigment, "visual purple," which sensitizes the eye for seeing in low light.

Then there is that little ball of cells which migrated from the skin and thrust itself into the mouth of the eye-stalk from the brain. It makes a lens there; it changes into glass-clear fibres, grouped with geometrical truth, locking together by toothed edges. The pencil of light let through must come to a point at the right distance for the length of the eye-ball which is to be. Not only must the lens be glass-clear but its shape must be optically right, and its substance must have the right optical refractive index. That index is higher than that of anything else which transmits light in the body. Its two curved surfaces back and front must be truly centred on one and the right axis, and each of the sub-spherical curvatures must be curved to the right degree, so that, the refractive index being right, light is brought to a focus on the retina and gives there a shaped image. The optician obtains glass of the desired refractive index and skilfully grinds its curvatures in accordance with the mathematical formulae required. With the lens of the eye, a batch of granular skin-cells are told off to travel from the skin to which they strictly belong, to settle down in the mouth of the optic cup, to arrange themselves in a compact and suitable ball, to turn into transparent fibres, to assume the right refractive index, and to make themselves into a subsphere with two correct curvatures truly centred on a certain axis. Thus it is they make a lens of the right size, set in the right place, that is, at the right distance behind the transparent window of the eye in front and the sensitive seeing screen of the retina behind. In short they behave as if fairly possessed.

I would not give a wrong impression. The optical apparatus of the eye is not all turned out with a precision equal to that of a first-rate optical workshop. It has defects which disarm the envy of the optician. It is rather as though the planet, producing all this as it does, worked under limitations. Regarded as a planet which "would," we yet find it no less a planet whose products lie open to criticism. On the other hand, in this very matter of the eye the process of its construction seems to seize opportunities offered by the peculiarity in some ways adverse of the material it is condemned to use. It extracts from the untoward situation practical advantages for its instrument which human craftsmanship could never in that way provide. Thus the cells composing the core of this living lens are denser than those at the edge. This corrects a focussing defect inherent in ordinary glass-lenses. Again, the lens of the eye, compassing what no glass-lens can, changes its curvature to focus near objects as well as distant when wanted, for instance, when we read. An elastic capsule is spun over it and is arranged to be eased by a special muscle. Further, the pupil—the camera stop—is self-adjusting. All this without our having even to wish it; without even our knowing anything about it, beyond that we are seeing satisfactorily.

The making of this eye out of self-actuated specks, which draw together and multiply and move as if obsessed with one desire, namely, to make the eye-ball. In a few weeks they have done so. Then, their madness over, they sit down and rest, satisfied to be life-long what they have made themselves, and, so to say, wait for death.

The chief wonder of all we have not touched on yet. Wonder of wonders, though familiar even to boredom. So much with us that we forget it all our time. The eye sends, as we saw, into the cell-and-fibre forest of the brain throughout the waking day continual rhythmic streams of tiny, individually evanescent, electrical potentials. This throbbing streaming crowd of electrified shifting points in the spongework of the brain bears no obvious semblance in space-pattern, and even in temporal relation resembles but a little remotely the tiny two-dimensional upside-down picture of the outside world which the eye-ball paints on the beginnings of its nerve-fibres to the brain. But that little picture sets up an electrical storm. And that electrical storm so set up is one which affects a whole population of brain-cells. Electrical charges having in themselves not the faintest elements of the visual—having, for instance, nothing of "distance," "right-side-upness," nor "vertical," nor "horizontal," nor "colour," nor "brightness," nor "shadow," nor "roundness," nor "square-ness," nor "contour," nor "transparency," nor "opacity," nor "near," nor "far," nor visual anything—yet conjure up all these. A shower of little electrical leaks conjures up for me, when I look, the landscape; the castle on the height, or, when I look at him, my friend's face, and how distant he is from me they tell me. Taking their word for it, I go forward and my other senses confirm that he is there.

It is a case of "the world is too much with us"; too banal to wonder at. Those other things we paused over, the building and shaping of the eye-ball, and the establishing of its nerve connections with the right points of the brain, all those other things and the rest pertaining to them we called in chemistry and physics and final causes to explain to us. And they did so, with promise of more help to come.

But this last, not the eye, but the "seeing" by the brain behind the eye? Physics and chemistry there are silent to our every question. All they say to us is that the brain is theirs, that without the brain which is theirs the seeing is not. But as to how? They vouchsafe us not a word. Their negation goes further—they assure us it is no concern of theirs at all. "That the eye is necessary to sight seems to me the notion of one immersed in matter." Such was this disparation to J. S. Mill.

But to return to the making of the eye. It seems clear that here is a subject which might well test the point of view say of Lucretius on the one hand, and our sixteenth-century physician, Fernel, on the other. Knowledge of much of its detail is, of course, new since either of them. At occasions something goes wrong. Fernel would not ask, but Omar Khayyám has: "And did the hand then of the Potter shake?" Thus, in the matter of the optic cup. Just within the lip of it, which holds the lens, the rim of the cup thins and becomes the circular iris which gives the eye what we call its colour, hazel, brown, grey, blue as the case may be. The circle of it is not at first complete because the cup is fissured at one place so that in its circular rim there is a gap. Later the groove closes and the iris becomes a perfect ring. But in some instances it does not so close; there is a gap in the iris extending from the pupil as a notch. The defect does not occur at random. It runs in families. In that great multitudinous creative dance which we traced, if things are to go right for the finale, the evolutions of the part-figures must keep step, or certain partners may arrive late at certain places for partners who will then already have moved on. A point we have to note is that in this great dance once a mistake is made there is no subsequent recovery. Moreover, the individual dancers seem blind themselves to any mistake which may have happened. Again, in the building of the nervous system where certain nerve-fibres have to grow far to join particular others also converging to a certain spot, their punctuality in keeping appointments counts for much. The time-keeping in fact is not exact; in consequence no two individuals of us have a make-up of spinal nerve-roots quite alike. This gives the surgeon trouble if he has to operate on us. That misfits of this kind happen suggests a fallible mechanism.

Success of the production of the infant creature is judged far more subtly by the truth of the working of the resultant life than by any test which inspection by the eye or microscope imposes. For instance there is its endowment with colour-sense. That is, we know, sometimes defective. There are born those unable to distinguish as do most of us between red and green. The eye and retina, and everything is normal in them to the minutest microscopic examination; nor is any part of the brain, visual or other, recognizably defective. The defect haunts particular family stocks. It is related to sex; it goes with maleness. To the geneticist that is a clue. Sex is a feature the development of which in the individual is traceable to a definite visible element in the egg. That element contains, along with potential sex, certain other "characters" which are called "sex-linked" because linked with the gene or genes of sex. Each "character" has its gene. Colour-vision is a "character" related to a gene. Normality in this respect may be wanting in one parent. The defect lies in a gene which is of those linked with sex. In males a chromosome y, from the father, partnering chromosome x from the mother, is small. It lacks duplicates of some genes in x, and so may not cover defect in x. But in females a second x-chromosome, from the father, may cover such defect. The mystery which at first seemed to deepen with knowledge of the strange preference for one sex, on further knowledge tends to clear.

It is less than a generation since Edouard Gley, at the end of an address inaugurating the academic year in Paris, remarked that Aristotle's causes had become largely Physics and Chemistry as a means of explanation in Biology. But, he added, one biological domain there is which it will never take over, the growth of the egg into a child.

There is the influence of one part of the growing embryo upon another part. We saw an instance in the eye-ball. A bud from the embryo-brain is the beginning of the eye. The skin over that bud dips down to meet it, and becomes the lens of the eye. Brain and skin, although separate, conspire and meet to build an eye. In the young tadpole the bud from the brain may be transplanted to a point distant from where the eye should be. At the new place the skin dips down to meet it there to form a lens for the eye which should not be there. At that new place the skin does just as would the skin of the right place. Again, if the skin from over the brain's eye-bud be replaced by skin from elsewhere, this latter skin, although not the right skin, dips down towards the eye-bud and forms a lens.

Again, if a piece of that part of the embryo which is to be the main nerve-cord be removed, and its place given to other skin and taken from a region not destined to be nerve-cord at all, the new graft not originally destined to be nerve-cord becomes nerve-cord. The embryo at this stage seems pervaded by some general invisible plan which compels each of its localities, whatever the provenance of the material there, to become what is demanded there as part of the immanent plan. Later on, the trend in the local part to be what it set out to be becomes too strong to permit change. Then, the rudiment beginning to be a limb, will be a limb whatever happens, and wherever the experimenter puts it.

There is a time when a certain restricted bit of the embryo, in what will be the embryo's back, has a curious power, as so-called "organizer." If it be transplanted to some part of another embryo, it there sets going and seems to direct a wholesale scheme of development, almost tantamount to starting a new embryo. Something like this at times happens naturally. There are two kinds of twins. One kind is traceable to the fertilizing of two eggs. The twins then are not more like each other than are other children of the same parentage. In the other kind of twins both come from one and the same fertilized egg. The egg implanting itself as usual and drawing nutriment from the mother, its primordial cell mass, probably at first as usual just one embryonic rudiment, then proceeds to start a second embryo. These twins are always puzzlingly alike. The Canadian quintuplets are of this kind. In their case the same fertilized egg produced an accessory embryo not once but four times over. The "organizer" explains how this might have happened.

A component of it is chemically akin to compounds now known to evoke cancerous growth. Its identification with this chemical group brings therefore the organization of the embryo into the same chemical picture as other growth, and that disease of growth, "rickets." Also with the chemical control of the menstrual cycle, and finally with the start and growth of cancer, misgrowth. There seems an underlying relation between them all. As our sixteenth-century physician would say, that bids fair for medicine. A critic of Edouard Gley would add, all looks like mechanism.

Our brief glimpse must not let us suppose that when the embryonic phase of life is over, this power of the parts of the body to "become" reaches its goal and ceases. Suppose a wound sever a nerve of my arm. The fibres of the nerve die down for their whole length between the point of severance and the muscles or skin they go to. The skin there has lost sensation; in my muscles there I have lost "my power." But at once after the injury the nerve-fibres start to regrow from their cut points, even far up the arm. For eighty years and more these, my nerve-fibres, have given no sign of growth. Yet after this wound each fibre, whether motor or sensory, would start again to grow stretching out toward its old goal in muscle or skin. There would be difficulties for it. A multitude of non-nervous cells busy on repair within the wound might spin scar-tissue across the path. Between these alien cells the regenerating nerve-fibre would thread a tortuous way, never uniting with any of them. This obstruction might take many days or weeks to traverse. Once through it the young nerve-fibre would press on and reach a region where the sheath-cells of the old dead fibres would lie altered beyond recognition. But they and the new growing nerve-fibre would, as it were, recognize each other. Tunnelling along endless chains of them, it would arrive finally, after weeks or months, at the wasted muscle-fibres which were its goal. These too it would, as it were, recognize forthwith. With them it would unite at once. It would pierce their covering membranes. It would re-establish with them junctions of characteristic pattern resembling the original which had died weeks or months before. Nor would one nerve-fibre of all the thousands join a muscle-fibre which another nerve-fibre had already begun to repair. When all the repair was done the nerve's growth would cease. The wasted muscle would recover; in my skin which had become insensitive, sensation would return.

Nerve-regeneration seems a return to the original phase of growth. Pieces of adult tissue which have long ceased growing, when removed from the body to artificial nutrient fluid, begin to grow. Epithelium, which in the body is not growing when thus removed, will then start growing. The cells then lose their adult specialization. In nerve-regeneration the sheath-cells and, to some extent, the muscle-cells which have lost their nerves lose likewise their specialized form. They regain it only when touch with the nerve-cell has been re-established.

As we saw, a scrap of the heart of the embryo-chick put into a glass tube thirty-seven years ago, protected from germs and fed, is growing still. Had it remained in its chick it would have died years since. All we can say is "final causes"—but that is no explanation. Whence comes the means and whence the provision? The eye prepared in darkness for seeing in the daylit world. The ear prepared in water for hearing in air. In the repair of the cut nerve, provision against a contingent accident possible enough which yet may never happen. The body never can suffer a wound without the tearing of some blood-vessels. That means loss of blood; and severe loss of blood can be fatal. The loss would always be severe and probably fatal if the bleeding did not stop. It would not stop, did not the blood solidify when and where and as it escapes. The blood clots and seals the point of escape. This solidifying is the work of an enzyme. The enzyme is traceable to a source in a particular gene. Some few of us are born deficient in this innate styptic. It is a defect which runs in families. It is sex-linked and that helps the geneticist to trace its gene.

Evidently the physics and chemistry of the cell can do much with the help of final causes. Chemistry and physics account for so much which the cell does, and for so much to which years ago physical science could at that time offer no clue, that it is justifiable to suppose that the still unexplained residue of the cell's behaviour will prove resoluble by chemistry and physics.

We can understand Keats' sighing against science, "there was an awful rainbow once in heaven!" Yet he was "to find," as has been written of him, "material in the scientific view of the world for the highest achievements of poetry." Could we foretell the rose-bud from its chemistry, would that make its beauty less? Surely the reverse, for we then know that such as the rose-bud are neither accident nor miracle. The final cause will stay as item of classification, but not as explanation. "Our task," Fernel says, "now that we have dealt with the excellent structure of the body, cannot stop there, because a man is a body and a mind together." The message is in so far something like one of Professor Whitehead's.

Erik H. Erikson

The following essay, written on the centenary of Sigmund Freud's birth by Erik Erikson, who is himself a distinguished psychoanalyst, is in essence a commemorative eulogy, a tribute to a great man. Its eulogistic character, directly manifested in the author's praise of Freud's intellectual achievement and personal heroism, finds equally significant expression in Erikson's approach itself, for it utilizes concepts derived from Freud's discoveries about the workings of the mind—discoveries that have permanently changed man's picture of himself.

Every new impingement of science—here defined as any systematized body of knowledge which aims to propose general laws—on man's conception of himself has initially been greeted with hostility and fear. Erikson introduces his account of Freud's accomplishment by comparing him to Darwin, whose findings destroyed the traditional view of man as a biologically unique creature, just as the discoveries of the sixteenth-century astronomers had destroyed the belief that man's earth was the center of the cosmos. These earlier scientific discoveries had indirectly altered man's views of his behavior; Freud, in applying the methods of science directly to human behavior, inevitably aroused not only scorn and misunderstanding from without but also more formidable opponents within his own personality, the most serious of them being the problem of the subject-object relationship. He found that when man as scientist attempts to apply to his own mind the same kind of dispassionate scrutiny he has learned to apply to objects outside himself, he encounters intellectual and emotional problems of extreme magnitude. Freud's greatness is that he overcame those problems and opened a new area to systematized knowledge. It is an area not wholly new to human knowledge, however. As Erikson points out, artists and thinkers had made significant expeditions into it before Freud; and it is an area not completely conquered for science, for psychoanalytic thought has just begun and its basic assumptions are still subject to controversy and revision. But Freud had expanded human frontiers—in literature and art as well as in science— and this expansion exemplifies the cogency of Lionel Trilling's refusal, in an essay later in this section, to accept the idea of a separation between the "two cultures" of science and literature.

THE FIRST PSYCHOANALYST

YALE CENTENARY ADDRESS

It is a solemn and yet always a deeply incongruous occasion when we select an anniversary to honor a man who in lonely years struggled through a unique experience and won a new kind of knowledge for mankind. To some of us, the field created by Sigmund Freud has become an absorbing profession, to some an inescapable intellectual challenge, to all the promise (or threat) of an altered image of man. But any sense of proprietary pride in the man to be honored this year should be sobered by the thought that we have no right to assume that we would have met his challenge with more courage than his contemporaries did in the days when his insights were new. It seems fitting to use his centenary to review some of the dimensions of lonely discovery.

It is not easy (unless it be all too easy) for a "Freudian" to speak of the man who *was* Freud, of a man who grew to be a myth before our eyes. I knew Freud when he was very old, and I was young. Being employed as a tutor in a family befriended to him I had the opportunity of seeing him on quiet occasions, with children and with dogs, and at outings in the mountains. I do not know whether I would have noticed Freud in a crowd. His notable features were not spectacular: the finely domed forehead, the dark, unfathomable eyes, and certain small indomitable gestures—they all had became part of that inner containment which crowns the old age of good fighters.

I was an artist then, which is a European euphemism for a young man with some talent, but nowhere to go. What probably impressed me most was the fact that this doctor of the mind, this expert of warped biography, had surrounded himself in his study with a small host of

From *The Yale Review*, XLVI, No. I (Autumn, 1956), pp. 40-62. Copyright Yale University Press.

little statues: those distilled variations of the human form which were created by the anonymous artists of the archaic Mediterranean. Certainly, of Freud's field, of conflict and complaint and confession, there was no trace in their art. This respect for form, so surprising in a man who had unearthed mankind's daimonic inner world, was also obvious in his love for proud dogs and for gaily bright children. I vaguely felt that I had met a man of rare dimensions, rare contradictions.

When I became a psychoanalyst myself, this same old man—now remote from the scene of training and gathering—became for me what he is for the world: the writer of superb prose, the author of what seems like more than one lifetime's collected works: a master, so varied in his grandiose one-sidedness that the student can manage to understand only one period of his work at a time. Strangely enough, we students knew little of his beginnings, nothing of that mysterious self-analysis which he alluded to in his writings. We knew people whom Freud had introduced into psychoanalysis, but psychoanalysis itself had, to all appearances, sprung from his head like Athena from the head of Zeus.

The early Freud became better known to us only a very few years ago, through the accidental discovery of intimate letters written before the turn of the century.[1] They permitted us to envisage Freud the beginner, the first, and for a decade, the only, psychoanalyst. It is to him that I would like to pay homage.

For orientation and comparison, let us consider the circumstances of another discovery of the nineteenth century, the discovery of a man who also was lonely and calumniated, and eventually recognized as a changer of man's image: Charles Darwin. Darwin came upon his evolutionary laboratory, the Galapagos Islands, on a voyage which was not part of an intended professional design. In fact, he had failed in medicine, not for lack of talent, it would seem, but partially because of an intellectual selectivity which forbade him to learn passively—a self-protective selectivity of the kind for which old Bernard Shaw, in retrospect, patted himself on the back when he said, "My memory rejects and selects; and its selections are not academic. . . . I congratulate myself on this."

Once embarked on the "Beagle," however, and on his way to his "laboratory," Darwin showed that dogged, that prejudiced persistence which is one condition for an original mind becoming a creative one. He now fully developed his superior gift, namely, "noticing things which

[1] See Sigmund Freud, *The Origins of Psychoanalysis. Letters to Wilhelm Fliess, Drafts and Notes (1887-1902)*, ed. Maria Bonaparte, Anna Freud, and Ernst Kris, tr. Eric Mosbacher and James Strachey (New York: Basic Books, 1954). Dr. Erikson has reviewed this publication in *The International Journal of Psychoanalysis*, Vol. XXXV (1955), 1-15.

easily escape attention, and observing them carefully." His physical stamina was inexhaustible. His mind proved ready for the laboratory, as the laboratory seemed to have waited for him. He could fully employ sweeping configurations of thought which had ripened in him: cutting across existing classifications, which assumed a parallel, linear origin of all species from a common pool of creation, he saw everywhere transitions, transmutations, variations, signs of a dynamic struggle for adaptation. The law of natural selection began to "haunt him." And he perceived that man must come under the same law. "I see no possible means of drawing the line and saying, here you must stop."

Darwin, at the age of twenty-seven, went home with his facts and theory, and traveled no more. He gave the scientific world a few papers primarily on geological subjects; then he withdrew to the country, to work, for twenty years, on *The Origin of Species*: he *made* it a long and lonely discovery. He now became physically incapacitated by insomnia, nausea, and chills. His father-doctor could not diagnose his disease, but declared the son too delicate for a career out in the world. The son became a life-long invalid. If his hypersensitivity was a sign of hereditary degeneracy, as some doctors believe, then there never was a degenerate guided more wisely in the utilization of his degeneracy by an inner genius of economy. For "I could . . . collect facts bearing on the origin of species . . . when I could do nothing else from illness." Not that Darwin did not realize what his restriction of his lifespace did to him: when, at the end, even Shakespeare seemed so "intolerably dull" as to nauseate him, he deplored the "curious and lamentable loss of the higher aesthetic tastes" and spoke of an "enfeeblement of the emotional part of our nature."

I do not wish to speculate here on the dynamics of a psycho-neurosis in a man like Darwin. But I do know that a peculiar malaise can befall those who have seen too much, who, in ascertaining new facts in a spirit seemingly as innocent as that of a child who builds with blocks, begin to perceive of the place of these facts in the moral climate of their day. "We physicists have known sin," Oppenheimer has said; but it does not take the use of scientific data for mankind's material destruction to make a scientist feel or behave as if he had sinned. It is enough to have persisted, with the naïveté of genius, on the dissolution of one of the prejudices on which the security and the familiarity of the contemporary image of man is built. But a creative man has no choice. He may come across his supreme task almost accidentally. But once the issue is joined, his task proves to be at the same time intimately related to his most personal conflicts, to his superior selective perception, and to the stubbornness of his one-way will: he must court sickness, failure, or insanity, in order to test the alternative whether the established world will crush him,

or whether he will disestablish a sector of this world's outworn funda-
ments and make place for a new one.

Darwin only dealt with man's biological origins. His achievement,
and his "sin," was a theory that made man part of nature. In comparing
Darwin's approach to nature with his approach to a man, a recent biographer remarks half-jokingly, "In any case, no man afflicted with a weak
stomach and insomnia has any business investigating his own kind."

As we now turn to Freud the psychological discoverer, I hope to
make the reader wonder whether anybody *but* one at least temporarily
afflicted with psychosomatic symptoms, one temporarily sick of his own
kind, could or would investigate his own species—provided only that he
had the inclination, the courage, and the mental means of facing his own
neurosis with creative persistence. A man, I will submit, could begin to
study man's inner world only by appointing his own neurosis that angel
who was to be wrestled with and not to be let go, until he would bless
the observer.

What was Freud's Galapagos, what species fluttered what kinds of
wings before his searching eyes? It has often been pointed out derisively:
his creative laboratory was the neurologist's office, the dominant species
hysterical ladies—"Fräulein Anna O.," "Frau Emmy v. N.," "Katarina"
(not a Fräulein, because she was a peasant).

Freud was thirty when, in 1886, he became the private doctor of such
patients. He had not expected to be a practitioner; he had, in fact, received his medical degree belatedly. His mind, too, had been "selective."
At the age of seventeen he had chosen medicine in preference to law and
politics, when he heard Goethe's "Ode to Nature": the unveiling of Nature's mysteries, not the healing of the sick, provided the first self-image
of a doctor. Then came *his* professional moratorium: as in an ascetic
reaction to a nature-philosophic indulgence he committed himself to the
physiological laboratory and to the monastic service of physicalistic
physiology. What geology was to Darwin, physiology was to Freud: a
schooling in method. The ideology of the physicalistic-physiologic method
of the time was formulated in an oath by two of its outstanding teachers,
DuBois Reymond and Brucke: "to put in power this truth: No other
forces than the common physical chemical ones are active within the
organism. . . . One has either to find the specific way or form of their
action by means of the physical mathematical method, or to assume new
forces equal in dignity to the chemical physical forces inherent in matter."
New forces equal in dignity: we will return to this phrase.

When Freud exchanged the academic monastery for the medical
parsonage, he had fully developed a style of work which would have
sufficed for an impressively productive life-time. He had published many

papers on physiological and neurological subjects, and had two major works in preparation. Thus, when he became a practicing neurologist, he left a future behind him. But he had married the girl who had waited for him, and he wanted a family, in fact, a large one; he had earned the right to have confidence in himself.

Yet, a future anticipated in a man's configurations of thought means more than time not yet spent. To give up the laboratory meant to relinquish a work-discipline and a work-ideology to which Freud had been deeply committed. The work of a specialist catering to the epidemiological market was lacking in what Freud nostalgically called an inner tyrant, i.e., a great principle. Luckily, he had met an older practitioner, Dr. Joseph Breuer, who had shown him that there was a laboratory hidden in the very practice of neurology.

Freud's new laboratory, then, were patients, mostly women, who brought him symptoms which only an overly-serious and searching observer could accept as constituting a field activated by dignified forces. These ladies suffered from neuralgic pains and anesthesias, from partial paralyses and contractions, from tics and convulsions, from nausea and finickiness, from the inability to see and from visual hallucinations, from the inability to remember and from painful floods of memory. Popular opinion judged these ladies to be spoiled, just putting on airs—"attention-getting" some of us would call it today. The dominant neuropathology of the day, however, assumed some of their disturbances to be a consequence of hereditary degenerative processes in the brain. Freud, too, had learned to treat these patients like partially decerebrated bundles, or like children without a will: he had learned to apply massage and electricity to the affected body part and to dominate the patient's will by hypnosis and suggestion. He might, for example, order the hypnotized patient to laugh out loud when encountering in the future a certain thought or person or place, the sight of which had previously caused a fit or a paralysis. The awakened patient did laugh out loud, but more often than not, she would become afflicted again, and in connection with something else.

But Freud, like Darwin, could not believe in linear descent—in this instance, of isolated symptoms from defects of the brain. In an array of symptoms he, too, looked for a common principle, a struggle for equilibrium, a clash of forces. And he was convinced that challenging phenomena must have a hidden history. As Freud listened to his hypnotized patients, he realized that they were urgently, desperately offering him series of memories which, seemingly fragmentary, were like variations in search of a theme—a theme which was often found in a historical model event.

Here no detail could be too trivial for investigation. A patient suffers from a persistent illusion of smelling burned pancakes. All right, the smell of burned pancakes shall be the subject of exhaustive analysis. As this smell is traced to a certain scene, the scene vividly remembered, the sensation disappears, to be replaced by the smell of cigars. The smell of cigars is traced to other scenes, in which a man in an authoritative position was present, and in which disturbing subjects had been mentioned in a connection which demanded that the patient control her feelings.

It fits our image of those Victorian days—a time when children in all, and women in most circumstances were to be seen but not heard—that the majority of symptoms would prove to lead back to events when violently aroused affects (love, sex, rage, fear) had come into conflict with narrow standards of propriety and breeding. The symptoms, then, were delayed involuntary communications: using the whole body as spokesman, they were saying what common language permits common people to say directly: "He makes me sick," "She pierced me with her eyes," "I could not swallow that insult," or, as the song has it, "I'm gonna wash that man right out of my hair." Freud the neurologist now became "haunted" by the basic conviction that any neurotic symptom, traced along a path of associated experiences (not of neurological pathways), would lead to the revival in memory of earlier and earlier conflicts, and in doing so would yield a complete history of its origin.

As Freud proceeded with his reconstruction of the past of his patients, a dangerous insight dawned on him: such conflicts as his patients revealed were, in principle, shared by all men. It would be hard, indeed, "to draw the line and say here you must stop." He became aware of the fact that man, in principle, does not remember or understand much of what is most significant in his childhood, and more, that he does not want to. Here, a mysterious *individual prehistory* seemed to loom up, as important for psychology as Darwin's biological prehistory was for biology.

But Darwin had at his disposal the whole tradition of an ancient science. For Freud's psychologic findings, there were, at first, only physiologic methods, his own speculations, and the sayings of writers and philosophers, who, in their way, it seemed, had known it all. Yet, it appears to be part of a creative man's beginnings that he may change his field and yet maintain the manner of work which became part of his first identity as a worker. Freud had investigated the nature of brain lesions by slicing the brains of young animals and foeti. He now investigated memories as representative cross sections of a patient's emotional condition. In successive memories, he traced trends which led, like pathways, to the traumatic past; there experiences of a disruptive nature loomed like lesions interfering with growth. Thus, the search for traumatic events in the individual's forgotten prehistory, his early childhood, replaced the search for lesions in early development.

Psychology, of course, is the preferred field for a transfer of configurations of thought from other fields. The nature of things, or better, man's logical approaches to things is such that analogies—up to a point—reveal true correspondences. But the history of psychology also reveals how consistently neglectful and belated man is in applying to his own nature methods of observation which he has tried out on the rest of nature. That man, the observer, is in some essential way different from the observed world, is clear. But this difference calls for a constant redefinition in the light of new modes of thought. Only thus can man keep wisely different rather than vainly so. Before Copernicus, vanity as well as knowledge insisted that the earth must be in the exact nodal center of God's universe. Well, we know now where we are. Before Darwin, man could claim a different origin from the rest of the animal world with whom he shares a slim margin of earth crust and atmosphere. Before Freud, man (that is, man of the male sex and of the better classes) was convinced that he was fully conscious of all there was to him, and sure of his divine values. Childhood was a mere training ground, in charge of that intermediary race, women.

In such a world female hysteria was implicitly acknowledged by men and men doctors as a symptom of the natural inferiority, the easy degeneracy, of women. When Freud presented to the Vienna Medical Society a case of *male* hysteria, the reaction of his colleagues convinced him that years of isolation lay ahead of him. He accepted it then and there: he never visited that society again. Yet, their reaction proved to be only one small aspect of a memorable crisis in which a new science was almost stillborn, by no means only because of professional isolation, but also because of disturbances in the instrument of observation, the observer's mind. Freud's early writings and letters permit us to see a *threefold crisis:* a crisis in therapeutic technique; a crisis in the conceptualization of clinical experience; and a personal crisis. I shall try to indicate it what way all three crises were, in essence, one, and were the necessary dimensions of discovery in psychology.

First, then, Freud's change in technique. The textbooks describe it as the replacement of the cathartic and the suggestive methods by the psychoanalytic one. In Freud's *Studies of Hysteria,* however, a pervasive change in the doctor-patient relationship is clearly described. Freud judged some of his patients to be outstanding in character and talents, rather than degenerate. He began to let himself be led by the sequence and the nature of their communications. With amused surprise he would admit that a hypnotized patient, in suggesting to him that he should stop interrupting her with his authoritative suggestions, had a point. She fortified her point by unearthing memories which he would not have suspected. He realized that in hypnosis the patients had at their disposal a depth of understanding and a freedom of affect which they did not marshal in normal life. This he had not imposed by suggestion: it was their judgment and their affect, and if they had it in hypnosis, it was part of them. Maybe, if he treated them like whole people, they would learn to realize the wholeness which was theirs. He now offered them a conscious and direct partnership: he made the patient's healthy, if submerged, part his partner in understanding the unhealthy part. Thus was established one basic principle of psychoanalysis, namely, that one can study the human mind only by engaging the fully motivated partnership of the observed individual, and by entering into a sincere contract with him.

But a contract has two partners, at least. The changed image of the patient changed the self-image of the doctor. He realized that habit and convention had made him and his fellow physicians indulge in an autocratic pattern, with not much more circumspection or justification than the very paternal authorities who he now felt had made the patients sick in the first place. He began to divine the second principle of psychoanalysis, namely, that you will not see in another what in principle you have not learned to recognize in yourself. The mental healer must divide himself as well as the patient into an observer and an observed.

The intellectual task faced here, namely, psychoanalytic insight and communication, was a massive one. Today, it is difficult to appreciate the psychosocial task involved. Freud had to relinguish a most important ingredient of the doctor role of the times: the all-knowing father role, which was safely anchored in the whole contemporary cult of the paternal male as the master of every human endeavor except the nursery and the kitchen. This should not be misunderstood: Freud did not, overnight, become a different man. Indeed, there are many who will see nothing in the nature of renunciation of paternalism in him. But we are not speaking here of opinions and roles in the modern sense, of personalities subject to change like the body styles of automobiles which retain little logical relation to the inner motor of the thing, nor to the laws of the road. True roles are a matter of a certain ideologic-esthetic unity, not of opinions and appearances. True change is a matter of worthwhile conflict, for it leads through the painful consciousness of one's position to a new conscience in that position. As Justice Holmes once said, the first step toward a truer faith is the recognition that *I*, at any rate, am *not* God. Furthermore, roles anchored in work-techniques are prepared in the intricacies of a man's life history. Whoever has suffered under and identified with a stern father, must become a stern father himself, or else find an entirely different measure of moral strength, an equal measure of strength.

Young Martin Luther's religious crisis is a transcendent example of the heights and the depths of this problem.

Freud, as we have seen, had sought a new inner tyrant in a work-ideology shared with esteemed minds. He had relinquished it. Now, he discarded the practicing neurologist's prevailing role of dominance and of license. This, then, is the first aspect of Freud's crisis: he had to create a new therapeutic role, for which there was no ideological niche in the tradition of his profession. He had to create it—or fail.

The *second* problem which isolated Freud in those years was the course taken by his search for the "energy of equal dignity" which might be the power behind a neurosis; for the mental mechanisms which normally maintain such power in a state of constancy; and for those inner conditions which unleash the destructiveness of that power. The power, as we saw, was first perceived as "affect," the disturbance in the machine, as a "damming up." A long treatise recently found with some of Freud's letters reveals the whole extent of Freud's conflict between the creative urge to say in psychological terms what only literature had known before him, and on the other hand, his desperate obedience to physiology. The treatise is called "A Psychology for Neurologists."[2] Freud introduces it thus: "The intention of this project is to furnish us with a psychology which shall be a natural science: its aim, that is, is to represent psychical processes as quantitatively determined states of specifiable material particles and so to make them plain and void of contradictions." Freud proceeds to develop a model of organization of these "particles," a sensitive machine for the management of qualities and quantities of excitation, such as are aroused by external and internal stimuli. Physical concepts are combined with histological concepts to create a kind of neuronic Golem, a robot, in which even consciousness and thought are mechanistically explainable on the basis of an over-all principle of inner constancy. Here, Freud, at the very beginning of his career as a psychologist, tried to create a mind-robot, a thinking-machine, in many ways related to the mechanical and economic as well as the physiological configurations of his day. As Freud wrote triumphantly to his friend: "Everything fell into place, the cogs meshed, the thing really seemed to be a machine which in a moment would run of itself." But one month after Freud had sent this manuscript to that friend, he recanted it. "All I was trying to do," he writes, "was to explain defense (against affect), but I found myself explaining something from the very heart of nature. I found myself wrestling with the whole of psychology. Now I want to hear no more of

2 See Freud, *The Origins of Psychoanalysis*, 336-445, where it is entitled "Project for a Scientific Psychology."

it." He now calls the psychology a "kind of aberration." This manuscript, found only accidentally, documents in a dramatic way the pains to which a discoverer will go *not* to haphazardly ignore the paths of his tradition, but follow them instead to their absurd limit, and to abandon them only when the crossroad of lone search is reached.

In the meantime, clinical work had brought Freud within sight of his crossroad. His patients, he had become convinced, were suffering primarily from the "damming up" of one irrepressible "affect," namely, sexual sensuality, the existence of which had been consistently denied by their overclothed parents, and suffered only with furtive shame and anemic degradation by many of their mothers. In the epidemiological fact of widespread female hysteria, Freud faced the specific symptoms of the Victorian age, the price paid, especially by women, for the hypocritical double standard of the sexes in the dominant classes, the masters or would-be masters of industrial power. However, the most glaring epidemiological fact (compare poliomyelitis, or juvenile delinquency) does not receive clarification until a seasoned set of theoretical configurations happens to suggest a specific approach. In introducing the energy concept of a sexual libido, which from birth onward is the fuel in everything we desire and love, and which our mind-machine must learn to transform according to our goals and ideals—in this concept Freud found at once the most fitting answer to the questions posed by his patients' memories, and the theory most consistent with his search for a "dignified force." But alas, it was also the most irrationally repugnant solution thinkable in his prudish times, and a solution of emotional danger to the observer. For, indeed, where "to draw the line"?

Here Freud's genetic fervor led to a faulty reconstruction. In the certainty of being on the right track, and yet shaken by inner and outer resistances, he overshot the mark. In search for a pathogenic Ur(-primal)-event, he was led to regard as historically real the patients' accounts of passive sexual experiences in the first years of childhood, and to consider the fathers of the patients the perpetrators of such events. He later confessed: "The analysis had led by the correct path to such infantile sexual traumas, and yet, these were not true. Thus, the basis of reality had been lost. At that time, I would gladly have dropped the whole thing." But finally, "I reflected that if hysterics trace back their symptoms to imaginary traumas, then this new fact signifies that they create such scenes in phantasy, and hence psychic reality deserves to be given a place next to actual reality." Freud would soon be able to describe psychic reality systematically as the domain of phantasy, dream, and mythology, and as the imagery and language of a universal unconscious, thus adding as a scientific dimension to the image of man what had been an age-old intuitive knowledge.

In the meantime, had his error detracted from the "dignity" of sexuality? It does not seem so. Knowing what we know today it is obvious that somebody had to come sometime who would decide that it would be better for the sake of the study of human motivation to call too many rather than too few things sexual, and then to modify the hypothesis implied by careful inquiry. For it was only too easy to do what had become civilization's "second nature," that is, in the face of man's sexual and aggressive drives ever again to beat a hasty retreat into romanticism and religionism, into secrecy, ridicule, and lechery. The patients' phantasies were sexual, and something sexual must have existed in those early years. Freud later called that something *psychosexuality*, for it encompasses the phantasies as well as the impulses, the psychology as well as the biology in the earliest stages of human sexuality.

Today one can add that Freud's error was not even as great as it seemed. First of all, sexual seductions of children do occur, and are dangerous to them. But more important, the general provocation and exploitation of the child by parent and grandparent for the sake of petty emotional relief, of suppressed vengefulness, of sensual self-indulgence, and sly righteousness must be recognized not only as evident in case histories, but as a universal potentiality often practiced and hypocritically rationalized by very "moral" individuals, indeed. Samuel Butler's *The Way of All Flesh* is probably the most forceful statement on record. What today is decried as "momism" in this country, existed in analogous form in the father's role in the Victorian world: it is only necessary to think of Hitler's official account of his father-hate and the appeal of this account for millions of young Germans, to know that here is a smoldering theme of general explosiveness. In finding access to the altogether fateful fact of man's prolonged childhood, Freud discovered that infantile man, in addition to and often under the guise of being trained, is being ruefully exploited, only to become in adulthood nature's most systematic and sadistic exploiter. Freud's search thus added another perspective of as yet unforeseeable importance to the image of man.

Yet, this discovery, too, had to pass through its lonely stage. Freud had made a significant mistake, and he was not one to shirk the responsibility for it either publicly or privately. He made it part of his self-analysis.

About the first self-analysis in history we know from the letters, already mentioned, which Freud wrote to Dr. Wilhelm Fliess of Berlin. The extent and the importance of Freud's friendship with Fliess was not even suspected until the letters revealed it.

The two doctors met for what they called their "congresses," long weekends in some European city or town. Their common heritage of education permitted them to roam in varied conversations, as they vigorously perambulated through the countryside. Freud seems to have shared Nietzsche's impression that a thought born without locomotion could not be much good. But among the theories discussed by the two doctors, there were many which never saw the light of publication. Thus, Fliess, for many years, was the first and only one to share Freud's thinking.

Psychoanalysts do not seem to like this friendship much; Fliess, after all, was not even a psychoanalyst. Some of us now read of Freud's affection for this man wishing we could emulate that biographer of Goethe who, in the face of Goethe's claim that at a certain time he had loved a certain lady dearly, remarks in a footnote: "here Goethe is mistaken." Freud, we now say, must have overestimated this friendship in an irrational, almost pathological way. But what, after all, do thinkers need friends for? So that they can share speculations, each alternately playing benevolent authority to the other, each be the other's co-conspirator, each be applauding audience, and cautioning chorus. Freud calls Fliess his *"Other one,"* to whom he can entrust what is not ready for "the *others*." Fliess, at any rate, seems to have had the stature and the wide education which permitted Freud to entrust him with "imaginings, transpositions, and guesses." That Freud's imaginings turned out to be elements of a true vision and a blueprint for a science, while Fliess' ended in a kind of mathematical mysticism, provides no reason to belittle the friendship. The value of a friend may sometimes be measured by the magnitude of the problem which we discard with him.

The friendship seems to have been unmarred by irrational disturbances, until, in 1894, Freud consulted Fliess in regard to his own symptoms and moods, which he condenses in the word *Herzelend*—something like "misery of the heart." Fliess had cauterized swellings in Freud's nose and had urged him to give up his beloved cigars. Suddenly, the intellectual communication appears jammed. "I have not looked at your excellent case histories," Freud writes, and indicates that his latest communication to Fliess "was abandoned in the middle of a sentence." He continues: "I am suspicious of you this time, because this heart business [*Herzangelegenheit*] of mine is the first occasion on which I have ever heard you contradict yourself." At that time, Freud speaks of his discoveries with the anguish of one who has seen a promised land which he must not set his foot on: "I have the distinct feeling," he writes, "that I have touched on one of the great secrets of nature." This tedium of thought seems to have joined the "heart misery" and was now joined by a mistrust of the friend. He wrote, "Something from the deepest depths of my own neurosis has ranged itself against my taking a further step in understanding of the neuroses, and you have somehow been involved."

Freud, at this point, had developed toward Fliess what later, when he understood it, he called a transference, that is, that peculiar mixture of overestimation and mistrust, which man is so especially ready to bestow on people in significant positions such as doctors and priests, leaders and kings, and other superiors, competitors, and adversaries. It is called transference, because, where it is neurotic, it is characterized by the blurring of an adult relationship through the transfer upon it of infantile loves and hates, dependencies and impotent rages. Transference thus also implies a partial regression to childish attitudes. It was this very area which, at that time, Freud was trying to understand in his patients. Yet, in Freud, it was quite obviously related to the processes of creativity. We have seen how young Freud, in his student days, had subdued an almost incestuous eagerness to "unveil nature" by the compensatory concentration on laboratory work. He had thus postponed a conflict by realizing only one part of his identity. But when, in his words, he "touched on one of the secrets of nature," he was forced to realize that other, that more creative identity. For any refuge to the established disciplines of scientific inquiry was, as the project proved, forever closed. It is in those moments when our divided selves threaten to drag each other down, that a friend, as Nietzsche said, becomes the life-saver which keeps us afloat and together; no wonder that here we can experience a desperate dependency comparable to that of a child on his father.

Freud thus discovered another principle in his new work, namely, that psychological discovery is accompanied by some irrational involvement of the observer, and that it cannot be communicated to another without a certain irrational involvement of both. Such is the stuff of psychology; here it is not enough to put on an armor of superiority or aloofness in the hope that, like the physicist's apron, it will protect vital organs against the radiation emanating from the observed. Here, only the observer's improved insight into himself can right the instrument, protect the observer, and permit the communication of the observed.

In his transference to Fliess, Freud recognized one of the most important transferences of all: the transfer of an early father-image on later individuals and events. And here we can recognize the pervasiveness in these crises of the great father theme. We saw this theme in Freud's determination not to play autocratic father to patients already crushed by autocracy; we recognized this theme as the core of his tendentious error in the genetic reconstruction of his patients' childhood; and we observe it in his filial reactions to Fliess. A dream, he now reported to Fliess, had clearly revealed to him the fact and the explanation for the fact, that an irrational wish to blame the fathers for their children's neuroses had dominated him.

Having established, then, both the actual and the fantastic aspects of a universal father-image, Freud now could break through to the first prehistoric Other of them all: the loving mother. He was free to discover the whole Oedipus complex, and to recognize it as a dominant theme in world literature and in mythologies around the world. Only then could he understand the full extent to which he, when sick and bewildered, had made a parent-figure out of Fliess, so that that mystic Other might help him analyze himself "as if he were a stranger." He concluded that "self-analysis is really impossible, otherwise there would be no illness. . . . I can only analyze myself with objectively acquired knowledge." This insight is the basis for what later became the training analysis, that is, the preventive and didactic psychoanalytic treatment of every prospective psychoanalyst.

The friendship, for other reasons too, had outlived itself. It ended when Freud, in a way, could least afford to lose it. It was after the appearance of *The Interpretation of Dreams.* Freud then, as later, considered this book his most fundamental contribution; he then also believed it to be his last. And, as he wrote, "not a leaf has stirred": for months, for years, there were no book reviews, no sales to speak of. Where there was interest, it was mostly disbelief and calumniation. At this time, Freud seems temporarily to have despaired of his medical way of life. Fliess offered a meeting at Easter. But this time Freud refused. "It is more probable that I shall avoid you," he writes. "I have conquered my depression, and now . . . it is slowly healing. . . . In your company . . . your fine and positive biological discoveries would rouse my innermost (impersonal) envy. . . . I should unburden my woes to you and come back dissatisfied . . . no one can help me in what depresses me, it is my cross, which I must bear. . . ." A few letters later, he refers to his patients' tendency to prolong the treatment beyond the acquisition of the necessary insight. "Such prolongation is a compromise between illness and health which patients themselves desire, and . . . the physician must therefore not lend himself to it." It is clear that he has now recognized such "prolongation and compromise" in his friendship as well, and that he will refuse to permit himself a further indulgence in the dependence on Fliess. But he will sorely miss him—"my one audience," as he calls him.

In the course of this friendship a balance was righted: "feminine" intuition, "childlike" curiosity, and "artistic" freedom of style were recognized and restored as partners of the masculine "inner tyrant" in the process of psychological discovery. And Fliess? According to him the friendship was shipwrecked on the age-old rock of disputed priorities: Freud, he said, envied him. And, indeed, Freud had expressed envy that Fliess worked "with light, not darkness, with the sun and not the unconscious." But it does not seem probable that Freud would have changed places.

These, then, were the dimensions of the crisis during which and through which psychoanalysis was born. But lest anyone form the faulty image of a lamentably torn and tormented man and physician, it must be reported that the Freud of those years was what today we would call an adjusted individual, and what then was a decent and an able one: a man who took conscientious care of all the patients who found their way to his door, who with devotion and joy raised a family of six children, who was widely read and well-groomed, traveled with curiosity, walked (or, as we would say, exercised) with abandon, loved good food and wine wisely, and his cigars unwisely. But he was not too adapted or too decent to approach a few things in life with decisive, with ruthless integrity. All of which in a way he could ill afford, for the times were bad for a medical specialist; it was the time of the first economic depression of the modern industrial era, it was a time of "poverty in plenty." Nor did the self-analysis "reform" or chasten Freud. Some of the vital conflicts which pervaded the friendship with Fliess remained lifelong, as did some of the early methodological habits: in *Totem and Taboo,* Freud again reconstructed—this time on the stage of history—an "event" which, though an unlikely happening in past actuality, yet proved most significant as a timeless theme. But that early period of Freud's work gave to the new science its unique direction, and with it gave its originator that peculiar unification of personal peculiarities which makes up a man's identity, becomes the cornerstone of his kind of integrity, and poses his challenge to contemporaries and generations to come.

The unique direction of the new science consisted of the introduction into psychology of a system of coördinates which I can only summarize most briefly. His early energy concept provided the *dynamic-economic* coördinate. A *topological* coördinate emerged from the refinement of that early mind-robot; while the *genetic* coördinate was established on the basis of the reconstruction of childhood. This is psychoanalysis; any insight and only insight traceable in these coördinates is psychoanalytic insight. But these coördinates can be understood only through systematic study.

Since those early days of discovery, psychoanalysis has established deep and wide interrelationships with other methods of investigation, with methods of naturalist observation, of somatic examination, of psychological experiment, of anthropological field work, and of scholarly research. If, instead of enlarging on all these, I have focused on the early days, and on the uniqueness of the original Freudian experience, I have done so because I believe that an innovator's achievement can be seen most dramatically in that moment when he, alone against historical adversity and inner doubts, and armed only with the means of persuasion, gives a new direction to human awareness—new in focus, new in method, and new in its inescapable morality.

The dimensions of Freud's discovery, then, are contained in a triad which, in a variety of ways, remains basic to the practice of psychoanalysis, but also to its applications. It is the triad of a *therapeutic contract,* a *conceptual design,* and *systematic self-analysis.*

In psychoanalytic practice, this triad can never become routine. As new categories of suffering people prove amenable to psychoanalytic therapy, new techniques come to life, new aspects of the mind find clarification, and new therapeutic roles are created. Today, the student of psychoanalysis receives a training psychoanalysis which prepares him for the emotional hazards of his work. But he must live with the rest of mankind, in this era of "anxiety in plenty," and neither his personal life nor the very progress of his work will spare him renewed conflicts, be his profession ever so recognized, ever so organized. Wide recognition and vast organization will not assure—they may even endanger—the basic triad, for which the psychoanalyst makes himself responsible, to wit: that as a clinician he accept his contract with the patient as the essence of his field of study and relinquish the security of seemingly more "objective" methods; that as a theorist he maintain a sense of obligation toward continuous conceptual redefinition and resist the lure of seemingly "deeper" philosophic short cuts; and finally, that as a humanist he put self-observant vigilance above the satisfaction of seeming professional omnipotence. The responsibility is great. For, in a sense, the psychoanalytic method must remain forever a "controversial" tool, a tool for the detection of that aspect of the total image of man which at a given time is being neglected or exploited, repressed or suppressed by the prevailing technology and ideology—including hasty "psychoanalytic" ideologies.

Freud's triad remains equally relevant in the applications of psychoanalysis to the behavioral sciences, and to the humanities. An adult studying a child, an anthropologist studying a tribe, or a sociologist studying a riot sooner or later will be confronted with data of decisive importance for the welfare of those whom he is studying, while the strings of his own motivation will be touched, sometimes above and sometimes well below the threshold of awareness. He will not be able, for long, to escape the necessary conflict between his emotional participation in the observed events and the methodological rigor required to advance his field and human welfare. Thus, his studies will demand, in the long run, that he develop the ability to include in his observational field his human obligations, his methodological responsibilities, and his own motivations. In doing so, he will, in his own way, repeat that step in scientific conscience which Freud dared to make.

That shift, however, cannot remain confined to professional partnerships such as the observer's to the observed, or the doctor's with his patient. It implies a fundamentally new morality in the adult's relationship to childhood: to the child within him, to his child before him, and to every man's children around him.

But the fields dealing with man's historical dimension are far apart in their appraisal of childhood. Academic minds whose long-range perspectives can ignore the everyday urgencies of the curative and educative arts, blithely go on writing whole world histories without any women and children in them, whole anthropologies without any reference to the varying styles of childhood. As they record what causal chain can be discerned in political and economic realities, they seem to shrug off as historical accidents due to "human nature" such fears and rages in leaders and masses as are clearly the residue of childish emotions now under study. True, these scholars may have been repelled by the first enthusiastic intrusion of doctors of the mind into their ancient disciplines. But their refusal to consider the historical relevance of human childhood can be due only to that deeper and more universal emotional aversion which Freud himself foresaw. On the other hand, it must be admitted that in clinical literature and in literature turned altogether clinical, aversion has given place to a faddish preoccupation with the more sordid aspects of childhood as the beginning and the end of human destiny.

Neither of these trends can hinder the emergence, in due time, of a new truth. The stream of world events, in all its historical lawfulness, is fed by the energies and thoughts of successive generations; and each generation brings to the existing historical trends its particular version of an inescapable conflict: the conflict with its individual "prehistories." This conflict helps to drive man toward the astonishing things he does—and it can be his undoing. It is a condition of man's humanity—and the prime cause of his bottomless inhumanity.

Freud not only revealed this conflict by dissecting the strains of its pathological manifestations. He also pointed to what is so largely and so regularly lost in the conflict: he spoke of "the child's radiant intelligence"—the naïve zest, the natural courage, the unconditional faith of childhood which are submerged by fearful teachings and by limited and limiting information.

Now and again, we are moved to say that a genius preserved in himself the clear eye of the child. But do we not all too easily justify man's ways and means by pointing to the occasional appearance of genius? Do we not know (and are we not morbidly eager to know) how tortured a genius can be by the very history of his ascendance, how often a genius is driven to destroy with one hand as he creates with the other?

In Freud, a genius turned a new instrument of observation back on his childhood, back on all childhood. He invented a specific method for the detection of that which universally spoils the genius of the child in every human being. In teaching us to recognize the daimonic evil in children, he urged us not to smother the creatively good. Since then, the nature of growth in childhood has been studied by ingenious observers over the world: never before has mankind known more about its own past—phylogenetic and ontogenetic. Thus, we may see Freud as a pioneer in a self-healing, balancing trend in human awareness. For now that technical invention readies itself really to conquer the moon, generations to come may well be in need of being more enlightened in their drivenness, and more conscious of the laws of individuality; they may well need to preserve more childlikeness in order to avoid utter cosmic childishness.

Freud, before he went into medicine, wanted to become a lawyer and politician, a lawmaker, a *Gesetzgeber*. When, in 1938, he was exiled from his country, he carried under his arm a manuscript on Moses, the supreme law-giver of the people whose unique fate and whose unique gifts he had accepted as his own. With grim pride he had chosen the role of one who opens perspectives on fertile fields to be cultivated by others. As we look back to the beginnings of his work, and forward to its implications, we may well venture to say: Freud the physician in finding a method of healing himself in the very practice of emotional cure has given a new, a psychological rationale for man's laws. He has made the decisive step toward a true interpenetration of the psychological with the technological and the political in the human order.

J. Robert Oppenheimer

In this essay an eminent physicist attempts to explain in general terms the nature and history of science—by which he means that form of knowledge which is based on objectively verifiable observations of phenomena. The motive behind the essay, however, is not merely informative. Oppenheimer is troubled, as so many thinkers of the last hundred years have been, by the growing tendency toward specialization in all human activities and by the fact that this has led to a breakdown of communication between scientists and those who are engaged in other types of intellectual endeavor. He does not, of course, simply lament the scientist's specialization or pretend that it is either possible or desirable to do away with it. His observations on the nature of scientific knowledge—its progressive and cumulative character, its free choice of objects of inquiry, its "branching reticular structure"—make it clear that that knowledge depends on specialization of an extreme sort. (He assumes that his readers can distinguish between science and technology.)

The complex world which intellectual specialization has created makes it impossible for any one man to sustain a view which does equal justice to all the varied activities of the modern mind, and Oppenheimer's observations on literature, art, and philosophy, although uttered with both the respect and the familiarity of a cultivated man, do seem to imply a partial failure to recognize that those disciplines have their valid difficulty comparable to that of science. Nevertheless, Oppenheimer aims, like Trilling, at the broad view which admits and rejoices in the multiplicity of the intellect. He specifically refutes, for example, both the claim that science is coextensive with modern culture and the claim that science has no connection with culture at all. He has no easy solution to the problem of lack of communication, but his final optimistic suggestion that the development of a new leisure may make for a truer cultural dialogue is, if vague, certainly provocative and at least possible, as is his implicit belief that scientific advance should lead to the ethical and social improvement of the race.

SCIENCE AND CULTURE

We live in an unusual world, marked by very great and irreversible changes that occur within the span of a man's life. We live in a time where our knowledge and understanding of the world of nature grows wider and deeper at an unparalleled rate; and where the problems of applying this knowledge to man's needs and hopes are new, and only a little illuminated by our past history.

Indeed it has always, in traditional societies, been the great function of culture to keep things rather stable, quiet, and unchanging. It has been the function of tradition to assimilate one epoch to another, one episode to another, even one year to another. It has been the function of culture to bring out meaning, by pointing to the constant or recurrent traits of human life, which in easier days one talked about as the eternal verities.

In the most primitive societies, if one believes the anthropologists, the principal function of ritual, religion, of culture is, in fact, almost to stop change. It is to provide for the social organism what life provides in such a magic way for living organisms, a kind of homeostasis, an ability to remain intact, to respond only very little to the obvious convulsions and alterations in the world around.

To-day, culture and tradition have assumed a very different intellectual and social purpose. The principal function of the most vital and living traditions to-day is precisely to provide the instruments of rapid change. There are many things which go together to bring about this alteration in man's life; but probably the decisive one is science itself. I will use that word as broadly as I know, meaning the natural sciences, meaning the historical sciences, meaning all those matters on which men can converse objectively with each other. I shall not continually repeat the distinction between science as an effort to find out about the world and understand it, on the one hand, and science, in its applications in technology, as an effort to do something useful with the knowledge so

From the October 1962 issue of *Encounter*. Reprinted by permission of the author.

acquired. But certain care is called for, because, if we call this the scientific age, we make more than one kind of oversimplification. When we talk about science to-day, we are likely to think of the biologist with his microscope or the physicist with his cyclotron; but almost certainly a great deal that is not now the subject of successful study will later come to be. I think we probably to-day have under cultivation only a small part of the terrain which will be natural for the sciences a century from now. I think of the enormously rapid growth in many parts of biology, and of the fact, ominous but not without hope, that man is a part of nature and very open to study.

The reason for this great change from a slowly moving, almost static world, to the world we live in, is the cumulative character, the firmness, the givenness of what has been learned about nature. It is true that it is transcended when one goes into other parts of experience. What is true on the scale of the inch and the centimeter may not be true on the scale of a billion light-years; it may not be true either of the scale of a one hundred billionth of a centimeter; but it stays true where it was proven. It is fixed. Thus everything that is found out is added to what was known before, enriches it, and does not have to be done over again. This essentially cumulative irreversible character of learning things is the hallmark of science.

This means that in man's history the sciences make changes which cannot be wished away and cannot be undone. Let me give two quite different examples. There is much talk about getting rid of atomic bombs. I like that talk; but we must not fool ourselves. The world will not be the same, no matter what we do with atomic bombs, because the knowledge of how to make them cannot be exorcised. It is there; and all our arrangements for living in a new age must bear in mind its omnipresent virtual presence, and the fact that one cannot change that. A different example: we can never have again the delusions about the centrality and importance of our physical habitat, now that we know something of where the earth is in the solar system, and know that there are hundreds of billions of suns in our galaxy, and hundreds of billions of galaxies within reach of the great telescopes of the world. We can never again base the dignity of man's life on the special character in space and time of the place where he happens to live.

These are irreversible changes; so it is that the cumulative character gives a paradigm of something which is, in other respects, very much more subject to question: the idea of human progress. One cannot doubt that in the sciences the direction of growth is progress. This is true both of the knowledge of fact, the understanding of nature, and the knowledge of skill, of technology, of learning how to do things. When one applies this to the human situation, and complains that we make great progress in automation and computing and space research but no comparable moral progress, this involves a total misunderstanding of the difference between the two kinds of progress. I do not mean that moral progress is impossible; but it is not, in any sense, automatic. Moral regress, as we have seen in our day, is just as possible. Scientific regress is not compatible with the continued practice of science.

It is, of course, true, and we pride ourselves on it that it is true, that science is quite international, and is the same (with minor differences of emphasis) in Japan, France, the United States, Russia. But culture is not international; indeed I am one of those who hope that, in a certain sense, it never quite will be, that the influence of our past, of our history, which is for different reasons and different peoples quite different, will make itself felt and not be lost in total homogeneity.

I cannot subscribe to the view that science and culture are co-extensive, that they are the same thing with different names; and I cannot subscribe to the view that science is something useful, but essentially unrelated to culture. I think that we live in a time which has few historical parallels, that there are practical problems of human institutions, their obsolescence and their inadequacy, problems of the mind and spirit which, if not more difficult than ever before, are different, and difficult. I shall be dealing with some traits of the sciences which contribute to the difficulty, and may here give a synopsis of what they are. They have to do with the question of why the scientific revolution happened when it did; with the characteristic growth of the sciences: with their characteristic internal structure: with the relation of discovery in the sciences to the general ideas of man in matters which are not precisely related to the sciences: with freedom and necessity in the sciences, and the question of the creative and the open character of science, its infinity: and with what direction we might try to follow in bringing coherence and order to our cultural life, in doing what it is proper for a group of intellectuals, of artists, of philosophers, teachers, scientists, statesmen to do to help refashion the sensibility and the institutions of this world, which need re-fashioning if we are at all to survive.

It is not a simple question to answer why the scientific revolution occurred when it did. It started, as all serious historians would agree, in the late Middle Ages and early Renaissance, and was very slow at first. No great culture has been free of curiosity and reflection, of contemplation and thought. "To know the causes of things" is something that serious men have always wanted, a quest that serious societies have sustained. No great culture has been free of inventive genius. If we think of the culture of Greece, and the following Hellenistic and Roman period, it is particularly puzzling that the scientific revolution did not occur then. The Greeks discovered something without which our contemporary world would not be what it is: standards of rigour, the idea of proof, the idea of logical necessity, the idea that one thing implies another. Without that, science is very nearly impossible, for unless there is a quasi-rigid structure of implication and necessity, then if something turns out not to be what one expected, one will have no way of finding out where the wrong point is: one has no way of correcting himself, of finding the error. But this is something that the Greeks had very early in their history. They were curious and inventive; they did not experiment in the scale of modern days, but they did many experiments; they had as we have only recently learned to appreciate a very high degree of technical and technological sophistication. They could make very subtle and complicated instruments; and they did, though they did not write much about it. Possibly the Greeks did not make the scientific revolution because of some flaw in communication. They were a small society, and it may be that there were not quite enough people involved.

In a matter of history, we cannot assign a unique cause, precisely because the event itself is unique; you cannot test, to see if you have it right. I think that the best guess is that it took something that was not present in Chinese civilisation, that was wholly absent in Indian civilisation, and absent also from Greco-Roman civilisation. It needed an idea of progress, not limited to better understanding for this idea the Greeks had. It took an idea of progress which has more to do with the human condition, which is well expressed by the second half of the famous Christian dichotomy—faith and works; the notion that the betterment of man's condition, his civility, had meaning; that we all had a responsibility to it, a duty to it, and to man. I think that it was when this basic idea of man's condition, which supplements the other worldly aspects of religion, was fortified and fructified between the 13th and 15th centuries by the re-discovery of the ancient world's scientists, philosophers, and mathematicians, that there was the beginning of the scientific age. By the 17th century there were a handful of men involved in improving human knowledge, or "useful knowledge" as the phrases went, so that new societies like the Royal Society and the Academy were formed, where people could talk to each other and bring to the prosecution of science that indispensable element of working together, of communication, of correcting the other fellow's errors and admiring the other fellow's skills, thus creating the first truly scientific communities.

Just before Newton, Hobbes wrote:

The Sciences are small power; because not eminent; and therefore, not acknowledged in any man, nor one at all, but in a few; and in them, but of a few things. For Science is of that nature, as none can understand it to be, but such as is good measure have attayned it.

Arts of publique use, as Fortification, making of Engines, and other Instruments of War; because they conferre to Defence, and Victory, are Power.

It was the next century that put science in a context of fraternity, even of universal brotherhood. It encouraged a political view which was egalitarian, permissive, pluralistic, liberal—everything for which the word "democratic" is to-day justly and rightly used. The result is that the scientific world of to-day is also a very large one: an open world in which, of course, not everybody does everything, in which not everybody is a scientist or a prime minister, but in which we fight very hard against arbitrary exclusion of people from any works, any deliberation, any discourse, any responsibility for which their talents and their interests suit them. The result is that we face our new problems, created by the practical consequences of technology, and the great intellectual consequences of science itself, in the context of a world of two or three billion people, an enormous society for which human institutions were not really ever designed. We are facing a world in which growth is characteristic, not just of the sciences themselves, but of the economy, of technology, of all human institutions; no one can open a daily paper without seeing the consequences.

One can measure scientific growth in a number of ways, but it is important not to mistake things. The excellence of the individual scientist does not change much with time. His knowledge and his power does, but not the high quality that makes him great. We do not look to anyone to be better than Kepler or Newton, any more than we look to anyone to be better than Sophocles, or to any doctrine to be better than the gospel according to St. Matthew. Yet one can measure things, and it has been done. One can measure how many people work on scientific questions: one can count them. One can notice how much is published.

These two criteria show a doubling of scientific knowledge in every ten years. Casimir calculated that if the *Physical Review* continued to grow as rapidly as it has between 1945 and 1960, it would weigh more than the earth during the next century. In fifteen years, the volume of chemical abstracts has quadrupled; in biology the changes are faster still. To-day, if you talk about scientists and mean by that people who have devoted their lives to the acquisition and application of new knowledge, then 93 per cent of us are still alive. This enormously rapid growth, sustained over two centuries, means, of course, that no man learned as a boy more than a small fraction in his own field of what he ought to know as a grown man.

There are several points to keep in mind. One would naturally think that if we are publishing so much, it must be trivial. I think that this is not true: any scientific community with sane people would protect itself against that: because we have to read what is published. The argument not to permit the accumulation of trivial, unimportant things which are not really new, which do not add to what was known before, is overwhelming.

The second point is that one may say that every new thing renders what was known before uninteresting, that one can forget as rapidly as one learns. That is in part true: whenever there is a great new understanding, a great new element of order, a new theory, or a new law of nature, then much that before had to be remembered in isolation becomes connected and becomes, to some extent, implied and simplified. Yet one cannot forget what went before, because usually the meaning of what is discovered in 1962 is to be found in terms of things that were discovered in 1955 or 1950 or earlier. These are the things in terms of which the new discoveries are made, the origins of the instruments that give us the new discoveries, the origins of the concepts in terms of which they are discovered, the origins of the language and the tradition.

A third point: if one looks to the future of something that doubles every ten years, there must come a time when it stops, just as *The Physical Review* cannot weigh more than the earth. We know that this will saturate, and probably at a level very much higher than to-day; there will come a time when the rate of growth of science is not such that in every ten years the amount that is known is doubled; but the amount that is added to knowledge then will be far greater than it is to-day. For this rate of growth suggests that, just as the professional must, if he is to remain professional, live a life of continuous study, so we may find a clue here also to the more general behaviour of the intellectual with regard to his own affairs, and those of his colleagues in somewhat different fields. In the most practical way a man will have some choice: he may choose to continue to learn about his own field in an intimate, detailed, knowledgeable way, so that he knows what there is to know about it. But then the field will not be very wide. His knowledge will be highly partial of science as a whole, but very intimate and very complete of his own field. He may, on the other hand, choose to know generally, superficially a good deal about what goes on in science, but without competence, without mastery, without intimacy, without depth. The reason for emphasising this is that the cultural values of the life of science almost all lie in the intimate view: here are the new techniques, the hard lessons, the real choices, the great disappointments, the great discoveries.

All sciences grow out of common sense, out of curiosity, observation, reflection. One starts by refining one's observation and one's words, and by exploring and pushing things a little further than they occur in ordinary life. In this novelty there are surprises; one revises the way one thinks about things to accommodate the surprises; then the old way of thinking gets to be so cumbersome and inappropriate that one realises that there is a big change called for, and one re-creates one's way of thinking about this part of nature.

Through all this one learns to say what one has done, what one has found, and to be patient and wait for others to see if they find the same things, and to reduce, to the point where it really makes no further difference, the normally overpoweringly vital element of ambiguity in human speech. We live by being ambiguous, by not settling things because they do not have to be settled, by suggesting more than one thing because their co-presence in the mind may be a source of beauty. But in talking about science one may be as ambiguous as ever until we come to the heart of it. Then we tell a fellow just what we did in terms that are intelligible to him, because he has been schooled to understand them, and we tell him just what we found and just how we did it. If he does not understand us, we go to visit him and help him; and if he still does not understand us, we go back home and do it over again. This is the way in which the firmness and solidity of science is established.

How then does it go? In studying the different parts of nature, one explores with different instruments, explores different objects, and one gets a branching of what at one time had been common talk, common sense. Each branch develops new instruments, ideas, words suitable for describing that part of the world of nature. This tree-like structure, all growing from the common trunk of man's common primordial experience, has branches no longer associated with the same question, nor the same words and techniques. The unity of science, apart from the fact that it all has a common origin in man's ordinary life, is not a unity of deriving one part from another, nor of finding an identity between one part and another, between let us say, genetics and topology, to take two impossible examples, where there is indeed some connection.

The unity consists of two things: first and ever more strikingly, an absence of inconsistency. Thus we may talk of life in terms of purpose and adaptation and function, but we have found in living things no tricks played upon the laws of physics and chemistry. We have found and I expect will find a total consistency, and between the different subjects, even as remote as genetics and topology, an occasional sharp mutual relevance. They throw light on each other; they have something to do with each other; often the greatest things in the sciences occur when two different discoveries made in different worlds turn out to have so much in common that they are examples of a still greater discovery.

The image is not that of an ordered array of facts in which every one follows somehow from a more fundamental one. It is rather that of a living thing: a tree doing something that trees do not normally do, occasionally having the branches grow together and part again in a great network.

The knowledge that is being increased in this extraordinary way is inherently and inevitably very specialised. It is different for the physicist, the astronomer, the micro-biologist, the mathematician. There are connections: there is this often important mutual relevance. Even in physics, where we fight very hard to keep the different parts of our subject from flying apart (so that one fellow will know one thing and another fellow will know another, and they do not talk to each other), we do not entirely succeed, in spite of a passion for unity which is very strong. The traditions of science are specialised traditions; this is their strength. Their strength is that they use the words, the machinery, the concepts, the theories, that fit their subjects; they are not encumbered by having to try to fit other sorts of things. It is the specialised traditions which give the enormous thrust and power to the scientific experience. This also makes for the problem of teaching and explaining the sciences. When we get to some very powerful general result which illuminates a large part of the world of nature, it is by virtue of its being general in the logical sense, of encompassing an enormous amount of experience in its concepts; and in its terminology it is most highly specialised, almost unintelligible except to the men who have worked in the field. The great laws of physics to-day, which do not describe everything (or we would be out of business) but which underlie almost everything that is ever noticed in ordinary human experience about the physical world, cannot be formulated in terms that can reasonably be defined without a long period of careful schooling. This is comparably true in other subjects.

One has then in these specialisations the professional communities in the various sciences. They are very intimate, work closely together, know each other throughout the world. They are always excited—sometimes jealous but usually pleased—when one member of the community makes a discovery. I think, for instance, that what we now call psychology will one day perhaps be many sciences, that there will be many different specialised communities practising them, who will talk with one another, each in their own profession and in their own way.

These specialised communities, or guilds, are a very moving experience for those who participate. There have been many temptations to see analogues in them for other human activities. One that we hear much discussed is this: "If physicists can work together in countries with different cultures, in countries with different politics, in countries of different religions, even in countries which are politically obviously hostile, is not this a way to bring the world together?"

The specialising habits of the sciences have, to some extent, because of the tricks of universities, been carried over to other work, to philosophy and to the arts. There is technical philosophy which is philosophy as a craft, philosophy for other philosophers, and there is art for the artists and the critics. To my mind, whatever virtues the works have for sharpening professional tools, they are profound misreadings, even profound subversions of the true functions of philosophy and art, which are to address themselves to the general common human problem. Not to everybody, but to anybody: not to specialists.

It is clear that one is faced here with formidable problems of communication, of telling people about things. It is an immense job of teaching on all levels, in every sense of the word, never ending.

It has often been held that the great discoveries in science, coming into the lives of men, affect their attitudes toward their place in life, their views, their philosophy. There is surely some truth in this.*

If discoveries in science are to have an honest effect on human thought and on culture, they have to be understandable. That is likely to be true only in the early period of a science, when it is talking about things which are not too remote from ordinary experience. Some of the great discoveries of this century go under the name of Relativity and Uncertainty, and when we hear these words we may think, "This is the way I felt this morning: I was relatively confused and quite uncertain": this is not at all a notion of what technical points are involved in these great discoveries, or what lessons.

I think that the reason why Darwin's hypothesis had such an impact was, in part, because it was a very simple thing in terms of ordinary life. We cannot talk about the contemporary discovery in biology in such language, or by referring only to things that we have all experienced.

Thus I think that the great effects of the sciences in stimulating and in enriching philosophical life and cultural interests have been necessarily confined to the rather early times in the development of a science. There is another qualification. Discoveries will really only resonate and change the thinking of men when they feed some hope, some need that pre-exists in the society. I think that the real sources of the Enlightenment, fed a little by the scientific events of the time, came in the re-discovery of the classics, of classic political theory, perhaps most of all of the Stoics. The hunger of the Eighteenth Century to believe in the power of reason, to wish to throw off authority, to wish to secularise, to take an

* Examples that are usually given include Newton and Darwin. Newton is not a very good example, for when we look at it closely we are struck by the fact that in the sense of the Enlightenment, the sense of a coupling of faith in scientific progress and man's reason with a belief in political progress and the secularisation of human life, Newton himself was in no way a Newtonian. His successors were.

optimistic view of man's condition, seized on Newton and his discoveries as an illustration of something which was already deeply believed in quite apart from the law of gravity and the laws of motion. The hunger with which the Nineteenth Century seized on Darwin had very much to do with the increasing awareness of history and change, with the great desire to naturalise man, to put him into the world of nature, which pre-existed long before Darwin and which made him welcome. I have seen an example in this century where the great Danish physicist Niels Bohr found in the quantum theory when it was developed thirty years ago this remarkable trait: it is consistent with describing an atomic system, only much less completely than we can describe large-scale objects. We have a certain choice as to which traits of the atomic system we wish to study and measure and which to let go; but we have not the option of doing them all. This situation, which we all recognise, sustained in Bohr his long-held view of the human condition: that there are mutually exclusive ways of using our words, our minds, our souls, any one of which is open to us, but which cannot be combined: ways as different, for instance, as preparing to act and entering into an introspective search for the reasons for action. This discovery has not, I think, penetrated into general cultural life. I wish it had; it is a good example of something that would be relevant, if only it could be understood.

Einstein once said that a physical theory was not determined by the facts of nature, but was a free invention of the human mind. This raises the question of how necessary is the content of science—how much is it something that we are free not to find—how much is it something that could be otherwise? This is, of course, relevant to the question of how we may use the words "objectivity" and "truth." Do we, when we find something, "invent" it or "discover" it?

The fact is, of course, just what one would guess. We are, of course, free in our tradition and in our practice, and to a much more limited extent individually to decide where to look at nature, and how to look at nature, what questions to put, with what instruments and with what purpose. But we are not the least bit free to settle what we find. Man must certainly be free to invent the idea of mass, as Newton did and as it has been refined and re-defined; but having done so, we have not been free to find that the mass of the light quantum or the neutrino is anything but zero. We are free in the start of things. We are free as to how to go about it; but then the rock of what the world is, shapes this freedom with a necessary answer. That is why ontological interpretations of the word "objective" have seemed useless, and why we use the word to describe the clarity, the lack of ambiguity, the effectiveness of the way we can tell each other about what we have found.

Thus in the sciences, total statements like those that involve the word "all," with no qualifications, are hardly ever likely to occur. In every investigation and extension of knowledge we are involved in an action; in every action we are involved in a choice; and in every choice we are involved in a loss, the loss of that we did not do. We find this in the simplest situations. We find this in perception, where the possibility of perceiving is co-extensive with our ignoring many things that are going on. We find it in speech where the possibility of understandable speech lies in paying no attention to a great deal that is in the air, among the sound waves, in the general scene. Meaning is always attained at the cost of leaving things out. We find it in the idea of complementarity here in a sharp form as a recognition that the attempt to make one sort of observation on an atomic system forecloses others. We have freedom of choice, but we have no escape from the fact that doing some things must leave out others.

In practical terms, this means, of course, that our knowledge is finite and never all-encompassing. There is always much that we miss, much that we cannot be aware of because the very act of learning, of ordering, of finding unity and meaning, the very power to talk about things means that we leave out a great deal.

Ask the question: *Would another civilisation based on life on another planet very similar to ours in its ability to sustain life have the same physics?* One has no idea whether they would have the same physics or not. We might be talking about quite different questions. This makes ours an open world without end. I had a Sanskritist friend in California who used to say mockingly that, if science were any good, it should be much easier to be an educated man now than it was a generation ago. That is because he thought the world was closed.

The things that make us choose one set of questions, one branch of enquiry rather than another are embodied in scientific traditions. In developed sciences each man has only a limited sense of freedom to shape or alter them; but they are not themselves wholly determined by the findings of science. They are largely of an aesthetic character. The words that we use: simplicity, elegance, beauty: indicate that what we grope for is not only more knowledge, but knowledge that has order and harmony in it, and continuity with the past. Like all poor fellows, we want to find something new, but not something too new. It is when we fail in that, that the great discoveries follow.

All these themes—the origin of science, its pattern of growth, its branching reticular structure, its increasing alienation from the common understanding of man, its freedom, the character of its objectivity and its openness—are relevant to the relations of science and culture. I believe that they can be and should be far more robust, intimate, and fruitful than they are to-day.

I am not here thinking of the popular subject of "mass culture." In broaching that, it seems to me one must be critical but one must, above all, be human; one must not be a snob; one must be rather tolerant and almost loving. It is a new problem; one must not expect it to be solved with the methods of Periclean Athens. In the problems of mass culture and, above all, of the mass media, it is not primarily a question of the absence of excellence. The modest worker, in Europe or in America, has within reach probably better music and more good music, more good art, more good writing than his predecessors have ever had. It seems rather that the good things are lost in such a stream of poor things, that the noise level is so high, that some of the conditions for appreciating excellence are not present. One does not eat well unless one is hungry; there is a certain frugality to the best cooking; and something of this sort is wrong with the mass media. But that is not now my problem.

Rather, I think loosely of what we may call the intellectual community: artists, philosophers, statesmen, teachers, men of most professions, prophets, scientists. This is an open group, with no sharp lines separating those that think themselves of it. It is a growing faction of all peoples. In it is vested the great duty for enlarging, preserving, and transmitting our knowledge and skills, and indeed our understanding of the interrelations, priorities, commitments, injunctions, that help men deal with their joys, temptations and sorrows, their finiteness, their beauty. Some of this has to do, as the sciences so largely do, with propositional truth, with propositions which say "If you do thus and so you will see this and that"; these are objective and can be checked and cross-checked; though it is always wise from time to time to doubt, there are ways to put an end to the doubt. This is how it is with the sciences.

In this community there are other statements which "emphasise a theme" rather than declare a fact. They may be statements of connectedness or relatedness or importance, or they may be in one way or another statements of commitment. For them the word "certitude," which is a natural norm to apply in the sciences, is not very sensible—depth, firmness, universality, perhaps more—but certitude, which applies really to verification, is not the great criterion in most of the work of a philosopher, a painter, a poet, or a playwright. For these are not, in the sense I have outlined, objective. Yet for any true community, for any society worthy of the name, they must have an element of community of being common, of being public, of being relevant and meaningful to man, not necessarily to everybody, but surely not just to specialists.

I have been much concerned that, in this world of change and scientific growth, we have so largely lost the ability to talk with one another, to increase and enrich our common culture and understanding. And so it is that the public sector of our lives, what we hold and have in common, has suffered, as have the illumination of the arts, the deepening of justice and virtue, and the ennobling power of our common discourse. We are less men for this. Never in man's history have the specialised traditions more flourished than to-day. We have our private beauties. But in those high undertakings when man derives strength and insight from public excellence, we have been impoverished. We hunger for nobility, the rare words and acts that harmonise simplicity with truth. In this default I see some connection with the great unresolved public problems—survival, liberty, fraternity.

In this default I see the responsibility that the intellectual community has to history and to our fellows: a responsibility which is a necessary condition for re-making human institutions as they need to be re-made to-day that there may be peace, that they may embody more fully those ethical commitments without which we cannot properly live as men.

This may mean for the intellectual community a very much greater effort than in the past. The community will grow; but I think that also the quality and the excellence of what we do must grow. I think, in fact, that with the growing wealth of the world, and the possibility that it will not all be used to make new committees, there may indeed be genuine leisure, and that a high commitment of this leisure is that we reknit the discourse and the understanding between the members of our community.

In this I think we have, all of us, to preserve our competence in our own professions, to preserve what we know intimately, to preserve our mastery. This is, in fact, our only anchor in honesty. We need also to be open to other and complementary lives, not intimidated by them and not contemptuous of them (as so many are to-day of the natural and mathematical sciences). As a start, we must learn again, without contempt and with great patience, to talk to one another; and we must hear.

Lionel Trilling

The year 1962 witnessed a violent controversy over the relations of science, literature, and culture; the principal antagonists were the English literary critic F. R. Leavis and the scientist and man of letters Sir Charles Snow.

The selection "Science, Literature and Culture" is a commentary on that dispute by one of America's most distinguished literary critics. Lionel Trilling is especially noted for his informed concern with the political and broadly social connections of literature, and appropriately enough he first gained prominence through a study of Matthew Arnold, the nineteenth-century poet and social thinker who first focused attention on the divided and divisive nature of modern culture. Trilling begins with a discussion of Arnold's views and thus places the Snow-Leavis controversy in a larger historical perspective, in terms of which he sees both men as guilty of oversimplification and inaccuracy. Intellectually disturbed by Snow's flat contention that the future belongs exclusively to the scientific mentality and by his denial to literature of that capacity for being a "criticism of life" which Arnold ascribed to it, Trilling is almost equally distressed by the moral narrowness and the distrust of the future expressed in Leavis' attack. But Trilling's tone is never strident, and, very much less rash in his assertions than either Snow or Leavis, he maintains throughout his essay a manner of judicious inquiry, even when refuting statements that seem to him manifestly irresponsible—as, for example, when he takes issue with Snow's charge that George Orwell, one of the most politically engaged of contemporary literary figures, shows "the strongest possible wish that the future shall not exist."

Trilling is a liberal and a humanist, and as such is committed to maintaining the best from past tradition and encouraging a future of desirable change. This double commitment lies behind his rejection of the radical claims of the narrow scientist and the narrow partisan of literary culture alike. It also lies behind his two central positive assertions: literature must continue to exercise freely its traditional function of criticizing and judging political behavior, and the current modern preoccupation of thinking in terms of "cultures" may profitably be modified by thinking sometimes in terms of the older and simpler abstraction of Mind.

Science, Literature and Culture

It is now nearly eighty years since Matthew Arnold came to this country on his famous lecture tour. Of his repertory of three lectures, none was calculated to give unqualified pleasure to his audience. The lecture on Emerson praised that most eminent of American writers only after it had denied that he was a literary figure of the first order. The lecture called "Numbers" raised disturbing questions about the relation of democracy to excellence and distinction. "Literature and Science" was the least likely to give offense, yet even this most memorable of the three *Discourses in America* was not without its touch of uncomfortableness.

Reprinted from *Commentary* (June 1962); copyright American Jewish Committee. Reprinted by permission of *Commentary* and the author.

In 1883 America was by no means committed—and, indeed, never was to be committed—to the belief that the right education for the modern age must be predominantly scientific and technical, and Arnold, when he cited the proponents of this idea, which of course he opposed, mentioned only those who were English. Yet his audiences surely knew that Arnold was warning them against what would seem to be the natural tendency of an industrial democracy to devalue the old "aristocratic" education in favor of studies that are merely practical..

Arnold wrote "Emerson" and "Numbers" especially for his American tour, but he had first composed "Literature and Science" as the Rede Lecture at Cambridge in 1882. Its original occasion cannot fail to have a peculiar interest at this moment, for C. P. Snow's *The Two Cultures and the Scientific Revolution,* around which so curious a storm rages in England, was the Rede Lecture of 1959.

Sir Charles did not mention his great predecessor in the lectureship, although his own discourse was exactly on Arnold's subject and took a line exactly the opposite of Arnold's. And F. R. Leavis, whose admiration of Arnold is well known and whose position in respect to the relative importance of literature and of science in education is much the same as Arnold's, did not mention Arnold either, when, in his recent Richmond Lecture at Downing College, he launched an attack of unexampled ferocity upon the doctrine and the author of *The Two Cultures.*

In its essential terms, the issue in debate has not changed since Arnold spoke. Arnold's chief antagonist was T. H. Huxley—it was he who, in his lecture on "Culture and Education," had said that literature should, and inevitably would, step down from its preeminent place in education, that science and not "culture" must supply the knowledge which is necessary for an age committed to rational truth and material practicality. What is more, Huxley said, science will supply the very basis of the assumptions of modern ethics. In effect Snow says nothing different.

The word "culture" had been Arnold's personal insigne ever since the publication of *Culture and Anarchy* in 1867 and Huxley made particular reference to the views on the value of humanistic study which Arnold had expressed in that book.* Arnold's reply in "Literature and Science" could not have been simpler, just as it could not have been more temperate, although it surely did not surpass in temperateness Huxley's statement of his disagreement with Arnold's ideas; the two men held each other in high admiration and were warm friends. Arnold said that he had

---

* Arnold, of course, did not use the word in the modern sense in which it is used by anthropologists, sociologists, and historians of thought and art; this is, more or less, the sense in which it is used by Snow. For Arnold, "culture" was "the best that has been thought and said in the world" and also an individual person's relation to this body of thought and expression. My own use of the word in this essay is not Arnold's.

not the least disposition to propose that science be slighted in education. Quite apart from its practical value, scientific knowledge is naturally a delight to the mind, no doubt engaging certain mental temperaments more than others but holding out the promise of intellectual pleasure to all. Yet of itself science does not, as Arnold put it, "serve" the instinct for conduct and the instinct for beauty, or at least it does not serve these instincts as they exist in most men. This service, which includes the relating of scientific knowledge to the whole life of man, is rendered by culture, which is not to be thought of as confined to literature—to *belles lettres*—but as comprising all the humane intellectual disciplines. When Dr. Leavis asserts the primacy of the humanities in education, he refers more exclusively to literature than Arnold did, but in general effect his position is the same.

It may seem strange, and a little tiresome, that the debate of eighty years ago should be instituted again today. Yet it is perhaps understandable in view of the "scientific revolution" about which Sir Charles tells us. This revolution would seem to be one of the instances in which a change of quantity becomes a change in kind—science can now do so much more and do it so much more quickly than it could a generation ago, let alone in the last century, that it has been transmuted from what the world has hitherto known. One of the consequences of this charge—to Sir Charles it is the most salient of all possible consequences—is the new social hope that is now held out to us, of life made better in material respects, not merely in certain highly developed countries but all over the world and among peoples that at the moment are, by Western standards, scarcely developed at all.

The new power of science perhaps justifies a contemporary revival of the Victorian question. But if we consent to involve ourselves in the new dialectic of the old controversy, we must be aware that we are not addressing ourselves to a question of educational theory, or to an abstract contention as to what kind of knowledge has the truest affinity with the human soul. We approach these matters only to pass through them. What we address ourselves to is politics, and politics of a quite ultimate kind, and to the disposition of the modern mind.

. . . . **II**

The Two Cultures has had a very considerable currency in England and America ever since its publication in 1959, and in England it was for a time the subject of lively discussion. Indeed, the general agreement in England that it was a statement of great importance, to the point of its being used as an assigned text in secondary schools, was what aroused Dr. Leavis to make his assault on the lecture this long after the first interest in it had subsided. The early discussions of *The Two Cultures* were of a substantive kind, but the concerns which now agitate the English in response to Dr. Leavis's attack have scarcely anything to do with literature and science, or with education, or with social hope. These matters have now been made a mere subordinate element in what amounts to a scandal over a breach of manners. The published comments on Dr. Leavis's attack on *The Two Cultures* were, with few exceptions, directed to such considerations as the exact degree of monstrousness which Dr. Leavis achieved in speaking of Sir Charles as he did; whether or not he spoke out of envy of Sir Charles's reputation; whether or not he has, or deserves to have, any real standing as a critic; or writes acceptable English; or represents, as he claims he does, "the essential Cambridge."

Dr. Leavis's Richmond Lecture, "The Significance of C. P. Snow," was delivered in the Hall of Downing College, Cambridge, on February 28 and published in the *Spectator* of March 9.* In the next week's issue of the *Spectator*, seventeen letters appeared, all defending Snow and most of them expressing anger at, or contempt for, Leavis. The following week brought fifteen more communications, of which eight expressed partisanship with Leavis; several of these deplored the tone of the previous week's correspondence. Many of the correspondents who defended Snow were of distinguished reputation; of the defenders of Leavis, the only one known to me was Mr. Geoffrey Wagner, who wrote from America to communicate his belief that the attack on Snow was much needed, for, despite a parody in *New Left Review* in which Snow appears as C. P. Sleet, despite, too, his own adverse criticism of Snow in the *Critic,* "the hosannas obediently continued on this side of the Atlantic, both from the Barzun-Trilling syndrome and the Book-of-the-Month Club, the worst of both worlds, as it were." Three of the writers of the Snow party touched upon the question of literature and science, the scientist J. D. Bernal, the historian of science Stephen Toulmin, and the literary critic G. S. Fraser. In a miasma of personality-mongering, their letters afforded a degree of relief, but they said little that was of consequence. Of the Leavis party two dons of the University of Birmingham in a joint letter touched rapidly but with some cogency on the relation between literature and science, deploring any attempt to prefer one above the other, concluding that if one must be preferred, it should be, for reasons not stated, literature.

From the *Spectator* letters, so many of them expressing small and rather untidy passions, there are no doubt conclusions to be drawn, of a sufficiently depressing sort, about the condition of cultural life at the

---

* In an editorial note, Dr. Leavis is quoted as saying, "The lecture was private and representatives of the press who inquired were informed that there was no admission and that no reporting was to be permitted. The appearance in newspapers of garbled reports has made it desirable that the lecture should appear in full."

moment. But no awareness that we may have of the generally bad state of intellectual affairs ought to blind us to the particular fault of Dr. Leavis in his treatment of Sir Charles Snow. Intelligent and serious himself, Dr. Leavis has in this instance been the cause of stupidity and triviality in other men.

There can be no two opinions about the tone in which Dr. Leavis deals with Sir Charles. It is a bad tone, an impermissible tone. It is bad in a personal sense because it is cruel—it manifestly intends to wound. It is bad intellectually because by its use Dr. Leavis has diverted attention, his own included, from the matter he sought to illuminate. The doctrine of *The Two Cultures* is a momentous one and Dr. Leavis obscures its massive significance by bringing into consideration such matters as Sir Charles's abilities as a novelist, his club membership, his opinion of his own talents, his worldly success, and his relation to worldly power. Anger, scorn, and an excessive consciousness of persons have always been elements of Dr. Leavis's thought—of the very process of his thought, not merely of his manner of expressing it. They were never exactly reassuring elements, but they could be set aside and made to seem of relatively small account in comparison with the remarkable cogency in criticism which Dr. Leavis so often achieved. But as they now appear in his valedictory address—for, in effect, that is what the Richmond Lecture was, since Dr. Leavis retires this year from his university post—they cannot be easily set aside, they stand in the way of what Dr. Leavis means to say.

And, indeed, our understanding of what he means to say is to be derived less from the passionate utterance of the lecture itself than from our knowledge of the whole direction of his career in criticism. That direction was from the first determined by Dr. Leavis's belief that the human faculty above all others to which literature addresses itself is the moral consciousness, which is also the source of all successful creation, the very root of poetic genius. The extent of his commitment to this idea results in what I believe to be a fault in his critical thought—he does not give anything like adequate recognition to those aspects of art which are gratuitous, which arise from high spirits and the impulse to play. One would suppose that the moral consciousness should, for its own purposes, take account of those aspects of art and life that do not fall within its dominion. But if the intensity of Dr. Leavis's commitment to the moral consciousness contrives to produce this deficiency of understanding, it is no less responsible for the accuracy and force which we recognize as the positive characteristics of his work. For Dr. Leavis, literature is what Matthew Arnold said it is, *the criticism of life*—he can understand it in no other way. Both in all its simplicity and in all its hidden complexity, he has made Arnold's saying his own, and from it he has drawn his strength.

If, then, Dr. Leavis now speaks with a very special intensity in response to *The Two Cultures*, we must do him the justice of seeing that the Rede Lecture denies, and in an extreme way, all that he has ever believed about literature—it is, in fact, nothing less than an indictment of literature on social and moral grounds. It represents literature as constituting a danger to the national well-being, and most especially when it is overtly a criticism of life.

Not only because Charles Snow is himself a practitioner of literature but also because he is the man he is, the statement that his lecture has this purport will be shocking and perhaps it will be thought scarcely credible. And I have no doubt that, in another mood and on some other occasion, Sir Charles would be happy to assert the beneficient powers of literature. But there can be no other interpretation of his lecture than that it takes toward literature a position of extreme antagonism.

The Two Cultures begins as an objective statement of the lack of communication between scientists and literary men. This is a circumstance that must have been often observed and often deplored. Perhaps nothing in our culture is so characteristic as the separateness of the various artistic and intellectual professions. As between, say, poets and painters, or musicans and architects, there is very little discourse, and perhaps the same thing could be remarked of scientists of different interests, say biologists and physicists. But the isolation of literary men from scientists may well seem to be the most extreme of these separations, if only because it is the most significant, for a reason which Sir Charles entirely understands: the especially close though never clearly defined relation of these two professions with our social and political life.

The even-handedness with which Sir Charles at first describes the split between the two "cultures" does not continue for long. He begins by telling us that scientists and literary men are equally to blame for the separation—they are kept apart by "a gulf of mutual incomprehension," by distorted images of each other which give rise to dislike and hostility. But as Sir Charles's lecture proceeds, it becomes plain that, although the scientists do have certain crudities and limitations, they are in general in the right of things and the literary men in the wrong of them. The matter which causes the scales to shift thus suddenly is the human condition. This, Sir Charles tells us, is of its nature tragic: man dies, and he dies alone. But the awareness of the ineluctably tragic nature of human life makes a moral trap, "for it tempts one to sit back, complacent in one's unique tragedy," paying no heed to the circumstances of everyday life, which, for the larger number of human beings, are painful. It is the literary men, we are told, who are the most likely, the scientists who are the least likely, to fall into this moral trap; the scientists "are inclined to be impatient to see if something can be done: and inclined to think that it can be done, until it's proved otherwise." It is their spirit, "tough and good and determined to fight it out at the side of their brother men," which has "made scientists regard the other [i.e. the literary] culture's social attitudes as contemptible."

"This is too facile," Sir Charles says in mild rebuke of the scientists, by which he of course means that essentially they are right. There follows a brief consideration of a question raised not by Sir Charles in his own person but by "a scientist of distinction" whom he quotes: Yeats, Pound, Wyndham Lewis, nine out of ten of those who have dominated literary sensibility in our time, weren't they not only politically silly, but politically wicked? Didn't the influence of all they represent bring Auschwitz that much nearer?" And Sir Charles in answer grants that Yeats was a magnanimous man and a great poet, but he will not, he says, defend the indefensible—"the facts . . . are broadly true." Sir Charles in general agrees, that is, that the literary sensibility of our time brought Auschwitz nearer. He goes on to say that things have changed considerably in the literary life in recent years, even if slowly, for "literature changes more slowly than science."

From the mention of Auschwitz onward, the way is open to the full assertion by Sir Charles of the virtues of the scientists. Although they are admitted to be sometimes gauche or stupidly self-assertive, although Sir Charles concedes of some of them that "the whole literature of the traditional culture doesn't seem relevant to [their] interests" and that, as a result, their "imaginative understanding" is diminished, he yet finds them to be men of a natural decency; they are free from racial feelings, they are lovers of equality, they are cooperative. And chief among their virtues, as Sir Charles describes them, is the fact that they "have the future in their bones."

Indeed, it turns out that it is the future, and not mere ignorance of each other's professional concerns, that makes the separation between the culture of science and the culture of literature. Scientists have the future in their bones. Literary men do not. Quite the contrary—"If the scientists have the future in their bones, then the traditional culture responds by wishing that the future did not exist." The future that the scientists have in their bones is understood to be nothing but a good future; it is very much like the History of the Marxists, which is always the triumph of the right, never possibly the record of defeat. In fact, to entertain the idea that the future might be bad is represented as being tantamount to moral ill-will—in a note appended to the sentence I have just quoted, Sir Charles speaks of George Orwell's *1984* as "the strongest possible wish that the future shall not exist."

It is difficult to credit the implications of this astonishing remark and to ascribe them to Sir Charles. As everyone recalls, Orwell's novel is an imagination of the condition of the world if the authoritarian tendencies which are to be observed in the present develop themselves—logically, as it were—in the future, the point being that it is quite within the range of possibility that this ultimate development should take place. In Orwell's representation of an absolute tyranny, science has a part, and a polemical partisan of science might understand this as the evidence of a literary man's malice toward science. But it is much more likely that, when Orwell imagined science as one of the instruments of repression, he meant to say that science, like everything else that is potentially good, like literature itself, can be perverted and debased to the ends of tyranny. Orwell was a man who, on the basis of actual and painful experience, tried to tell the truth about politics, even his own politics. I believe that he never gave up his commitment to socialism, but he refused to be illusioned in any way he could prevent; it lay within the reach of his mind to conceive that even an idealistic politics, perhaps especially an idealistic politics, can pervert itself. To say of such a man that he wishes that the future—the presumably good future—shall not exist is like saying that intelligence wishes that the future shall not exist.

Having characterized the culture of literature, or, as he sometimes calls it, "the traditional culture," by its hostility to the future, Sir Charles goes on to say that "it is the traditional culture, to an extent remarkably little diminished by the emergence of the scientific one, which manages the western world." This being so, it follows that the traditional culture must be strictly dealt with if the future is to be brought into being: what is called "the existing pattern" must be not merely changed but "broken." Only if this is done shall we be able to educate ourselves as we should. As for the need to educate ourselves: "To say, we have to educate ourselves or perish is perhaps a little more melodramatic than the facts warrant. To say, we have to educate ourselves or watch a steep decline in our lifetime is about right." And Sir Charles indicates our possible fate by the instance—he calls it an "historical myth"—of the Venetian Republic in its last half century. "Its citizens had become rich, as we did, by accident. They had acquired immense political skill, just as we have. A good many of them were tough-minded, realistic, patriotic men. They knew, just as clearly as we know, that the current of history had begun to flow against them. Many of them gave their minds to working out ways to keep going. It would have meant breaking the pattern into which they had been crystallized. They were fond of the pattern, just as we are fond of ours. They never found the will to break it."

I quoted without comment Sir Charles's statement of the idea on which, we may say, the whole argument of *The Two Cultures* is based: "It is the traditional culture, to an extent remarkably little diminished

by the emergence of the scientific one, which manages the western world."
It is a bewildering statement. In what way can we possibly understand it?
That the Western world is managed by some agency which is traditional
is of course comprehensible. And we can take in the idea that this agency
may be described, for particular purposes of explanation, in terms of a
certain set of mind, a general tendency of thought and feeling which,
being pervasive, is hard to formulate, and that this is to be called "a culture." But for Sir Charles, the words "traditional" and "literary" are inter-
changeable, and that this culture, as we agree to call it, is *literary*, that it
bears the same relation to actual literary men and their books that what
is called the "scientific culture" bears to scientists and their work in laboratories, is truly a staggering thought. The actions of parliaments and
congresses and cabinets in directing the massive affairs of state, the nego-
tiations of embassies, the movement of armies and fleets, the establishment of huge scientific projects for the contrivance of armaments and of
factories for the production of them, the promises made to citizens, and
the choices made by voters at the polls—these, we are asked to believe,
are in the charge of the culture of literature. What can this mean?

It can of course be said that literature has some part in the management of the Western world, a part which is limited but perhaps not
wholly unimportant. If, for example, we compare the present condition
of industrial England with the condition of industrial England in the
early 19th century, we can say that the present condition is not, in human
respects, anything like what men of good will might wish it to be, but
that it is very much better than it was in the early years of the Industrial
Revolution. And if we then ask what agencies brought about the improvement, we can say that one of them was literature. Certain literary men
raised the "Condition of England Question" in a passionate and effective
way and their names are still memorable to us—Coleridge, Carlyle, Mill
(I take him to be a man of letters; he was certainly a good literary critic),
Dickens, Ruskin, Arnold, William Morris. They made their effect only
upon individuals, but the individuals they touched were numerous, and
by what they said they made it ever harder for people to be indifferent
to the misery around them or to the degradation of the national life in
which they came to think themselves implicated. These literary men
helped materially, some would say decisively, to bring about a change in
the state of affairs. This is not exactly management, but it is a directing
influence such as literature in the modern time often undertakes to have
and sometimes does have.

Yet in Sir Charles's opinion this directing influence of the literary
men of the 19th century deserves no praise. On the contrary, his description of their work is but another count in the indictment of the culture

of literature. Speaking of the response which literary men made to the Industrial Revolution, he says, "Almost everywhere ... intellectual persons did not comprehend what was happening. Certainly the writers didn't. Plenty of them shuddered away, as though the right course for a man of feeling was to contract out; some, like Ruskin and William Morris and Thoreau and Emerson and Lawrence, tried various kinds of fancies, which were not much in effect more than screams of horror. It is hard to think of a writer of high class who really stretched his imaginative sympathy, who could see at once the hideous back-streets, the smoking chimneys, the internal price—and also the prospects of life that were opening out for the poor. . . ."

Nothing could be further from the truth. No great English writer of the 19th century, once he had become aware of the Industrial Revolution, ever contracted out. This is not the place to rehearse the miseries that were acquiesced in by those who comforted the world and their own consciences with the thought of "the prospects of life that were opening out for the poor." It is enough to say that there were miseries in plenty, of a brutal and horrifying kind, by no means adequately suggested by phrases like "the hideous back-streets, the smoking chimneys, the internal price." (Auschwitz, since it has been mentioned, may be thought of as the development of the conditions of the factories and mines of the earlier Industrial Revolution.) If the writers "shuddered away," it was not in maidenly disgust with machines and soot; if they uttered "screams of horror," it was out of moral outrage at what man had made of man—and of women and little children. Their emotions were no different from those expressed by Karl Marx in his chapter on the Working Day, nor from those expressed in Blue Books by the factory inspectors, those remarkable men of the middle class whom Marx, in a moving passage of *Capital,* praises and wonders at for their transcendence of their class feelings.

I have mentioned Matthew Arnold among those writers who made the old conditions of the Industrial Revolution ever less possible. Like many of his colleagues in this undertaking, he did entertain "fancies"— they all found modern life ugly and fatiguing and in some way false, and they set store by certain qualities which are no doubt traditional to the point of being archaic.* But Arnold's peculiar distinction as a literary critic is founded on the strong sensitivity of his response to the modern situation. He uniquely understood what Hegel had told the world, that

---

* Emerson doesn't deserve Sir Charles's scorn on this point. His advice to the American scholar was that he should respond positively to the actual and the modern, and he was inclined to take an almost too unreserved pleasure in new forms of human energy and ingenuity. As for Thoreau, his quarrel was not with factories but with farms—and families.

the French Revolution marked an absolute change in the condition of man. For the first time in history, Hegel said, Reason—or Idea, or Theory, or Creative Imagination—had become decisive in human destiny. Arnold's argument in "Literature and Science" was the affirmation of the French Revolution; he was speaking on behalf of the illumination and refinement of that Reason by which man might shape the conditions of his own existence. This is the whole purport of his famous statement, "Literature is the criticism of life."

That saying used to have a rough time of it, perhaps because people found the word criticism narrow and dour and wished to believe that life was worthier of being celebrated than criticized. But less and less, I think, will anyone find the ground on which to quarrel with it. Whatever else we also take literature to be, it must always, for us now, be the criticism of life.

But it would seem to be precisely the critical function of literature that troubles Sir Charles. And perhaps that is why, despite all that he says about the need to educate ourselves, he does not make a single substantive proposal about education.

If we undertake to say what the purpose of modern education is, our answer will surely be suggested by Arnold's phrase, together with the one by which he defined the particular function of criticism: "to see the object as in itself it really is." Whenever we undertake to pass judgment on an educational enterprise, the import of these two phrases serves as our criterion: we ask that education supply the means for a criticism of life and teach the student to try to see the object as in itself it really is. Yet when Sir Charles speaks of the need to break the "existing pattern" and to go on to a right education, he does not touch upon any such standard of judgment. Although he would seem to be the likeliest person in the world to speak intelligently about the instruction in science of students who do not intend to be scientists, actually he says nothing more on the subject than that ignorance of the Second Law of Thermodynamics is equivalent to ignorance of Shakespeare, or that the Yang-Lee experiment at Columbia should have been a topic of general conversation at college High Tables.

Nor does he propose anything for the education of the scientist, except, of course, science. He does say that scientists need to be "trained not only in scientific but in human terms," but he does not say how. Scientists—but eventually one begins to wonder if they are really scientists and not advanced technologists and engineers—are to play a decisive part in the affairs of mankind, but nowhere does Sir Charles suggest that, if this is so, they will face difficulties and perplexities and that their education should include the study of books—they need not be "literary," they need not be "traditional": they might be contemporary works of history, sociology, anthropology, psychology, philosophy—which would raise the difficult questions and propose the tragic complexity of the human condition, which would suggest that it is not always easy to see the object as in itself it really is.

Well, it isn't beyond belief that a professional corps of high intellectual quality, especially if it is charged with great responsibility, should learn to ask its own questions and go on to make its own ethos, perhaps a very good one. But Sir Charles would seem to be asking for more than the right of scientists to go their own way. What he seems to require for scientists is the right to go their own way *with no questions asked*. The culture of literature, having done its worst, must now be supplanted and is not ever to play the part of a loyal opposition. How else are we to understand Sir Charles's contempt for the irresponsibility of the literary mind, his curious representation of the literary culture as having the management of the Western world, that is to say, as being answerable for all the anomalies, stupidities, and crimes of the Western world, for having made the "existing pattern" which must now be broken if the West is to survive or at least not suffer steep decline? It is manifest that the literary culture has lost the right to ask questions.

No one could possibly suppose of Charles Snow that he is a man who wants to curtail the rights of free criticism. The line which he takes in *The Two Cultures* is so far from the actuality of his temperament in this respect that we can only suppose that he doesn't mean it, not in all the extravagance of its literalness. Or we suppose that he means it at the behest of some large preoccupation of whose goodness he is so entirely convinced that he will seek to affirm it even in ways that would take him aback if the preoccupation were not in control of his thought. And this, I think, is the case. I believe that the position of *The Two Cultures* is to be explained by Sir Charles's preoccupation—it has become almost the best-known thing about him—with a good and necessary aim, with the assuring of peace, which is to say, with the compounding of the differences between the West and the Soviet Union. It is an aim which, in itself, can of course only do Sir Charles credit, yet it would seem to have implicit in it a strange desperate method of implementing itself.

For the real message of *The Two Cultures* is that an understanding between the West and the Soviet Union could be achieved by the culture of scientists, which reaches over factitious national and ideological differences. The field of agreement would be the scientists' common perception of the need for coming together to put the possibilities of the scientific revolution at the disposal of the disadvantaged of all nations. The bond between scientists, Sir Charles has told us, is virtually biological: they all have the future in their bones. Science brings men together in despite of all barriers—speaking of the way in which the very wide differences in the class origins of English scientists were overcome to make the scientific culture of England (and seeming to imply that this is a unique grace of scientists, that English men of letters never had differences of class to overcome), Sir Charles says, "Without thinking about it, they respond alike. That is what a culture means." And in the same way, "without thinking about it," the scientists of the West and the scientists of the Soviet Union may be expected to "respond alike." And, since "that is what a culture means," they will have joined together in an entity which will do what governments have not done, the work of relieving the misery of the world. But in the degree to which science naturally unites men, literature separates them, and the scientists of the world cannot form this beneficent entity until we of the West break the existing pattern of our traditional culture, the literary culture, which is self-regarding in its complacent acceptance of tragedy, which is not only indifferent to human suffering but willing to inflict it, which asks rude and impertinent questions about the present and even about the future.

It is a point of view that must, I suppose, in desperate days, have a show of reason. In desperate days, it always seems wise to throw something or someone overboard, preferably Jonah or Arion, the prophet or the poet. Mr. G. S. Fraser, for example, seems to understand what Sir Charles wants, and he is rather willing to go along with him, rather open to the idea that the achievement of peace may require some adverse judgment on literature. "It does not matter," he says, "whether we save the real Cambridge within the actual Cambridge . . .; what we want to save is our actual human world with all the spots on it. This will not be done by teaching English at universities; men like Snow, at home both in Russia and America, and in a simple blunt way trying to teach these two blunt simple giants to understand each other may in the end prove greater benefactors than Dr. Leavis."

No, the world will not be saved by teaching English at universities, nor, indeed, by any other literary activity. It is very hard to say what will save the world, and pretty surely it is no one single thing. But we can be perfectly certain that the world will not be saved by denying the actualities of the world. Among these actualities politics is one. And it can be said of *The Two Cultures* that it communicates the strongest possible wish that we should forget about politics. It mentions national politics once, speaking of it as the clog upon the activity of scientists, as the impeding circumstance in which they must work. But the point is not developed and the lecture has the effect of suggesting that the issue is not between the abilities and good intentions of scientists and the inertia or bad will of governments; the issue is represented as being between the good culture of science and the bad culture of literature.

In this denial of the actuality of politics, Sir Charles is at one with the temper of intellectuals today—we all want politics not to exist, we all want that statement of Hegel's to be absolutely and immediately true, we dream of Reason taking over the whole management of the world, and soon. No doubt a beneficent eventuality, but our impatience for it is dangerous if it leads us to deny the actuality of politics in the present. While we discuss, at Sir Charles's instance, the relative merits of scientific Philosopher Kings as against literary Philosopher Kings, politics goes on living its own autonomous life, of which one aspect is its massive resistance to Reason. What is gained by describing the resistance to Reason as other than it is, by thinking in the specious terms of two opposing "cultures"?

But of course the fact is that politics is not finally autonomous. It may be so massively resistant to Reason that we are led to think of its resistance as absolute—in bad times we conceive politics to be nothing but power. Yet it cannot be said—at least not so long as politics relies in any degree upon ideology—that politics is never susceptible to such Reason as is expressed in opinion, only that it is less susceptible in some nations and at some times than in other nations and at other times. And nowhere and at no time is politics exempt from moral judgment, whether or not that judgment is effectual. But if we make believe, as *The Two Cultures* does, that politics does not exist at all, then it cannot be the object of moral judgment. And if we deny all authority to literature, as *The Two Cultures* does, going so far as to say that the great traditional agency of moral awareness is itself immoral, then the very activity of moral judgment is impugned, except for that single instance of it which asserts the rightness of bringing the benefits of science to the disadvantaged of the world. In short, Sir Charles, seeking to advance the cause of understanding between the West and the Soviet Union, would seem to be saying that this understanding will come if we conceive both that politics cannot be judged (because it does not really exist) and that it should not be judged (because the traditional agency of judgment is irresponsible).

. . . . **III**

I judge *The Two Cultures* to be a book which is mistaken in a very large way indeed. And I find the failure of Dr. Leavis's criticism of it to consist in his addressing himself not to the full extent of its error but to extraneous matters. From reading the Richmond Lecture one gains the impression that the substance of the Rede Lecture is extremely offensive to Dr. Leavis, that all his sensibilities are outraged by it: we conclude that Sir Charles wants something which is very different from what Dr. Leavis wants, and that Dr. Leavis thinks that what Sir Charles wants is crude and vulgar. But we can scarcely suppose from Dr. Leavis's response that what Sir Charles says has a very wide reference—for all we can tell, he might have been proposing a change in the university curriculum which Dr. Leavis is repelling with the violence and disgust that are no doubt often felt though not expressed at meetings of curriculum committees. For Dr. Leavis, who has always attached great importance to educational matters, the proposed change is certainly important beyond the university. He understands it both as likely to have a bad effect on the national culture and as being the expression of something already bad in the national culture. But this, we suppose, he would feel about any change in the curriculum.

In short, Dr. Leavis, in dealing with the Rede Lecture, has not seen the object as in itself it really is, just as Sir Charles, in dealing with the culture of literature in its relation to politics, has not seen the object as in itself it really is.

An example of the inadequacy of Dr. Leavis's criticism of *The Two Cultures* is his response to what Sir Charles says, in concert with the distinguished scientist, about the political posture of the great writers of the modern period. That statement, if we stop short of its mention of Auschwitz—which makes a most important modification—certainly does have a color of truth. It is one of the cultural curiosities of the first three decades of the 20th century that, while the educated people, the readers of books, tended to become ever more liberal and radical in their thought, there is no literary figure of the very first rank (although many of the next rank) who, in his work, makes use of or gives credence to liberal or radical ideas. I remarked on this circumstance in an essay of 1946. "Our educated class," I said, "has a ready if mild suspiciousness of the profit motive, a belief in progress, science, social legislation, planning, and international cooperation, perhaps especially where Russia is in question. These beliefs do great credit to those who hold them. Yet it is a comment, if not on our beliefs then on our way of holding them, that not a single first-rate writer has emerged to deal with these ideas, and the emotions that are consonant with them, in a great literary way.... If we name those writers who, by the general consent of the most serious criticism, by consent too of the very class of educated people of which we speak, are thought of as the monumental figures of our time, we see that to these writers the liberal ideology has been at best a matter of indifference. Proust, Joyce, Lawrence, Yeats, Mann [as novelist], Kafka, Rilke, Gide [also as novelist]—all of them have their own love of justice and the good life, but in not one of them does it take the form of a love of the ideas and emotions which liberal democracy, as known by our educated class, has declared respectable." To which it can be added that some great writers have in their work given credence or utterance to conservative and even reactionary ideas, and that some in their personal lives maintained a settled indifference to all political issues, or a disdain of them. No reader is likely to derive political light either from the works or the table-talk of a modern literary genius, and some readers (of weak mind) might even be led into bad political ways.

If these writers are to be brought to the bar of judgment, anyone who speaks as their advocate is not, as Sir Charles says, defending the indefensible. The advocacy can be conducted in honest and simple ways. It is not one of these ways to say that literature is by its nature or by definition innocent—it is powerful enough for us to suppose that it has the possibility of doing harm. But the ideational influence of literature is by no means always as direct as, for polemical purposes, people some- times say it is. As against the dismay of Sir Charles and the distinguished scientist at the reactionary tendencies of modern literary geniuses, there is the fact—a bald one—that the English poets who learned their trade from Yeats and Eliot, or even from Pound, have notably had no sympathy with the social ideas and attitudes of their poetical masters.

Every university teacher of literature will have observed the circum- stance that young people who are of radical social and political opinion are virtually never troubled by the opposed views or the settled indiffer- ence of the great modern writers. This is not because the young exempt the writer from dealing with the serious problems of living, or because they see him through a mere aesthetic haze. It is because they know—and quite without instruction—that, in D. H. Lawrence's words, they are to trust the tale and not the teller of the tale. They perceive that the tale is always on the side of their own generous impulses. They know that, if the future is in the bones of anyone, it is in the bones of the literary genius, and exactly because the present is in his bones, exactly because the past is in his bones. They know that if a work of literature has any true artistic existence, it has value as a criticism of life; in whatever com- plex way it has chosen to speak, it is making a declaration about the qualities that life should have, about the qualities life does not have but should have. They feel, I think, that it is simply not possible for a work of literature that comes within the borders of greatness *not* to ask for more energy and fineness of life, and, by its own communication of aware- ness, bring these qualities into being. And if, in their experience of such a work, they happen upon an expression of contempt for some idea which they have connected with political virtue, they are not slow to under- stand that it is not the idea in its ideal form that is being despised, but the idea as it passes current in specious form, among certain and par- ticular persons. I have yet to meet the student committed to an altruistic politics who is alienated from Stephen Daedalus by that young man's disgust with political idealism, just as I have yet to meet the student from the most disadvantaged background who feels debarred from what Yeats can give him by the poet's slurs upon shopkeepers or by anything else in his inexhaustible fund of snobbery.

If ever a man was qualified to state the case for literature, and far more persuasively than I have done, it is Dr. Leavis. His career as a critic and a teacher has been devoted exactly to the exposition of the idea that literature presents to us "the possibilities of life," the qualities of energy and fineness that life might have. And it is, of course, the intention of the Richmond Lecture to say just this in answer to Sir Charles's indictment. Yet something checks Dr. Leavis. When it is a question of the defense, not of literature in general, but of modern literature, he puts into counter-vailing evidence nothing more than a passage in which Lawrence says something, in a wry and grudging way, on behalf of social equality. This does not meet the charge; against it Sir Charles might cite a dozen instances in which Lawrence utters what Sir Charles—and perhaps even Dr. Leavis himself—would consider "the most imbecile expressions of anti-social feeling."

There is only one feasible approach to the anti-social utterances of many modern writers, and that is to consider whether their expressions of anti-social feeling are nothing but imbecile. It is the fact, like it or not, that a characteristic cultural enterprise of our time has been the questioning of society itself, not its particular forms and aspects but its very essence. To this extreme point has the criticism of life extended itself. Of the ways of dealing with this phenomenon, that of horror and dismay, such as Sir Charles's, is perhaps the least useful. Far better, it seems to me, is the effort to understand what this passionate hostility to society implies, to ask whether it is a symptom, sufficiently gross, of the decline of the West, or whether it is not perhaps an act of critical energy on the part of the West, an act of critical energy on the part of society itself— the effort of society to identify in itself that which is but speciously good, the effort to understand afresh the nature of the life it is designed to foster. I would not anticipate the answer, but these questions make, I am sure, the right way to come at the phenomenon.

It is not the way that Dr. Leavis comes at the phenomenon, despite his saying that the university study of literature must take its stand on the "intellectual-cultural frontier." Of the two D. H. Lawrences, the one who descended from the social-minded 19th century and who did, in some sort, affirm the social idea, and the other, for whom the condition of salvation was the total negation of society, Dr. Leavis can be comfortable only with the former. For the fact is that his commitment to the intellectual-cultural frontier is sincere but chiefly theoretical; he has, as is well known, sympathy with very few modern writers, and he therefore cannot in good grace come to their defense against Sir Charles's characterization of them.

Mr. Walter Allen, writing in the *New York Times Book Review*, has accurately remarked on "the common areas of agreement" between Dr. Leavis and Sir Charles. "One would expect . . . that Snow would be sympathetic to Leavis's emphasis on the all-importance of the moral center of literature," Mr. Allen says. "Both have attacked experiment in literature. Neither of them, to put it into crude shorthand, are Flaubert-and-Joyce men." The similarities go further. In point of social background the two men are not much apart, at least to the untutored American eye. Both spring from the provincial middle class in one or another of its strata, and whatever differences there may have been in the material advantages that were available or lacking to one or the other, neither was reared in the assumption of easy privilege. From these origins they derived, we may imagine, their strong sense of quotidian actuality and a respect for those who discharge the duties it imposes, and a high regard for the domestic affections, a quick dislike of the frivolous and merely elegant. Neither, as I have suggested, has any least responsiveness to the tendencies of modern thought or literature which are existential or subversive. A lively young person of advanced tastes would surely say that if ever two men were committed to England, Home, and Duty, they are Leavis and Snow—he would say that in this they are as alike as two squares.

There is one other regard, an especially significant one, in which they are similar. This is their feeling about social class. One of the chief interests of Sir Charles's novels is their explicitness about class as a determinative of the personal life, and in this respect *The Two Cultures* is quite as overt as the novels—its scientists make a new class by virtue of their alienation from the old class attitudes, and Sir Charles's identification of literary men with the traditional culture which supposedly manages the Western world implies that they are in effect the representatives of an aristocratic ruling class, decadent but still powerful. The work of Dr. Leavis is no less suffused by the idea of social class, even though its preoccupation with the subject is far less explicit. To my recollection, Dr. Leavis does not make use of any of the words which denote the distinctions of English society—he does not refer to an aristocracy, a gentry, an upper-middle or lower-middle or working class. For him a class defines itself by its idea of itself—that is, by its tastes and style. Class is for him a cultural entity. And when he conceives of class power, as he often does, it is not economic or political power but, rather, cultural power that he thinks of. It is true that cultural power presents itself to his mind as being in some way suggestive of class power, but the actualities of power or influence are for him always secondary to the culture from which they arose or to which they give rise.

And indeed, no less than Sir Charles, Dr. Leavis is committed to the creation of a new class. This, we might even say, is the whole motive of his work. The social situation he would seem to assume is one in which there is a fair amount of mobility which is yet controlled and limited by the tendency of the mobile people to allow themselves to be absorbed into one of the traditional classes. As against the attraction exerted by a quasi-aristocratic, metropolitan upper-middle class, Dr. Leavis has taken it to be his function to organize the mobile people, those of them who are gifted and conscious, into a new social class formed on the basis of its serious understanding of and response to literature, chiefly English literature. In this undertaking he has by no means been wholly unsuccessful. One has the impression that many of the students he has trained think of themselves, as they take up their posts in secondary schools and universities, as constituting at least a social cadre.

The only other time I wrote about Dr. Leavis I remarked that the Cromwellian Revolution had never really come to an end in England and that Dr. Leavis was one of the chief colonels of the Roundhead party. His ideal readers are people who "are seriously interested in literature," and it is on their behalf that he wages war against a cultural-social class which, when it concerns itself with literature, avows its preference for the qualities of grace, lightness, and irony, and deprecates an overt sincerity and seriousness. "To a polished nation," said Gibbon, "poetry is an amusement of the fancy, not a passion of the soul," and all through his career it is against everything that Gibbon means by a polished nation and might mean by a polished class that Dr. Leavis has set his face. Bloomsbury has been his characteristic antagonist. But now, in Charles Snow, he confronts an opponent who is as Roundhead as himself, and as earnest and *intentional*.

To this confrontation Dr. Leavis is not adequate. It is not an adequate response to the massive intention of *The Two Cultures* for Dr. Leavis to meet Sir Charles's cultural preferences with his own preferences; or to seek to discredit Sir Charles's ideas chiefly by making them out to be vulgar ideas or outmoded (Wellsian) ideas; or to offer, as against Sir Charles's vision of a future made happier by science, the charms of primitive peoples "with their marvellous arts and skills and vital intelligence." I do not mean to say that Dr. Leavis does not know where Sir Charles goes wrong in the details of his argument—he is as clear as we expect him to be in rebuking that quite massive blunder about the Victorian writers. Nor, certainly, do I mean that Dr. Leavis does not know what the great fundamental mistake of Sir Charles's position is—he does, and he can be eloquent in asserting against a simplistic confidence in a scientific "future" the need of mankind, in the face of a rapid advance of science and technology, "to be in full intelligent possession of its full humanity (and 'possession' here means, not confident ownership of that which belongs to *us*—our property, but a basic living deference towards that to which, opening as it does into the unknown and itself immeasurable, we know we belong)." But such moments of largeness do not save the Richmond Lecture from its general aspect of dealing with an issue that is essentially parochial. For example, of the almost limitless political implications of Sir Charles's position it gives no evidence of awareness. And if we undertake to find a reason for the inadequacy of Dr. Leavis's response, we will find, I think, that it is the same as the reason which accounts for Sir Charles having been in the first place so wholly mistaken in what he says—both men set too much store by the idea of *culture* as a category of thought.

The concept of culture is an idea of great attractiveness and undoubted usefulness. We may say that it begins in the assumption that all human expressions or artifacts are indicative of some considerable tendencies in the life of social groups or sub-groups, and that what is indicative is also causative—all cultural facts have their consequences. To think in cultural terms is to consider human expressions not only in their overt existence and avowed intention, but in, as it were, their secret life, taking cognizance of the desires and impulses which lie behind the open formulation. In the judgments which we make when we think in the category of culture we rely to a very large extent upon the style in which an expression is made, believing that style will indicate, or betray, what is not intended to be expressed. The aesthetic mode is integral to the idea of culture, and our judgments of social groups are likely to be made chiefly on an aesthetic basis—we like or do not like what we call their life-styles, and even when we judge moralities, the criterion by which we choose between two moralities of, say, equal strictness or equal laxness is likely to be an aesthetic one.

The concept of culture affords to those who use it a sense of the liberation of their thought, for they deal less with abstractions and mere objects, more with the momentous actualities of human feelings as these shape and condition the human community, as they make and as they indicate the quality of man's existence. Not the least of the attractions of the cultural mode of thought are the passions which attend it—because it assumes that all things are causative or indicative of the whole of the cultural life, it proposes to us those intensities of moralized feeling which seem appropriate to our sense that all that is good in life is at stake in every cultural action. An instance of mediocrity or failure in art or thought is not only what it is but also a sin, deserving to be treated as such. These passions are vivifying; they have the semblance of heroism.

And if we undertake to say what were the circumstances that made the cultural mode of thought as available and as authoritative as it now is, we must refer to Marx, and to Freud, and to the general movement of existentialism, to all that the tendencies of modernity imply of the sense of contingency in life, from which we learn that the one thing that can be disputed, and that is worth disputing, is preference or taste. The Rede Lecture and the Richmond Lecture exemplify the use to which the idea of culture can be put in shaking the old certainties of class, in contriving new social groups on the basis of taste. All this does indeed give the cultural mode of thought a very considerable authority. Yet sometimes we may wonder if it is wholly an accident that so strong an impulse to base our sense of life, and our conduct of the intellectual life, chiefly upon the confrontations of taste should have developed in an age dominated by advertising, the wonderful and terrible art which teaches us that we define ourselves and realize our true being by choosing the right style. In our more depressed moments we might be led to ask whether there is a real difference between being The Person Who defines himself by his commitment to one or another idea of morality, politics, literature, or city-planning, and being The Person Who defines himself by wearing trousers without pleats.

We can, I suppose, no more escape from the cultural mode of thought than we can escape from culture itself. Yet perhaps we must learn to cast a somewhat colder eye upon it for the sake of whatever regard we have for the intellectual life, for the possibility of rational discourse. Sir Charles envisages a new and very powerful social class on the basis of a life-style which he imputes to a certain profession in contrast with the life-style he imputes to another profession, and he goes on from there to deny both the reality of politics and the possibility of its being judged by moral standards. Dr. Leavis answers him with a passion of personal scorn which obscures the greater part of the issue and offers in contradiction truth indeed but truth so hampered and hidden by the defenses of Dr. Leavis's own choice in life-styles that it looks not much different from a prejudice. And the *Spectator* correspondents exercise their taste in life-styles and take appropriate sides. It is at such a moment that our dispirited minds yearn to find comfort and courage in the idea of Mind, that faculty whose ancient potency our commitment to the idea of culture denies. To us today, Mind must inevitably seem but a poor gray thing, for it always sought to detach itself from the passions (but not from the emotions, Spinoza said, and explained the difference) and from the conditions of time and place. Yet it is salutary for us to contemplate it, whatever its grayness, because of the bright belief that was once attached to it, that it was the faculty which belonged not to professions, or to social classes, or to cultural groups, but to Man, and that it was possible for men, and becoming to them, to learn its proper use, for it was the means by which they could communicate with each other.

It was on this belief that science based its early existence, and it gave to the men who held it a character which is worth remarking. Sir Charles mentions Faraday among those scientists who over-rode the limitations of social class to form the "scientific culture" of England. This is true only so far as it can be made consonant with the fact that Faraday could not have imagined the idea of a "scientific culture" and would have been wholly repelled by it. It is told of Faraday that he refused to be called a *physicist;* he very much disliked the new name as being too special and particular and insisted on the old one, *philosopher,* in all its spacious generality: we may suppose that this was his way of saying that he had not over-ridden the limiting conditions of class only to submit to the limitations of profession. The idea of Mind which had taught the book-binder's apprentice to embark on his heroic enterprise of self-instruction also taught the great scientist to place himself beyond the specialness of interest which groups prescribe for their members. Every personal episode in Tyndall's classic account of his master, *Faraday as a Researcher,* makes it plain that Faraday undertook to be, in the beautiful lost sense of the word, a *disinterested* man. From his belief in Mind, he derived the certitude that he had his true being not as a member of this or that profession or class, but as—in the words of a poet of his time—"a man speaking to men."

No one now needs to be reminded of what may befall the idea of Mind in the way of excess and distortion. The literature of the 19th century never wearied of telling us just this, of decrying the fatigue and desiccation of spirit which result from an allegiance to Mind that excludes impulse and will, and desire and preference. It was, surely, a liberation to be made aware of this, and then to go on to take serious account of those particularities of impulse and will, of desire and preference, which differentiate individuals and groups—to employ what I have called the cultural mode of thought. We take it for granted that this, like any other mode of thought, has its peculiar dangers, but there is cause for surprise and regret that it should be Sir Charles Snow and Dr. Leavis who have jointly demonstrated how far the cultural mode of thought can go in excess and distortion.

Albert Camus

Throughout his tragically short life (1913-1960), the Algerian-born French novelist Albert Camus exemplified the capacity for social criticism and politial judgment that Trilling ascribes to the literary artist. Like George Orwell, he was an example of the "engaged" writer, but his creative gifts, displayed in his novels *The Stranger* and *The Plague,* his plays, and such speculative works of nonfiction as *The Rebel,* exceeded Orwell's in both variety and intensity. Camus was incapable of withdrawing, in the name of art, from the physical and moral realities of our unfortunate century, and the following expression of savage indignation over the suppression of the Hungarian revolution of 1956 attests to this fact.

His essay is of its very nature emotional and polemical; its dominant note is a noble and sustained anger—not only at Soviet tyranny but also at those in the West who condoned that tyranny through the lie of abstraction and those others, more numerous, who applauded the revolution but did nothing to support it. Camus' emotion has intellectual roots in ideas which he had spent his life formulating, ideas which had led earlier to his association with the existentialists Jean-Paul Sartre and Simone de Beauvoir. The most important of those ideas is that individual freedom is the necessary condition of any possible self-fulfillment and that culture itself is finally to be defined as the product of a creativity founded only in freedom. Intellectual awareness is not always matched, however, by moral perception, and Camus stood nearly alone among his existentialist contemporaries in reacting as he did to the suppression of Hungary. For him, philosophical conviction was supported by personal honesty and a capacity for direct emotional reaction.

KADAR HAD HIS DAY OF FEAR

> *The Hungarian Minister of State Marosan, whose name sounds like a program, declared a few days ago that there would be no further counter-revolution in Hungary. For once, one of Kadar's Ministers has told the truth. How could there be a counter-revolution since it has already seized power? There can be no other revolution in Hungary.*

I am not one of those who long for the Hungarian people to take up arms again in an uprising doomed to be crushed under the eyes of an international society that will spare neither applause nor virtuous tears before returning to their slippers like football enthusiasts on Saturday evening after a big game. There are already too many dead in the stadium, and we can be generous only with our own blood. Hungarian blood has proved to be so valuable to Europe and to freedom that we must try to spare every drop of it.

But I am not one to think there can be even a resigned or provisional

Reprinted from *Resistance, Rebellion and Death* by Albert Camus by permission of Alfred A. Knopf, Inc. Copyright 1960 by Alfred A. Knopf, Inc.

compromise with a reign of terror that has as much right to be called socialist as the executioners of the Inquisition had to be called Christians. And, on this anniversary of liberty, I hope with all my strength that the mute resistance of the Hungarian people will continue, grow stronger, and, echoed by all the voices we can give it, get unanimous international opinion to boycott its oppressors. And if that opinion is too flabby or selfish to do justice to a martyred people, if our voices also are too weak, I hope that the Hungarian resistance will continue until the counter-revolutionary state collapses everywhere in the East under the weight of its lies and its contradictions.

. . . . The Bloody and Monotonous Rites

For it is indeed a counter-revolutionary state. What else can we call a regime that forces the father to inform on his son, the son to demand the supreme punishment for his father, the wife to bear witness against her husband—that has raised denunciation to the level of a virtue? Foreign tanks, police, twenty-year-old girls hanged, committees of workers decapitated and gagged, scaffolds, writers deported and imprisoned, the lying press, camps, censorship, judges arrested, criminals legislating, and the scaffold again—is this socialism, the great celebration of liberty and justice?

No, we have known, we still know this kind of thing; these are the bloody and monotonous rites of the totalitarian religion! Hungarian socialism is in prison or in exile today. In the palaces of the State, armed to the teeth, slink the petty tyrants of absolutism, terrified by the very word "liberty," maddened by the word "truth"! The proof is that today, the 15th of March, a day of invincible truth and liberty for all Hungarians, was for Kadar simply a long day of fear.

For many years, however, those tyrants, aided in the West by accomplices who were not obliged by anything or anyone to show such zeal, cloaked their true actions in a heavy smoke screen. When something could be seen through the screen, they or their Western interpreters explained to us that everything would be all right in ten generations or so, that meanwhile everyone was joyfully heading toward the future, that the deported had made the mistake of getting in the way of traffic on the magnificent road of progress, that the executed agreed completely as to their own suppression, that the intellectuals declared themselves delighted with their pretty gag because it was dialectical, and that the proletariat were charmed with their own work because, if they worked overtime for wretched wages, this was in the proper direction of history.

Alas, the people themselves spoke up! They began to talk in Berlin, in Czechoslovakia, in Poznan, and eventually in Budapest. All at once, everywhere, intellectuals tore off their gags. And together, with a single voice, they said that instead of progress there was regression, that the killings had been useless; the deportations useless, the enslavements useless, and that henceforth, to be sure of making real progress, truth and liberty had to be granted to all.

Thus, with the first shout of insurrection in free Budapest, learned and shortsighted philosophies, miles of false reasonings and deceptively beautiful doctrines were scattered like dust. And the truth, the naked truth, so long outraged, burst upon the eyes of the world.

Contemptuous teachers, unaware that they were thereby insulting the working classes, had assured us that the masses could readily get along without liberty if only they were given bread. And the masses themselves suddenly replied that they didn't have bread but that, even if they did, they would still like something else. For it was not a learned professor but a Budapest blacksmith who wrote: "I want to be considered an adult eager to think and capable of thought. I want to be able to express my thoughts without having anything to fear and I want, also, to be listened to."

As for the intellectuals who had been told and shouted at that there was no truth other than the one that served the cause, this is the oath they took at the grave of their comrades assassinated by that cause: "Never again, not even under threat and torture, nor under a misunderstood love of the cause, will anything but the truth issue from our mouths." (Tibor Meray at the grave of Rajk.)

. . . . The Scaffold Does Not Become Any More Liberal

After that, the case is closed. The slaughtered people are our people. What Spain was for us twenty years ago Hungary will be today. The subtle distinctions, the verbal tricks, and the clever considerations with which people still try to cloak the truth do not interest us. The competition we are told about between Rakosi and Kadar is unimportant. The two are of the same stamp. They differ only by the number of heads to their credit, and if Rakosi's total is more impressive, this will not be so for long.

In any event, whether the bald killer or the persecuted persecutor rules over Hungary makes no difference as to the freedom of that country. I regret having to play the role of Cassandra once more and having to disappoint the fresh hopes of certain ever hopeful colleagues, but there is no possible evolution in a totalitarian society. Terror does not evolve except toward a worse terror, the scaffold does not become any more liberal, the gallows are not tolerant. Nowhere in the world has there been a party or a man with absolute power who did not use it absolutely.

The first thing to define totalitarian society, whether of the Right or of the Left, is the single party, and the single party has no reason to destroy itself. This is why the only society capable of evolution and liberalization, the only one that deserves both our critical and our active support is the society that involves a plurality of parties as a part of its structure. It alone allows one to denounce, hence to correct, injustice and crime. It alone today allows one to denounce torture, disgraceful torture, as contemptible in Algiers as in Budapest.

. . . . **What Budapest Was Defending**

The idea, still voiced among us, that a party, because it calls itself proletarian, can enjoy special privileges in regard to history is an idea of intellectuals tired of their advantages and of their freedom. History does not confer privileges: it lets them be snatched away.

And it is not the function of intellectuals or of workers to glorify even slightly the right of the stronger and the *fait accompli*. The truth is that no one, neither individual nor party, has a right to absolute power or to lasting privileges in a history that is itself changing. And no privilege, no supreme reason can justify torture or terror.

On this point Budapest again showed us the way. Hungary conquered and in chains (which our false realists compare with commiseration to Poland), still on the edge of equilibrium, has done more for freedom and justice than any people in twenty years. But, for that lesson to reach and convince those in the West who close their eyes and ears, the Hungarian people (and we shall never be consoled for this) had to shed their own blood, and it is already drying up in people's memories.

At least we shall try to be faithful to Hungary as we have been to Spain. In Europe's present solitude, we have but one way of being so—which is never to betray, at home or abroad, that for which the Hungarian combatants died and never to justify even indirectly, at home or abroad, what killed them.

The untiring insistence upon freedom and truth, the community of the worker and the intellectual (who are still stupidly warring here, as tyranny aims to keep them doing), and, finally, political democracy as a necessary and indispensable (though surely not sufficient) condition of economic democracy—this is what Budapest was defending. And in doing so, the great city in insurrection reminded Western Europe of its forgotten truth and greatness. It made short work of that odd feeling of inferiority that debilitates most of our intellectuals but that I, for one, refuse to feel.

374   SCIENCE, LITERATURE AND CULTURE

........Reply to Shepilov

The defects of the West are innumerable, its crimes and errors very real. But in the end, let's not forget that we are the only ones to have the possibility of improvement and emancipation that lies in free genius. Let's not forget that when totalitarian society, by its very principles, forces the friend to denounce his friend, Western society, despite its wanderings from the path of virtue, always produces a race of men who uphold honor in life—I mean men who stretch out their hands even to their enemy to save him from suffering or death.

When Minister Shepilov on his return from Paris dares to write that "Western art is bound to tear the human soul apart and to form butchers of every sort," it is time to reply to him that at least our writers and artists have never butchered anyone and that yet they are generous enough not to blame the theory of socialist realism for the massacres ordered by Shepilov and those who resemble him.

The truth is that there is room for everything among us, even for evil, and even for Shepilov's writers. There is room also for honor, for the freedom to desire, for the adventure of the mind. Whereas there is room for nothing in Stalinist culture except for edifying sermons, colorless life, and the catechism of propaganda. To any who still had any doubts about this, the Hungarian writers have just shouted the truth before choosing permanent silence today when they are ordered to lie.

It will be hard for us to be worthy of so many sacrifices. But we must try to do so in a Europe at last united, by forgetting our quarrels, by getting rid of our own errors, by multiplying our creations and our solidarity. And to those who wanted to humble us and persuade us that history could justify a reign of terror, we shall reply by our real faith that we share, as we now know, with Hungarian writers, Polish writers, and even, indeed, with Russian writers, who are also gagged.

Our faith is that throughout the world, beside the impulse toward coercion and death that is darkening history, there is a growing impulse toward persuasion and life, a vast emancipatory movement called culture that is made up both of free creation and of free work.

Our daily task, our long vocation is to add to that culture by our labors and not to subtract, even temporarily, anything from it. But our proudest duty is to defend personally to the very end, against the impulse toward coercion and death, the freedom of that culture—in other words, the freedom of work and of creation.

The Hungarian workers and intellectuals, beside whom we stand today with so much impotent grief, realized that and made us realize it. This is why, if their suffering is ours, their hope belongs to us too. Despite their destitution, their exile, their chains, it took them but a single day to transmit to us the royal legacy of liberty. May we be worthy of it!

FRANC-TIREUR, 18 March 1957

William Butler Yeats

We live in an age with an innate fondness for viewing the artistic imagination (when it views it at all) solely in terms of its practical, social, and ultimately transitory functions. Such a critic as Trilling, and such novelists as Camus and Orwell, although they are aware of the uniquensss of art, its special and irreplaceable contributions to life, prefer to center their attention on the relation between the artist and his social milieu, the world of action. The drama critic Kenneth Tynan goes much further than they in denying to literature, effectively, any function except the socially useful, and in so doing he speaks for a very large segment of the ostensibly literate public. In a climate of opinion like ours, the statement of William Butler Yeats, one of the greatest of twentieth-century poets, makes a special claim on our attention. It is a piece of prose that requires concentration as well as attention if we are to understand it, for Yeats, an instinctive aristocrat in his art as in his life, displays in his prose the very qualities of intense compression of statement and rich allusiveness of diction that distinguish his poetry. The important distinctions that he makes ought not to be taken as constituting a rejection of either social involvement or political action (Yeats, an Irishman, was himself active in the cultural and political struggles of his country). They are rather there to affirm the solitary nature of the search for truth which is at the heart of the greatest poetry. In the most ideal society imaginable, man will remain a being who lives and dies alone, and it is in his aloneness, Yeats reminds us that he creates.

RHETORICIANS, SENTIMENTALISTS, AND POETS

We make out of the quarrel with others, rhetoric, but of the quarrel with ourselves, poetry. Unlike the rhetoricians, who get a confident voice from remembering the crowd they have won or may win, we sing amid our uncertainty; and, smitten even in the presence of the most

From *Essays* by William Butler Yeats (New York, The Macmillan Company). Reprinted by permission of the publisher. Copyright 1912, 1918 by The Macmillan Company. Renewed 1939 and 1946 by Bertha Georgie Yeats.

high beauty by the knowledge of our solitude, our rhythm shudders. I think, too, that no fine poet, no matter how disordered his life, has ever, even in his mere life, had pleasure for his end. Johnson and Dowson, friends of my youth, were dissipated men, the one a drunkard, the other a drunkard and mad about women, and yet they had the gravity of men who had found life out and were awakening from the dream; and both, one in life and art and one in art and less in life, had a continual preoccupation with religion. Nor has any poet I have read of or heard of or met with been a sentimentalist. The other self, the anti-self or the antithetical self, as one may choose to name it, comes but to those who are no longer deceived, whose passion is reality. The sentimentalists are practical men who believe in money, in position, in a marriage bell, and whose understanding of happiness is to be so busy whether at work or at play, that all is forgotten but the momentary aim. They find their pleasure in a cup that is filled from Lethe's wharf, and for the awakening, for the vision, for the revelation of reality, tradition offers us a different word—ecstasy. An old artist wrote to me of his wanderings by the quays of New York, and how he found there a woman nursing a sick child, and drew her story from her. She spoke, too, of other children who had died: a long tragic story. "I wanted to paint her," he wrote, "if I denied myself any of the pain I could not believe in my own ecstasy." We must not make a false faith by hiding from our thoughts the causes of doubt, for faith is the highest achievement of the human intellect, the only gift man can make to God, and therefore it must be offered in sincerity. Neither must we create, by hiding ugliness, a false beauty as our offering to the world. He only can create the greatest imaginable beauty who has endured all imaginable pangs, for only when we have seen and foreseen what we dread shall we be rewarded by that dazzling unforeseen wing-footed wanderer.

E. M. Forster

This address by the celebrated British novelist E. M. Forster, author of *A Passage to India* and *Howard's End,* may usefully be viewed as an expansion and elaboration of the conception of art expressed in distilled form by Yeats. Forster's tone of witty urbanity is appropriate to the occasion of his address, a meeting of a group professionally interested in arts and letters, yet there can be no mistaking the deep seriousness of what he has to say. Simultaneously a master of his own art of fiction and a conscious and articulate defender of civilization in its broadest sense, Forster is too shrewd to be taken in by either of the opposed oversimplifications which monotonously make their appearance in discussions of literature. Those oversimplifications maintain that literary values are narrowly and solely aesthetic and have nothing to do with life itself, and that literature can only be justified by its positive contribution to society and ought thus to be conceived of either as propaganda or as a branch of sociology. Too much a humanist to maintain that art and life are completely separate, Forster is too much an artist to accept the idea that art and life are synonymous. The value of a literary work, for him, resides ultimately in its form, in the separate world which it makes. It is interesting to compare his observations on literary form with those made by Sir Kenneth Clark on form in the art of painting, especially in view of Forster's approving quotation from Sir Kenneth in refuting the naive attitude toward art which sometimes springs from a misunderstanding of democratic ideals. His total view of the function of art may also be meaningfully compared with those of Gottfried Benn, for example, or contrasted with those of Orwell and Oppenheimer. Very often an individual's attitude toward art operates as the expression of an attitude toward life, as the epitome of an entire philosophy.

ART FOR ART'S SAKE

AN ADDRESS DELIVERED BEFORE THE AMERICAN ACADEMY OF
ARTS AND LETTERS IN NEW YORK

I believe in art for art's sake. It is an unfashionable belief, and some of my statements must be of the nature of an apology. Fifty years ago I should have faced you with more confidence. A writer or a speaker who chose "Art for Art's Sake" for his theme fifty years ago could be sure of being in the swim, and could feel so confident of success that he sometimes dressed himself in esthetic costumes suitable to the occasion—in an embroidered dressing-gown, perhaps, or a blue velvet suit with a Lord Fauntleroy collar; or a toga, or a kimono, and carried a poppy or a lily or a long peacock's feather in his mediaeval hand. Times have changed. Not thus can I present either myself or my theme today. My aim rather is to ask you quietly to reconsider for a few minutes a phrase which has been much misused and much abused, but which has, I believe, great importance for us—has, indeed, eternal importance.

Now we can easily dismiss those peacock's feathers and other affectations—they are but trifles—but I want also to dismiss a more dangerous heresy, namely the silly idea that only art matters, an idea which has

From *Two Cheers for Democracy*, copyright, 1951, by E. M. Forster. Reprinted by permission of Harcourt, Brace & World, Inc.

somehow got mixed up with the idea of art for art's sake, and has helped to discredit it. Many things, besides art, matter. It is merely one of the things that matter, and high though the claims are that I make for it, I want to keep them in proportion. No one can spend his or her life entirely in the creation or the appreciation of masterpieces. Man lives, and ought to live, in a complex world, full of conflicting claims, and if we simplified them down into the esthetic he would be sterilised. Art for art's sake does not mean that only art matters, and I would also like to rule out such phrases as "The Life of Art," "Living for Art," and "Art's High Mission." They confuse and mislead.

What does the phrase mean? Instead of generalising, let us take a specific instance—Shakespeare's *Macbeth,* for example, and pronounce the words, "*Macbeth* for *Macbeth's* sake." What does that mean? Well, the play has several aspects—it is educational, it teaches us something about legendary Scotland, something about Jacobean England, and a good deal about human nature and its perils. We can study its origins, and study and enjoy its dramatic technique and the music of its diction. All that is true. But *Macbeth* is furthermore a world of its own, created by Shakespeare and existing in virtue of its own poetry. It is in this aspect *Macbeth* for *Macbeth's* sake, and that is what I intend by the phrase "art for art's sake." A work of art—whatever else it may be—is a self-contained entity, with a life of its own imposed on it by its creator. It has internal order. It may have external form. That is how we recognise it.

Take for another example that picture of Seurat's which I saw two years ago in Chicago—"*La Grande Jatte.*" Here again there is much to study and to enjoy: the pointillism, the charming face of the seated girl, the nineteenth-century Parisian Sunday sunlight, the sense of motion in immobility. But here again there is something more; "*La Grande Jatte*" forms a world of its own, created by Seurat and existing by virtue of its own poetry: "*La Grande Jatte*" pour "*La Grande Jatte*": l'art pour l'art. Like *Macbeth* it has internal order and internal life.

It is to the conception of order that I would now turn. This is important to my argument, and I want to make a digression, and glance at order in daily life, before I come to order in art.

In the world of daily life, the world which we perforce inhabit, there is much talk about order, particularly from statesmen and politicians. They tend, however, to confuse order with orders, just as they confuse creation with regulations. Order, I suggest, is something evolved from within, not something imposed from without; it is an internal stability, a vital harmony, and in the social and political category it has never existed except for the convenience of historians. Viewed realistically, the past is really a series of *dis*orders, succeeding one another by discoverable laws, no doubt, and certainly marked by an increasing growth of human inter-

MONTANA STATE UNIVERSITY

©1985 CSA, Inc. Dsn.402

MONTANA STATE UNIVERSITY

©1985 CSA, Inc. Dsn.402

ference, but disorders all the same. So that, speaking as a writer, what I hope for today is a disorder which will be more favourable to artists than is the present one, and which will provide them with fuller inspirations and better material conditions. It will not last—nothing lasts—but there have been some advantageous disorders in the past—for instance, in ancient Athens, in Renaissance Italy, eighteenth-century France, periods in China and Persia—and we may do something to accelerate the next one. But let us not again fix our hearts where true joys are not to be found. We were promised a new order after the first world war through the League of Nations. It did not come, nor have I faith in present promises, by whomsoever endorsed. The implacable offensive of Science forbids. We cannot reach social and political stability for the reason that we continue to make scientific discoveries and to apply them, and thus to destroy the arrangements which were based on more elementary discoveries. If Science would discover rather than apply—if, in other words, men were more interested in knowledge than in power—mankind would be in a far safer position, the stability statesmen talk about would be a possibility, there could be a new order based on vital harmony, and the earthly millennium might approach. But Science shows no signs of doing this: she gave us the internal combustion engine, and before we had digested and assimilated it with terrible pains into our social system, she harnessed the atom, and destroyed any new order that seemed to be evolving. How can man get into harmony with his surroundings when he is constantly altering them? The future of our race is, in this direction, more unpleasant than we care to admit, and it has sometimes seemed to me that its best chance lies through apathy, uninventiveness, and inertia. Universal exhaustion might promote that Change of Heart which is at present so briskly recommended from a thousand pulpits. Universal exhaustion would certainly be a new experience. The human race has never undergone it, and is still too perky to admit that it may be coming and might result in a sprouting of new growth through the decay.

I must not pursue these speculations any further—they lead me too far from my terms of reference and maybe from yours. But I do want to emphasise that order in daily life and in history, order in the social and political category, is unattainable under our present psychology.

Where is it attainable? Not in the astronomical category, where it was for many years enthroned. The heavens and the earth have become terribly alike since Einstein. No longer can we find a reassuring contrast to chaos in the night sky and look up with George Meredith to the stars, the army of unalterable law, or listen for the music of the spheres. Order is not there. In the entire universe there seem to be only two possibilities for it. The first of them—which again lies outside my terms of reference— is the divine order, the mystic harmony, which according to all religions is available for those who can contemplate it. We must admit its possibility, on the evidence of the adepts, and we must believe them when they say that it is attained, if attainable, by prayer. "O thou who changest not, abide with me," said one of its poets. *"Ordina questo amor, o tu che m'ami,"* said another: "Set love in order, thou who lovest me." The existence of a divine order, though it cannot be tested, has never been disproved.

The second possibility for order lies in the esthetic category, which is my subject here: the order which an artist can create in his own work, and to that we must now return. A work of art, we are all agreed, is a unique product. But why? It is unique not because it is clever or noble or beautiful or enlightened or original or sincere or idealistic or useful or educational—it may embody any of those qualities—but because it is the only material object in the universe which may possess internal harmony. All the others have been pressed into shape from outside, and when their mould is removed they collapse. The work of art stands up by itself, and nothing else does. It achieves something which has often been promised by society, but always delusively. Ancient Athens made a mess—but the *Antigone* stands up. Renaissance Rome made a mess—but the ceiling of the Sistine got painted. James I made a mess—but there was *Macbeth*. Louis XIV—but there was *Phèdre*. Art for art's sake? I should just think so, and more so than ever at the present time. It is the one orderly product which our muddling race has produced. It is the cry of a thousand sentinels, the echo from a thousand labyrinths; it is the lighthouse which cannot be hidden: *c'est le meilleur témoignage que nous puissions donner de notre dignité. Antigone* for *Antigone's* sake, *Macbeth* for *Macbeth's,* "La Grande Jatte" pour "La Grande Jatte."

If this line of argument is correct, it follows that the artist will tend to be an outsider in the society to which he has been born, and that the nineteenth-century conception of him as a Bohemian was not inaccurate. The conception erred in three particulars: it postulated an economic system where art could be a full-time job, it introduced the fallacy that only art matters, and it overstressed idiosyncrasy and waywardness—the peacock-feather aspect—rather than order. But it is a truer conception than the one which prevails in official circles on my side of the Atlantic— I don't know about yours: the conception which treats the artist as if he were a particularly bright government advertiser and encourages him to be friendly and matey with his fellow citizens, and not to give himself airs.

Estimable is mateyness, and the man who achieves it gives many a pleasant little drink to himself and to others. But it has no traceable connection with the creative impulse, and probably acts as an inhibition on it. The artist who is seduced by mateyness may stop himself from doing the one thing which he, and he alone, can do—the making of something out of words or sounds or paint or clay or marble or steel or film which has internal harmony and presents order to a permanently disarranged planet. This seems worth doing, even at the risk of being called uppish by journalists. I have in mind an article which was published some years ago in the London *Times,* an article called "The Eclipse of the Highbrow," in which the "Average Man" was exalted, and all contemporary literature was censured if it did not toe the line, the precise position of the line being naturally known to the writer of the article. Sir Kenneth Clark, who was at that time director of our National Gallery, commented on this pernicious doctrine in a letter which cannot be too often quoted. "The poet and the artist," wrote Clark, "are important precisely because they are not average men; because in sensibility, intelligence, and power of invention they far exceed the average." These memorable words, and particularly the words "power of invention," are the Bohemian's passport. Furnished with it, he slinks about society, saluted by a brickbat and now by a penny, and accepting either of them with equanimity. He does not consider too anxiously what his relations with society may be, for he is aware of something more important than that—namely the invitation to invent, to create order, and he believes he will be better placed for doing this if he attempts detachment. So round and round he slouches, with his hat pulled over his eyes, and maybe with a louse in his beard, and—if he really wants one—with a peacock's feather in his hand.

If our present society should disintegrate—and who dare prophesy that it won't?—this old-fashioned and démodé figure will become clearer: the Bohemian, the outsider, the parasite, the rat—one of those figures which have at present no function either in a warring or a peaceful world. It may not be dignified to be a rat, but many of the ships are sinking, which is not dignified either—the officials did not build them properly. Myself, I would sooner be a swimming rat than a sinking ship—at all events I can look around me for a little longer—and I remember how one of us, a rat with particularly bright eyes called Shelley, squeaked out, "Poets are the unacknowledged legislators of the world," before he vanished into the waters of the Mediterranean.

What laws did Shelley propose to pass? None. The legislation of the artist is never formulated at the time, though it is sometimes discerned by future generations. He legislates through creating. And he creates through his sensitiveness and his power to impose form. Without form the sensitiveness vanishes. And form is as important today, when the human race is trying to ride the whirlwind, as it ever was in those less agitating days of the past, when the earth seemed solid and the stars fixed, and the discoveries of science were made slowly, slowly. Form is not tradition. It alters from generation to generation. Artists always seek a new technique, and will continue to do so as long as their work excites them.

But form of some kind is imperative. It is the surface crust of the internal harmony, it is the outward evidence of order.

My remarks about society may have seemed too pessimistic, but I believe that society can only represent a fragment of the human spirit, and that another fragment can only get expressed through art. And I wanted to take this opportunity, this vantage ground, to assert not only the existence of art, but its pertinacity. Looking back into the past, it seems to me that that is all there has ever been: vantage grounds for discussion and creation, little vantage grounds in the changing chaos, where bubbles have been blown and webs spun, and the desire to create order has found temporary gratification, and the sentinels have managed to utter their challenges, and the huntsmen, though lost individually, have heard each other's calls through the impenetrable wood, and the lighthouses have never ceased sweeping the thankless seas. In this pertinacity there seems to me, as I grow older, something more and more profound, something which does in fact concern people who do not care about art at all.

In conclusion, let me summarise the various categories that have laid claim to the possession of Order.

(1) The social and political category. Claim disallowed on the evidence of history and of our own experience. If man altered psychologically, order here might be attainable; not otherwise.

(2) The astronomical category. Claim allowed up to the present century, but now disallowed on the evidence of the physicists.

(3) The religious category. Claim allowed on the evidence of the mystics.

(4) The esthetic category. Claim allowed on the evidence of various works of art, and on the evidence of our own creative impulses, however weak these may be, or however imperfectly they may function. Works of art, in my opinion, are the only objects in the material universe to possess internal order, and that is why, though I don't believe that only art matters, I do believe in Art for Art's Sake.

[1949]

C. G. Jung

We have suggested that a thinker's attitude toward art may serve as an epitome of his entire attitude toward life. In his essay on the relations of psychology and literature, the great Swiss psychologist Carl G. Jung (1875-1961) presents a point of view with profound implications for many areas of thought.

In its scope the essay is typical of the work of a man who has deeply influenced not only the practice of psychoanalysis but also philosophy, art, literature, and criticism (the school of literary criticism known as "myth-criticism" or "archetypal criticism," for example, owes its origin to his insights).

Jung begins with the assumption that a work of art is "something in and for itself," and in so doing he implicitly aligns himself with Forster and others who, with whatever modifications, believe in "art for art's sake." His position is at variance with that of Oppenheimer, who seems to allow art only a kind of ancillary function to the great collective work of science, and with that of the "engaged" artists and critics who emphasize the social utility of art. He disagrees also, and very crucially, with his early master Freud, who had viewed art as a neurotic manifestation significant primarily as a symptom of psychic disturbance.

As Jung investigates what he calls "visionary" literature, the type of literature that he finds most important for psychological knowledge, one begins to perceive the larger dimensions of his disagreement with Freud and with Freud's commitment to the strict rationalism and determinism which, until our own time, have been central to scientific inquiry. Jung's concept of a "collective unconscious" which may be tapped by the great visionary artist is obviously derived from the initial Freudian concept of the unconscious, but it sets limits to the reach of science that neither Freud nor his modern disciples would be willing to admit.

Jung's theory of literature is clearly part of an attempt to achieve some new synthesis of thought which will allow a place for the mysterious, the religious, and the imaginative—for all those qualities which a strictly scientific orientation tends to abolish or at least to minimize. He attempts, as a modern intellectual, to recapture some of the mythic, timeless sense of existence known to cultures earlier than ours, that sense of existence examined in the last essay of this volume by Carl Kerényi. In so doing, Jung sacrifices some of the power of objective demonstration which science insists is essential to valid knowledge, but he liberates, perhaps, a unifying power that we cannot wholly lose without losing our humanity.

PSYCHOLOGY AND LITERATURE

It is obvious enough that psychology, being the study of psychic processes, can be brought to bear upon the study of literature, for the human psyche is the womb of all the sciences and arts. We may expect psychological research, on the one hand, to explain the formation of a work of art, and on the other to reveal the factors that make a person artistically creative. The psychologist is thus faced with two separate and distinct tasks, and must approach them in radically different ways.

In the case of the work of art we have to deal with a product of complicated psychic activities—but a product that is apparently intentional and consciously shaped. In the case of the artist we must deal with

From *Modern Man in Search of a Soul* by Carl Jung. Reprinted by permission of Harcourt, Brace & World, Inc.

the psychic apparatus itself. In the first instance we must attempt the psychological analysis of a definitely circumscribed and concrete artistic achievement, while in the second we must analyse the living and creative human being as a unique personality. Although these two undertakings are closely related and even interdependent, neither of them can yield the explanations that are sought by the other. It is of course possible to draw inferences about the artist from the work of art, and *vice versa,* but these inferences are never conclusive. At best they are probable surmises or lucky guesses. A knowledge of Goethe's particular relation to his mother throws some light upon Faust's exclamation: "The mothers— mothers—how very strange it sounds!" But it does not enable us to see how the attachment to his mother could produce the Faust drama itself, however unmistakably we sense in the man Goethe a deep connection between the two. Nor are we more successful in reasoning in the reverse direction. There is nothing in *The Ring of the Nibelungs* that would enable us to recognize or definitely infer the fact that Wagner occasionally liked to wear womanish clothes, though hidden connections exist between the heroic masculine world of the Nibelungs and a certain pathological effeminacy in the man Wagner.

The present state of development of psychology does not allow us to establish those rigorous causal connections which we expect of a science. It is only in the realm of the psycho-physiological instincts and reflexes that we can confidently operate with the idea of causality. From the point where psychic life begins—that is, at a level of greater complexity—the psychologist must content himself with more or less widely ranging descriptions of happenings and with the vivid portrayal of the warp and weft of the mind in all its amazing intricacy. In doing this, he must refrain from designating any one psychic process, taken by itself, as "necessary." Were this not the state of affairs, and could the psychologist be relied upon to uncover the causal connections within a work of art and in the process of artistic creation, he would leave the study of art no ground to stand on and would reduce it to a special branch of his own science. The psychologist, to be sure, may never abandon his claim to investigate and establish causal relations in complicated psychic events. To do so would be to deny psychology the right to exist. Yet he can never make good this claim in the fullest sense, because the creative aspect of life which finds its clearest expression in art baffles all attempts at rational formulation. Any reaction to stimulus may be causally explained; but the creative act, which is the absolute antithesis of mere reaction, will for ever elude the human understanding. It can only be described in its manifestations; it can be obscurely sensed, but never wholly grasped. Psychology and the study of art will always have to turn to one another for help, and the one will not invalidate the other. It is an important principle of psychology that psychic events are derivable. It is a principle in the study of art that a psychic product is something in and for itself whether the work of art or the artist himself is in question. Both principles are valid in spite of their relativity.

. . . . .I. The Work of Art

There is a fundamental difference of approach between the psychologist's examination of a literary work, and that of the literary critic. What is of decisive importance and value for the latter may be quite irrelevant for the former. Literary products of highly dubious merit are often of the greatest interest to the psychologist. For instance, the so-called "psychological novel" is by no means as rewarding for the psychologist as the literary-minded suppose. Considered as a whole, such a novel explains itself. It has done its own work of psychological interpretation, and the psychologist can at most criticize or enlarge upon this. The important question as to how a particular author came to write a particular novel is of course left unanswered, but I wish to reserve this general problem for the second part of my essay.

The novels which are most fruitful for the psychologist are those in which the author has not already given a psychological interpretation of his characters, and which therefore leave room for analysis and explanation, or even invite it by their mode of presentation. Good examples of this kind of writing are the novels of Benoît, and English fiction in the manner of Rider Haggard, including the vein exploited by Conan Doyle which yields that most cherished article of mass-production, the detective story. Melville's *Moby Dick,* which I consider the greatest American novel, also comes within this class of writings. An exciting narrative that is apparently quite devoid of psychological exposition is just what interests the psychologist most of all. Such a tale is built upon a groundwork of implicit psychological assumptions, and, in the measure that the author is unconscious of them, they reveal themselves, pure and unalloyed, to the critical discernment. In the psychological novel, on the other hand, the author himself attempts to reshape his material so as to raise it from the level of crude contingency to that of psychological exposition and illumination—a procedure which all too often clouds the psychological significance of the work or hides it from view. It is precisely to novels of this sort that the layman goes for "psychology"; while it is novels of the other kind that challenge the psychologist, for he alone can give them deeper meaning.

I have been speaking in terms of the novel, but I am dealing with a psychological fact which is not restricted to this particular form of literary art. We meet with it in the works of the poets as well, and are confronted with it when we compare the first and second parts of the Faust drama. The love-tragedy of Gretchen explains itself; there is nothing that the psychologist can add to it that the poet has not already said in better words. The second part, on the other hand, calls for explanation. The prodigious richness of the imaginative material has so overtaxed the poet's formative powers that nothing is self-explanatory and every verse adds to the reader's need of an interpretation. The two parts of *Faust* illustrate by way of extremes this psychological distinction between works of literature.

In order to emphasize the distinction, I will call the one mode of artistic creation *psychological,* and the other *visionary.* The psychological mode deals with materials drawn from the realm of human consciousness—for instance, with the lessons of life, with emotional shocks, the experience of passion and the crises of human destiny in general—all of which go to make up the conscious life of man, and his feeling life in particular. This material is psychically assimilated by the poet, raised from the commonplace to the level of poetic experience, and given an expression which forces the reader to greater clarity and depth of human insight by bringing fully into his consciousness what he ordinarily evades and overlooks or senses only with a feeling of dull discomfort. The poet's work is an interpretation and illumination of the contents of consciousness, of the ineluctable experiences of human life with its eternally recurrent sorrow and joy. He leaves nothing over for the psychologist, unless, indeed, we expect the latter to expound the reasons for which Faust falls in love with Gretchen, or which drive Gretchen to murder her child! Such themes go to make up the lot of humankind; they repeat themselves millions of times and are responsible for the monotony of the police-court and of the penal code. No obscurity whatever surrounds them, for they fully explain themselves.

Countless literary works belong to this class: the many novels dealing with love, the environment, the family, crime and society, as well as didactic poetry, the larger number of lyrics, and the drama, both tragic and comic. Whatever its particular form may be, the psychological work of art always takes its materials from the vast realm of conscious human experience—from the vivid foreground of life, we might say. I have called this mode of artistic creation psychological because in its activity it nowhere transcends the bounds of psychological intelligibility. Everything that it embraces—the experience as well as its artistic expression—belongs to the realm of the understandable. Even the basic experiences themselves, though non-rational, have nothing strange about them; on the contrary, they are that which has been known from the beginning of time —passion and its fated outcome, man's subjection to the turns of destiny, eternal nature with its beauty and its horror.

The profound difference between the first and second parts of *Faust* marks the difference between the psychological and the visionary modes of artistic creation. The latter reverses all the conditions of the former. The experience that furnishes the material for artistic expression is no longer familiar. It is a strange something that derives its existence from the hinterland of man's mind—that suggests the abyss of time separating us from pre-human ages, or evokes a super-human world of contrasting light and darkness. It is a primordial experience which surpasses man's understanding, and to which he is therefore in danger of succumbing. The value and the force of the experience are given by its enormity. It arises from timeless depths; it is foreign and cold, many-sided, demonic and grotesque. A grimly ridiculous sample of the eternal chaos—a *crimen laesae majestatis humanae,* to use Nietzsche's words—it bursts asunder our human standards of value and of aesthetic form. The disturbing vision of monstrous and meaningless happenings that in every way exceed the grasp of human feeling and comprehension makes quite other demands upon the powers of the artist than do the experiences of the foreground of life. These never rend the curtain that veils the cosmos; they never transcend the bounds of the humanly possible, and for this reason are readily shaped to the demands of art, no matter how great a shock to the individual they may be. But the primordial experiences rend from top to bottom the curtain upon which is painted the picture of an ordered world, and allow a glimpse into the unfathomed abyss of what has not yet become. Is it a vision of other worlds, or of the obscuration of the spirit, or of the beginning of things before the age of man, or of the unborn generations of the future? We cannot say that it is any or none of these.

> Shaping—re-shaping—
> The eternal spirit's eternal pastime.*

We find such vision in *The Shepherd of Hermas,* in Dante, in the second part of *Faust,* in Nietzsche's Dionysian exuberance, in Wagner's *Nibelungenring,* in Spitteler's *Olympischer Frühling,* in the poetry of William Blake, in the *Ipnerotomachia* of the monk Francesco Colonna, and in Jacob Boehme's philosophic and poetic stammerings. In a more restricted and specific way, the primordial experience furnishes material for Rider Haggard in the fiction-cycle that turns upon *She,* and it does the same for Benoît, chiefly in *L'Atlantide,* for Kubin in *Die Andere Seite,* for Meyrink in *Das Grüne Gesicht*—a book whose importance we should not undervalue—for Goetz in *Das Reich ohne Raum,* and for Barlach in *Der Tote Tag.* This list might be greatly extended.

* *Gestaltung, Umgestaltung,*
  Des ew'gen Sinnes ew'ge Unterhaltung. (Goethe.)

In dealing with the psychological mode of artistic creation, we never need ask ourselves what the material consists of or what it means. But this question forces itself upon us as soon as we come to the visionary mode of creation. We are astonished, taken aback, confused, put on our guard or even disgusted—and we demand commentaries and explanations. We are reminded in nothing of everyday, human life, but rather of dreams, night-time fears and the dark recesses of the mind that we sometimes sense with misgiving. The reading public for the most part repudiates this kind of writing—unless, indeed, it is coarsely sensational—and even the literary critic feels embarrassed by it. It is true that Dante and Wagner have smoothed the approach to it. The visionary experience is cloaked, in Dante's case, by the introduction of historical facts, and, in that of Wagner, by mythological events so that history and mythology are sometimes taken to be the materials with which these poets worked. But with neither of them does the moving force and the deeper significance lie there. For both it is contained in the visionary experience. Rider Haggard, pardonably enough, is generally held to be a mere inventor of fiction. Yet even with him the story is primarily a means of giving expression to significant material. However much the tale may seem to overgrow the content, the latter outweighs the former in importance.

The obscurity as to the sources of the material in visionary creation is very strange, and the exact opposite of what we find in the psychological mode of creation. We are even led to suspect that this obscurity is not unintentional. We are naturally inclined to suppose—and Freudian psychology encourages us to do so—that some highly personal experience underlies this grotesque darkness. We hope thus to explain these strange glimpses of chaos and to understand why it sometimes seems as though the poet had intentionally concealed his basic experience from us. It is only a step from this way of looking at the matter to the statement that we are here dealing with a pathological and neurotic art—a step which is justified in so far as the material of the visionary creator shows certain traits that we find in the fantasies of the insane. The converse also is true; we often discover in the mental output of psychotic persons a wealth of meaning that we should expect rather from the works of a genius. The psychologist who follows Freud will of course be inclined to take the writings in question as a problem in pathology. On the assumption that an intimate, personal experience underlies what I call the "primordial vision"—an experience, that is to say, which cannot be accepted by the conscious outlook—he will try to account for the curious images of the vision by calling them cover-figures and by supposing that they represent an attempted concealment of the basic experience. This, according to his view, might be an experience in love which is morally or aesthetically incompatible with the personality as a whole or at least with certain fictions of the conscious mind. In order that the poet, through his ego, might repress this experience and make it unrecognizable (unconscious), the whole arsenal of a pathological fantasy was brought into action. Moreover, this attempt to replace reality by fiction, being unsatisfactory, must be repeated in a long series of creative embodiments. This would explain the proliferation of imaginative forms, all monstrous, demonic, grotesque and perverse. On the one hand they are substitutes for the unacceptable experience, and on the other they help to conceal it.

Although a discussion of the poet's personality and psychic disposition belongs strictly to the second part of my essay, I cannot avoid taking up in the present connection this Freudian view of the visionary work of art. For one thing, it has aroused considerable attention. And then it is the only well-known attempt that has been made to give a "scientific" explanation of the sources of the visionary material or to formulate a theory of the psychic processes that underlie this curious mode of artistic creation. I assume that my own view of the question is not well known or generally understood. With this preliminary remark, I will now try to present it briefly.

If we insist on deriving the vision from a personal experience, we must treat the former as something secondary—as a mere substitute for reality. The result is that we strip the vision of its primordial quality and take it as nothing but a symptom. The pregnant chaos then shrinks to the proportions of a psychic disturbance. With this account of the matter we feel reassured and turn again to our picture of a well-ordered cosmos. Since we are practical and reasonable, we do not expect the cosmos to be perfect; we accept these unavoidable imperfections which we call abnormalities and diseases, and we take it for granted that human nature is not exempt from them. The frightening revelation of abysses that defy the human understanding is dismissed as illusion, and the poet is regarded as a victim and perpetrator of deception. Even to the poet, his primordial experience was "human—all too human," to such a degree that he could not face its meaning but had to conceal it from himself.

We shall do well, I think, to make fully explicit all the implications of that way of accounting for artistic creation which consists in reducing it to personal factors. We should see clearly where it leads. The truth is that it takes us away from the psychological study of the work of art, and confronts us with the psychic disposition of the poet himself. That the latter presents an important problem is not to be denied, but the work of art is something in its own right, and may not be conjured away. The question of the significance to the poet of his own creative work—of his regarding it as a trifle, as a screen, as a source of suffering or as an achievement—does not concern us at the moment, our task being to interpret the work of art psychologically. For this undertaking it is essential that we give serious consideration to the basic experience that underlies it—namely, to the vision. We must take it at least as seriously as we do the experiences that underlie the psychological mode of artistic creation, and no one doubts that they are both real and serious. It looks, indeed, as if the visionary experience were something quite apart from the ordinary lot of man, and for this reason we have difficulty in believing that it is real. It has about it an unfortunate suggestion of obscure metaphysics and of occultism, so that we feel called upon to intervene in the name of a well-intentioned reasonableness. Our conclusion is that it would be better not to take such things too seriously, lest the world revert again to a benighted superstition. We may, of course, have a predilection for the occult; but ordinarily we dismiss the visionary experience as the outcome of a rich fantasy or of a poetic mood—that is to say, as a kind of poetic license psychologically understood. Certain of the poets encourage this interpretation in order to put a wholesome distance between themselves and their work. Spitteler, for example, stoutly maintained that it was one and the same whether the poet sang of an Olympian Spring or to the theme: "May is here!" The truth is that poets are human beings, and that what a poet has to say about his work is often far from being the most illuminating word on the subject. What is required of us, then, is nothing less than to defend the importance of the visionary experience against the poet himself.

It cannot be denied that we catch the reverberations of an initial love-experience in *The Shepherd of Hermas,* in the *Divine Comedy* and in the *Faust* drama—an experience which is completed and fulfilled by the vision. There is no ground for the assumption that the second part of *Faust* repudiates or conceals the normal, human experience of the first part, nor are we justified in supposing that Goethe was normal at the time when he wrote *Part I,* but in a neurotic state of mind when he composed *Part II. Hermas,* Dante and Goethe can be taken as three steps in a sequence covering nearly two thousand years of human development, and in each of them we find the personal love-episode not only connected with the weightier visionary experience, but frankly subordinated to it. On the strength of this evidence which is furnished by the work of art itself and which throws out of court the question of the poet's particular psychic disposition, we must admit that the vision represents a deeper and more impressive experience than human passion. In works of art of this nature—and we must never confuse them with the artist as a person —we cannot doubt that the vision is a genuine, primordial experience, regardless of what reason-mongers may say. The vision is not something derived or secondary, and it is not a symptom of something else. It is true symbolic expression—that is, the expression of something existent in its own right, but imperfectly known. The love-episode is a real experience really suffered, and the same statement applies to the vision. We need not try to determine whether the content of the vision is of a physical, psychic or metaphysical nature. In itself it has psychic reality, and this is no less real than physical reality. Human passion falls within the sphere of conscious experience, while the subject of the vision lies beyond it. Through our feelings we experience the known, but our intuitions point to things that are unknown and hidden—that by their very nature are secret. If ever they become conscious, they are intentionally kept back and concealed, for which reason they have been regarded from earliest times as mysterious, uncanny and deceptive. They are hidden from the scrutiny of man, and he also hides himself from them out of *deisidae-monia*. He protects himself with the shield of science and the armour of reason. His enlightenment is born of fear; in the day-time he believes in an ordered cosmos, and he tries to maintain this faith against the fear of chaos that besets him by night. What if there were some living force whose sphere of action lies beyond our world of every day? Are there human needs that are dangerous and unavoidable? Is there something more purposeful than electrons? Do we delude ourselves in thinking that we possess and command our own souls? And is that which science calls the "psyche" not merely a question-mark arbitrarily confined within the skull, but rather a door that opens upon the human world from a world beyond, now and again allowing strange and unseizable potencies to act upon man and to remove him, as if upon the wings of the night, from the level of common humanity to that of a more than personal vocation? When we consider the visionary mode of artistic creation, it even seems as if the love-episode had served as a mere release—as if the personal experience were nothing but the prelude to the all-important "divine comedy."

It is not alone the creator of this kind of art who is in touch with the night-side of life, but the seers, prophets, leaders and enlighteners also. However dark this nocturnal world may be, it is not wholly unfamiliar. Man has known of it from time immemorial—here, there, and everywhere; for primitive man today it is an unquestionable part of his picture of the cosmos. It is only we who have repudiated it because of our fear of superstition and metaphysics, and because we strive to construct a conscious world that is safe and manageable in that natural law holds in it the place of statute law in a commonwealth. Yet, even in our midst, the poet now and then catches sight of the figures that people the night-world—the spirits, demons and gods. He knows that a purposiveness outreaching human ends is the life-giving secret for man; he has a presentiment of incomprehensible happenings in the pleroma. In short, he sees something of that psychic world that strikes terror into the savage and the barbarian.

From the very first beginnings of human society onward man's efforts to give his vague intimations a binding form have left their traces. Even in the Rhodesian cliff-drawings of the Old Stone Age there appears, side by side with the most amazingly life-like representations of animals, an abstract pattern—a double cross contained in a circle. This design has turned up in every cultural region, more or less, and we find it today not only in Christian churches, but in Tibetan monasteries as well. It is the so-called sun-wheel, and as it dates from a time when no one had thought of wheels as a mechanical device, it cannot have had its source in any experience of the external world. It is rather a symbol that stands for a psychic happening; it covers an experience of the inner world, and is no doubt as lifelike a representation as the famous rhinoceros with the tick-birds on its back. There has never been a primitive culture that did not possess a system of secret teaching, and in many cultures this system is highly developed. The men's councils and the totem-clans preserve this teaching about hidden things that lie apart from man's daytime existence —things which, from primeval times, have always constituted his most vital experiences. Knowledge about them is handed on to younger men in the rites of initiation. The mysteries of the Graeco-Roman world performed the same office, and the rich mythology of antiquity is a relic of such experiences in the earliest stages of human development.

It is therefore to be expected of the poet that he will resort to mythology in order to give his experience its most fitting expression. It would be a serious mistake to suppose that he works with materials received at second-hand. The primordial experience is the source of his creativeness; it cannot be fathomed, and therefore requires mythological imagery to give it form. In itself it offers no words or images, for it is a vision seen "as in a glass, darkly." It is merely a deep presentiment that strives to find expression. It is like a whirlwind that seizes everything within reach and, by carrying it aloft, assumes a visible shape. Since the particular expression can never exhaust the possibilities of the vision, but falls far short of it in richness of content, the poet must have at his disposal a huge store of materials if he is to communicate even a few of his intimations. What is more, he must resort to an imagery that is difficult to handle and full of contradictions in order to express the weird paradoxicality of his vision. Dante's presentiments are clothed in images that run the gamut of Heaven and Hell; Goethe must bring in the Blocksberg and the infernal regions of Greek antiquity; Wagner needs the whole body of Nordic myth; Nietzsche returns to the hieratic style and recreates the legendary seer of prehistoric times; Blake invents for himself indescribable figures, and Spitteler borrows old names for new creatures of the imagination. And no intermediate step is missing in the whole range from the ineffably sublime to the perversely grotesque.

Psychology can do nothing towards the elucidation of this colourful imagery except bring together materials for comparison and offer a terminology for its discussion. According to this terminology, that which appears in the vision is the collective unconscious. We mean by collective unconscious, a certain psychic disposition shaped by the forces of heredity; from it consciousness has developed. In the physical structure of the body we find traces of earlier stages of evolution, and we may expect the human psyche also to conform in its make-up to the law of phylogeny. It is a fact that in eclipses of consciousness—in dreams, narcotic states and cases of insanity—there come to the surface psychic products or contents that show all the traits of primitive levels of psychic development. The images themselves are sometimes of such a primitive character that we might suppose them derived from ancient, esoteric teaching. Mythological themes clothed in modern dress also frequently appear. What is of particular importance for the study of literature in these manifestations of the collective unconscious is that they are compensatory to the conscious attitude. This is to say that they can bring a one-sided, abnormal, or dangerous state of consciousness into equilibrium in an apparently purposive way. In dreams we can see this process very clearly in its positive aspect. In cases of insanity the compensatory process is often perfectly obvious, but takes a negative form. There are persons, for instance, who have anxiously shut themselves off from all the world only to discover one day that their most intimate secrets are known and talked about by everyone.*

If we consider Goethe's *Faust*, and leave aside the possibility that it is compensatory to his own conscious attitude, the question that we must answer is this: In what relation does it stand to the conscious outlook of his time? Great poetry draws its strength from the life of mankind, and we completely miss its meaning if we try to derive it from personal factors. Whenever the collective unconscious becomes a living experience and is brought to bear upon the conscious outlook of an age, this event is a creative act which is of importance to everyone living in that age. A work of art is produced that contains what may truthfully be called a message to generations of men. So *Faust* touches something in the soul of every German. So also Dante's fame is immortal, while *The Shepherd of Hermas* just failed of inclusion in the New Testament canon. Every period has its bias, its particular prejudice and its psychic ailment. An epoch is like an individual; it has its own limitations of conscious outlook, and therefore requires a compensatory adjustment. This is effected by the collective unconscious in that a poet, a seer or a leader allows himself to be guided by the unexpressed desire of his times and shows the

---

* See my article: "Mind and the Earth," in *Contributions to Analytical Psychology.* Harcourt, Brace & World, Inc., New York, 1928.

way, by word or deed, to the attainment of that which everyone blindly craves and expects—whether this attainment results in good or evil, the healing of an epoch or its destruction.

It is always dangerous to speak of ones own times, because what is at stake in the present is too vast for comprehension. A few hints must therefore suffice. Francesco Colonna's book is cast in the form of a dream, and is the apotheosis of natural love taken as a human relation; without countenancing a wild indulgence of the senses, he leaves completely aside the Christian sacrament of marriage. The book was written in 1453. Rider Haggard, whose life coincides with the flowering-time of the Victorian era, takes up this subject and deals with it in his own way; he does not cast it in the form of a dream, but allows us to feel the tension of moral conflict. Goethe weaves the theme of Gretchen-Helen-Mater-Gloriosa like a red thread into the colourful tapestry of Faust. Nietzsche proclaims the death of God, and Spitteler transforms the waxing and waning of the gods into a myth of the seasons. Whatever his importance, each of these poets speaks with the voice of thousands and ten thousands, foretelling changes in the conscious outlook of his time.

. . . . II. The Poet

Creativeness, like the freedom of the will, contains a secret. The psychologist can describe both these manifestations as processes, but he can find no solution of the philosophical problems they offer. Creative man is a riddle that we may try to answer in various ways, but always in vain, a truth that has not prevented modern psychology from turning now and again to the question of the artist and his art. Freud thought that he had found a key in his procedure of deriving the work of art from the personal experiences of the artist.* It is true that certain possibilities lay in this direction, for it was conceivable that a work of art, no less than a neurosis, might be traced back to those knots in psychic life that we call the complexes. It was Freud's great discovery that neuroses have a causal origin in the psychic realm—that they take their rise from emotional states and from real or imagined childhood experiences. Certain of his followers, like Rank and Stekel, have taken up related lines of enquiry and have achieved important results. It is undeniable that the poet's psychic disposition permeates his work root and branch. Nor is there anything new in the statement that personal factors largely influence the poet's choice and use of his materials. Credit, however, must certainly be given to the Freudian school for showing how far-reaching this influence is and in what curious ways it comes to expression.

* See Freud's essay on Jensen's *Gradiva* and on Leonardo da Vinci.

Freud takes the neurosis as a substitute for a direct means of gratification. He therefore regards it as something inappropriate—a mistake, a dodge, an excuse, a voluntary blindness. To him it is essentially a shortcoming that should never have been. Since a neurosis, to all appearances, is nothing but a disturbance that is all the more irritating because it is without sense or meaning, few people will venture to say a good word for it. And a work of art is brought into questionable proximity with the neurosis when it is taken as something which can be analysed in terms of the poet's repressions. In a sense it finds itself in good company, for religion and philosophy are regarded in the same light by Freudian psychology. No objection can be raised if it is admitted that this approach amounts to nothing more than the elucidation of those personal determinants without which a work of art is unthinkable. But should the claim be made that such an analysis accounts for the work of art itself, then a categorical denial is called for. The personal idiosyncrasies that creep into a work of art are not essential; in fact, the more we have to cope with these peculiarities, the less is it a question of art. What is essential in a work of art is that it should rise far above the realm of personal life and speak from the spirit and heart of the poet as man to the spirit and heart of mankind. The personal aspect is a limitation—and even a sin—in the realm of art. When a form of "art" is primarily personal it deserves to be treated as if it were a neurosis. There may be some validity in the idea held by the Freudian school that artists without exception are narcissistic—by which is meant that they are undeveloped persons with infantile and auto-erotic traits. The statement is only valid, however, for the artist as a person, and has nothing to do with the man as an artist. In his capacity of artist he is neither auto-erotic, nor hetero-erotic, nor erotic in any sense. He is objective and impersonal—even inhuman—for as an artist he is his work, and not a human being.

Every creative person is a duality or a synthesis of contradictory aptitudes. On the one side he is a human being with a personal life, while on the other side he is an impersonal, creative process. Since as a human being he may be sound or morbid, we must look at his psychic make-up to find the determinants of his personality. But we can only understand him in his capacity of artist by looking at his creative achievement. We should make a sad mistake if we tried to explain the mode of life of an English gentleman, a Prussian officer, or a cardinal in terms of personal factors. The gentleman, the officer and the cleric function as such in an impersonal rôle, and their psychic make-up is qualified by a peculiar objectivity. We must grant that the artist does not function in an official capacity—the very opposite is nearer the truth. He nevertheless resembles the types I have named in one respect, for the specifically artistic disposition involves an overweight of collective psychic life as against the personal. Art is a kind of innate drive that seizes a human being and makes him its instrument. The artist is not a person endowed with free will who seeks his own ends, but one who allows art to realize its purposes through him. As a human being he may have moods and a will and personal aims, but as an artist he is "man" in a higher sense—he is "collective man"—one who carries and shapes the unconscious, psychic life of mankind. To perform this difficult office it is sometimes necessary for him to sacrifice happiness and everything that makes life worth living for the ordinary human being.

All this being so, it is not strange that the artist is an especially interesting case for the psychologist who uses an analytical method. The artist's life cannot be otherwise than full of conflicts, for two forces are at war within him—on the one hand the common human longing for happiness, satisfaction and security in life, and on the other a ruthless passion for creation which may go so far as to override every personal desire. The lives of artists are as a rule so highly unsatisfactory—not to say tragic—because of their inferiority on the human and personal side, and not because of a sinister dispensation. There are hardly any exceptions to the rule that a person must pay dearly for the divine gift of the creative fire. It is as though each of us were endowed at birth with a certain capital of energy. The strongest force in our make-up will seize and all but monopolize this energy, leaving so little over that nothing of value can come of it. In this way the creative force can drain the human impulses to such a degree that the personal ego must develop all sorts of bad qualities—ruthlessness, selfishness and vanity (so-called "auto-erotism")—and even every kind of vice, in order to maintain the spark of life and to keep itself from being wholly bereft. The auto-erotism of artists resembles that of illegitimate or neglected children who from their tenderest years must protect themselves from the destructive influence of people who have no love to give them—who develop bad qualities for that very purpose and later maintain an invincible egocentrism by remaining all their lives infantile and helpless or by actively offending against the moral code or the law. How can we doubt that it is his art that explains the artist, and not the insufficiencies and conflicts of his personal life? These are nothing but the regrettable results of the fact that he is an artist—that is to say, a man who from his very birth has been called to a greater task than the ordinary mortal. A special ability means a heavy expenditure of energy in a particular direction, with a consequent drain from some other side of life.

It makes no difference whether the poet knows that his work is begotten, grows and matures with him, or whether he supposes that by taking thought he produces it out of the void. His opinion of the matter does not change the fact that his own work outgrows him as a child its mother. The creative process has feminine quality, and the creative work arises from unconscious depths—we might say, from the realm of the mothers. Whenever the creative force predominates, human life is ruled and moulded by the unconscious as against the active will, and the conscious ego is swept along on a subterranean current, being nothing more than a helpless observer of events. The work in process becomes the poet's fate and determines his psychic development. It is not Goethe who creates *Faust,* but *Faust* which creates Goethe. And what is *Faust* but a symbol? By this I do not mean an allegory that points to something all too familiar, but an expression that stands for something not clearly known and yet profoundly alive. Here it is something that lives in the soul of every German, and that Goethe has helped to bring to birth. Could we conceive of anyone but a German writing *Faust* or *Also sprach Zarathustra?* Both play upon something that reverberates in the German soul—a "primordial image," as Jacob Burckhardt once called it—the figure of a physician or teacher of mankind. The archetypal image of the wise man, the saviour or redeemer, lies buried and dormant in man's unconscious since the dawn of culture; it is awakened whenever the times are out of joint and a human society is committed to a serious error. When people go astray they feel the need of a guide or teacher or even of the physician. These primordial images are numerous, but do not appear in the dreams of individuals or in works of art until they are called into being by the waywardness of the general outlook. When conscious life is characterized by one-sidedness and by a false attitude, then they are activated—one might say, "instinctively"—and come to light in the dreams of individuals and the visions of artists and seers, thus restoring the psychic equilibrium of the epoch.

In this way the work of the poet comes to meet the spiritual need of the society in which he lives, and for this reason his work means more to him than his personal fate, whether he is aware of this or not. Being essentially the instrument for his work, he is subordinate to it, and we have no reason for expecting him to interpret it for us. He has done the best that in him lies in giving it form, and he must leave the interpretation to others and to the future. A great work of art is like a dream; for all its apparent obviousness it does not explain itself and is never unequivocal. A dream never says: "You ought," or: "This is the truth." It presents an image in much the same way as nature allows a plant to grow, and we must draw our own conclusions. If a person has a nightmare, it means either that he is too much given to fear, or else that he is too exempt from it; and if he dreams of the old wise man it may mean that he is too pedagogical, as also that he stands in need of a teacher. In a subtle way both meanings come to the same thing, as we perceive when we are able to let the work of art act upon us as it acted upon the artist. To grasp its meaning, we must allow it to shape us as it once shaped him. Then we understand the nature of his experience. We see that he has drawn upon the healing and redeeming forces of the collective psyche that underlies consciousness with its isolation and its painful errors; that he has penetrated to that matrix of life in which all men are embedded, which imparts a common rhythm to all human existence, and allows the individual to communicate his feeling and his striving to mankind as a whole.

The secret of artistic creation and of the effectiveness of art is to be found in a return to the state of *participation mystique*—to that level of experience at which it is man who lives, and not the individual, and at which the weal or woe of the single human being does not count, but only human existence. This is why every great work of art is objective and impersonal, but none the less profoundly moves us each and all. And this is also why the personal life of the poet cannot be held essential to his art—but at most a help or a hindrance to his creative task. He may go the way of a Philistine, a good citizen, a neurotic, a fool or a criminal. His personal career may be inevitable and interesting, but it does not explain the poet.

Thomas Mann

In the pages that follow, one of the greatest of twentieth-century novelists, the German Thomas Mann, comments on the work of the Russian writer whom many critics consider the greatest of all novelists. Mann's eminence in modern letters rests not only on his novels and short stories but also, to a lesser degree, on his essays and his literary criticism. His essay on Tolstoy, entirely typical of his approach as a critic, provides an interesting contrast with the essay by Bernard Knox which follows it. Knox, the professional academic critic, centers his attention on the texture of the literary work itself, and he formulates his reading of the work from that texture, without overt consideration of the personality of Sophocles or the conditioning effect of his historical milieu. Mann, the creative artist momentarily engaged in the critical function, moves instinctively into a sympathetic identification with Tolstoy, and he arrives at his reading of *Anna Karenina* partly in terms of his own familiarity with the springs of creativity, as they exist in himself and as they must have existed in Tolstoy. Indeed, the creative and critical functions are never decisively separated in Mann; repeatedly he expresses his critical perceptions by devices that are native to the poet or the writer of fiction, as at the beginning of this essay, where his impressionistic and lyrical evocation of setting leads into a metaphor in which the sea is equated with the spirit of epic literature.

Mann's treatment of Tolstoy, however, has ramifications which extend beyond *Anna Karenina;* his essay summons up again the argument over the proper
relations of imagination, reason, and morality which is carried on in other terms
elsewhere in this volume. The great irony of Tolstoy's career is that he,
supremely gifted as the natural, instinctive artist who renders without moralistic
comment the rich complexities of character and life, was driven by an inner
compulsion to a severely moralistic position which ended in the rejection of art
itself. Mann is admirably suited to investigate that irony, for his own creative
work, exemplified in his famous novels *Buddenbrooks, The Magic Mountain,*
and *Doctor Faustus,* has consistently concerned itself with the ironic tension
between "spirit" and "nature" which he finds basic to human experience.

*A*NNA KARENINA

1939

Today high tide is at ten. The waters rush up the narrowing strand, carrying foam-bubbles and jelly-fish—primitive children of an
unnatural mother, who will abandon them on the sands to death by
evaporation. The waves run up, almost to the foot of my beach-chair;
sometimes I must lift away my plaid-wrapped legs as the waters encroach
and threaten to cover them. My heart responds blithely, though also with
utter respect, to these sportive little tricks the mighty ocean plays me;
my sympathy, a deep and tender, primitive, soul-extending stirring, is
far indeed from any annoyance.

No bathers yet. They await the midday warmth to wade out into
the ebbing tide, little flutters and shrieks escaping them as they begin
their pert yet fearful toying with the vast. Coast-guards in cork jackets,
lynx-eyed, tooting their horns, watch over all this amateurish frivolity.
My "workshop" here surpasses any I know. It is lonely; but even were it
livelier, the tumultuous surf so shuts me in, and the sides of my admirable
beach-chair, seat and cabin in one, familiar from my youth up, is so
peculiarly protective that there can be no distraction. Beloved, incomparably soothing and suitable situation—it recurs in my life again and
again, as by a law. Beneath a sky where gently shifting continents of
cloud link the blue depths, rolls the sea, a darkening green against the
clear horizon, oncoming in seven or eight foaming white rows of surf
that reach out of sight in both directions. There is superb activity farther
out, where the advancing waves hurl themselves first and highest against

Reprinted from *Essays of Three Decades* by Thomas Mann, by permission of Alfred
A. Knopf, Inc. Copyright 1947 by Alfred A. Knopf, Inc.

the bar. The bottle-green wall gleams metallic as it mounts and halts and curls over, then shatters with a roar and an explosion of foam down, down, in ever recurrent crash, whose dull thunder forms the deep ground-bass to the higher key of the boiling and hissing waves as they break nearer in. Never does the eye tire of this sight nor the ear of this music.

A more fitting spot could not be for my purpose: which is to recall and to reflect upon the great book whose title stands at the head of my paper. And here by the sea there comes to mind inevitably an old, I might almost say an innate association of ideas: the spiritual identity of two elementary experiences, one of which is a parable of the other. I mean the ocean and the epic. The epic, with its rolling breadth, its breath of the beginnings and the roots of life, its broad and sweeping rhythm, its all-consuming monotony—how like it is to the sea, how like to it is the sea! It is the Homeric element I mean, the story going on and on, art and nature at once, naïve, magnificent, material, objective, immortally healthy, immortally realistic! All this was strong in Tolstoy, stronger than in any other modern creator of epic art; it distinguishes his genius, if not in rank, yet in essence, from the morbid manifestation, the ecstatic and highly distorted phenomenon, that was Dostoyevsky. Tolstoy himself said of his early work *Childhood* and *Boyhood:* "Without false modesty, it is something like the Iliad." That is the merest statement of fact; only on exterior grounds does it fit still better the giant work of his maturity, *War and Peace.* It fits everything he wrote. The pure narrative power of his work is unequalled. Every contact with it, even when he wished no longer to be an artist, when he scorned and reviled art and only employed it as a means of communicating moral lessons; every contact with it, I say, rewards the talent that knows how to receive (for there is no other) with rich streams of power and refreshment, of creative primeval lustiness and health. Seldom did art work so much like nature; its immediate, natural power is only another manifestation of nature itself; and to read him again, to be played upon by the animal keenness of this eye, the sheer power of this creative attack, the entirely clear and true greatness, unclouded by any mysticism, of this epic, is to find one's way home, safe from every danger of affectation and morbid trifling; home to originality and health, to everything within us that is fundamental and sane.

Turgenyev once said: "We have all come out from under Gogol's *Mantle"*—a fiendishly clever pun which puts in a phrase the extraordinary uniformity and unity, the thick traditionalism of Russian literature as a whole. Actually, they are all there simultaneously, its masters and geniuses, they can put out their hands to each other, their life-spans in great part overlap. Nikolai Gogol read aloud some of *Dead Souls* to the great Pushkin, and the author of *Yevgeny Onyegin* shook with laughter—and then suddenly grew sad. Lermontov was the contemporary of both. Turgenyev, as one may easily forget, for his frame, like Dostoyevsky's, Lieskov's, and Tolstoy's, belongs to the second half of the nineteenth century, came only four years later than Lermontov into the world and ten before Tolstoy, whom he adjured in a touching letter expressing his faith in humanistic art, "to go back to literature." What I mean by thick traditionalism is illustrated by an anecdote that most significantly connects Tolstoy's artistically finest work, *Anna Karenina,* with Pushkin.

One evening in the spring of 1873, Count Leo Nikolayevich entered the room of his eldest son, who was reading aloud to his old aunt Pushkin's *Stories of Byelkin;* the father took the book and read: "The guests assembled in the country house." "That's the way to begin," he said; went into his study and wrote: "In the Oblonsky house great confusion reigned." That was the original first sentence from *Anna Karenina.* The present beginning, the *aperçu* about happy and unhappy families, was introduced later. That is a marvellously pretty little anecdote. He had already begun much and brought much to triumphant conclusion. He was the fêted creator of the Russian national epos, in the form of a modern novel, the giant panorama *War and Peace.* And he was about to excel both formally and artistically this chef-d'œuvre of his thirty-five years in the work he had now in hand, which one may with an easy mind pronounce the greatest society novel of world literature. And here he was, restlessly prowling about the house, searching, searching, not knowing how to begin. Pushkin taught him, tradition taught him, Pushkin the classic master, from whose world his own was so remote, both personally and generally speaking. Pushkin rescued him, as he hesitated on the brink; showed him how one sets to, takes a firm grip, and plumps the reader *in medias res.* Unity is achieved, the continuity of that astonishing family of intellects which one calls Russian literature is preserved in this little piece of historical evidence.

Merezhkovsky points out that historically and pre-modernly only Pushkin among these writers really possesses charm. He inhabits a sphere by himself, a sensuously radiant, naïve, and blithely poetic one. But with Gogol there begins what Merezhkovsky calls critique: "the transition from unconscious creation to creative consciousness"; for him that means the end of poetry in the Pushkin sense, but at the same time the beginning of something new. The remark is true and perceptive. Thus did Heine speak of the age of Goethe, an æsthetic age, an epoch of art, an objective-ironic point of view. Its representative and dominant figure had been the Olympian; it died with his death. What then began was a time of taking sides, of conflicting opinions, of social consolidation, yes, of politics and, in short, of morals—a morality that branded as frivolous every purely æsthetic and universal point of view.

In Heine's comments, as in Merezhkovsky's, there is feeling for temporal change, together with feeling for its opposite, the timeless and perpetual. Schiller, in his immortal essay, reduced it to the formula of the sentimental and the naïve. What Merezhkovsky calls "critique" or "creative consciousness," what seems to him like contrast with the unconscious creation of Pushkin, as the more modern element, the future on the way, is precisely what Schiller means by the sentimental in contrast to the naïve. He too brings in the temporal, the evolutional, and—"*pro domo*," as we know—declares the sentimental, the creativeness of conscious critique, in short the moralistic, to be the newer, more modern stage of development.

There are now two things to say: first, Tolstoy's original convictions were definitely on the side of the æsthetic, of pure art, the objectively shaping, anti-moralistic principle; and second, in him took place that very cultural and historical change which Merezhkovsky speaks of, that move away from Pushkin's simplicity towards critical responsibility and morality. Within his own being it took such a radical and tragic form that he went through the severest crises and much anguish and even so could not utterly repudiate his own mighty creativeness. What he finally arrived at was a rejection and negation of art itself as an idle, voluptuous, and immoral luxury, admissible only in order to make moral teachings acceptable to men, even though dressed in the mantle of art.

But to return to the first position: we have his own unequivocal declarations to the effect that a purely artistic gift stands higher than one with social significance. In 1859, when he was thirty-one years old, he gave, as a member of the Moscow society of Friends of Russian Literature, an address in which he so sharply emphasized the advantages of the purely art element in literature over all the fashions of the day that the president of the society, Khomyakov, felt constrained to rejoin that a servant of pure art might quite easily become a social reformer even without knowing or willing it. Contemporary criticism saw in the author of *Anna Karenina* the protagonist of the art for art's sake position, the representative of free creativeness apart from all tendentiousness or doctrine. Indeed, it considered this naturalism the characteristically new thing; the public must in time grow up to it, though at present they had got used, in the works of others, to the presentation of political and social ideas in the form of art. In point of fact, all this was only one side of the business. As an artist and son of his time, the nineteenth century, Tolstoy was a naturalist, and in this connection he represented—in the sense of a trend—the new. But as an intellectual he was beyond (or rather, he struggled amid torments to arrive beyond) the new, to something further still, on the other side of his, the naturalistic century. He was reaching after conceptions of art which approached much nearer to "mind" (*Geist*), to knowledge, to "critique" than to nature. The commentators of 1875, impressed by the first chapters of *Anna Karenina* as they appeared in a Russian magazine, the *Messenger*, seeking benevolently to prepare the way with the public for the naturalism of the work, did not dream that the author was in full flight towards an anti-art position, which was already hampering his work on his masterpiece and even endangering its completion.

This development was to go very far, the vehemence of its consistency shrank from nothing: neither from the anti-cultural nor even from the absurd. Before long, he was to regret in public having written *Childhood* and *Youth,* the work of his freshest youthful hours—so poor, so insincere, so literary, so sinful was this book. He was to condemn root and branch the "artist twaddle" with which the twelve volumes of his works were filled, to which "the people of our day ascribe an undeserved significance." It was the same undeserved significance that they ascribed to art itself— for instance, to Shakespeare's plays. He went so far—one must set it down with respect and a sober face, or at least with the smallest, most non-committal smile—as to put Mrs. Harriet Beecher Stowe, the author of *Uncle Tom's Cabin,* far above Shakespeare.

We must be at pains to understand this. Tolstoy's hatred for Shakespeare dated from much earlier than is usually supposed. It signified rebellion against nature, the universal, the all-affirming. It was jealousy of the morally tormented for the irony of the absolute creator, it meant the straining away from nature, naïveté, moral indifference, towards *"Geist"* in the moralistically critical sense of the word; towards moral valuations and edifying doctrine. Tolstoy hated himself in Shakespeare, hated his own vital bearish strength, which was originally like Shakespeare's, natural and creatively a-moral; though his struggles for the good, the true and right, the meaning of life, the doctrine of salvation, were after all only the same thing in another and self-denying form. The immensity of his writings sometimes resulted in a gigantic clumsiness which forces a respectful smile. And yet it is precisely the paradoxically ascetic application of a titanic helplessness arising from a primeval force that, viewed as art, gives his work that huge moral *élan,* that Atlas-like moral muscle-tensing and flexing which reminds one of the agonized figures of Michelangelo's sculpture.

I said that Tolstoy's hatred of Shakespeare belongs to an earlier period than is generally thought. But all that which later made his friends and admirers like Turgenyev weep, his denial of art and culture, his radical moralism, his highly questionable pose of prophet and confessor in his last period—all that begins much further back, it is quite wrong to imagine this process as something suddenly occurring in a crisis of con-version in later life, coincident with Tolstoy's old age. The same kind of mistake occurs in the popular opinion that Richard Wagner suddenly got religion—whereas the matter was one of a development vastly and fatally consistent and inevitable, the direction of which is clearly and unmistakably traceable in *The Flying Dutchman* and in *Tannhäuser*. The judgment of the Frenchman, Vogüé, was entirely correct when, on the news that the great Russian writer was now "as though paralysed by a sort of mystic madness," Vogüé declared that he had long ago seen it coming. The course of Tolstoy's intellectual development had been present in the seed in *Childhood* and *Boyhood* and the psychology of Levin in *Anna Karenina* had marked out the path it would take.

So much is true, that Levin is Tolstoy, the real hero of the mighty novel, which is a glorious, indestructible signpost on the woeful Way of the Cross the poet was taking; a monument of an elemental and creative bear-strength, which was first heightened and then destroyed by the inner ferment of his subtilizing conscience and his fear of God. Yes, Levin is Tolstoy—almost altogether Tolstoy, this side Tolstoy the artist. To this character Tolstoy transferred not only the important facts and dates of his own life: his experiences as a farmer, his romance and betrothal (which are completely autobiographic), the sacred, beautiful, and aweful experiences of the birth of his first child, and the death of his brother—which forms a pendant of equal and boundless significance—not only there but in his whole inner life, his crises of conscience, his groping after the whole duty of man and the meaning of life, his painful wrestling over the good life, which so decisively estranged him from the doings of urban society; his gnawing doubts about culture itself or that which his society called culture, doubts of all this brought him close to the anchorite and nihilist type. What Levin lacks of Tolstoy is only just that he is not a great artist besides. But to estimate *Anna Karenina* not only artistically but also humanly, the reader must saturate himself with the thesis that Constantin Levin himself wrote the novel. Instead of being the man with the pointer, indicating the incomparable beauty of the painting as a whole, I shall do better to speak of the conditions of difficulty and stress under which the work came to birth.

That is the right word: it came to birth; but there did not lack much for it not to be born. A work of this kind, so all of one piece and that piece so absorbing, so complete in the large and in the small, makes us suppose that its creator gave himself utterly to it with entire and devoted heart and, like one driven to self-expression, committed it, so to speak, in one gush to paper. That is a misapprehension; although, even so, the origin of *Anna Karenina* does in fact lie in the happiest, most harmonious period of Tolstoy's life. The years in which he worked on it belong to the first decade and a half of his marriage with the woman whose literary image is Kitty Shtcherbatsky and who later suffered so much from her Lievotshka—until at last just before his death the old man broke away and ran. It is she who, in addition to her constant pregnancies, and her abundant activities as mistress of the farm, as mother and housewife, copies *War and Peace* seven times with her own hand—that first colossal intellectual harvest of the period that brought the doubting, brooding man relative peace in the patriarchal animalism of marriage and family life in the country. It was the period at which the poor Countess looked so yearningly back when Leochen had become "the prophet of Yasnaya Polyana" and succeeded under self-torture, and even so up to the end never quite succeeded, in brooding to death all his sensual and instinctive passions: family, nation, state, church, club, and chase, at bottom the whole life of the body, but most particularly art, which for him quite essentially meant sensuality and the body's life.

Well, those fifteen years were a good, happy time, though from a later, higher point of view, good only in a low and animal sense. *War and Peace* had made Tolstoy the "great writer of Russia," and as such he went to work to write a new historical and national epos. He had in mind a novel about Peter the Great and his times. And for months he carried on conscientious and comprehensive studies for it in the libraries and archives of Moscow. "Lievotshka reads and reads," it says in the Countess's letters. Did he read too much? Did he take in too much, did he spoil his appetite? Oddly enough, it turned out that the Czar reformer, the imperial compeller of civilization, was at bottom an unsympathetic figure to Tolstoy. To hold the position he had achieved as the national epic-writer, he had wanted to repeat his performance in *War and Peace*. It would not come off; the material unexpectedly resisted him. After endless preparatory labour he flung the whole thing away, sacrificed his whole investment of time and study, and turned to something quite different: the passion and stumbling of *Anna Karenina*, the modern novel of St. Petersburg and Moscow high society.

The first onset, by dint of Pushkin's help, was fresh and blithe. But before long Tolstoy got stuck, though the reader in his untrammelled enjoyment would never guess it. For weeks and months the work only dragged on or did not go at all. What was the trouble? Household cares, children's illnesses, fluctuations in his own health—oh, no, these were all nothing compared with a piece of work like *Anna Karenina*—or they ought to be. What is really disturbing is doubt of the importance and personal urgency of what we are doing. Might we not do better to learn Greek, to get some fundamental knowledge of the New Testament? Then the schools for the children of peasants we have founded. Should they not claim more of our time and thought? Is not the whole of belles-lettres folly? And is it not our duty or even much more consistent with our deepest need to bury ourselves in theological and philosophical studies in order to find at last the meaning of life? That contact with the mystery of death which he had had when his older brother died had made a strong impression on Tolstoy's own vitality, powerful to the point of mysticism, which demanded spiritual wrestling, not in a literary way but in something confessional on the pattern of Saint Augustine and Rousseau. Such a book, sincere as far as human power could make it, weighed on his mind and gave him increasing distaste for writing novels. Actually, he would never have finished *Anna Karenina* if it had not begun appearing in the *Rusky Vyestnik (Russian Messenger)* of Katkov. The fact made him responsible to the publisher and the reading public. In January 1875 and the following three months successive numbers of the novel appeared in the magazine. Then they left off, because the author had no more to deliver. The first months of the next year produced a few fragments, then seven months' pause. Then in December one more number. What we find simply enchanting, what we cannot imagine as originating in anything except a state of prolonged inspiration—Tolstoy groaned over. "My tiresome, horrible *Anna Karenina*," he wrote from Samara, where he was drinking mares' milk. *Sic!* Literally. "At last," he wrote in March 1876, "I was driven to finish my novel, of which I am sick to death." Of course in the process the enthusiasm and eagerness came back by fits and starts. But it was just at such times that the writing was prone to go more slowly—owing to fastidious artistry that caused endless filing and remodelling and improving out of a stylistic perfectionism which still shows through the most inadequate translation. This amazing saint took his art the more seriously the less he believed in it.

The publication dragged on, with constant interruptions, as far as the eighth book. Then it stopped, for now the thing had become political and the national epic-writer of Russia had in the latest number expressed himself so heretically about Slavophilism, the current enthusiasm for the Bulgarian, Serbian, Bosnian brothers in their fight for freedom against the Turks, the much ado over the volunteers and the patriotic nonsense uttered by Russian society, that Katkov dared not print it. He demanded cuts and changes, which the author in high dudgeon refused to make. Tolstoy had the final numbers printed separately with a note on the disagreement.

What I have boldly called the greatest society novel in all literature is an anti-society novel. The Bible text: "Vengeance is mine, I will repay, saith the Lord," stands at its head. The moral momentum of the work was certainly the desire to lash society for the cold, cruel rebuff inflicted by it on a woman who goes astray through passion but is fundamentally proud and high-minded, instead of leaving to God the punishment for her sins. Indeed, society might well do just that, for after all it is society and its irrevocable laws that God too avails Himself of to exact the payment. It shows the fatal and inevitable character of Anna's doom that it proceeds inscrutably, step by step, up to the frightful end out of her affront to the moral law. So there is a certain contradiction in the author's original moral motive, in the complaint he lodges against society. One asks oneself in what way would God punish if society did not behave as it does? Custom and morality, how far are they distinguishable, how far are they—in effect—one and the same, how far do they coincide in the heart of the socially circumscribed human being? The question hovers unanswered over the whole novel. But such a work is not compelled to answer questions. Its task is to bring them out, to enrich the emotions, to give them the highest and most painful degree of questionableness. Thus it will have performed its task, and in this case the story-teller's love for his creature leaves no doubt at all, no matter how much suffering he painfully and relentlessly visits on her.

Tolstoy loves Anna very much, one feels that. The book bears her name; it could bear no other. But its hero is not Anna's lover, the strong, decent, chivalrous, and somewhat limited officer of the Guards, Count Vronsky. Nor is it Alexander Alexandrovich, Anna's husband, with whatever profound skill Tolstoy has modelled this incomparable, at once repellent and superior, comic and touching cuckold. No, the hero is another person altogether, who has as good as nothing to do with Anna's lot, and whose introduction in a way twists the theme of the novel and almost pushes its first motive into second place. It is Constantin Levin, the introspective man, the author's image—he, no other, with his brooding and scrutinizing, with the peculiar force and obstinate resistance of his critical conscience, that makes the great society novel into an anti-society novel.

What an extraordinary fellow he is, this surrogate of the author! What in the French *pièce à thèse* is called the *raisonneur*—Levin is that in Tolstoy's society world. Yet how un-French! To amount to something as a critic of society, one must, I suppose, be in society oneself; but precisely that he is not in the least, this tortured, radically remote *raisonneur,* despite his native right to move in the highest circles. Strong and shy, defiant and dubious, with an intelligence of great anti-logical, natural, even helpless abundance, Levin is at bottom convinced that decency, uprightness, seriousness, and sincerity are possible only in singleness, in dumb isolation, each for himself; and that all social life turns him into a chatterer, a liar, and a fool. Observe him in the salons of Moscow, or on cultural occasions when he has to make conversation, play a social part, express "views." Such a coming-together of people seems to him banal, he sees himself a blushing fool, a prattler, a parrot. This Rousseauian quite sincerely considers all urban civilization, with the intellectual and cultural goings-on bound up in it, a sink of iniquity. Only life in the country is worthy of a man—though not the country life that the city man in sentimental relaxation finds "charming." Levin's learned brother, for instance, even boasts in a way that he enjoyed such an un-intellectual occupation as fishing. No, what Levin means is the real, serious life on the land, where you have to work hard, where the human being dwells truly and perforce at the heart of that nature whose "beauty" the guest from civilization sentimentally admires from outside.

Levin's morality and conscientiousness are strongly physical, having reference to the body and bound up with it. "I need physical exercise," he says to himself, "otherwise my character suffers." He resolves to help the peasants with the mowing and it gives him the highest moral and physical pleasure (a splendid and Tolstoyan chapter). His scorn of the "intellectual" or, better, his disbelief in it, estranging him as a product of civilization, involving him in contradictions, is radical. It leads him, when he has to come right down to it, into paradoxes, into opinions hard to express among civilized beings. Take for instance popular education— or, worse still, any education at all. Levin's position towards it is the same as his position towards nature: "The same people whom you say you love."—"I never said that," thought Constantin Levin.—"Why should I bother my head about schools where I shall never send my own children and where the peasants will never send theirs either? And on top of that, I am not even convinced that it is necessary to send them!"—"You can make better use of a peasant and labourer who can read and write than of one who cannot."—"No, ask anybody you like," countered Constantin Levin decisively; "a worker with some schooling is distinctly worse."— "Do you admit that education is a blessing for the people?"—"Yes, that I admit," responded Levin thoughtlessly, and saw at once that what he had said was not really just what he thought.—Very bad! A difficult, dangerous case! He recognizes the blessings of "education," because what he "really" thinks about it, in the nineteenth century, cannot be put into words and for that reason may even be unthinkable.

Of course he moves in the thought-channels of his century, and they in a certain way are scientific. He "observes humanity, not as something standing outside of zoological law but as something dependent on its environment, and he proceeds from this dependence in order to discover the laws lying at the base of its development." So at least the scholar understands him; and it is no other than Taine to whom he there makes acknowledgment, good, great nineteenth century. But there is something in him that either goes back behind the scientific spirit of his epoch or goes on beyond it, something desperately bold, inadmissible, impossible in conversation. He lies on his back and looks up at the high and cloudless sky. "Do I not know that that is infinite space and not a round vault? But however I screw up my eyes and strain my sight I cannot see it not round and not bounded; and in spite of my knowledge about infinite space I am incontestably right when I see a solid blue dome, and more right than when I strain my eyes to see beyond it. . . . Can this be faith?"

But whether faith or the new realism, it is no longer the scientific spirit of the nineteenth century. In a sort of way it recalls Goethe. And Levin-Tolstoy's sceptical, realistic, rebellious attitude towards patriotism, towards the Slavic brethren and the war volunteers, does the same. He declines to share in the enthusiasm, he is solitary in the midst of it, precisely as Goethe was at the time of the Freiheitskrieg—although in both cases something new, the democratic, joined the national movement and for the first time the popular will conditioned the conduct of the government. That too is nineteenth-century; and Levin, or Lievotshka, as the poor Countess called him, could simply not do with the truths of his time. He called them comfortless. He is a step further on; I cannot help calling it a very dangerous step, which, if not safeguarded by the profoundest love of truth and human sympathy, can quite easily lead to black reaction and barbarism. Today it takes no forlorn, single-handed courage to throw overboard the scientific discipline of the nineteenth century and surrender to the "mythus," the "faith"—in other words, to a paltry and culture-destroying vulgarity. Masses of people do it today; but it is not a step forward, it is a hundred miles backwards. Such a step will be in a forward direction only when it is taken for humanity's sake, only if another step follows it straightway, moving from the new realism of the solid blue vault to the neither old nor new but humanly eternal idealism of truth, freedom, and knowledge. Today there are some desperately stupid ideas about reaction in the air.

A digression—but a necessary one. Levin, then, cannot do with the ideals of his epoch, he cannot live with them. What I call his physical morality and conscientiousness is shaken to the depths by the experience of the physically transcendent and transparent mysteries of birth and death; and all that the times teach him about organisms and their destruction, about the indestructibility of matter and the laws of conservation of energy, about evolution, and so forth, all that looks to him not only like utter ignorance of the whole problem of the meaning of life but also like a kind of thinking that makes it impossible for him to get the knowledge he needs. That in infinite time, infinite space, infinite matter, and organism, a cell frees itself; that it persists for a while and then bursts and that this bubble is he himself, Levin; that seems to him like the malicious mockery of some demon. It cannot indeed be refuted; it must be overcome some other way, that one may not be driven to shoot oneself.

What to his profounder necessities looks like a mortal lie and a kind of thinking which is no sort of instrument for the apprehension of

truth—that actually is the naturalistic materialism of the nineteenth century, whose inspiration is honest love of truth, despite the comfortless
pessimism that is its necessary aura. The honesty must be preserved; but
a little illumination is required in order to do justice to life and its deeper
concerns. So there is real humour in the fact that in *Anna Karenina* a
simple little peasant shows the brooding man the way out of his despair.
This little peasant teaches him, or recalls to his mind, something he has
always known: true, he says, living for our physical well-being and in
order to fill our bellies is natural and inborn and laid upon us all. But
even so, it is not righteous or even important. What we have to do is to
live for the "truth," "for our souls," "as God wills," for "the Good." How
wonderful that this necessity is laid upon us just as naturally inborn and
imposed as the need to fill our bellies! Wonderful indeed; for the sure
conviction common to all men that it is shameful to live only for the
belly, and that one must rather live for God, for the true and the good,
has nothing to do with reason, but quite the contrary. It is reason that
makes us care for the body and in its interest to exploit our neighbours
all we can. Knowledge of the good, asserts Levin, does not lie in the
realm of reason; the good stands outside the scientific chain of cause and
effect. The good is a miracle, because it is contrary to reason and yet
everyone understands it.

There is something outside of and beyond the melancholy science of
the nineteenth century, which resigned all attempt to give meaning to
life. There is a spiritual factor, a spiritual need. And Levin is enchanted
and soothed by this absurdly simple statement of the human being's
supra-reasonable obligation to be good. In his joy he forgets that also
that melancholy materialistic naturalistic science of the nineteenth century had, after all, as motive power, human striving for the good. He
forgot that it was stern and bitter love of truth that made it deny meaning to life. It too, denying God, lived for God. That, too, is possible, and
Levin forgets it. Art he does not need even to forget; he knows, it seems,
nothing about it, obviously thinking of it only as the society prattle of
the "cultured" about painting, the Luccas, Wagner, and so on. Here is the
difference between him and Leo Tolstoy. Tolstoy knew art; he has suffered frightfully from and for it, achieved mightier things in it than the
rest of us can hope to achieve. Perhaps it was just the violence of his
artist personality that made him fail to see that knowledge of the good
is just the opposite of a reason to deny art. Art is the most beautiful,
austerest, blithest, most sacred symbol of all supra-reasonable human
striving for good above and beyond reason, for truth and fullness. The
breath of the rolling sea of epic would not so expand our lungs with
living air if it did not bring with it the astringent quickening spice of
the spiritual and the divine.

Bernard Knox

Sophocles' *Oedipus Tyrannos* ranks with its sequel *Oedipus at Colonus* as one of the peaks of Greek tragic drama and as one of the supreme achievements of world literature. It provided Aristotle with the basis on which he formulated the earliest and still most influential theory of tragedy. More than two thousand years later Sigmund Freud, finding in its presentation of a man who unknowingly kills his father and weds his mother a definitive representation of disturbing universal conflicts in the human unconscious, used its insights to clarify the new concepts of psychoanalysis. One of the greatest of classical works of art, it creates its own world in the manner described by Forster and at the same time arouses in those who witness it that sense of the mysterious and terrible which Jung ascribes to visionary literature. Its meanings are inexhaustible; its value is permanent.

To his analysis of the play, Bernard Knox, formerly of Yale University and now Director of The Center for Hellenic Studies in Washington, D. C., brings both a scholar's knowledge of language, history and culture and a critic's imaginative sensitivity to subtleties of meaning and poetic technique. His study is an admirable example of the modern critical method of close textual analysis: noting the specific contributions which word and image make to character and action, his interpretation is capable of doing justice to the complexity as well as the grandeur of Sophocles' vision of human destiny. As Aristotle and Freud in their different ways knew, that vision holds in suspension an awareness of man's greatness and an awareness of his limitations; it possesses, in short, that paradoxical double focus which almost defines tragic art. Knox's close reading of the text, always true to the facts of Greek culture in the fifth century B.C., is true also the facts of life in the twentieth century A.D. Oedipus as man-the-measurer, master of the world, is obviously relevant to modern man, but so too is Oedipus as the swollen-footed outcast, heir to the curse of his own nature.

SOPHOCLES' OEDIPUS

Sophocles' Oedipus is not only the greatest creation of a major poet and the classic representative figure of his age: he is also one of the long series of tragic protagonists who stand as symbols of human aspiration and despair before the characteristic dilemma of Western civilization—the problem of man's true stature, his proper place in the universe.

In the earlier of the two Sophoclean plays which deal with the figure of Oedipus, this fundamental problem is raised at the very beginning of the prologue by the careful distinctions which the priest makes in defin-

Reprinted by permission of the author.

ing his attitude toward Oedipus, the former savior of Thebes, its absolute ruler, and its last hope of rescue from the plague. "We beg your help," he says, "regarding you not as one equated to the gods, θεοῖσι . . . οὐκ ἰσούμενον, but as first of men."

"Not equated to the gods, but first of men." The positive part of the statement at any rate is undeniably true. Oedipus is *tyrannos* of Thebes, its despotic ruler. The Greek word corresponds neither to Shelley's "Tyrant" nor to Yeats' "King": tyrannos is an absolute ruler, who may be a bad ruler, or a good one (as Oedipus clearly is), but in either case he is a ruler who has seized power, not inherited it. He is not a king, for a king succeeds only by birth; the tyrannos succeeds by brains, force, influence. "This absolute power, τυραννίς," says Oedipus in the play "is a prize won with masses and money." This title of Oedipus, tyrannos, is one of the most powerful ironies of the play, for, although Oedipus does not know it, he is not only tyrannos, the outsider who came to power in Thebes, he is also the legitimate king by birth, for he was born the son of Laius. Only when his identity is revealed can he properly be called king: and the chorus refers to him by this title for the first time in the great ode which it sings after Oedipus knows the truth.

But the word tyrannos has a larger significance. Oedipus, to quote that same choral ode, is a παράδειγμα, a paradigm, an example to all men; and the fact that he is tyrannos, self-made ruler, the proverbial Greek example of worldly success won by individual intelligence and exertion, makes him an appropriate symbol of civilized man, who was beginning to believe, in the 5th century B.C., that he could seize control of his environment and make his own destiny, become, in fact, equated to the gods. "Oedipus shot his arrow far beyond the range of others"— the choral ode again—"and accomplished the conquest of complete prosperity and happiness."

Oedipus became tyrannos by answering the riddle of the Sphinx. It was no easy riddle, and he answered it, as he proudly asserts, without help from prophets, from bird-signs, from gods; he answered it alone, with his intelligence. The answer won him a city and the hand of a queen. And the answer to the Sphinx's riddle was—Man. In Sophocles' own century the same answer had been proposed to a greater riddle. "Man," said Protagoras the sophist, "is the measure of all things."

Protagoras' famous statement is the epitome of the critical and optimistic spirit of the middle years of the 5th century; its implications are clear—man is the center of the universe, his intelligence can overcome all obstacles, he is master of his own destiny, tyrannos, self-made ruler who has the capacity to attain complete prosperity and happiness.

In an earlier Sophoclean play, *Antigone,* the chorus sings a hymn to this man the conqueror. "Many are the wonders and terrors, and nothing more wonderful and terrible than man." He has conquered the sea, "this creature goes beyond the white sea pressing forward as the swell crashes about him"; and he has conquered the land, "earth, highest of the gods . . . he wears away with the turning plough." He has mastered not only the elements, sea and land, but the birds, beasts, and fishes; "through knowledge and technique," sings the chorus, he is yoker of the horse, tamer of the bull. "And he has taught himself speech and thought swift as the wind and attitudes which enable him to live in communities and means to shelter himself from the frost and rain. Full of resources he faces the future, nothing will find him at a loss. Death, it is true, he will not avoid, yet he has thought out ways of escape from desperate diseases. His knowledge, ingenuity and technique are beyond anything that could have been foreseen." These lyrics describe the rise to power of *anthropos tyrannos;* self-taught he seizes control of his environment, he is master of the elements, the animals, the arts and sciences of civilization. "Full of resources he faces the future"—an apt description of Oedipus at the beginning of our play.

And it is not the only phrase of this ode which is relevant; for Oedipus is connected by the terms he uses, and which are used to and about him, with the whole range of human achievement which has raised man to his present level. All the items of this triumphant catalogue recur in the *Oedipus Tyrannos;* the images of the play define him as helmsman, conqueror of the sea, and ploughman, conqueror of the land, as hunter, master of speech and thought, inventor, legislator, physician. Oedipus is faced in the play with an intellectual problem, and as he marshals his intellectual resources to solve it, the language of the play suggests a comparison between Oedipus' methods in the play and the whole range of sciences and techniques which have brought man to mastery, made him tyrannos of the world.

Oedipus' problem is apparently simple: "Who is the murderer of Laius?" but as he pursues the answer the question changes shape. It becomes a different problem: "Who am I?" And the answer to this problem involves the gods as well as man. The answer to the question is not what he expected, it is in fact a reversal, that *peripeteia* which Aristotle speaks of in connection with this play. The state of Oedipus is reversed from "first of men" to "most accursed of men"; his attitude from the proud ἀρκτέον "I must rule" to the humble πειστέον, "I must obey." "Reversal" says Aristotle, "is a change of the action into the opposite," and one meaning of this much disputed phrase is that the action produces the opposite of the actor's intentions. So Oedipus curses the murderer of Laius and it turns out that he has cursed himself. But this reversal is not confined to the action; it is also the process of all the great images of the play which identify Oedipus as the inventive, critical spirit of his century.

As the images unfold, the enquirer turns into the object of enquiry, the hunter into the prey, the doctor into the patient, the investigator into the criminal, the revealer into the thing revealed, the finder into the thing found, the savior into the thing saved ("I was saved, for some dreadful destiny"), the liberator into the thing released ("I released your feet from the bonds which pierced your ankles" says the Corinthian messenger), the accuser becomes the defendant, the ruler the subject, the teacher not only the pupil but also the object lesson, the example. A change of the action into its opposite, from active to passive.

And the two opening images of the Antigone ode recur with hideous effect. Oedipus the helmsman, who steers the ship of state, is seen, in Tiresias' words, as one who "steers his ship into a nameless anchorage," "who" in the chorus' words "shared the same great harbour with his father." And Oedipus the ploughman—"How," asks the chorus, "how could the furrows which your father ploughed bear you in silence for so long?"

This reversal is the movement of the play, parallel in the imagery and the action: it is the overthrow of the tyrannos, of man who seized power and thought himself "equated to the gods." The bold metaphor of the priest introduces another of the images which parallel in their development the reversal of the hero, and which suggest that Oedipus is a figure symbolic of human intelligence and achievement in general. He is not only helmsman, ploughman, inventor, legislator, liberator, revealer, doctor—he is also equator, mathematician, calculator; "equated" is a mathematical term, and it is only one of a whole complex of such terms which present Oedipus in yet a fresh aspect of man tyrannos. One of Oedipus' favorite words is "measure" and this is of course a significant metaphor: measure, mensuration, number, calculation—these are among the most important inventions which have brought man to power. Aeschylus' Prometheus, the mythical civilizer of human life, counts number among the foremost of his gifts to man. "And number, too, I invented, outstanding among clever devices." In the river valleys of the East generations of mensuration and calculation had brought man to an understanding of the movements of the stars and of time: in the histories of his friend Herodotus Sophocles had read of the calculation and mensuration which had gone into the building of the pyramids. "Measure"—it is Protagoras' word: "Man is the measure of all things." In this play man's measure is taken, his true equation found. The play is full of equations, some of them incomplete, some false; the final equation shows man equated not to the gods but to himself, as Oedipus is finally equated to himself. For there are in the play not one Oedipus but two.

One is the magnificent figure set before us in the opening scenes, tyrannos, the man of wealth and power, first of men, the intellect and energy which drives on the search. The other is the object of the search, a shadowy figure who has violated the most fundamental human taboos, an incestuous parricide, "most accursed of men." And even before the one Oedipus finds the other, they are connected and equated in the name which they both bear, Oedipus. Oedipus—Swollen-foot; it emphasizes the physical blemish which scars the body of the splendid tyrannos, a defect which he tries to forget but which reminds us of the outcast child this tyrannos once was and the outcast man he is soon to be. The second half of the name πούς, "foot," recurs throughout the play, as a mocking phrase which recalls this other Oedipus. "The Sphinx forced us to look at what was at our feet," says Creon. Tiresias invokes "the dread-footed curse of your father and mother." And the choral odes echo and re-echo with this word. "Let the murderer of Laius set his foot in motion in flight." "The murderer is a man alone with forlorn foot." "The laws of Zeus are high-footed." "The man of pride plunges down into doom where he cannot use his foot."

These mocking repetitions of one-half the name invoke the unknown Oedipus who will be revealed: the equally emphatic repetition of the first half emphasizes the dominant attitude of the man before us. *Oidi*— "swell," but it is also *Oida*, "I know," and this word is often, too often, in Oedipus' mouth. His knowledge is what makes him tyrannos, confident and decisive; knowledge has made man what he is, master of the world. Οἶδα, "I know"—it runs through the play with the same mocking persistence as πούς, "foot," and sometimes reaches an extreme of macabre punning emphasis.

When the messenger, to take one example of many, comes to tell Oedipus that his father, Polybus, is dead, he enquires for Oedipus, who is in the palace, in the following words:

> "Strangers, from you might I learn where
> is the palace of the tyrannos Oedipus,
> best of all, where he is himself if you know where."

Here it is in the Greek:

ἆρ' ἄν παρ' ὑμῶν ὦ ξένοι μάθοιμ' ὅπου   (oimopou)
τὰ τοῦ τυράννου δώματ' ἐστὶν Οἰδίπου   (oidipou)
μάλιστα δ' αὐτὸν εἴπατ' εἰ κάτισθ' ὅπου   (isthopou)

Those punning rhyming line-endings. μάθοιμ' ὅπου, Οἰδίπου, κάτισθ' ὅπου, "learn where," "Oedipus," "know where," unparalleled elsewhere in Greek tragedy, are a striking example of the boldness with which Sophocles uses language: from the "sweet singer of Colonus" they are somewhat unexpected, they might almost have been written by the not-so-sweet singer of Trieste-Zürich-Paris.

Οἶδα, the knowledge of the tyrannos, ποὑς, the swollen foot of Laius' son—in the hero's name the basic equation is already symbolically present, the equation which Oedipus will finally solve. But the priest in the prologue is speaking of a different equation, ἰσοὑμενον, "We beg your help, not as one equated to the gods . . ." It is a warning, and the warning is needed. For although Oedipus in the opening scenes is a model of formal and verbal piety, the piety is skin-deep. And even before he declares his true religion, he can address the chorus, which has been praying to the gods, with godlike words. "What you pray for you will receive, if you will listen to and accept what I am about to say."

The priest goes on to suggest a better equation: he asks Oedipus to equate himself to the man he was when he saved Thebes from the Sphinx. "You saved us then, be now the equal of the man you were." This is the first statement of the theme, the double Oedipus; here there is a contrast implied between the present Oedipus who is failing to save his city from the plague and the successful Oedipus of the past who answered the riddle of the Sphinx. He must answer a riddle again, be his old self, but the answer to this riddle will not be as simple as the answer to the first. When it is found, he will be equated, not to the foreigner who saved the city and became tyrannos, but to the native-born king, the son of Laius and Jocasta.

Oedipus repeats the significant word, "equal," ὅστις ἐξ ἴσου νοσεῖ. "Sick as you are, not one of you has sickness equal to mine," and he adds a word of his own, his characteristic metaphor. He is impatient at Creon's absence. "Measuring the day against the time (ξυμμετροὑμενον χρόνῳ), I am worried . . ." And then as Creon approaches, "He is now commensurate with the range of our voices" — ξὑμμετρος γὰρ ὡς κλὑειν.

Here is Oedipus the equator and measurer, this is the method by which he will reach the truth: calculation of time and place, measurement and comparison of age and number and description—these are the techniques which will solve the equation, establish the identity of the murderer of Laius. The tightly organized and relentless process by which Oedipus finds his way to the truth is the operation of the human intellect in many aspects; it is the investigation of the officer of the law who identifies the criminal, the series of diagnoses of the physician who identifies the disease—it has even been compared by Freud to the process of psychoanalysis—and it is also the working out of a mathematical problem which will end with the establishment of a true equation.

The numerical nature of the problem is emphasized at once with Creon's entry. "One man of Laius' party escaped," says Creon, "he had only one thing to say." "What is it?" asks Oedipus. "One thing might find a way to learn many." The one thing is that Laius was killed not by one man but by many. This sounds like a problem in arithmetic, and Oedipus undertakes to solve it. But the chorus which now comes on stage has no such confidence: it sings of the plague with despair, but it makes this statement in terms of the same metaphor; it has its characteristic word which, like the priest and like Oedipus, it pronounces twice. The chorus' word is ἀνάριθμος, "numberless," "uncountable." "My sorrows are beyond the count of number," and later, "uncountable the deaths of which the city is dying." The plague is something beyond the power of "number . . . outstanding among clever devices."

The prologue and the first stasimon, besides presenting the customary exposition of the plot, present also the exposition of the metaphor. And with the entry of Tiresias, the development of the metaphor begins, its terrible potentialities are revealed. "Even though you are tyrannos," says the prophet at the height of his anger, "you and I must be made equal in one thing, at least, the chance for an equal reply," ἐξισωστέον τὸ γοῦν ἴσ᾿ ἀντιλέξαι. Tiresias is blind, and Oedipus will be made equal to him in this before the play is over. But there is more still. "There is a mass of evil of which you are unconscious which shall equate you to yourself and your children."

ἃ σ᾿ ἐξισώσει σοί τε καὶ τοῖς σοῖς τέκνοις.

This is not the equation the priest desired to see, Oedipus present equated with Oedipus past, the deliverer from the Sphinx, but a more terrible equation reaching farther back into the past, Oedipus son of Polybus and Merope equated to Oedipus son of Laius and Jocasta; "equate you with your own children," for Oedipus is the brother of his own sons and daughters. In his closing words Tiresias explains this mysterious line, and connects it with the unknown murderer of Laius. "He will be revealed, a native Theban, one who in his relationship with his own children is both brother and father, with his mother both son and husband, with his father, both marriage-partner and murderer. Go inside and reckon this up, λογίζου, and if you find me mistaken in my reckoning, ἐψευσμένον, then say I have no head for prophecy."

Tiresias adopts the terms of Oedipus' own science and throws them in his face. But the new equations are beyond Oedipus' understanding, he dismisses them as the ravings of an unsuccessful conspirator with his back to the wall. Even the chorus, though disturbed, rejects the prophet's words and resolves to stand by Oedipus.

After Tiresias, Creon: after the prophet, the politician. In Tiresias, Oedipus faced a blind man who saw with unearthly sight; but Creon's vision, like that of Oedipus, is of this world. They are two of a kind, and Creon talks Oedipus' language. It is a quarrel between two calculators. "Hear an equal reply," says Creon, and "Long time might be measured since Laius' murder." "You and Jocasta rule in equality of power." And finally "Am I not a third party equated, ἰσοῦμαι, to you two?" Creon and Oedipus are not equal now, for Creon is at the mercy of Oedipus, begging for a hearing; but before the play is over Oedipus will be at the mercy of Creon, begging kindness for his daughters, and he then uses the same word. "Do not equate them with my misfortunes."

μηδ' ἐξισώσῃς τάσδε τοῖς ἐμοῖς κακοῖς

With Jocasta's intervention the enquiry changes direction. In her attempt to comfort Oedipus, whose only accuser is a prophet, she indicts prophecy in general, using as an example the unfulfilled prophecy about her own child, who was supposed to kill Laius. The child was abandoned on the mountain-side and Laius was killed by robbers where three wagon roads meet. "Such were the definitions, διώρισαν, made by prophetic voices," and they were incorrect. But Oedipus is not, for the moment, interested in prophetic voices. "Where three wagon roads meet." He once killed a man at such a place and now in a series of swift questions he determines the relation of these two events. The place, the time, the description of the victim, the number in his party, five, all correspond exactly. His account of the circumstances includes Apollo's prophecy that he would kill his father and be his mother's mate. But this does not disturb him now. That prophecy has not been fulfilled, for his father and mother are in Corinth, where he will never go again. "I measure the distance to Corinth by the stars," ἄστροις . . . . ἐκμετρούμενος. What does disturb him is that he may be the murderer of Laius, the cause of the plague, the object of his own solemn excommunication. But he has some slight ground for hope. There is a discrepancy in the two events. It is the same numerical distinction which was discussed before, whether Laius was killed by one man or many. Jocasta said robbers and Oedipus was alone. This distinction is now all-important, the key to the solution of the equation. Oedipus sends for the survivor who can confirm or deny the saving detail. "If he says the same number as you then I am not the murderer. For one cannot equal many."

οὐ γὰε γένοιτ' ἂν εἷς γε τοῖς πολλοῖς ἴσος

which may fairly be rendered, "In no circumstances can one be equal to more than one." Oedipus' guilt or innocence rests now on a mathematical axiom.

But a more fundamental equation has been brought into question, the relation of the oracles to reality. Here are two oracles, both the same, both unfulfilled; the same terrible destiny was predicted for Jocasta's son, who is dead, and for Oedipus, who has avoided it. One thing is clear to Jocasta. Whoever turns out to be Laius' murderer, the oracles are wrong. "From this day forward I would not, for all prophecy can say, turn my head this way or that." If the equation of the oracles with reality is a false equation, then religion is meaningless. Neither Jocasta nor Oedipus can allow the possibility that the oracles are right, and they accept the consequences, as they proceed to make clear. But the chorus cannot, and it now abandons Oedipus the calculator and turns instead to those "high-footed laws, which are the children of Olympus and not a creation of mortal man." It calls on Zeus to fulfill the oracles. "If these things do not coincide," ἁρμόσει, if the oracles do not equal reality, then "the divine order is overthrown," ἔρρει τὰ θεῖα. The situation and future of two individuals has become a test of divine power: if they are right, sings the chorus, "why reverence Apollo's Delphi, the center of the world? Why join the choral dance?" τί δεῖ με χορεύειν; and with this phrase the issue is brought out of the past into the present moment in the theater of Dionysus. For this song itself is also a dance, the choral stasimon which is the nucleus of tragedy and which reminds us that tragedy itself is an act of religious worship. If the oracles and the truth are not equated the performance of the play has no meaning, for tragedy is a religious ritual. This phrase is a tour de force which makes the validity of the performance itself depend on the dénouement of the play.

The oracles are now the central issue; the murder of Laius fades into the background. A messenger from Corinth brings news, news which will be greeted, he announces, "with an equal amount of sorrow and joy." "What is it," asks Jocasta, "which has such double power?" Polybus is dead. The sorrow equal to the joy will come later; for the moment there is only joy. The oracles are proved wrong again: Oedipus' father is dead. Oedipus can no more kill his father than the son of Laius killed his. "Oracles of the gods, where are you now?" Oedipus is caught up in Jocasta's exaltation, but it does not last. Only half his burden has been lifted from him. His mother still lives. He must still measure the distance to Corinth by the stars, still fear the future.

Both Jocasta and the messenger now try to relieve him of this last remaining fear. Jocasta makes her famous declaration in which she rejects fear, providence, divine and human alike, and indeed any idea of order or plan. Her declaration amounts almost to a rejection of the law of cause and effect: and it certainly attacks the basis of human calculation. For her, the calculation has gone far enough: it has produced an acceptable result; let it stop here. "Why should man fear?" she asks. "His life is governed by the operation of chance. Nothing can be accurately foreseen. The best rule is to live blindly, at random, εἰκῇ, as best one can." It is a statement which recognizes and accepts a meaningless universe.

420	SCIENCE, LITERATURE AND CULTURE

And Oedipus would agree, but for one thing. His mother lives. He must still fear.

Where Jocasta failed the messenger succeeds. He does it by destroying the equation on which Oedipus' life is based. And he uses familiar terms. "Polybus is no more your father than I, but equally so." Oedipus' question is indignant: "How can my father be equal to a nobody, to zero? τῷ μηδενί." The answer—"Polybus is not your father, neither am I." But that is as far as the Corinthian's knowledge goes; he was given the child Oedipus by another, a shepherd, one of Laius' men. And now the two separate equations begin to merge. "I think," says the chorus, "that that shepherd was the same man that you already sent for." The eyewitness to the death of Laius. He was sent for to say whether Laius was killed by one or many, but he will bring more important news. He will finally lift from Oedipus' shoulders the burden of fear he has carried since he left Delphi. Chance governs all. Oedipus' life history is the operation of chance; found by one shepherd, passed on to another, given to Polybus who was childless, brought up as heir to a kingdom, self-exiled from Corinth he came to Thebes a homeless wanderer, answered the riddle of the Sphinx, and won a city and the hand of a queen. And that same guiding chance will now reveal to him his real identity. Jocasta was right. Why should he fear?

But Jocasta has already seen the truth. Not chance, but the fulfillment of the oracle; the prophecy and the facts coincide (ἀρμόσει), as the chorus prayed they would. Jocasta is lost, but she tries to save Oedipus, to stop the enquiry. But nothing can stop him now. Her farewell to him expresses her agony and knowledge by its omissions: she recognizes but cannot formulate the dreadful equation which Tiresias stated. "ἰού, ἰού, δύστηνε, Unfortunate. This is the only name I can call you." She cannot call him husband. The three-day-old child she sent out to die on the mountain-side has been restored to her, and she cannot call him son.

Oedipus hardly listens. He in his turn has scaled the same heights of confidence from which she has toppled, and he goes higher still. "I will know my origin, burst forth what will." He knows that it will be good. Chance governs the universe and Oedipus is her son. Not the son of Polybus, nor of any mortal man but the son of fortunate chance. In his exaltation he rises in imagination above human stature. "The months, my brothers, have defined, διώρισαν, my greatness and smallness"; he has waned and waxed like the moon, he is one of the forces of the universe, his family is time and space. It is a religious, a mystical conception; here is Oedipus' real religion, he is equal to the gods, the son of chance, the only real goddess. Why should he not establish his identity?

The solution is only a few steps ahead. The shepherd is brought on. "If I, who never met the man, may make an estimate (σταθμᾶσθαι),

I think this is the shepherd who has been the object of our investigation (ζητοῦμεν). In age he is commensurate σύμμετρος with the Corinthian here." With this significant prologue he plunges into the final calculation.

The movement of the next sixty lines is the swift ease of the last stages of the mathematical proof: the end is half foreseen, the process an automatic sequence from one step to the next until Oedipus tyrannos and Oedipus the accursed, the knowledge and the swollen foot, are equated. "It all comes out clear," he cries. τὰ πάντ' ἂν ἐξήκοι σαφῆς. The prophecy has been fulfilled. Oedipus knows himself for what he is. He is not the measurer but the thing measured, not the equator but the thing equated. He is the answer to the problem he tried to solve. The chorus sees in Oedipus a παράδειγμα, an example to mankind. In this self-recognition of Oedipus, man recognizes himself. Man measures himself and the result is not that man is the measure of all things. The chorus, which rejected number and all that it stood for, has learned to count; and states the result of the great calculation. "Generations of man that must die, I add up the total of your life and find it equal to zero." ἴσα καὶ τὸ μηδὲν ζώσας ἐναριθμῶ.

The overthrow of the tyrannos is complete. When Oedipus returns from the palace he is blind, and, by the terms of his own proclamation, an outcast. It is a terrible reversal, and it raises the question, "Is it deserved? How far is he responsible for what he has done? Were the actions for which he is now paying not predestined?" No. They were committed in ignorance, but they were not predestined, merely predicted. An essential distinction, as essential for Milton's Adam as for Sophocles' Oedipus. His will was free, his actions his own, but the pattern of his action is the same as that of the Delphic prophecy. The relation between the prophecy and Oedipus' actions is not that of cause and effect. It is the relation suggested by the metaphor, the relation of two independent entities which are equated.

Yet no man can look on Oedipus without sympathy. In his moment of exaltation—"I am the son of fortune"—he is man at his blindest, but he is also man at his most courageous and heroic: "Burst forth what will, I will know." And he has served, as the chorus says, to point a moral. He is a paradigm, a demonstration. True, Oedipus, the independent being, was a perfectly appropriate subject for the demonstration. But we cannot help feeling that the gods owe Oedipus a debt. Sophocles felt it too, and in his last years wrote the play which shows us the nature of the payment, *Oedipus at Colonus*.

This play deals with Oedipus' reward, and the reward is a strange one. How strange can be seen clearly if we compare Oedipus with another great figure who also served as the subject of a divine demonstration, Job. After his torment Job had it all made up to him. "The Lord gave Job twice as much as he had before. For he had 14,000 sheep, and 6,000 camels and 1,000 yoke of oxen and 1,000 she-asses. He had also 7 sons and 3 daughters. And after this lived Job an hundred and forty years, and saw his sons and his sons' sons, even four generations." This is the kind of reward we can understand—14,000 sheep, 6,000 camels—Job, to use an irreverent comparison, hit the patriarchal jackpot. Oedipus' reward includes no camels or she-asses, no long life, in fact no life at all, his reward is death. But a death which Job could never imagine. For in death Oedipus becomes equated to the gods. The ironic phrase with which the first play began has here a literal fulfillment. Oedipus becomes something superhuman, a spirit which lives on in power in the affairs of men after the death of the body. His tomb is to be a holy place, for the city in whose territory his body lies will win a great victory on the field where Oedipus lies buried. By his choice of a burial place he thus influences history, becomes a presence to be feared by some and thanked by others. But it is not only in his grave that he will be powerful. In the last hours of his life he begins to assume the attributes of the divinity he is to become; the second play, *Oedipus at Colonus*, puts on stage the process of Oedipus' transition from human to divine.

"Equated to the gods." We have not seen the gods, but we know from the first play what they are. That play demonstrated that the gods have knowledge, full complete knowledge, the knowledge which Oedipus thought he had. He was proved ignorant; real knowledge is what distinguishes god from man. Since the gods have knowledge their action is confident and sure. They act with the swift decision which was characteristic of Oedipus but which was in him misplaced. Only a god can be sure, not a man. And their action is just. It is a justice based on perfect knowledge, is exact and appropriate, and therefore allows no room for forgiveness—but it can be angry. The gods can even mock the wrongdoer as Athene does Ajax, as the echoes of his name mocked Oedipus. This sure, full, angry justice is what Oedipus tried to administer to Tiresias, to Creon, but his justice was based on ignorance and was injustice. These attributes of divinity—knowledge, certainty, justice—are the qualities Oedipus thought he possessed—and that is why he was the perfect example of the inadequacy of human knowledge, certainty, and justice. But in the second play Oedipus is made equal to the gods, he assumes the attributes of divinity, the attributes he once thought his, he becomes what he once thought he was. This old Oedipus seems to be equal to the young, confident in his knowledge, fiercely angry in his administration of justice, utterly sure of himself—but this time he is justified. These are not the proper attitudes for a man, but Oedipus is turning into something more than man; now he knows surely, sees clearly, the gods give Oedipus back his eyes, but they are eyes of superhuman vision. Now in his transformation, as then, in his reversal, he serves still as an example. The rebirth of the young, confident Oedipus in the tired old man emphasizes the same lesson; it defines once more the limits of man and the power of gods, states again that the possession of knowledge, certainty, and justice is what distinguishes god from man.

The opening statement of Oedipus shows that as a man he has learned the lesson well. "I have learned acquiescence, taught by suffering and long time." As a man Oedipus has nothing more to learn. With this statement he comes to the end of a long road. The nearby city whose walls he cannot see is Athens, and here is the place of his reward, his grave, his home. The welcome he receives is to be ordered off by the first arrival; he has trespassed on holy ground, the grove of the Eumenides. He knows what this means, this is the resting place he was promised by Apollo, and he refuses to move. His statement recalls the tyrannos, a characteristic phrase: "In no circumstances will I leave this place." The terms of his prayer to the goddesses of the grave foreshadow his transition from body to spirit. "Pity this wretched ghost of Oedipus the man, this body that is not what it once was long ago."

As a body, as a man, he is a thing to be pitied; he is blind, feeble, ragged, dirty. But the transformation has already begun. The first comer spoke to him with pity, even condescension, but the chorus of citizens which now enters feels fear. "Dreadful to see, dreadful to hear." When they know his identity their fear changes to anger, but Oedipus defends his past. He sees himself as one who was ignorant, who suffered rather than acted. But now he is actor, not sufferer. He comes with knowledge, and power. "I come bringing advantage to this city."

He does not yet know what advantage. His daughter Ismene comes to tell him what it is, that his grave will be the site of a victory for the city that shelters him. And to tell him that his sons and Creon, all of whom despised and rejected him, now need him, and will come to beg his help. Oedipus has power over the future and can now reward his friends and punish his enemies. He chooses to reward Athens, to punish Creon and his own sons. He expresses his choice in terms which show a recognition of human limitations; Athens' reward, something which lies within his will, as an intention; his sons' punishment, something over which he has no sure control, as a wish. "May the issue of the battle between them lie in my hands. If that were to be, the one would not remain king, nor the other win the throne."

Theseus, the king of Athens, welcomes him generously, but when he learns that Thebes wants Oedipus back and that he refuses to go, Theseus reproaches the old man. "Anger is not what your misfortune calls for." And the answer is a fiery rebuke from a superior. "Wait till you hear what I say, before you reproach me." Oedipus tells Theseus that he bring

424 SCIENCE, LITERATURE AND CULTURE

victory over Thebes at some future time, and Theseus, the statesman, is confident that Athens will never be at war with Thebes. Oedipus reproaches him in his turn. Such confidence is misplaced. No man should be so sure of the future: "Only to the gods comes no old age or death. Everything else is dissolved by all-powerful time. The earth's strength decays, the body decays, faith dies, mistrust flowers and the wind of friendship changes between man and man, city and city." No man can be confident of the future. Man's knowledge is ignorance. It is the lesson Oedipus learned in his own person and he reads it to Theseus now with all the authority of his blind eyes and dreadful name—but he does not apply it to himself. For he goes on to predict the future. He hands down the law of human behavior to Theseus speaking already as a *daemon,* not one subject to the law but one who administers it. And with his confident prediction, his assumption of sure knowledge, goes anger, but not the old human anger of Oedipus tyrannos. As he speaks of Thebes' future defeat on the soil where he will be buried, the words take on an unearthly quality, a daemonic wrath.

> ἵν' οὑμὸς εὕδων καὶ κεκρυμμένος νέκυς
> ψυχρὸς ποτ' αὐτῶν θερμὸν αἷμα πίεται
> εἰ Ζεὺς ἔτι Ζεὺς χὠ Διὸς Φοῖβος σαφής.

"There my sleeping and hidden corpse, cold though it be, will drink their warm blood, if Zeus is still Zeus and Apollo a true prophet." What before was wish and prayer is now prediction. But the prediction is qualified: "if Apollo be a true prophet." He does not yet speak in the authority of his own name. That will be the final stage.

And when it comes, he speaks face to face with the objects of his anger. Creon's condescending and hypocritical speech is met with a blast of fury that surpasses the anger he had to face long ago in Thebes. The final interview is a repetition of the first. In both Creon is condemned, in both with the same swift vindictive wrath, but this time the condemnation is just. Oedipus sees through to the heart of Creon, he knows what he is: and Creon proceeds to show the justice of Oedipus' rejection by revealing that he has already kidnapped Ismene, by kidnapping Antigone, and laying hands on Oedipus himself. Oedipus is helpless, and only the arrival of Theseus saves him. This is the man who is being equated to the gods, not the splendid tyrannos, the man of power, vigor, strength, but a blind old man, the extreme of physical weakness, who cannot even see, much less prevent, the violence that is done him.

Physical weakness, but a new height of spiritual strength. This Oedipus judges justly and exactly, knows fully, sees clearly—his power is power over the future, the defeat of Thebes, the death of his sons, the terrible reversal of Creon. One thing Creon says to Oedipus clarifies the nature of the process we are witnessing. "Has not time taught you wisdom?" Creon expected to find the Oedipus of the opening scene of the play, whom time had taught acquiescence, but he finds what seems to be the tyrannos he knew and feared. "You harm yourself now as you did then," he says, "giving way to that anger which has always been your defeat." He sees the old Oedipus as equal to the young. In one sense they are, but in a greater sense they are no more equal than man is equal to the gods.

With the next scene the whole story comes full circle. A suppliant begs Oedipus for help. Our last sight of Oedipus is like our first. This suppliant is Polynices, his son, and the comparison with the opening scene of the first play is emphasized by the repetitions of the priest's speech—words, phrases, even whole lines—which appear in Polynices' appeal to his father. It is a hypocritical speech which needs no refutation. It is met with a terrible indictment which sweeps from accusation through prophecy to a climax which, with its tightly packed explosive consonants resembles not so much human speech as a burst of daemonic anger:

$$\theta\alpha\nu\epsilon\hat{\imath}\nu \ \kappa\tau\alpha\nu\epsilon\hat{\imath}\nu \ \theta'\upsilon\phi' \ o\hat{\upsilon}\pi\epsilon\rho \ \dot{\epsilon}\xi\epsilon\lambda\dot{\eta}\lambda\alpha\sigma\alpha\iota$$
$$\tau o\iota\alpha\hat{\upsilon}\tau' \ \dot{\alpha}\rho\hat{\omega}\mu\alpha\iota \ \kappa\alpha\grave{\iota} \ \kappa\alpha\lambda\hat{\omega} \ \tau\grave{o} \ \mathrm{T}\alpha\rho\tau\dot{\alpha}\rho o\upsilon$$
$$\sigma\tau\upsilon\gamma\nu\grave{o}\nu \ \pi\alpha\tau\rho\hat{\omega}o\nu \ \check{\epsilon}\rho\epsilon\beta o\varsigma \ \dot{\omega}\varsigma \ \sigma' \ \dot{\alpha}\pi o\iota\kappa\dot{\iota}\sigma\eta$$

"Kill and be killed by the brother who drove you out. This is my curse, I call on the hideous darkness of Tartarus where your fathers lie, to prepare a place for you . . ." This is a superhuman anger welling from the outraged sense of justice not of a man but of the forces of the universe themselves.

Creon could still argue and resist, but to this speech no reply is possible. There can be no doubt of its authority. When Polynices discusses the speech with his sisters, the right word for it is found. Oedipus speaks with the voice of an oracle. "Will you go to Thebes and fulfill his prophecies? ($\mu\alpha\nu\tau\epsilon\dot{\upsilon}\mu\alpha\tau\alpha$)" says Antigone. Oedipus who fought to disprove an oracle has become one himself. And his son now starts on the same road his father trod. "Let him prophecy. I do not have to fulfill it." Polynices leaves with a phrase that repeats his mother's denunciation of prophets. "All this is in the power of the divinity $\dot{\epsilon}\nu \ \tau\hat{\omega} \ \delta\alpha\dot{\iota}\mu o\nu\iota$, it may turn out this way or that." In the power of a god—in the power of chance—whatever he means, he does not realize the sense in which the words are true. The daemon, the divinity, in whose power it lies is Oedipus himself.

Oedipus has stayed too long. Power such as this should not walk the earth in the shape of a man. The thunder and lightning summon him, and the gods reproach him for his delay. "You Oedipus, you, why do we hesitate to go? You have delayed too long."

> ὦ οὗτος οὗτος Οἰδίπους τί μέλλομεν
> χωρεῖν; πάλαι δὴ τἀπὸ σοῦ βραδύνεται.

These strange words are the only thing the gods say in either play. And as was to be expected of so long delayed and awful a statement, it is complete and final. The hesitation for which they reproach Oedipus is the last shred of his humanity, which he must now cast off. Where he is going vision is clear, knowledge certain, action instantaneous and effective; between the intention and the act there falls no shadow of hesitation or delay. The divine "we"—"Why do *we* hesitate to go"—completes and transcends the equation of Oedipus with the gods; his identity is merged with theirs. And in this last moment of his bodily life they call him by his name, *Oidipous,* the name which contains in itself the lesson of which not only his action and suffering but also his apotheosis serve as the great example—*oida*—that man's knowledge, which makes him master of the world, should never allow him to think that he is equated to the gods, should never allow him to forget the foot, *pous,* the reminder of his true measurement, his real identity.

Part Five

A CONTROVERSY ON
DRAMA AND LIFE

The lively journalistic exchange in the following pages was occasioned by the production in London in 1958 of two plays by the Rumanian dramatist Ionesco, who now lives in Paris and writes in French. Ionesco, together with the Irish Samuel Beckett, the French Jean Genêt, the English Harold Pinter, the Swiss Max Frisch, and the Americans Jack Gelber and to some extent Edward Albee, is associated with the writing of a kind of contemporary drama that some critics have called "the theatre of the absurd." Although differing significantly from each other—and they do not in any sense think of themselves as a group—these dramatists share a common fondness for a technique of fantasy and a common obsession with the theme of the difficulty, or even the impossibility, of communication between human beings. Kenneth Tynan, one of the most articulate and forceful of modern drama critics, is at present committed to both a social position and an attitude toward art which render him hostile to the assumptions of a dramatist like Ionesco, and he makes the nature of his commitment clear in the drama review that initiates the controversy. Tynan, as a man who is dedicated to improving the world, is inclined to support only one type of writing for the stage—social realism of the sort that he describes in his review. His objections to Ionesco's art (and, as he makes clear in his later piece, to the art of even such a major writer as Strindberg) are at least as much moral as aesthetic: it does not inculcate socially beneficial attitudes, it does not have "traceable roots in life," and it denies such "humanist" values as "logic and belief in man." His attitude is an extreme version of the "engagement" discussed by several of the writers in an earlier section of this volume.

Reality and *humanism* are complex words, however, as Ionesco makes clear in the open letter in which he replies to Tynan. He has, his letter indicates, his own kind of commitment—to the hallucinatory reality of his own fantasy—and he believes that it, too, expresses something which is "common to all mankind." Ionesco's "humanism" has to do not with the logic of discourse but with the exploration of the individual self: like Tynan's "humanism" it has one aspect of the European past behind it.

To some extent, the argument between Tynan and Ionesco is the argument between the intellectual who believes that art should try to approach the condition of science and the artist who denies that scientific concepts or methods are relevant to his work at all. This contrast emerges most powerfully in the comments on Sophocles and Freud made by the two antagonists. For Ionesco, "it was not Sophocles who was inspired by Freud but, obviously, the other way around." For Tynan, "Freud merely found in Sophocles confirmation of a theory he had formed on a basis of empirical evidence." The respective attitudes toward the claims of the artistic imagination and the scientific intelligence are clear: Tynan and Ionesco must disagree, for they locate reality in different places and make extreme—and exclusive—claims for each.

Four years after the original controversy, in reviewing a book of Tynan's collected drama criticism, the novelist and drama critic Nigel Dennis commented on the dispute both directly and indirectly. Like the original antagonists, Dennis is capable of mounting a polemical attack without losing either his urbanity or his courtesy, but he is perhaps an even more dangerous man to have as an opponent. This is true partly because, making less ambitious claims for an exclusive insight into reality, he is free to make more precise observations on the actual functions of creation and criticism. In the course of his essay-review he pays measured tribute to Tynan's gifts as a critic and as a force in British intellectual life, but his final position is firmly opposed to Tynan's activism and simplified political orientation. In his last paragraph we find, for the only time in the controversy, the familiar phrase "art for art's sake," but it is clear in context that Dennis means the same thing by it that Forster does—not that art has no connection with life, but that art makes its contribution to life only by fulfilling its own nature as art. (This, incidentally, is exactly what pure science insists upon for itself too—see the essay by Oppenheimer—and only those who confuse science and technology, its application in daily life, attempt to deny to science its need to fulfill its own nature.) Dennis states further his belief that the responsible critic must make his judgments not on the basis of the virtue of the artist's intention but solely on the basis of the solidity of his achievement.

Suggested Further Readings:

Aristotle, *The Poetics*

Sophocles, *Oedipus*
Shakespeare, *Hamlet*
Strindberg, *Five Plays*
Tennessee Williams, *The Glass Menagerie*
Samuel Beckett, *Waiting for Godot*
Eugene Ionesco, *Four Plays*

IONESCO: MAN OF DESTINY? · by Kenneth Tynan

The French theatre, about which I prophesied glumly some months ago, has now entered upon a state of emergency. An alarming article in the current issue of *Arts* reveals that during the first five months of this year the box-office receipts at Parisian theatres declined, compared with the same period last year, by nearly two-fifths. Nor can the political situation be blamed for the drop; even during last month's national earthquake the established hits, such as M. Achard's "Patate," continued to play to full houses.

The fact to be faced is brutal and simple: French audiences are drifting away from the theatre because they feel the theatre is drifting away from them. They are frankly bored with it: and the immediate prospect reflects their boredom. Thirty-two theatres, an unprecedented number, will close this summer. Only twelve have elected to brave the drought, most of them peddling the theatrical equivalent of scented water-ices. "Cocktail Sexy" will hold the fort at the Capucines; at the Grand-Guignol, "L'Ecole du Strip-tease." At only one small theatre will you find, throughout the dog-days, the work of a French author of serious repute. Who is the man capable of inspiring such unique managerial confidence? Nobody but M. Ionesco, founder and headmaster of *l'ecole du strip-tease intellectuel, moral et social.*

Faith in the drawing-power of this anarchic wag seems to be shared by the English Stage Company, who last week offered a double bill of *The Chairs* and *The Lesson* (Royal Court). Neither play is new to London: "The Chairs" is a Court revival, and the Arts Theatre taught us our lesson in 1955. The point of the programme is to demonstrate the versatility of Joan Plowright, who sheds seventy years during the interval; and to celebrate this nimble girl's return from Broadway, where she appeared in both plays under Tony Richardson's direction. Yet there was more in the applause than a mere welcome home. It had about it a blind, deafening intensity: one felt present at the consecration of a cult. Not, let me add, a Plowright cult: staggeringly though she played the crumbling hag in the first play, she simpered a little too knowingly as the crammer's prey in the second. No: this was an Ionesco cult, and in it I smell danger.

Ever since the Fry-Eliot "poetic revival" caved in on them, the ostriches of our theatrical intelligentsia have been seeking another faith. Anything would do as long as it shook off what are known as "the fetters of realism." Now the broad definition of a realistic play is that its char-

Originally published in the June 22, 1958 issue of *The Observer*. Reprinted here from *Curtains* by Kenneth Tynan. Copyright 1961 by Kenneth Tynan. Reprinted by permission of Atheneum Publishers.

acters and events have traceable roots in life. Gorki and Chekhov, Arthur Miller and Tennessee Williams, Brecht and O'Casey, Osborne and Sartre have all written such plays. They express one man's view of the world in terms of people we can all recognise. Like all hard disciplines, realism can easily be corrupted. It can sink into sentimentality (N. C. Hunter), half-truth (Terence Rattigan), or mere photographic reproduction of the trivia of human behaviour. Even so, those who have mastered it have created the lasting body of twentieth-century drama: and I have been careful not to except Brecht, who employed stylised production techniques to set off essentially realistic characters.

That, for the ostriches, was what ruled him out of court. He was too real. Similarly, they preferred Beckett's "Fin de Partie," in which the human element was minimal, to "Waiting for Godot," which not only contained two tramps of mephitic reality but even seemed to regard them, as human beings, with love. Veiling their disapproval, the ostriches seized on Beckett's more blatant verbal caprices and called them "authentic images of a disintegrated society." But it was only when M. Ionesco arrived that they hailed a messiah. Here at last was a self-proclaimed advocate of *anti-theatre:* explicitly anti-realist, and by implication anti-reality as well. Here was a writer ready to declare that words were meaningless and that all communication between human beings was impossible. The aged (as in "The Chairs") are wrapped in an impenetrable cocoon of hallucinatory memories; they can speak intelligibly neither to each other nor to the world. The teacher in "The Lesson" can "get through" to his pupil only by means of sexual assault, followed by murder. Words, the magic innovation of our species, are dismissed as useless and fraudulent.

———————•———————

Ionesco's is a world of isolated robots, conversing in cartoon-strip balloons of dialogue that are sometimes hilarious, sometimes evocative, and quite often neither, on which occasions they become profoundly tiresome. (As with shaggy-dog stories, few of M. Ionesco's plays survive a second hearing; I felt this particularly with "The Chairs.") This world is not mine, but I recognise it to be a valid personal vision, presented with great imaginative aplomb and verbal audacity. The peril arises when it is held up for general emulation as the gateway to the theatre of the future, that bleak new world from which the humanist heresies of faith in logic and belief in man will forever be banished.

M. Ionesco certainly offers an "escape from realism": but an escape into what? A blind alley, perhaps, adorned with *tachiste* murals. Or a self-imposed vacuum, wherein the author ominously bids us observe the absence of air. Or, best of all, a funfair ride on a ghost train, all skulls and hooting waxworks, from which we emerge into the far more intimidating clamour of diurnal reality. M. Ionesco's theatre is pungent and exciting, but it remains a diversion. It is not on the main road; and we do him no good, nor the drama at large, to pretend that it is. Mr. Richardson's productions are ideally lurid; George Devine looked a bit rusty in the first half, but Edgar Wreford, repeating his Oxford Playhouse performance, is superbly disgusting in the second. The music, an airborne plunking that deserves a less earthbound epithet than *concrete,* is by John Addison.

A REPLY TO KENNETH TYNAN

THE PLAYWRIGHT'S ROLE · by Eugene Ionesco

I was of course honoured by the article Mr. Tynan devoted to my two plays, "The Chairs" and "The Lesson," in spite of the strictures it contained, which a critic has a perfect right to make. However, since some of his objections seem to me to be based on premises that are not only false but, strictly speaking, outside the domain of the theatre, I think I have the right to make certain comments.

In effect, Mr. Tynan says that it has been claimed, and that I myself have approved or supported this claim, that I was a sort of "messiah" of the theatre. This is doubly untrue because I do not like messiahs and I certainly do not consider the vocation of the artist or the playwright to lie in that direction. I have a distinct impression that it is Mr. Tynan who is in search of messiahs. But to deliver a message to the world, to wish to direct its course, to save it, is the business of the founders of religions, of the moralists or the politicians who, incidentally, as we know only too well, make a pretty poor job of it. A playwright simply writes plays, in which he can offer only a testimony, not a didactic message—a personal, affective testimony of his anguish and the anguish of others or, which is rare, of his happiness—or he can express his feelings, comic or tragic, about life.

A work of art has nothing to do with doctrine. I have already written elsewhere that any work of art which was ideological and nothing else would be pointless, tautological, inferior to the doctrine it claimed to illustrate, which would already have been expressed in its proper language, that of discursive demonstration. An ideological play can be no more than the vulgarisation of an ideology. In my view, a work of art has

From the June 29, 1958 issue of *The Observer*. Reprinted by permission of the author.

its own unique system of expression, its own means of directly apprehending the real.

———•———

Mr. Tynan seems to accuse me of being deliberately, explicitly, anti-realist; of having declared that words have no meaning and that all language is incommunicable. That is only partly true, for the very fact of writing and presenting plays is surely incompatible with such a view. I simply hold that it is difficult to make oneself understood, not absolutely impossible, and my play "The Chairs" is a plea, pathetic perhaps, for mutual understanding. As for the idea of reality, Mr. Tynan seems (as he also made clear in an interview published in *Encounter*) to acknowledge only one plane of reality: what is called the "social" plane, which seems to me to be the most external, in other words the most superficial. That is why I think that writers like Sartre (Sartre the author of political melodramas), Osborne, Miller, Brecht, etc., are simply the new *auteurs du boulevard,* representatives of a left-wing conformism which is just as lamentable as the right-wing sort. These writers offer nothing that one does not know already, through books and political speeches.

But that is not all: it is not enough to be a social realist writer, one must also, apparently, be a militant believer in what is known as progress. The only worth-while authors, those who are on the "main road" of the theatre, would be those who thought in a certain clearly defined way, obeying certain pre-established principles or directives. This would be to make the "main road" a very narrow one; it would considerably restrict the planes of reality (which are innumerable) and limit the field open to the investigations of artistic research and creation.

I believe that what separates us all from one another is simply society itself, or, if you like, politics. This is what raises barriers between men, this is what creates misunderstanding.

If I may be allowed to express myself paradoxically, I should say that the true society, the authentic human community, is extra-social—a wider, deeper society, that which is revealed by our common anxieties, our desires, our secret nostalgias. The whole history of the world has been governed by these nostalgias and anxieties, which political action does no more than reflect and interpret, very imperfectly. No society has been able to abolish human sadness, no political system can deliver us from the pain of living, from our fear of death, our thirst for the absolute; it is the human condition that directs the social condition, not vice versa.

This "reality" seems to me much vaster and more complex than the one to which Mr. Tynan and many others want to limit themselves. The problem is to get to the source of our malady, to find the non-conventional language of this anguish, perhaps by breaking down this "social" language which is nothing but clichés, empty formulas, and slogans. The "robot" characters Mr. Tynan disapproves of seem to me to be precisely those who belong *solely* to this or that *milieu* or social "reality," who are prisoners of it, and who—being no more than social, seeking a solution to their problems only by so-called social means—have become impoverished, alienated, empty. It is precisely the conformist, the *petit-bourgeois,* the ideologist of *every* society who is lost and dehumanised. If anything needs demystifying it is our ideologies, which offer ready-made solutions (which history quickly overtakes and refutes) and a language that congeals *as soon as it is formulated.* It is these ideologies which must be continually re-examined in the light of our anxieties and dreams, and their congealed language must be relentlessly split apart in order to find the living sap beneath.

To discover the fundamental problem common to all mankind, I must ask myself what *my* fundamental problem is, what *my* most ineradicable fear is. I am certain, then, to find the problems and fears of literally everyone. That is the true road, into my own darkness, our darkness, which I try to bring to the light of day.

———————•———————

It would be amusing to try an experiment, which I have no room for here but which I hope to carry out some day. I could take almost any work of art, any play, and guarantee to give it in turn a Marxist, a Buddhist, a Christian, an Existentialist, a psycho-analytical interpretation and "prove" that the work subjected to each interpretation is a perfect and exclusive illustration of each creed, that it confirms this or that ideology beyond all doubt. For me this proves another thing: that every work of art (unless it is a pseudo-intellectualist work, a work already comprised in some ideology that it merely illustrates, as with Brecht) is outside ideology, is not reducible to ideology. Ideology circumscribes without penetrating it. The absence of ideology in a work does not mean an absence of ideas: on the contrary it fertilises them. In other words, it was not Sophocles who was inspired by Freud but, obviously, the other way round. Ideology is not the source of art. A work of art is the source and the raw material of ideologies to come.

What, then, should the critic do? Where should he look for his criteria? Inside the work itself, its universe and its mythology. He must look at it, listen to it, and simply say whether it is true to its own nature. The best judgment is a careful exposition of the work itself. For that, the work must be allowed to speak, uncoloured by preconception or prejudice.

Whether or not it is on the "main road"; whether or not it is what you would like it to be—to consider this is already to pass judgment, a judgment that is external, pointless and false. A work of art is the expression of an incommunicable reality that one tries to communicate— and which sometimes can be communicated. That is its paradox, and its truth.

IONESCO AND THE PHANTOM · by Kenneth Tynan

M. Ionesco's article on "The Playwright's Role" is discussed elsewhere in these pages by Mr. Toynbee and several readers. I want to add what I hope will not be a postscript, for this is a debate that should continue.

As I read the piece I felt first bewilderment, next admiration, and finally regret. Bewilderment at his assumption that I wanted drama to be forced to echo a particular political creed, when all I want is for drama to realise that it is a *part* of politics, in the sense that every human activity, even buying a packet of cigarettes, has social and political repercussions. Then, admiration: no one could help admiring the sincerity and skill with which, last Sunday, M. Ionesco marshalled prose for his purposes. And ultimately, regret: regret that a man so capable of stating a positive attitude towards art should deny that there was any positive attitude worth taking towards life. Or even (which is crucial) that there was an umbilical connection between the two.

————•————

The position towards which M. Ionesco is moving is that which regards art as if it were something different from and independent of everything else in the world; as if it not only did not but *should* not correspond to anything outside the mind of the artist. This position, as it happens, was reached some years ago by a French painter who declared that, since nothing in nature exactly resembled anything else, he proposed to burn all of his paintings which in any way resembled anything that already existed. The end of that line, of course, is Action Painting.

M. Ionesco has not yet gone so far. He is stuck, to pursue the analogy, in an earlier groove, the groove of cubism, which has fascinated him so

Originally published in the July 6, 1958 issue of *The Observer*. Reprinted here from *Curtains* by Kenneth Tynan. Copyright 1961 by Kenneth Tynan. Reprinted by permission of Atheneum Publishers.

much that he has begun to confuse ends and means. The cubists employed distortion to make discoveries about the nature of objective reality. M. Ionesco, I fear, is on the brink of believing that his distortions are more valid and important than the external world it is their proper function to interpret. To adapt Johnson, I am not yet so lost in drama criticism as to forget that plays are the daughters of earth, and that things are the sons of heaven. But M. Ionesco is in danger of forgetting; of locking himself up in that hall of mirrors which in philosophy is known as solipsism.

Art is parasitic on life, just as criticism is parasitic on art. M. Ionesco and his followers are breaking the chain, applying the tourniquet, aspiring as writers to a condition of stasis. At their best, of course, they don't succeed: the alarming thing is that they try. As in physiology, note how quickly the brain, starved of blood, produces hallucinations and delusions of grandeur. "A work of art," says M. Ionesco, "is the source and the raw material of ideologies to come." O hubris! Art and ideology often interact on each other; but the plain fact is that both spring from a common source. Both draw on human experience to explain mankind to itself; both attempt, in very different ways, to assemble coherence from seemingly unrelated phenomena; both stand guard for us against chaos. They are brothers, not child and parent. To say, as M. Ionesco does, that Freud was inspired by Sophocles is the direst nonsense. Freud merely found in Sophocles confirmation of a theory he had formed on a basis of empirical evidence. This does not make Sophocles a Freudian, or vice versa: it is simply a pleasing instance of fraternal corroboration.

You many wonder why M. Ionesco is so keen on this phantom notion of art as a world of its own, answerable to none but its own laws. Wonder no more: he is merely seeking to exempt himself from any kind of value-judgment. His aim is to blind us to the fact that we are all in some sense critics, who bring to the theatre not only those "nostalgias and anxieties" by which, as he rightly says, world history has largely been governed, but also a whole series of new ideas—moral, social, psychological, political—through which we hope some day to free ourselves from the rusty hegemony of *Angst*. These fond ideas, M. Ionesco quickly assures us, do not belong in the theatre. Our job, as critics, is just to hear the play and "simply say whether it is true to its own nature." Not, you notice, whether it is true to ours: or even relevant: for we, as an audience, have forfeited our right to a hearing as conscious, sentient beings. "Clear evidence of cancer here, sir." "Very well, leave it alone—it's being true to its own nature."

———————•———————

Whether M. Ionesco admits it or not, every play worth serious consideration is a statement. It is a statement addressed in the first person singular to the first person plural; and the latter must retain the right of dissent. I am rebuked in the current *Encounter* for having disagreed with the nihilistic philosophy expressed in Strindberg's "Dream Play": "The important thing," says my interviewer, "seems to me to be not the rightness of Strindberg's belief, but rather how he has expressed it. . . ." Strindberg expressed it very vividly, but there are things more important than that. If a man tells me something I believe to be an untruth, am I forbidden to do more than congratulate him on the brilliance of his lying?

Cyril Connolly once said, once and wanly, that it was closing time in the gardens of the West; but I deny the rest of that suavely cadenced sentence, which asserts that "from now on an artist will be judged only by the resonance of his solitude or the quality of his despair." Not by me he won't. I shall, I hope, respond to the honesty of such testimonies: but I shall be looking for something more, something harder: for evidence of the artist who is not content with the passive role of a symptom, but concerns himself, from time to time, with such things as healing. M. Ionesco correctly says that no ideology has yet abolished fear, pain or sadness. Nor has any work of art. But both are in the business of trying. What other business is there?

———•———

DOWN ON THE SIDE OF LIFE · *by Nigel Dennis*

Nobody will deny that there is an approved method of expressing sharp disagreement with an important person. One begins by declaring a profound gratitude for his existence, and one continues gratefully for at least a page, listing the person's astonishing qualities and explaining exactly why the world would be poor without him. By the time one has reached the second page it is clear to the reader—or should be, if the work has not been botched—that far from being merely poor without this titan, the world would be so poverty-stricken as to constitute a dead loss. And this is the moment when the critic, as if anxious to re-assure the world that its fate does not hang upon this single, priceless life, takes up his scythe and starts mowing down the golden harvest which he has nourished with such respect. He reminds his readers that even the stoutest of titans is not without weaknesses, and these he begins to list. There is a weakness in the head, apparently, about which little can be done. The stuff which has gone into the feet is largely grey and clammy. The heart is all right, if you like your hearts spongy. After a good deal of this, the reader begins to feel braver, for he sees that the man's talent has a good

From the April 1962 issue of *Encounter*. Reprinted by permission of the author.

deal of sham in it and that the world can struggle on without him after all. And by the end of the article—if the article has been properly written—the reader should have the feeling that this lonely struggle is not only possible but extremely desirable. For it is better to stumble on alone than accept leadership from one of whom we can say now with confidence that it were better if he had never been born.

Mr. Kenneth Tynan was born in Birmingham in 1927. If he had not taken this initial step the world would not necessarily be better but it would certainly be more at ease. This is a hard thing to say because Mr. Tynan, in a famous bicker with M. Ionesco, declared that his business in life was the healing of suffering, and no man that sees his work in such a golden light can enjoy being feared by others as a bigoted dentist. Yet such is the case without a doubt. Mr. Tynan has spent ten years using sharp, unpleasant instruments for the advancement of humanity. He has done so in the name of "realism," but this has always been a form of romantic idealism. As in the case of his favourite critic, Bernard Shaw, the pursuit of a dream has been represented by the dreamer as a practical preference for the useful. And, again like Shaw, Mr. Tynan has not found it easy to shape his natural romanticism into an utilitarian likeness. If now, at last, he has found peace on the rock of Brecht, it is because this playwright above all found ways in which imagination, romanticism and mawkishness could be made to seem hard-headed, radical and practical.

There are two reasons why Mr. Tynan's collected reviews* are interesting. The first is that they record the history of his own quest; the second, that this quest was concurrent with a similar march in the English theatre. The reviews cover the period from 1950 to 1960, and during this time the transformation of the drama was matched by the transformation of Mr. Tynan. Both transformations are to be applauded, so long as they do not stunt themselves by becoming permanent. Mr. Tynan is more vulnerable than the theatre in this respect because he has reached his goal and made up his mind. The theatre, not having a mind, never reaches any goal and just goes where fashion pushes it.

The fashion when Mr. Tynan began reviewing was perfectly conventional—as it will be again, no doubt, before long. The fashion Mr. Tynan wanted to impose was more exciting: he loved "the theatre of fantasy and shock" and believed that "this sad age needs to be dazzled, shaped, and spurred by the spectacle of heroism . . . If heroic plays take the stage, life may produce, in honest emulation, its own poor heroes of flesh and fact." Today, ten years later, Mr. Tynan believes he has dropped all this, for he has come to regard the theatre "as a branch of sociology as well as a means of self-expression." The change is not so great as Mr. Tynan thinks,

* *Curtains.* By Kenneth Tynan. (Longmans, 42s.)

for in both points of view the importance of artistry is less than the importance of being earnest. The shaping of real life heroes is no less sociological than the shaping of radical realists; all that has happened is that the social reformer wishes now to reform in a different way. One stresses this point because it is important to understand that the young missionary's attitude to the arts was the same as the mature missionary's; the playwright's aim must be socially beneficial and a play is to be judged largely by the directions it takes and the conclusions it reaches.

The conclusions reached by the plays Mr. Tynan saw in his early years as a critic were so drab, pointless and uninteresting that the reader of his reviews can feel nothing but sympathy for what Mr. Tynan's enthusiasm had to suffer. All through these years he searched passionately and honourably for *interesting* plays; he soon forgot, one may guess, to demand plays that would shape heroes, since such plays were nonexistent; all he asked was to be excited into feeling that life was worth living. His rudeness when faced week after week by the most ordinary kinds of plays was well justified and well expressed—indeed, very few plays were as dramatic as Mr. Tynan's reviews of them. The real play, one felt, was taking place not on the stage but in Mr. Tynan's aisle seat, and the theatre's ignominy rarely failed to be the *Observer's* triumph. Then, as for many years afterwards, Mr. Tynan looked to eloquent words for vitality, and when a play failed to provide these, Mr. Tynan's insults never failed to make good the lack. Faced, as he was very occasionally, with a playwright who enjoyed words, or, as happened much more frequently, an actor who spoke well and acted forcefully and subtly, Mr. Tynan's prose rose to the occasion almost too gratefully. "Miss Bloom's candour is as still as a smoke-ring and as lovely"; "Hector's scenes . . . ring in the mind like doubloons flung down on marble"; ". . . the manic riot of his prose . . . builds a verbal bawdy-house where words mate and couple on the wing, like swifts." This has been cleaned up in recent years: Mr. Tynan's adjectives still couple, but more on the ground; his increased severity of mind has been accepted by his wings.

One of the nicest and most natural things about Mr. Tynan's first five years of critical quest was his spasmodic hope, which burst out in directions which may seem strange now but were perfectly reasonable then. In *The Deep Blue Sea* he detected "a heart-pricking strength of purpose with which I had never before credited Mr. Rattigan," while Charles Morgan's *The River Line* was "incontestably the finest play since *The Deep Blue Sea*." Graham Greene's *The Living Room* was the work of "a potentially great dramatist" and "the best first play of its (English) generation," while Noel Coward's "best things" were credited with "the

staccato, blind impulsiveness of a machine gun." "I have heard him
accused," said Mr. Tynan, "of having enervated English comedy. . . . The
truth, of course, is the opposite: Coward took sophistication out of the
refrigerator and set it bubbling on the hob." Mr. Tynan is not to be
blamed if the Coward manner has ceased to bubble, the Rattigan heart
to prick, and the Greene potential become fit only for Mr. Tynan's power
of parody. He judged by what he saw and had no way of guessing that in
a year or two he would discover the plays that really mattered to him.
In 1954, he could still imply the object of his quest by saying: "Our
dramatists . . . will wear gags and blinkers, spread half-truths and smoke-
screens—anything rather than stare life in the face." But what "life" was
exactly, and what it should look like on the stage, was still a puzzle to
him and he propounded various solutions which, by their variance with
one another, suggest that each was snatched at hopefully but was destined,
like the chosen playwrights, to be discarded.

"The greatest plays are those which convince us that men can occasionally
speak like angels."
"Good drama, of whatever kind, has but one mainspring—the human being
reduced by ineluctable process to a state of desperation."
"I shall reserve my cheers for the play in which man among men, not against
men, is the well-spring of tragedy."
"Let the Hjalmars of the world keep their illusions: no price is too high for
the postponement of despair."
"For me the two parts of *Henry IV* are the twin summits of Shakespeare's
achievements. Lime-hungry actors have led us always to the tragedies, where a
single soul is spotlit and its agony explored; but these private torments dwindle
beside the Henries, great public plays in which a whole nation is under scrutiny
and on trial."
"By all the known criteria, Samuel Beckett's *Waiting For Godot* is a dramatic vacuum . . . [But it appeals] to a definition of drama much more fundamental than any in the books. A play, it asserts and proves, is basically a means
of spending two hours in the dark without being bored."

This has always been the *whimsical* side of Mr. Tynan, for better
and for worse. His dogmatic lurches in conflicting directions have done
much to keep his mind open, and much to confuse the minds of his
readers. And he has experienced the same fitfulness when he has tried to
define his function as a critic.

"I see myself predominantly as a lock. If the key, which is the work of art,
fits snugly into my mechanism of bias and preference, I click and rejoice; if not
I am helpless. . . . Sometimes . . . a masterpiece . . . batters down the door, and
enters unopposed; and when that happens . . . I cave in *con amore.*"

This is all very feminine; but it shows a certain sloppiness. A critic
can be didactic or helpless, but it is wrong for him to play the former

and plead the latter. His brain should be active all the time—particularly if, as Mr. Tynan declares elsewhere: "The true critic cares little for here and now . . . his real rendezvous is with posterity."

The arrival of *Mother Courage* (1955) was the turning point for Mr. Tynan and his lock. Brecht's "epic" view coincided exactly with Mr. Tynan's preference for the epical Shakespeare, and because "behind its every line . . . there beats a passionate desire to improve the human condition," Mr. Tynan's questing humanitarianism was satisfied as well. He had not liked "propaganda" before, but now, he found, he did, particularly as Brecht's helped towards "the postponement of despair." And a year later, the arrival of *Look Back in Anger* completed Mr. Tynan's quest. Everything was there—the stream of words that Mr. Tynan had always loved, the absence of drawing-room refinements, the spirit of young England expressed in "the drift towards anarchy [and] instinctive Leftishness," plus the thrill of seeing "the sex war and the class war on . . . one and the same stage." "Jimmy Porter," Mr. Tynan wrote joyously, "is the completest young pup in our literature since Hamlet, Prince of Denmark." This remains the most puzzling of all his comparisons.

In the years that have followed this happy moment, Mr. Tynan has been much more settled. The advancement of humanity has been his principal dramatic test and he has had very decided ideas about what advancement is and what it is not. Mr. Beckett and M. Ionesco, both of whom made excellent first impressions on Mr. Tynan, have gone the way of Terence Rattigan and Noel Coward: far from postponing human despair they have expressed it. For the same reason, Pirandello's theories have been rejected as "at once frivolous and despondent" and Strindberg's "nihilistic philosophy" as "untruth." Propaganda, desirable when radically directed, has become "special pleading" and objectionable when emitted by a Roman Catholic such as Mr. Greene, while the "inner anguish" of the writer which once made O'Neill commendable has become selfish in Tennessee Williams. The drama of T. S. Eliot cannot be countenanced, partly because it is too "glacial," but chiefly because it is phrased in verse, a medium which Mr. Tynan considers as impractical as the "lofty, lapidary, 'mandarin' style of writing," which is now superseded by "Prose that has its feet on the ground." More recently, Mr. Tynan has dismissed Aeschylus on the grounds that Freud's interpretations have explained the problems that vexed the Greeks.

This makes an interesting list of unsatisfactory playwrights, particularly if one turns to see which plays and playwrights Mr. Tynan admires and for what reasons he admires them. Brecht, of course, is the first of these, first in the line of today's "true healers," first among those who would substitute public trials for private agonies. But the other favourites are a mixed lot. After seeing Mr. Wesker's *Roots*, Mr. Tynan "stumbled out in a haze of emotion, on a sticky, baking July evening." Mr. Brendan Behan's *The Hostage* excited his hopes for humanity by providing "a life-embracing chorus called 'There's no place on earth like the world' " and "a rousing number entitled 'Oh death, where is thy sting-a-ling-a-ling, oh grave, thy victoree!' " A "penetrating freshness of . . . vision" combined with innate "respect for ordinary people" in *The Summer of the Seventeenth Doll* gave a place in the theatre to the "simple human being" for the first time since the English drama "lost sight of it in the fifteenth century." *South Pacific*—"the first musical romance I have ever seen which was seriously involved in an adult subject"—allowed Mary Martin to "[pour] her voice directly into that funnel to the heart . . ." and broke Mr. Tynan down: "I wept . . ." (this, admittedly, was in 1951). As for Miss Pearl Buck's *A Desert Incident*, Mr. Tynan admitted that "it would be awfully easy to write a flip, sardonic review of it." But he could not do so because though it was a perfectly awful play, Miss Buck had chosen "the most important subject in the world"—the atomic bomb—"and though she handled it vaguely and emotionally, she came down on the side of life."

These are not, of course, the only contemporary writers whom Mr. Tynan has liked: his odd collection includes Arthur Miller (whose prose is "gnarled, whorled in its gleaming like a stick of oak"), N. F. Simpson ("pure plutonium . . . rarer than gold"), M. Genet (whose *The Balcony* "is a theatrical experience as startling as anything since Ibsen's revelation . . . that there was such a thing as syphilis"); Miss Shelagh Delaney ("a Lancashire girl who is well over six feet tall" and displays "a boisterous appetite for tomorrow"). But they help to show that in deciding to "come down on the side of life," Mr. Tynan has become more like a key than a lock. Active, keen and vigorous, he goes to the theatre to find out if a play is prepared to corroborate his opinions. The lock is now, as it were, removed from the critic and screwed onto the playwright.

Two points may be stressed in this respect. The first is that every critic must recognise in himself the spirit of didacticism that inspires Mr. Tynan; the second is that Mr. Tynan's particular brand of it has nearly always gone with an intelligence that has done more good than harm. One may detest many of the reasons Mr. Tynan gives for disliking a play, but only rarely does one fail to agree with his dislike of it. The trouble is that it is only the rare occasions that really matter, there being so few good writers and good plays, and it is upon these rarities that Mr. Tynan's uplifting dogma bears down very hardly indeed.

Instead of arguing against the sociological approach, let us accept Mr. Tynan's criterion and agree that the healing of suffering and the advancement of humanity are essential elements of good art. The first thing we must do in adopting this attitude is to make clear to ourselves precisely what virtues are best fitted to fulfilling this honourable aim. Goodness of heart and the desire to go on living are, we decide, among those virtues, and as they are present in Miss Pearl Buck, we refuse to put her bad writing to the test of critical intelligence. As Strindberg, however, seems not to care very much about the joys of living or the continuance of the human race, we ignore any quality that may be present in his writing and deny him the handshake we have given to Miss Buck. Other virtues which we feel will advance humanity are racy gusts of colloquial language and a cheery gift of optimistic song: these qualities allow Mr. Brendan Behan and Rogers and Hammerstein a place beside Miss Buck that must be denied to such as Pirandello and Mr. T. S. Eliot. The postponement of despair being another helpful virtue in the advancement of humanity, we can include Mr. Samuel Beckett for one play and throw him out for another; while M. Ionesco, who strongly deters human advancement by doubting the possibility of human communication, cannot ever hold to our heart the highly communicative funnel of Miss Mary Martin or fill us with the boisterous optimism of Miss Shelagh Delaney. But perhaps we value above all a certain radical passion for plain people and must always love the zeal with which a dramatist sets out to show the ruinous effects of capitalism and capitalists upon such persons; in this case, Brecht must not only be our most-favoured dramatist but must never be inspected with critical care. If there is any badness in his goodness, it must be overlooked, much as the goodness in Miss Buck's badness must *not* be overlooked.

It will be seen that though the following of such a star may heal and advance humanity in some respects, it may set it back considerably in others. To begin with, it entails a general lowering of artistic standards, to allow the good-hearted fumblers a place in the pantheon. It sets such a high value upon optimism that this likeable trait becomes not only an obligatory tenet but the principal test of intellect and intelligence. It restricts the writer to a view of life that has been laid down by the critic, and it restricts the critic to a fixed range of perception beyond which he cannot allow himself to see or think. None of this is likely to be advantageous to humanity.

The sociological criterion of art is identical to the "realistic" manner of making art. Both the sociologist and the realist like a direct approach to virtue and a straightforward boosting of human endeavour. They expect the playwright to aim his work at social betterment of an obvious kind—the levelling of classes, the banning of atomic bombs, the curing of syphilis, the reforming of unjust conditions. They argue that since people must hope in order to live, the playwright must encourage them to hope, and they assume that all such hope is best expressed by playwrights whose minds do not outrun the bedside manner of a provincial doctor.

The playwright, unfortunately, does not usually believe that this is the best way of doing good work. He thinks that art for art's sake is of first importance, for reasons that seem sensible and obvious to him. In the first place, he wants to maintain the highest possible standard in his writing and to express as well as he possibly can a view of life which he finds interesting and even absorbing. If, like Strindberg, he finds his own view alarming and horrible, he goes to enormous pains to present it as such, caring not at all how much he depresses his audience or how bad an impression he makes on optimistic people. As for his style, he either chooses the one that comes best from him or the one that is best suited to his material; what he does not do on any account is to set out to duplicate an existing style. If he is convinced that there is a place for poetry in the theatre, he will struggle to write dramatic poetry, regardless of how often he is told that this is not the right way nowadays. If he finds that the theatre is abounding in racy vernacular and breezy songs about death's stings, he may well turn to a prose of extreme coldness and "mandarin" hauteur, this being a precise and intelligent form of expression and a highly effective way of snubbing verbose exhilaration. Finally, if most of his contemporaries are hard at work promoting miscegenation, denouncing capitalism and inspiring immense quantities of hope, he will feel that this is just the time to work out his own point of view as clearly as possible and carry his highly individual thoughts as far as they will go, even if they frighten him to death.

This is art for art's sake. This is what goes on in an ivory tower. Does it heal pain? Does it advance humanity? Well, let us not claim too much for it. Let us just say rather drily that it promotes independence, personal honesty, intelligence, high standards of art and thoughtfulness. These qualities can encourage the critic to attempt, "in honest emulation," a standard of criticism which posterity will think is worth a rendezvous.

Part Six

SOME ARTS
AND ARTISTS

Aristotle's *Poetics*, which has remained for more than 2,000 years one of the most significant investigations into the nature of the art of literature (see the introductory note to the selection by Bernard Knox, p. 411), raises a number of questions which have eternal relevance to the other arts of man as well. The Greek philosopher's definition of literary art as an "imitation" of nature, for example, has often been cited by critics of the various arts, both by those who believe that art should be, as it were, a photographic copy of observed reality, a "slice of life," as it has sometimes been called, and those who, like Forster and Mann, believe that art should "imitate" nature by creating, like nature, a world of its own. Several of Aristotle's other provocative suggestions (such as that poetry—by which he means all imaginative literature—is truer than history, since it is more general) give one the impression that the philosopher would agree not with the naive realists but with those who support the independent function of art, whatever its medium.

The debate has a continuing relevance, as Sir Kenneth Clark's essay on modern painting and architecture makes abundantly clear, but serious reflection will lead us to the conclusion that the relationship between any form of art and the life which gives it sustenance is far from simple. The artist, as Jung's essay in Section IV proposes, is not bound irrevocably to material fact, as is the scientist, but one may well question the idea that the artist can sever himself from ordinary experience as radically as many modern artists have tried to sever themselves. One may question, at any rate, whether their work will prove as enduring as much work of the past.

But the art of the past can pose problems as complex as that of the present, especially in view of changing conceptions of the functions of art. In some periods of history, for example, the whole question of the nature of art has not posed itself as strongly as in others. The western Europeans of the fourteenth and fifteenth centuries, the object of Huizinga's inquiry, stressed the social and decorative aspects of art and paid scant attention to its independent potentialities: as Huizinga points out, the medieval artist cannot really be separated from his milieu. But since the time of the Renaissance, the autonomy of art has been a fact of Western civilization, a fact with moral as well as purely aesthetic implications.

The problem of the moral function of art is in some cases closely related to the problem of imitation: many hostile comments on modern painting imply simply that representational realism is a kind of moral duty devolving on the painter, and a whole long tradition in Western literary criticism regards moralization as an aspect of valid "imitation." The latter issue is touched on significantly by several of the authors of Section IV, particularly Forster and Mann, and no purpose would be served by rehearsing their comments here. Rather we should like first to approach the over-all problem of the nature and function of art in terms of the art of music, one of the highest of arts, but one which poses very special problems for the aesthetician who is inclined to oversimplified doctrines of imitation or moralization.

Music, as W. H. Auden's essay reminds us, cannot be conceived of as an imitative art in any simple sense. Program music, based on the imitation of sounds occurring in nature, has been quite properly regarded by most music lovers as a minor variety of musical expression. The pastoral movement of Beethoven's Sixth Symphony is not the equal of the great movements of his Third, Fifth, or Ninth, and the tone poems of Richard Strauss seldom reach the greatness of the same composer's operas. By the same token, music which is bound to some historical episode cannot achieve the independence and universality of music which is not: Tschaikovsky's "1812 Overture" is an effective piece of occasional music, but few musicians would think of placing it in the same category with the symphonies or concerti of Mozart. Many of the observations on literature in Sections IV and V (Trilling, Yeats, Forster, Jung, Mann, Ionescu, Dennis) insist that literature of necessity must fulfill its own nature rather than the dictates of science or society, and it is obvious that a similar self-fulfillment is obligatory for music. Such a conception underlies W. H. Turner's whole description of the music of Mozart, with his emphasis on the formal perfection and the meaningful ambiguity of content which he finds in that music. The same conception is implied in Igor Stravinsky's firsthand remarks on the process of musical creation—a process which begins "not with infinite possibilities but with choice." The historian, like Johan Huizinga, may validly find in the art of the past the record of a whole civilization, the traces of a whole stage of human experience, but for the artist himself creation is a completely individual and completely lonely process—as Yeats tells us in his essay in Section IV and as Rilke maintains with great eloquence in his account of the sculptor Rodin. In this process the artist—whether composer, painter, sculptor, or poet—creates a formal order which is, despite the creator's isolation, an imitation of nature in its totality. For nature too is a formal order, although one which neither artist nor scientist can fully seize and comprehend.

From this formal order (the kind posited by Forster as the purpose of art) comes the "exalted happiness" which Clark sees art as evoking and which Turner locates to an extreme degree in Mozart's music. Clearly, the achievement of form is something which commentators on the various artistic media agree is central to art, and it has much to do with that often-misunderstood phrase "art for art's sake" which occurs in several of the essays of this volume. The relationship between form and content is a complex one: in art of the highest and most fully achieved sort, such as the music of Mozart, form and content have been identified to such a degree that it is impossible to separate them, and the same kind of identification, Clark points out, existed in the painting of such great periods as the Renaissance and the seventeenth century.

Painting and music, as Auden's essay demonstrates, originate in radically different areas of human experience, areas which may be equated with the organ of perception and the organ of expression: man paints because he has eyes to see the world outside him; man composes because he has a voice to utter the world inside him. This distinction may well account for the fact that the external world has historically been more important for painting than for music, for the fact that "imitation" in the simple sense has had a significance for painting and sculpture which it could never have for music (or, indeed, for literature). It may also in part account for the breakdown between the relations of content and form which Clark finds characteristic of the plastic arts in the modern age, an age which has seen such a notable turning away from representation. The musician, by the very terms of his medium, which is simultaneously emotional and mathematical, cannot proceed to the extremes of many modern painters. He can give his whole allegiance neither to "the blot" nor to "the diagram."

But Clark has another, and larger, explanation of current tendencies in the plastic arts, one which relates his essay quite closely to those of Oppenheimer and Trilling in Section IV: the massive achievements of science in the last hundred years have brought about a marked specialization in all areas of intellectual endeavor and have also constituted what Clark calls a "deflection" of creative energy away from its former artistic channels. (Like Sherrington, he recognizes no absolute barrier between different forms of thought and creativity.) But he concludes with an observation which has continuing relevance—that the scientist's task, however much it calls on the same kind of imagination and energy as the artist's, can by definition never be involved with the questions of value which are central to the artist's. For that reason Clark does not believe that the current split between form and content, between inner world and outer, will be permanent, and this faith unites him to the other writers on art represented in this section.

Suggested Further Readings:

Aristotle, *Poetics*
Longinus, *On the Sublime*
George Bernard Shaw, *On Music and Musicians*
Sir Kenneth Clark, *The Nude*

W. J. Turner

Nowhere is the unique quality of human life more specifically mani- fested than in the creation of art; nowhere does art assume more transcendent and absolute form than in music. It is obvious that the specific experience of music cannot be described or even, in any full sense, analyzed. To tell someone, for example, what a certain tune is, it is natural to hum or whistle the tune, not to attempt the impossible task of finding a verbal equivalent for it. Hence the criticism of music, unlike the criticism of literature, is seldom entirely satisfac- tory and is often quite inadequate. In the next three selections, a musicologist, a major modern composer, and a poet with a strong interest in music manage in quite different ways to say significant things about that art. All three seem to feel that the area in which it is possible to speak meaningfully about music lies neither in vague impressionism nor in formal technical analysis (although such analysis can certainly be important to the specialist, who can read the language of musical notation) but rather in the investigation of the kinds of psychological reality made accessible by music in its uniqueness.

The excerpt from W. J. Turner's biography of Mozart makes perhaps the closest approach to the attempt to suggest in words the quality of music, and some of Turner's metaphors are very happily chosen to recall to the listener some- thing of the ineffable quality of Mozart's work. But Turner is essentially con- cerned with speculation on the psychology of genius, and in the life as well as the work of Mozart—possibly the most extraordinary example of pure genius to be found in history—he has rich material for his speculation.

Like E. M. Forster and Sir Kenneth Clark, Turner has no sympathy with the naive proposition that the man of genius is simply the ordinary man plus some specific and limited skill. For him Mozart was unquestionably a superior human being, whose "mind of large general powers," as he says in quoting Dr. Johnson's generic definition of genius, was "accidentally determined to some particular direction." He finds in the disastrous material circumstances of Mozart's life—his desperate poverty, his lack of concern with practical affairs, his tragically early death—the inevitable concomitants of a life that has realized its absolute vision to such a degree that ordinary reality has become insignificant. Turner's observa- tions on Mozart's music as music—its universality and its perfection of form, its simplicity and its demonic quality, its combination of playfulness and ultimate melancholy—assume added meaning in the context of his theory of genius. What he is finally saying is that Mozart's art is so perfect that it reproduces the entire natural creation: given his terms, there is neither sentimentality nor exaggeration in Turner's suggestion that the source of Mozart's music is the love of God.

THE GENIUS OF MOZART

It is my belief that the essential nature of genius is always the same whatever its sphere of manifestation. Therefore we can truly speak of the nature of genius apart from whether, in its objective materialization, it takes the form of music, poetry, mathematics, painting, or any other nonrealistic abstraction invented by the human mind. This "essence" of genius is vividly suggested in the well-known saying of Goethe's:

"That glorious hymn *Veni, Creator Spiritus,* is really an appeal to genius. That is why it speaks so powerfully to men of intellect and power."

But we must be careful to discriminate between the emotion—however deep—expressed in the prayer: *Veni, Creator!* which voices the desire for the coming of the creative spirit, and the actual non-emotional functioning of the creative spirit when it has indeed come and *is* actually present.

Within historical times, at all epochs when there has been a pure apprehension of things rather than a mere Philistine interest in things, men and women have naturally regarded all exceptional powers as divine and coming from a spiritual source. Mozart's highly gifted musical sister, referring to her brother, speaks of "the talent given to him by God." This may be accepted as voicing the instinctive popular recognition that genius is not only born and not made by industry applied to a talent; but also that it rather possesses the person than is possessed by him. A man "possessed" necessarily acts otherwise than always sensibly and in his own interests; he can never achieve that purely reasonable goal of all self-education because he is controlled by, rather than in control of, a natural force. But this natural force which possesses him is not without its laws, it is not irresponsible; if it were, then genius would be the same thing as madness, to which it is admittedly akin. Is there a fundamental law of genius, and if so what is it? Goethe has perhaps formulated it in his saying:

'The first and last thing required of genius is the love of truth."

Reprinted from *Mozart: The Man and His Works* by W. J. Turner, by permission of Alfred A. Knopf, Inc. Copyright 1938 by Alfred A. Knopf, Inc.

This love of truth is quite a different thing from the love of truths and must be clearly distinguished from it. The love of truths is the necessary and useful passion of all unoriginating minds for rules, formulas, prescriptions, and methods which are of proved utility and can be passed on to others. The "truth" of "truths" is purely pragmatic; it is therefore limited to time, place, and occasion, which it must fit, and it is this fittingness that constitutes its truth. What, then, is this other "truth" about which Pilate asked his famous question? Now, I would answer very simply that it can be nothing else but the love of God.

A light on the meaning of this comes from what may be considered as a very odd quarter—namely, Schopenhauer. Schopenhauer has said in *The World as Will and Idea* that the fundamental condition of genius is an abnormal predominance of sensibility over the will and reproductive power. I believe that here we have a clue to that opposition between self-assertion, the will of the individual ego—which is an uncreative thing reproducing only itself—and the selflessness of creative genius, which is in itself a pure love of God. In the case of Mozart his most striking characteristic is his abnormal or supernormal sensibility. Mozart as a boy burst into tears when he was overpraised. Can one imagine the type which Keats has so well distinguished from men of genius, but which, I think, he not too happily describes as "men of power"—can one think of such a one, an Edison ("Genius is one per cent inspiration and ninety-nine per cent perspiration"), a Napoleon, or a Stalin, bursting into tears at lavish praise?

The modesty of men of genius is not ignorance. This has been well noted by the observation of Miguel de Unamuno that there is "a certain characteristic common to all those whom we call geniuses. Each of them has a consciousness of being a man apart." The modest Mozart calmly informs his father in a letter from Vienna how the Archduke Maximilian had remarked that such a man as he (Mozart) does not come into the world more than once in a hundred years. I am convinced that this remark made about himself did not in the least surprise Mozart because he knew it already and here we have the key to what might seem—and actually did seem to Mozart's father, Leopold—a baffling change in his nature.

"As a boy you were excessively modest and serious," complains Leopold in a letter to his son, "but now you turn everything to joking; your character seems to have entirely changed." Actually what had happened was that, after puberty and his contact as an adult with the rest of the world and the prolonged practice of his art among other musicians, Mozart had come to a fuller realization of himself and his powers and now knew himself for what he was. Nothing could depress him, nothing seemed serious to him compared with this overwhelming secret of which he had become conscious that he was born to the happiness of praising

God in music. A rose-bush bursting into blossom does not need advice and Mozart, in whom this hidden joyous creativeness now was fully functioning, could not take anything else seriously at all.

But, even so, this love of God is only the energy, the mainspring of genius. We have more to discover when we examine its functioning. It is here pertinent to recall what Samuel Johnson had to say of genius because of the Doctor's colossal common sense and uncommon penetration. Johnson said: "The true genius is a mind of large general powers, accidentally determined to some particular direction." This, as far as it goes, is certainly true. The word *genius* ought not to be applied to gifted men of a minor category in whom their particular talent seems to derive from an absence of other possibly inhibiting qualities—that is, from a minus rather than a plus endowment as human beings. Indeed, this is the deciding factor between talent and genius. The true genius is always a great man in the fullest meaning of the word *great*. He is a superior man, a man in every respect above the average, a man who includes, comprehends, and surpasses the majority. And as he surpasses them in goodness he can surpass them in badness—"Genius," said Emerson, "even as it is the greatest good is the greatest harm." And why is the man of genius capable of the greatest evil as of the greatest good? Because of the predominance of his sensibility: "A person of genius should marry a person of character," once wrote that curious American writer Oliver Wendell Holmes, and this remark, though its biological inferences are probably not sound, is useful as a perhaps unconscious testimony of the fundamental principle of genius—which Schopenhauer has enunciated and which Keats discovered for himself—that there is a certain antithesis or repulsion or incompatibility between genius and what we call "character," in that genius is of its very nature unstable and chameleon-like by virtue of its supersensitive universality. Here we may recall the unconscious testimony of Schachtner on Mozart: "I believe . . . he might have become a profligate —he was so ready to yield to every attraction which offered."

Actually, the man of genius is kept from subsiding into evil by force of that mysterious attraction which we may find symbolized in the myth of the good and the evil angels—on the one side Michael and his fellows, who were faithful, and on the other Satan and his fellows, who instead of loving God turned to hating Him because they loved themselves more. It is significant that no poet has succeeded in portraying the antithesis of Satan so vividly as Milton has portrayed Satan; but to do so it would be necessary to indicate clearly that Michael (taking Michael as the antithesis) contained all the potentialities of Satan. In other words, if a poet is to create a convincing symbol of goodness he must succeed in making it include evil—comprehending, assimilating, and consuming it.

The man of genius is a man of good and evil and that is the explanation why Mozart, who wrote the Isis and Osiris chorus of *Die Zauberflöte,* the *Ave Verum,* and numerous other pieces of the purest single-minded ecstasy, also wrote the Queen of Night music, *Don Giovanni, Così fan Tutte, Figaro,* and other, wholly instrumental, works in which the elements of darkness and light are both present.

But beyond all this the man of genius not only possesses a mind of larger general powers, but has as its foundation a physical vitality much above the normal. We do not know exactly what is meant by "vitality," but we can feel it, and we feel it in the work of all men of genius. This extra vitality, it may be, is connected with their double intellect—which Schopenhauer considered to be a chief characteristic. There is the normal consciousness functioning in life purposively for the usual practical ends of the individual in his environment and as a social animal and there is the extra consciousness which is dominant and is always dealing with generalities and creating a synthesis which has no practical bearing whatever and is of no use to the genius as a man, but rather a hindrance. And as a man of genius grows older he comes to realize that his genius is nothing but a hindrance and a handicap to his success as an individual man, struggling for the usual aims of the individual—his livelihood and security in the society of his fellows, to say nothing of personal happiness and repose in human relationship.

There is one aspect of genius to which I shall only make the briefest reference and it is that I believe that *intellectually* all men of genius are hermaphroditic. How this comes about and what the particular nature of this synthesis of masculine and feminine elements is I do not wish to discuss here. Mozart (and, as far as we know, also Shakespeare) was passionately fond of women and had not got either the physical or the psychological traits of either of the two main classes of homosexuals who are unattracted by women. Nevertheless, there is a duality of intellect in Mozart which is very striking indeed, just as there is in Shakespeare, and it is this which gives his work its extraordinary comprehensiveness.

It remains to draw attention to a certain characteristic of Mozart's music which does not obviously apply to all his works but is nevertheless a general quality which pervades all and of which he himself was certainly aware and to which he was referring when he said that music, whatever the intensity of the passions and thoughts it was expressing, must always remain music. I cannot do better than extract something of what I have said before on this point, with certain emendations that increased experience has suggested to me.

Mr. Bernard Shaw once remarked that nothing could be more uncharacteristic of Mozart than the portraits of the beautiful young man exhibited above his name in all the music-shops of the world today. These portraits show Mozart as the most handsome, the most regular-featured of all great composers. Such "classic" proportions seem at first sight to be peculiarly appropriate to a composer who is universally admired as the classic of classics. Where else in music shall we find those qualities of serenity, limpidity, simplicity, lucidity, which we concentrate in one adjective, *Mozartian?* It is impossible in music to find a parallel to that flawless perfection. Whether we take a whole opera—such as *Le Nozze de Figaro*—or a mere scrap scribbled impromptu on the page of a visitor's book—such as the Gigue written in 1789 for the Leipzig organist Engel—we are confronted with a completely finished musical composition in which there is not a superfluous bar, not a redundant or meaningless note. There is no "waste" in Mozart—no overlapping, no exaggeration, no strain, no vagueness, no distortion, no suggestion. He is so pure that he seems often meaningless. His music *disappears,* like the air we breathe on a transparent day. All those who have really appreciated Mozart will admit that at one time or another they have felt certain Mozart masterpieces as one would feel a still, bright, perfect, cloudless day. Such a day has no meaning, none of the suggestiveness, the "atmosphere," the character of a day of cloud or storm, or of any day in which there is a mixture of warring elements whose significance has yet to appear. Such a day does not provoke or in the faintest degree suggest one mood rather than another. It is infinitely protean. It means just what you mean. It is intangible, immaterial—fitting your spirit like a glove. Thus, as Sir Charles Stanford has said, when you are a child, Mozart speaks to you as a child—no music could be more simple, more childlike—but when you are a man, you find to your astonishment that this music which seemed childlike is completely adult and mature. At every age this pure, pellucid day, this intangible transparency, awaits you and envelops you in its unruffled light. Then suddenly there will pass through you a tremor of terror. A moment comes when that tranquillity, that perfection, will take on a ghastly ambiguity. That music still suggests nothing, nothing at all; it is just infinitely ambiguous. Then you may remember the phrase of a German critic who wrote of the "demoniacal clang" of Mozart. Then you look at a genuine portrait of Mozart, and instead of that smooth, regular young beauty you see a straight jutting profile with a too prominent nose and an extraordinary salience of the upper lip, and for an instant you feel as if you have had a revelation. But that revelation escapes you as suddenly as it came, and you are left face to face with a mask whose directness and clarity are completely baffling.

One may speak often of a movement of Mozart just as a mathematician might speak of a beautiful proposition. Whereas in the music of most composers it is a case of content *and* structure, it is with Mozart a case of structure only, for there is no perceptible content—*ubi materia ibi geometria.* This is strikingly shown in the overture to *Le Nozze de Figaro.*

I would suggest to the reader that he should buy the phonograph records of this overture and of Rossini's overture to *Il Barbiere di Siviglia* and compare them. The difference is astonishing. Rossini was born the year after Mozart's death; he also had the advantage of following instead of preceding Beethoven and he was a composer of striking natural genius. But, after *Figaro,* listen to his *Il Barbiere di Siviglia* overture, with its alluring tunefulness over its easy *tum-ti, tum-ti, tum-ti bass,* and you will be struck with its straggling formlessness. Its tunes are very engaging, but you can carry them away with you and hear them mentally on a penny whistle, a cornet, or any instrument you like. They are like bright threads in a common-place piece of stuff which you can pull out without compunction as there is no design to spoil. But you can do nothing of the sort with the *Figaro* overture. There are no bright threads to pull out. There is no melodic content as such. You cannot even hear the music in your memory apart from the rush of the strings and the accents of the wood-wind. It cannot be played upon the piano. Take away a note of it and the whole is completely disintegrated. Nor can anyone put his hand upon his heart and say what feeling that music arouses in his breast. It is completely without expression, as expression is vulgarly understood; but the oftener you hear it, the more excited you become, the more passionate grow your asseverations that there was never music like this before or since. Its effect upon the mind is out of all proportion to its impingement on the senses. To hear it is as though one had been present at a miracle and had seen a mountain of matter blown into a transparent bubble and float vanishing into the sky. Your desire to hear that overture again and again and again is the simple but intense desire to see the miracle repeated. It is an astonishing experience, and it is an experience which Mozart is constantly giving us.

It would be useless to attempt to explain this peculiar intellectual gift which was Mozart's to a degree that separates him from all other composers. It must just be stated and left. But there are certain facts known about Mozart which are so relevant to this point that they should be mentioned now. He was exceptionally good at dancing and playing billiards, which were his two chief pleasures. He was small, but his limbs, feet, and hands were beautifully proportioned. He composed away from any musical instrument entirely in his head and could complete the whole of a work, from the first note to the last, and then write it down—often weeks or more later—from memory. Thus the overture to *Don Giovanni,* which was written on the night of October 28, 1787 for the first performance of the opera in Prague on the next day, while his wife kept him awake by telling him fairy-stories, was not composed on that night but merely copied out from memory. He would often compose at meals, and while composing would take his napkin by two corners and continually fold and refold it very neatly and exactly. To me this is all extraordinarily illuminating. Conciseness—even conciseness so unparalleled and amazing as Mozart's—is not surprising in a composer who could work in this way. One also cannot but think that his invariable serenity and good temper—upon which all who knew him have left comment—was yet another sign of perfect physical and mental poise. It is on record that Mozart never used glasses and that his eyesight was perfect at his death in spite of the strain which manuscript music imposes. This, also, is not without significance. Mozart's mental grip never loosens; he never abandons himself to any one sense; even at his most ecstatic moments his mind is vigorous, alert, and on the wing. It is from this astounding elasticity that his conciseness largely derives. Most artists are unable to tear themselves away from their most delightful discoveries; they linger on them and handle them fondly, but not Mozart. He dives unerringly on to his finest ideas like a bird of prey, and once an idea is seized he soars off again with undiminished power.

It is not astonishing that a mind so well balanced as Mozart's should show so great a sense of humor. In this he surpasses all other composers and, as the sense of humour is essentially intellectual, it is natural that Mozart, the most intellectual of composers, should be the greatest master of comic opera. But what might be altogether unexpected is his power to make one's flesh creep. Nothing has ever been written of such truly diabolical verve as the aria for the Queen of the Night in *Die Zauberflöte*. It is the rarest event to find a light soprano who can sing this at all; it is certain that we shall never have it sung so as to do full justice to its startling cold-blooded ferocity. And yet that aria has the smooth, glassy surface of a mere bit of coloratura virtuosity; but it is the surface of ice beneath which is a fathomless black water. This sinister ambiguity is a quality quite apart from the more familiar power of striking the imagination which he shows in the music which announces and accompanies the entrance of the statue at the supper-party in the last act of *Don Giovanni*.[1] Yet I would like to insist that there is another and even more troubling quality in Mozart's music. Linked with the "demoniacal clang," which is probably the result of that bareness which makes Mozart's music appear a mere rhythmical skeleton beside the work of more sensuous composers such as Brahms and Wagner (but a skeleton of electric vitality!), there is

[1] This is an example of Gluck's precept of using music to enforce the dramatic situation such as was, possibly, within the power of Gluck himself to achieve. But that complex and subtle musical propriety which consists in writing ensemble music in which a number of characters are differentiated psychologically and yet have their separate musical expression coherently combined in a convincing and harmonious form, absolutely beautiful in its proportions and meaning, was not so highly developed by Gluck as by Mozart, for whom music was not a means of enforcing the expression of the poetry but was the very expression and poetry itself.

a profoundly disturbing melancholy. It is never active in Mozart's work as it is frequently in the work of Tchaikovsky, in Brahms, in Chopin, and even in Beethoven. It is a still, unplumbed melancholy underlying even his brightest and most vivacious movements. It is this that gives his music that ambiguity to which I have drawn attention, an ambiguity which makes one sometimes find a peculiar, all-pervading, transparent gloom in Mozart's music. I am not even sure that *gloom* and *melancholy* are the right words to use. Mozart is very mysterious—far more mysterious than Beethoven, because his music *seems* to express much less of his human character. But the mystery lies also in Mozart himself and there for the present we will let it remain.

Igor Stravinsky

In passing from Turner's essay to Stravinsky's reflections, we move from an attempt to understand the nature of musical genius to a direct confrontation of the mind of musical genius. Igor Stravinsky, who was born in Russia in 1882 but has spent most of his life either in France or the United States, has been a dominant force in modern music. Composing in a wide variety of forms and styles, he has at different stages in his career been important both as an innovator and as a traditionalist, and in both capacities he has exerted a powerful influence on other composers.

Music, rather than words, constitutes the true language of Stravinsky's thought, and it is perhaps for that reason that he makes no attempt to present us with an orderly verbal statement of his views on music or on the over-all significance of his work as a composer. Instead, he provides us with a series of random and seemingly unconnected observations in an associative, rather than a logical, pattern. When we look at these observations closely, however, we perceive a definite consistency in their concerns. Time, pure duration, is, as Stravinsky has noted elsewhere, the medium with which the composer works, and time is the central subject of his reflections here. He considers not only musical time, which constitutes simultaneously a linear progression and a permanent ideal form, but also historical time, the conditioning factor of all art, from which somehow the great artist, like Beethoven, wrests a permanence which, liberating him from time, makes his work "contemporary."

Behind Stravinsky's preoccupation with time turned into ideal form lies a set of traditional idealistic attitudes which emerge philosophically in his expression of a Platonic attitude toward the relation of soul and body and religiously in his simple belief that his talent is the gift of God. The latter statement may well remind us of Turner's religious interpretation of the genius of Mozart, and it suggests, whatever our own religious views, something of the mystery at the heart of artistic creation.

My REFLECTIONS ON BEING EIGHTY

I was born out of time in the sense that by temperament and talent I would have been more suited for the life of a small Bach living in anonymity and composing regularly for an established service and for God.

I did weather the world I have lived in—weathered it well, you will say—and I have survived, though not uncorrupted, the corruption of spirit in the musical business world of publishers, conductors, music festivals, recordings, publicity, television, critics (with whom my real argument is that the person who practises the vocation of music should not be judged by the person who has no vocation and does not understand musical practice, and to whom music must therefore be of an infinitely less fundamental consequence) and all of the misunderstandings about performance the word concerts has come to mean. But the small Bach might have composed three times as much music.

Now, at 80, I have found new joy in Beethoven. The Great Fugue, for example, now seems to me the most perfect miracle in music—and how right Beethoven's friends were when they convinced him to detach it from opus 130!

It is also the most absolutely contemporary piece of music I know, and contemporary forever, a statement that might surprise students of my own later music because the Great Fugue is all variation and development and my later music is generally canonic and therefore "static" and "objective"—in fact, the antithesis of Beethoven's fugue. (Students of my music would expect me to cite something like Josquin's great Ferrara motet *Hic me sidereo* as my "favourite" piece, or so I imagine.)

Hardly birthmarked by its age, the Great Fugue is, in rhythm alone, more subtle than any music of my own century—what subtlety in the notation ♩ as Herr Webern knew. But it is pure interval music, this fugue, and I love it beyond everything.

———•———

The dualism widens, my self and my body, as though I had become a demonstration instrument in a platonic argument. The container is

Originally published in the June 17, 1962 issue of *The Observer*. Copyright 1963 by Igor Stravinsky, from *Dialogues and a Diary* by Igor Stravinsky under the title "Thoughts of an Octogenarian." Reprinted by permission of Doubleday & Company, Inc.

more foreign each day, and more of a penance. I wish to walk faster but my unwilling partner will not execute the wish, and one imminent tomorrow it will refuse to move at all, at which time I shall insist upon an even sharper distinction between the alien form instrument and myself.

———————•———————

I regard my talent as God-given and I pray to Him daily for the strength to use it. When I discovered that I had been made the custodian of this gift, in my earliest childhood, I pledged myself to God to be worthy of it, but I have received uncovenanted mercies all my life. The custodian has too often kept faith on his own all-too-worldly terms.

———————•———————

What about the much publicised infinity of possibilities in connection with this new art material, electronically produced sound? With few exceptions (notably Milton Babbitt's *Vision and Prayer,* which is worth the rule) "infinite possibilities" have meant collages of radio static, rubber suction, organ burbling, machine-gunning and other equally interesting rackets.

Not infinite possibilities but choice is the beginning of art. But the sound lab. is already part of the musical super-market. I know a composer of an older generation who wanted "something electronic, kind of middle range, bassoon-trombone like"—these were his only instructions to the sound engineer who, nevertheless, flipped a toggle switch, made a few connections, and gave the composer of the older generation an envelope containing the tape of the desired noise. The composition—I heard it— sounded like electronic Brahms.

———————•———————

In a 60-year span of creative activity (today more, I think, than in Sophocles's, or Voltaire's, or even Goethe's day) the great feat is merely to "stay with it." (Perhaps no one can be *primus inter pares* at present and the historical centre was held only once and that by Schoenberg from 1906 to 1912.) I was born to a world that explained itself almost entirely in dogmatic terms, and I have lived, through several changes of management, to a world that explains itself in psychoanalytic terms.

I was born to causality and determinism and I have survived to probability theory and chance. I was educated by simple "fact": the trigger one squeezed was what shot the gun; and I have had to learn that in fact the universe of anterior contributing possibilities was responsible. I was also born to a nonprogressivist notion of the practice of my art and on this point, though I have lived into a society that pursues the opposite idea, I have not been able to change.

I do not understand the composer who says we must analyse the evolutionary tendency of the whole musical situation and go from there. I have never consciously analysed any musical "situation" and I can "go" only where my musical appetites lead me.

⸻ • ⸻

And how is one to know what "the whole musical situation" is? I am one of the aldermanic figures among composers today and one still considered to be capable of invention in at least some departments of musical technique. Yet recently trying to read an essay on current techniques by a foremost scholiast of supra-serial music I discovered that I understood hardly a word.

Whether I am a forefront or rear guard or road-hog composer is beside the point—which is the disparity between the doer and the explainer. I have not been able to "keep up" even in my own specialised and ever-narrowing preserves. And since everything one writes is already out of date on publication, the professional literature of the future (which is now) can consist only of summaries and supplements: the developments in the field during the previous week. Dr. Toynbee's last book was called "Volume Twelve, Reconsiderations." And Volume Thirteen? Further Reconsiderations? And so on.

⸻ • ⸻

"Mortify the past." The past as a wish that creates the probability pattern of the future? Did John of the Cross mean that and the fear of changing the past which is the fear of the present? I have to "mortify the past" every time I sit at the piano to compose, but I do not wish to go back anyway, or to relive a day of my life. Yet I have in the last few years relived much, I think because my four cerebral thromboses have unshuttered the remotest reaches of memory and enabled me to roam in the Phoenix Park of childhood as I could not do a decade ago.

But I do not go there now, in the threat of time, because I wish to return. (My subconscious may be trying to close the circle but I want to go on rectilinearly, as always: the dualism again.) I am like the mountain-climber who tugs on his rope simply to see how and where it is tied. The archaeologist's dream—Renan's—of the whole past recaptured is only another of my visions of purgatory.

———————•———————

My agenbite of inwit is that I do not know, am not aware, while composing, of any question of value. I love with my whole being whatever I am now composing, and with each new work I always feel that I have just found the way, just begun to compose. I love all of my children of course, and like any father I favour the backward and imperfectly formed ones. But I am only excited by the newest—Don Juanism—and the youngest—nymphetism.

I believe that my best work is still to be written (I want to write a string quartet and a television opera) but "best" means nothing to me while I am composing and comparisons of that sort made by other people about my music are to me invidious or simply absurd.

———————•———————

Were Eliot and myself merely trying to refit old ships while "the other side," Webern, Schoenberg, Joyce, Klee sought new forms of travel? I think that distinction, much traded on a generation ago, has disappeared. Our era is a unity of which we are all a part. Of course we seemed, Eliot and myself, to have exploited an apparent discontinuity, to have made art out of the *disjecta membra,* the quotations of other poets and composers, the references to earlier styles (hints of earlier and other creation), the detritus that betokened a wreck. But we used it, and anything that came to hand, to rebuild. We did not invent new conveyors, new means of travel. But the true business of the artist *is* to refit old ships. He can say again, in his way, only what has already been said.

W. H. Auden

Like Thomas Mann, the poet W. H. Auden is a creative artist who is also noted for his perceptive and original contributions to criticism. Auden, who was born in England in 1907 but has been an American citizen since 1946, is distinguished not only for his literary criticism but also for his criticism of music. His interest in music led in 1951 to his writing, in collaboration with Chester Kallman, the libretto for Stravinsky's opera *The Rake's Progress*. Since then he has written other original libretti, notably *Elegy for Young Lovers*, the music of which is by the young German composer Hans-Werner Henze. He has also translated the libretti of several Mozart operas.

Auden's treatment of music recalls Stravinsky's both in its concentration on time as the defining quality of the art and in its form as a series of brilliant fragments rather than as a reasoned argumentative whole in the manner of Knox and other more conventional critics. (Auden observes elsewhere that he "prefers a critic's notebook to his treatises.") He is a master of this difficult aphoristic form, which in less skillful hands could easily degenerate into incoherence or pomposity.

Despite the seeming casualness of his approach, Auden's remarks on music are distinguished by a speculative intricacy which makes them essentially more philosophical than those of either Turner or Stravinsky. When he distinguishes between the internal nature of opera and that of nonmusical drama, for instance, or when he points out that music differs from painting in that it originates in the organ of expression rather than in the organ of perception, he suggests lines of thought that lead us deep into the essence of the musician's art.

$\mathcal{N}$OTES ON MUSIC AND OPERA

Opera consists of significant situations in artificially arranged sequence.

GOETHE

Singing is near miraculous because it is the mastering of what is otherwise a pure instrument of egotism: the human voice.

HUGO VON HOFMANNSTHAL

What is music about? What, as Plato would say, does it imitate? Our experience of Time in its twofold aspect, natural or organic repetition, and historical novelty created by choice. And the full development of music as an art depends upon a recognition that these two aspects are different and that choice, being an experience confined to man, is more significant than repetition. A succession of two musical notes is an act of choice; the first causes the second, not in the scientific sense of making it occur necessarily, but in the historical sense of provoking it, of providing it with a motive for occurring. A successful melody is a self-

Copyright 1952 by W. H. Auden. Reprinted from *The Dyer's Hand,* by W. H. Auden, by permission of Random House, Inc.

determined history; it is freely what it intends to be, yet is a meaningful whole, not an arbitrary succession of notes.

Music as an art, i.e., music that has come to a conscious realization of its true nature, is confined to Western civilization alone and only to the last four or five hundred years at that. The music of all other cultures and epochs bears the same relation to Western music that magical verbal formulas bear to the art of poetry. A primitive magic spell may be poetry but it does not know that it is, nor intend to be. So, in all but Western music, history is only implicit; what it thinks it is doing is furnishing verses or movements with a repetitive accompaniment. Only in the West has chant become song.

Lacking a historical consciousness, the Greeks, in their theories of music, tried to relate it to Pure Being, but the becoming implicit in music betrays itself in their theories of harmony in which mathematics becomes numerology and one chord is intrinsically "better" than another.

Western music declared its consciousness of itself when it adopted time signatures, barring and the metronome beat. Without a strictly natural or cyclical time, purified from every trace of historical singularity, as a framework within which to occur, the irreversible historicity of the notes themselves would be impossible.

In primitive proto-music, the percussion instruments which best imitate recurrent rhythms and, being incapable of melody, can least imitate novelty, play the greatest role.

The most exciting rhythms seem unexpected and complex, the most beautiful melodies simple and inevitable.

Music cannot imitate nature: a musical storm always sounds like the wrath of Zeus.

A verbal art like poetry is reflective; it stops to think. Music is immediate, it goes on to become. But both are active, both insist on stopping or going on. The medium of passive reflection is painting, of passive immediacy the cinema, for the visual world is an immediately given world where Fate is mistress and it is impossible to tell the difference between a chosen movement and an involuntary reflex. Freedom of choice lies, not in the world we see, but in our freedom to turn our eyes in this direction, or that, or to close them altogether.

Because music expresses the opposite experience of pure volition and subjectivity (the fact that we cannot shut our ears at will allows music to assert that we cannot *not* choose), film music is not music but a technique for preventing us from using our ears to hear extraneous noises and it is bad film music if we become consciously aware of its existence.

Man's musical imagination seems to be derived almost exclusively from his primary experiences—his direct experience of his own body, its tensions and rhythms, and his direct experience of desiring and choosing —and to have very little to do with the experiences of the outside world brought to him through his senses. The possibility of making music, that is, depends primarily, not upon man's possession of an auditory organ, the ear, but upon his possession of a sound-producing instrument, the vocal cords. If the ear were primary, music would have begun as program pastoral symphonies. In the case of the visual arts, on the other hand, it is a visual organ, the eye, which is primary for, without it, the experiences which stimulate the hand into becoming an expressive instrument could not exist.

The difference is demonstrated by the difference in our sensation of motion in musical space and visual space.

An increase in the tension of the vocal cords is conceived in musical space as a going "up," a relaxation as a going "down." But in visual space it is the bottom of the picture (which is also the foreground) which is felt as the region of greatest pressure and, as the eye rises up the picture, it feels an increasing sense of lightness and freedom.

The association of tension in hearing with up and seeing with down seems to correspond to the difference between our experience of the force of gravity in our own bodies and our experience of it in other bodies. The weight of our own bodies is felt as inherent in us, as a personal wish to fall down, so that rising upward is an effort to overcome the desire for rest in ourselves. But the weight (and proximity) of other objects is felt as weighing down on us; they are "on top" of us and rising means getting away from their restrictive pressure.

All of us have learned to talk, most of us, even, could be taught to speak verse tolerably well, but very few have learned or could ever be taught to sing. In any village twenty people could get together and give a performance of *Hamlet* which, however imperfect, would convey enough of the play's greatness to be worth attending, but if they were to attempt a similar performance of *Don Giovanni,* they would soon discover that there was no question of a good or a bad performance because they could not sing the notes at all. Of an actor, even in a poetic drama, when we say that his performance is good, we mean that he simulates by art, that is, consciously, the way in which the character he is playing would, in real life, behave by nature, that is, unconsciously. But for a singer, as for a ballet dancer, there is no question of simulation, of singing the composer's notes "naturally"; his behavior is unabashedly and triumphantly art from beginning to end. The paradox implicit in all drama, namely, that emotions and situations which in real life would be sad or painful are on the stage a source of pleasure becomes, in opera, quite explicit. The singer may be playing the role of a deserted bride who is about to kill herself, but we feel quite certain as we listen that not only we, but also she, is having a wonderful time. In a sense, there can be no tragic opera because whatever errors the characters make and whatever they suffer, they are doing exactly what they wish. Hence the feeling that *opera seria* should not employ a contemporary subject, but confine itself to mythical situations, that is, situations which, as human beings, we are all of us necessarily in and must, therefore, accept, however tragic they may be. A contemporary tragic situation like that in Menotti's *The Consul* is too actual, that is, too clearly a situation some people are in and others, including the audience, are not in, for the latter to forget this and see it as a symbol of, say, man's existential estrangement. Consequently the pleasure we and the singers are obviously enjoying strikes the conscience as frivolous.

On the other hand, its pure artifice renders opera the ideal dramatic medium for a tragic myth. I once went in the same week to a performance of *Tristan und Isolde* and a showing of *L'Eternal Retour,* Jean Cocteau's movie version of the same story. During the former, two souls, weighing over two hundred pounds apiece, were transfigured by a transcendent power; in the latter, a handsome boy met a beautiful girl and they had an affair. This loss of value was due not to any lack of skill on Cocteau's part but to the nature of the cinema as a medium. Had he used a fat middle-aged couple the effect would have been ridiculous because the snatches of language which are all the movie permits have not sufficient power to transcend their physical appearance. Yet if the lovers are young and beautiful, the cause of their love looks "natural," a consequence of their beauty, and the whole meaning of the myth is gone.

> The man who wrote the Eighth Symphony has a right to rebuke the man who put his rapture of elation, tenderness, and nobility into the mouths of a drunken libertine, a silly peasant girl, and a conventional fine lady, instead of confessing them to himself, glorying in them, and uttering them without motley as the universal inheritance.
>
> (BERNARD SHAW.)

Shaw, and Beethoven, are both wrong, I believe, and Mozart right. Feelings of joy, tenderness and nobility are not confined to "noble" characters but are experienced by everybody, by the most conventional, most stupid, most depraved. It is one of the glories of opera that it can demonstrate this and to the shame of the spoken drama that it cannot. Because we use language in everyday life, our style and vocabulary become identified with our social character as others see us, and in a play, even a verse play, there are narrow limits to the range in speech possible for any character beyond which the playwright cannot go without making the character incredible. But precisely because we do not communicate by singing, a song can be out of place but not out of character; it is just as credible that a stupid person should sing beautifully as that a clever person should do so.

If music in general is an imitation of history, opera in particular is an imitation of human willfulness; it is rooted in the fact that we not only have feelings but insist upon having them at whatever cost to ourselves. Opera, therefore, cannot present character in the novelist's sense of the word, namely, people who are potentially good *and* bad, active *and* passive, for music is immediate actuality and neither potentiality nor passivity can live in its presence. This is something a librettist must never forget. Mozart is a greater composer than Rossini but the Figaro of the *Marriage* is less satisfying, to my mind, than the Figaro of the *Barber* and the fault, is, I think, Da Ponte's. His Figaro is too interesting a character to be completely translatable into music, so that co-present with the Figaro who is singing, one is conscious of a Figaro who is not singing but thinking to himself. The barber of Seville, on the other hand, who is not a person but a musical busybody, goes into song exactly with nothing over.

Again, I find *La Bohéme* inferior to *Tosca,* not because its music is inferior, but because the characters, Mimi in particular, are too passive; there is an awkward gap between the resolution with which they sing and the irresolution with which they act.

The quality common to all the great operatic roles, e.g., Don Giovanni, Norma, Lucia, Tristan, Isolde, Brünnhilde, is that each of them is a passionate and willful state of being. In real life they would all be bores, even Don Giovanni.

In recompense for this lack of psychological complexity, however, music can do what words cannot, present the immediate and simultaneous relation of these states to each other. The crowning glory of opera is the big ensemble.

The chorus can play two roles in opera and two only, that of the mob and that of the faithful, sorrowing or rejoicing community. A little of this goes a long way. Opera is not oratorio.

Drama is based on the Mistake. I think someone is my friend when he really is my enemy, that I am free to marry a woman when in fact she is my mother, that this person is a chambermaid when it is a young nobleman in disguise, that this well-dressed young man is rich when he is really a penniless adventurer, or that if I do this such and such a result will follow when in fact it results in something very different. All good drama has two movements, first the making of the mistake, then the discovery that it was a mistake.

In composing his plot, the librettist has to conform to this law but, in comparison to the dramatist, he is more limited in the kinds of mistake he can use. The dramatist, for instance, procures some of his finest effects from showing how people deceive themselves. Self-deception is impossible in opera because music is immediate, not reflective; whatever is sung is the case. At most, self-deception can be suggested by having the orchestral accompaniment at variance with the singer, e.g., the jolly tripping notes which accompany Germont's approach to Violetta's deathbed in *La Traviata*, but unless employed very sparingly such devices cause confusion rather than insight.

Again, while in the spoken drama the discovery of the mistake can be a slow process and often, indeed, the more gradual it is the greater the dramatic interest, in a libretto the drama of recognition must be tropically abrupt, for music cannot exist in an atmosphere of uncertainty; song cannot walk, it can only jump.

On the other hand, the librettist need never bother his head, as the dramatist must, about probability. A credible situation in opera means a situation in which it is credible that someone should sing. A good libretto plot is a melodrama in both the strict and the conventional sense of the word; it offers as many opportunities as possible for the characters to be swept off their feet by placing them in situations which are too tragic or too fantastic for "words." No good opera plot can be sensible for people do not sing when they are feeling sensible.

The theory of "music-drama" presupposes a libretto in which there is not one sensible moment or one sensible remark: this is not only very difficult to manage, though Wagner managed it, but also extremely exhausting on both singers and the audience, neither of whom may relax for an instant.

In a libretto where there are any sensible passages, i.e., conversation not song, the theory becomes absurd. If, for furthering the action, it becomes necessary for one character to say to another "Run upstairs and fetch me a handkerchief," then there is nothing in the words, apart from their rhythm, to make one musical setting more apt than another. Wherever the choice of notes is arbitrary, the only solution is a convention, e.g., *recitativo secco*.

In opera the orchestra is addressed to the singers, not to the audience. An opera-lover will put up with and even enjoy an orchestral interlude on condition that he knows the singers cannot sing just now because they are tired or the scene-shifters are at work, but any use of the orchestra by itself which is not filling in time is, for him, wasting it. Leonora III is a fine piece to listen to in the concert hall, but in the opera house, when it is played between scenes one and two of the second act of *Fidelio,* it becomes twelve minutes of acute boredom.

If the librettist is a practicing poet, the most difficult problem, the place where he is most likely to go astray, is the composition of the verse. Poetry is in its essence an act of reflection, of refusing to be content with the interjections of immediate emotion in order to understand the nature of what is felt. Since music is in essence immediate, it follows that the words of a song cannot be poetry. Here one should draw a distinction between lyric and song proper. A lyric is a poem intended to be chanted. In a chant the music is subordinate to the words which limit the range and tempo of the notes. In song, the notes must be free to be whatever they choose and the words must be able to do what they are told.

The verses of *Ah non credea* in *La Sonnambula,* though of little interest to read, do exactly what they should: suggest to Bellini one of the most beautiful melodies ever written and then leave him completely free to write it. The verses which the librettist writes are not addressed to the public but are really a private letter to the composer. They have their moment of glory, the moment in which they suggest to him a certain melody; once that is over, they are as expendable as infantry to a Chinese general: they must efface themselves and cease to care what happens to them.

There have been several composers, Campion, Hugo Wolf, Benjamin Britten, for example, whose musical imagination has been stimulated by poetry of a high order. The question remains, however, whether the listener hears the sung words as words in a poem, or, as I am inclined to believe, only as sung syllables. A Cambridge psychologist, P. E. Vernon, once performed the experiment of having a Campion song sung with nonsense verses of equivalent syllabic value substituted for the original; only six per cent of his test audience noticed that something was wrong. It is precisely because I believe that, in listening to song (as distinct from chant), we hear, not words, but syllables, that I am not generally in favor of the performances of operas in translation. Wagner or Strauss in English sounds intolerable, and would still sound so if the poetic merits of the translation were greater than those of the original, because the new syllables have no apt relation to the pitch and tempo of the notes with which they are associated. The poetic value of the words may provoke a composer's imagination, but it is their syllabic values which determine the kind of vocal line he writes. In song, poetry is expendable, syllables are not.

"History," said Stephen Dedalus, "is the nightmare from which I must awake." The rapidity of historical change and the apparent powerlessness of the individual to affect Collective History has led in literature to a retreat from history. Instead of tracing the history of an individual who is born, grows old and dies, many modern novelists and short story writers, beginning with Poe, have devoted their attention to timeless passionate moments in a life, to states of being. It seems to me that, in some modern music, I can detect the same trend, a trend towards composing a static kind of music in which there is no marked difference between its beginning, its middle and its end, a music which sounds remarkably like primitive proto-music. It is not for me to criticize a composer who writes such music. One can say, however, that he will never be able to write an opera. But, probably, he won't want to.

The golden age of opera, from Mozart to Verdi, coincided with the golden age of liberal humanism, of unquestioning belief in freedom and progress. If good operas are rarer today, this may be because, not only have we learned that we are less free than nineteenth-century humanism imagined, but also have become less certain that freedom is an unequivocal blessing, that the free are necessarily the good. To say that operas are more difficult to write does not mean that they are impossible. That would only follow if we should cease to believe in free will and personality altogether. Every high C accurately struck demolishes the theory that we are the irresponsible puppets of fate or chance.

R. M. Rilke

One of the great formative experiences in the life of the Prague-born German poet Rainer Maria Rilke (1875-1926) was his friendship with the French sculptor August Rodin. In the following letter, written to his wife shortly after he first made Rodin's acquaintance, the young poet writes about certain insights he has gotten into the nature of Rodin's work, its "basic element." This element, of course, has to do with arrangements in space (just as music has to do with arrangements in time). But more particularly, the element has to do with the molding or shaping of matter—the *plastic* aspects of the art—according to the form which that matter really has and which Rodin's genius permits him to see. *Le modelé*, Rodin's phrase, is here all-important to Rilke, and though he does not define it precisely he suggests in a number of ways what it means. The reader senses that the idea of *le modelé* has perhaps accidentally opened up for Rilke ways into the very different art of poetry, though he does not say this. Certainly the point of view expressed in the latter half of the letter, that the artist must choose either his work or happiness (the vaguely unhappy household at Rodin's, like Tolstoy's "unedifying" household, seems to lead Rilke to this conclusion more than anything Rodin says), suggests that the young poet is posing a choice for himself.

Our age in general no longer regards letter writing as a form of literature. We can no longer understand those great, formal letter writers (Mme. de Sévigné, Walpole, Chesterfield) for whom the personal reason for writing a letter was little more than an occasion seized upon for the expression of quite impersonal matters, and we clearly do not emulate them by polishing, revising, and recopying a number of times any letters we may write. We have not, however, lost an interest in private lives, and more volumes of personal letters have been published in our time than in any other. Such a personal letter as this one by Rilke should be read therefore with the understanding that its author did not—at least consciously—intend it to be seen by any eyes other than those of his wife. Yet since it was written by one of the great poets of our century it is bound to be of interest to others. Furthermore, for Rilke, too, the letter was more than just a way of telling his wife what he had been doing recently; we see quite plainly that he is working out on paper, chiefly for himself, certain ideas on aesthetics and also facing certain probabilities about his own destiny as an artist.

A LETTER WRITTEN AFTER A VISIT WITH RODIN

To Clara Rilke   11 rue Toullier, Paris
                                             September 5, 1902

. . . I believe much has now been revealed to me at Rodin's recently. After a *déjeuner* that passed no less uneasily and strangely than the one I last mentioned, I went with Rodin into the garden, and we sat down on a bench which looked out wonderfully far over Paris. It was still and beautiful. The little girl (it is probably Rodin's daughter), the little girl had come with us without Rodin's having noticed her. Nor did the child seem to expect it. She sat down not far from us on the path and looked slowly and sadly for curious stones in the gravel. Sometimes she came over and looked at Rodin's mouth when he spoke, or at mine, if I happened to be saying something. Once she also brought a violet. She laid it bashfully with her little hand on that of Rodin and wanted to put it in his hand somehow, to fasten it somehow to that hand. But the hand was as though made of stone, Rodin only looked at it fleetingly, looked past it, past the shy little hand, past the violet, past the child, past this whole little moment of love, with a look that clung to the things that seemed continually to be taking shape in him.
He spoke of art, of art dealers, of his lonely position and said a great

Reprinted from *Letters of Rainer Maria Rilke,* Vol. I. Translated by Jane Bannard Greene and M. D. Herter Norton. By permission of W. W. Norton & Company, Inc. Copyright 1945 by W. W. Norton & Company, Inc.

deal that was beautiful which I rather sensed than understood, because he often spoke very indistinctly and very rapidly. He kept coming back to beauty which is everywhere for him who rightly understands and wants it, to things, to the life of these things—*de regarder une pierre, le torse d'une femme* . . . And again and again to work. Since physical, really difficult manual labor has come to count as something inferior—he said, work has stopped altogether. I know five, six people in Paris who really work, perhaps a few more. There in the schools, what are they doing year after year—they are "composing." In so doing they learn nothing at all of the nature of things. *Le modelé* (ask your Berlitz French woman sometime how one could translate that, perhaps it is in her dictionary). I know what it means: it is the character of the surfaces, more or less in contrast to the contour, that which fills out all the contours. It is the law and the relationship of these surfaces. Do you understand, for him there is *only le modelé* . . . in all things, in all bodies; he detaches it from them, makes it, after he has learned it from them, into an independent thing, that is, into sculpture, into a plastic work of art. For this reason, a piece of arm and leg and body is for him a whole, an entity, because he no longer thinks of arm, leg, body (that would seem to him too like subject matter, do you see, too—novelistic, so to speak), but only of a *modelé* which completes itself, which is, in a certain sense, finished, rounded off. The following was extraordinarily illuminating in this respect. The little girl brought the shell of a small snail she had found in the gravel. The flower he hadn't noticed,—this he noticed immediately. He took it in his hand, smiled, admired it, examined it and said suddenly: *Voilà le modelé grec.* I understood at once. He said further: *Vous savez, ce n'est pas la forme de l'objet, mais: le modelé.* . . . Then still another snail shell came to light, broken and crushed . . . :—*C'est le modelé gothique-renaissance,* said Rodin with his sweet, pure smile! . . . And what he meant was more or less: It is a question for me, that is for the sculptor par excellence, of seeing or studying not the colors or the contours but that which constitutes the plastic, the surfaces. The character of these, whether they are rough or smooth, shiny or dull (not in color but in character!). Things are infallible here. This little snail recalls the greatest works of Greek art: it has the same simplicity, the same smoothness, the same inner radiance, the same cheerful and festive sort of surface. . . . And herein things are infallible! They contain laws in their purest form. Even the *breaks* in such a shell will again be of the same kind, will again be *modelé grec.* This snail will always remain a whole, as regards its *modelé,* and the smallest piece of snail shell is still always *modelé grec.* . . . Now one notices for the first time what an advance his sculpture is. What must it have meant to him when he first felt that no one had ever yet looked for this basic element of plasticity! He had to find it: a thousand things offered it to him: above all the nude body. He had to transpose it, that is to make it into *his* expression, to become accustomed to saying *everything* through the *modelé* and *not otherwise*. Here, do you see, is the second point in this great artist's life. The first was that he had discovered a new basic element of his art, the second, that he wanted nothing more of life than to express himself fully and all that is his through this element. He married, *parce qu'il faut avoir une femme,* as he said to me (in another connection, namely when I spoke of groups who join together, of friends, and said I thought that only from solitary striving does anything result anyway, then he said it, said: *Non, c'est vrai, il n'est pas bien de faire des groupes, les amis s'empêchent. Il est mieux d'être seul. Peut-être avoir une femme—parce qu'il faut avoir une femme)* . . . something like that.—Then I spoke of you, of Ruth, how sad it is that you must leave her,—he was silent for a while and said then, with wonderful seriousness he said it: . . . *Oui, il faut travailler, rien que travailler. Et il faut avoir patience.* One should not think of wanting to make something, one should try only to build up one's own medium of expression and to say everything. One should work and have patience. Not look to right nor left. Should draw all of life into this circle, have *nothing* outside of this life. Rodin has done so. *J'ai donné ma jeunesse,* he said. It is certainly so. One must sacrifice the other. Tolstoy's unedifying household, the discomfort of Rodin's rooms: it all points to the same thing: that one must choose either this or that. Either happiness or art. *On doit trouver le bonheur dans son art* . . . R. too expressed it something like that. And indeed it is all so clear, so clear. The great men have all let their lives become overgrown like an old road and have carried everything into their art. Their lives are stunted like an organ they no longer need.

. . . You see, Rodin has lived nothing that is not in his work. Thus it grew around him. Thus he did not lose himself; even in the years when lack of money forced him to unworthy work, he did not lose himself, because what he experienced did not remain a plan, because in the evenings he immediately made real what he had wanted during the day. Thus everything always became real. That is the principal thing—not to remain with the dream, with the intention, with the being-in-the-mood, but always forcibly to convert it all into things. As Rodin did. Why has he prevailed? Not because he found approbation. His friends are few, and he is, as he says, on the Index. But his work was there, an enormous, grandiose reality, which one cannot get away from. With it he wrested room and right for himself. One can imagine a man who had felt, wanted all that in himself, and had waited for better times to do it. Who would respect him; he would be an aging fool who had nothing more to hope for. But to make, to make is the thing. And once something is there, ten or twelve things are there, sixty or seventy little records about one, all made now out of this, now out of that impulse, then one has already won a piece of ground on which one can stand upright. Then one no longer loses one-self. When Rodin goes about among his things, one feels how youth, security, and new work flow into him continually from them. He cannot be confused. His work stands like a great angel beside him and protects him . . . his great work! . . .

J. Huizinga

The essays by Stravinsky and Auden, both attempts to understand and express the nature of aesthetic experience as embodied in the art of music, and Rilke's letter, with its comparable reflections on sculpture, are all distinguished by their analytic and speculative qualities. Behind them lies the precedent of several centuries of conscious thought about aesthetics. The present selection, "Art and Life," reminds us of the fact that prior to the Renaissance (when many of the ideals and values of classical civilization were at last revived in new forms), western European man had a much more instinctive, less intellectual attitude toward beauty and regarded art itself as merely adjunctive to a variety of social functions both sacred and profane. The book from which it comes, *The Waning of the Middle Ages,* is essentially a study of the fourteenth and fifteenth centuries in France and the Netherlands, a period which its author, the great Dutch cultural historian, J. Huizinga (1872-1945), regards as the *close* of the Middle Ages, not, as a number of historians had done, as the beginning of the Renaissance. "Such a view," Huizinga writes in his Preface, "presented itself to the author of this volume, whilst endeavoring to arrive at a genuine understanding of the art of the brothers Van Eyck and their contemporaries, that is to say, to grasp its meaning by seeing it in connection with the entire life of their times." In order then, to pursue this "view," as he modestly puts it, he turns, like other cultural historians, to all of the surviving art of the period (and even on occasion to descriptions of some objects which have disappeared), to literature, to music, but above all to the visual arts, not only painting and sculpture but even to costume, to gew-gaws of every sort, all of which help to reveal "the relation of artistic production to social life." Quite aside from his particular thesis about the period under discussion, everything in Huizinga demonstrates a general truth of considerable importance: that there is a deep though far from simple connection between any society and the art that it produces.

Huizinga does not of course talk only about art; indeed the number and variety of lively historical anecdotes which fill his pages bring the late Middle Ages before our eyes in a very direct and concrete way. We expect any good historian to have mastery over his material, but only the great historian manages to make us feel that the past whose culture he evokes is still somehow present. Huizinga does just this, as does Kerényi, another cultural historian with whom he has much in common (note in particular the uses both make of the idea of "festivals"). A portion of Kerényi's work on Greek and Roman religion closes this volume.

Art and Life

If a man of culture of 1840 had been asked to characterize French civilization in the fifteenth century in a few words, his answer would probably have been largely inspired by impressions from Barante's *Histoire des Ducs de Bourgogne* and Hugo's *Notre Dame de Paris*. The picture called up by these would have been grim and dark, scarcely illuminated by any ray of serenity and beauty.

The experiment repeated to-day would yield a very different result. People would now refer to Joan of Arc, to Villon's poetry, but above all to the works of art. The so-called primitive Flemish and French masters— Van Eyck, Rogier van der Weyden, Foucquet, Memling, with Claus Sluter, the sculptor, and the great musicians—would dominate their general idea of the epoch. The picture would altogether have changed its colour and tone. The aspect of mere cruelty and misery as conceived by romanticism, which derived its information chiefly from the chronicles, would have made room for a vision of pure and naïve beauty, of religious fervour and profound mystic peace.

It is a general phenomenon that the idea which works of art give us of an epoch is far more serene and happy than that which we glean in reading its chronicles, documents, or even literature. Plastic art does not lament. Even when giving expression to sorrow or pain it transports them to an elegiac sphere, where the bitter taste of suffering has passed away, whereas the poets and historians, voicing the endless griefs of life, always keep their immediate pungency and revive the harsh realities of bygone misery.

Now, our perception of former times, our historical organ, so to say, is more and more becoming visual. Most educated people of to-day owe their conception of Egypt, Greece, or the Middle Ages, much more to the sight of their monuments, either in the original or by reproductions, than to reading. The change of our ideas about the Middle Ages is due less to a weakening of the romantic sense than to the substitution of artistic for intellectual appreciation.

Still, this vision of an epoch resulting from the contemplation of works of art is always incomplete, always too favourable, and therefore fallacious. It has to be corrected in more than one sense. Confining ourselves to the period in question, we first have to take into consideration

From *The Waning of the Middle Ages* by J. Huizinga (London, Edward Arnold Publishers, Ltd.). Reprinted by permission of the publisher.

the fact that, proportionately, far more of the written documents than of the monuments of art have been preserved. The literature of the declining Middle Ages, with some few exceptions, is known to us fairly completely. We have products of all genres: the most elevated and the most vulgar, the serious and the comic, the pious and the profane. Our literary tradition reflects the whole life of the epoch. Written tradition, moreover, is not confined to literature: official records, in infinite number, enable us to augment almost indefinitely the accuracy of our picture.

Art, on the contrary, is by its very nature limited to a less complete and less direct expression of life. Moreover, we only possess a very special fraction of it. Outside ecclesiastical art very little remains. Profane art and applied art have only been preserved in rare specimens. This is a serious want, because these are just the forms of art which would have most clearly revealed to us the relation of artistic production to social life. The modest number of altar-pieces and tombs teaches us too little in this respect; the art of the epoch remains to us as a thing apart from the history of the time. Now, really to understand art, it is of great importance to form a notion of the function of art in life; and for that it does not suffice to admire surviving masterpieces, all that has been lost asks our attention too.

Art in those times was still wrapped up in life. Its function was to fill with beauty the forms assumed by life. These forms were marked and potent. Life was encompassed and measured by the rich efflorescence of the liturgy: the sacraments, the canonical hours of the day and the festivals of the ecclesiastical year. All the works and all the joys of life, whether dependent on religion, chivalry, trade or love, had their marked form. The task of art was to adorn all these concepts with charm and colour; it is not desired for its own sake, but to decorate life with the splendour which it could bestow. Art was not yet a means, as it is now, to step out of the routine of everyday life to pass some moments in contemplation; it had to be enjoyed as an element of life itself, as the expression of life's significance. Whether it served to sustain the flight of piety or to be an accompaniment to the delights of the world, it was not yet conceived as mere beauty.

Consequently, we might venture the paradox that the Middle Ages knew only applied art. They wanted works of art only to make them subservient to some practical use. Their purpose and their meaning always preponderated over their purely æsthetic value. We should add that the love of art for its own sake did not originate in an awakening of the craving for beauty, but developed as a result of superabundant artistic production. In the treasuries of princes and nobles, objects of art accumulated so as to form collections. No longer serving for practical use, they were admired as articles of luxury and of curiosity; thus the taste for art was born which the Renaissance was to develop consciously.

In the great works of art of the fifteenth century, notably in the altar-pieces and tombs, the nature of the subject was far more important than the question of beauty. Beauty was required because the subject was sacred or because the work was destined for some august purpose. This purpose is always of a more or less practical sort. The triptych served to intensify worship at the great festivals and to preserve the memory of the pious donors. The altar-piece of the Lamb by the brothers Van Eyck was opened at high festivals only. Religious pictures were not the only ones which served a practical purpose. The magistrates of the towns ordered representations of famous judgments to decorate the law courts, in order to solemnly exhort the judges to do their duty. Such are the judgment of Cambyses, by Gerard David, at Bruges; that of the Emperor Otto, by Dirk Bouts, at Louvain; and the lost pictures by Rogier van der Weyden, once at Brussels.

The following example may serve to illustrate the importance attached to the subjects represented. In 1384 an interview took place at Lelinghem for the purpose of bringing about an armistice between France and England. The duke of Berry had the naked walls of the old chapel, where the negotiating princes were to meet, covered with tapestry representing battles of antiquity. But John of Gaunt, duke of Lancaster, as soon as he saw them on entering, demanded that these pictures of war should be removed, because those who aspire to peace ought not to have scenes of combat and of destruction before their eyes. The tapestries were replaced by others representing the instruments of the Passion.

The importance of the subject is closely connected with the artistic value in the case of portraits, which even now preserve some moral significance, as souvenirs or heirlooms, because the sentiments determining their use are as vital as ever. In the Middle Ages portraits were ordered for all sorts of purposes, but rarely, we may be certain, to obtain a masterpiece of art. Besides gratifying family affection and pride, the portrait served to enable betrothed persons to make acquaintance. The embassy sent to Portugal by Philip the Good in 1428, to ask for the hand of a princess, was accompanied by Jan van Eyck, with orders to paint her portrait. Court chroniclers liked to keep up the fiction that the royal fiancé had fallen in love with the unknown princess on seeing her portrait—for instance, Richard II of England when courting the little Isabelle of France, aged six. Sometimes it is even said that a selection was made by comparing portraits of different parties. When a wife had to be found for the young Charles VI, according to the *Religieux de Saint Denis,* the choice lay between a Bavarian, an Austrian and a Lorraine duchess. A painter of talent was sent to the three courts; three portraits were submitted to the king, who chose the young Isabella of Bavaria, judging her by far the most beautiful.

Nowhere was the practical use of works of art weightier than in connection with tombs, by far the most important domain of the sculpture of the epoch. The wish to have an effigy of the deceased was so strong that it claimed satisfaction even before the construction of the tomb. At the burial of a man of rank, he is represented either by a living man or by an effigy. At the funeral service of Bertrand du Guesclin, at Saint Denis, "four men-at-arms, armed cap-à-pie, mounted on four chargers, well appointed and caparisoned, representing the dead man as he was alive," entered the church. An account of the Polignacs of 1375 relating to a funeral ceremony shows the item: "Six shillings to Blaise for representing the dead knight at the funeral." At royal interments a figure of leather, in state dress, represented the deceased. Great pains were taken to obtain a good likeness. Sometimes there is more than one of these effigies in the cortège. Visitors to Westminster Abbey know these figures. Perhaps the origin of making funeral masks, which began in France in the fifteenth century, is to be found here.

As all art was more or less applied art, the distinction between artists and craftsmen did not arise. The great masters in the service of the courts of Flanders, of Berry, or of Burgundy, each of them an artist of a very marked personality, did not confine themselves to painting pictures and to illuminating manuscripts; they were not above colouring statues, painting shields and staining banners, or designing costumes for tournaments and ceremonies. Thus Melchior Broederlam, court painter to the first duke of Burgundy, after holding the same position in the household of his father-in-law, the count of Flanders, puts the finishing touches to five sculptured chairs for the palace of the counts. He repairs and paints some mechanical apparatus at the castle of Hesdin, used for wetting the guests with water by way of a surprise. He does work on a carriage for the duchess. He directs the sumptuous decoration of the fleet which the duke had assembled at Sluys in 1387 for an expedition against the English, which, however, did not take place. So, too, at wedding festivities and funeral ceremonies court painters were laid under contribution. Statues were painted in Jan van Eyck's workshop. He himself made a sort of map of the world for Duke Philip, on which the towns and the countries were painted with marvellous delicacy. Hugo van der Goes designed posters advertising a papal indulgence at Ghent. When the Archduke Maximilian was a prisoner at Bruges in 1488, the painter Gerard David was sent for, to decorate with pictures the wickets and shutters of his prison.

Of all the handiwork of the masters of the fifteenth century, only a portion of a very special nature has survived: some tombs, some altarpieces and portraits, numerous miniatures, also a certain number of objects of industrial art, comprising vessels used in religious worship, sacerdotal dress and church furniture, but of secular work, except woodwork and chimneys, scarcely anything is left. How much more should we know of the art of the fifteenth century if we could compare the bathing and hunting pieces of Jan van Eyck and Rogier van der Weyden with their *pietàs* and madonnas. It is not only profane pictures we lack. There are whole departments of applied art of which we can hardly even form a conception. For this we lack the power to compare with the priestly vestments that have been preserved, the court costumes with their precious stones and tiny bells, that have perished: we lack the actual sight of the brilliantly decorated war-ships of which miniatures give us but a conventional and clumsy representation. Froissart, who, as a rule, is little susceptible to impressions of beauty, fairly exults in his descriptions of the splendours of a decked-out fleet, with its streamers, gay with blazonry, floating from the mast-heads, and some reaching to the water. The ship of Philippe le Hardi, decorated by Broederlam, was painted azure and gold; large heraldic shields surrounded the pavilion of the castle; the sails were studded with daisies and the initials of the duke and the duchess, and bore the motto *Il me tarde*. The nobles vied with each other in lavishing money on the decoration of their vessels. Painters had a good time of it, says Froissart; there were not enough of them to go round, and they got whatever prices they asked. According to him, many nobles had their ship-masts entirely covered with gold leaf. Guy de la Trémoïlle spent £2,000 on decorations. "And all this was paid by the poor people of France. . . ."

These lost products of decorative art would have revealed to us, above all, extravagant sumptuousness. This trait is characteristic of the epoch; it is to be found equally in the works which we do possess, but as we study these only for the sake of their beauty, we pay little attention to this element of splendour and of pomp, which no longer interests us, but which was just what people of that time prized most.

Burgundo-French culture of the expiring Middle Ages tends to oust beauty by magnificence. The art of this period exactly reflects this spirit. All that we cited above as characteristic of the mental processes of the epoch: the craving to give a definite form to every idea, and the over-crowding of the mind with figures and forms systematically arranged—all this reappears in art. There, too, we find the tendency to leave nothing without form, without figure, without ornament. The flamboyant style of architecture is like the postlude of an organist who cannot conclude. It decomposes all the formal elements endlessly; it interlaces all the details; there is not a line which has not its counter-line. The form develops at the expense of the idea, the ornament grows rank, hiding all the lines and all the surfaces. A *horror vacui* reigns, always a symptom of artistic decline.

All this means that the border-line between pomp and beauty is being obliterated. Decoration and ornament no longer serve to heighten the natural beauty of a thing; they are overgrowing it and threaten to stifle it. The further we get away from pure plastic art, the more this rankness of formal decorative motifs is accentuated. This may be very clearly observed in sculpture. In the creation of isolated figures this overgrowth of forms does not occur: the statues of Moses' well and the "plourants" of the tombs are as sober as the figures of Donatello. But where sculpture is performing a decorative function we at once find the overgrowth. In looking at the tabernacle of Dijon, every one will be struck by a lack of harmony between the sculpture of Jacques de Baerze and the painting of Broederlam. The picture, painted for its own sake, is simple and sober; the reliefs, on the contrary, in which the purpose is decorative, are complicated and overloaded. We notice the same contrast between painting and tapestry. Textile art, even when representing scenes and figures, remains limited by its technique to decorative conception and expression; hence we find the same craving for excessive ornamentation.

In the art of costume, the essential qualities of pure art, that is to say, measure and harmony, vanish altogether, because splendour and adornment are the sole objects aimed at. Pride and vanity introduce a sensual element incompatible with pure art. No epoch ever witnessed such extravagance of fashion as that extending from 1350 to 1480. Here we can observe the unhampered expansion of the æsthetic sense of the time. All the forms and dimensions of dress are ridiculously exaggerated. The female head-dress assumes the conical shape of the "hennin," a form evolved from the little coif, keeping the hair under the kerchief. High and bombed foreheads are in fashion, with the temples shaved. Low-necked dresses make their appearance. The male dress had features still more bizarre—the immoderate length of the points of the shoes, called "poulaines," which the knights at Nicopolis had to cut off, to enable them to flee; the laced waists; the balloon-shaped sleeves standing up at the shoulders; the too long "houppelandes" and the too short doublets; the cylindrical or pointed bonnets; the hoods draped about the head in the form of a cock's comb or a flaming fire. A state costume was ornamented by hundreds of precious stones.

The taste for unbridled luxury culminated in the court fêtes. Every one has read the descriptions of the Burgundian festivities at Lille in 1454, at which the guests took the oath to undertake the crusade, and at Bruges in 1468, on the occasion of the marriage of Charles the Bold with Margaret of York. It is hard to imagine a more absolute contrast than that of these barbarous manifestations of arrogant pomp and the pictures of the brothers Van Eyck, Dirk Bouts and Rogier van der Weyden, with their sweet and tranquil serenity. Nothing could be more insipid and ugly than the "entremets," consisting of gigantic pies enclosing complete orchestras, full-rigged vessels, castles, monkeys and whales, giants and dwarfs, and all the boring absurdities of allegory. We find it difficult to regard these entertainments as something more than exhibitions of almost incredible bad taste.

Yet we must not exaggerate the distance separating the two extreme forms of the art of the fifteenth century. In the first place, it is important to realize the function of festivals in the society of that time. They still preserved something of the meaning they have in primitive societies, that of the supreme expression of their culture, the highest mode of a collective enjoyment and an assertion of solidarity. At epochs of great renovations of society, like that of the French Revolution, we see that festivals resume this social and æsthetic function.

Modern man is free, when he pleases, to seek his favourite distractions individually, in books, music, art or nature. On the other hand, at a time when the higher pleasures were neither numerous nor accessible to all, people felt the need of such collective rejoicings as festivals. The more crushing the misery of daily life, the stronger the stimulants that will be needed to produce that intoxication with beauty and delight without which life would be unbearable. The fifteenth century, profoundly pessimistic, a prey to continual depression, could not forgo the emphatic affirmation of the beauty of life, afforded by these splendid and solemn collective rejoicings. Books were expensive, the country was unsafe, art was rare; the individual lacked the means of distraction. All literary, musical and artistic enjoyment was more or less closely connected with festivals.

Now festivals, in so far as they are an element of culture, require other things than mere gaiety. Neither the elementary pleasures of gaming, drinking and love, nor luxury and pomp as such, are able to give them a framework. The festival requires style. If those of modern times have lost their cultural value, it is because they have lost style. In the Middle Ages the religious festival, because of its high qualities of style founded on the liturgy itself, for a long time dominated all the forms of collective cheerfulness. The popular festival, which had its own elements of beauty in song and dance, was linked up with those of the Church. It is towards the fifteenth century that an independent form of civil festival with a style of its own disengages itself from the ecclesiastical one. The "rhetoricians" of Northern France and the Netherlands are the representatives of this evolution. Till then only princely courts had been able to equip secular festivals with form and style, thanks to the resources of their wealth and the social conception of courtesy.

Nevertheless, the style of the courtly festival could not but remain greatly inferior to that of religious festivals. In the latter worship and rejoicing in common were always the expression of a sublime thought, which lent them a grace and dignity that even the excesses of their frequently burlesque details could not affect. On the other hand, the ideas glorified by the secular feast were nothing more than those of chivalry and of courtly love. The ritual of chivalry, no doubt, was rich enough to give these festivities a venerable and solemn style. There were the accolade, the vows, the chapters of the orders, the rules of the tournaments, the formalities of homage, service and precedence, all the dignified proceedings of kings-at-arms and heralds, all the brightness of blazonry and armour. But this did not suffice to satisfy all aspirations. The court fêtes were expected to visualize in its entirety the dream of the heroic life. And here style failed. For in the fifteenth century the apparatus of chivalrous fancy was no longer anything but vain convention and mere literature.

The staging of the amazing festivities of Lille or of Bruges is, so to say, applied literature. The ponderousness of material representation destroyed the last remainder of charm which literature with the lightness of its airy reveries had hitherto preserved. The unfaltering seriousness with which these monstrous pageants were organized is truly Burgundian. The ducal court seems to have lost, by its contact with the North, some qualities of the French spirit. For the preparation of the banquet of Lille, which was to crown and conclude a series of banquets which the nobles provided, each in his turn, vying with each other in magnificence, Philip the Good appointed a committee, presided over by a knight of the Golden Fleece, Jean de Lannoy. The most trusted counsellors of the duke— Antoine de Croy, the chancellor Nicolas Rolin himself—were frequently present at the sessions of the committee, of which Olivier de la Marche was a member. When the latter in his memoirs comes to this chapter, a feeling of awe still comes over him. "Because great and honourable achievements deserve a lasting renown and perpetual remembrance...," thus he begins the narrative of these memorable things. It is needless to reprint it here, as it belongs to the *loci communes* of historical literature.

Even from across the sea people came to view the gorgeous spectacle. Besides the guests, a great number of noble spectators were present at the feast, disguised for the most part. First every one walked about to admire the fixed show-pieces; later came the "entremets," that is to say, representations of "personnages" and tableaux vivants. Olivier himself played the important part of Holy Church, making his appearance in a tower on the back of an elephant, led by a gigantic Turk. The tables were loaded with the most extravagant decorations. There were a rigged and ornamented carack, a meadow surrounded by trees with a fountain, rocks, and a statue of Saint Andrew, the castle of Lusignan with the fairy Mélusine, a bird-shooting scene near a windmill, a wood in which wild beasts walked about, and, lastly, a church with an organ and singers, whose songs alternated with the music of the orchestra of twenty-eight persons, which was placed in a pie.

The problem for us is to determine the quality of taste or bad taste to which all this bears witness. It goes without saying that the mythological and allegorical tenor of these "entremets" cannot interest us. But what was the artistic execution worth? What people looked for most was extravagance and huge dimensions. The tower of Gorcum represented on the table of the banquet of Bruges in 1468 was 46 feet high. La Marche says of a whale, which also figured there: "And certainly this was a very fine entremets, for there were more than forty persons in it." People were also much attracted by mechanical marvels: living birds flying from the mouth of a dragon conquered by Hercules, and such-like curiosities, in which, to us, any idea of art is altogether lacking. The comic element was of a very low class: boars blow the trumpet in the tower of Gorcum; elsewhere goats sing a motet, wolves play the flute, four large donkeys appear as singers—and all this in honour of Charles the Bold, who was a good musician.

I would not, however, suggest that there may not have been many an artistic masterpiece among these pretentious and ridiculous curiosities. Let us not forget that the men who enjoyed these Gargantuan decorations were the patrons of the brothers Van Eyck and of Rogier van der Weyden—the duke himself, Rolin, the donor of the altars of Beaune and of Autun, Jean Chevrot, who commissioned Rogier to paint "The Seven Sacraments," now at Antwerp. What is more, it was the painters themselves who designed these show-pieces. If the records do not mention Jan van Eyck or Rogier as having contributed to similar festivities, they do give the names of the two Marmions and Jacques Daret. For the fête of 1468 the services of the whole corporation of painters were requisitioned; they were summoned in haste from Ghent, Brussels, Louvain, Tirlemont, Mons, Quesnoy, Valenciennes, Douai, Cambray, Arras, Lille, Ypres, Courtray, Oudenarde, to work at Bruges. It is impossible to believe that their handiwork was ugly. The thirty vessels decorated with the arms of the duke's domains, the sixty images of women dressed in the costumes of their country, "carrying fruit in baskets and birds in cages. . . ." I should be ready to give more than one mediocre church-picture to see them.

We may go further, at the risk of being thought paradoxical, and affirm that we have to take this art of show-pieces, which has disappeared without leaving a trace, into account, if we would thoroughly understand the art of Claus Sluter.

Of all the forms of art, sepulchral sculpture is most fettered by the exigencies of its purpose. The sculptors charged with making the ducal tombs were not left free to create beautiful things; they had to exalt the glory of the deceased prince. The painter can always give free rein to his imagination; he is never obliged to limit himself strictly to commissioned work. It is probable, on the other hand, that the sculptor of this epoch rarely worked except on specified tasks. The motifs of his art, moreover, are limited in number and fixed by a rigorous tradition. It is true that painters and sculptors are equally servants of the ducal household; Jan van Eyck, as well as Sluter and his nephew, Claus de Werve, bore the title of "varlet de chambre," but for the two latter, the service is far more real than for the painters. The two great Dutchmen whom the irresistible attraction of French art life drew for good from their native country were completely monopolized by the duke of Burgundy. Claus Sluter inhabited a house at Dijon which the duke placed at his disposal; there he lived as a gentleman, but at the same time as a servant of the court. His nephew and successor, Claus de Werve, is the tragic type of an artist in the service of princes: kept back at Dijon year after year, to finish the tomb of Jean sans Peur, for which the financial means were never forthcoming, he saw his artistic career, so brilliantly begun, ruined by fruitless waiting.

Thus the art of the sculptor at this epoch is a servile art. On the other hand, sculpture is generally little influenced by the taste of an epoch, because its means, its material and its subjects are limited and little subject to change. When a great sculptor appears, he creates everywhere and always that *optimum* of purity and simplicity which we call classic. The human form and its drapery are susceptible of few variations. The masterpieces of carving of the different ages are very much alike, and, for us, Sluter's work shares this eternal identity of sculpture.

Nevertheless, on examining it more closely, we notice that especially the art of Sluter bears the marks of being influenced by the taste of the time (not to call it Burgundian taste) as far as the nature of sculpture permits. Sluter's works have not been preserved as they were, and as the master intended them to be. We must picture the well of Moses as it was in 1418, when the papal legate granted an indulgence to whosoever should come to visit it in a pious spirit. It must be remembered that the well is but a fragment, a part of a calvary with which the first duke of Burgundy of the house of Valois intended to crown the well of his Carthusian monastery of Champmol. The principal part, that is to say, the crucified Christ with the Virgin, Saint John and Mary Magdalen, had almost completely disappeared before the French Revolution. There remains only the pedestal, surrounded by the statues of the six prophets who predicted the death of the Saviour, with a cornice supported by angels. The whole composition is in the highest degree a representation, "une œuvre parlante," a show, closely related as such to the tableaux vivants or the "personnages" of the princely entries and of the banquets. There, too, the subjects were borrowed, for choice, from the prophecies relating to the coming of Christ. Like these "personnages," the figures surrounding the well hold scrolls containing the text of their predictions. It rarely happens in sculpture that the written word is of such importance. We can only fully realize the marvellous art here displayed in *hearing* these sacred and solemn words. *Immolabit eum universa multitudo filiorum Israel ad vesperum;* this is Moses' sentence. *Foderunt manus meas et pedes meos, dinumeraverunt omnia ossa mea;* this is David's. Jeremiah says: *O vos omnes qui transitis per viam, attendite et videte si est dolor sicut dolor meus.*[1] Isaiah, Daniel, Zachariah, all announce the death of the Lord. It is like a threnody of six voices rising up to the cross. Now in this feature lies the essence of the work. The gestures of the hands by which the attention is directed to the texts are so emphatic, and there is an expression of such poignant grief on the faces, that the whole is in some danger of losing the *ataraxia* which marks great sculpture. It appeals too directly to the spectator. Compared with the figures of Michelangelo, those of Sluter are too expressive, too personal. If more had come down to us of the calvary supported by the prophets than the head and the torso of Christ, of a stark majesty, this expressive character would be still more evident.

The spectacular character of the calvary of Champmol also came into prominence in the luxurious decorations of the work. We must picture it in all its polychrome splendour, for Jean Malouel, the artist, and Herman of Cologne, the gilder, were not sparing of vivid colours and brilliant effects. The pedestals were green, the mantles of the prophets were gilt, their tunics red and azure with golden stars. Isaiah, the gloomiest of all, wore a dress of goldcloth. The open spaces were filled with golden suns and initials. The pride of blazonry displayed itself not only round the columns below the figures, but on the cross itself, which was entirely gilt. The extremities of the arms of the cross, shaped like capitals, bore the coats of arms of Burgundy and Flanders. Can one ask for better proof of the spirit in which the duke conceived this great monument of his piety? As a crowning "bizarrerie," a pair of spectacles of gilded brass, the work of Hannequin de Hacht, were placed on Jeremiah's nose.

This serfdom of a great art controlled by the will of a princely patron is tragic, but it is at the same time exalted by the heroic efforts of the great sculptor to shake off his shackles. The figures of the "plourants" around the sarcophagus had for a long time been an obligatory motif

[1] Exodus xii. 6: "And the whole assembly of the congregation of Israel shall kill it in the evening." Psalm xxii. 16, 17: "They pierced My hands and My feet. They told all My bones." Lamentations of Jeremiah i. 12: "All ye that pass by, behold, and see if there be any sorrow like unto My sorrow."

in Burgundian sepulchral art. These weeping figures were not meant to express grief in general; the sculptor was bound to give a faithful representation of the funeral cortège with the dignitaries present at the burial. But the genius of Sluter and his pupils succeeded in transforming this motif into the most profound expression of mourning known in art, a funeral march in stone.

Is it so certain, after all, that we are right in thinking of the artist as struggling with the lack of taste and refinement of his patron? It is quite possible that Sluter himself considered Jeremiah's spectacles a very happy find. In the men of that epoch artistic taste was still blended with the passion for what is rare or brilliant. In their simplicity they could enjoy the bizarre as if it were beauty. Objects of pure art and articles of luxury and curiosity were equally admired. Long after the Middle Ages the collections of princes contained works of art mixed up indiscriminately with knick-knacks made of shells and of hair, wax statues of celebrated dwarfs and such-like articles. At the castle of Hesdin, where side by side with art treasures the "engins d'esbatement" (contrivances for amusement) usual in princely pleasure-grounds were found in abundance, Caxton saw a room ornamented with pictures representing the history of Jason, the hero of the Golden Fleece. The artist is unknown, but was probably a distinguished master. To heighten the effect, a "machinerie" was annexed which could imitate lightning, thunder, snow and rain, in memory of the magic arts of Medea.

In the shows at the entries of princes inventive fancy stuck at nothing. When Isabella of Bavaria made her entry into Paris in 1389, there was a white deer with gilt antlers, and a wreath round its neck, stretched out on a "lit de justice," moving its eyes, antlers, feet, and at last raising a sword. At the moment when the queen crossed the bridge to the left of Notre Dame, an angel descended "by means of well-constructed engines" from one of the towers, passed through an opening of the hangings of blue taffeta with golden fleurs-de-lis which covered the bridge, and put a crown on her head. Then the angel "was pulled up again as if he had returned to heaven of his own accord." Philip the Good and Charles VIII were treated to similar descents. Lefèvre de Saint Remy greatly admired the spectacle of four trumpeters and twelve nobles on artificial horses, "sallying forth and caracoling in such a way that it was a fine thing to see."

Time the destroyer has made it easy for us to separate pure art from all these gewgaws and bizarre trappings, which have completely disappeared. This separation which our æsthetic sense insists upon, did not exist for the men of that time. Their artistic life was still enclosed within the forms of social life. Art was subservient to life. Its social function was to enhance the importance of a chapel, a donor, a patron, or a festival, but never that of the artist. Fully to realize its position and scope in this respect is now hardly possible. Too little of the material surroundings in which art was placed, and too few of the works of art themselves, have come down to us. Hence the priceless value of the few works by which private life, outside courts and outside the Church, is revealed to us. In this respect no painting can compare with the portrait of Jean Arnolfini and of his wife, by Jan van Eyck, in the National Gallery. The master, who, for once, need not portray the majesty of divine beings nor minister to aristocratic pride, here freely followed his own inspiration: it was his friends whom he was painting on the occasion of their marriage. Is it really the merchant of Lucca, Jean Arnoulphin, as he was called in Flanders, who is represented? Jan van Eyck painted this face twice (the other portrait is at Berlin); we can hardly imagine a less Italian-looking physiognomy, but the description of the picture in the inventory of Margaret of Austria, "Hernoul le fin with his wife in a chamber," leaves little room for doubt. However this may be, the persons represented were friends of Van Eyck; he himself witnesses to it by the ingenious and delicate way in which he signs his work, by an inscription over the mirror: *Johannes de Eyck fuit hic,* 1434.

"Jan van Eyck was here." Only a moment ago, one might think. The sound of his voice still seems to linger in the silence of this room. All that tenderness and profound peace, which only Rembrandt was to recapture, emanate from this picture. That serene twilight hour of an age, which we seemed to know and yet sought in vain in so many of the manifestations of its spirit, suddenly reveals itself here. And here at last this spirit proves itself happy, simple, noble and pure, in tune with the lofty church music and the touching folk-songs of the time.

So perhaps we imagine a Jan van Eyck escaping from the noisy gaiety and brutal passions of court life, a Jan van Eyck of the simple heart, a dreamer. It does not require a great effort of fancy to call up the "varlet de chambre" of the duke, serving the great lords against his will, suffering all the disgust of a great artist obliged to belie his sublime ideal of art by contributing to the mechanical devices of a festival.

Nothing, however, justifies us in forming such a conception of his personality. This art, which we admire, bloomed in the atmosphere of that aristocratic life, which repels us. The little we know of the lives of fifteenth-century painters shows them to us as men of the world and courtiers. The duke of Berry was on good terms with his artists. Froissart saw him in familiar conversation with André Beauneveu in his marvellous castle of Mehun sur Yevre. The three brothers of Limburg, the great illuminators, come to offer the duke, as a New Year's present, a surprise in the shape of a new illuminated manuscript, which turned out to be "a dummy book, made of a block of white wood painted to look like a book, in which there were no leaves and nothing was written." Jan van Eyck, without doubt, moved constantly in court circles. The secret diplomatic missions entrusted to him by the duke required a man of the world. He passed, moreover, for a man of letters, reading classic authors and studying geometry. Did he not, by an innocent whim, disguise in Greek letters his modest device, *Als ik kan* (As I can)?

The intellectual and moral life of the fifteenth century seems to us to be divided into two clearly separated spheres. On the one hand, the civilization of the court, the nobility and the rich middle classes: ambitious, proud and grasping, passionate and luxurious. On the other hand, the tranquil sphere of the "devotio moderna," of the *Imitation of Christ,* of Ruysbroeck and of Saint Colette. One would like to place the peaceful and mystic art of the brothers Van Eyck in the second of these spheres, but it belongs rather to the other. Devout circles were hardly in touch with the great art that flourished at this time. In music they disapproved of counterpoint, and even of organs. The rule of Windesheim forbade the embellishment of the singing by modulations, and Thomas à Kempis said: "If you cannot sing like the nightingale and the lark, then sing like the crows and the frogs, which sing as God meant them to." The music of Dufay, Busnois, Okeghem, developed in the chapels of the courts. As to painting, the writers of the "devotio moderna" do not speak of it; it was outside their range of thought. They wanted their books in a simple form and without illuminations. They would probably have regarded the altar-piece of the Lamb as a mere work of pride, and actually did so regard the tower of Utrecht Cathedral.

The great artists generally worked for other circles than those of the devout townspeople. The art of the brothers Van Eyck and of their followers, through it sprang up in municipal surroundings and was fostered by town circles, cannot be called a bourgeois art. The court and the nobility exercised too powerful an attraction. Only the patronage of princes permitted the art of miniature to raise itself to the degree of artistic refinement which characterizes the work of the brothers of Limburg and the artists of the Hours of Turin. The employers of the great painters were, besides the princes themselves, the great lords, temporal or spiritual, and the great upstarts with whom the Burgundian epoch abounds, all gravitating towards the court. The ground for the difference between Franco-Flemish and Dutch art in this period lies in the fact that the latter still preserves some traits of simple soberness recalling the little out-of-the-way towns, such as Haarlem, where it was born. And even Dirk Bouts went south and painted at Louvain and Brussels.

Among the patrons of fifteenth-century art may be named Jean Chevrot, bishop of Tournay, whom a scutcheon designates as the donor of that work of touching and fervent piety, now at Antwerp, "The Seven Sacraments." Chevrot is the type of the court prelate; as a trusted counsellor of the duke, he was full of zeal for the affairs of the Golden Fleece and for the crusade. Another type of donor is represented by Pierre Bladelin, whose austere face is seen on the Middelburg altar-piece, now at Berlin. He was the great capitalist of those times; from the post of receiver of Bruges, his native town, he rose to be paymaster-general of the duke. He introduced control and economy into the ducal finances. He was appointed treasurer of the Golden Fleece and knighted. He was sent to England to ransom Charles of Orléans. The duke wished to charge him with the administration of the finances of the expedition against the Turks. He employed his wealth, which was the wonder of his contemporaries, on works of embankment and the founding of a new town in Flanders, to which he gave the name of Middelburg, after the town in Zeeland of that name.

Other notable donors—Judocus Vydt, the canon Van de Paele, the Croys, the Lannoys—belonged to the very rich, noble or burgher, ancient or new, of their time. Most famous of all is Nicolas Rolin, the chancellor, "sprung from little people," jurist, financier, diplomat. The great treaties of the dukes, from 1419 to 1435, are his work. "He used to govern everything quite alone and manage and bear the burden of all business by himself, be it of war, be it of peace, be it of matters of finance." By methods which were not above suspicion he amassed enormous wealth, which he spent on all sorts of pious and charitable foundations. Nevertheless, people spoke with hatred of his avarice and pride, and had no faith in the devotional feelings which inspired his pious works. This man whom we see in the Louvre kneeling so devoutly in the picture painted for him by Jan van Eyck for Autun, his native town, and again in that by Rogier van der Weyden, destined for his hospital of Beaune, passed for a mind only set on earthly things. "He always harvested on earth," says Chastellain, "as though the earth was to be his abode for ever, in which his understanding erred and his prudence abased him, when he would not set bounds to that, of which his great age showed him the near end." This is corroborated by Jacques du Clercq in these terms: "The aforesaid chancellor was reputed one of the wise men of the kingdom, to speak temporally; for as to spiritual matters, I shall be silent."

Are we, then, to look for a hypocritical expression in the face of the donor of La Vierge au Chancelier Rolin? Let us remember, before condemning him, the riddle presented by the religious personality of so many other men of his time, who also combined rigid piety with excesses of pride, of avarice and of lust. The depths of these natures of a past age are not easily sounded.

In the piety interpreted by the art of the fifteenth century, the extremes of mysticism and of gross materialism meet. The faith pictured here is so direct that no earthly figure is too sensual or too heavy to ex-

press it. Van Eyck may drape his angels and divine personages with ponderous and stiff brocades, glittering with gold and precious stones; to call
up the celestial sphere he has no need of the flowing garments and sprawling limbs of the baroque style.

Yet neither this art nor this faith is primitive. By using the term
primitive to designate the masters of the fifteenth century we run the risk
of a misunderstanding. They are primitive in a purely chronological
sense, in so far as, for us, they are the first to come, and no older painting
is known to us. But if to this designation we attach the meaning of a
primitive spirit, we are egregiously mistaken. For the spirit which this art
denotes is the same which we pointed out in religious life: a spirit rather
decadent than primitive, a spirit involving the utmost elaboration, and
even decomposition, of religious thought through the imagination.

In very early times the sacred figures had been seen as endlessly remote: awful and rigid. Then, from the twelfth century downward, the
mysticism of Saint Bernard introduced a pathetic element into religion,
which contained immense possibilities of growth. In the rapture of a new
and overflowing piety people tried to share the sufferings of Christ by the
aid of the imagination. They were no longer satisfied with the stark and
motionless figures, infinitely distant, which romanesque art had given to
Christ and His Mother. All the forms and colours which imagination
drew from mundane reality were now lavished by it upon the celestial
beings. Once let loose, pious fancy invaded the whole domain of faith
and gave a minutely elaborate shape to every holy thing.

At first verbal expression had been in advance of pictorial and plastic
art. Sculpture was still adhering to the formal rigidity of preceding ages,
when literature undertook to describe all the details, both physical and
mental, of the drama of the cross. A sort of pathetic naturalism arose, for
which the *Meditationes vitae Christi,* early attributed to Saint Bonaven-
tura, supplied the model. The nativity, the childhood, the descent from
the cross, each received a fixed form, a vivid colouring. How Joseph of
Arimathea mounted the ladder, how he had to press the hand of the Lord
in order to draw out the nail, was all described in minute detail.

In the meantime, towards the end of the fourteenth century, pictorial
technique had made so much progress that it more than overtook literature in the art of rendering these details. The naïve, and at the same time
refined, naturalism of the brothers Van Eyck was a new form of pictorial
expression; but viewed from the standpoint of culture in general, it was
but another manifestation of the crystallizing tendency of thought which
we noticed in all the aspects of the mentality of the declining Middle
Ages. Instead of heralding the advent of the Renaissance, as is generally
assumed, this naturalism is rather one of the ultimate forms of development of the medieval mind. The craving to turn every sacred idea into

precise images, to give it a distinct and clearly outlined form, such as we observed in Gerson, in the *Roman de la Rose,* in Denis the Carthusian, controlled art, as it controlled popular beliefs and theology. The art of the brothers Van Eyck closes a period.

Sir Kenneth Clark

In this essay, Sir Kenneth Clark, one of the ranking art historians of our time, addresses himself to a topic which continues to arouse passionate, if not always well-informed, opinion: Modern Art. (In the last decade alone two Presidents of the United States and the Premier of the Soviet Union have added their voices to the general mutter.) Sir Kenneth, ignoring a great many superficial points on which argument is frequently wasted, begins with the two basic assumptions that modern art is "a true and vital expression of our day" and that it "differs radically from any art which has preceded it." The whole essay is, in effect, an attempt to substantiate these assumptions, and it is only most indirectly and subtly that the author evaluates the *intrinsic* worth of modern art as measured against the great art of the past. (It should be noted that while most of the authors in this volume and the editors have generally used the word "art" to refer to all of the arts, Sir Kenneth frequently uses it to refer only to painting.)

His approach, like Huizinga's, is necessarily both analytical and historical, and the metaphor that gives the essay its title and basic structure functions brilliantly in both. The blot (disorder, free association, imagination, intuition, sensory perception) and the diagram (order, control, intellect, rational analysis, abstraction)—to give some very quick synonyms—these oppositions, according to Leonardo, who invented the metaphor, unite in art (and by implication, according to Sir Kenneth, only when they do is the greatest art produced). Half of the author's task, then, is to show that the blot and the diagram, both as concepts and functions, are basic to art, and indeed to any supreme human activity; the other half is to show how, historically, they have pulled apart until in our own day they are completely disunited, the blot having become painting and the diagram architecture. In the course of detailing all the factors which have led to this—some of which have come from within the art of painting itself, but many more from a general change in the human spirit—Sir Kenneth reminds us of many of the basic issues which have recurred in this volume, as they recur in the world we live in: the effect on our thinking, our personal lives, and our general culture of the spectacular power of science, of an industrialized and mass society, of the findings of such new learnings as psychology, of politics, of global war, and so on.

Again, Sir Kenneth's essay reminds us indirectly of the virtues of the enlightened mind, especially in his own demonstrated capacity for detachment, for making fair judgments, because if we look at the last few paragraphs we shall see just how much he feels *is* missing in modern art, above all that harmonious balance between intellect and the imagination which produced the greatest art of the past.

$\mathcal{T}$HE BLOT AND THE DIAGRAM

I have been told to "look down from a high place over the whole extensive landscape of modern art." We all know how tempting high places can be, and how dangerous. I usually avoid them myself. But if I must do as I am told, I shall try to find out why modern art has taken its peculiar form, and to guess how long that form will continue.

I shall begin with Leonardo da Vinci, because although all processes are gradual, he does represent one clearly marked turning point in the history of art. Before that time, the painters' intentions were quite simple; they were first of all to tell a story, secondly to make the invisible visible, and thirdly to turn a plain surface into a decorated surface. Those are all very ancient aims, going back to the earliest civilisations, or beyond; and for three hundred years painters had been instructed how to carry them out by means of a workshop tradition. Of course, there had been breaks in that tradition—in the fourth century, maybe, and towards the end of the seventh century; but broadly speaking, the artist learnt what he could about the technique of art from his master in his workshop, and then set up shop on his own and tried to do better.

As is well known, Leonardo had a different view of art. He thought that it involved both science and the pursuit of some peculiar attribute called beauty or grace. He was, by inclination, a scientist: he wanted to find out how things worked, and he believed that this knowledge could be stated mathematically. He said "Let no one who is not a mathematician read my works," and he tried to relate this belief in measurement to his belief in beauty. This involved him in two rather different lines of thought, one concerned with magic—the magic of numbers—the other with science. Ever since Pythagoras had discovered that the musical scale could be stated mathematically, by means of the length of the strings, etc., and so had thrown a bridge between intellectual analysis and sensory perception, thinkers on art had felt that it should be possible to do the same for painting. I must say that their effort had not been very rewarding; the modulus, or golden section, and the logarithmic spiral of shells are practically the only undisputed results. But Leonardo lived at a time when it was still possible to hope great things from perspective, which should not only define space, but order it harmoniously; and he also inherited a belief that ideal mathematical combinations could be derived from the proportions of the human body. This line of thought may be

Originally published for the Reed and Barton Design Lecture. Subsequently published in the January 1963 issue of *Encounter*. Reprinted by permission of the author.

called the *mystique* of measurement. The other line may be called *the use* of measurement. Leonardo wished to state mathematically various facts related to the act of seeing. How do we see light passing over a sphere? What happens when objects make themselves perceptible on our retina? Both these lines of thought involved him in drawing diagrams and taking measurements, and for this reason were closely related in his mind. No painter except perhaps Piero della Francesca has tried more strenuously to find a mathematical statement of art, nor has had a greater equipment for doing so.

But Leonardo was also a man of powerful and disturbing imagination. In his notebooks, side by side with his attempts to achieve *order* by mathematics, are drawings and descriptions of the most violent scenes of *dis*order which the human mind can conceive—battles, deluges, eruptions. And he included in his treatise on painting advice on how to develop this side of the artistic faculty also. The passages in which he does so have often been quoted, but they are so incredibly foreign to the whole Renaissance idea of art, although related to a remark in Pliny, that each time I read them, they give me a fresh surprise. I will, therefore, quote them again.

I shall not refrain from including among these precepts a new and speculative idea, which although it may seem trivial and almost laughable, is none the less of great value in quickening the spirit of invention. It is this: that you should look at certain walls stained with damp or at stones of uneven colour. If you have to invent some setting you will be able to see in these the likeness of divine landscapes, adorned with mountains, ruins, rocks, woods, great plains, hills and valleys in great variety; and then again you will see there battles and strange figures in violent action, expressions of faces and clothes and an infinity of things which you will be able to reduce to their complete and proper forms. In such walls the same thing happens as in the sound of bells, in whose strokes you may find every named word which you can imagine.

Later he repeats this suggestion in slightly different form, advising the painter to study not only marks on walls, but also "the embers of the fire, or clouds or mud, or other similar objects from which you will find most admirable ideas . . . because from a confusion of shapes the spirit is quickened to new inventions."

I hardly need to insist on how relevant these passages are to modern painting. Almost every morning I receive cards inviting me to current exhibitions, and on the cards are photographs of the works exhibited. Some of them consist of blots, some of scrawls, some look like clouds, some like embers of the fire, some are like mud—some of them are mud; a great many look like stains on walls, and one of them, I remember, consisted of actual stains on walls, photographed and framed. Leonardo's famous passage has been illustrated in every particular. And yet I doubt if he would have been satisfied with the results, because he believed that we must somehow unite the two opposite poles of our faculties. Art itself was the connection between the diagram and the blot.

Now in order to prevent the impression that I am taking advantage of a metaphor, as writers on art are often bound to do, I should explain how I am going to use these words. By "diagram" I mean a rational statement in a visible form, involving measurements, and usually done with an ulterior motive. The theorem of Pythagoras is proved by a diagram. Leonardo's drawings of light striking a sphere are diagrams; but the works of Mondrian, although made up of straight lines, are not diagrams, because they are not done in order to prove or measure some experience, but to please the eye. That they look like diagrams is due to influences which I will examine later. But diagrams can exist with no motive other than their own perfection, just as mathematical propositions can.

By "blots" I mean marks or areas which are not intended to convey information, but which, for some reason, seem pleasant and memorable to the maker, and can be accepted in the same sense by the spectator. I said that these blots were not intended to convey information, but of course they do, and that of two kinds. First, they tell us through association, about things we had forgotten; that was the function of Leonardo's stains on walls, which as he said, quickened the spirit of invention, and it can be the function of man-made blots as well; and secondly a man-made blot will tell us about the artist. Unless it is made entirely accidently, as by spilling an inkpot, it will be a commitment. It is quite difficult to make a non-committal blot. Although the two are connected, I think we can distinguish between analogy blots and gesture blots.

Now let me try to apply this to modern art. Modern art is not a subject on which one can hope for a large measure of agreement, but I hope I may be allowed two assumptions. The first is that the kind of painting and architecture which we call, with varying inflections of the voice, "modern," is a true and vital expression of our own day; and the second assumption is that it differs radically from any art which has preceded it. Both these assumptions have been questioned. It has been said that modern art is "a racket" engineered by art dealers, who have exploited the incompetence of artists and the gullibility of patrons, that the whole thing is a kind of vast and very expensive practical joke. Well, fifty years is a long time to keep up a hoax of this kind, and during these years modern art has spread all over the free world and created a complete international style. I don't think that any honest-minded historian, whether he liked it or not, could pretend that modern art was the result of an accident or a conspiracy. The only doubt he could have would be whether it is, so to say, a long-term or a short-term movement. In the history of

art there are stylistic changes which appear to develop from purely internal causes, and seem almost accidental in relation to the other circumstances of life and society. Such, for example, was the state of art in Italy
(outside Venice) from about 1530 to 1600. When all is said about the
religious disturbances of the time, the real cause of the Mannerist style
was the domination of Michelangelo, who had both created an irresistible
style and exhausted its possibilities. It needed the almost equally powerful pictorial imagination of Caravaggio to produce a counter-infection,
which could spread from Rome to Spain and the Netherlands and prepare the way for Rembrandt. I can see nothing in the history of man's
spirit to account for this episode. It seems to me to be due to an internal
and specifically artistic chain of events which are easily related to one another, and comprehensible within the general framework of European
art. On the other hand, there are events in the history of art which go far
beyond the interaction of styles and which evidently reflect a change in
the whole condition of the human spirit. Such an event took place towards the end of the fifth century, when the Hellenistic-Roman style
gradually became what we call Byzantine; and again in the early thir-
teenth century, when the Gothic cathedrals shot up out of the ground.
In each case the historian could produce a series of examples to prove
that the change was inevitable. But actually it was nothing of the sort;
it was wholly unpredictable, and was part of a complete spiritual revolution.

Whether we think that modern art represents a transformation of
style or a change of spirit depends to some extent on my second assumption, that it differs radically from anything which has preceded it. This
too has been questioned; it has been said that Léger is only a logical development of Poussin, or Mondrian of Vermeer. And it is true that the
element of design in each has something in common. If we pare a Poussin
down to its bare bones, there are combinations of curves and cubes which
are the foundations of much classical painting, and Léger had the good
sense to make use of them. Similarly, in Vermeer there is a use of rec-
tangles, large areas contrasted with very narrow ones, and a feeling for
shallow recessions, which became the preferred theme of Mondrian. But
such analogies are trifling compared with the differences. Poussin was a
very intelligent man who thought deeply about his art, and if anyone had
suggested to him that his pictures were praise-worthy solely on account
of their construction, he would have been incredulous and affronted.

So let us agree that the kind of painting and architecture which we
find most representative of our times—say, the painting of Jackson Pol-
lock and the architecture of the Lever building—is deeply different from
the painting and architecture of the past; and is *not* a mere whim of

fashion, but the result of a great change in our ways of thinking and feeling.

How did this great change take place and what does it mean? To begin with, I think it is related to the development upon which all industrial civilisation depends, the differentiation of function. Leonardo was exceptional, almost unique in his integration of functions—the scientific and the imaginative. Yet he fore-shadowed more than any other artist their disintegration, by noting and treating in isolation the diagrammatic faculty and the blot-making faculty. The average artist took the unity of these faculties for granted. They were united in Leonardo, and in lesser artists, by *interest or pleasure in the thing seen*. The external object was like a magnetic pole which drew the two faculties together. At some point the external object became a negative rather than a positive charge. Instead of drawing together the two faculties, it completely dissociated them; architecture went off in one direction with the diagram, painting went in the other direction with the blot.

This disintegration was related to a radical change in the philosophy of art. We all know that such changes, however harmless they sound when first enunciated, can have drastic consequences in the world of action. Rulers who wish to maintain the *status quo* are well advised to chop off the heads of all philosophers. What Hilaire Belloc called the "remote and ineffectual don" is more dangerous than the busy columnist with his eye on the day's news. The revolution in our ideas about the nature of painting seems to have been hatched by a don who was considered remote and ineffectual even by Oxford standards—Walter Pater. It was he (inspired, I believe, by Schopenhauer) who first propounded the idea of the aesthetic sensation, intuitively perceived.

> In its primary aspect [Pater said] a great picture has no more difficult message for us than an accidental play of sunlight and shadow for a few moments on the wall or floor; in itself, in truth, a space of such fallen light, caught, as in the colours of an Eastern carpet, but refined upon and dealt with more subtly and exquisitely than by nature itself.

It is true that his comparison with an Eastern carpet admits the possibility of "pleasant sensations" being arranged or organised; and Pater confirms this need for organisation a few lines later, when he sets down his famous dictum that "all art constantly aspires towards the condition of music." He does not believe in blots uncontrolled by the conscious mind. But he is very far from the information-giving diagram.

This belief that art has its origin in our intuitive rather than our rational faculties, picturesquely asserted by Pater, was worked out historically and philosophically, in the somewhat wearisome volumes of Benedetto Croce, and owing to his authoritative tone, he is usually considered the originator of a new theory of aesthetics. It was, in fact, the reversion to a very old idea. Long before the Romantics had stressed the importance of intuition and self-expression, men had admitted the Dionysiac nature of art. But philosophers had always assumed that the frenzy of inspiration must be controlled by law and by the intellectual power of putting things into harmonious order. And this general philosophic concept of art as a combination of intuition and intellect had been supported by technical necessities. It was necessary to master certain laws and to use the intellect in order to build the Gothic cathedrals, or set up the stained glass windows of Chartres or cast the bronze doors of the Florence Baptistry. When this bracing element of craftsmanship ceased to dominate the artist's outlook, as happened soon after the time of Leonardo, new scientific disciplines had to be invented to maintain the intellectual element in art. Such were perspective and anatomy. From a purely artistic point of view, they were unnecessary. The Chinese produced some of the finest landscapes ever painted, without any systematic knowledge of perspective. Greek figure sculpture reached its highest point before the study of anatomy had been systematised. But from the Renaissance onwards, painters felt that these two sciences made their art intellectually respectable. They were two ways of connecting the diagram and the blot.

In the nineteenth century, belief in art as a scientific activity declined, for a quantity of reasons. Science and technology withdrew into specialisation. Voltaire's efforts to investigate the nature of heat seem to us ludicrous; Goethe's studies of botany and physics a waste of a great poet's time. In spite of their belief in inspiration, the great Romantics were aware of the impoverishment of the imagination which would take place when science had drifted out of reach, and both Shelley and Coleridge spent much time in chemical experiments. Even Turner, whose letters reveal a singular lack of analytic faculty, annotated Goethe's theories of colour, and painted two pictures to demonstrate them. No good. The laws which govern the movement of the human spirit are inexorable. The enveloping assumption, within which the artist has to function, was that science was no longer approachable by any but the specialist. And gradually there grew up the idea that all intellectual activities were hostile to art.

I have mentioned the philosophic development of this view by Croce. Let me give one example of its quiet acceptance by the official mind. The British Council sends all over the world, even to Florence and Rome, exhibitions of children's art—the point of these children's pictures being that they have no instruction of any kind, and do not attempt the troublesome task of painting what they see. Well, why not, after all? The results are quite agreeable—sometimes strangely beautiful; and the therapeutic effect on the children is said to be excellent. It is like one of those small harmless heresies which we are shocked to find were the object of persecution by the Mediaeval Church. When, however, we hear admired modern painters saying that they draw their inspiration from the drawings of children and lunatics, as well as from stains on walls, we recognise that we have accomplices in a revolution.

The lawless and intuitive character of modern art is a familiar theme and certain historians have said that it is symptomatic of a decline in Western civilisation. This is journalism—one of those statements that sound well to-day and nonsense to-morrow. It is obvious that the development of physical science in the last hundred years has been one of the most colossal efforts the human intellect has ever made. But I think it is also true that human beings can produce, in a given epoch, only a certain amount of creative energy, and that this is directed to different ends and different times—music in the eighteenth century is the obvious example; and I believe that the dazzling achievements of science during the last seventy years have deflected far more of those skills and endowments which go to the making of a work of art than is usually realised. To begin with, there is the sheer energy. In every moulding of a Renaissance palace we are conscious of an immense intellectual energy, and it is the absence of this energy in the nineteenth-century copies of Renaissance buildings which makes them seem so dead. To find a form with the same vitality as a window moulding of the Palazzo Farnese I must wait till I get back into an aeroplane, and look at the relation of the engine to the wing. That form is alive, not (as used to be said) because it is functional—many functional shapes are entirely uninteresting—but because it is animated by the breath of modern science.

The deflections from art to science are the more serious because these are not, as used to be supposed, two contrary activities, but in fact draw on many of the same capacities of the human mind. In the last resort each depends on the imagination. Artist and scientist alike are both trying to give concrete form to dimly apprehended ideas. Dr. Bronowski has put it very well: "All science is the search for unity in hidden likenesses, and the starting point is an image, because then the unity is before our mind's eye." Even if we no longer have to pretend that a group of stars looks like a plough or a bear, our scientists still depend on humanly comprehensible images, and it is striking that the valid symbols of our time, invented to embody some scientific truth, have taken root in the popular imagination. Do those red and blue balls connected by rods really resemble a type of atomic structure? I am too ignorant to say. I accept the symbol just as an early Christian accepted the Fish or the Lamb, and I find it echoed or even (it would seem) anticipated in the work of modern artists like Kandinsky and Miró.

Finally, there is the question of popular interest and approval. We have grown accustomed to the idea that great artists can work in solitude and incomprehension; but that was not the way things happened in the Renaissance or the seventeenth century, still less in ancient Greece. The pictures carried through the streets by cheering crowds, the *Te Deum* sung on completion of a public building—all this indicates a state of opinion in which men could undertake great works of art with a confidence quite impossible to-day. The research scientist, on the other hand, not only has millions of pounds worth of plant and equipment for the asking, he has principalities and powers waiting for his conclusions. He goes to work, as Titian once did, confident that he will succeed because the strong tide of popular admiration is flowing with him.

But although science has absorbed so many of the functions of art and deflected (I believe) so many potential artists, it obviously cannot be a *substitute* for art. Its mental processes may be similar, but its ends are different. There have been three views about the purpose of art. First that it aims simply at imitation; secondly that it should influence human conduct; and thirdly that it should produce a kind of exalted happiness. The first view, which was developed in ancient Greece, must be reckoned one of the outstanding failures of Greek thought. It is simply contrary to experience, because if the visual arts aimed solely at imitating things they would be of very little importance; whereas the Greeks above all people knew that they were important, and treated them as such. Yet such was the prestige of Greek thought that this theory of art was revived in the Renaissance, in an uncomfortable sort of way, and had a remarkable recrudescence in the nineteenth century. The second view, that art should influence conduct and opinions, is more respectable, and held the field throughout the Middle Ages; indeed the more we learn about the art of the past and motives of those who commissioned it, the more important this particular aim appears to be; it still dominated art theory in the time of Diderot. The third view, that art should produce a kind of exalted happiness, was invented by the Romantics at the beginning of the nineteenth century (well, perhaps *invented* by Plotinus, but given currency by the Romantics), and gradually gained ground until by the end of the century it was believed in by almost all educated people. It has held the field in Western Europe till the present day. Leaving aside the question which of these theories is correct, let me ask which of them is most likely to be a helpful background to art (for that is all that a theory of æsthetics can be) in an age when science has such an overwhelming domination over the human mind. The first aim must be reckoned *by itself* to be pointless, since science has now discovered so many ways of imitating appearances, which are incomparably more accurate and convincing than even the most realistic picture. Painting might defend itself against the daguerreotype, but not against Cinerama.

The popular application of science has also, it seems to me, invalidated the second aim of art, because it is quite obvious that no picture can influence human conduct as effectively as a television advertisement. It is quite true that in totalitarian countries artists are still instructed to influence conduct. But that is either due to technical deficiencies, as in China, where in default of T.V., broadsheets and posters are an important way of communicating with an illiterate population; or, in Russia, to a philosophic time-lag. The fact is that very few countries have had the courage to take Plato's advice and exclude works of art altogether. They have, therefore, had to invent some excuse for keeping them on, and the Russians are still using the pretext that paintings and sculpture can influence people in favour of socialist and national policies, although it must have dawned on them that these results can be obtained far more effectively by the cinema and television.

So it seems to me that of these three possible purposes of art—imitation, persuasion, or exalted pleasure—only the third still holds good in an age of science; and it must be justified very largely by the fact that it is a feeling which is absent from scientific achievements—although mathematicians have told us that it is similar to the feeling aroused by their finest calculations. We might say that in the modern world the art of painting is defensible only in so far as it is complementary to science.

We are propelled in the same direction by another achievement of modern science, the study of psychology. That peeling away of the psyche, which was formerly confined to spiritual instructors, or the great novelists, has become a commonplace of conversation. When a good, solid, external word like Duty is turned into a vague, uneasy, internal word like Guilt, one cannot expect artists to take much interest in good, solid, external objects. The artist has always been involved in the painful process of turning himself inside out, but in the past his inner convictions have been of such a kind that they can, so to say, re-form themselves round an object. But, as we have seen, even in Leonardo's time, there were certain obscure needs and patterns of the spirit, which could discover themselves only through less precise analogies—the analogies provided by stains on walls or the embers of a fire. Now, I think that in this inward-looking age, when we have become so much more aware of the vagaries of the spirit, and so respectful of the working of the unconscious, the artist is more likely to find his point of departure in analogies of this kind. They are more exciting because they, so to say, take us by surprise, like forgotten smells; and they seem to be more profound because the memories they awaken have been deeply buried in our minds. Whether Jung is right in believing that this free, undirected, illogical form of mental activity will allow us to pick up, like a magic radio station, some deep memories of our race which can be of universal interest, I do not know. The satisfaction we derive from certain combinations of shape and colour does seem to be inexplicable even by the remotest analogies, and may perhaps involve inherited memories. It is not yet time for the art-historian to venture in to that mysterious jungle. I must, however, observe that our respect for the unconscious mind not only gives us an interest in analogy blots, but in what I called "gesture blots" as well. We recognise how free and forceful such a communication can be, and this aspect of art has become more important in the last ten years. An apologist of modern art has said: "What we want to know is not what the world looks like, but what we mean to each other." So the gesture blot becomes a sort of ideogram, like primitive Chinese writing. Students of Zen assure us it is a means of communication more direct and complete than anything which our analytic system can achieve. Almost 2,000 years before Leonardo looked for images in blots, Lao-tzu had written:

> *The Tao is something blurred and indistinct.*
> *How indistinct! How blurred!*
> *Yet within are images,*
> *How blurred! How indistinct!*
> *Yet within are things.*

I said that when the split took place between our faculties of measurement and intuition, *architecture* went off with the diagram. Of course architecture had always been involved with measurement and calculation, but we tend to forget how greatly it was also involved with the imitation of external objects. "The question to be determined," said Ruskin, "is whether architecture is a frame for the sculpture, or the sculpture an ornament of the architecture." And he came down on the first alternative. He thought that a building became architecture only in so far as it was a frame for figurative sculpture. I wonder if there is a single person alive who would agree with him. And yet Ruskin had the most sensitive eye and the keenest analytic faculty that has ever been applied to architecture. Many people disagreed with him in his own day; they thought that sculpture should be subordinate to the total design of the building. But that anything claiming to be architecture could dispense with ornament altogether never entered anyone's head till a relatively short time ago.

A purely diagrammatic architecture is only about thirty years older than a purely blottesque painting; yet it has changed the face of the world and produced in every big city a growing uniformity. Perhaps because it is a little older, perhaps because it seems to have a material justification, we have come to accept it without question. People who are still puzzled or affronted by action painting are proud of the great steel and glass boxes which have arisen so miraculously in the last ten years. And yet these two are manifestations of the same state of mind. The same difficulties of function, the same deflection from the external object, and the same triumph of science. Abstract painting and glass box architecture are related in two different ways. There is the direct relationship of style—the kind of relationship which painting and architecture had with one another in the great consistent ages of art like the 13th and 17th centuries. For modern architecture is not simply functional; at its best it has a style which is almost as definite and as arbitrary as Gothic. And this leads me back to my earlier point: that diagrams can be drawn in order to achieve some imagined perfection, similar to that of certain mathematical propositions. Thirty years after Pater's famous dictum, painters in Russia, Holland, and France began to put into practice the theory that "all art constantly aspires to the condition of music"; and curiously enough this Pythagorean mystique of measurement produced a style—the style which reached its purest expression in the Dutch painter, Mondrian. And through the influence of the *Bauhaus,* this became the leading style of modern architecture.

The other relationship between contemporary architecture and painting appears to be indirect and even accidental. I am thinking of the visual impact when the whole upper part of a tall glass building mirrors the clouds or the dying embers of a sunset, and so becomes a frame for a marvellous, moving Tachiste picture. I do not think that future historians of art will find this accidental at all, but will see it as the culmination of a long process beginning in the Romantic period, in which, from Wordsworth and De Quincey onwards, poets and philosophers recognised the movement of clouds as the symbol of a newly discovered mental faculty.

Such, then, would be my diagnosis of the present condition of art. I must now, by special request, say what I think will happen to art in the future. I think that the state of affairs which I have called the blot and the diagram will last for a long time. Architecture will continue to be made up of glass boxes and steel grids, without ornament of any kind. Painting will continue to be subjective and arcane, an art of accident rather than rule, of stains on walls rather than of calculation, of inscape rather than of external reality.

This conclusion is rejected by those who believe in a social theory of art. They maintain that a living art must depend on the popular will, and that neither the blot nor the diagram is popular; and, since those who hold a social theory of art are usually Marxists, they point to Soviet Russia as a country where all my conditions obtain—differentiation of function, the domination of science and so forth—and yet what we call modern art has gained no hold. This argument does not impress me. There is, of course, nothing at all in the idea that Communist doctrines inevitably produce social realism. Painting in Yugoslavia, in Poland and Hungary is in the same modern idiom as painting in the United States, and shows remarkable vitality. Whereas the official social realism of the U.S.S.R., except for a few illustrators, lacks life or conviction, and shows no evidence of representing the popular will. In fact Russian architecture has already dropped the grandiose official style, and I am told that this is now taking place in painting also. In spite of disapproval amounting to persecution, experimental painters exist and find buyers.

I doubt if the Marxists are even correct in saying that the blot and the diagram are not popular. The power, size, and splendour of, say, the Seagram building in New York makes it as much the object of pride and wonder as great architecture was in the past. And one of the remarkable things about Tachisme is the speed with which it has spread throughout the world, not only in sophisticated centres, but in small local art societies. It has become as much an international style as Gothic in the 14th and Baroque in the 17th centuries. I recently visited the exhibition of a provincial academy in the north of England, a very respectable body then celebrating its hundred and fiftieth anniversary. A few years ago it had been full of Welsh mountain landscapes, and scenes of streets and harbours, carefully delineated. Now practically every picture was in the Tachiste style, and I found that many of them were painted by the same artists, often quite elderly people, who had previously painted the mountains and streets. As works of art, they seemed to me neither better nor worse. But I could not help thinking that they must have been less trouble to do, and I reflected that the painters must have had a happy time releasing the Dionysiac elements in their natures. However, we must not be too cynical about this. I do not believe that the spread of action painting is due solely to the fact that it is easy to do. Cubism, especially synthetic Cubism, also looks easy to do, and never had this immense diffusion. It remained the style of a small élite of professional painters and specialised art lovers; whereas Tachisme has spread to fabrics, to the decoration of public buildings, to the backgrounds of television programmes, to advertising of all kinds. Indeed the closest analogy to action painting is the most popular art of all—the art of jazz. The trumpeter who rises from his seat as one possessed, and squirts out his melody like a scarlet scrawl against a background of plangent dashes and dots, is not as a rule performing for a small body of intellectuals.

Nevertheless, I do not think that the style of the blot and the diagram will last forever. For one thing, I believe that the imitation of external reality is a fundamental human instinct which is bound to reassert itself. In his admirable book on sculpture called *Aratra Pentelici*, Ruskin describes an experience which many of us could confirm. "Having been always desirous," he says,

"that the education of women should begin in learning how to cook, I got leave, one day, for a little girl of eleven years old to exchange, much to her satisfaction, her schoolroom for the kitchen. But as ill fortune would have it, there was some pastry toward, and she was left unadvisedly in command of some delicately rolled paste; whereof she made no pies, but an unlimited quantity of cats and mice. . . .
"Now [he continues] you may read the works of the gravest critics of art from end to end; but you will find, at last, they can give you no other true account of the spirit of sculpture than that it is an irresistible human instinct for the making of cats and mice, and other imitable living creatures, in such permanent form that one may play with the images at leisure."

I cannot help feeling that he was right. I am fond of works of art, and I collect them. But I do not want to hang them on the wall simply in order to get an electric shock every time that I pass them. I want to hold them, and turn them round and re-hang them—in short, to play with the images at leisure. And, putting aside what may be no more than a personal prejudice, I rather doubt if an art which depends solely on the first impact on our emotions is permanently valid. When the shock is exhausted, we have nothing to occupy our minds. And this is particularly troublesome with an art which depends so much on the unconscious, because, as we know from the analysis of dreams, the furniture of our unconscious minds is even more limited, repetitive, and commonplace than that of our conscious minds. The blots and stains of modern painting depend ultimately on the memories of things seen, memories sunk deep in the unconscious, overlaid, transformed, assimilated to a physical condition, but memories none the less. *Ex nihilo nihil fit*. It is not possible for a painter to lose all contact with the visible world.

At this point the apes have provided valuable evidence. There is no doubt that they are Tachiste painters of considerable accomplishment. I do not myself care for the work of Congo the chimp, but Sophie, the Rotterdam gorilla, is a charming artist, whose delicate traceries remind me of early Paul Klee. As you know, apes take their painting seriously. The patterns they produce are not the result of mere accident, but of intense, if short-lived, concentration, and a lively sense of balance and space-filling. If you compare the painting of a young ape with that of a human child of relatively the same age, you will find that in the first, expressive, pattern-making stage, the ape is superior. Then, automatically and inexorably the child begins to draw *things*—man, house, truck, etc. This the ape never does. Of course his Tachiste paintings are far more attractive than the child's crude conceptual outlines. But they cannot develop. They are monotonous and ultimately rather depressing.

The difference between the child and the ape does not show itself in æsthetic perception, or in physical perception of any kind, but in the child's power to form a concept. Later, as we know, he will spend his time trying to adapt his concept to the evidence of physical sensation; in that struggle lies the whole of style. But the concept—the need to draw a line round his thought—comes first. Now it is a truism that the power to form concepts is what distinguishes man from the animals; although the prophets of modern society, Freud, Jung, D. H. Lawrence, have rightly insisted on the importance of animal perceptions in balanced human personality, the concept-forming faculty has not declined in modern man. On the contrary, it is the basis of that vast scientific achievement which, as I said earlier, seems almost to have put art out of business.

Now if the desire to represent external reality depended solely on an interest in visual sensation, I would agree that it might disappear from art and never return. But if, as the evidence of children and monkeys indicates, it depends primarily on the formation of concepts, which are then modified by visual sensation, I think it is bound to return. For I consider the human faculty of forming concepts at least as "inalienable" as "life, liberty, and the pursuit of happiness...."

I am not, of course, suggesting that the imitation of external reality will ever again become what it was in European art from the mid-17th to the late 19th centuries. Such a subordination of the concept to the visual sensation was altogether exceptional in the history of art. Much of the territory won by modern painting will, I believe, be held. For example, freedom of association, the immediate passage from one association to another—which is so much a part of Picasso's painting and Henry Moore's sculpture, is something which has existed in music since Wagner and in poetry since Rimbaud and Mallarmé. (I mean existed consciously; of course it underlies all great poetry and music.) It need not be sacrificed in a return to external reality. Nor need the direct communication of intuition, through touch and an instinctive sense of materials. This I consider pure gain. In the words of my original metaphor, both the association blot and the gesture blot can remain. But they must be given more nourishment: they must be related to a fuller knowledge of the forms and structures which impress us most powerfully, and so become part of our concept of natural order. At the end of the passage in which Leonardo tells the painter that he can look for battles, landscapes, and animals in the stains on walls, he adds this caution, "But first be sure that you know all the members of all things you wish to depict, both the members of the animals and the members of landscapes, that is to say of rocks, plants, and so forth." It is because one feels in Henry Moore's sculpture this knowledge of the members of animals and plants, that his work, even at its most abstract, makes an impression on us different from that of his imitators. His figures are not merely pleasing examples of design, but seem to be a part of nature, "rolled round in Earth's diurnal course with rocks and stones and trees."

Those lines of Wordsworth lead me to the last reason why I feel that the intuitive blot and scribble may not dominate painting forever. Our belief in the whole purpose of art may change. I said earlier that we now believe it should aim at producing a kind of exalted happiness: this really means that art becomes an end in itself. Now it is an incontrovertible fact of history that the greatest art has always been *about* something, a means of communicating some truth which is assumed to be more important than the art itself. The truths which art has been able to communicate have been of a kind which could not be put in any other way. They have been ultimate truths, stated symbolically. Science has achieved its triumph precisely by disregarding such truths, by not asking unanswerable questions, but sticking to the question "how." I confess it looks to me as if we shall have to wait a long time before there is some new belief which requires expression through art rather than through statistics or equations. And until this happens, the visual arts will fall short of the greatest epochs, the ages of the Parthenon, the Sistine Ceiling, and Chartres Cathedral.

I am afraid there is nothing we can do about it. No amount of goodwill and no expenditure of money can affect that sort of change. We cannot even dimly foresee when it will happen or what form it will take. We can only be thankful for what we have got—a vigorous, popular, decorative art, complementary to our architecture and our science, somewhat monotonous, somewhat prone to charlatanism, but genuinely expressive of our time.

Part Seven

A POSTSCRIPT ON CULTURE: LIFE AND DEATH

Most of the essays in this book have concerned themselves, more or less directly, with problems of the present, and some of them have manifested overtly the desire to influence the future. Our two concluding essays are devoted to the past, and to the study of ways of thought and life which are long since dead. They may seem thus to stand in contrast to the earlier essays, but a few moments' thought will suggest several ways in which their relationship is one of fulfillment rather than of contrast. (1) The earlier essays, however contemporary their subject matter, have consistently revealed the awareness of the continuing power of the past which is one of the characteristic dispositions of the humanistic tradition. Toynbee and Shaw affirm in different ways their belief in ever-repeated historical patterns; Wilson, Warren, and de Rougemont dig into the past to find the roots of present-day experience; Erikson and Jung suggest the values in the investigation of the individual past which is also the universal past; the writers on art and literature know that in the aesthetic realm nothing authentic can either grow old or be entirely new (see especially Knox and Stravinsky). (2) The two concluding essays, although they deal with a past civilization, have really come into being because of the authors' conviction that the vital power of that civilization continues, and will continue, to assert itself in the experience of living man. (3) Finally, both essays can validly be regarded as explorations, as attempts to extend the frontiers of human understanding. We live in an age in which the exploration of space is both a practical concern and a governing symbol for contemporary experience (in this respect being analogous to the exploration of the globe in the later Renaissance). But there are other kinds of space which twentieth-century man is engaged in exploring—as chartless, vast, and challenging as the interplanetary: one is the historical space which Miss Hamilton (like Huizinga) investigates; another is the psychological space which Kerényi (like Jung) takes as his province.

Edith Hamilton asserts most directly the relevance of ancient Greek civilization to our own: "We think and feel differently because of what a little Greek town did during a century or two, twenty-four hundred years ago." There is a long precedent for her assertion, one practically as long as Western civilization itself. The Renaissance of the fifteenth and sixteenth centuries, for example, is almost defined by its rediscovery of Greek art and its attempts to model its own art and life upon it, and European philosophy and political thought have, to a large degree, pursued directions first pointed out by Plato and Aristotle. Every age finds Greek culture "modern"; every age finds in its riches reinforcement for its own defining values. It is not surprising, then, that Miss Hamilton, as a twentieth-century thinker, praises the Greeks in particular for their rationalism, their development of scientific method, their commitment to freedom of thought, inquiry, and expression, and their refusal to allow knowledge to become the exclusive possession of any specialized caste. There may be a degree of oversimplification in her account—one would not guess, from her essay, that Athens was a slave-holding society—but the antithesis which she points to between Greek culture and the despotic, priest-ridden, and life-despising societies elsewhere in the ancient world is both instructive and provocative, and it has a special timeliness in view of the present confrontation between the West and the burgeoning societies of Asia and the Near East. For these societies, despite current revolutionary attempts to modernize themselves (especially in China and Egypt) are still strongly affected by the traditional Eastern assumption that the invisible world is vastly more important than the visible—in short, by what Miss Hamilton calls "spirit" as opposed to "mind." "Mind" operates on the perceptible world outside one's self; "spirit" regards as real only the inner world. For Miss Hamilton, the classical Greek refusal to conceive of the two worlds as separate provides the West with its values and the entire world with an ideal to be emulated.

The most immediately striking distinction between Miss Hamilton's essay and Karl Kerényi's is that, whereas she stresses the similarity between Greek culture and our own, he stresses the differences, in part because his interest lies in the primitive origins of Greek religious thought rather than, like hers, in the full fruition of Greek culture in the fifth century B.C. Kerényi's discipline is comparative religion, a field which, in our century, requires a profound knowledge of a number of related fields— psychology, anthropology, philosophy, theology, linguistics, and the history of art and literature. Deeply versed in all these areas (as the wide range of his footnotes indicates), Kerényi brings to his study of the Greek mind a special capacity for psychological insights, developed in part during his long association with the psychoanalytic thinker Carl Jung, as well as an imaginative sympathy with ways of thought foreign to his own. From these related capacities comes his remarkable ability to feel his way, without either condescension or arrogance, into the ancient mind— to understand, for example, that religious ideas, in contrast to philosophical ideas, exist not to answer questions but to express perceptions, that mythology is not (as Miss Hamilton at one point implies) a set of naive fairy tales but a way of using the imagination in order to grasp in their totality the complex realities of existence.

Kerényi's essay, the last chapter of his book on the religion of the Greeks and the Romans, deals with the Greek conception of death. One of his major points is that that conception was religious rather than philosophical, but in elucidating it he is obliged to bring into play the intellectual discipline of philosophy itself. Like the great psychologists who influenced him, Freud and Jung, he uses the rational intellect to illuminate the irrational. His account of the Greek feeling for the inter-relationship of life and death frequently employs the technical philosophical vocabulary developed by European metaphysicians over the past 300 years. This vocabulary contributes to the difficulty of a piece which in any case makes heavy demands on the intellect of its readers, but it helps Kerényi to bring very distant ideas into focus for the reader who is energetic enough to follow him.

If Kerényi has a philosopher's gift for making distinctions, he has also a poet's gift for responding to the great intuitive formulations of the ancient mind. We see this quality especially near the end of the essay, in the eloquent passage in which he evokes the Greek conception of a border-region between being and nonbeing, a region which is at once the abode of death and the source of ever-renewed life. Associating this conception both with primitive fertility ritual and with modern theories concerning the death wish which accompanies normal death fear, Kerényi clearly also reacts to the image itself as to a valid representation of the condition of life.

Only life makes death possible as a real idea; if it were not for its opposite, life, death would not exist even as an idea, just as, if it were not for death, man would not have his vivid and poignant awareness of the reality and joy of life—with these observations Kerényi emphasizes an aspect of the Greek spirit which Miss Hamilton also notes, in her remarks on the splendidly vigorous sense of the joy of life which breaks into even the darkest of Greek tragedies. On the deepest level there is no contradiction between the interpretations of Kerényi and Hamilton, for the whole implied motive of Kerényi's sensitive and learned investigation is the illumination of the human mind, which does not change in its essentials, and a clear motive of Miss Hamilton's book is the attempt to discover what it was that the Greeks had and we have lost—that balance between the claims of "mind" and those of "spirit" for which she commends them in the final paragraph of her essay.

Through this balance, as manifested in the nonphilosophical modes of myth and ritual, the Greeks, as Kerényi says, "extended the concept of being even into the realm of nonbeing." They confronted, without dishonesty or terror, the fact of death—a fact never to be conjured away, by reason or faith, by science or imagination—and through their confrontation they affirmed the reality of life and beauty. Therein, Hamilton and Kerényi would agree, lies a large part of their human greatness, their eternal value.

Suggested readings:

Plato, *Socrates' Apology*
Sophocles, *Oedipus Rex*

Edith Hamilton

Born in Germany of American parents in 1867, Edith Hamilton was educated at Bryn Mawr College, Pennsylvania, and did further study at Leipzig and Munich. After teaching at Bryn Mawr College for several years, she became head of the Bryn Mawr School in Baltimore and retained that post until 1922. Her writings, which continued until her death in 1963, include *The Greek Way* (1930), from which our selection is taken, *The Roman Way* (1932), and many contributions to learned journals.

The first third of the twentieth century witnessed a significant expansion of classical studies: Sir James Frazer, in his influential book *The Golden Bough*, related Greco-Roman myth to the findings of the new science of anthropology; Sir Arthur Evans investigated the ancient civilization of Crete; and Jane Harrison placed the study of Greek religion on a new basis. Edith Hamilton's work is both less specialized and less original than that of these figures, but it nevertheless has great merit as a general survey of Greco-Roman civilization in the light of modern research and theory.

EAST AND WEST

Five hundred years before Christ in a little town on the far western border of the settled and civilized world, a strange new power was at work. Something had awakened in the minds and spirits of the men there which was so to influence the world that the slow passage of long time, of century upon century and the shattering changes they

Reprinted from *The Greek Way* by Edith Hamilton. By permission of W. W. Norton & Company, Inc. Copyright 1930, 1942 by W. W. Norton & Company, Inc.

brought, would be powerless to wear away that deep impress. Athens had entered upon her brief and magnificent flowering of genius which so molded the world of mind and of spirit that our mind and spirit to-day are different. We think and feel differently because of what a little Greek town did during a century or two, twenty-four hundred years ago. What was then produced of art and of thought has never been surpassed and very rarely equalled, and the stamp of it is upon all the art and all the thought of the Western world. And yet this full stature of greatness came to pass at a time when the mighty civilizations of the ancient world had perished and the shadow of "effortless barbarism" was dark upon the earth. In that black and fierce world a little centre of white-hot spiritual energy was at work. A new civilization had arisen in Athens, unlike all that had gone before.

What brought this new development to pass, how the Greeks were able to achieve all they did, has significance for us to-day. It is not merely that Greece has a claim upon our attention because we are by our spiritual and mental inheritance partly Greek and cannot escape if we would that deep influence which worked with power through the centuries, touching with light of reason and grace of beauty the wild Northern savages. She has a direct contribution for us as well. The actual Greek remains are so few and so far away, so separated from us by space and a strange, difficult language, they are felt to be matters for the travellers and the scholars and no more. But in truth what the Greeks discovered, or rather how they made their discoveries and how they brought a new world to birth out of the dark confusions of an old world that had crumbled away, is full of meaning for us to-day who have seen an old world swept away in the space of a decade or two. It is worth our while in the confusions and bewilderments of the present to consider the way by which the Greeks arrived at the clarity of their thought and the affirmation of their art. Very different conditions of life confronted them from those we face, but it is ever to be borne in mind that though the outside of human life changes much, the inside changes little, and the lesson-book we cannot graduate from is human experience. Great literature, past or present, is the expression of great knowledge of the human heart; great art is the expression of a solution of the conflict between the demands of the world without and that within; and in the wisdom of either there would seem to be small progress.

Of all that the Greeks did only a very small part has come down to us and we have no means of knowing if we have their best. It would be strange if we had. In the convulsions of that world of long ago there was no law that guaranteed to art the survival of the fittest. But this little remnant preserved by the haphazard of chance shows the high-water mark reached in every region of thought and beauty the Greeks entered. No sculpture comparable to theirs; no buildings ever more beautiful; no writings superior. Prose, always late of development, they had time only to touch upon, but they left masterpieces. History has yet to find a greater exponent than Thucydides; outside of the Bible there is no poetical prose that can touch Plato. In poetry they are all but supreme; no epic is to be mentioned with Homer; no odes to be set beside Pindar; of the four masters of the tragic stage three are Greek. Little is left of all this wealth of great art: the sculptures, defaced and broken into bits, have crumbled away; the buildings are fallen; the paintings gone forever; of the writings, all lost but a very few. We have only the ruin of what was; the world has had no more than that for well on to two thousand years; yet these few remains of the mighty structure have been a challenge and an incitement to men ever since and they are among our possessions to-day which we value as most precious. There is no danger now that the world will not give the Greek genius full recognition. Greek achievement is a fact universally acknowledged.

The causes responsible for this achievement, however, are not so generally understood. Rather is it the fashion nowadays to speak of the Greek miracle, to consider the radiant bloom of Greek genius as having no root in any soil that we can give an account of. The anthropologists are busy, indeed, and ready to transport us back into the savage forest where all human things, the Greek things, too, had their beginnings; but the seed never explains the flower. Between those strange rites they point us to through the dim vistas of far-away ages, and a Greek tragedy, there lies a gap they cannot help us over. The easy way out is to refuse to bridge it and dismiss the need to explain by calling the tragedy a miracle, but in truth the way across is not impassable; some reasons appear for the mental and spiritual activity which made those few years in Athens productive as no other age in history has been.

By universal consent the Greeks belong to the ancient world. Wherever the line is drawn by this or that historian between the old and the new the Greeks' unquestioned position is in the old. But they are in it as a matter of centuries only; they have not the hall-marks that give title to a place there. The ancient world, in so far as we can reconstruct it, bears everywhere the same stamp. In Egypt, in Crete, in Mesopotamia, wherever we can read bits of the story, we find the same conditions: a despot enthroned, whose whims and passions are the determining factor in the state; a wretched, subjugated populace; a great priestly organization to which is handed over the domain of the intellect. This is what we know as the Oriental state to-day. It has persisted down from the ancient world through thousands of years, never changing in any essential. Only in the last hundred years—less than that—it has shown a semblance of change, made a gesture of outward conformity with the demands of the modern world. But the spirit that informs it is the spirit of the East that never changes. It has remained the same through all the ages down from the antique world, forever aloof from all that is modern. This state and this spirit were alien to the Greeks. None of the great civilizations that preceded them and surrounded them served them as model. With them something completely new came into the world. They were the first Westerners; the spirit of the West, the modern spirit, is a Greek discovery and the place of the Greeks is in the modern world.

The same cannot be said of Rome. Many things there pointed back to the old world and away to the East, and with the emperors who were gods and fed a brutalized people full of horrors as their dearest form of amusement, the ancient and the Oriental state had a true revival. Not that the spirit of Rome was of the Eastern stamp. Common-sense men of affairs were its product to whom the cogitations of Eastern sages ever seemed the idlest nonsense. "What is truth?" said Pilate scornfully. But it was equally far removed from the Greek spirit. Greek thought, science, mathematics, philosophy, the eager investigation into the nature of the world and the ways of the world which was the distinguishing mark of Greece, came to an end for many a century when the leadership passed from Greece to Rome. The classical world is a myth in so far as it is con- ceived of as marked by the same characteristics. Athens and Rome had little in common. That which distinguishes the modern world from the ancient, and that which divides the West from the East, is the supremacy of mind in the affairs of men, and this came to birth in Greece and lived in Greece alone of all the ancient world. The Greeks were the first intel- lectualists. In a world where the irrational had played the chief role, they came forward as the protagonists of the mind.

The novelty and the importance of this position are difficult for us to realize. The world we live in seems to us a reasonable and compre- hensible place. It is a world of definite facts which we know a good deal about. We have found out a number of rules by which the dark and tre- mendous forces of nature can be made to move so as to further our own purposes, and our main effort is devoted to increasing our power over the outside material of the world. We do not dream of questioning the importance of what acts, on the whole, in ways we can explain and turn to our advantage. What brings about this attitude is the fact that, of all the powers we are endowed with, we are making use pre-eminently of the reason. We are not soaring above the world on the wings of the imagina- tion or searching into the depths of the world within each one of us by the illumination of the spirit. We are observing what goes on in the world around us and we are reasoning upon our observations. Our chief and characteristic activity is that of the mind. The society we are born into is built upon the idea of the reasonable, and emotional experience and intuitive perception are accorded a place in it only if some rational account can be given of them.

When we find that the Greeks, too, lived in a reasonable world as a result of using their reason upon it, we accept the achievement as the natural thing that needs no comment. But the truth is that even to-day our point of view obtains only within strict limits. It does not belong to the immense expanse and the multitudinous populations of the East. There what goes on outside of a man is comparatively unimportant and completely undeserving of the attention of the truly wise. The observing reason which works on what we of the West call the facts of the real world, is not esteemed in the East. This conception of human values has come down from antiquity. The world in which Greece came to life was one in which the reason had played the smallest role; all that was important in it belonged to the realm of the unseen, known only to the spirit.

That is a realm in which outside fact, everything that makes up this visible, sensible, audible world, plays only an indirect part. The facts of the spirit are not seen or felt or heard; they are experienced; they are peculiarly a man's own, something that he can share with no one else. An artist can express them in some sort, partially at best. The saint and the hero who are most at home in them can put them into words—or pictures or music—only if they are artists, too. The greatest intellect cannot do that through the intellect. And yet every human being has a share in the experiences of the spirit.

Mind and spirit together make up that which separates us from the rest of the animal world, that which enables a man to know the truth and that which enables him to die for the truth. A hard and fast distinction between the two can hardly be made; both belong to the part of us which, in Platonic phraseology, draws us up from that which is ever dragging down or, in the figure Plato is fondest of, that which gives form to the formless. But yet they are distinct. When St. Paul in his great definition says that the things that are seen are temporal and the things that are not seen are eternal, he is defining the realm of the mind, the reason that works from the visible world, and the realm of the spirit that lives by the invisible.

In the ancient world before Greece the things that are not seen had become more and more the only things of great importance. The new power of mind that marked Greece arose in a world facing toward the way of the spirit. For a brief period in Greece East and West met; the bias toward the rational that was to distinguish the West, and the deep spiritual inheritance of the East, were united. The full effect of this meeting, the immense stimulus to creative activity given when clarity of mind is added to spiritual power, can be best realized by considering what had happened before Greece, what happens, that is, when there is great spiritual force with the mind held in abeyance. This is to be seen most clearly in Egypt where the records are fullest and far more is known than about any other nation of antiquity. It is materially to the point, therefore, to leave Greece for a moment and look at the country which had had the greatest civilization of all the ancient world.

In Egypt the centre of interest was the dead. The ruling world-power, a splendid empire—and death a foremost preoccupation. Countless numbers of human beings for countless numbers of centuries thought of death as that which was nearest and most familiar to them. It is an extraordinary circumstance which could be made credible by nothing less considerable than the immense mass of Egyptian art centred in the dead. To the Egyptian the enduring world of reality was not the one he walked in along the paths of every-day life but the one he should presently go to by the way of death.

There were two causes working in Egypt to bring about this condition. The first was human misery. The state of the common man in the ancient world must have been wretched in the extreme. Those tremendous works that have survived through thousands of years were achieved at a cost in human suffering and death which was never conceived of as a cost in anything of value. Nothing so cheap as human life in Egypt and in Nineveh, as nothing more cheap in India and China to-day. Even the well-to-do, the nobles and the men of affairs, lived with a very narrow margin of safety. An epitaph extant of a great Egyptian noble holds him up to admiration in that he was never beaten with whips before the magistrate. The lives and fortunes of all were completely dependent upon the whims of a monarch whose only law was his own wish. One has but to read the account Tacitus gives of what happened under the irresponsible despotism of the early Roman emperors to realize that in the ancient world security must have been the rarest of goods.

In such conditions men, seeing little hope for happiness in this world, turned instinctively to find comfort in another. Only in the world of the dead could there be found security and peace and pleasure which a man, by taking thought all his life for, might attain. No concern of earthly living could count to him in comparison or be esteemed as real in comparison. Little profit for him there to use his mind, his reasoning powers. They could do nothing for him in the one matter of overwhelming importance, his status in the world to come. They could not give him hope when life was hopeless or strength to endure the unendurable. People who are terrified and hard pressed by misery do not turn to the mind for their help. This instinctive recoil from the world of outside fact was enormously reinforced by the other great influence at work upon the side of death and against the use of the mind, the Egyptian priesthood.

Before Greece the domain of the intellect belonged to the priests.

They were the intellectual class of Egypt. Their power was tremendous. Kings were subject to it. Great men must have built up that mighty organization, great minds, keen intellects, but what they learned of old truth and what they discovered of new truth was valued as it increased the prestige of the organization. And since Truth is a jealous mistress and will reveal herself not a whit to any but a disinterested seeker, as the power of the priesthood grew and any idea that tended to weaken it met with a cold reception, the priests must fairly soon have become sorry intellectualists, guardians only of what seekers of old had found, never using their own minds with freedom.

There was another result no less inevitable: all they knew must be kept jealously within the organization. To teach the people so that they would begin to think for themselves, would be to destroy the surest prop of their power. No one except themselves must have knowledge, for to be ignorant is to be afraid, and in the dark mystery of the unknown a man cannot find his way alone. He must have guides to speak to him with authority. Ignorance was the foundation upon which the priest-power rested. In truth, the two, the mystery and those who dealt in it, reinforced each other in such sort that each appears both the cause and the effect of the other. The power of the priest depended upon the darkness of the mystery; his effort must ever be directed toward increasing it and opposing any attempt to throw light upon it. The humble role played by the reason in the ancient world was assigned by an authority there was no appeal against. It determined the scope of thought and the scope of art as well, with an absolutism never questioned.

We know of one man, to be sure, who set himself against it. For a few years the power of the Pharaoh was pitted against the power of the priests and the Pharaoh won out. The familiar story of Akhenaton, who dared to think for himself and who built a city to enshrine and propagate the worship of the one and only God, might appear to point to a weakness in the great priestly body, but the proof is, in point of fact, rather the other way about. The priests were men deeply learned and experienced in human nature. They waited. The man of independent thought had only a very brief reign—did his contests with the priests wear him out, one wonders?—and after his death nothing of what he had stood for was allowed to remain. The priests took possession of his successor. They erased his very name from the monuments. He had never really touched their power.

But whatever their attitude to this autocrat or that, autocratic government never failed to command the priests' allegiance. They were ever the support of the throne as well as the power above it. Their instinct was sure: the misery of the people was the opportunity of the priest. Not only an ignorant populace but one subjugated and wretched was their guarantee. With men's thoughts directed more and more toward the unseen world, and with the keys to it firmly in their own grasp, their terrific power was assured.

When Egypt ended, the East went on ever farther in the direction Egypt had pointed. The miseries of Asia are a fearful page of history. Her people found strength to endure by denying any meaning and any importance to what they could not escape. The Egyptian world where dead men walked and slept and feasted was transmuted into what had always been implicit in its symbolism, the world of the spirit. In India, for centuries the leader of thought to the East, ages long since, the world of the reason and the world of the spirit were divorced and the universe handed over to the latter. Reality—that which we have heard, which we have seen with our eyes and our hands have handled, of the Word of life—was dismissed as a fiction that had no bearing upon the Word. All that was seen and heard and handled was vague and unsubstantial and forever passing, the shadow of a dream; only that was real which was of the spirit. This is always man's way out when the facts of life are too bitter and too black to be borne. When conditions are such that life offers no earthly hope, somewhere, somehow, men must find a refuge. Then they fly from the terror without to the citadel within, which famine and pestilence and fire and sword cannot shake. What Goethe calls the inner universe, can live by its own laws, create its own security, be sufficient unto itself, when once reality is denied to the turmoil of the world without.

So the East found a way to endure the intolerable, and she pursued it undeviatingly through the centuries, following it to its farthest implications. In India the idea of truth became completely separated from outside fact; all outside was illusion; truth was an inner disposition. In such a world there is little scope for the observing reason or the seeing eye. Where all except the spirit is unreal, it is manifest folly to be concerned with an exterior that is less than a shadow.

It is easy to understand how in these conditions the one department of the intellect that flourished was mathematics. Nothing is less likely to react practically upon life or to intrude into the domain of theology than the world of the ideal revealed to the mathematical imagination. Pure mathematics soars into a region far removed from human wretchedness and no priest ever troubled himself about the effects of free inquiry along mathematical lines. There the mind could go where it pleased. "Compared with the Egyptians we are childish mathematicians," observes Plato. India, too, made notable contributions in this field. But, sooner or later, if the activity of the mind is restricted anywhere it will cease to function even where it is allowed to be free. To-day in India the triumph of the spirit over the mind is complete, and wherever Buddhism, the great product of the Indian spirit, has prevailed, the illusoriness of all that is of this earth and the vanity of all research into its nature is the centre of the faith.

As in Egypt, the priests saw their opportunity. The power of the Brahmans, the priestly caste, and of the great Buddhist hierarchy, is nothing less than stupendous. The circle is complete: a wretched populace with no hope save in the invisible, and a priesthood whose power is bound up with the belief in the unimportance of the visible so that they must forever strive to keep it an article of faith. The circle is complete in another sense as well: the wayfarer sheltering for the night in an abandoned house does not care to mend the roof the rain drips through, and a people living in such wretchedness that their one comfort is to deny the importance of the facts of earthly life, will not try to better them. India has gone the way of the things that are not seen until the things that are seen have become invisible.

That is what happens when one course is followed undeviatingly for ages. We are composite creatures, made up of soul and body, mind and spirit. When men's attention is fixed upon one to the disregard of the others, human beings result who are only partially developed, their eyes blinded to half of what life offers and the great world holds. But in that antique world of Egypt and the early Asiatic civilizations, that world where the pendulum was swinging ever farther and farther away from all fact, something completely new happened. The Greeks came into being and the world, as we know it, began.

MIND AND SPIRIT

Egypt is a fertile valley of rich river soil, low-lying, warm, monotonous, a slow-flowing river, and beyond, the limitless desert. Greece is a country of sparse fertility and keen, cold winters, all hills and mountains sharp cut in stone, where strong men must work hard to get their bread. And while Egypt submitted and suffered and turned her face toward death, Greece resisted and rejoiced and turned full-face to life. For somewhere among those steep stone mountains, in little sheltered valleys where the great hills were ramparts to defend and men could have security for peace and happy living, something quite new came into the world; the joy of life found expression. Perhaps it was born there, among the

Reprinted from *The Greek Way* by Edith Hamilton. By permission of W. W. Norton & Company, Inc. Copyright 1930, 1942 by W. W. Norton & Company, Inc.

shepherds pasturing their flocks where the wild flowers made a glory on the hillside; among the sailors on a sapphire sea washing enchanted islands purple in a luminous air. At any rate it has left no trace anywhere else in the world of antiquity. In Greece nothing is more in evidence. The Greeks were the first people in the world to play, and they played on a great scale. All over Greece there were games, all sorts of games; athletic contests of every description: races—horse-, boat-, foot-, torch-races; contests in music, where one side outsung the other; in dancing—on greased skins sometimes to display a nice skill of foot and balance of body; games where men leaped in and out of flying chariots; games so many one grows weary with the list of them. They are embodied in the statues familiar to all, the disc thrower, the charioteer, the wrestling boys, the dancing flute players. The great games—there were four that came at stated seasons—were so important, when one was held, a truce of God was proclaimed so that all Greece might come in safety without fear. There "glorious-limbed youth"—the phrase is Pindar's, the athlete's poet —strove for an honor so coveted as hardly anything else in Greece. An Olympic victor—triumphing generals would give place to him. His crown of wild olives was set beside the prize of the tragedian. Splendor attended him, processions, sacrifices, banquets, songs the greatest poets were glad to write. Thucydides, the brief, the severe, the historian of that bitter time, the fall of Athens, pauses, when one of his personages has conquered in the games, to give the fact full place of honor. If we had no other knowledge of what the Greeks were like, if nothing were left of Greek art and literature, the fact that they were in love with play and played magnificently would be proof enough of how they lived and how they looked at life. Wretched people, toiling people, do not play. Nothing like the Greek games is conceivable in Egypt or Mesopotamia. The life of the Egyptian lies spread out in the mural paintings down to the minutest detail. If fun and sport had played any real part they would be there in some form for us to see. But the Egyptian did not play. "Solon, Solon, you Greeks are all children," said the Egyptian priest to the great Athenian. At any rate, children or not, they enjoyed themselves. They had physical vigor and high spirits and time, too, for fun. The witness of the games is conclusive. And when Greece died and her reading of the great enigma was buried with her statues, play, too, died out of the world. The brutal, bloody Roman games had nothing to do with the spirit of play. They were fathered by the Orient, not by Greece. Play died when Greece died and many and many a century passed before it was resurrected.

To rejoice in life, to find the world beautiful and delightful to live in, was a mark of the Greek spirit which distinguished it from all that had gone before. It is a vital distinction. The joy of life is written upon everything the Greeks left behind and they who leave it out of account fail to reckon with something that is of first importance in understanding how the Greek achievement came to pass in the world of antiquity. It is not a fact that jumps to the eye for the reason that their literature is marked as strongly by sorrow. The Greeks knew to the full how bitter life is as well as how sweet. Joy and sorrow, exultation and tragedy, stand hand in hand in Greek literature, but there is no contradiction involved thereby. Those who do not know the one do not really know the other either. It is the depressed, the gray-minded people, who cannot rejoice just as they cannot agonize. The Greeks were not the victims of depression. Greek literature is not done in gray or with a low palette. It is all black and shining white or black and scarlet and gold. The Greeks were keenly aware, terribly aware, of life's uncertainty and the imminence of death. Over and over again they emphasize the brevity and the failure of all human endeavor, the swift passing of all that is beautiful and joyful. To Pindar, even as he glorifies the victor in the games, life is "a shadow's dream." But never, not in their darkest moments, do they lose their taste for life. It is always a wonder and a delight, the world a place of beauty, and they themselves rejoicing to be alive in it.

Quotations to illustrate this attitude are so numerous, it is hard to make a choice. One might quote all the Greek poems there are, even when they are tragedies. Every one of them shows the fire of life burning high. Never a Greek poet that did not warm both hands at that flame. Often in the midst of a tragedy a choral song of joy breaks forth. So Sophocles, of the three tragedians the soberest, the most severe, sings in the *Antigone* of the wine-god, "with whom the stars rejoice as they move, the stars whose breath is fire." Or in the *Ajax* where "thrilling with rapture, soaring on wings of sudden joy," he calls to "Pan, O Pan, come, sea-rover, down from the snow-beaten mountain craig. Lord of the dance the gods delight in, come, for now I, too, would dance. O joy!" Or in the *Oedipus Coloneus,* where tragedy is suddenly put aside by the poet's love of the out-of-door world, of the nightingale's clear thrilling note and the stainless tide of pure waters and the glory of the narcissus and the bright-shining crocus, "which the quire of the muses love and Aphrodite of the golden rein." Passages like these come again and again, lifting the black curtain of tragedy to the full joy of life. They are no artifice or trick to heighten by contrast. They are the natural expression of men who were tragedians indeed but Greeks first, and so thrillingly aware of the wonder and beauty of life, they could not but give it place.

The little pleasures, too, that daily living holds, were felt as such keen enjoyment: "Dear to us ever," says Homer, "is the banquet and the harp and the dance and changes of raiment and the warm bath and love and sleep." Eating and drinking have never again seemed so delightful as in the early Greek lyrics, nor a meeting with friends, nor a warm fire of a winter's night—"the stormy season of winter, a soft couch after dinner by the fire, honey-sweet wine in your glass and nuts and beans at your elbow"—nor a run in the springtime "amid a fragrance of woodbine and leisure and white poplar, when the plane-tree and the elm whisper together," nor a banqueting hour, "moving among feasting and giving up the soul to be young, carrying a bright harp and touching it in peace among the wise of the citizens." It is a matter of course that comedy should be their invention, the mad, rollicking, irresponsible fun of the Old Comedy, its verve and vitality and exuberant, overflowing energy of life. A tomb in Egypt and a theatre in Greece. The one comes to the mind as naturally as the other. So was the world changing by the time the fifth century before Christ began in Athens.

"The exercise of vital powers along lines of excellence in a life affording them scope" is an old Greek definition of happiness. It is a conception permeated with energy of life. Through all Greek history that spirit of life abounding moves. It led along many an untried way. Authoritarianism and submissiveness were not the direction it pointed to. A high-spirited people full of physical vigor do not obey easily, and indeed the strong air of the mountains has never been wholesome for despots. The absolute monarch-submissive slave theory of life flourishes best where there are no hills to give a rebel refuge and no mountain heights to summon a man to live dangerously. When history begins in Greece there is no trace of the ancient state. The awful, unapproachable sacred potentate, Pharaoh of Egypt, priest-king of Mesopotamia, whose absolute power none had questioned for thousands of years, is nowhere in the scene. There is nothing that remotely resembles him in Greece. Something we know of the Age of the Tyrants in Greek history but what we know most clearly is that it was put a stop to. Abject submission to the power on the throne which had been the rule of life in the ancient world since kings began, and was to be the rule of life in Asia for centuries to come, was cast off by the Greeks so easily, so lightly, hardly more than an echo of the contest has come down to us.

In the *Persians* of Aeschylus, a play written to celebrate the defeat of the Persians at Salamis, there is many an allusion to the difference between the Greek way and the Oriental way. The Greeks, the Persian queen is told, fight as free men to defend what is precious to them. Have they no master? she asks. No, she is told. No man calls Greeks slaves or vassals. Herodotus in his account adds, "They obey only the law." Something completely new is here. The idea of freedom has been born. The conception of the entire unimportance of the individual to the state, which had persisted down from earliest tribal days and was universally accepted in all the ancient world, has given place in Greece to the conception of the liberty of the individual in a state which he defends of his own free will. That is a change not worked by high spirit and abounding vigor alone. Something more was at work in Greece. Men were thinking for themselves.

One of the earlier Greek philosophic sayings is that of Anaxagoras: "All things were in chaos when Mind arose and made order." In the ancient world ruled by the irrational, by dreadful unknown powers, where a man was utterly at the mercy of what he must not try to understand, the Greeks arose and the rule of reason began. The fundamental fact about the Greek was that he had to use his mind. The ancient priests had said, "Thus far and no farther. We set the limits to thought." The Greeks said, "All things are to be examined and called into question. There are no limits set to thought." It is an extraordinary fact that by the time we have actual, documentary knowledge of the Greeks there is not a trace to be found of that domination over the mind by the priests which played such a decisive part in the ancient world. The priest plays no real part in either the history or the literature of Greece. In the *Iliad* he orders a captive taken back to appease an angry god and stop a pestilence, and is given a grudging obedience—with the backing of the pestilence, but that is his sole appearance on the scene. The Trojan War is fought out by gods and men with no intermediaries. A prophet or two appears in the tragedies but for evil oftener than for good. In the *Agamemnon* of Aeschylus, a hundred years before Plato, there is a criticism of the dark powers exercised by the ministers of religion which goes with precision to the heart of the matter:

> And, truly, what of good
> ever have prophets brought to men?
> Craft of many words,
>   only through
> evil your message speaks.
>   Seers bring aye
> terror, so to keep
>   men afraid.

The conclusion might be drawn from the words that something of that sort of power was in fact wielded then by priest and prophet, but what is certainly true is that the poet who spoke them to a great audience, with the most important priests sitting in the front-row seats, won for himself not disapproval but the highest mark of favor the people could give. There is nothing clearer and nothing more astonishing than the strict limits the Greeks set to the power of the priests. Priests in numbers there were and altars and temples, and at a time of public danger, disrespect shown to the forms of religion would arouse even in Athens superstition and popular fury, but the place of the priest in Greece was in the background. The temple was his and the temple rites, and nothing else.

The Greek kept his formal religion in one compartment and everything that really mattered to him in another. He never went to a priest for guidance or advice. Did he want to know how to bring up his children or what Truth was, he went to Socrates, or to the great sophist Protagoras, or to a learned grammarian. The idea of consulting a priest would never have occurred to him. The priests could tell him the proper times and the proper forms for sacrifices. That was their business and only that. In the *Laws,* written in Plato's old age and on the whole in a spirit of reaction against his earlier revolts, the entire subject of religion is discussed without a single reference to a priest. The *Laws,* it should perhaps be pointed out, is not written for the ideal state, the heavenly pattern of the *Republic,* but is addressed to the ideas and feelings of the Greeks of that day. The Athenian, who is the chief speaker, often meets with criticism from the two other personages of the dialogue when he proposes an innovation, but they accept without a word of surprise or dissent a statement that those who talk loosely about the gods and sacrifices and oracles, should be admonished by—members of the governing Council! These are to "converse with them touching the improvement of their soul's health." There is not a suggestion from any of the three that a priest might be of use here. Furthermore, "Before a man is prosecuted for impiety the guardians of the law shall determine if the deed has been done in earnest or only from childish levity." It was clearly not the idea that in matters touching the life and liberty of a Greek citizen the priest should have a voice. At the end of the argument the priest's proper domain is briefly indicated: "When a man is disposed to sacrifice, let him place his offerings in the hands of the priests and priestesses who have under their care the holy rite." That is the sum total of what the speakers hold to be the priest's part in religion, and he has no part in anything except religion. Even more noteworthy as illustrating the Greek point of view is the Athenian's characterization as "monstrous natures" of those "who say they can conjure the dead and bribe the gods with sacrifices and prayers"—in other words, those who used magic and tried to obtain favors from heaven by practices not unknown in the most civilized lands today.

No doubt the oracles, at Delphi notably, played a prominent role in Greece, but none of the oracular sayings that have come down to us bear the familiar priestly stamp. Athens seeking guidance from the Delphic priestess at the time of the Persian invasion is not told to sacrifice hecatombs to the god and offer precious treasure to the oracle, but merely to defend herself with wooden walls, a piece of acute worldly wisdom, at least as interpreted by Themistocles. When Crœsus the rich, the king of Lydia, sent to Delphi to find out if he would succeed in a war against Persia and paved his way by magnificent gifts, any priests in the world except the Greeks would have made their profit for their church by an intimation that the costlier the offering the surer his success, but the only answer the Greek holy of holies gave him was that by going to war he would destroy a great empire. It happened to be his own, but, as the priestess pointed out, she was not responsible for his lack of wit, and certainly there was no intimation that if he had given more, things would have turned out better. The sentences which Plato says were inscribed in the shrine at Delphi are singularly unlike those to be found in holy places outside of Greece. *Know thyself* was the first, and *Nothing in excess* the second, both marked by a total absence of the idiom of priestly formulas all the world over.

Something new was moving in the world, the most disturbing force there is. "All things are at odds when God lets a thinker loose on this planet." They were let loose in Greece. The Greeks were intellectualists; they had a passion for using their minds. The fact shines through even their use of language. Our word for school comes from the Greek word for leisure. Of course, reasoned the Greek, given leisure a man will employ it in thinking and finding out about things. Leisure and the pursuit of knowledge, the connection was inevitable—to a Greek. In our ears Philosophy has an austere if not a dreary sound. The word is Greek but it had not that sound in the original. The Greeks meant by it the endeavor to understand everything there is, and they called it what they felt it to be, the *love* of knowledge:

How charming is divine philosophy—

In the world of antiquity those who practiced the healing art were magicians, priests versed in special magic rites. The Greeks called their healers physicians, which means those versed in the ways of nature. Here in brief is an exemplification of the whole trend of the Greek mind, its swing away from antiquity and toward modernity. To be versed in the ways of nature means that a man has observed outside facts and reasoned about them. He has used his powers not to escape from the world but to think himself more deeply into it. To the Greeks the outside world was real and something more, it was interesting. They looked at it attentively and their minds worked upon what they saw. This is essentially the scientific method. The Greeks were the first scientists and all science goes back to them.

In nearly every field of thought "they took the first indispensable steps." The statement means more than is apparent on the surface. The reason that antiquity did not give birth to science was not only because fact tended to grow more and more unreal and unimportant. There was an even more cogent cause: the ancient world was a place of fear. Magical forces ruled it and magic is absolutely terrifying because it is absolutely incalculable. The minds of those who might have been scientists had been held fast-bound in the prison of that terror. Nothing of all the Greeks did is more astonishing than their daring to look it in the face and use their minds about it. They dared nothing less than to throw the light of reason upon dreadful powers taken completely on trust everywhere else, and by the exercise of the intelligence to banish them. Galileo, the humanists of the Renaissance, are glorified for their courage in venturing beyond the limits set by a power that could damn their souls eternally, and in demanding to know for themselves what the universe was like. No doubt it was high courage, great and admirable, but it was altogether beneath that shown by the Greeks. The humanists ventured upon the fearful ocean of free thought under guidance. The Greeks had preceded them there. They chanced that great adventure all alone.

High spirit and the energy of great vital powers had worked in them to assert themselves against despotic rule and to refuse to submit to priestly rule. They would have no man to dictate to them and being free from masters they used their freedom to think. For the first time in the world the mind was free, free as it hardly is to-day. Both the state and religion left the Athenian free to think as he pleased.

During the last war a play would have had short shrift here which showed up General Pershing for a coward; ridiculed the Allies' cause; brought in Uncle Sam as a blustering bully; glorified the peace party. But when Athens was fighting for her life, Aristophanes did the exact equivalent of all these things many times over and the Athenians, pro- and anti-war alike, flocked to the theatre. The right of a man to say what he pleased was fundamental in Athens. "A slave is he who cannot speak his thought," said Euripides. Socrates drinking the hemlock in his prison on the charge of introducing new gods and corrupting the youth is but the exception that proves the rule. He was an old man and all his life he had said what he would. Athens had just gone through a bitter time of crushing defeat, of rapid changes of government, of gross mismanagement. It is a reasonable conjecture that he was condemned in one of those sudden panics all nations know, when the people's fears for their own safety have been worked upon and they turn cruel. Even so, he was condemned by a small majority and his pupil Plato went straight on teaching in his name, never molested but honored and sought after. Socrates was the only man in Athens who suffered death for his opinions. Three others were forced to leave the country. That is the entire list and to compare it with the endless list of those tortured and killed in Europe during even the last five hundred years is to see clearly what Athenian liberty was.

The Greek mind was free to think about the world as it pleased, to reject all traditional explanations, to disregard all the priests taught, to search unhampered by any outside authority for the truth. The Greeks had free scope for their scientific genius and they laid the foundations of our science to-day.

Homer's hero who cried for more light even if it were but light to die in, was a true Greek. They could never leave anything obscure. Neither could they leave anything unrelated. System, order, connection, they were impelled to seek for. An unanalyzed whole was an impossible conception for them. Their very poetry is built on clarity of ideas, with plan and logical sequence. Great artists though they were, they would never give over trying to understand beauty as well as to express it. Plato is speaking as a typical Greek when he says that there are men who have an intuitive insight, an inspiration, which causes them to do good and beautiful things. They themselves do not know why they do as they do and therefore they are unable to explain to others. It is so with poets and, in a sense, with all good men. But if one could be found who was able to add to his instinct for the right or the beautiful, a clear idea of the reason for its rightness or beauty, he would be among men what a living man would be in the dead world of flitting shades. That statement is completely Greek in its conception of values. There never were people farther from the idea of the contemplation of beauty as a rest to the mind. They were not in the world to find rest for their mind in anything. They must analyze and reflect upon everything. Any general term they found themselves using must be precisely realized and the language of all philosophy is their creation.

But to leave the intellectuality of the Greeks here would be to give only half of the picture. Even in Greece Science and Philosophy wore a sober look, but the Greeks did not think soberly about the exercise of the intellect. "Thoughts and ideas, the fair and immortal children of the mind," as a Greek writer calls them, were a delight to them. Never, not in the brightest days of the Renaissance, has learning appeared in such a radiant light as it did to the gay young men of imperial Athens. Listen to one of them talking to Socrates, just waked up in the early dawn by a persistent hammering at his door: "What's here?" he cries out, still half asleep. "O Socrates," and the voice is that of a lad he knows well, "Good news, good news!" "It ought to be at this unearthly hour. Well, out with it." The young fellow is in the house now. "O Socrates, Protagoras has come. I heard it yesterday evening. And I was going to you at once but it was so late—" "What's it all about—Protagoras? Has he stolen something of yours?" The boy bursts out laughing. "Yes, yes, that's just it. He's robbing me of wisdom. He has it—wisdom, and he can give it to me. Oh, come and go with me to him. Start now." That eager, delightful boy in love with learning can be duplicated in nearly every dialogue of Plato. Socrates has but to enter a gymnasium; exercise, games, are forgotten.

A crowd of ardent young men surround him. Tell us this. Teach us that, they clamor. What is Friendship? What is Justice? We will not let you off, Socrates. The truth—we want the truth. "What delight," they say to each other, "to hear wise men talk!" "Egypt and Phœnicia love money," Plato remarks in a discussion on how nations differ. "The special characteristic of our part of the world is the love of knowledge." "The Athenians," said St. Luke, "and the strangers sojourning there spend their time in nothing else but to tell or to hear some new thing." Even the foreigners caught the flame. That intense desire to know, that burning curiosity about everything in the world—they could not come into daily contact with it and not be fired. Up and down the coast of Asia Minor St. Paul was mobbed and imprisoned and beaten. In Athens "they brought him unto the Areopagus, saying, 'May we know what this new teaching is?' "

Aristotle, the model scientist, the man of cool head and detached observation, unbiased, impersonal, does not display any dispassionate aloofness in his consideration of reason. He so loves it and delights in it that when it is the theme of discourse he cannot be held within the sober bounds of the scientific spirit. His words must be quoted, they are so characteristically Greek:

Since then reason is divine in comparison with man's whole nature, the life according to reason must be divine in comparison with (usual) human life. Nor ought we to pay regard to those who exhort us that as men we ought to think human things and keep our eyes upon mortality: nay, as far as may be, we should endeavor to rise to that which is immortal, and live in conformity with that which is best, in us. Now, what is characteristic of any nature is that which is best for it and gives most joy. Such to man is the life according to reason, since it is this that makes him man.

Love of reason and of life, delight in the use of the mind and the body, distinguished the Greek way. The Egyptian way and the way of the East had led through suffering and by the abnegation of the intellect to the supremacy of the spirit. That goal the Greeks could never come within sight of. Their own nature and the conditions of their life alike, shut them off from it, but they knew the way of the spirit no less. The all-sufficing proof that the world of the spirit was where the flame of their genius burned highest is their art. Indeed their intellectuality has been obscured to us precisely by virtue of that transcendent achievement. Greece means Greek art to us and that is a field in which the reason does not rule. The extraordinary flowering of the human spirit which resulted in Greek art shows the spiritual power there was in Greece. What marked the Greeks off from Egypt and India was not an inferior degree of spirituality but a superior degree of mentality. Great mind and great spirit combined in them. The spiritual world was not to them another world from the natural world. It was the same world as that known to the mind. Beauty and rationality were both manifested in it. They did not see the conclusions reached by the spirit and those reached by the mind as opposed to each other. Reason and feeling were not antagonistic. The truth of poetry and the truth of science were both true.

It is difficult to illustrate this conception of reality by isolated quotations, but the attitude of the greatest of Greek scientists may serve as an example. Aristotle was in one sense the typical scientist, a man endowed with extraordinary powers of observation and of reasoning upon his data, preoccupied with what he could see and what he could know. Anywhere else and at any other time he would have been the man of pure reason, viewing with condescension if not contempt conclusions reached in any way except that of the mind. But to Aristotle the Greek the way of the spirit was also important, and the scientific method sometimes to be abandoned in favor of the poetic method. In his well-known statement in the *Poetics* that poetry has a higher truth than history since it expresses truth of general application whereas that of history is partial and limited, he is not speaking as a scientist nor would the statement commend itself to the scientific mind outside of Greece. There is no evidence, again, of the scientist's point of view in the great passage where he sets forth the reason for the work of his life, his search into the nature of all living things:

The glory, doubtless, of the heavenly bodies fills us with more delight than the contemplation of these lowly things, but the heavens are high and far off, and the knowledge of celestial things that our senses give us, is scanty and dim. Living creatures, on the contrary, are at our door, and if we so desire we may gain full and certain knowledge of each and all. We take pleasure in a statue's beauty; should not then the living fill us with delight? And all the more if in the spirit of the love of knowledge we search for causes and bring to light evidences of meaning. Then will nature's purpose and her deep-seated laws be revealed in all things, all tending in her multitudinous work to one form or another of the beautiful.

Did ever scientist outside of Greece so state the object of scientific research? To Aristotle, being a Greek, it was apparent that the full purpose of that high enterprise could not be expressed in any way except the way of poetry, and, being a Greek, he was able so to express it.

Spirituality inevitably brings to our mind religion. Greek religion is known to us chiefly or only as a collection of fairy tales, by no means always edifying. This is to belie the immense hold the Greeks had on things spiritual. It would have been impossible for the nation that produced the art and the poetry of Greece to have a permanently superficial view of religion, just as it would have been impossible for them not to use their minds on Homer's gods and goddesses. Those charming stories which came down from a time when men had a first-hand knowledge of nature now forever lost, were never, it is true, anathematized with book and bell and public recantation. That was not the Greek way. They loved them and their fancy played with them, but they found their way through them to what underlies all religion, East or West. Aeschylus will speak like a prophet of Israel, and the Zeus he praises Isaiah would have understood:

> Father, Creator, mighty God,
> great craftsman, with his hand he fashioned man.
> Ancient in wisdom, working through all things,
> into safe harbor guiding all at last. . . .
> With whom the deed and word are one,
> to execute with swiftness all the ends
> conceived in the deep counsels of his mind.

"Ye men of Athens," said St. Paul on the Areopagus, "I perceive that in all things ye are too superstitious"—so the Bible version runs, but the last word could quite as accurately be translated "in dread of the divine power," a meaning borne out by the reason St. Paul gives for his use of it: "For as I passed by and beheld your devotions I found an altar with this inscription, *To the Unknown God."* The words carry us far away from the gay company of the Olympians. They go back to the poet who had written, "Through thick and shadowed forests stretch the pathways of his purpose, beyond our power to search out." That altar to the Unknown God who is past our power to search out, could have been raised only by men who had gone beneath the pleasant surface of comfortable orthodoxies and easy certainties. A single sentence of Socrates, spoken when he was condemned to death, shows how the Greek could use his mind upon religion, and by means of human wisdom joined to spiritual insight could sweep aside all the superficialities and see through to the thing that is ultimate in religion: "Think this certain, that to a good man no evil can happen, either in life or in death." These words are the final expression of faith.

There is a passage in Socrates' last talk with his friends before his death, which exemplifies with perfect fidelity that control of the feelings by the reason, and that balance between the spirit and the mind, which belonged to the Greek. It is the last hour of his life and his friends who have come to be with him to the end have turned the talk upon the immortality of the soul. In such a moment it would be natural to seek only for comfort and support and let calm judgment and cool reason loosen their hold. The Greek in Socrates could not do that. His words are:

At this moment I am sensible that I have not the temper of a seeker after knowledge; like the vulgar, I am only a partisan. For the partisan, when he is engaged in a dispute, cares nothing about the rights of the question, but is anxious only to convince his hearers. And the difference between him and me at the present moment is only this—that while he seeks to convince his hearers that what he says is true, I am seeking to convince myself; to convince my hearers is a secondary matter with me. And do but see how much I have to gain by this. For if what I say is true, then I do well to believe it; and if there be nothing after death, still, I shall save my friends from grief during the short time that is left me, and my ignorance will do me no harm. This is the state of mind in which I approach the argument. And I would ask you to be thinking of the truth and not of Socrates. Agree with me if I seem to you to speak the truth; or, if not, withstand me might and main that I may not deceive you as well as myself in my desire, and like the bee leave my sting in you before I die. And now let us proceed.

Thus in Greece the mind and the spirit met on equal terms.

Karl Kerenyi

Karl Kerényi was born in Temesvár, Hungary, in 1897, and was educated in Budapest. His early interests included literature, philosophy, and theology, but his major contributions to learning have been in the fields of comparative religion and mythology, in which his work takes a place beside that of Jane Harrison.

Since World War II he has lived in Switzerland, where he has been closely associated with Carl Jung, with whom he collaborated on a number of historico-psychological studies of myth. Kerényi's writings, which continue to appear at the present time, constitute a notable example of the new synthesis of learning in the twentieth century, a synthesis which is expanding our understanding of history, psychology, and society in a wide variety of ways.

EPILOGUE: THE RELIGIOUS IDEA OF NON-EXISTENCE

. . . . 1

One human experience from which attempts have been made to derive not merely ancient religion but all religion is death. We have been offered statements like this: "All faith is faith in another world, the fate

From the book *The Religion of the Greeks and Romans* by Karl Kerényi. Translated by Christopher Holme. Copyright Thames and Hudson 1962. Reprinted by permission of E. P. Dutton & Co., Inc.

of the soul after death constitutes in all religions the centre of religious thought."[408] No doubt this is an extreme generalisation. Yet here, at the end of a book which has sought to understand the ancient religions as "religions of the certainty of the universe," certainty, that is, of the non-human foundations of the world of men, we must give some consideration to the question how the "other world" is regarded in these and similar religions of "this world." We have spoken of the fundamental outlines of the ancient religion without having said a word about Greek and Roman notions of the soul. There is need of a new, exhaustive treatment of this subject,[409] and we shall be making only a small, though indispensable, step towards it if we now deal with the question here.

Death was taken very seriously by the ancient Greeks and Romans. It was not doubted that man is subject to death as to a ruler over existence. It would be easy to say that religious man in antiquity was always preoccupied with the problem of death and that it was his religion, with its ideas about death, which first gave him answers to it. In reality the ideas of the most ancient Greek philosophers have not been transmitted to us in such a form that we can say what *questions* they asked and how they asked them. The art of asking questions was a much later achievement of ancient philosophy than that of *viewing* and *stating* what was important in the world. Philosophic ideas existed before philosophic questions were asked. Ideas do not presuppose the asking of questions, especially not child-like questions. There is no justification for assuming that such questions were in fact asked by serious thinkers of antiquity. Questions are first formulated for the benefit of ignorant people and schoolchildren after knowledge and vision have already been consolidated. Or they emerge when the solid foundations begin to dissolve.

Least of all do religious ideas exist in order to answer questions. Religions are not solutions of primeval problems. Rather they add considerably to the number of problems. The religious ideas and the mythological accounts of them themselves become assumptions on which questions and answers are based. Even when a god has appeared to a man, he can put questions about that appearance. All the more will questions be put as the end of a religion is approached. In the end the gods and all religious ideas become "questionable." In their original, living, valid form religious ideas belong to a quite different sphere from the asking of questions and posing of problems or from the giving of answers and solutions. They do, however, show a certain similarity with the oldest philosophic ideas in that they do, like them, contain an attitude of man to

[408] C. Schmidt, "Gespräche Jesu mit seinen Jüngern nach der Auferstehung," in *Text u. Unters.* 43, 455.

[409] Erwin Rhode's once-famous work, *Psyche*, is now partly obsolete. It was made so by W. F. Otto, *Die Manen* (2nd ed., Darmstadt, 1958).

the world. The reality of the world manifests itself in them in one of the forms which the world itself offers. It shows itself to man, who as knower and perceiver confronts both form and content and holds firm what is offered him, as one aspect of the world, a sort of idea of the world.

We have learnt to know this attitude of ancient religious man as the attitude of *aidos* and *sebas* or else as the attitude of observance, of regulating one's life according to rule, of *religio*. In its highest form, the Greek, it is in contact with the attitude of the philosopher. However, the *noein* of the philosopher is directed at a special transparency of the world, at penetrating to naked being. This was particularly the case in archaic Greek philosophy. Plato and Aristotle did at least give pride of place to "wonder" as the origin of philosophy.[410] *Thaumazein, thauma,* and *thambos* are connected with *sebas,* but on the evidence of the Greek language they had no religious consequences.[411] Yet not even *thauma* originally meant what was there to provoke questions and make a starting point for philosophising, but only that which it was worth while to view.[412] The archaic philosopher was not the man of *thaumazein* in this sense, but nor was he in the later, Socratic sense. Without putting questions he was convinced of the necessity of holding fast to the one essential thing in the world, its meaning and its truth, the *logos* and the *aletheia.* And all he did was to proclaim this essential thing as the man who looks out over the many particular aspects of the world and thinks about them, about the gods. He was the man, as we have put it, of ultimate penetration.

The ideas of ancient religion about death are not answers to questions. They express the attitude of ancient man to the reality of death and are founded in the idea of death itself, on the knowledge of death, and they particularise that knowledge. Men are mortal. This is how the most general and the simplest knowledge of death has always had to be formulated. Yet this knowledge, insofar as it represents a *religious idea,* is not the mere result of an inference which can be reached by thinking and which is formulated purely as thought. It is a knowledge which wakes a peculiar "echo" in us, even when it proceeds from experiences of human society. It is only through this echo, through our knowledge of the fact that this simplest and most general knowledge of death concerns *us too,* that its effect on us is so convincing. It becomes like the other world realities, a festal idea—as the idea of death always is.[413] Only this echo is for us the token that death belongs to the realities at all.

---

[410] Plat. *Teaet.* 155d; Arist. *Met.* 982b.11.

[411] *cf.* above, p. 113.

[412] θαῦμα ἰδέσθαι

[413] "That deep shudder which we are too ready to call fear, whereas it may also be the expression of a most solemn and sublime mood." W. F. Otto, *The Homeric Gods,* p. 143.

It cannot be denied. If there is any reality in the world then death is one, a mighty, spiritual reality which leaves no one "cold." It is not like any other subject of knowledge, but touches everyone with dread. If the study of religion attempted to ignore this fact and to treat the idea of death only as a logical inference and not as a psychic reality, it could rightly be accused of unreality, of detaching itself from all actuality, and therewith also of being unscientific. What is real in the case is the death of an individual, the very one who has the idea about death. It is this which seems to provide a clear and firm foundation for ideas of death in general. The difficulties for the view of ancient religion taken by this book seem to begin when we look for the objective content of these ideas. For it is not the world which seems to be expressed in them but thoughts which go much further than that, having to do with a world beyond this one and lying far outside it. Ideas about death seem to represent an exclusive, one-sided affair of the soul, so that there is *nothing* corresponding to them in the world, unless it be in some supernatural order of things.

This is how it *seems*. For the simplest knowledge of death which is at the same time a psychic reality for us, because it also includes our own death, can probably be taken as a *firm* foundation for all religious ideas of death. It cannot, however, be maintained that it is a *clear* idea for the religious man or for the science of religion. There is one reproach which can be levelled at all earlier research into notions about the soul and the world beyond. It has neglected the important distinction between a man's own death and that of *another*. The first to make this distinction were Rilke and recent philosophers. If I quote them in what follows, it is not in adherence to any particular school of philosophy but simply to make use of their clear-cut formulations in order to throw light on a universal human topic.

. . . . 2

Even if we wanted to choose, as the starting point for an investigation of the religious idea of death, experiences of the soul which belong in the domain of parapsychology, we should still have to start from the reality of death and its given content of ideas, with their apparent contradictions. We have to say with Max Scheler, "The first condition for a life after death is death itself." It was this philosopher who remarked, no doubt rightly, that the chief reason why modern man is not much interested in a life after death is that, essentially, he denies death.[414] The definitions of death given by natural science are in fact uncertain.[415] The medical view is that the departure of life can be delayed *ad infinitum*.

414 *Schriften aus dem Nachlass* I (Berlin, 1933), 8.

415 *cf.* G. Perthes, *Über den Tod* (2nd ed., Stuttgart, 1927).

That is why Scheler begins his examination of the after-life by elaborating a theory of the knowledge of death. This is probably the only correct scientific procedure. It was expressed by Heidegger perhaps even more sharply: "We cannot even ask at all, with sense or reason, what is *after death*, until we have understood death in its complete ontological essence."[416] This methodological principle and the axiom of the priority of death over the after-life is just as valid when our subject of consideration is not the life after death in general, but the ideas of ancient religion about death and the after-life.

Religious knowledge is far ahead of philosophic knowledge in directness. Heidegger correctly recognised that the problem presenting itself for his "existential" analysis could be most directly illuminated from a primary source—the views of death among "primitives" and their actual behaviour towards death in cult and magic.[417] One of the most genuinely prehistoric views of death, that which we find in the labyrinth image, to give only one example, shows how much richer, more complex, and meaningful a mythological idea can be than an ancient philosophical one.[418]

The ancient philosopher conceives death as a "polar" opposite of life, connected with it in such a way that the one can only be present in the absence of the other. For Heraclitus this form of connection was equivalent to a deeper identity—let the name of the "bow" (*biós* equated with *bíos*) be "life," but let its work be "death." Or to take an example from the archaic Greek religion, let Dionysus and Hades be the same.[419] In Plato's *Phaedo* this opposition is the guarantee that death can do nothing to the soul. The one excludes the other, understanding *psyche* in the sense of "soul" and "life."[420] Epicurus takes his stand on this exclusiveness of life when he says: "When we are present, death is not present, and when death is present we are not."[421] On the other hand, mythological narratives of the origin of death are everywhere found as part of the myth of the origin of the normal life of humanity.[422] Death is neither identical with life nor does it exclude it, but it belongs to it as an essential component—a component of the infinite lifeline of the tribe, which is continued by every death, in the succession life-death-life. This idea of the relatedness of life and death as a beginning and a setting, followed

416 *Sein und Zeit* I, 238.

417 *op. cit.*, 247.

418 *cf.* my *Labyrinth-Studien* (2nd ed., Zurich, 1950).

419 Fr. 48 and 15 Diels.

420 105c-e.

421 *Ad Menec.* 125.

422 African examples in H. Baumann, *Schöpfung und Urzeit des Menschen im Mythos der afrikanischen Völker* (Berlin, 1936), 268 *ff.*; H. Abrahamsson, *The Origin of Death. Studies in African Mythology* (Uppsala, 1951).

in succession by a new beginning, could be derived from the heavenly bodies, especially the moon, or from plant growth and the generation of animals. It is experienced in divine Forms which die and are yet eternal, especially in moon-like goddesses.

. . . . 3

The idea here indicated of "life-death-life" stands over the difference between "one's own" and "another's death," but does not exclude this or the mythological ideas based on it. Above all it does not exclude the idea of the Hades frontier. The determination that death has occurred is on the one hand a practical matter—today a medico-legal one. Theoretical science with its definitions, as we have seen, is uncertain on this point. On the other hand the determination of death is also a religious and mythological matter. With the consciousness that death has occurred, truth in the form of myth springs up in the soul of the survivor. This truth is now the frontier which finally divides the dead from the living, no matter how near or how far the place where they are laid to rest or thought to be.[423] The one thing about the realm of the dead which is today still unshakably real is its frontier. It has a psychic reality, but not *only* a psychic one. It becomes noticeable, beyond all dispute, when someone dies. Attic grave urns (lekythoi) show the dead as in life, at home with their relations and friends, receiving them, adorning themselves. But in the same picture the grave too is visible, and Hermes or Charon in an Acherontian landscape.[424] For the one who crosses the frontier the realm of the dead has sprung up in his life, at home. For the survivors the frontier is there, invisible.

What does it consist of, this psychic reality? What is this inconceivable something, so hard to determine scientifically and yet fatally real, for which the only appropriate determination is the mythological "frontier of Hades"? The dead body and the transformation of a living man into a corpse belong to the world and not to the soul. The "death of another" is not an internal concern of man except insofar as it awakens that peculiar "echo." However real the Hades frontier may be for a living man, what he experiences in it is only the "death of another." His "own death" is yet more real for him, it is the really real thing from which the other death, the death of another, gets its psychic reality. There is a difference between the two deaths which is directly experienced by all of us, even when it is not even admitted by us and for that reason not clearly imagined. This difference has been given a precise philosophical formu-

423 *cf.* my article in *Hermes* 66 (1931), 418.
424 *cf.* E. Buschor in *Münchener Jahrb. bild. Künste* 2 (1925), 167 *ff.*

lation: "We do not in any real sense experience the death of others but are at most 'present' at it."[425] What is real and primary is the psychic reality conveyed to us by that echo. To quote the philosopher further, "Death, if it 'is' at all, is essentially my death."[426] Only as "one's own death" does death have any psychic reality.

But is the idea of "one's own death" conceivable at all from its subjective, spiritual side? From the objective side, of course it is conceivable. Objectively, the world contains, first as a possibility, then as its fulfilment, our own death, just as it contains in the past all completed death and all the dead.[427] But how is it with our own *perishable nature?* Is it at all possible for us to have a *direct* attitude to it? Can we directly experience "our own death" in our own life, or read it in the book of the world, as we read there the idea of the inter-connectedness of life and death?

The saying of Epicurus argues against it. "Death is no concern of ours. For when we are present, death is not present, and when death is present, we are not." And yet it was Epicurus in particular for whom death in an important fashion was always present. His thorough treatment of the subject was criticised in this sense by his ancient opponents.[428] But it is not until much later times that we find a special *sense* of "one's own death." Rilke was the first who spoke of it as the "great death," the death "which everyone has in him," "of which we are nothing but the husk and the leaf." For, he said, "this is the fruit on which everything depends."[429] But we must first acquaint ourselves with the bare facts as they are experienced by modern man. We shall find Scheler's "theory of the knowledge of death" in some measure suitable for this purpose. We shall not use his system of thought to *prove* that "our own death" is for us the primary one. His genuine experience is shared as *living* experience by every one of us, however paradoxical that may sound. But we may succeed in making this experience intelligible, rather as we did with the experience of the festival, and in endowing it with some needed clarity.

A man, even if he were the only living thing on earth, in some sort of way would know that death was going to overtake him—so runs Scheler's train of thought.[430] The certainty of this is involved in every phase of life, however small, and in the structure of his experience. The "idea and nature of death" is one of the constituent elements of all vital consciousness. We experience and see in every indivisible moment of our

425 *Sein und Zeit* 239.

426 *op. cit.,* 240.

427 According to W. F. Otto, *The Homeric Gods,* 142 *ff.,* this "having-been" *is* the Homeric Hades.

428 Cic. *De Nat. Deor.* 240.

429 The quotations are from the *Stundenbuch.*

430 *op. cit.,* 9 *ff.*

life process something "passing" and something "coming." In every present moment we are affected by the feeling that something in general is
"passing away" and that something else in general is "to be expected,"
independently of what it may contain. The total extent of what is "passing" and what is "to come," with the advance of the life process, is always
being distributed afresh in a characteristic direction. That which is passing increases, while that which is to come decreases. The extent of what
is present existence gets more and more strongly "compressed" between
these two. For the child the present is a broad, bright surface of the most
colourful existence. This surface decreases in extent with every advance
of the life process. It becomes smaller and smaller, more and more compressed. For the young person the future is there like a broad, bright
corridor stretching out into the invisible distance. But with every piece
of life that is lived there is perceptibly less room for life still to be lived.
The livable life is steadily consumed while life already lived increases.
This is the "direction of death." We experience it, in the natural structure of every living moment, as a sense of an increasing difference between
two lengths. The future shrinks as the past grows longer. Death is not
just an empirical constituent of our experience, but it is of the nature
of every life experience, our own among them, that it has the direction of
death. Death belongs to the form and structure, internal and external,
of every life as it is given, our own among the rest. It is not a frame which
has by chance been added to the picture of particular psychic and physiological processes, but a frame that is itself part of the picture. Without it
the picture would not be a picture of life.

The modern philosopher speaks to us men of today in our own language. He remains in the realm of the subjective, and at that is not even
exhaustive. In every life he ignores its spiritual content, which for an
individual who sees life hurrying away from him with advancing age may
well be of most value.[431] By contrast with this philosopher we may turn
to a man much richer in the experience of life—Berdyaev, who says, "Suffering passes, the having suffered never passes. . . . Victory may indeed be
achieved over what has been experienced, and yet that experience is still
in our possession as a permanent enhancement and extension of the
reality of our spiritual life. What has once been lived through cannot
possibly be effaced. That which has been continues to exist in a transfigured form. Man is by no means a completely finished product. Rather
he moulds and creates himself in and through his experience of life."[432]
Yet insofar as man is a living being, the structure of his life corresponds
exactly to that idea of the interconnection of life and death in which this
important, natural component of life is to be found. What Goethe would

431 W. F. Otto's criticism of Scheler.
432 N. Berdyaev, *Freedom and the Spirit* (London, 1935), vii.

call the entelechy, or full development, of the spiritual form of an individual may give promise of something more than one single, unique life,
yet everyone in his life must experience "his own death." Once he has
attained a state of spiritual fulfilment, he may perhaps contemplate the
world with the openness of mind of the ancients, culminating in their
theoria or *religio*. Yet there too he cannot fail to read the message that
human existence is in its nature transitory.

Scheler describes the death-direction from the point of view of a man
turned in on himself. For the ancients the corresponding description,
although it also included a man's *own* death, would have to be a description not of his inner life, but of the world of men. This is the world
which contracts around us in our experience of the death-direction,
indeed independently of our actual experience, and which in its relation
to ourselves approaches closer and closer to rejection and complete negation. In our experience of our own death a real aspect of the world reveals
itself to us, announcing non-existence, the total absence of room for life.
It is not easy to formulate the idea of non-existence philosophically and
the task of doing so was left for relatively late times. But in the study of
religions this philosophically "difficult" idea of non-existence is the very
one which can serve as a model to show how an ancient religious idea is
constructed, for it is one which is at the heart of many mythological tales,
incorporated in images of the gods and descriptions of another world.

. 4

We say the religious idea of non-existence. Could we not just as well talk
of the "myth of non-existence," a myth worked into particular mythical
tales, incorporated in images of the gods and descriptions of another
world? It can be done. The choice of the word "idea" instead of "myth,"
however, gives more prominence to the visual appearance, while "myth"
emphasises the content of what is stated or appears as a picture.[433] When
the dying Greek invokes "the gates of Hades,"[434] this is a *picture,* but not
only a picture. It is also the viewing and naming of a reality. In particular, since an "after life" in Hades is not necessarily implied by it nor
self-evident in it, the reality viewed is that of non-existence. It is real
because the impending non-existence of the speaker is an actual part of
the world. It will be that he will not be! Nor is the god Hades himself
only an image. He too is an "actual" god. Because of him and in company with him the other death deities of the ancient world, which do not
guarantee an "after life" but only the reality of death, we are forced to

---

433 *cf.* my *Griechische Miniaturen,* 148 *ff.*

434 Aesch. *Agam.* 1291; *cf.* Hom. *Il.* 5.646, 9.313.

recognise that the ancient religious view, in its unreflective fashion, includes non-existence among the forms of existence, that it extends the all-embracing realm of being to non-being itself.[435] It is rare for an ancient "religious idea" to be found in such exemplary form as here, where its content—non-existence—although really there for us all in the world, is conceivable *only* as an idea and *only* in pictorial form, by the one who experiences and knows it, and only by him.

There is a big series of Roman tomb inscriptions which describe the reality of death as a world of negation and privation—a world of evil, of darkness, of stillness, of cold, of ugliness. A survey made in the spirit of these interpretations[436] yielded the following statement: "The mythical view clothes even non-existence with a shape and gives a form to nothing-ness. The Greek and Roman belief in immortality is almost always treated by historians of religion as if we here had to do with ideas about an actual afterlife in the grave or in the underworld—a mistake which more than anything else shows up the immense gulf dividing the ancient from the modern view. For these ideas are far removed from a belief in immortality. On the contrary, they are direct forms of expression of the human condition in death." The apotheosis of the dead which we encoun-ter in archaic and then in later imperialistic times was something quite different. This too was a highly contradictory idea. Generally speaking, the state of death is described in the tomb inscriptions as something objective. It appears as a paraphrase for "objective non-existence," the thing we are headed for as we move in the direction of death.

These paraphrases have nothing to do with a capacity or incapacity for abstraction. The withdrawal of itself which life in fact performs was expressed by analogy, in terms of existence. It is quite in the spirit of Greece and of antiquity when Plato says, "Non-Existence in some sense exists."[437] The language of the unreflected experience of life puts for "non-existence"—"death." Yet death too has its place assigned to it in the Greek conception of the universe. Death and its domain are bounded. The world which contains *our* non-existence therein displays one of its aspects, whether a monstrous, beast-like, or man-like, or even a motherly face, or only emptiness and cold and gloom—an aspect at any rate which we know and recognise. We know it from inside as a capacity of the world to undergo a transformation which for us is final. The dread of this change springs from the negation and privation which it means for us. And what makes it all the more dreadful is that it does not face us

435 *cf.* my lecture *Dionysos und das Tragische in der Antigone* (Frankfurt a. M., 1935), 9 *f.*

436 A. Brelich, *Aspetti della morte nelle inscrizioni sepolcrali dell' impero Romano* (Budapest, 1937), 8.

437 Soph. 241d τὸ μὴ ὂν ἔστι κατά τι.

with the possibility that the existence of the world itself could be shattered, but only with our own reduction to nothingness. For in this aspect
of the world there is displayed to everyone his own death. The death-
aspect of the world is, in a primary and immediate fashion, identical with
the experience that the whole universe stands before us, but with diminishing room for ourselves. Some room in another world is not excluded
by this knowledge, yet it must be more appropriate to the state of death
than to that of life.

We recognise this non-existence in the *death of others*. The transformation of those who have just died, which announces that they have
crossed the frontier of Hades, is the external counterpart of that transformation which we all gradually undergo and experience in the direction of death. Our internal experience finds an external support and
justification. It announces itself in that "echo" of which we have spoken.
It is at the same time evoked and completed by the external experience,
just as our idea of a fruit which we have known only in its unripe state
is completed by the sight of the ripe fruit. Parmenides said that the dead
body does not indeed perceive light or warmth or sounds because its fire
has gone out but that it does perceive cold and silence and whatever else
is opposed to them.[438] This cold and quiet, the state of being dead, is
experienced by us only exceptionally. The dead experience it for ever.
In them the world accomplishes and shows us the "ripe fruit."

Yet Epicurus too had right on his side when he said, "When we are
present, death is not present, and when death is present we are not." The
transformation is so thorough and complete that anyone who has undergone it is no longer the self that he was. Being dead means being quite
other, the death direction is the direction towards the "quite other." This
quite-other is contained in the world. It is a feature of the death-face of
the world. It is what distinguishes it, together with all the gods which
are its aspects and everyone of which represents a special face of the
world, from mortal creatures. What makes the world "quite other" is just
this quality, that it supports non-existence lightly and eternally, while
for living creatures it is the occasion of the most complete of all their
transformations, so complete that it does not even exclude the notion of
apotheosis, that the dead may become gods. Yet for living man the shock
of the "quite other" remains, for it includes also his own coming other-
ness. Here we encounter one of the fundamental elements of all religion,
but only *one* among many.

The idea of non-existence as a world aspect is only *one* among many
aspects of the universe to which it is related. First let us grasp the idea
itself. It is evoked, or is echoed, in songs and stories, as ideas are evoked,
not as a sum of internal and external experiences, but as a unity. It is the

---

[438] Theophr. *De sensu* 3.

unity of our own death, cherished and ripening in us, and of the world's death towards which every living creature is moving and which in our own death concerns us too. Thus it is expressed in a song of the Dinka by the Upper Nile:[439]

> On the day when God created all things,
>> he created the sun
> and the sun rises and sets and returns again,
>> he created the moon
> and the moon rises and sets and returns again,
>> he created the stars
> and the stars rise and set and return again,
>> he created man
> and man comes forth, goes into the earth,
>> and does not return again.

That is the death-face of the world which it turns to men. This face intruded also into the maize festival of the Cora Indians. "They appear only once, my younger brethren. Do they not die really for ever? But I never die, I shall appear continually." Such an intrusion of the death-face of the world does not have the effect of something alien in the festive atmosphere. Where divinity is present to man, this difference too is present—mortality in its purest form, a form of non-existence contrasted with the existence of the gods. This characteristic of the festal phenomenon corresponds to the festal character of the phenomenon of death.

The inherent festiveness of Nature, its eternal and periodic character, which makes Nature itself the primal calendar, the true festival calendar, also causes the death-face of the world to appear. Evidence of this is to be found not only in primitive poetry but also in the classics. The joy of life in Catullus's *Vivamus mea Lesbia* acquires a special festivity from the reminder which it gives of the death-face of the world. It has playful licence, intensity, and seriousness all at the same time:

> *Soles occidere et redire possunt,*
> *Nobis cum semel occidit brevis lux*
> *Nox est perpetua una dormienda.*

> Suns may set and still return,
> When our brief light has set, for us
> There's one perpetual night of sleep.

For the classical treatment of the same divine appearance we have the two spring poems of Horace, *Solvitur acris hiems* and *Diffugere nives*. The experience of the divine found by the poet in the seasons of the year is realised not so much through the images of particular gods, or at any

[439] Cited by Scheler from Frobenius.

rate not only by this means, but in his concluding argument. It is particularly sharp and clear in the second poem:

> *Damna tamen celeres reparant caelestia lunae;*
>   *nos ubi decidimus,*
> *quo pius Aeneas, quo Tullus dives et Ancus,*
>   *pulvis et umbra sumus.*

> Swift-following moons make good their heavenly losses.
>   When we are dead and gone
> the way of pious Aeneas, rich Tullus, Ancus,
>   we'll be but dust and shade.

The death-face of the world is clear for all to see.

. 5

On the other hand, it is never or almost never this face alone by which
man is confronted. The rising up of the death idea does not mean
the sinking of the opposite idea which is necessarily connected with it, the
idea of life.

By this we must understand not an abstraction, not a mere concept.
Just as in the idea of death the reality of non-existence appears in one
aspect of the world, its death-face, so in the idea of life there appears the
reality of existence as an aspect of the world. If non-existence shows itself
in this world as pure negation and privation, yet in this same experience,
the experience of death, there accumulates on the other side everything
that is positive, and the life face of the world comes into view. If all these
positive things, light, heat, gaiety, sound, did not evoke the idea of life,
then there would be in the world no mode of appearance for death at
all, there would be no "idea" for non-existence. And not only that! If by
an experiment of thought we were to think life out of the world, then
there would no longer be any force or power left for non-existence. If we
had not known life, we should never have experienced the power of
death. It is only by life that non-existence has been raised to the rank
of a reality which appears in the world and is powerful there.

The one idea leads inevitably to the other. Life makes the idea of
death possible, even powerful, and the idea of death enables life in all its
reality, its strength and power, to become actual. As the room for livable
life steadily contracts about every mortal creature, our first thought might
be that the grey and gloomy colours would increasingly dominate his
landscape. But it is rather the other way round. The contraction causes
all the colours of life, all that the world has to show, to glow more
brightly.[440] The experience of this polarity may vary from one individual

440 *cf.* Soph. *Ant.* 809 *ff.*

to another. The *fact* that it is experienced is just as much an ingredient of the structure of all living things, and consequently of the structure of the world, as the death direction. And it is not merely an external and literal manifestation, in which the idea of life and the idea of death appear together as the colourful splendour of the world. It is an aspect of the world in which we can fully participate without distinguishing between external vision and internal experience. To the slumbering and fitful consciousness of life the idea of death comes at times like water thrown on a dying fire, at times like oil to stir it into a blaze.

Yet this idea of life, the reality which so to speak blazes up in its fullest intensity under the pressure of death, is not to be confused with notions of another world. It is an essence, really existent and irreplaceable. We experience it simply as life, undiluted by its no less real opposite. Indeed we only experience what real existence is when we face that condition which is its total negation—the state of death. And this thing whose place can be taken only by something other, never by something like, is in truth irreplaceable.

. . . . 6

The ideas of ancient religion, like the idea of death or the idea of life, are not only themselves aspects of the world, but also have various aspects of their own. We have only to consider in how many deities the life-aspect of the world appears. And the negation of existence in death, the pure privation of non-existence, may well be repugnant to us in comparison with all the positive gifts of life, its feelings and experience. Yet life too can be so painful and agonising that the purely negative aspect, the world of Hades, may appear mild and beneficent by contrast. There is a natural fear of death, and death is bitter for it. But there is also, just as natural, our urge towards death, which can build itself up into a longing for death. For this longing non-existence is sweet, and the mild and beneficent face of non-existence corresponds to it.

The bitterness and the sweetness of death are both realities. Poets give accounts of them as credible as those they give of love. Death was listed as one of the muses of great lyric poetry.[441] This was doubtless the case, too, in the period we are considering, though we have lost the choral songs which were sung in honour of Persephone, the goddess of death. But the *fact* that she is beautiful, though she may also be the sender of the dreaded Gorgon head,[442] should give students of religion food for thought. We should learn from the ancient artists and more recent poets that there is more in the case than a wish for some outward embellish-

441 F. Brunetière.

442 *Od.* 11.634-5; *pulchra Prosperpina* Verg. *Aen.* 6.142.

ment of death. True, students of religion are more inclined to follow natural science than poetry, but that would lead us here into a blind alley.

For natural science, natural death is really inconceivable. Anthropology has taught us that there are primitive peoples who are unwilling to consider death as a natural end.[443] Even in cases of natural death they look for an evil will which was the cause of death. This remarkable attitude can be explained psychologically. It is always tempting to explain away an unpleasant and well-known fact by a lie. One such fact is our inevitable natural death. Moreover, psychic research has drawn attention to the fact that even in cases of natural death the survivors have a feeling of guilt. The separation of a living creature from life appears always as an injustice of which we are helpless spectators. The propitiation of the dead is found among the mourning ceremonies of many societies. We can easily understand how the guilt may be pushed off on to some foreign magician.

On the other hand, there is nothing which could excuse the student of religion from concerning himself with that human behaviour in the face of death which is *really felt* as death. To do this, he is not absolutely obliged to make use of the experiences of poets. Psychology and biology have arrived at a common conclusion[444] that there is not only a life instinct—and the fear of death bound up with it—but also a death instinct. The existence of this instinct follows from the structure of the living creature. "Life instinct" and "death instinct" are nothing but scientific terms for the fact that every living thing is continually in process of construction and destruction. These two, construction and destruction, can be thought of as two tracks, one directed upwards, the other downwards. But both together coincide with the direction of death. Construction proceeds just as much in the direction of death as destruction. It is really only *one* track, along which the living creature moves, and no one can tell at what point of life the movement begins to go downward. From the beginning the track is a track and not a stopping place. It is the track of life and therewith also the slope of death. "Movement," "track," "slope," are obvious metaphors. Their real meanings are: "movement"—"life"; "life track"—"keeping oneself alive"; "slope of death"—"giving oneself over to death."[445]

Life and death instinct together, inseparably joined to one another, make up the nature of the living creature. They are two aspects of the living creature, which could just as well be called the "dying creature." In one and the same individual the "dying creature" can even assume the

[443] Lévy-Bruhl, *Les fonctions mentales dans les sociétés inférieurs* (Paris, 1922), 321.

[444] S. Freud, *Beyond the Pleasure Principle* (Vol. 18 of the Standard Edition; London, 1955).

[445] *Dionysos und das Tragische in der Antigone,* 13.

predominance over the "living creature"—in advanced years or in illness or, what is not the same, in tragic circumstances. Both creatures which make up the *one* living-dying creature, have their own fears and long-ings—fear of death and longing for life, fear of life and longing for death. The bitterness of death is connected with the first pair, the sweetness of death with the second.

Both are possible because man as a living and dying creature is in continual, structural contact with his own death, and yet has no direct experience of it as an actual state. Only the dead man experiences the state of death. However, we have the possibility of hurrying ahead along the track which is both the track of life and the slope of death and anticipating the end, not in reality but in dream and imagination. But there is a reason even for the anxious and wishful pictures of a dreaming or imagining mind. The reason is given by the track, which is at the same time a slope and has for its end an unwished-for, even terrifying, break, which can yet appear as a longed-for goal. But however this end may appear to the anticipating soul, whether dreadful or longed-for, the subject matter of the pictures in which it shows itself cannot be taken from death itself. Non-existence contains nothing. That being-other is something different from any experience of life. Thus it is that even those fancies which make death seem pleasant come from life. The end is so imagined as if it were a continuation, wished for or not.

Such an "as if," felt by everyone whether they admit it or no, sets a clear distinction between all notions of another world and the memories and experiences we have of the real world. Behind the experiences of life there stands the world as an uninterrupted, continuous background, here and now and always. Notions of another world are strictly no more than imaginative projections of the soul as, questioning and fearful, it antici-pates the end. They take the soul into the "other world," the world "beyond" the end, which it has not yet reached. The background to such notions is neither this world nor that "other world," for they do not refer to this world, which is here and now, and the other world to which they do refer is not here and now. That is why notions of the Beyond can never be confused with the knowledge that everyone has in himself about life—unless perhaps in exceptional states of ecstasy. But whence could such notions be generated if not from the storehouse of the soul and from possibilities of the mind, all of which form part of the content of this world?

In preference to the dreadful aspect of death we choose, quite natu-rally and unconsciously, its other, seductive aspect. The horrors of death are partly the fears of the soul as it anticipates the end. They are partly due, here and now, to the fact that the advance of privation and nega-tion, that aspect of the world in which death shows itself, is in fact horrifying. To set against the fears of the soul we have its pleasant expectations and longings. These are as well founded as the fears and like them have a deep-lying cause and are supported by a real aspect of the world. For the natural inclination towards death of every living creature is balanced by the soul's capacity for self-deception, here stimulated by the fear of death itself. Thus hopes of another world arise, with sounds and colours more compelling than anything else the soul can dream of, even in its finest and deepest moments.

It is characteristic of other-world notions that even the most seductive among them are not powerful enough to prevent the dread aspect of death from presenting itself as a possibility which we ourselves shall perhaps escape, but to which *others* will all the more certainly fall victim. In this unequal distribution of the other world the demand for justice has played a varying part. It depends on the particular ethical mission of the religion to which the promise of an after-life belongs. Alongside "Paradiso" even in antiquity there stands "Inferno," to satisfy the requirement of an unavoidable polarity. Not till the terrors of death had been philosophically "overcome" were the soul's anxieties, at least in theory, removed. In this case, it is true, the loss of "Inferno" has entailed that of "Paradiso" too. Other-world notions of this crude kind, however, were in ancient religion secondary or peripheral phenomena. What is primary and central from the viewpoint of ancient religion is the comprehension of the reality of death, its complete acknowledgement, not its anticipatory veiling with pictures, dreadful or pleasant, of another world. It was this acknowledgement which figured in the cults of the ancient death deities.

. 7

Objective non-existence, realised in the death of living creatures, has appeared to us, as it necessarily did also to the ancients, in two aspects, as a dreaded end, and as a confining framework for all living creatures, on which they begin and on which, just as naturally, they cease to exist, as if arrived at a destination down a pleasant slope. On the other hand, for ancient man non-existence had another characteristic, different from those with which we are familiar. The modern idea of non-existence is completely empty. For ancient religious man non-existence, as the enclosing framework of organic life, was both full and empty at the same time.

It is not a logically bounded, exactly defined idea, like the non-existence of the philosophers, but a reality bordering on all living things. It is only in its border region that it can be comprehended at all, for its real core remains the inconceivable. In its border region, however, we do approach this inconceivable. We do it by intermediate stages, just as we approach non-existence. Between the light of day and the complete absence of light, for which the Greeks had the name Erebos, there is night. Before the fully formed state of an organism there is the germ. As ground of every living movement there is the resting earth. But where is the frontier between night, the germinal state, the earth in motherly repose, and a realm of non-existence conceived as lightless, germless, and *totally* dead?

We can indicate a domain of reality lying midway, so to speak, between the domain of wholly negative, pure non-existence and the domain of total existence, containing within itself every stage and every possibility. This intermediate realm of all the small life that swarms in darkness is the bottommost layer in the great realm of life.[446] As the domain of incompleteness and motherly protection it is not closed to the realm of non-existence. For ancient man, indeed, it was so much a part of this realm that non-existence itself was joined to it. For non-existence could not be conceived as a sheer yawning void, but only as completely and inseparably bound up with the idea of mother earth and as one of her aspects. Thus it was that the fullness of germination itself became an aspect of non-existence.

We may speak here of a root aspect of existence.[447] "The roots of the earth and of the sea," the two realms of swarming and germinating creatures, according to Hesiod[448] would be visible to the Titans in Tartaros if it were not for the total darkness called Erebos. It is a motherly domain which bore the world and now supports it and is always capable of bearing it anew. In terms of the labyrinth idea, the endless line of life, it is a stage before and after life. It was only for the philosopher among the Greeks, and not before him, that pure non-existence could be separated from existence, the *me on* from the *on*. Ancient religion worshipped the gods of heaven and of the underworld, the Olympic and the Chthonic deities. Their world was even more of a single whole than the world of later pantheistic philosophy. Non-existence had its place in it as a reality of the soul, a "being-other" for man. In it both existence and non-existence were equally powerful, and capable of appearing in a rout of divine figures which surrounded and penetrated the universal whole with radiance and meaning.

---

[446] *cf.* my remarks in *Gnomon* 1933, 305 *f.*
[447] *Dionysos und das Tragische in der Antigone*, 10.
[448] *Theog.* 728.

APPENDIXES

- # APPENDIX I
A GENERIC TABLE OF CONTENTS

The following table is not meant to be either definitive or exhaustive. A number of selections have been placed in more than one category, and a number of other categories might also be designed. The table aims only to suggest a possible approach for the instructor who may wish to use the volume as an introduction to the study of the forms of expository writing.

1. **ESSAYS**
   GOTTFRIED BENN, Art and the Third Reich
   GEORGE ORWELL, Politics and the English Language
   BERTRAND RUSSELL, Machines and Emotion
   HANNAH ARENDT, The Crisis in Education
   ERIK ERIKSON, The First Psychoanalyst
   ROBERT OPPENHEIMER, On Science and Culture
   LIONEL TRILLING, Science, Literature, and Culture
   CARL JUNG, Psychology and Literature
   SIR KENNETH CLARK, The Blot and the Diagram

2. **FORMAL TREATISES**
   ELIAS CANETTI, The Crowd
   CARL KERÉNYI, Epilogue: The Religious Idea of Non-Existence

3. **SOCIAL COMMENTARY**
   ROBERT PENN WARREN, On Segregation
   JOHN K. GALBRAITH, Inequality
   DENNIS DE ROUGEMONT, The Breakdown of Marriage
   JOHN P. CONRAD, The Swedish Paradox
                   The American Nightmare
                   What Lenin Foresaw

4. **THESES**
   ORTEGA Y GASSET, The Revolt of the Masses
   ALDOUS HUXLEY, Overpopulation

5. **REFLECTIONS**
   SYBILLE BEDFORD, Some Faces of Justice
   IGOR STRAVINSKY, Reflections on Being Eighty
   W. H. AUDEN, Notes on Music and Opera

6. **CONTROVERSIAL DISCOURSE**
   MARY MC CARTHY, The Contagion of Ideas
   VIRGINIA WOOLF, Shakespeare's Sister
   ALBERT CAMUS, Kadar Had His Day of Fear
   KENNETH TYNAN, Ionesco: Man of Destiny?
                  Ionesco and the Phantom
   EUGENE IONESCO, The Playwright's Role
   NIGEL DENNIS, Down on the Side of Life

7. **FORMAL CONTROVERSY**
   KENNETH TYNAN, Ionesco: Man of Destiny?
                  Ionesco and the Phantom
   EUGENE IONESCO, The Playwright's Role

8. **POLEMIC**
   MARY MC CARTHY, The Contagion of Ideas
   KENNETH TYNAN, Ionesco and the Phantom

9. **SCIENTIFIC DISCOURSE**
   SIR CHARLES SHERRINGTON, The Wisdom of the Body

10. **JOURNALS**
    GERALD BRENAN, Cordova
    SYBILLE BEDFORD, Some Faces of Justice

11. **TRAVEL NARRATIVE**
    GERALD BRENAN, Cordova

12. **JOURNALISTIC REPORTS**
    RAYMOND ARON, Polymorphous Violence
    ALAN MOOREHEAD, Belsen

13. **NOTES**
    GEORGE BERNARD SHAW, Notes to *Caesar and Cleopatra*

14. **PUBLIC ADDRESSES**
    MARY MC CARTHY, The Contagion of Ideas
    ERIK ERIKSON, The First Psychoanalyst
    E. M. FORSTER, Art for Art's Sake

15. **EDITORIAL**
    ALBERT CAMUS, Kadar Had His Day of Fear

16. **LETTERS**
    JOHN WAIN, Answer to a Letter from Joe
    EUGENE IONESCO, The Playwright's Role
    RAINIER MARIA RILKE, A Letter Written after a Visit with Rodin

17. **OPEN LETTERS**
JOHN WAIN, Answer to a Letter from Joe
EUGENE IONESCO, The Playwright's Role

18. **LITERARY CRITICISM**
E. M. FORSTER, Art for Art's Sake
WILLIAM BUTLER YEATS, Rhetoricians, Sentimentalists, and Poets
BERNARD KNOX, Sophocles' *Oedipus*
THOMAS MANN, *Anna Karenina*

19. **ART CRITICISM**
J. HUIZINGA, Art and Life
RAINIER MARIA RILKE, A Letter Written after a Visit with Rodin
SIR KENNETH CLARK, The Blot and the Diagram

20. **MUSIC CRITICISM**
W. J. TURNER, The Genius of Mozart
IGOR STRAVINSKY, Reflections on Being Eighty
W. H. AUDEN, Notes on Music and Opera

21. **BOOK REVIEW**
NIGEL DENNIS, Down on the Side of Life

22. **DRAMA REVIEW**
KENNETH TYNAN, Ionesco: Man of Destiny?

23. **HISTORY**
EDMUND WILSON, The Partnership of Marx and Engels
ARNOLD TOYNBEE, The Present Point in History
J. HUIZINGA, Art and Life
EDITH HAMILTON, East and West
                    Mind and Spirit

24. **BIOGRAPHY**
ERIK ERIKSON, The First Psychoanalyst
W. J. TURNER, The Genius of Mozart

25. **AUTOBIOGRAPHY**
ARTHUR KOESTLER, Portrait of the Author as a Comrade
DIANA ATHILL, Beckton Manor
SIMONE DE BEAUVOIR, Life at the Sorbonne

26. **RECOLLECTION PIECE**
DIANA ATHILL, Beckton Manor

ADDITIONAL WORKS BY AUTHORS IN THIS VOLUME

Listed below are other *expository* works by some of the authors in this volume, works which have a particular relevance to the major themes which have been under discussion. It is included for the convenience of those who wish to do further, independent reading. The parenthetical numbers after each entry suggest some of the connections to the various sections of *Culture and Crisis*.

Following the expository works is a selected list of works of *imaginative literature*—novels, poems, plays—by a number of the authors in this volume. Again, it is included for the convenience of those who want to read further on their own.

EXPOSITION

ARENDT, HANNAH	*The Origins of Totalitarianism* (I, II)
AUDEN, W. H.	*The Enchaféd Flood* (IV, V)
DE BEAUVOIR, SIMONE	*The Second Sex* (III)
BRENAN, GERALD	*Spanish Labyrinth* (I, II)
CAMUS, ALBERT	*The Myth of Sisyphus* (II)
CLARK, SIR KENNETH	*The Nude* (VI)
	Landscape into Art (VI)
FORSTER, E. M.	*Aspects of the Novel* (IV)
	The Hill of Devi (II, III)
GALBRAITH, JOHN K.	*American Capitalism* (I, II, III)
	The Great Crash (III)
HAMILTON, EDITH	*The Roman Way* (II, VII)
	The Echo of Greece (II, VII)
HUIZINGA, J.	*Homo Ludens* (VI, VII)
HUXLEY, ALDOUS	*The Devils of Loudon* (III)
	On Art and Artists (IV, VI)
JUNG, CARL	*The Archetypes and the Collective Unconscious* (III, IV)
KERÉNYI, CARL	*The Gods of the Greeks* (IV, VI, VII)
	The Heroes of the Greeks (IV, VI, VII)
KOESTLER, ARTHUR	*The Yogi and the Commissar and Other Essays* (II, III)
	The Lotus and the Robot (III, VII)
MC CARTHY, MARY	*The Stones of Florence* (VI)
	Sights and Spectacles (V)

MANN, THOMAS — *Last Essays* (I, II, IV)
MOOREHEAD, ALAN — *The Traitors* (II)
ORTEGA Y GASSET — *The Dehumanization of Art and Other Essays* (II, IV)
ORWELL, GEORGE — *Critical Essays* (II, IV)
RUSSELL, BERTRAND — *Authority and the Individual* (I, II)
SHAW, GEORGE BERNARD — *A Young Woman's Guide to Socialism* (II, III)
— *The Preface to Saint Joan* (I, II, V)
TOYNBEE, ARNOLD — *A Study of History* (I, IV, VII)
TRILLING, LIONEL — *The Liberal Imagination* (II, III, IV)
WOOLF, VIRGINIA — *Three Guineas* (II, III)
— *The Common Reader* (IV)
YEATS, WILLIAM BUTLER — *The Autobiography of William Butler Yeats* (IV)
WILSON, EDMUND — *Patriotic Gore* (I, II, III)

IMAGINATIVE LITERATURE

AUDEN, W. H. — *The Collected Poems of W. H. Auden*
DE BEAUVOIR, SIMONE — *The Mandarins*
BEDFORD, SYBILLE — *A Legacy*
— *A Favourite of the Gods*
CAMUS, ALBERT — *The Stranger*
— *The Plague*
DENNIS, NIGEL — *Cards of Identity*
FORSTER, E. M. — *Howard's End*
— *A Passage to India*
HUXLEY, ALDOUS — *Antic Hay*
— *Point Counterpoint*
IONESCO, EUGENE — *Four Plays*
KOESTLER, ARTHUR — *Darkness at Noon*
MC CARTHY, MARY — *The Group*
MANN, THOMAS — *Buddenbrooks*
— *Death in Venice*
— *The Magic Mountain*
— *Dr. Faustus*
ORWELL, GEORGE — *1984*
RILKE, RAINIER MARIA — *Selected Poems*
— *Sonnets to Orpheus*
SHAW, GEORGE BERNARD — *The Selected Plays of Bernard Shaw*
WAIN, JOHN — *Hurry on Down*
WARREN, ROBERT PENN — *All the King's Men*
WOOLF, VIRGINIA — *Mrs. Dalloway*
— *To the Lighthouse*
— *The Waves*
YEATS, WILLIAM BUTLER — *The Selected Poems of William Butler Yeats*

INDEX TO AUTHORS AND TITLES